SOFTWARE EVOLUTION
AND FEEDBACK

SOFTWARE EVOLUTION AND FEEDBACK

Theory and Practice

Edited by

Nazim H. Madhavji
University of Western Ontario, Canada

Juan C. Fernández-Ramil
The Open University, UK

and

Dewayne E. Perry
The University of Texas at Austin, USA

John Wiley & Sons, Ltd

Copyright © 2006   John Wiley & Sons Ltd, The Atrium, Southern Gate, Chichester,
West Sussex PO19 8SQ, England

Telephone (+44) 1243 779777

Email (for orders and customer service enquiries): cs-books@wiley.co.uk
Visit our Home Page on www.wiley.com

All Rights Reserved. No part of this publication may be reproduced, stored in a retrieval system or transmitted in any form or by any means, electronic, mechanical, photocopying, recording, scanning or otherwise, except under the terms of the Copyright, Designs and Patents Act 1988 or under the terms of a licence issued by the Copyright Licensing Agency Ltd, 90 Tottenham Court Road, London W1T 4LP, UK, without the permission in writing of the Publisher. Requests to the Publisher should be addressed to the Permissions Department, John Wiley & Sons Ltd, The Atrium, Southern Gate, Chichester, West Sussex PO19 8SQ, England, or emailed to permreq@wiley.co.uk, or faxed to (+44) 1243 770620.

This publication is designed to provide accurate and authoritative information in regard to the subject matter covered. It is sold on the understanding that the Publisher is not engaged in rendering professional services. If professional advice or other expert assistance is required, the services of a competent professional should be sought.

Other Wiley Editorial Offices

John Wiley & Sons Inc., 111 River Street, Hoboken, NJ 07030, USA

Jossey-Bass, 989 Market Street, San Francisco, CA 94103-1741, USA

Wiley-VCH Verlag GmbH, Boschstr. 12, D-69469 Weinheim, Germany

John Wiley & Sons Australia Ltd, 42 McDougall Street, Milton, Queensland 4064, Australia

John Wiley & Sons (Asia) Pte Ltd, 2 Clementi Loop #02-01, Jin Xing Distripark, Singapore 129809

John Wiley & Sons Canada Ltd, 22 Worcester Road, Etobicoke, Ontario, Canada M9W 1L1

Wiley also publishes its books in a variety of electronic formats. Some content that appears in print may not be available in electronic books.

Library of Congress Cataloging-in-Publication Data:

Software evolution and feedback : theory and practice / edited by Nazim H. Madhavji ... [et al.].
   p. cm.
 Includes bibliographical references and index.
 ISBN-13: 978-0-470-87180-5 (cloth : alk. paper)
 ISBN-10: 0-470-87180-6 (cloth : alk. paper)
 1. Computer software – Development. I. Madhavji, Nazim H.
 QA76.76.D47S66135 2006
 005.1 – dc22
                                                   2006006500

British Library Cataloguing in Publication Data

A catalogue record for this book is available from the British Library

ISBN-13: 978-0-470-87180-5
ISBN-10: 0-470-87180-6

Typeset in 10/12pt Times by Laserwords Private Limited, Chennai, India
Printed and bound in Great Britain by Antony Rowe Ltd, Chippenham, Wiltshire
This book is printed on acid-free paper responsibly manufactured from sustainable forestry
in which at least two trees are planted for each one used for paper production.

To Ilen and Sasha for their love and energy to dad. – Nazim H. Madhavji
To Karine, my wife and my blessing. – Juan C. Fernández-Ramil
To my wife Faith for her loving patience. – Dewayne E. Perry

Contents

Foreword	xix
Preface	xxi
Acknowledgements	xxvii
Editors' Biographies	xxix
List of Contributors	xxxi

PART ONE SOFTWARE EVOLUTION   1

1 Software Evolution   7
Meir Lehman and Juan C. Fernández-Ramil

1.1 Introduction	7
1.1.1 Evolution	7
1.1.2 Interpretation of the Term Evolution in the Context of Software	8
1.2 The Evolution of Large Software Systems	8
1.2.1 Early Work	8
1.2.2 Large Programs	9
1.3 Program Classification	10
1.3.1 The SPE Program Classification Schema	10
1.3.2 S-type Applications and Software	10
1.3.3 E-type Applications and Software	12
1.3.4 P-type Situations and Software	13
1.4 The Inevitability of Evolution	13
1.5 Levels of Software-Related Evolution	14
1.6 *Ab Initio* Implementation or Change	16
1.6.1 Process Steps	16
1.6.2 The LST Paradigm	17
1.6.3 Phenomenological Analysis of Real-World Computer Usage	18
1.6.4 Theoretical Underpinning	18
1.6.5 The Value of Formalisms and of Verification	19
1.6.6 Bounding	20
1.6.7 The Consequence: Continual System Evolution	21

	1.6.8 Summary	21
	1.6.9 Principle of Software Uncertainty	22
1.7	Software Systems Evolution	22
	1.7.1 Early Work	22
	1.7.2 FEAST	23
	1.7.3 The Growth Trend	24
	1.7.4 Evolution Drivers	25
	1.7.5 Relationship Between the Above Levels of Evolution	26
	1.7.6 Evolutionary Development	26
1.8	Evolution of the Application and Its Domain	27
1.9	Process Evolution	28
	1.9.1 Software Processes as Systems	28
	1.9.2 Process Improvement	28
	1.9.3 The Theoretical Approach	29
	1.9.4 Evolving Specifications	30
	1.9.5 The Empirical Approach	30
	1.9.6 Laws of Software Evolution	30
	1.9.7 The Ephemeral Process	31
1.10	Process Model Evolution	32
	1.10.1 The Nature of the Software Process	32
	1.10.2 Process Models	32
	1.10.3 Software Process Models	33
	1.10.4 Process Improvement	33
	1.10.5 Links Between Process and Process Model Evolution	35
1.11	Relationships Between Levels	35
	1.11.1 The Software/Software Process Contrast	35
	1.11.2 The Software Process/Process Model Contrast	36
1.12	Conclusions	37
1.13	Acknowledgments	37
	References	37

2	**A Nontraditional View of the Dimensions of Software Evolution**	**41**
	Dewayne E. Perry	
2.1	Introduction	41
2.2	The Domains	42
	2.2.1 The Real World and Its Model	42
	2.2.2 The Model and the Derived Specification	43
	2.2.3 Theory	43
2.3	Experience	44
	2.3.1 Feedback	45
	2.3.2 Experimentation	46
	2.3.3 Understanding	46
2.4	Process	47
	2.4.1 Methods	47
	2.4.2 Technology	48
	2.4.3 Organization	48
2.5	Summary	49
2.6	Acknowledgments	50
	References	51

3	**IT Legacy Systems: Enabling Environments That Reduce the Legacy Problem: A Complexity Perspective**	**53**
	Professor Eve Mitleton-Kelly	
3.1	Introduction	53
3.2	The Legacy Problem	55
	3.2.1 Feedback	56
	3.2.2 Co-evolution	56
	3.2.3 The Social Ecosystem	57
3.3	The Two Case Studies	58
	3.3.1 Business and Market	60
	3.3.2 Organisation and Management	61
	3.3.3 Technology	62
	3.3.4 Interactions between the Various Elements	62
3.4	The Socio-Technical Enabling Environment	64
	3.4.1 The Bank's Enabling Environment	64
	3.4.2 The Building Society and Some Complexity Principles	66
3.5	Summary and Conclusions	68
3.6	Acknowledgements	69
	References	69
4	**Facets of Software Evolution**	**71**
	Roland T. Mittermeir	
4.1	Introduction	71
4.2	What is Software?	72
	4.2.1 Software: A Technical Artefact	72
	4.2.2 Software: A Utility	72
	4.2.3 Software: A Text, Reflecting Reality	73
	4.2.4 Software is Information	74
4.3	Evolution	75
	4.3.1 Principles	75
	4.3.2 Evolution Drivers	76
4.4	Strata of Software-Size and Complexity	77
	4.4.1 Module	77
	4.4.2 Design Unit	78
	4.4.3 Architecture	79
	4.4.4 System	80
	4.4.5 System-of-Systems	80
	4.4.6 Discussion	81
4.5	Approaches to (R-)evolve	82
	4.5.1 Changes in Modules	83
	4.5.2 Modifying Design Units	84
	4.5.3 Evolution on the Architectural Level	84
	4.5.4 System-Level Evolution	84
	4.5.5 Evolution of Systems-of-Systems	85
4.6	An Example	86
	4.6.1 A System-of-Systems?	86
	4.6.2 System-Level Changes	87
	4.6.3 Architectural Decisions	88
	4.6.4 Design Units	88

	4.6.5 Modules	90
	4.6.6 Discussion	91
4.7	Summary	91
	References	92

5 Evolution in Software Systems: Foundations of the SPE Classification Scheme — 95
Stephen Cook, Rachel Harrison, Meir M. Lehman and Paul Wernick

5.1	Introduction	95
5.2	Background and Related Work	96
	5.2.1 Software Evolution	96
	5.2.2 Stakeholders, Architecture and Software Evolution	104
	5.2.3 Hermeneutics and Software Evolution	108
	5.2.4 Requirements Analysis, Paradigms and Hermeneutics	113
5.3	SPE+	115
	5.3.1 Introduction	115
	5.3.2 The SPE+ Taxonomy	115
	5.3.3 Validation of SPE+	123
5.4	Conclusions and Future Research	125
5.5	Acknowledgements	126
	References	127

6 A Simple Model of Software System Evolutionary Growth — 131
Władysław M. Turski

	References	141

7 Statistical Modelling of Software Evolution Processes — 143
Tetsuo Tamai and Takako Nakatani

7.1	Introduction	143
7.2	Approach	145
	7.2.1 Measurement	145
	7.2.2 Case Studies	145
	7.2.3 Metrics	146
7.3	Observed Evolution Patterns	146
	7.3.1 Stable Statistic Model	147
	7.3.2 Exceptional Data	150
	7.3.3 Discontinuous Change	150
	7.3.4 Class Tree Characteristics	151
7.4	Distribution Model	153
	7.4.1 Negative Binomial Distribution	153
	7.4.2 Evolution of Model Parameters	155
	7.4.3 Larger Case Study	157
7.5	Discussions	159
	References	160

8 Software Requirements Changes Due to External Factors — 161
Vic Nanda and Nazim H. Madhavji

8.1	Introduction	161
	8.1.1 Organisation of This Chapter	162

8.2	Congruence Evaluation System (CES): A Case Study	163
	8.2.1 CES Context and Key Events	*163*
	8.2.2 Contribution, Relevance and Applicability of This Case Study	*163*
	8.2.3 CES: Background and Implementation Strategy	*164*
	8.2.4 Analysis of CES Capabilities	*165*
	8.2.5 The Impact of Environmental Evolution	*167*
	8.2.6 Threats to Validity	*176*
8.3	Lessons Learnt and Conclusions	177
	References	177
	Appendix A: An Instrument to Assess System Deficiencies	178
	Appendix B: An Instrument to Assess Environment Evolution	179
9	**Understanding Open Source Software Evolution**	**181**
	Walt Scacchi	
9.1	Introduction	181
9.2	Empirical Studies of Software Evolution	182
	9.2.1 Studies of the Laws of Software Evolution	*182*
	9.2.2 Other Empirical Studies of Software Evolution	*183*
9.3	Evolutionary Patterns in Open Source Software	184
	9.3.1 Types of Entities for Studying F/OSS Evolution	*185*
	9.3.2 Patterns in Open Source Software Evolution Studies	*186*
9.4	Evolution Models and Theories	194
9.5	Do We Need New or Revised Models, Laws or Theories for Open Source Software Evolution?	197
	9.5.1 Embracing the Feedback Control Systems Ontology	*197*
	9.5.2 Alternative Ontologies for F/OSS Evolution	*198*
9.6	Conclusions	200
9.7	Acknowledgements	202
	References	202
10	**Structural Analysis of Open Source Systems**	**207**
	Andrea Capiluppi, Maurizio Morisio and Juan C. Fernández-Ramil	
10.1	Introduction	207
10.2	Related Work	208
10.3	Rationale	209
10.4	Approach	210
10.5	Attributes Studied	211
	10.5.1 Source Code Size	*211*
	10.5.2 Code Structure	*212*
	10.5.3 Modification Types	*212*
10.6	Evolution of Code Structure	213
	10.6.1 Horizontally Expanding	*213*
	10.6.2 Vertically Shrinking	*215*
	10.6.3 Vertically Expanding	*216*
10.7	Summary	218
10.8	Current and Future Work	219
10.9	Acknowledgements	220
	References	220
	Appendix	222

11	**A Study of Software Evolution at Different Levels of Granularity**	**223**
	Elizabeth Burd	
11.1	Introduction	223
11.2	Existing Studies of Software Evolution	225
11.3	Case Study Approach	228
11.4	Results	230
	11.4.1 The System Level	230
	11.4.2 Level 2, The Function Level	233
	11.4.3 Level 3, The Data Level	236
	11.4.4 Comparing Levels	242
11.5	General Recommendations	244
11.6	Conclusions	245
	References	246
12	**The Role of Ripple Effect in Software Evolution**	**249**
	Sue Black	
12.1	Introduction	249
12.2	Impact Analysis	250
12.3	Software Maintenance and Software Maintenance Models	252
12.4	Background on the Ripple Effect	254
	12.4.1 Computation of the Ripple Effect	255
	12.4.2 The REST Software Tool	258
12.5	Links Between Ripple Effect and the Laws of Software Evolution	260
	12.5.1 First Law – Continuing Change	261
	12.5.2 Second Law – Growing Complexity	262
	12.5.3 Third Law – Self Regulation	263
	12.5.4 Fourth Law – Conservation of Organisational Stability	263
	12.5.5 Fifth Law – Conservation of Familiarity	263
	12.5.6 Sixth Law – Continuing Growth	264
	12.5.7 Seventh Law – Declining Quality	264
	12.5.8 Eighth Law – Feedback System	264
12.6	Conclusions	265
12.7	Further Work	266
12.8	Acknowledgements	266
	References	266
13	**The Impact of Software-Architecture Compliance on System Evolution**	**269**
	R. Mark Greenwood, Ken Mayes, Wykeen Seet, Brian C. Warboys,	
	Dharini Balasubramaniam, Graham Kirby, Ron Morrison and Aled Sage	
13.1	Introduction	269
13.2	Evolution and Compliance	270
13.3	A Generic Scheduling Problem	271
	13.3.1 A ProcessWeb Example	272
	13.3.2 Programming Around Poor Compliance	273
13.4	Compliance Through Configuration	273
	13.4.1 Trade-offs in Configuration	275
13.5	Exploiting an Analytical Model	277
	13.5.1 A First Analytical Model for ProcessWeb	277

13.6	Discussion	278
13.7	Acknowledgements	280
	References	280

14 Comparison of Three Evaluation Methods for Object-Oriented Framework Evolution — 281
Michael Mattsson

14.1	Introduction	281
14.2	Object-oriented Frameworks	285
	14.2.1 The Studied Frameworks	285
14.3	Methods and Results	287
	14.3.1 Evolution Identification Using Historical Information	287
	14.3.2 Stability Assessment	293
	14.3.3 Distribution of the Development Effort	300
14.4	Method Comparison	305
	14.4.1 Change-prone Modules	305
	14.4.2 Framework Deployment	306
	14.4.3 Change Impact Analysis	306
	14.4.4 Benchmarking	306
	14.4.5 Requirements Management	307
	14.4.6 Some Comments	307
14.5	Related Work	308
14.6	Conclusion	309
	References	310

15 Formal Perspectives on Software Evolution: From Refinement to Retrenchment — 313
Michael Poppleton and Lindsay Groves

15.1	Introduction	313
15.2	Program Refinement	314
15.3	Modifying Refinements by Adapting Derivations	320
15.4	A Compositional Approach to Program Modification	322
15.5	Retrenchment	324
	15.5.1 Refinement – a Relational Perspective	325
	15.5.2 The Need to Generalise Refinement	327
	15.5.3 Retrenchment: Generalising Refinement	330
	15.5.4 Retrenchment for Software Evolution	332
15.6	Conclusions	335
	References	336

16 Background and Approach to Development of a Theory of Software Evolution — 339
Meir M. Lehman and Juan C. Fernández-Ramil

16.1	Software Evolution	339
16.2	Global Views of Evolution	340
	16.2.1 Two Approaches	340
	16.2.2 The Verbal Approach	341

	16.2.3 The Nounal Approach	342
	16.2.4 Mutual Support of the Two Views	342
	16.2.5 Process Improvement	342
16.3	The Case for Theory	343
16.4	Theory Development	345
16.5	A World View	346
	16.5.1 Real-World Program Relationship	346
	16.5.2 Assumptions	347
16.6	Example	349
	16.6.1 Introduction	349
	16.6.2 Preliminary Definitions	349
	16.6.3 Observations	350
	16.6.4 Inferences	351
	16.6.5 Guidelines	351
16.7	The Theory	352
16.8	Organisation of Theory Development	352
16.9	Goals	352
16.10	Related Work	353
16.11	Final Remarks	354
16.12	Acknowledgements	355
	References	355

PART TWO FEEDBACK   359

17 Difficulties with Feedback Control in Software Processes   363
Meir M. Lehman, Dewayne E. Perry and Wlad Turski

17.1	Introduction	363
17.2	Feedback and Control	365
17.3	Technology versus Sociology	366
17.4	Manifesto and Model	367
17.5	Influence versus Control	370
	17.5.1 Immaturity	371
	17.5.2 Feedback Overload	371
	17.5.3 Step Functions versus Regulation	371
	17.5.4 Design versus Production	372
17.6	Examples of Feedback Control	373
17.7	Summary	373
17.8	Acknowledgments	374
	References	375

18 Governing Software Evolution through Policy-oriented Feedback   377
Nazim H. Madhavji and Josée Tassé

18.1	Introduction	377
18.2	The Policy-Checking Mechanism	379
	18.2.1 Controlling System Growth	379
	18.2.2 Re-engineering Change-Prone Modules	381
	18.2.3 Discussion	383
18.3	The Contextual Framework	384
	18.3.1 New-Release Development	384

	18.3.2 Roles, Communication and Feedback	386
	18.3.3 The Framework Architecture	387
18.4	Technological Support	389
	18.4.1 Policy-Checking Mechanism	389
	18.4.2 Framework	390
18.5	Evaluation	391
18.6	Related Work	393
18.7	Conclusions	394
	References	394

19	**Feedback in Requirements Discovery and Specification: A Quality Gateway for Testing Requirements**	**397**
	Suzanne Robertson	
19.1	Contents of the Requirements Specification	397
19.2	Project Drivers	399
	19.2.1 Producers	400
	19.2.2 Consumers	401
	19.2.3 Sponsors	402
	19.2.4 Subject Matter Consultants	403
	19.2.5 Technical Consultants	404
	19.2.6 Influencers	404
	19.2.7 Project-Sociology Analysis	405
19.3	Contents of Individual Requirements	405
19.4	Keeping Track of Connections	407
19.5	The Quality Gateway	408
19.6	Lessons Learnt	409
19.7	Conclusion	410
	References	410

20	**Requirements Risk and Software Reliability**	**411**
	Norman F. Schneidewind	
20.1	Introduction	411
	20.1.1 Requirements Changes and Software Evolution	412
	20.1.2 Objectives	412
	20.1.3 Methods	413
20.2	Background	413
20.3	Selected Measurement Research Projects	414
20.4	Approach to Analyzing Requirements Risk	415
	20.4.1 Categorical Data Analysis	416
20.5	Risk Factors	418
	20.5.1 Space Shuttle Flight Software Requirements Change Risk Factors	418
20.6	Solutions to Risk Analysis Example	420
	20.6.1 Categorical Data Analysis	420
	20.6.2 Dependency Check on Risk Factors	422
	20.6.3 Identification of Modules that Caused Failures	422
20.7	Future Trends	423
20.8	Conclusions	424
20.9	Acknowledgments	424
	References	424

21	**Combining Process Feedback with Discrete Event Simulation Models to Support Software Project Management**	**427**
	David Raffo and Joseph Vandeville	
21.1	Introduction	427
21.2	Providing Up-to-Date Process Feedback	428
	21.2.1 Feedback in Simulation Models	428
	21.2.2 Metrics Repository	429
21.3	Discrete Event Simulation Models	431
21.4	Combining Process Feedback with the Discrete Model	433
	21.4.1 Comparing Statistical Process Control with Outcome Based Control Limits	433
21.5	Illustrative Example	434
	21.5.1 The Scenario Under Consideration	434
	21.5.2 Determining the Performance of the Baseline Process	436
	21.5.3 Use of the Model and Metrics for Quantitative Process Feedback Management	437
	21.5.4 Assessing the Implications of Feedback and Developing an Action Plan (Is the Process in Control?)	438
	21.5.5 Taking Corrective Action and Assessing the Impact of the Changes	439
21.6	Conclusions	440
21.7	Acknowledgements	440
	References	440

22	**A Feedforward Capability to Improve Software Reestimation**	**443**
	William W. Agresti	
22.1	Introduction	443
	22.1.1 Reestimation: State of the Practice	443
	22.1.2 Objective	445
	22.1.3 Related Research	446
22.2	A Feedforward Capability	446
	22.2.1 Feedforward Estimation in Other Domains	447
	22.2.2 Feedforward Estimation in Software Development	448
	22.2.3 Operation of a Feedforward Model	449
22.3	Example Uses of the Feedforward Concept	452
	22.3.1 Feedforward Capability Integrated with a Software Estimation Tool	452
	22.3.2 The Role of a Feedforward Capability in Risk Management	453
22.4	Conclusion	454
22.5	Acknowledgements	455
	Appendix	455
	References	458

23	**Modelling the Feedback Part of the Software Process in Software Resource Estimation**	**459**
	Juan C. Fernández-Ramil and Sarah Beecham	
23.1	Introduction	459
23.2	The Evidence of Feedback	460
23.3	The Need for a Taxonomy	461
23.4	Feedback as a Cost Factor	461
23.5	Cost Estimation as a 'System Identification' Problem	461
23.6	Why do Algorithmic Cost Estimation Approaches such as COCOMO 'Work'?	464

23.7	Approaches to Model 'Feedback' in Cost Estimation Models	465
23.8	Indirect Black-Box Modelling and Feedback-Related Cost Factors	466
23.9	Final Remarks	468
23.10	Acknowledgments	468
	References	469

24 Value-Based Feedback in Software and Information Systems Development — 471
Barry Boehm and LiGuo Huang

24.1	Introduction	471
24.2	Feedback Control of Software Development: Four Primary Feedback Cycles	472
	24.2.1 Feedback Cycle 1: Project Scoping	472
	24.2.2 Feedback Cycle 2: Project Execution	473
	24.2.3 Feedback Cycle 3: Model Update	474
	24.2.4 Feedback Cycle 4: Organizational Productivity Improvement	475
24.3	Using 'EV' for Feedback Control of Software Development and Evolution	476
	24.3.1 An Earned Value System Example	477
24.4	Real Earned-Value Feedback Control	478
	24.4.1 Business-Case and Benefits-Realized Monitoring and Control	479
24.5	Value-Based Feedback Control: An Order Processing Example	481
	24.5.1 Business Case Analysis: Costs, Benefits and Return on Investment	482
	24.5.2 Value-Based Monitoring and Control	485
24.6	Conclusions and Future Challenges	487
24.7	Acknowledgments	488
	References	488

25 Expert Estimation of Software Development Cost: Learning through Feedback — 489
Magne Jørgensen and Dag Sjøberg

25.1	Introduction	489
25.2	Estimation Learning	490
25.3	Estimation Feedback and Process Guidelines	493
	25.3.1 Increase the Motivation for Learning Estimation Skills	494
	25.3.2 Reduce the Impact from Estimation-Learning Biases	495
	25.3.3 Ensure a Fit Between the Estimation Process and Type of Feedback	495
	25.3.4 Provide Learning Situations	496
25.4	Experiment: Application of the Guidelines	497
	25.4.1 Background	498
	25.4.2 Experiment Design	499
	25.4.3 Results	501
25.5	Summary	503
25.6	Acknowledgement	503
	References	503

26 Self-Adaptive Software: Internalized Feedback — 507
Robert Laddaga, Paul Robertson and Howard Shrobe

26.1	Introduction	507
	26.1.1 Some Software Life Cycle Concepts	508
	26.1.2 Brief Introduction to Self-Adaptive Software	509
	26.1.3 Introduction of Binding of Function Call to Function Value	510

26.2	Historical Perspective	510
	26.2.1 Dynamic Versus Static Binding	510
	26.2.2 Language and Compiler Development	512
	26.2.3 Performance Trade-Offs	514
	26.2.4 The Concept of Software Application Evolution	514
	26.2.5 A Note about Software Ecology	515
26.3	Self-Adaptive Software	517
	26.3.1 Concepts	517
	26.3.2 Technology Requirements and Opportunities	518
26.4	Applications of Self-Adaptive Software	521
	26.4.1 Recent Application Work	522
	26.4.2 Vision Systems	522
	26.4.3 Face Recognition	528
	26.4.4 Pervasive Computing	530
26.5	Conclusion	535
	References	536
27	**Rules and Tools for Software Evolution Planning and Management**	**539**
	Meir M. Lehman and Juan C. Fernández-Ramil	
27.1	Introduction	539
27.2	Laws of Software Evolution	541
27.3	*S*- and *E*-Type Program Classification	542
	27.3.1 Basic Properties	542
	27.3.2 Implications of the SPE Program Classification Scheme	542
27.4	First Law: Continuing Change	543
27.5	Second Law: Increasing Complexity	545
27.6	Third Law: Self Regulation	547
27.7	Fourth Law: Conservation of Organisational Stability	549
27.8	Fifth Law: Conservation of Familiarity	550
27.9	Sixth Law: Continuing Growth	551
27.10	Seventh Law: Declining Quality	552
27.11	Eighth Law: Feedback System	554
27.12	The FEAST Hypothesis	556
27.13	The Principle of Software Uncertainty	557
27.14	Conclusions	559
27.15	Acknowledgements	560
	References	560
Index		**565**

Foreword

The topic of software evolution and feedback as it relates to software development is often misunderstood. To make matters worse, the term 'evolution' was not used until the 1970s. Thus, the topic is only recently getting its just due within the software engineering community.

Change is endemic to software systems. Requirements change, environments change – and so must the systems that are built. The problem is that often researchers and practitioners do not have sufficient information and understanding about why and how systems progressively change over time. Research has shown that more than 80% of life-cycle costs are incurred after a system is delivered. Therefore, there are significant economic reasons to possess a better understanding of why and how systems evolve.

A pioneer in the field of software evolution, Meir 'Manny' Lehman has spent a lifetime conducting research into this difficult topic, and continues to do so. He has also been successful in getting others involved, and the fruits of their collective labor are found within these pages. This book brings together extensive works from significant evolution researchers.

With the publication of this book, readers will now be able to go to one authoritative source to obtain critical information about evolution, including patterns of change, feedback issues and feedback mechanisms. The time is right for this book, as there are no books in print that specifically address software evolution.

This book is a must-read for anyone in the software engineering community. Every software maintenance researcher, practitioner, graduate student and instructor needs to clear space on their bookshelf for a copy, as it will be an invaluable resource you will come back to again and again.

Thomas M. Pigoski
Pensacola, Florida

Preface

'All is flux, nothing stays still'
Heraclitus (540–480 B.C.)
From Diogenes Laertius, Lives of Eminent Philosophers.

About the field of software evolution and feedback

Since the advent of electronic computers, the growing software development community is increasingly faced with not only how to create a new software application (or system) of the desired quality attributes (e.g., reliability, performance, security, interoperability, portability, etc.) within shrinking timeframes and budgets, but also, following initial development, how to upgrade it so that the users find it satisfactory for their continued and changing needs. In this respect, software is arguably different from most other kinds of products of human endeavor in that a software system needs to be upgraded, time after time, to keep the users satisfied with it in their continually changing operational contexts. In contrast, most other forms of human-made products (though not necessarily their blueprints) do not have to be so modified to keep the users satisfied. Instead, these products are typically repaired to obtain more use from them, or discarded or replaced. From this, a reality with respect to software is that if it is not changed adequately with time then it is probably 'dying' if not already dead.

In 'Software Maintenance and Evolution: a Roadmap'[1], Bennett and Rajlich lucidly depict a *staged* life-cycle model of a software system. According to this model, following the initial development of a system, it sequentially goes through the stages of evolution, servicing, phase-out and closedown. Though all the stages are critical from the business point of view, the evolution stage is where most of the challenges are in research and practice.

This book is concerned mainly with the evolution of a system following its initial development. It encompasses concern for the manner in which a given system (or a class of systems) progressively changes *over time*, for example, from the point of view of the system's size, features, structure and design entropy, documentation size, agent-roles and technological support needed to keep it current, average time or budget needed to add a new unit of software measure (e.g., function point or line of code) into the system and so forth. It also encompasses concern for the technology needed to change the system over time, for example, methods, techniques, tools and processes that not only facilitate the

---

[1] See 'The Future of Software Engineering', Anthony Finkelstein (Ed.), ACM Press 2000.

change at hand but also are sensitive to the long-term 'health' of the software system. The term software *evolution* was coined by Lehman and colleagues in the 1970s, whose work has started and, has since, significantly fueled this field.

In software engineering, any kind of change following the initial development or delivery of a software system is widely referred to as software *maintenance* (see, for example, the standards: IEEE 1219 and ISO/IEC 14764). Typically, this includes corrective, adaptive, perfective and preventive changes. Though for practical reasons it is at times difficult to classify a given change among these cleanly (e.g., a corrective change might involve substantial adaptation[2]), it is generally the *adaptive* aspect (to maintain user's satisfaction with a system in the changing environment) that is of most concern in this book.

From an economic point of view, system adaptation soaks up most of the 80%, or so, of the post-delivery, noncorrective software costs in the life of a software system. There is thus a significant economic reason to improve the science of system adaptation (both managerial and technical aspects) and of adaptive technologies so that, ultimately, the running systems would be healthier, last longer, and would result in increased benefits to the end-users, customers and other stakeholders.

In his eloquent description on Software Maintenance, as part of the 'Software Engineering Body of Knowledge (SWEBOK)' sponsored by the IEEE Computer Society, Pigoski identifies maintenance techniques such as program comprehension, reverse engineering, re-engineering and impact analysis. Also, in the cited 'Software Maintenance and Evolution: a Roadmap', Bennett and Rajlich identify yet other areas of importance such as linking software attributes to maintainability, change and system validation. While all such topics are considered to help in the analysis and implementation of the change at hand, they do not generally consider the dimension of *time* spanning multiple releases of a software system and are thus *not* represented in this book. Do note, however, that there is an emergence of interest in linking topics such as code exploration and visualization and aspect-oriented software development to software evolution as visualized over multiple releases. The field is indeed not staying still!

Nonetheless, as the technologies and development paradigms have changed over time, for example, from main-frames to workstations to web and pervasiveness; or from solely closed-source (or proprietary) development to increasingly open-source (or community-based) development; or from fine-grained (or lines-of-code based) development to coarse-grained (or component based) development to loosely coupled system integration; or from purely function orientation to the emergence of service orientation; or from traditional life-cycle models to the emergence of agile methods and no doubt other such transitions and advances, so has the intricacy of what constitutes the field of software evolution. In turn, this has presented an open-ended opportunity to researchers and practitioners alike to grasp new challenges in software evolution with innovations in system design, development technologies and management.

Software evolution would arguably be nonexistent without the impetus for change, which results from a wide variety of reasons, such as technological changes; new needs of the stakeholders; changes in laws, rules and regulations and others. Thus, an important driver here is *feedback* concerning the relevance of an existing system in its operationally

---

[2] See Chapin N, Hale J.E, Khan K.M, Ramil J.F and Tan W.G: Types of Software Evolution and Software Maintenance, *Journal of Software Maintenance and Evolution: Research and Practice*, v. 13, issue 1, Jan-Feb. 2001, pp. 1–30.

changing contexts. Gathered typically from the field of use, such feedback consists of, amongst other things, where the system is failing to meet the expectations and what new functional, nonfunctional and behavioral features are needed to keep the system current.

As can be easily imagined, feedback involves not only the 'what' (as in the type of information fed back from the field to development) but also other dimensions described above: the processes needed to effectively feed back, monitor and control information, the organizational structures and technologies needed to support the processes, the roles played by people in the feedback processes, the cost and benefits of feedback, and so forth. Opportunities for innovation in research and practice abound here as well, as new paradigms and technologies are embraced by society. Let us end this description on evolution and feedback with Lehman's Eighth law, which says that evolution processes are multi-level, multi-loop, multi-agent feedback systems.

About this book

This book provides a depth of material in the field of software evolution and feedback. It focuses on the concepts, theory and practice underlying the numerous changes a system typically undergoes to keep it in productive use over its lifetime.

In particular, this book describes the phenomenological underpinnings; concepts in the software products and software organizations that encircle evolutionary changes; patterns of change discovered through statistical analysis of object-oriented systems; how requirements change over time due to external factors; characteristics of open-source software evolution; the role of ripple effects; the relationship between software architectures and software evolution; the evolution of object-oriented frameworks; formal aspects of software evolution; feedback issues in the software process; use of policies to guide software evolution; feedback in requirements elicitation; the role of metrics that characterize the risk of making requirements changes; how process feedback can be combined with discrete event simulation models to support software project management; feedback and feed-forward capabilities to aid software estimation and learning; self-adaptive software through internalized feedback, and rules and tools for software system process planning and management.

While, clearly, not every conceivable topic in the field of evolution and feedback could possibly be treated in any book of this nature, the coverage provided by the book's 27 chapters is significant. The scope, however, is constrained not only by the lack of body of knowledge in many areas of evolution and feedback but also by other considerations such as time and effort required to create the content, and the size and cost of the book. Still, in what appears in between the covers, many chapters are original, written specifically for this book, while others are significant revisions of earlier publications.

In fact, the book has several goals:

- To capture and disseminate a substantial body of knowledge in the area of software evolution and feedback that represents a cross-section of modern research.
- To promote the book's subject in a learning environment.
- To promote critical thinking on different topics in software evolution and feedback.
- To precipitate ways to improve the practice of software development and evolution.
- To precipitate further research in this field.

These goals are pursued through different means. For example, the different perspectives of the field of software evolution and feedback are brought together in this book through the contributions made by numerous researchers of international standing. There are presentation slides that ease the dissemination of the book's content in a learning or group environment, and suggested questions, model responses and discussion points to promote critical thinking and dialogue within a group. Also, improved understanding of the life of a software system after its initial development can help improve practice through adoption of new concepts, technical and managerial processes, technologies and organizational structures in the workplace. Lastly, researchers now have a significant source of knowledge in the area of software evolution and feedback, all in one book, to support their investigation.

Level and readership

The book is intended for researchers in software engineering; senior practitioners and consultants in the software industry who face software evolution challenges; graduate students and junior practitioners enrolled in software engineering, computer science, IT and related courses; Masters and Doctoral thesis students in software engineering and computer science; advanced undergraduate students undertaking enrichment studies and final-year projects in software engineering and instructors of software engineering courses.

Reading guide

It is the described duality of evolution and feedback that underlies the structure of this book. Chapters 1 to 16 are 'evolution' centered; whereas chapters 17 to 27 are 'feedback' centered though both these topics are often discussed in the same chapter. Within these partitions, the chapters are organized from more conceptual to more concrete content. Do note that the book has not been structured to follow any particular route map. It is conceivable that one could read from beginning to end though this may not be a typical reading pattern. Other suggestions to consider are to read the abstracts to select desired chapters, to read chapters involving the same author or the same topic together or to use the index terms to read the related chapters.

Note to the students and instructors, and support material

Though the book is not designed to steer any particular course as laid out by a software engineering curriculum (see, e.g., the Unit 'EVO – Evolution' in 'Computing Curriculum – Software Engineering, May 2004', The Joint Task Force on Computing Curricula, IEEE Computer Society and Association for Computing Machinery), it is a valuable reference for instructors and students for selecting specific topics on evolution and feedback and fitting them into their own frameworks for learning. The support material of presentation slides and discussion questions and responses are particularly useful for enhancing the learning experience. For access, please see the website: www.wiley.com/go/softwareevolution.

Likewise, senior undergraduate and graduate students are particularly encouraged to undertake 'enrichment studies' where possible, suitably guided by supervising instructors and involving specific topics of interest covered in the book. Of course, additional sources of information (see below) would add to the richness of such studies. In supervising such studies over many years, our experience suggests that students obtain a deep knowledge of the subject area and tend to have competitive advantage for employment and entrance in advanced degree programs over others who have not conducted such studies.

Online and related resources

Here, we list, in no particular order, additional resources that may enhance the learning experience:

- Journal of Software Maintenance and Evolution – Research and Practice, Wiley.
- IEEE International Conference on Software Maintenance (ICSM).
- IEEE European Conference on Software Maintenance and Reengineering (CSMR).
- International Workshop on Principles of Software Evolution (IWPSE).
- International Workshop on Evolution of Large-scale Industrial Software Applications (ELISA).
- IEEE International Workshop on Web Site Evolution (WSE).
- International Workshop on Evaluation & Evolution of Component Composition (EECC).
- IEEE International Workshop on Program Comprehension (IWPC).
- Feedback, Evolution And Software Technology (FEAST): http://www.cs.mdx.ac.uk/staffpages/mml/feast2/papers.html (last access: 20/1/2006)
- Research Links to Explore and Advance Software Evolution (RELEASE).
- Research Institute for Software Evolution (RISE), Durham, England.
- Consortium for Software Engineering (CSER), Canada.
- IEEE Transactions on Software Engineering (TSE).
- ACM Transactions on Software Engineering and Methodology (TOSEM)
- Requirements Engineering Journal, Springer-Verlag.
- Journal of Systems and Software, Elsevier.
- International Conference on Software Engineering (ICSE)
- IEEE International Requirements Engineering Conference (RE).
- ACM Sigsoft Foundations of Software Engineering (FSE)
- Asia-Pacific Software Engineering Conference (APSEC).
- IEEE/ACM International Conference on Automated Software Engineering (ASE).
- ACM Sigsoft Software Engineering Notes (SEN)

Why this book?

Studies of software evolution and feedback should be central to our knowledge, understanding and practice of software development. Yet, ironically, it has received relatively little attention in the field of software engineering, which tends to focus more on initial development. While a small number of other texts on the subject of software evolution or software maintenance are known, they are either no longer available in print form (e.g., M.M. Lehman and L.A. Belady, Academic Press, 1985) or address the general topics in software maintenance (e.g., J. Martin and C. McClure, Prentice-Hall, 1983; G. Parikh, John Wiley & Sons, 1986; L.J. Arthur, John Wiley & Sons, 1988; T.M. Pigoski, John

Wiley & Sons, 1996; A.A. Takang and P.A. Grubb, Int. Thomson Computer Press, 1996; and general software engineering texts). There is thus a huge gap in the area of software evolution and feedback that this book in part attempts to fill.

The story of the book

This book has humble beginnings. One day, following the fourth 'Feedback, Evolution And Software Technology'(FEAST 2000) workshop, which was held in June 2000, Lehman (who was the initiator and chair of the series of four FEAST workshops between 1994 and 2000) invited me to produce the proceedings of the last FEAST workshop based on the accepted position and full papers. Upon analysis of these pre-prints (which were edited by Fernández-Ramil), it seemed to me that there was little new to be gained by producing a hardcopy proceedings because the pre-prints were already available on FEAST's website. Instead, I proposed a completely new effort in creating an edited book of chapters, involving authors active in the field of software evolution and not necessarily restricted to only those involved with FEAST.

Seeing this as a possible follow-up book to the Lehman–Belady's book of 1985, Lehman supported the proposed idea but not without cautionary advise on the complexity and volume of the task that would necessarily follow this decision. Despite my guarded optimism, I still underestimated the effort it would take to bring together the works of diverse researchers, many of whom had to start from scratch to submit their chapter. I have no doubt that this effort would have been even more arduous had it not been for the support by the co-editors (Fernández-Ramil and Perry) and Lehman throughout this project. Working with the contributors over numerous iterations, the book has taken nearly five years of elapsed time to complete. It is worth mentioning that a significant contributor to this span of time was that several of us changed institutions and, in one case, changed country as well. While the task has been monumental, it has been a worthwhile experience, the results of which, I hope, will serve the researchers, practitioners and learners in the field.

London, Ontario, January 2006.

Nazim H. Madhavji

Acknowledgements

This book is the result of many people's contributions and we are truly indebted to all of them.

We would first like to thank deeply all the contributors of the chapters in this book. It was our pleasure to work and interact with them. Without their efforts, clearly, this book would not have been possible. They are thus the unsung heroes of this book! They also provided the supporting material (presentation slides and questions and responses or discussion points) to enhance the learning experience.

The lustre on the chapters is in part credited to the anonymous reviewers to whom we are quite indebted. Their feedback was sincerely appreciated by the contributors and by the editors of course, and it helped to improve the individual chapters considerably and, hence, also the book overall.

We also thank sincerely Wiley's most friendly and supportive staff for being patient with us, for it did take its time to bring the book to fruition. Their expert advice was crucial in helping us to size and structure the book and in designing the cover. In addition, they took practically all the burden away in formatting and standardizing the chapters for consistency and coordinating with the many contributors throughout the production process. All such work has contributed immensely to the book's quality.

These acknowledgements would not be complete without looking back at the roots. This book rests fundamentally on the recognition and success of foundational work in the field of software evolution and feedback. Starting with Lehman and Belady's seminal work on *system growth dynamics*, which ignited the field of software evolution in the 1970s, Lehman and colleagues have since formulated a set of *laws* of software evolution and are in search for a theory of software evolution. This has influenced the work of many other researchers as evidenced by the diversity of the topics represented in this book.

Finally, we are most grateful to our respective institutions and Madhavji would like to thank the Natural Science and Engineering Research Council (NSERC) of Canada for partially supporting this work.

Nazim H. Madhavji
Juan C. Fernández-Ramil
Dewayne E. Perry

Editors' Biographies

Nazim H. Madhavji is a Professor in the Department of Computer Science at the University of Western Ontario, Canada. From 2000 to 2002, he held a Chair in Software Engineering at the University of Otago, Dunedin, New Zealand. From 1983 to 2000, he was with the School of Computer Science, McGill University, Montreal, Canada.

His research interests are in software requirements, software architectures, software evolution, software processes, software quality and measurements, empirical studies and intersection of all of these areas. He has published in scholarly journals and conferences in these areas and teaches at Western in these subjects and gives seminars and courses in the private sector. He led a number of research projects involving large corporations in Canada.

He has edited a book (with El Emam) on software processes (IEEE Computer Society Press, 1999); was a Guest Editor of journal issues: IEE/BCS Software Engineering Journal (Sept. 1991), IEEE Transactions on Software Engineering (Dec. 1993) and Journal of Software Process: Improvement and Practice (1998); and was, for many years, Chair of the IEEE Computer Society's TCSE Committee on Software Process.

He is on the Editorial Boards of the Journal of Software Maintenance and Evolution and the Journal of Software Process Improvement and Practice; and has been on the organizing and program committees of a number of software engineering conferences and workshops. He is a member of the IEEE Computer Society.

Juan C. Fernández-Ramil has been a Lecturer since 2001 at The Open University. Born in Caracas and raised partly in La Coruña, Spain, and in Caracas, he started professional work in 1986 with assignments at a re-instrumentation project at the Puerto La Cruz Oil Refinery in Venezuela and at a local phone equipment manufacturer. In 1988 he joined Lagoven, a large oil company, where we participated in several plant modernization and informatization projects. In 1995 he came to the United Kingdom as a British Council-Fundayacucho Chevening Scholar to study Control Systems and Information Technology at UMIST, Manchester. In 1996 he was attracted by the software evolution field, working first as a Research Assistant and then as a Research Fellow at the Imperial College London, as a member of the UK EPSRC funded Feedback, Evolution And Software Technology, FEAST, team led by M. M. Lehman. His interests include theoretical and empirical laws of software evolution, their practical implications, estimation methods and application of simulation modelling to empirical studies. He has recently led the UK EPSRC-funded project Continual Resource ESTimation for Evolving Software – CRESTES GR/S90782/01 (2004–2005). He has presented tutorials on software evolution themes at the ICSM, ESEC-FSE and PROFES conferences and has been a panelist at ICSM. He has served in program committees including ICSE, ESEC-FSE, ICSM, CSMR and Prosim. He has reviewed submissions to several journals, including IEEE Transactions on Software Engineering and the Journal of Software Maintenance and Evolution: Research and Practice. He is currently a member of the ACM and of the ERCIM Working Group on Software Evolution. He holds a BSc degree in Electronic Engineering, first in his class, Cum Laude (1986), a Master in Management Engineering (1993), both from the Simon Bolivar University, Caracas, Venezuela, and a PhD degree (2003) from the Computing Dept, Imperial College London.

Dewayne E. Perry is the Motorola Regents Chair of Software Engineering at The University of Texas at Austin and the Director of the Empirical Software Engineering Laboratory (ESEL).

The first half of his computing career was spent as a professional programmer and a consulting software architect and designer. The next 16 years were spent as a software engineering research MTS at Bell Laboratories in Murray Hill, NJ. He has been at UT Austin since 2000.

His research interests include empirical studies in software engineering, software architecture and software development processes. He is particularly interested in the process of transforming requirements into architectures and the creation of dynamic, self-managing and reconfigurable architectures.

He is a member of ACM SIGSOFT and the IEEE Computer Society, has been Co-Editor in Chief of Wiley's Software Process: Improvement & Practice as well as an associate editor of IEEE Transactions on Software Engineering, and has served as organizing chair, program chair and program committee member on various software engineering conferences.

List of Contributors

William W. Agresti
Department of Information Technology
Johns Hopkins University
Rockville, Maryland, USA

Dharini Balasubramaniam
Department of Computer Science
University of St Andrews
North Haugh, UK

Sue Black
School of Computing, Information Systems and Mathematics
South Bank University
London, UK

Barry Boehm
Computer Science Department
University of Southern California
Los Angeles, California, USA

Elizabeth Burd
Department of Computer Science
University of Durham
Durham, UK

Andrea Capiluppi
Dipartimento di Automatica e Informatica
Politecnico di Torino
Torino, Italy

Stephen Cook
School of Computer Science, Cybernetics & Electronic Engineering
University of Reading
Whiteknights, UK

R. Mark Greenwood
School of Computer Science
University of Manchester
Manchester, UK

Lindsay Groves
School of Mathematics, Statistics and Computer Science
Victoria University of Wellington
Wellington, New Zealand

Rachel Harrison
Department of Computer Science
University of Reading
Reading, UK

LiGuo Huang
Computer Science Department
University of Southern California
Los Angeles, California, USA

Magne Jørgensen
Simula Research Laboratory
Norway

Graham Kirby
Department of Computer Science
University of St Andrews
North Haugh, UK

Robert Laddaga
Massachusetts Institute of Technology (MIT)
Cambridge, Massachusetts, USA

Meir M. Lehman
School of Computing
Middlesex University
London, UK

Nazim H. Madhavji
Department of Computer Science
University of Western Ontario
Ontario, Canada

Michael Mattsson
Blekinge Institute of Technology
Department of Software Engineering and Computer Science
Ronneby, Sweden

Ken Mayes
School of Computer Science
University of Manchester
Manchester, UK

Eve Mitleton-Kelly
London School of Economics
London, UK

Roland T. Mittermeir
Institut für Informatik-Systeme
Universität Klagenfurt
Austria

Maurizio Morisio
Dipartimento di Automatica e Informatica
Politecnico di Torino
Torino, Italy

Ron Morrison
Department of Computer Science
University of St Andrews
North Haugh, UK

Vivek Nanda
CHS IT Quality Manager
Motorola Corporation
Horsham, Pennsylvania, USA

Takako Nakatani
S-Lagoon Co.,Ltd.
Chiba, Japan

Dewayne E. Perry
Electrical and Computer Engineering
The University of Texas at Austin
Austin, TX, USA

Michael R. Poppleton
School of Electronics and Computer Science
University of Southampton
Southampton, UK

Juan C. Fernández-Ramil
Computing Department
Faculty of Maths and Computing and Centre for Research in computing
The Open University
Walton Hall, Milton Keynes, UK

David Raffo
School of Business
Portland State University
Portland, Oregon, USA

Paul Robertson
Massachusetts Institute of Technology (MIT)
Cambridge, Massachusetts, USA

Suzanne Robertson
The Atlantic Systems Guild Ltd.
London UK

Aled Sage
Department of Computer Science
University of St Andrews
North Haugh, UK

Walt Scacchi
Institute for Software Research
University of California
Irvine, California USA

Norman F. Schneidewind
Naval Postgraduate School
California, USA

Wykeen Seet
School of Computer Science
University of Manchester
Manchester, UK

Dag Sjøberg
Simula Research Laboratory
Norway

Howard E. Shrobe
Massachusetts Institute of Technology (MIT)
Cambridge, Massachusetts, USA

Tetsuo Tamai
Graduate School of Arts and Sciences
University of Tokyo
Tokyo, Japan

Josée Tassé
Department of Applied Statistical & Computer Sciences
University of New Brunswick
New Brunswick, Canada

Władysław M. Turski
Institute of Informatics
Warsaw University
Warsaw, Poland

Joseph Vandeville
Northrop Grumman Corporation
Integrated Systems Sector
Melbourne, Florida, USA

Brian C. Warboys
School of Computer Science
University of Manchester
Manchester, UK

Paul Wernick
Department of Computer Science
University of Hertfordshire
Hatfield, England

Part One

Software Evolution

This part of the book covers the chapters with a strong focus on 'evolution'. The abstracts below give an overview of the chapters that follow.

Chapter 1: Software Evolution

This chapter discusses *evolution* in the context of software, software technology, the software process and related domains, describing various properties, aspects and implications of the phenomenon as observed and studied over many years.

Chapter 2: A Nontraditional View of the Dimensions of Software Evolution

Software evolution is usually considered in terms of corrections, improvements and enhancements. While helpful, this approach does not take into account the fundamental dimensions of well-engineered software systems (the domains, experience and process) and how they themselves evolve and affect the evolution of systems for which they are the context. Each dimension is discussed and provided with examples to illustrate its various aspects and to summarize how evolution in that dimension affects system evolution. This holistic approach provides a deep understanding of evolution and how evolution might be effectively managed.

Chapter 3: IT Legacy Systems: Enabling Environments That Reduce the Legacy Problem: A Complexity Perspective

Information Technology (IT) 'legacy' systems are often seen as a problem, particularly when they are *systems that no longer support the current business objectives or are inhibiting future developments* (for example, the creation of new financial products). Many IT legacy systems are old, but there is evidence that new systems quickly become 'legacy' in the sense that they do not fully support current and future business objectives. Because the reasons for the emergence of legacy systems are not fully understood, the same behaviour is repeated. One such reason is the mistaken belief that legacy is merely a technical issue involving only computer software and hardware. This, however, is often not the case. Legacy is a socio-technical issue with the 'socio' part playing a greater role than is recognized. This chapter will use two case studies to illustrate this assertion and to suggest ways of creating an enabling environment that may reduce the legacy problem. Complexity theory will be used to provide some insights and three concepts will be introduced: co-evolution, feedback and social ecosystem.

Chapter 4: Facets of Software Evolution

Research on software evolution focuses, on the one hand, on empirical investigations that study changes in long-living software systems, and on the other hand, on methods and tools supporting and controlling software evolution. The results of this research do not, however, always fully hit home. One reason for this might be that misunderstandings arise when people argue on the basis of the token semantics of the word *evolution*. This chapter attempts to contribute to the understanding of software evolution by considering the relationship between software, its producers and its users. To do so, it first analyses the precise meanings of the words *software* and *evolution*. On the basis of these definitions a stratification of the artefacts under consideration is proposed, which shows the different consequences of evolution in the various strata. On the basis of the consideration that the evolutionary nature of software depends on the way how software engineers can cope with changing requirements, the categories *module, design unit, architecture, system* and *system-of-system* are introduced as reference points for different evolutionary options. The chapter concludes with an example demonstrating how arguments raised on these categories are reflected in a particular case.

Chapter 5: Evolution in Software Systems: Foundations of the SPE Classification Scheme

The SPE taxonomy of evolving software systems, first proposed by Lehman in 1980, is re-examined in this work. The primary concepts of software evolution are related to generic theories of evolution, particularly Dawkins' concept of replicator, to the hermeneutic tradition in philosophy and to Kuhn's concept of paradigm. These concepts provide the foundations that are needed for understanding the phenomenon of software evolution and for refining the definitions of the SPE categories. In particular, this work argues that a software system should be defined as of type P if its controlling stakeholders have made a strategic decision that the system must comply with a single paradigm in its representation of domain knowledge. The proposed refinement of SPE is expected to provide a more productive basis, for developing testable hypotheses and models about possible differences in the evolution of E- and P-type systems, than is provided by the original scheme.

Chapter 6: A Simple Model of Software System Evolutionary Growth

With some arbitrary but natural assumptions, a simple model for software evolutionary growth is constructed. The model is found to be in agreement with empirical data. Its application to some hypothetical growth scenarios yields surprisingly realistic patterns.

Chapter 7: Statistical Modelling of Software Evolution Processes

A number of interesting phenomena can be observed when the evolution of an object-oriented software system is analysed over a series of versions or releases. This chapter proposes a framework for the study of object-oriented software, reports the results of empirical case studies and presents the evolution patterns discovered through the analysis. The results include the observation that within a given class tree the size of classes measured in lines of code appears to follow a negative binomial distribution. The empirically fitted values of the distribution parameters p and k are linearly related when observed over versions. A visualisation approach to monitor the evolution of object-oriented applications is offered.

Chapter 8: Software Requirements Changes Due to External Factors

This chapter describes how changes in the environment of a software system can affect the requirements for a software system over a period. A case study is presented along with an *instrument* (a questionnaire) used to investigate the impact of such changes over a period of four years in the environment of a software system. During this study, the state of the system's requirements, as well as that of the environment, were assessed at different times during system development and re-development. From this experience, the key contribution of this chapter is a detailed insight into how environmental changes can lead to requirements changes that, in turn, can result in software evolution. Also, three observations made are: (a) it *is* possible to construct an instrument to periodically assess environmental changes; (b) the use of such an instrument can facilitate timely identification of new requirements, which can help in prolonging the longevity of the system; and (c) many new requirements *germinate* slowly, as opposed to dramatically, during the changes in the environment.

Chapter 9: Understanding Open Source Software Evolution

This chapter examines the evolution of free/open-source software (F/OSS) and how their evolutionary patterns compare to prior studies of software evolution of proprietary (or closed-source) software. F/OSS development focuses attention to systems like the GNU/Linux operating system, Apache Web server and Mozilla Web browser, though there are now thousands of F/OSS projects underway. As these systems are being ever more widely used, questions regarding their evolution are of considerable interest. This chapter is organized around four themes. First, it presents a brief survey of empirical studies of software evolution. Second, it presents selected data and evidence that has begun to appear that characterizes change and evolution patterns associated with the evolution of F/OSS. Third, it presents a brief review of models and theories of evolution from domains outside of software. The fourth and last section addresses whether it is necessary to reconsider the models, laws and theory and how they can be modified and supplemented to better account for the observations and findings emerging in studies of new software development processes and environments, such as those associated with the development of F/OSS.

Chapter 10: Structural Analysis of Open Source Systems

Understanding how software systems evolve is one of the most intriguing issues in empirical studies of software engineering. In the study presented in this chapter, we take 25 software systems released as Open Source, and observe their evolution, recognizing some evolutionary patterns. In particular, we analysed the structure of the source folders, visualising them as a tree containing branches (source folders) and leaves (source files). In doing so, we have been able to distinguish three main evolution patterns, basically related to how the folders evolve on a vertical and horizontal dimension. We have called them *horizontal expansion, vertical expansion and vertical shrinking*. The chapter briefly discusses three Open Source Software (OSS) systems that exemplify each of the three evolution patterns found.

Chapter 11: A Study of Software Evolution at Different Levels of Granularity

The chapter presents a case study with a unique slant on the study of evolution by presenting examples at different levels of granularity. The three levels investigated are the system level, which shows gross changes in the application such as frequency of changes, the function level showing the changes to the architecture of the system and finally the data level showing changes in data complexity. This chapter argues that studying evolution at three levels provides a fuller and more in depth understanding of the process of software evolution. The higher levels can be used to provide essential data for the cost benefit analysis and hence justification of preventative maintenance, but additional studies at the lower levels provide concrete examples in a form suitable to demonstrate to the management the problems that need to be dealt with. This chapter adopts the stance that ultimately prevention is better than cure. Therefore, lessons learned from the study of the process of evolution are used to formulate a number of recommendations that can, if followed, assist software developers to produce software that will ultimately be more supportive of the process of software evolution.

Chapter 12: The Role of Ripple Effect in Software Evolution

The ripple effect, as described in this chapter, measures source code from two points of view: (a) impact, or how likely it is that a change to a particular module is going to cause problems in the rest of a program or system; (b) the complexity of a particular module, program or software system. One specific use of the ripple effect is to measure the complexity of the first version of a system, then use this as a benchmark for comparison with subsequent releases of the system. If the system becomes more complex over time, (which it probably would be expected to), ripple effect can be used to highlight where that increase in complexity is occurring and steps taken to minimise unnecessary complexity. As ripple effect is used during the maintenance of software systems, several software maintenance models are described, which include accounting for ripple effect as one of their stages. Ripple effect as part of a suite of software measures can be used to address the decline of systems over time by providing change data that facilitates the optimal modelling of system trends.

Chapter 13: The Impact of Software-Architecture Compliance on System Evolution

This chapter discusses how the evolution of a software system is influenced by its underlying system architecture. When the architecture is flexible, and can change dynamically, evolution may be more easily accommodated than would otherwise be the case. Compliant architectures, which are those that may be tailored to fit the needs of particular applications, fit this description. The degree of compliance can be measured by the goodness of fit of the application to the architecture. This degree of compliance can be used to monitor and inform the evolutionary development of the system. In this chapter, the scheduling policy of Process*Web*, a multi-user process support system, is used as an example. The 'goodness of fit' of the scheduling policy, and its impact on the evolution of the system, are discussed. Finally, the monitoring of a system's degree of compliance is discussed in order that its evolution may be better understood.

Chapter 14: Comparison of Three Evaluation Methods for Object-Oriented Framework Evolution

Object-oriented frameworks, a kind of reusable design asset, have become a common software reuse technology in object-oriented software development. As with all software, object-oriented frameworks tend to evolve. Once the framework has been deployed, new versions of a framework cause high maintenance cost for the products built with the framework since all products need to be updated. This fact in combination with the high costs of developing and evolving an object-oriented framework due to its future reuse makes it important to have controlled and predictable evolution of the functionality and costs of the framework. This chapter presents three methods that provide management with information that will make it possible to make well-informed decisions about the evolution of the framework: (i) Evolution identification using historical information, (ii) Stability assessment and (iii) Distribution of development effort. The methods have been applied to between one to three different frameworks, both in the proprietary and the commercial domains.

Chapter 15: Formal Perspectives on Software Evolution: From Refinement to Retrenchment

The discipline of formal methods is concerned with the use of mathematical techniques to capture precise system specifications, and to transform these into verifiably correct programs. As these techniques mature, formal methods researchers are now taking a broader view of software development, and considering how evolution of such specifications and programs may be formally supported. This chapter discusses various ways in which formal methods can contribute to the evolutionary development of verifiably correct software. This discussion centres around model-based specification notations and associated development techniques, as exemplified by VDM, Z, B and the refinement calculus. The chapter begins by introducing the refinement calculus and outlining two ways in which program refinement can support evolutionary development. The chapter then introduces a recent generalisation of refinement, called *retrenchment*. Some of the factors motivating this generalisation are shown to be relevant to the evolution problem, and a sketch of a potential retrenchment-based method for modelling evolution is drawn. Discussion is supported by considering elements of realistic examples.

Chapter 16: Background and Approach to Development of a Theory of Software Evolution

Studies of software evolution since 1968 have yielded an empirical, data-derived body of knowledge that includes industrial data, generalizations about that data, observed behavioural patterns and invariants of industrial software process evolution systems and attributes. The phenomenon and its main characteristics are discussed in Chapters 1 and 27 of this book. These observations and the generalizations derived from them provide the basis for a set of axioms and theorems, a starting point for the development of a Theory of Software Evolution. The theory is illustrated by a statement and outline proof of a Principle of Software Uncertainty. As a theory is developed and the theorems proven, their interpretation provides support for laws, rules and guidelines already developed, yields others, guides good practice in software evolution planning, management and control and suggests a more responsive and effective evolution process and improved products. This is of major significance in a world evermore dependent on computers and software that must be continually evolved to maintain it compatible with a changing world.

1

Software Evolution

Meir Lehman and Juan C. Fernández-Ramil

This chapter is a revised version of the paper by Lehman MM and Ramil JF, Software Evolution and Software Evolution Processes, Annals of Software Engineering, special issue on Software Process-based Software Engineering, vol. 14, 2002, pp. 275–309, with kind permission of Springer Science and Business Media.

1.1 Introduction

1.1.1 Evolution

Evolution describes a phenomenon that is widespread across many domains. Natural species, societies, cities, concepts, theories, ideas all evolve over time, each in its own context. The term reflects a process of *progressive*, for example beneficial, change in the attributes of the evolving entity or that of one or more of its constituent elements. What is accepted as progressive must be determined in each context.

It is also appropriate to apply the term evolution when long-term change trends are beneficial even though isolated or short sequences of changes may appear degenerative. Thus it may be regarded as the antithesis of decay. For example, an entity or a collection of entities may be said to be evolving if their value or fitness is increasing over time; Individually or collectively they are becoming more meaningful, more complete or more adapted to a changing environment.

In most situations, evolution results from concurrent changes in several, even many, of the properties of the evolving entity or collection of entities. Individual changes are generally small relative to the entity as a whole, but even then their impact may be significant. In areas such as software, many allegedly independent changes may be implemented in parallel. As changes occur as a part of the overall evolution, properties no longer appropriate may be removed or may disappear and new properties may emerge.

The evolution phenomena as observed in different domains vary widely. To distinguish between domains, one may start by classifying them according to their most evident characteristics. A study of common factors shared by subsets of their entities, distinctions between them and their individual evolutionary patterns may suggest specific relationships between evolution and other properties and indicate how individual patterns and trends are driven, directed and even controlled.

One could, perhaps, increase understanding of software evolution by studying instances of the phenomenon in other domains. The discussion here is, however, limited to the computing and software fields.

1.1.2 Interpretation of the Term Evolution in the Context of Software
The term *evolution in the context of software* may be interpreted in two distinct ways, discussed more fully in Chapter 16 [Lehman and Ramil 2001b]. The most widespread view is that the important evolution issues in software engineering are those that concern the *means* whereby it may be directed, implemented and controlled. Matters deserving attention and the investment of resources relate to *methods, tools* and *activities* whereby software and the systems it controls may be implemented from conception to realisation and usage, and then evolved to adapt it to changing operational environments. One is seeking continuing satisfactory execution with maximum confidence in the results at minimum cost and delay in a changing world.

Means include mechanisms and tools whereby evolution may be achieved according to plan in a systematic and controlled manner. The focus of this approach, termed the *verbal* approach, is on the *how* of software evolution. Work addressing these issues has been widely presented and discussed, for example, at a series of meetings titled Principles of Software Evolution (e.g. IWPSE 2004).

An alternative approach may also be taken. This less common, but equally, important view seeks an understanding of the *nature* of the evolution phenomenon, what drives it, its impact, and so on. It is a *nounal* view investigating the *what* and *why* of evolution. Far fewer investigators (e.g. Lehman *et al.* 1969–2002, Chong Hok Yuen 1981, Kemerer and Slaughter 1999, Antón and Potts 2001, Nanda and Madhavji 2002, Capiluppi *et al.* 2004) have adopted it. It is driven by the realisation that more insight into and better understanding of the evolution phenomenon must lead to improved methods and tools for its planning, management and implementation. It will, for example, help identify areas in which research effort is most likely to yield significant benefit. The need for *understanding* and its significance will become clearer when the nature of, at least, the industrial software evolution process as a multi-loop, multi-level, multi-agent feedback system (Lehman 1994) is appreciated. Failure to fully appreciate that fact and its consequences can result in unexpected, even anti-intuitive responses when software is executed and used.

There is a view that the term evolution should be restricted to software *change* (e.g. Mittermeir 2006). However, under this interpretation, important activities such as defect fixing, functional extension and restructuring would be implicitly excluded. Other authors have interpreted evolution as a stage in the operational lifetime of a software system, intermediate between initial implementation and a stage called *servicing* (Bennett and Rajlich 2000, Rajlich and Bennett 2000). These and still other interpretations are covered by the areas of evolution presented below. They are, therefore, not separately identified in the present chapter.

1.2 The Evolution of Large Software Systems
1.2.1 Early Work
As stated in Lehman's first law of software evolution, (Lehman 1974), it is now generally accepted (e.g. Bennett and Rajlich 2000, Pfleeger 2001, Cook *et al.* 2006) that

E-type[1] software must be continually adapted and changed if it is to remain satisfactory in use. Universal experience that software requires continual *maintenance* (as evolution was then termed) was first publicly discussed at the Garmisch Conference[2] (Naur and Randell 1968) and viewed as a matter of serious concern.

At about that time, Lehman reported on his study of the IBM programming process (Lehman 1969), though his report did not become generally available till much later (Lehman and Belady 1985). *Inter alia*, the report examined and modelled the continuing change process being applied to IBM's OS360-370 operating system. Preliminary models of that system's evolution were derived from measures and models of release properties. Refined versions of these were subsequently proposed as tools for planning, management and control of sequences of releases (Belady and Lehman 1972, Lehman 1974, 1980).

Recognition of the software process as a feedback system brought the realisation that the study of the process and its evolution must consider that fact, if more effective management and process improvement was to be achieved. This observation triggered an investigation of the phenomenon initially termed *Program Growth Dynamics* (Belady and Lehman 1972) and later *Program Evolution Dynamics* (Lehman 1974). The resultant study produced not only fundamental insights into the nature and properties of the software *process* but also into those of its products. Early studies concentrated on OS360-370 release data; later studies involved other systems (Lehman 1980, Lehman and Belady 1985). All in all, the results of these studies greatly increased understanding of the software evolution phenomenon and identified practices and tools for its support (Lehman 1980).

1.2.2 Large Programs

Lehman and Belady's early work on software growth dynamics and evolution concluded that evolution is intrinsic to *large* programs. This adjective has been variously interpreted as applying to programs ranging in size from 50 and 500 thousand of lines of code (Klocs). Subsequently, Lehman suggested that such an arbitrary boundary was not very useful in the evolution context. It appeared highly unlikely that one could identify, even approximately, a single bound over a spectrum of programs such that those on either side of the divide displayed different properties. Moreover, if size were a major factor in determining evolutionary properties, one would expect these to change for programs of different size.

Moreover, it was seen as unlikely that all would appear at around the same loc level, independently of, for example, application, organisational, managerial, process and computational factors. Any of these might relate to the emergence of disciplined evolutionary behaviour. As a result of considerations such as these, Lehman suggested that the observed phenomena were more likely to be linked to properties related to characteristics of software development, usage and application environments and processes or of their products. He, therefore proposed that a program should be termed *large* if '... it had been developed or maintained in a management structure involving at least two groups' (Lehman 1979), that is, subject to, at least, two levels of direct management. This property appeared sufficient to explain many of the observed evolution dynamics properties of the systems studied.

---

[1] Defined later in this chapter.
[2] See statement by H. R. Gillette in the Garmisch conference report, P. Naur and B. Randell eds. (1968), p. 111 in the original version.

This definition followed from the recognition of the fact that development by an individual or small group subject to the direct control of a single individual, is quite different to one in which there are two or more management levels. When a single manager is in day-to-day control the focus of goals and activities will be a matter of ongoing discussion and decision within the group, subject to a final approval by the manager. With two or more groups and managers at two or more levels of management, each level, each manager, each group will develop its individual goals, understanding, language, interpretations etc. Communication between the members of any individual group will tend to be continual and informal. Between groups and levels it will tend to be discontinuous and more formal. This will cause divergence of the terminologies, technologies, interpretations, goals, and so on as perceived and applied in and by the separate groups. Such divergence is clearly a major source of the 'large program problem' (Brooks 1975) and that problem, in turn, appears to be one of the drivers of software evolution. It must also be recognised that in cooperative multi-group activity, it is human nature for individual groups and their managers to seek to optimise their own immediate results, overlooking or ignoring the impact on other groups and on the overall, long-term consequence.

Furthermore, programs developed by the joint effort of multiple groups are functionally rich and structurally complex. Their effective development and use requires the application and integration of many skills and approaches and communication between participants. It was thought at one time (Lehman 1979) that the resultant activities will favour the emergence of evolutionary characteristics associated with programs that have traditionally been termed *large*. This further supported the above definition of *largeness*. However, the latter was still considered unsatisfying as a complete explanation for the intrinsic need for software evolution.

1.3 Program Classification

1.3.1 The SPE Program Classification Schema

Despite the revised definition, the concept of *largeness* appeared unsatisfactory as the fundamental basis for a study of software evolution. To address these concerns, a program classification scheme, not involving a concept of size was proposed. Initially, this defined programs of types S, P and E (Lehman 1980, 1982, Pfleeger 2001) as discussed below. The third is the most closely related to a discussion of software evolution. Though not a *defining* property of the phenomenon, it has been shown as inevitable for that class of program if users are to remain satisfied with the results of its use. Subsequently, it was realised that the classification is equally relevant to computer applications, application domains, application and computing systems and so on (Lehman 1991).

1.3.2 S-type Applications and Software
1.3.2.1 Definition

A program is defined as being of type S if it can be shown that it satisfies the necessary and sufficient condition that it is *correct* in the full mathematical sense relative to a pre-stated formal *specification* (Lehman 1980, 1982). Thus a demonstration, by means of *proof* for example, that it satisfies the specification (Hoare 1969, 1971), suffices for contractual completion and program acceptance. Where it is possible, for example with the exception of systems where decidability issues arise (Apt and Kozen 1986), demonstration of correctness is also a matter of mathematical skill and the availability of appropriate tools. The proof demonstrates that program properties satisfy the specification *in its entirety*. Such verification suffices for program acceptability if the specification is satisfactory to intended users and meets their requirements. That is, the specification will have been validated and accepted. Completion of verification then justifies contractual acceptance of the program.

The definition assumes implicitly that a specification can be predetermined before development begins and that, once fixed, learning during the course of the subsequent process is restricted to determination of methods of solution and the choice of a *best* method (in the context of constraints applying in the solution domain). Implementation is driven purely by the implementers' knowledge, understanding and experience.

The designation S was applied to S-type systems to indicate the role played by the *specification* in determining product properties.

1.3.2.2 Validation

The above implies that verification with respect to the specification completes the S-type development process. If satisfaction of the specification by the final program product is (contractually) accepted as sufficient by both developer and client, verification leads directly to acceptance. Practical application of the S-type development process, however, requires that the specification is *valid* in the context of its intented use. Validation of a specification is, in general, nontrivial.

1.3.2.3 The S-type in a Changing Domain

Even if initially satisfactory, changes in the use of an S-type program or in its operational environments or circumstances can cause it to become unsatisfactory. In this event, the specification, the problem or both must be revised. By definition, this means that a *new* program based on a *new* specification is being implemented. However, the new derivation is likely to be based on previous versions of the specification and program, that is, the latter are modified rather than recreated. Conceptually, however, evolution of S-type programs is restricted to the initial development. It consists of a discrete sequence of processes each of which includes specification revision, program derivation and verification.

1.3.2.4 Formal Specification

Application of the S-type concept is limited to formally specifiable problems. It also requires that a procedure for computation of the solution is known or can be developed within budgetary and time constraints. In other words, there are four conditions that the S-type program must satisfy in order to be legitimately termed as such. First, the problem can be rigorously, that is, formally, stated. Second, the problem must be solvable algorithmically. Third, it must be feasible to prove that the program is correct with respect to the formal specification. Last, but not least, the specification must be complete, that is, final for the moment (see Section 1.3.2.3), in terms of the stakeholders' current requirements. It must explicitly state *all* functional and nonfunctional requirements of concern to the stakeholders and, in particular, clients and users. Nonfunctional requirements include the range and precision of variables, maximum storage space, execution time limits, and so on.

1.3.2.5 The S-type in Practice

S-type domains are exemplified by, though not restricted to, those in which it is required to compute values of mathematical functions or formally defined transformations as, for example, in program compilers or proof procedures. This is so because in these domains the development process may be followed in its purest form. Its use in other domains is more limited, but nevertheless retains both theoretical and practical importance. Its theoretical importance arises from the fact that the S-type represents an ideal, specification-driven, development process where the developers exercise maximum intellectual control on the program properties of interest. One example of its practical importance is briefly discussed in Section 1.3.3.2. In the vast majority of domains, however, the S-type program process cannot be implemented for a variety of reasons: The most common, the difficulty of creating a formal specification which is complete and final, in the sense implied above. It is then that the E-type discussed below becomes relevant.

1.3.3 E-type Applications and Software
1.3.3.1 Definition

Type E programs were originally defined as 'programs that mechanise a human or societal activity' (Lehman 1980). The definition was subsequently amended to include all programs that 'operate in or address a problem or activity of the real world'.

A key property of the type is that the system becomes an integral part of the domains within which it operates and that it addresses. It must reflect within itself all those properties of the domains that in any way affect the outcome of computations. Thus, to remain satisfactory as applications, domains and their properties change, E-type programs must be continually changed and updated. They must be *E*volved. Software evolution is a direct consequence and reflection of ongoing changes in a dynamic real world. Operating systems, databases, transaction systems, control systems are all instances of the type, even though they may include elements that are of type S in isolation.

1.3.3.2 S-Type Programs in the Real World

S-type elements can also contribute greatly to an E-type system despite the fact that it is addressing a real-world application. Given the appropriate circumstances, their use can provide important quality and evolvability benefits. Once embedded, they will, of course be subject to all the evolutionary pressures that the host system is subject to, even though shielded by other system elements. As the latter are changed to reflect an evolving application, changing application and operational domains (hard and soft) under which it operates, the S-type program will also require adaptation by changes to its specification and, possibly, its interfaces. One cannot always expect it to remain static, a matter that is particularly important in considering component-based architectures and the use of components typically termed *Commercial Off-The-Shelf* (COTS) (Lehman and Ramil 2000b).

1.3.3.3 Domain and System Bounds

The number of properties of an E-type application and of the domains in which it is developed, evolved, operated, executed and used is unbounded. Clearly they cannot be explicitly identified, enumerated or uniquely defined. Hence, selection of those to be reflected in the system requires abstraction. Properties and behaviours considered irrelevant in the circumstances or to domains of interest will be discarded. Their exclusion may be explicit or implicit, conscious or unconscious, by commission or omission, recorded or unrecorded, momentarily valid or invalid. Those excluded will be unbounded in number since only a bounded number can be addressed and adopted. Moreover, each exclusion involves at least one assumption[3]. To complicate matters, the practical bounds of the many domains involved will, in general, be fuzzy and will change as knowledge and deeper understanding of the application, operational domains and acceptable solutions accumulate during development and as the intended application and the operational domains evolve. As discussed in the next section, feedback plays a central role in this process.

1.3.4 P-type Situations and Software

A further class, type P, was also defined (Lehman 1980). The type was conceived as addressing problems that appear to be fully specifiable but where the users' *concern* is with the correctness of the results of execution in the domains where they are to be *used* rather than being relative to a specification. Such programs will clearly satisfy the definition of one or other of the other types. Hence, in the context of the present discussion, their separate classification is redundant. However Cook *et al.* have recently proposed a redefinition of the type P, conceptually faithful to the initial description of the classification, but making the type P distinct from the other two types (Cook *et al.* 2006).

1.4 The Inevitability of Evolution

The *intrinsic* evolutionary nature of real-world computer usage (Lehman 1991) and, hence, of E-type software was recognised long ago (e.g. Lehman 1980, Lehman and Belady 1985, Lehman 1991, 1994). Continual correction, adaptation, enhancement and extension of any system operating in the real world was clearly necessary to ensure that it adequately reflected the state at the time of execution of all application and domain properties which influenced the real-world outcome of the problem being solved or the application being supported. It was also self evident that such change or evolution must be planned, directed and managed.

Information on the evolution of a variety of systems of differing sizes, from different application areas, developed in significantly different industrial organisations and with distinct user populations has been acquired over many years (e.g. Lehman and Parr 1976, Lehman and Belady 1985, FEAST 2001). From the very start the study demonstrated that software evolution is a phenomenon that can be observed, measured and analysed (Lehman 1980), with *feedback* playing a major role in determining the behaviour (Belady and Lehman 1972). A more complete picture and wider implications became clear over a longer period (Lehman 1994).

Figure 1.1 is the original example of supporting evidence showing a steady OS/360-370 growth trend with a superimposed ripple. The latter was interpreted as indicating feedback stabilisation and constituted the source of the suggestion that feedback plays a major role

---

[3] See Chapter 16 (Lehman and Ramil 2001b) in this book for a further discussion on the topic of assumptions.

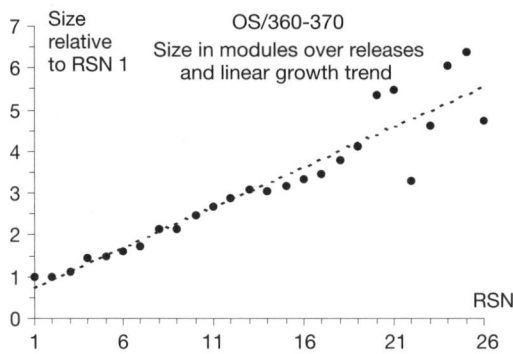

Figure 1.1 The growth of OS/360-370 over releases as a function of release sequence number (RSN)

in controlling software growth. The growth pattern following the release with sequence number 20 reinforced this conclusion being typical of the behaviour of a system[4] with excessive positive feedback. The excessive feedback here was reflected by a growth rate from RSN 20 to RSN 21, more than three times as great as any previously observed. Similar behaviour was also observed in the other systems studied (FEAST 2001), though with differences in detail.

All in all, the observations and measurements over the years on many systems confirm and advance the 1971 hypothesis (Belady and Lehman 1972) that in the long term '... the rate of growth of a system is self-regulatory, despite the fact that over the years many different causes control the selection of work implemented in each release, budgets vary, number of users reporting faults or desiring new function change, economic conditions vary and management attitudes towards system enhancement, frequency of releases and improving methodology and tool support all change'.

The feedback observation was formalised in the FEAST (*F*eedback, *E*volution *A*nd *S*oftware *T*echnology) hypothesis (Lehman 1994, FEAST 2001). This states that, in general and certainly for *mature*[5] processes, software evolution processes are multi-agent, multi-level, multi-loop feedback systems. They must be seen and treated as such if sustained improvement is to be achieved. Implications of the hypothesis have been discussed in a number of publications (FEAST 2001).

1.5 Levels of Software-Related Evolution

Evolution phenomena in software-related domains are not confined to programs and related artefacts such as specifications, designs and documentation. Applications, definitions, goals, paradigms, algorithms, languages, usage practices, the sub-processes and processes of software evolution and so on, also evolve. These evolving entities interact, impact and affect one another. If their evolution is to be disciplined, the respective evolution processes must be planned, driven and controlled. To be mastered, they must be understood and mastered individually and jointly.

---

[4] In general, a feedback system is a system in which the output modifies its input.

[5] For a discussion of the process *maturity* concept and its practical assessment see Paulk *et al.* (1993) and Zahran (1997).

In the first instance, however, one must focus on individual aspects. The consequences of interactions between the various levels of evolution require more insight than is presently available. It is mentioned here only in passing, even though it is a topic that requires further investigation.

Further discussion of software evolution is ordered by a simple classification scheme summarised below and discussed in more detail in the following sections:

I. The *development* process implements a new program or *software system* or applies *changes* to an existing system. On the basis of some identified need or desire, it yields a new artefact. The stimuli and feedback mechanisms that drive and direct this process yield gradual evolution of the application and its implementing system to adapt them to a changing environment with changing needs, opportunities and desires.

At the start of an E-type system development, knowledge and understanding of the details of the application to be supported or the problem to be solved and of approaches and methods for their solution are often undefined, even arbitrary (Turski 1981). The relative benefits of alternatives often cannot be established except through trials. Results of the latter are unlikely to be comprehensive or conclusive. The development process is a learning process in many dimensions that includes both the *matter* being addressed and the *manner* in which it is addressed. Feedback from development, change experience and evaluation of results drive the evolution process.

II. At a somewhat higher level, consider a *sequence* of *versions, releases* or *upgrades* of a program or software system each of which is the output of such a process. These incorporate changes that rectify or remove defects, implement desired improvements or extensions to system functionality, performance, quality and so on. These are made available to users by means of what is commonly termed a *release* process (Basili *et al.* 1996).

Generally intended to produce improvements to the program, the release process is often referred to as program *maintenance*. Over the years, however, it has been recognised that the term is inappropriate, even misleading, in the software context. After all, in other contexts, the term describes an activity that, in general, rectifies aging, wear, tear and other deterioration that has developed in an artefact. The purpose is to return the latter as closely as possible to a former, even pristine, state. But software as such is not subject to wear and tear. In itself, it does not deteriorate. The deterioration that software users and others sense is due to changes in its environment, in the purpose for which it was acquired, the properties of the application, those of the operational domains and the emergence of competitive products. Deterioration or misbehaviour can often be associated with assumptions implicitly or explicitly reflected in the software. These would have become invalid as a result of such external changes.

Thus one must accept that in the software context, the term *maintenance* is incompatible with common usage. What happens with software is that it is changed or adapted to *maintain* it satisfactorily in changed domains and under new circumstances as judged by stakeholders such as users. Software is *evolved* to *maintain* embedded assumptions and its compatibility valid with respect to the world as it is now. Only in this sense, is the use of the term *maintenance* appropriate in the software context.

III. The areas supported by *E*-type software also evolve. *Activities* in these may range from pure computation to embedded computers to cooperative computer-supported integrated human-machine activity. We refer to such activities generically as *application* areas. Introduction to use of successive software versions by the user community as in II inevitably changes the activity supported. It also changes the operational domain. Changes may be driven and include needs, opportunities, functionality, procedures and so on. In general, they require further changes to the system to achieve satisfactory operation. Installation and operation of an *E*-type system, drives an unending process of joint system and application evolution.

IV. The *process* of software evolution also evolves. The term refers to the aggregate of all activities involved in implementing evolution in any of the above levels. It is variously estimated that between 60 and 95% of lifetime expenditure on a software system is incurred after first release (Pigoski 1996), that is, in area II evolution (can even exceed 95% in, for example, defence applications). Hence, there is good reason to improve the process of evolution, to achieve lower costs, improved quality and faster response to user needs for change and so on.

Human dependence on computers and on the software that gives them functional and computational power is increasing at ever growing rates. Process improvement is also essential to reduce societal exposure to the consequences of high costs, computer malfunction and delays in adaptation to changing circumstances. All these and many other causes demand improvement of the means whereby evolution is achieved. And the improvement achieved must produce gains in areas such as quality, cost and response times in meeting the needs of the application areas and domains concerned. The process evolves, driven by experience and technological advances.

V. The software evolution process is a complex multi-loop feedback system[6]. Achieving full understanding and mastery of it remains a distant goal. *Modelling*, using a variety of approaches, is an essential tool for study, control and improvement of the process (Potts 1984). *Models* facilitate reasoning about it, exploration of alternatives and assessment of the impact of change, for example. As the process and understanding of it evolve, so must its models.

1.6 *Ab Initio* Implementation or Change

1.6.1 Process Steps

Ab initio implementation of a program or changes to an existing program is achieved by interacting individuals and teams in a series of discrete steps, using a variety of, generally computer-based tools. Their joint action over a period of weeks, months or even years produces the desired program or a new *version* or *release* of an existing program. The many steps or stages in such development differ widely. The first published model of the software process, the Waterfall model (Royce 1970) and its subsequent refinements (e.g. Boehm 1976, 1988), used terms such as *requirements development, specification, high-level design, detailed design, coding, unit test, integration, system test, documentation* and so on to describe these activities.

---

[6] In a multi-loop feedback system, the inputs are influenced by the outputs by many different routes or 'loops'.

Their execution is not purely sequential. Overlapping and iteration between steps in reaction to feedback or changes external to the system are inevitable as, for a variety of reasons, is repetition. Thus, execution of any step may reveal an error in an earlier step, suggest an improvement to the detailed design or reveal the impact of an underlying assumption that requires attention. The latter may relate to the application, a procedure being implemented, the current realisation, domain characteristics and so on.

Steps will, normally, operate at different conceptual and linguistic levels of abstraction and will require alternative transformation techniques. Their aggregated impact is that of a refinement process that systematically transforms an application concept into an operational software system. Program development was indeed recognised and termed *successive refinement* by Wirth (Wirth 1971). Thus even this process may be viewed as *evolutionary* because it progressively evolves the application concept to gradually produce the desired program. At the process level, it is conceptually equivalent to a process known as the *LST transformation*.

1.6.2 The LST Paradigm

The LST process, was described by its authors (Lehman *et al.* 1984) as a sequence of *transformation* steps driven by human creative and analytic power and moderated by developing experience, insight and understanding. At first sight, the paradigm may be considered abstract and remote from the complex reality of industrial software processes. This is, however, far from the truth. A brief description will suffice to clarify this in the context of the *practical* significance of the *SPE* classification (described in Section 1.3) and reveal some issues that emerge during *ab initio* software development.

LST views each step of the implementation process as the transformation of a specification into a model of that specification, in other words, of a design into an implementation. The transformation steps include verification, a demonstration that the relationship between the implemented output and the specification is *correct* in the strict mathematical sense. In this form, it is, therefore, only applicable to *S*-type applications where the formal specification, can be *complete* and, by definition, express *all* the properties the program is required to possess to be deemed satisfactory and acceptable. Only in this context is mathematical *correctness* meaningful and relevant.

The paradigm, however, also requires a process of *validation* – termed *beauty contest* in the LST paper – to complete each step. It is needed to confirm (or otherwise) at each stage of refinement that the process is heading towards a product that will satisfy the *purpose* for which it is being developed. The model fails validation if some weakness or defect is revealed, which implies that the final product is unlikely to be satisfactory in the context of the intended purpose. Unsatisfactory features may have arisen during transformation by the introduction of properties undesirable in the context of the intended purpose though not excluded by the current specification. Such features may even prove to be incompatible with the purpose, their nonexclusion by the specification reflecting an oversight or error in the latter.

The source of validation failure must be identified and rectified by modification of the specification. That is, the previous specification must be replaced by a new one[7]. When

---

[7] Though, in practice, it may be derived by modification of a previous version.

both verification and validation are successful, the new model becomes the specification of the next transformational refinement step and the process continues.

Verification is a powerful tool where applicable but can only be applied to completely and formally specified elements. It will be shown below that for programs operating in and addressing real-world applications in real-world domains, their properties cannot all be formally or completely specified. Hence the pure LST process cannot be used. Individually and collectively, however, these nonformalisable properties influence the computational process, its behaviour and its outputs and contribute to the level of user satisfaction and program quality. As already observed, it is the satisfaction with the results of program execution that concerns E-type users, not the correctness of the software. Without verification, validation becomes even more crucial. The process whereby they are implemented is, at best, a pseudo-LST process.

This distinction leads directly to a further observation relating to the use of component-based architectures, reuse and COTS. The benefits these are expected to yield implicitly assume that the elements are correct with respect to a stated specification. In a malleable, evolutionary E-type domain, S-type components must be maintained compatible with all of the domains in which they operate and are embedded (Lehman and Ramil 2000b); their specification must be continually updated. This is not straightforward. As Turski has affirmed '... the problem of adopting existing software to evolving specifications remains largely unsolved, perhaps is algorithmically not solvable in full generality ...' (Turski 2000). In the real world of constant change and evolving systems, reliance on the use of standardised components, reuse and COTS is difficult and hazardous, likely to negate the benefits of their alleged use.

1.6.3 Phenomenological Analysis of Real-World Computer Usage

Clearly, pseudo-LST process cannot be *guaranteed* to produce a program that is satisfactory whenever executed. This observation reflects the nature of the real world and of people. Satisfaction depends upon the state of the former and the needs, desires, reactions and judgements of the latter when *using* the results of execution. Relative to a world that is forever changing, formal specification and demonstration of correctness where applicable, is bound to the period at which the specification was developed and accepted. Behaviour considered satisfactory even yesterday may not meet the conditions, needs and desires of today. Later satisfaction cannot be *guaranteed* unless it is demonstrated that the definitions, values and assumptions underlying the formulation and correctness demonstration are still valid. *Testing* and other means of validation may increase *confidence* in the likelihood of satisfaction from subsequent execution. But even this is not absolute, As Dijkstra said 'Testing can only demonstrate the presence of defects, never their absence' (Dijkstra 1972b). In the real world of 'now' a claim of demonstrated correctness (even in its everyday sense) of an E-type program with respect to the specification as it was, is, at best, a statement about the likelihood of satisfaction from subsequent execution. Any assertion of *absolute* or *lasting*, satisfaction is meaningless.

1.6.4 Theoretical Underpinning

The above reasoning is phenomenological. Closer examination provides a basis for formalising its conclusions. Programs and their specifications are products of human activity.

As such, they are essentially *bounded* in themselves and in the number of real-world properties that they reflect. Real-world applications and domains are themselves unbounded in the number of their properties. Specifications and programs therefore, cannot reflect them in their entirety. Knowingly and unknowingly, an unbounded number of real-world properties are discarded during the abstraction that produces the specification and permeates the subsequent development process. Moreover, each abstraction involves at least one assumption. An unbounded number of assumptions are therefore reflected in any E-type system (and in each of its E-type elements). Moreover, assumptions reflected in the system may become invalid, for example, as discarded properties become relevant. Ignoring this possibility adds further assumptions. Admittedly, most of the assumptions embedded in the system will be and remain totally irrelevant, but some will inevitably become irritants very possibly error or other, misbehaviour. All program elements that reflect such assumptions will require rectification. However carefully and to whatever detail software specifications and their implementations are developed the time for which they remain valid will be limited.

Contractually, one may be able to protect the developers from responsibility for resultant failure to achieve satisfactory results. Users will, in general, be unaware of the fact that the program can only address foreseen changes that permit corrective procedures to be included in the software and/or usage procedures. Usage will be judged as satisfactory or otherwise on the basis of the results of execution but depends on the properties the program *has*, not those it *should* have to satisfy and reflect the *current* states of the application and the operational domains. Even in special cases where a real-world program has and is correct against a formal specification, the use of the term correctness of a bounded program relative to an unbounded domain is wrong. Formal *correctness* of a program or system has only limited value.

1.6.5 The Value of Formalisms and of Verification

Nevertheless, formalisms and specifications can play an important role in the development and evolution of E-type applications (van Lamsweerde 2000). Other than momentarily, systems, software or otherwise, cannot, in general, be better, than the foundations on which they are built. A demonstrably *correct* element does not provide any permanent indication that the system as a whole is valid or will be satisfactory to its users. Nor can correctness prove that a specification on which the demonstration is based is sufficient or correct to ensure satisfactory operation. But the greater the number of system elements that can be shown to be correct relative to a precise and complete specification, the greater the likelihood that the system will prove to be satisfactory, at least for a while. Demonstration, by whatever means, of the correctness of an element with respect to its specification can assist in the isolation, characterisation and minimisation of uncertainties and inconsistencies (Lehman 1989, 1990). It will then also assist systematic and controlled evolution of the system and its parts as and when required.

Some researchers have highlighted the need to accompany a formal specification with a precise, informal definition of its interpretation in the domains of interest (van Lamsweerde 2000). The systematic development and maintenance of these is a worthwhile activity in the context of E-type evolution. It is referred to briefly later in the next section when the role of assumptions is addressed.

1.6.6 Bounding

Abstraction is a bounding process. It determines the operational range of E-type systems. The bounds required for such systems are, generally, imprecise, even unclear and subject to change. Some of the boundaries will be well defined by prior practice or related experience, for example. Others are adopted on the basis of compromise or recognised constraints. Still others will be uncertain, undecidable or verging on the inconsistent. This situation may be explicitly acknowledged or remain unrecognised until exposed by chance or during system operation. Since applications and the domains to which they apply and in which they operate are dynamic, always changing, and E-type system (in particular) must be continually reviewed and, where necessary, changed to ensure continuing validity of execution results in all situations that may legitimately arise.

In the context of evolution, *fuzziness* of bounds arises from several sources. The first relates to the, in general, unlimited, number of potential application properties from which those to be implemented and supported must be selected. The detail of system functional and nonfunctional properties and system behaviour also cannot be uniquely determined. A limited set must be selected for implementation on the basis of the current state of knowledge and understanding, experience, managerial and legal directives and so on.

Precise bounds of the operational domains are, in general, equally undetermined. The uncertainty is overcome by provisionally selecting boundaries within which the system is to operate to provide satisfactory solutions at some level of precision and reliability, in some defined time frame, at acceptable cost. Inevitably however, once a system is operational, the need or desire to change or extend the area of validity, whether of domains or of behaviours, will inevitably arise. Without such changes, exclusions will become performance inhibitors, irritants and sources of system failure. In summary, the potential set of properties and capabilities to be included in a system is, in general, unbounded and not uniquely selectable. Even a set that appears reasonably complete may well exceed what can be accommodated within the resources and time allocated for system implementation. As implemented, system boundaries will be arbitrary, largely determined by many individual and group decision makers. Inevitably, the system will need to be continually evolved by modifying or extending domains it defines, and explicitly or implicitly assumes, so as to satisfy changing constraints, newly emerging needs or changed environmental circumstances.

But, unlike those of the domain, once developed and installed, system boundaries become solid, increasingly difficult and costly to change, interpret and respect, fault prone, slow to modify. A user requiring a facility not provided by the system may, in the first instance, use stand-alone software to satisfy individual or local needs. This may be followed by direct coupling of such software tightly to the system for greater convenience in cooperative execution. But problems such as additional execution overhead, time delays, performance and reliability penalties and sources of error will emerge, however the desired or required function is invoked and the results of execution passed to the main system. Omissions become onerous; a source of performance inhibitors and user dissatisfaction. A request for system extension will eventually follow.

The history of automatic computation is rich with examples of functions first developed and exploited as stand-alone application software, migrating inwards to become, at least conceptually, part of an operating or run time system and ultimately integrated into some larger application system or, at the other extreme, into hardware (chips). This is exemplified by the history of language and graphics support. The evolving computing system is an *expanding universe* with an inward drift of function from the domains to the core of the system. The drift is driven by feedback about the effectiveness, strengths, weaknesses, precision, convenience and potential of the system as recognised during its use and the application of results.

1.6.7 The Consequence: Continual System Evolution

Properties such as those mentioned make implementation and use of an E-type system a learning experience. Its evolution is driven, in part, by the ongoing experiences of those that interact with or use the results of execution directly or indirectly, of those who observe, experience or are affected by its use as well as those who develop or maintain it. The system must reflect any and all properties and behaviours of the application being implemented or supported, the domains in which the application is being executed, pursued and supported, and everything that affects the results of execution. It must be a *model-like reflection*[8] of the application and its many operational domains.

However as repeatedly observed, the latter are unbounded in the number of their properties. They, therefore, cannot be known entirely by humans during the conscious and unconscious abstraction and reification decisions that occur from conception onwards. The learning resulting from development, use and evolution plays a decisive role in the changes that must be implemented throughout its lifetime in the nature and pattern of its inevitable evolution.

Evolution of E-type applications, systems, software and usage practices is clearly intrinsic to computer usage. Serious software suppliers and users experience the phenomenon as a continuing need to acquire successive versions, releases and upgrades of used software to ensure that the system maintains its validity, applicability, viability and value in an ever-changing world. Development and adaptation of such systems cannot be covered by an exhaustive and complete theory if only because of human involvement in the applications, the partially arbitrary nature of procedures in business, manufacturing, government, the service sector and so on, and the potential unboundedness of the domain boundaries (Turski 1981). Inherently, therefore, the software evolution process is, at least to some extent, *ad hoc*.

1.6.8 Summary

In summary, every E-type program is a bounded, discrete and static reflection of an unbounded, dynamic application and its operational domain. The boundaries and

---

[8] In accepted mathematical usage the term *model* is valid when formally describing, for example, a required relationship between a program *specification*, the *application*, operational *domains* to which it relates and the *program* derived from it. The specification is derived from application and domain statements by an abstraction process. The program is, in turn, derived from the specification by reification. The program, application and domains will, however, possess additional properties. These must not be incompatible with the specification but are not necessarily compatible with one another. The program is, therefore, *not* a model of the application and its domains. The term *model-like reflection* is used here to convey the relationships which do exist. Software maintenance may then be viewed as 'maintaining reflective validity between the program and application' as the latter and its operational domains evolve.

other attributes of the latter are first determined in initial planning and adjusted, during development, by technology, time, business and operational considerations and constraints. Some are determined explicitly in processes such as requirements analysis and specification, others as a result of explicit or implicit assumptions adopted and embedded in the system during the evolution process. Fixing the detailed properties of human/system interfaces or interactions between people and the operational system must include trial and error. The fine design detail cannot be based on either one-off observation and requirements elicitation or on intuition, conjecture or statistics alone. It arises from continuing human experience, judgement and decision by development staff, users and so on. Development changes perception and understanding of the application itself, of facilities that may be offered, of how incompatibilities may be resolved, what requirements should be satisfied by the solution, possible solutions, and so on. In combination, such considerations drive the process onwards, by experience and learning-based feedback, to its final goal, a satisfactory operational system.

1.6.9 Principle of Software Uncertainty

The preceding discussions have shown how the processes of abstraction and bounding each generate a bounded number of assumptions that are reflected in the specifications and programs. The latter are a subset of the unbounded number of assumptions made, implicitly or explicitly, during the above processes and that relate, *inter alia*, to the states and behaviours of the various domains addressed by the program and within which it operates. The real world is dynamic, always changing and the rate of change is also likely to be significantly affected by the development, installation and use of the computing system. Inevitably, members of this bounded, embedded, assumption set will become invalid as a result of changes in the real world. This principle follows that every E-type system is likely to reflect a number of invalid assumptions. Since they are, in general, not identified, the consequences in execution are not known. Hence the outcome of every E-type program or system execution is uncertain. This observation has been formalised in a Principle of Software Uncertainty. It has been discussed in several papers (e.g. Lehman 1989, 1990), more recently as an example of potential theorems in the development of a theory of software evolution (Lehman and Ramil 2000a, 2001b).

1.7 Software Systems Evolution

1.7.1 Early Work

The decision whether, when and how to upgrade a system will be taken by the organisation owning a product though often forced on them by others, clientele, for example. Their considerations will involve many factors: business, economic, technical and even social. Each version or release that emerges from the evolution process which implements their decision is an adaptation, improvement (in some sense) and/or extension of the system, and represents one element of the ongoing evolution. The sequence of releases transforms the system away from one satisfying the original concept to one that successively supports the ever-changing and emerging circumstances, needs and opportunities in a dynamic world. If conditions to support evolution do not exist, then the system will gradually lapse into uselessness as a widening gap develops between the real world as mirrored by the program and the real world as it now is (First Law of Software Evolution, Lehman, 1974).

Recognition of software evolution, its identification as a disciplined phenomenon and its subsequent study was triggered by a 1968/1969 report entitled *The Programming Process* (Lehman 1969). *Inter alia*, the study examined empirical data on the growth of the IBM OS/360-370 operating system. As analysed in a number of papers since then, it concluded that system evolution, as measured, for example, by growth in size over successive releases, displayed regularity that was unlikely to have been primarily determined by human management decision. Instead, the regularity appears to be due to feedback via many different routes. The empirical data that first suggested this conclusion was illustrated and was briefly discussed in Section 1.4, Figure 1.1. The figure plots system size measured in numbers of modules – a surrogate for the functional power of the system – against *release sequence number* (RSN) up to and including the period of instability preceding its break-up into the VS/1 and VS/2 systems.

The growth trend of OS/360-370, when plotted over releases, was close to linear[9] up to RSN 20. A superimposed ripple suggested self-stabilisation around that trend, *self* because no indication could be found that management sought linear growth. In fact, there was no evidence that growth considerations played any part in defining individual release content.

This stabilisation phenomenon provided the first empirical evidence that feedback was playing a role in determining the growth rate of functional power or other attributes of evolving systems. The conclusion was strengthened (Belady and Lehman 1972) by the post RSN 21 instability. By the same reasoning, this was attributed to excessive *positive* feedback, as reflected in the excessive incremental growth[10] from RSN 20 to RSN 21.

1.7.2 FEAST

Follow-on studies in the 1970s and 1980s (Lehman and Belady 1985) produced further evidence of similar evolutionary behaviour and led eventually to eight *Laws of Software Evolution* that encapsulated these invariants (Lehman 1974, 1978, 1980, Lehman et al. 1997). Following formulation of the FEAST hypothesis (Lehman 1994) successive studies, FEAST/1 and/2, were undertaken to further explore the evolution phenomenon (FEAST 2001). Figure 1.2 provides just one example of the similarity between the observation of the growth of OS/360-370 (Figure 1.1) and observations some 30 years later. Discussion of those results can be found in some of the publications listed on the FEAST web pages (FEAST 2001).

Attention should also be drawn to some of the differences in the evolution patterns of the systems studied. For example, five of the FEAST systems display *declining* growth rate trends appropriately modelled by an inverse square model of the form $S_{i+1} = S_i + E/S_i^2$ where S_i is the predicted size of the release with sequence number 'i', with size measured in appropriate units and E is a model parameter as determined from data on the growth history of the system (Turski 1996). Moreover, for all five of these systems, the precision of the trend model was increased by breaking up the growth data and by estimating the model over two or more sequential segments. The recovery of the growth rate, at break points such as that visible in Figure 1.2 may be assumed to indicate improvements in the evolution process or restructuring of the evolving system. In fact, the figure appears to

---

[9] As noted later, this early result was subsequently refined but this does not affect the basic reasoning.

[10] Three-and-a-half times as great as the previously largest growth increment.

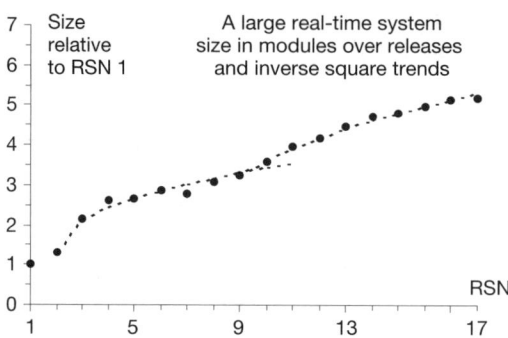

Figure 1.2 Growth trend of one of the systems studied in the FEAST projects (dots) with inverse square models fitted to two individual segments (dashes). The start of segment 1 at RSN 2 provides a slightly better fit than a model fitted starting at RSN 1

provide empirical support for the evolutionary stages concept (Bennett and Rajlich 2000, Rajlich and Bennett 2000).

These five systems exemplify release level evolution. Phenomenological reasoning as summarised above suggests that, in principle, similar behaviour is to be expected from *all* real-world software systems. The data studied in FEAST was, however, all obtained from systems developed and evolved using variations or extensions of the classical waterfall process paradigm. Use of newer approaches, *object oriented, open source, agile* and *extreme programming*, *component-based architecture*, and *implementation* introduces new situations. But the all-pervading influences of factors such as the role of learning, feedback, environmental changes, the impact of computer integration and usage on needs and usage patterns and the consequences of assumptions in a dynamic real world reflected in the software suggest that paradigm changes will, at most, have an impact on the detail of the software evolution phenomenon. The evolution of specific software under the newer approaches is currently a topic of study and some results have been reported [e.g. Godfrey and Tu 2000, Lehman and Ramil 2000b, Succi *et al.* 2001, Bauer and Pizka 2003, Capiluppi *et al.* 2004]. A discussion of current results cannot be included here.

The sixth system studied under FEAST involved *ab initio development* of a defence system. Moreover, in that system, the size of the executable code was externally constrained by the memory capacity of the computer used in the application and alternative metrics were unavailable. Hence it was concluded that the comparison of this system to the other five could not contribute to the present study. It is mentioned here for the sake of completeness.

1.7.3 The Growth Trend

The observed inverse square growth trend is consistent with a hypothesis that declining growth rate may be attributed, at least in part, to growing complexity of the evolving system and application as change is applied upon change. The growth in complexity may, of course, be compensated by growing familiarity with the system, improved training, expertise, documentation and tools, by re-engineering, system restructuring, *refactoring* (Fowler 1999) and, more generally, *anti-regressive* activity (Lehman 1974). System dynamics models (Forrester 1961) reproducing this phenomenon suggest that sufficient anti-regressive activity can yield close to linear growth (following an initial increasing growth rate as briefly discussed below) (Lehman *et al.* 2002).

The results of these investigations have been widely reported (FEAST 2001). The systems studied were industrially evolved systems stemming from different development organisations, addressing different application areas in differing operational environments and of widely different sizes. The conclusions suggested some relatively minor modification of earlier overall results and strengthened conviction in the universality of the phenomenon of E-type software evolution. As stated by the first (continuing change) and sixth (continuing growth) laws, such systems must be continually adapted, changed and extended, that is, evolved, if they are to remain of value to users and profitable to the organisations in charge of their evolution.

More recently it has been realised that the inverse square model, while valid over an extended period of the system life cycle, or over segments, is not the last word. Re-examination of existing data and its interpretation indicates that growth rates at the start of a development or at the initiation of a new growth segment are increasing, even approaching the exponential. If, as appears likely, this conclusion is sustained then it is more appropriate to replace the segmented inverse square growth model with an S-curve, initial increasing rate that gradually approaches linearity and then decreases into, possibly, inverse square growth.

1.7.4 Evolution Drivers

Observations and insights that suggested the laws of software evolution support the observation that feedback plays a major role in driving and controlling release processes (Lehman and Belady 1985, chap. 16; Lehman 1991). Sources of feedback include *defect reports* from the field, *domain changes* due to installation, operation and use of the system, changing user *needs*, new *opportunities*, advances in technology, even the economic climate. At a more abstract level, experience changes user *perception*, *understanding*, underlying application *detail*, system *concepts*, *abstractions* and *assumptions*. A need and demand for change emerges. The always-emerging needs are conveyed back to suppliers and demands action on their part. But the response can rarely be immediate since it requires informed selection and approval that requires technical, business and, economic judgements with moderation of the needs and priorities of many different users. As is to be expected from a feedback system, the resultant delays cause further distortion of the evolution process.

The information required to support this process propagates along paths involving human interpretation, judgement and decision; hence there are significant delays. All involved are liable to have an impact on the information and on feedback characteristics. Many will contribute to the change process and not all are developers or user communities exploiting insight gained from their usage and experience. But in all cases information is the principal driver, with the characteristics of the feedback path influencing its significance: that is, process-internal feedback paths are relatively short and involve people who are experts in the application, the development process and the target system. Their feedback is based on individual interpretation. In control-theoretic terms it can be interpreted as low-level amplification, delay, noise and distortion. But long external *user-* and *business-based* loops are likely to be primary determinants of *release dynamics* characteristics.

1.7.5 Relationship Between the Above Levels of Evolution

Sections 1.6 and 1.7 of this chapter each addresses one area of software evolution. Section 1.6 covers the activity of *development* of an entire system *ab initio* or of a change to an existing system. Section 1.7 addresses the continual adaptation of a developed system to changing circumstances, needs and ambitions. The two areas are related: The second area also requires planning, development, specification, design and implementation of desired changes and additions. Such implementation will then involve evolution activity such as the one considered in the first area. But as briefly stated in Section 1.1.1, relative to the system as a whole, the amount of change in any one release of a software system is generally small even though locally many individual elements or components may be changed or replaced by newly developed or acquired alternatives.

1.7.6 Evolutionary Development

Attention may also be drawn to development approaches that constitute an amalgamation of the two above areas. As an example, consider Gilb's Evolutionary Development approach (Gilb 1981, 1988). In this approach, *ab initio* development and fielding of complex (in some sense) systems in a sequence of releases each involving a new component or chunk of functionality. In this way, the complexity of the task undertaken in any release interval is greatly reduced. Moreover, by fielding the *'in development'* system to users, the latter becomes progressively exposed to a system of increasing functionality and power. Learning and reaction, that is, user feedback, can be taken into account well before development is completed. Hence the degree and complexity of validation and of rework may be reduced. Regression testing and revalidation, on the other hand, is likely to have to be increased.

Application of the approach depends on being able to architect the system so that constituent parts may be interconnected, part by part, to yield a sequence of viable systems of increasing functionality and power. The parts are developed, installed and, ideally, introduced into use in a predetermined order. The latter is, however, very likely to require modification as a result of, for example, unanticipated difficulties in completing some elements, a need for redesign, introduction of new requirements, domain changes and so on.

The system is not evolved continuously but by leaps and bounds. Constituent parts are progressively exposed to system internal interactions and to usage. Hence, some interface errors and undesirable or incorrect internal interactions will be detected sooner than would be the case if real-world operation were to await completion of the entire system. On the other hand, any benefit from this may be reduced or even reversed as development later in the evolution process takes note of changes in the operational domains, reflects these in the current design and implementation activity but fails to adjust older part of the system. That is wrong of course, but very likely to occur.

It is likely that where a system structure can be decomposed to yield a viable process and a usable system at each stage of the development, the approach can provide clear net benefit. It has been industrially applied in practice but we are not aware of any empirical assessment of its effectiveness in relation to more conventional development approaches. It must, however, be accepted that a major problem in real-world system development is that of uncertainty and risk associated with fixing the properties of the system. Related to this is the lack of a theoretical framework to guide selection of system properties during requirements analysis, specification and design. Many decisions are, therefore, arbitrary and not fully validated or rejected until the system has been fielded and is in regular use. It is not now clear how effectively evolutionary development addresses these issues although potentially it might well be more effective in this respect than the more classical approaches. Detailed assessment of the approach is required to determine its dependency on the nature of the application, development and other environments and what, if any, changes are required to ensure maximum benefit from the approach.

1.8 Evolution of the Application and Its Domain

Continuing evolution is not confined to the software or even to a wider *system* within which the software may be embedded. It is inherent in the very nature of computer *application*. This is illustrated by a study of long-term *feature* evolution in the telephone industry (Antón and Potts 2001). The activity that software supports and the problems solved also evolve. Such evolution is, in part, driven by human aspiration for improvement and growth. But more subtle forces are also at play. The very installation and use of the system changes both the activity being supported and the domains within which it is pursued. When installed and operational, the output of the process that evolved the software changes the attributes of the application and the domains that defined the process in the first place. As illustrated by Figure 1.3, the development process in association with the application and the operational domains as defined and bounded, clearly constitute a feedback loop. Depending on the manner in which and the degree to which changes impact use of the system and loop characteristics such as amplification, attenuation and delays, the overall feedback at this level can be negative or positive, leading to stabilisation, continuous controlled growth and/or instability.

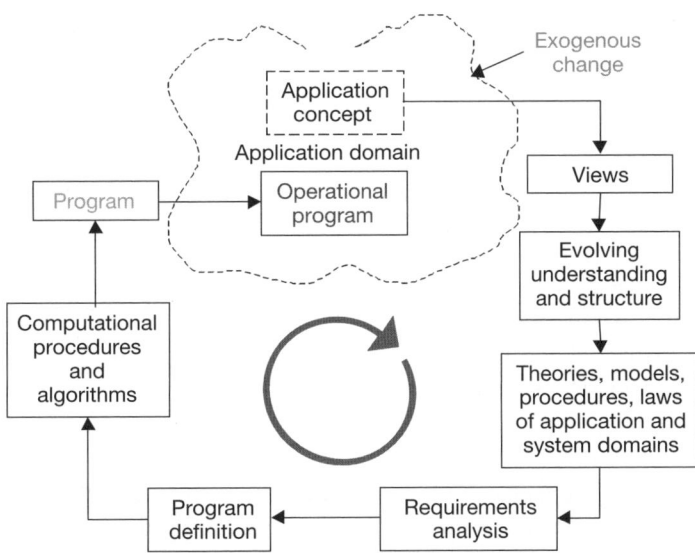

Figure 1.3 Evolution of the application in its domains as an iterative feedback system. Process steps are illustrative. Internal process loops are not shown

In many instances, however, the phenomenon of application evolution is more complex than indicated in the preceding paragraph. In particular, it may not be self-contained but a phenomenon of *co-evolution*. As government, business and other organisations make ever greater use of computers for administration, internal and external communication, marketing, security, technical activity and so on, the various applications become inextricably interdependent, sharing and exchanging data, invoking services from one another, making demands on common manpower resources and budgets. The inescapable trend is towards the integration of services, internal and external, with the goal, for example, of minimising the need for human involvement in information handling and communication, avoidance of delays and errors and increases in safety and security. And such integration is seen as needing to gradually extend to clients' systems, their customers and suppliers and service organisations, banks for example.

With this scenario, the rate at which an organisation can grow and be adapted to changing conditions and advancing technology depends on the rate at which it can evolve the software systems that support its activities. More generally, in the world of today, and even more of tomorrow, organisations will become interdependent. This will happen, whatever their activity or sphere of operation, however disparate the domains within which they operate, the activities they pursue, the technologies they employ and the computer software which links, coordinates and ties all together. All co-evolve, each one advancing only at a rate that can be accommodated by the others. And those rates depend not only on the various entities involved but also on the processes pursued and the extent to which these can be improved. Software is at the very heart of this co-evolution. Change to any element almost inevitably implies software changes elsewhere.

1.9 Process Evolution

1.9.1 Software Processes as Systems

Software processes are the aggregate of all activities in developing or evolving software and of the relationships between them. If correctly executed, they transform an application concept into a satisfactory operational system. Improvement of the process is achieved by improvement of its inputs, its parts and of their interactions. The parts themselves implement and support technical, operational and managerial activity. At some level, process steps can be seen as elements in a successive transformation paradigm (e.g. LST as in Section 1.6.2).

But enactment of a software process requires a wide variety of interacting activities and entities. Many of these are outside the core transformational steps but are nevertheless, needed to address fuzziness in the application concept, to enable the orderly interaction of many stakeholders and to ensure that the required outcome is achieved within relevant quality, schedule and economic constraints.

1.9.2 Process Improvement

Over the past decade, computers and the software that gives them their functional capability, have penetrated ever more deeply into the very fabric of society, individually and collectively. The world at large has become more and more dependent on the *timely* availability of *satisfactorily operating* software with the reliability and at a *cost* that is commensurate with the *value* that the software is to yield on *execution*. But, as repeatedly observed, E-type software must be adapted and extended as the world changes to yield satisfactory results whenever or wherever, within the accepted and supported bounds, the system is executed. Errors or delays in this continuing process can yield significant cost and/or performance penalties due to incorrect or unacceptable behaviour. They can even constrain or throttle organisations limited by out-of-date capabilities and *legacy* software. The extent, number and severity of problems experienced is certainly, at least in part, related to the nature and quality of the process by which the software is developed, maintained and evolved.

As variously practised today, that process is far from perfect, expensive, the source of many delays and with its products displaying major defects and deficiencies. The need for improvement is widely accepted. Major investment is being made in developing and applying software *process improvement* techniques (Zahran 1997). The methods used have been formalised, developed and applied using paradigms such as SPICE (El Eman *et al*. 1997), Bootstrap (Kuvaja *et al*. 1994) ISO 9000 and its derivatives, CMM (Paulk *et al*. 1993) and more recently CMMi (Ahern *et al*. 2001). All are being explored and applied the world over.

A major element of this search for improvement involves the development of new programming paradigms and languages. These include Object Orientation, Component-Based Architecture, Java, UML, Agile and Extreme. These new technologies involve significant changes in approach and/or development practices to earlier practice. They also cross-fertilise one another and, in turn, suggest or demand changes to or extensions of the processes in which they feature. Hence, software evolution processes also evolve. In the absence of a comprehensive scientific framework for software technology, such evolution is primarily driven and directed by experience, emerging insight, inventiveness and feedback.

1.9.3 The Theoretical Approach

Process improvement may be based on theory or be empirical. The first approach is exemplified by the work of WG 2.3 (Gries 1978). That group has been meeting formally since 1971 as an IFIP working group, to discuss its members' views and work on various aspects of programming methodology. The approach is bottom–up, based on both fundamental thinking about the nature and goals of the basic program development task and how it is or could be approached by individuals seeking solutions of a problem. The group's many positive results extended earlier work by their members. These included Dijkstra's much quoted observation that 'GOTOs are considered harmful' (Dijkstra 1968b), the concepts and procedures of structured programming (Dijkstra 1972a), the concepts of program correctness proving (Dijkstra 1968a, Hoare 1969, 1971) and successive refinement (Wirth 1971). The approach has provided basic concepts of modern programming methods, but relate in the first instance to S-type programs. As a result they are most significant at the heart of programming process improvement. They provide, for example, a basis for individual programmer practice (Humphrey 1997) that seeks to develop defect-free code.

In summary, the wider importance of the theoretical approach relates in the main to the use of S-type elements to implement and evolve E-type systems. The resultant methods and techniques are primarily relevant to the development of individual elements within such systems. Any demonstration of correctness is limited by the fact that, in the total system context, the individual element must be, and be maintained, correct in the context of an intrinsically incomplete specification. The value of this, if achieved, is unquestionable. The use of precise specifications with correct implementations at any level provides value. But as the application, its domains and the system in which elements are embedded and integrated evolve some, at least, will have to be adapted to the changing environment in which they operate. It will become increasingly difficult to maintain them correctly. The use of formal methods wherever possible is, at most, a partial answer to maintaining an *E*-type system satisfactorily.

1.9.4 Evolving Specifications
The theory-based approach has also identified another fundamental software evolution problem, the consequences of evolution at the specification level. As already stated in Section 1.6.2, '... the problem of adopting existing software to evolving specifications remains largely unsolved, perhaps is algorithmically not solvable in full generality ...' (Turski 2000). More generally, an open problem in program implementation relates to the achievement of evolutionary approaches, in which, for example, unforeseen changes and updates to an *existing* specification can be cheaply and safely reflected in an *existing* model of that specification, including the operational program. That problem too may not be solvable in full generality.

1.9.5 The Empirical Approach
The empirical approach must be seen as being parallel to and in support of the theoretical approach. It is essential if the methods and techniques developed in relation to the latter are to make a significant contribution to the evolution of large program systems. Empiricism in the software evolution area is exemplified by Lehman's early work (Lehman and Belady 1985), the work of the FEAST group (Lehman *et al.* 1994–2002, FEAST 2001) and that of Kemerer (Kemerer and Slaughter 1999). All these exploit observation, measurement, modelling and interpretation of actual industrially developed and evolved software systems. This permits the development of black and white box (e.g. system dynamics) models. Reasoning about the findings leads to the gradual development of an empirical theory, and this in turn must be tied in with the low-level approach.

It is not possible to discuss the findings of these empirical studies further here and the interested are referred to the referenced literature. It is, however, worthy of note that the eight laws of Software Evolution, as outlined briefly below, are a direct outcome of such empirical observation and interpretation over a period of some 30 years. The observations brought together here provide a basis for development of a formal Theory of Software Evolution (Lehman 2000, Lehman and Ramil 2000a, 2001b), indeed they constitute an informal, for the moment partial, theory. They also lead to practical rules for software release planning, management and control (Lehman and Ramil 2001a).

1.9.6 Laws of Software Evolution
The, currently eight, Laws, as listed below (Figure 1.4), were formulated in the decade following the mid-seventies. They were derived from direct observation and measurement of the evolution of a number and variety of systems. As such, they were viewed as reflecting specific, largely individual, behaviour and regarded as independent of one

Software Evolution

No.	Name	Statement
1	Continuing Change	An E-type system must be continually adapted, else it becomes progressively less satisfactory in use
2	Increasing Complexity	As an E-type system is changed its complexity increases and becomes more difficult to evolve unless work is done to maintain or reduce the complexity
3	Self Regulation	Global E-type system evolution is feedback regulated
4	Conservation of Organisational Stability	The work rate of an organisation evolving an E-type software system tends to be constant over the operational lifetime of that system or phases of that lifetime
5	Conservation of Familiarity	In general, the incremental growth (growth rate trend) of E-type systems is constrained by the need to maintain familiarity
6	Continuing Growth	The functional capability of E-type systems must be continually enhanced to maintain user satisfaction over system lifetime
7	Declining Quality	Unless rigorously adapted and evolved to take into account changes in the operational environment, the quality of an E-type system will appear to be declining
8	Feedback System	E-type evolution processes are multi-level, multi-loop, multi-agent feedback systems

Figure 1.4 The Laws of Software Evolution

another. Relationships between them, though not ruled out, were not investigated. However, following formulation of the observed feedback phenomenon as formalised in the eighth law[11], the likelihood of a structured relationship rooted in that law was accepted and awaits development as an integral part of the formal development of a Theory of Software Evolution. More complete discussion of the laws may be found in a number of publications (Lehman 1974, 1978, 1980, Lehman and Belady 1985, Lehman et al. 1997, Lehman and Ramil 2001a).

1.9.7 The Ephemeral Process
Any instance of the process is *transient, ephemeral*. Once executed, it is gone forever. It will normally have been pre-planned in outline, detail being filled in as progress is made. But unanticipated circumstances and conditions are the norm; budgets and schedules change, new requirements, functional or performance problems arise. All these, and many more, lead to process adjustments, adaptations and, though to be avoided, changes *on the*

---

[11] It is of interest to note that this phenomenon was second only to recognition of continual evolution as a phenomenon and was already referred to in 1972 (Belady and Lehman 1972).

fly. Triggered by observation of results or consequences of past activity or by perception of what lies ahead, such unplanned changes are often the result of crisis action and local reaction. They may result in a change to planned process activity or a need to backtrack or iterate. Thus they tend to be error prone, hence undesirable. In any event there is a complex mixture of feedback and *feed forward* of information based on individual and collective interpretation, intellectual judgement and decision by humans that determines how to proceed. The greater part of this is based on what is perceived, what is experienced, what is anticipated and challenges that arise.

Absolute predictability is not possible when people are involved in a process. Some degree of freedom must exist, otherwise their activity could and would be mechanised. The freedom relates to what is done, how it is done, what is not done and by what it is replaced. The potential for process definition and pre-planning is limited in extent, level of detail, precision and repeatability. It can only be enforced at a comparatively coarse level of granularity. Enforcement of a process specified at a high level of detail may appear desirable in specific circumstances as in life-critical medical or aerospace applications. But it must be accepted that rigid enforcement and application may itself result in problems, defect injection, inadequate treatment of unforeseen circumstances, high cost or serious time delays. Any of these can result from, for example, a misunderstanding of aspects of the situation, incorrect anticipation of the future or delays while authorisation to deviate is obtained.

Most development environments are subject to strong resource, schedule, budget and other constraints. Reliance on a process that can and will be carried out as planned is likely to prove naive in the extreme. Even in a single project, the process will evolve dynamically *in vitro*, as well as *in vivo* through pre-planning.

1.10 Process Model Evolution

1.10.1 The Nature of the Software Process

Real-world processes are very complex. As a multi-level, multi-loop, multi-agent feedback system with many of its mechanisms involving unpredictable decision taking by humans, the process is likely to display the nonintuitive or even anti-intuitive behaviour observed in feedback systems (Forrester 1961). Understanding how they act and interact requires models that reflect feedback mechanisms that can be used to validate them by observation and measurement of real-world properties and events.

1.10.2 Process Models

Models are used in many different areas and many different ways to facilitate and advance understanding of a phenomenon, activity or process. They are indeed essential as vehicles for communication and reasoning, providing, for example, means for systematic and disciplined examination, evaluation, comparison and improvement. As simulators or enactment tools they permit preliminary measurement, exploration and evaluation of proposed changes (Tully 1989). In all these areas, their role can be greatly enhanced if they are formal. In the absence of a formal representation, results are difficult to obtain or validate using theoretical reasoning.

As the applications they reflect become larger, more complex and more integrated, models must be evolved to remain of continuing value. This is particularly the case for models of the software process. With feedback producing pressure for continuing change and direct human involvement, the full *consequences* of introduction and use of computers and software is essentially unpredictable. It has already been stressed that software must remain compatible with the human reactions and volatile applications and domains that it addresses and in which it operates. The result is continual pressure for change to applications, interfaces, domains and processes involved and to the application of changes to any of these. As a consequence, software processes and models of them must also be changed and evolved to cope with the demands made of them, for the role they can play in maintaining and improving the reliability, timeliness, cost effectiveness and, above all, reliability of the process product. One must also consider that there are inherent limitations in modelling processes involving human action and decisions in a dynamic world (Lehman 1977).

1.10.3 Software Process Models

In considering the role and potential of models in the software process, one must take the dynamic, feedback-dependant nature of the latter into account. Models must reflect its structure. This fact was briefly described and explored, in a number of papers in the 1970s and 1980s (Lehman and Belady 1985) using very simple models. This early work came to the forefront with the first International Process Workshop (Potts 1984) and its successors. Later instances of this series were dominated by discussions of *process programming* and process program models. Interest in this approach was triggered by Osterweil's keynote address at ICSE 9 in 1987. Serious questions about it were, however, raised by Lehman in his response to that talk. (Lehman 1987). Sometime later *behavioural, system dynamics* (Forrester 1961) and other types of process models, were proposed by Abdel-Hamid and Madnick for the management of software development (Abdel-Hamid and Madnick 1991).

1.10.4 Process Improvement

At the highest level of abstraction, process improvement relates to a variety of performance and product quality, more generally *reliability*, factors as well as those relating to cost and elapsed time, more generally *productivity* factors. These include the reduction of time to detect, analyse and correct defects of any sort and the reliable release of a correction to users. An overall goal must be the reduction in the total number and frequency of justified defect reports, and their rate of submission once the system is in use. In this context, behavioural process models that address these concerns can be useful (e.g. Lehman *et al.* 2002).

Process evolution to achieve such improvement proceeds slowly and is implemented in incremental steps. Such steps will tend to be implemented locally as, for example, in the insertion of a new activity between two existing steps, or code inspection between coding and testing. In other instances the new activity will be out of the main line of development seeking out and verifying, for example, program elements that have been formally specified. As in the two instances cited, such an improvement may be of great local significance with both inspection and verification adding to the underlying quality of the system being developed. As such it makes a definite contribution to the overall value of the system, one that must be welcomed. But in terms of contribution to the overall quality or other attributes of the system as perceived by system beneficiaries, users and other stakeholders, this low-level activity will be taken for granted as it would in any other engineering discipline. It does not directly provide the visible benefit that stakeholders expect in a system. Programming standards and software validation techniques have, in general, advanced to the point where code stability and quality is largely taken for granted.

Incremental improvement at the process step level, for example, has, in general, little global impact on stakeholders in general, and individual and organisational users in particular.

Unless process changes take the multi-level feedback structure of the process into account, any benefit is likely to be overlooked, an illustration of the anti-intuitive behaviour of such systems. Multi-level loop structures tend to be largely hierarchical but may also involve loops, cutting across level boundaries. Whatever the case, one will have loops within loops; more generally, feedback-generated responses that control and moderate the behaviour and output of other loop mechanisms. Every process locality with its feedback loops will lie within others that drive and control the more extensive process and its interaction with the operational domains. If feedback is negative, encompassing loops will attenuate, even suppress, the effects of inner, more local changes. The potential impact of improvements, whatever their significance in the isolation of their process neighbourhood, will be small outside. Positive feedback, while having the potential to amplify some process property, may ultimately cause instability in the behaviour or a property of the domain it controls. The instability of OS/360-370 growth illustrated occurring after RSN 20 as illustrated in Section 1.4, Figure 1.1 represents an example of this effect. To constitute a visible and measurable global improvement and to provide benefit to the stakeholders and user communities, a process improvement must have visible, preferably measurable, impact outside the programming process. Only such impact, has meaning and value in the real world (Lehman 1994).

Models can be used to develop and evaluate proposed software process improvements. However, if they are to be of value in their reflection of the likely properties of the process after change and in the consequences of its implementation, they may well be more difficult, costly and error prone to implement than is the process change itself. It is not sufficient that the model reflects the change with sufficient precision. A framework must be provided to provide a realistic environment for its validation, assessment of the proposed change and evaluation. In addition, one must provide mechanisms to adjust, and in some sense optimise, the change. And in any event, the full global consequences of a process change are not straightforward to predict or to evaluate in the presence of feedback, whether before implementation or after. Process models have a role in and a contribution to make to software engineering but these are likely to be rather limited, barring some major advances in process modelling and the use of models.

One final note on process model evolution must be made. However exploited, the information that drives improvement is garnered from observation and previous experience. Model evolution is also feedback driven. The flow will be from within the organisation, from other software developers and from process experts and practitioners (Lehman 1991). Disciplined and directed effort in process improvement is typified by the work of the Software Engineering Institute at Carnegie Mellon University (Humphrey 1989). Their work does not explicitly focus on process models or feedback direction and control. But those, in essence, are among the issues addressed and exploited.

1.10.5 Links Between Process and Process Model Evolution

What is the nature of the linkage between evolution of a process and that of its model? Where impetus for change comes from a need to adapt a process to specific conditions or circumstances, model evolution is a consequence of process evolution. The likely consequence or benefit of a process change may possibly be assessed by implementing, exploring and comparing alternative changes through model enactment before incorporating the selected change in the process. Evaluation of changes to the model can drive process change. Where this is not done, changes made to the process, whether premeditated or on the fly must be reflected in a change to the model if the latter is to retain its validity and value. If, on the other hand, the pressure for evolution comes from recognition of a need for improvement, the process model can play a seminal role. It may then influence the design and evaluation of the change before implementation. Such evaluation must, however, include the benefits that would result and the investment required for their implementation.

1.11 Relationships Between Levels

1.11.1 The Software/Software Process Contrast

There are clearly interactions between the various aspects and levels of evolution of individual roles and evolution patterns as discussed. But this must not be interpreted as indicating that there are similarities between their evolutionary behaviour. The reverse is, in fact, the case. Software process evolution, for example, clearly differs significantly from that of the software itself. Similarly, there is a fundamental difference in the relationships between a software process and its models on the one hand and between E-type software and the problem or application processes of which the software is a model-like reflection on the other.

Wherein lie the differences? E-type software is concerned with some application process and the application of program execution to the real world (Lehman 1991). Given that operational domain, one develops and evolves systems to be used by a changing population of (largely anonymous) people and organisations with differing degrees of understanding, skill and experience. The concern will, in general, be with user community behaviour. Only in exceptional instances can code make provision for individual misuse, and that only if such misuse can and has been anticipated.

An essential ingredient of successful software design is, therefore, insulation of the system from user behaviour. Computer applications evolve, *inter alia*, in response to the changes in their software and in the domains. This is so, even though the former may have been inspired by observation of real-world processes influenced or controlled by its execution. There is directed interaction from the software to the application. Though a model-like reflection of the application, it is often the software that forces evolution. Software changes drive application changes while co-evolving with it.

1.11.2 The Software Process/Process Model Contrast

In direct contrast, when software development processes and the models that describe them are considered, the focus of concern is the process even though a model was the source of evolutionary change. A proposed change and its consequences may indeed be explored by use of a model and be evaluated by its enactment. The process may even be guided to some extend by a model-based support environment (Taylor *et al.* 1988). Nevertheless, the real concern remains with the process *in execution*. Humans interpret specifications, process directives, choose directions, take decisions, follow and apply methods. The proof of the pudding lies in the eating. The process model is a broad-brush tool to permit reasoning about the process but the consequences of process execution depend on the processes as executed through the specific actions of individuals. It is the dependability, quality, ease of use, timeliness and robustness of the process, which is of direct concern.

Process models are incomplete; at best a high-level guide to the process. They do not and cannot provide a precise and complete representation of the process actually followed. If, mistakenly, they are accepted as precise and complete they become straightjackets. They constitute a constraint in domains where the unexpected and unanticipated is a daily occurrence. This must be contrasted with executable software. Once acknowledged, the software is relied upon to provide a precise, detailed, complete representation of the actuality required or desired. Software *defines the process of computation* completely. The language that determines it possesses a formal semantics with no ambiguity. Where the process cannot be predetermined, alternatives must be identified and automated, tests devised to select that which is to be followed. The process definition is absolute in the context of that language[12].

Process models, on the other hand are, as already observed, a *partial* reflection of the desired process. It is the *product* of that process that is of concern. Changes to the model are incidental to the ultimate purpose and interest in pursuing the process. They describe changes, proposed or implemented; concepts to be translated into reality by people. They are evaluated in terms of their *impact* on the process *in execution*. A process change may be conceived and incorporated in a model. The acid test comes with the *execution* of an instance of the *process*. Determination of its improvement or deterioration, success or failure, is judged on the basis of *product* attributes.

There are also other significant differences. For example, process quality, productivity and cost concerns relate to the process, not its model. For software, the reverse is the case. Quality, productivity and cost concerns as visualised by the software engineer relate to the software as a reflection of the application in its domain, not to the application itself. Concern about such factors does arise but these must, in the first place, be addressed by application experts. Deficiencies will, in general, be overcome, in the first instance, by changes to system requirements and specification, to be reflected in changes to future versions of the software.

Consider, finally, the time relationship between model and process changes and the nature of the feedback loops that convey the interactions. For the process the keyword is *immediacy,* whereas for software there is, in general, significant relative delay in feedback. One could go on listing the differences. The analysis as given suffices to indicate

---

[12] The use of, for example, statistical tests, random number generators or other random choices is no exception to this general rule. It is also predetermined, though the path taken cannot be predicted except in a probabilistic sense.

that the thesis (Osterweil 1987) that 'software processes are software too' must not be taken literally.

1.12 Conclusions

The brief discussion of evolutionary development at the end of Section 1.7 indicates that the classification of areas of evolution proposed in this chapter is not as precise as one might have hoped for. There are other examples and in introducing one more in these concluding remarks, a more general point can be made. Luqi's Evolution by Rapid Prototyping (Luqi 1989) also combines views from areas of *ab initio* development and release-based evolution. This suggests that there might be advantages in simultaneously addressing these, and indeed, other areas described in this chapter. In particular, it must be recognised that the lowest level of evolution as outlined is used to implement the evolution of the individual entities in the other areas. Thus, while compartmentalisation has very clear benefits as an aid to understanding, it remains arbitrary to some extent. It is certain that in industrial situations, for example, evolution over several levels will occur concurrently. Consideration and management of each and of the interactions between them must be coordinated to ensure maximum benefit.

The objective of this chapter has been to expose the wider and crucial role of evolution and feedback in a number of domains related to software. Only recently has serious thought been given to this topic and firm conclusions must await further directed and intensive study. Though not sufficiently structured, the analysis presented here constitutes an outline Theory of Software Evolution (Lehman and Ramil 2000a, 2001b). Formal development and presentation of such a theory should not be long delayed.

In summary, feedback drive and control plays a major, critical and unavoidable role in software technology. The characteristics of individual phenomena are functions of the properties of the feedback loops. As a phenomenon, evolution occurs at different levels in the computing and software domains. There is still much to be learned in this area and the nature, impact and control of evolution at all levels must become a major focus of future research and development.

1.13 Acknowledgments

Many thanks are due to industrial collaborators and academic colleagues for many discussions, particularly during two EPSRC supported FEAST projects (1996–2001). Over the years these have helped to prune, sharpen and extend the concepts and ideas presented.

References

References indicated with an "*" were reprinted in Lehman and Belady, 1985.

T.K. Abdel-Hamid and S.E. Madnick (1991), *Software Project Dynamics – An Integrated Approach*, Prentice Hall, Englewood Cliffs, NJ, 264.

D. Ahern, A. Clouse and R. Turner (2001), *CMMi Distilled – An Introduction to Multi-discipline Process Improvement, SEI Series in Software Engineering*, Addison-Wesley, Reading, MA.

A. Antón and C. Potts (2001), Functional Paleontology: System Evolution as the User Sees It, *23rd International Conference on Software Engineering*, Toronto, Canada, 12–19 May, pp. 421–430.

K.R. Apt and D. Kozen (1986), Limits for Automatic Program Verification of Finite-State Concurrent Systems, *Inf. Process. Lett.*, vol. 22, no. 6, pp. 307–309.

V.R. Basili, L. Briand, S. Condon, W. Melo and J. Valett (1996), Understanding and Predicting the Process of Software Maintenance Releases, *18th International Conference on Software Engineering*, Berlin, Germany, March 25–29.

A. Bauer and M. Pizka (2003), The Contribution of Free Software to Software Evolution, *Proceedings of the International Workshop on Principles of Software Evolution (IWPSE)*, Helsinki, Finland, Sept. 2003.

*L.A. Belady and M.M. Lehman (1972), An Introduction to Growth Dynamics, in W. Freiburger (ed.), *Statistical Computer Performance Evaluation*, Academic Press, New York, pp. 503–511.

K.H. Bennett and V.T. Rajlich (2000), Software Maintenance and Evolution: A Roadmap, in A. Finkelstein (ed.), *The Future of Software Engineering*, ACM Order Nr. 592000-1, June 4–11, ICSE, Limerick, Ireland, pp. 75–87.

B.W. Boehm (1976), Software Engineering, *IEEE Trans. Comput.*, vol. C-25, no. 12, pp. 1226–1241.

B.W. Boehm (1988), A Spiral Model of Software Development and Enhancement, *Computer*, vol. 21, May 1988, pp. 61–72.

F. Brooks (1975), *The Mythical Man-Month*, Addison-Wesley, Reading, MA.

A. Capiluppi, M. Morisio and J.F. Ramil (2004), The Evolution of Source Folder Structure in actively evolved Open Source Systems, *Metrics 2004 Symposium*, Chicago, Ill.

C.K.S. Chong Hok Yuen (1981), *Phenomenology of Program Maintenance and Evolution*, PhD thesis, Department of Computing, Imperial College.

S. Cook, R. Harrison, M.M. Lehman and P. Wernick (2006), Evolution in Software Systems: Foundations of the SPE Classification Scheme, *J. Softw. Maint. Evol.*, vol. 18, no. 1, pp. 1–35.

E.W. Dijkstra (1968a), A Constructive Approach to the Problem of Program Correctness, *BIT*, vol. 8, no. 3, pp. 174–186.

E.W. Dijkstra (1968b), GOTO Statement Considered Harmful, Letter to the Editor, *Commun. ACM*, vol. 11, no. 11, Nov. 1968, pp. 147–148.

E.W. Dijkstra (1972a), Notes on Structured Programming, in O.J. Dahl, E.W. Dijkstra and C.A.R. Hoare (eds.), *Structured Programming*, Academic Press, pp. 1–82.

E.W. Dijkstra (1972b), The Humble Programmer, ACM Turing Award Lecture, *Commun. ACM*, vol. 15, no. 10, Oct. 1972, pp. 859–866.

K. El Eman, J.N. Drouin and W. Melo (1997), *SPICE: The Theory and Practice of Software Process Improvement and Capability Determination*, IEEE Computer Society Press, Los Alamitos, CA, p. 450.

FEAST (2001), *Feedback, Evolution And Software Technology*, http://www.doc.ic.ac.uk/~mml/feast/ <as of Oct. 2001> See also http://www.cs.mdx.ac.uk/staffpages/mml <as of Feb 2004>.

J.W. Forrester (1961), *Industrial Dynamics*, MIT Press, Cambridge, MA.

M. Fowler (1999), *Refactoring: Improving the Design of Code*, Addison-Wesley, New York.

T. Gilb (1981), Evolutionary Development, *ACM Softw. Eng. Notes*, vol. 6, no. 2, April, 1981, p. 17.

T. Gilb (1988), *Principles of Software Engineering Management*, Addison-Wesley, Wokingham, United Kingdom.

M.W. Godfrey and Q. Tu (2000), Evolution in Open Source Software: A Case Study, *Proceedings International Conference on Software Maintenance, ICSM 2000*, 11–14 Oct. 2000, San Jose, CA, pp. 131–142.

D. Gries (1978), *Programming Methodology – A Collection of Articles by Members of IFIP WG2.3*, Springer-Verlag, New York, p. 437.

C.A.R. Hoare (1969), An Axiomatic Basis for Computer Programming, *Commun. ACM*, vol. 12, no. 10, pp. 576–583.

C.A.R. Hoare (1971), Proof of a Program FIND, *Commun. ACM*, vol. 14, no. 1, pp. 39–45.

W.S. Humphrey (1989), *Managing the Software Process*, Addison-Wesley, Reading, MA.

W.S. Humphrey (1997), *Introduction to the Personal Software Process(SM)*, Addison-Wesley, Reading, MA.

IWPSE. (2004), *Proceedings International Workshop on Principles of Software Evolution*, Kyoto, Japan, 6–7 Sept. http://iwpse04.wakayama-u.ac.jp/ <as of July 2004>.

C.F. Kemerer and S. Slaughter (1999), An Empirical Approach to Studying Software Evolution, *IEEE Trans. Softw. Eng.*, vol. 25, no. 4, July/August 1999, pp. 493–509.

S. Kuvaja, P. Koch, L. Mila, A. Krzanik, S. Bicego and G. Saukkonen (1994), *Software Process Assessment and Improvement – The Bootstrap Approach*, Blackwell.

*M.M. Lehman (1969), *The Programming Process*, IBM Research Report RC2722M, IBM Research Center, Yorktown Heights, New York.

*M.M. Lehman (1974), Programs, Cities, Students – Limits to Growth, *Imp. Coll. Inaug. Lect. Ser.*, vol. 9, 1970–1974, pp. 211–229; also in Gries, 1978.

*M.M. Lehman (1977), Human Thought and Action as an Ingredient of System Behaviour, in R. Duncan and M. Weston Smith (eds.), *Encyclopedia of Ignorance*, Pergamon Press, Oxford, England.

*M.M. Lehman (1978), Laws of Program Evolution–Rules and Tools for Programming Management, *Proceedings of the Infotech State of the Art Conference, Why Software Projects Fail*, London, England, April 9–11, 1978, pp. 1V1–1V25.

M.M. Lehman (1979), The Environment of Design Methodology, in T.A Cox (ed.), *Proceedings of Symposium on Formal Design Methodology*, Cambridge, UK, Apr. 9–12, 1979, pp. 17–38; STL Ltd, Harlow, Essex, 1980.

*M.M. Lehman (1980), Program Life Cycles and Laws of Software Evolution, *Proc. IEEE Spec. Iss. on Softw. Eng.*, vol. 68, no. 9, Sept. 1980, pp. 1060–1076.

*M.M. Lehman (1982), *Program Evolution, Symposium on Empirical Foundations of Computer and Information Sciences, 1982, Japan Information Center of Science and Technology*, published in J. Info. Proc. and Management, 1984, Pergamon Press, reprinted as chapter 2 in (Lehman and Belady 1985).

M.M. Lehman (1987), Process Models, Process Programs, Programming Support, *Invited Response to a Keynote Address by Lee Osterweil, Proceedings of the Ninth International Conference on Software Engineering*, Monterey, CA, March 30–April 2, pp. 14–16.

M.M. Lehman (1989), Uncertainty in Computer Application and its Control Through the Engineering of Software, *J. Softw. Maint. Res. Pract.*, vol. 1, no. 1, pp. 3–27.

M.M. Lehman (1990), Uncertainty in Computer Application, *Commun. ACM*, vol. 33, no. 5, pp. 584–586.

M.M. Lehman (1991), Software Engineering, the Software Process and Their Support, *IEE Softw. Eng. J.* Special Issue on Software Environ Factories, vol. 6, no. 5, pp. 243–258.

M.M. Lehman (1994), Feedback in the Software Evolution Process, *CSR Eleventh Annual Workshop on Software Evolution: Models and Metrics*, 7–9 Sept. 1994, Workshop Proceedings, Information and Software Technology, Special Issue on Software Maintenance, Elsevier, Dublin, NC, 1996, pp. 681–686.

M.M. Lehman (2000), *These – Towards a Theory of Software Evolution*, EPSRC Proposal, Case for Support Part 2, Department of Computing, ICSTM, 11 Dec.

M.M. Lehman and F.N. Parr (1976), Program Evolution and its Impact on Software Engineering, *Proceedings of the 2nd ICSE*, San Francisco, pp. 350–357.

M.M. Lehman and L.A. Belady (1985), *Program Evolution – Processes of Software Change*, Academic Press, London.

M.M. Lehman and J.F. Ramil (2000a), Towards a Theory of Software Evolution – And its Practical Impact, in Katayama T, Tamai T and Yonezaki N, (eds.), invited talk, *Proceedings ISPSE 2000, Kanazawa, Japan*, IEEE Computer Society Press, Los Alamitos, CA, pp. 2–11.

M.M. Lehman and J.F. Ramil (2000b), Software Evolution in the Age of Component Based Software Engineering, *IEE Softw.*, special issue on Component Based Software Engineering, vol. 147, no. 6, pp. 249–255; earlier version as Tech. Rep. 98/8, Imperial College, London, June 1998.

M.M. Lehman and J.F. Ramil (2001a), Rules and Tools for Software Evolution Planning and Management, *Ann. Softw. Eng. Spec. Issue Softw. Manage.*, vol. 11, pp. 15–44.

M.M. Lehman and J.F. Ramil (2001b), *An Approach to a Theory of Software Evolution*, IWPSE 2001. A revised version as *Background and Approach to Development of a Theory of Software Evolution*.

M.M. Lehman, G. Kahen and J.F. Ramil (2002), Behavioural Modelling of Long-lived Evolution Processes: Some Issues and an Example, *J. Softw. Maint. Res. Pract.*, vol. 14, no. 5, pp. 335–351.

M.M. Lehman, Stenning V. and Turski W.M. (1984), Another Look at Software Design Methodology, *ACM SigSoft. Softw. Eng. Notes*, vol. 9, no. 2, pp. 38–53.

M.M. Lehman, D.E. Perry, J.F. Ramil, W.M. Turski and P. Wernick (1997), Metrics and Laws of Software Evolution – The Nineties View, *Proceedings of the 4th International Symposium on Software Metrics, Metrics 97*, Albuquerque, New Mexico, pp. 20–32; Also in K. El Eman and N.H. Madhavji (eds.) (1999), *Elements of Software Process Assessment and Improvement*, IEEE Computer Society Press, pp. 343–368.

Luqi (1989), Software Evolution through Rapid Prototyping, *IEEE Comput.*, vol. 22, no. 5, pp. 13–25.

R.T. Mittermeir (2006), *Facets of Software Evolution*.

V. Nanda and N.H. Madhavji (2002), The Impact of Environmental Evolution on Requirements Changes, *Proceedings International Conference on Software Maintenance*, Montreal, Canada, pp. 452–461.

P. Naur and B. Randell (1968), *Software Engineering – Report on a Conference Sponsored by the NATO Science Committee*, Garmisch, Germany, Scientific Affairs Division; NATO, Brussels, Belgium, 1969, http://homepages.cs.ncl.ac.uk/brian.randell/NATO/ <as of July 2004>.

L. Osterweil (1987), Software Processes are Software Too, *Proceedings of the 9th International Conference on Software Engineering*, IEEE Computer Society Press, Monterey, CA, Pub. 767, pp. 2–13.

M.C. Paulk, B. Curtis, M.B. Chrissis and C. Weber (1993), *Capability Maturity Model for Software*, Version 1.1. Technical Report CMU/SEI-93-TR-24, Software Engineering Institute.

S.L. Pfleeger (2001), *Software Engineering – Theory and Practice*, 2nd Ed, Prentice Hall, Upper Saddle River, NJ, pp. 659.

T.M. Pigoski (1996), *Practical Software Maintenance*, Wiley, p. 384.

C. Potts (ed.), (1984), *Proceedings of the Software Process Workshop*, IEEE Computer Society Press, Egham, Surrey, Feb., Order No. 587.

V.T. Rajlich and K.H. Bennett (2000), A Staged Model for the Software Life Cycle, *Computer*, vol. 33, no. 7, July 2000, pp. 66–71.

W.W. Royce (1970), Managing the Development of Large Software Systems, *Proceedings of IEEE Westcon*, Los Angeles, CA, pp. 1–9.

G. Succi, J. Paulson and A. Eberlein (2001), Preliminary Results from an Empirical Study on the Growth of Open Source and Commercial Software Products, *EDSER-3 Wkshop, Co-located with ICSE 2001*, May 14–15, Toronto, Canada.

R.N. Taylor, F.C. Belz, L.A. Clarke, L. Osterweil, R.W. Selby, J.C. Wileden, A.L. Wolf and M.Young (1988), *Foundations for the Arcadia Environment Architecture*, SIGSOFT Software Engineering Notes, ACM Press, New York, vol. 13, no. 5, pp. 1–13.

C. Tully (1989), Representing and Enacting the Software Process, *Proceedings of the 4th International Software Process Workshop*, ACM SIGSOFT Software Engineering Notes, ACM Press, June 1989.

W.M. Turski (1981), Specification as a Theory with Models in the Computer World and in the Real World, *Infotech State Art Rep.* vol. 9, no. 6, pp. 363–377.

W.M. Turski (1996), A Reference Model for the Smooth Growth of Software Systems, *IEEE Trans. Softw. Eng.*, vol. 22, no. 8, pp. 599–600.

W.M. Turski (2000), An Essay on Software Engineering at the Turn of the Century, in T. Maibaum (ed.), *Fundamental Approaches to Software Engineering, Proceedings of the Third International Conference FASE 2000. LNCS 1783*, Springer-Verlag, Berlin, Germany, pp. 1–20.

A. van Lamsweerde 2000, Formal Specification: a Roadmap, in A. Finkelstein (ed.), *22nd International Conference on software Engineering, The Future of Software Engineering*, ACM Press, Limerick, Ireland, Order No. 592000-1, pp. 149–159.

N. Wirth (1971), Program Development by Stepwise Refinement, *Commun. ACM*, vol. 14, no. 4, pp. 221–222.

S. Zahran (1997), *Software Process Improvement – Practical Guidelines for Business Success*, SEI Series in Software Engineering, Addison-Wesley, Harlow, England.

2

A Nontraditional View of the Dimensions of Software Evolution

Dewayne E. Perry

Based on "Dimensions of Software Evolution" by Dewayne E. Perry which appeared as an Invited Keynote Paper, International Conference on Software Maintenance 1994, Victoria BC. (c) 1994 IEEE.

2.1 Introduction

The evolution of software systems is usually thought of in terms of the kinds of changes that are made. While the overall motivation of evolution is adaptation, software changes are usually partitioned into three general classes: corrections, improvements and enhancements. Corrections tend to be fixes of coding errors, but may also range over design, architecture and requirements errors. Improvements tend to be things like increases in performance, usability, maintainability and so forth. Enhancements are new features or functions that are generally visible to the users of the system.

This approach is too limiting and does not consider important sources of evolution that affect how systems evolve. To understand software evolution properly, one must take a wholistic view – that is, one must consider *everything* that is involved in well-engineered software systems. There are three interrelated ingredients required for well (software)-engineered systems:

- the domains,
- experience and
- process.

Moreover, these three ingredients are the sources, or dimensions, of software evolution. The critical issue is that each of these dimensions evolves, sometimes independently, sometimes synergistically with other dimensions. It is only by getting to know these dimensions and how they evolve that a deep understanding of software system evolution can be reached. With this understanding, the evolution of our systems can be managed more effectively.

In the subsequent sections, each of these dimensions will be discussed in turn. While precise definitions of these dimensions will not be given, a number of examples will be provided for each to illustrate their various aspects. Finally, a summary will be given of the important lessons to be learnt from each dimension about software evolution.

2.2 The Domains

In building and evolving software systems, there are a number of domains that are pertinent: The 'real world', which provides the context domain for the model and specification of the system, and various theoretical subdomains, which provide foundational underpinnings for the system.

In the subsequent subsections, the real world, the model of the real world, the specification of the system derived from the model, and foundational theories and algorithms will be discussed. How these elements interact with each other and how each of these elements evolves and affects the evolution of the software system will be discussed.

2.2.1 The Real World and Its Model

The real world is of primary importance in any software system. It is, ultimately, the originating point of the system. The first attempts to introduce specific software systems are usually those systems that imitate what already exists in the real world. This imitation is the starting point from which the system evolves.

In the real world, there are objects and processes. From this basis, a model is derived of the application domain for our system together with the selected objects and their associated theories. It is this model that is the abstraction basis for the system specification, which then becomes reified into an operational system [Lehman84].

Thus, both the real world and the model of it exist together, with the latter obviously tied closely to the former. It is at this point that one should note the following sources of evolution: changes in the real world and changes in the model.

By its very nature, the model is an abstraction of the real world. The real world provides an uncountable number of observations – that is, one can always make more observations. A subset of these observations is used as the basis for the system model. Over time, further observations of the world are taken and as a result often change what is considered to be relevant. These changes provide some of the stimulus to change the model.

The real world also provides a richer set of objects than what is needed for the model. To keep the model within some reasonable bounds, one must select objects in the world for inclusion in the model and, hence, leave some objects out of the model. It is these excluded objects that become bottlenecks and irritants in the operational system, and thus cause the model to change (Lehman's First Law, and as most of these kinds of changes are additive, Lehman's Sixth Law as well [Lehman91])

The real world evolves in two important distinct ways: Independently of the system and as a consequence of the system being operational in that real world. In the first case, these changes may affect the model or even affect the operational system. If the system model has an object 'bus conductor' and its associated theory of behavior, and that object in the real world changes (that is, bus conductors behave differently), then the theory must change to mirror the change in the real world. If the system depends on parts of the real world as its context and they change (as for example, hardware often does), then the system evolves as well.

The more fundamental of the two kinds of real-world evolution is that set of changes that happen in the real world as a result of introducing the operational system into it. This introduction inherently perturbs the world and changes it, so that the model of the world is now out of step with the actual world [LB80]. By its very nature, the model must include a model of the system itself as part of the world. This is inherently unstable and is an intrinsic source of evolution. This closed-loop source of evolution is more interesting than the open-loop (that is, independent changes) source and more difficult to understand and manage.

The real world and the abstracted application model of the real world are fundamental sources of system evolution because they are intrinsically evolving themselves.

2.2.2 The Model and the Derived Specification

From the model of the real world, one uses abstraction to initially derive the specification of the system to be built. This specification is then reified through the software development processes into an operational system, which then becomes part of the real world [Lehman84]. How this cycle is an intrinsic source of evolution both in the real world and in our model of that world has been discussed above.

Given the intrinsic evolutionary nature of the model that is the source of the system specification, it will come as no surprise that the specification will evolve as well. The various objects and their behavior, which evolve in the model will have to evolve in the specification.

Equally obvious is the fact that the operational system must evolve to accommodate the evolving specification, since the fundamental relationship between the operational system and the specification is one of correct implementation. It is not a matter at this point whether the theory of the system – the specification – is right or wrong, but whether the operational system implements that theory.

The relationship between the specification and the implementation is the best understood of the various ingredients that are discussed in this chapter: When the specification evolves, the system must evolve as well.

2.2.3 Theory

In the reification of the specification into an operational system, one appeals to a number of different theoretical domains that are relevant either because of the domain of the real world or because of the various architectural and design domains used to reify the specification. It is likely that these underlying theories will evolve independently throughout the life of the system.

Some theories are stable, that is, they have reached a point where they are well understood and defined. For example, the language theory used as the basis of programming language parsing [HU79] is well understood and our understanding of how to use that theory is well established [AU72]. There are parser generators of various sorts (for example, yak) to automatically produce parsers from a language specification. Hence, one no longer worries about how to produce the front ends of compilers.

However, some theories are not as well established and are much less stable. For example, the theory of machine representation is not so well understood. There are the beginnings of such a theory, and it has been used as the basis of generating compiler back ends [PQCC80]. The introduction of this kind of theory had the initial effect of evolving the standard architecture of a compiler as well as evolving the way we think about, describe and build compilers.

More practical examples of theory stability and evolution are those of structured programming [DDH72] and process improvement [Humphrey89]. The theory of structured programming is now well understood. It has been stable for more than a decade (though, unfortunately, there still seem to be many that do not understand the theory or its practice). The theory of process improvement is still in its evolutionary phase. There are only the beginnings of this theory and there is much yet to discover and establish.

There is yet a third category of theoretical underpinnings: Those aspects of the model or system for which there is only very weak theory or no theory at all. Many of the real-world domains have, at best, only weak theories and many have none other than what is established in the specification. It is in this category that one experiences substantial, and seemingly arbitrary, changes. There is very little guidance and thus it is very difficult to find suitable theories to serve in the implementation and evolution of the operational system.

Closely allied to the various theories, are the algorithms that perform various transformations on the domains or determine various facts about those domains. As with their attendant theories, some of these algorithms are stable. For example, there is a well-established set of sorting algorithms [Knuth73] that have well-known properties so that they can be used both efficiently and appropriately where and when needed in software systems. Alternatively, there are algorithms that are known to be optimal. In either case, there is no need for improvement, and hence, no need for evolution, provided the appropriate algorithm is used.

Analogous to theories that are still evolving, are algorithms that are evolving as well. This usually means that the complexity bounds are improving either by reducing that complexity in the worst case or in the average case [HS78].

In some cases, there are domains that are very hard and must be satisfied with algorithms that are at best approximations [HS78]. In other cases, problems are inherently undecidable as in, for example, various forms of logic. For these problems, there are algorithms that may not terminate, that is, they may not find a solution. Or in the cases where there is little or no theory, such as in banking, one makes some approximations and sees how well they work [Turski81]. In all of these cases, there is a constant search for circumstances in which one can improve the performance of the algorithms, in which one can find subcases for which there are workable algorithms, or in which one can move from approximate to definitive algorithms.

Thus, independent of the real world and the specification, there are theories and algorithms which evolve and which can be used to reify the specifications into an operational system. The benefits of this evolution are germane to the implemented system.

2.3 Experience

Of fundamental and critical importance in the enterprise of building and evolving a software system, is judgment. While some aspects of the abstraction and reification process proceed from logical necessity, most of this process depends on judgment. Unfortunately, good judgment is only gained by insight into a rich set of experience.

One gains experience in a number of different ways: Some through various forms of feedback, some from various forms of experimentation, and some with the accumulation of knowledge about various aspects relevant to the system. Each of these forms of experience is discussed in turn.

2.3.1 Feedback

Feedback is, of course, one of the primary results of introducing the implemented software system into the real world. There is an immediate response to the system from those affected by it. However, there are various other important forms of feedback as well: both internal and external, planned and unplanned.

A major form of unplanned feedback is gotten from the modelers, specifiers and reifyers of the system. For example, in the process of evolving the model by abstracting essential objects and behaviors from the real world, there are various paths of feedback between the people evolving that model. This is the interaction that is typical of group design efforts. Similarly, these interacting feedback loops exist when defining the specification and reifying that specification into an operational system.

At various transformation points from one representation to another, there are various paths of feedback from one group of people to another. For example, while going from the model to the specification, there is feedback about both the abstractions and the abstraction process from those trying to understand the specification. While going from the specification to the operational system, there is feedback about both the specification and the specification process.

At the various validation points of the system, there are explicitly planned feedback paths. That is the purpose of various forms of validation: To provide specific feedback about the validated portion of the system representation (model, specification or reification).

Prior to delivering the operational system into general use, one plans carefully controlled use to provide user feedback. Typically, one controls the feedback loop by limiting the number of people exposed to the system. For example, there are alpha and beta tests of the system for this reason. In both tests, one limits the population to 'friendly' users to optimize the amount of useful feedback, that is, feedback that will result in improvements – and minimize the amount of useless feedback, that is, feedback that is essentially noise.

The difference between alpha and beta testing is the number of users involved. The focus of the alpha test is to remove as many of the remaining problems as possible by means of a small population of users. The focus of the beta testing is the removal of a much smaller set of problems that usually require a much larger set of users to find. Once a certain threshold has been reached, the system is then provided to the complete set of users.

Thus, feedback provides a major source of experience about modeling, specifying and reifying software systems. Some of that feedback is immediate, some of it is delayed. In all cases, this set of feedback is one of the major sources of corrections, improvements and enhancements to the system.

Feedback also provides us with experience about the system evolution process itself. Not only does one learn facts about various artifacts in evolving the operational system, but also one learns facts about the methods and techniques we use in evolving those artifacts.

2.3.2 Experimentation

Whereas feedback provides information as a by-product of normal work, experimentation seeks to provide information by focusing on specific aspects of either the system or the process. The purpose of experimentation is to create information for the sake of understanding, insight and judgment. The purpose of feedback is to provide corrective action. They both are concerned about understanding and corrective action, but their emphases are complimentary.

Experiments are divided into three classes: scientific experiments, statistical experiments and engineering experiments. Each has a different set of goals and each provides us with a different class of experience.

In scientific experiments, there are well-designed experiments in which one has a specific set of hypotheses to test and a set of variables to control. The time and motion studies of Perry, Staudenmayer and Votta [PSV94], the Perpich *et al.* work about on-line inspections [PPPVW02], and the design studies of Guindon [Guindon90] are examples of these kinds of experiments. These approaches exemplify basic experimental science. One increases one's understanding by means of the experiment and generates new hypotheses because of that increased experience and understanding.

In statistical experiments, there is a set of data about which one makes assumptions. Those assumptions are then evaluated by means of statistical analysis. In these cases, one is experimenting with ideas, that is, one performs conceptual experiments. Votta's work on inspections [Votta93], the Leszak *et al.* work on root causes [LPS02], and Lehman and Belady's work on evolution [LB85] are examples of these kinds of experiments. Knowledge is increased by analyzing existing sets of data and extracting useful information from them.

In engineering experiments, one generally builds something to see how useful it is or whether it exhibits a desired property. This form of experiment is usually called *prototyping*. In a real sense, it is a miniature version of the full evolution process or operational system, depending on whether one is experimenting with aspects of the process or the system. For example, the database community made effective use of this approach over about a decade or so in the realization of relational databases as practical systems. Here, one finds an interesting interaction between theory and experiment. Codd [Codd70] initially defined relational theory. While clean and elegant, it was the general wisdom that it would never be practical. However, a decade of engineering experimentation in storage and retrieval structures [GR93] in conjunction with advances in theories of query optimization have resulted in practical relational databases in more or less ubiquitous use today.

Thus, there are various forms of experimentation that provide us with focused knowledge about both software processes and software systems. The evolution of this knowledge is a source of evolution for both software systems and our software processes.

2.3.3 Understanding

Thus, there are a number of important ways in which to expand knowledge by means of experience: of knowledge of the real world and the model of it, of the supporting theoretical domains, of the system specification, of the software systems, its structure and representation and of the software evolution process (see also the section on 'Process' below).

However, knowledge itself is valueless without understanding. While knowledge expands, it is understanding that evolves. It is the combination of experience and understanding of that experience that forms the basis of judgment and rejudgment. It is judgment that is the source of both the assumptions and the choices that one makes in building and evolving software systems. And, as understanding evolves, some of those assumptions and choices may be invalidated.

Thus, the evolution of understanding and judgment is a fundamental source of the evolution of software systems and processes.

2.4 Process

Process, in a general sense, is composed of three interrelated and interacting ingredients: methods, technologies and organizations. Methods embody the wisdom of theory and experience. Technology provides automation of various parts of the processes. And, organizations bound, support or hinder effective processes. In some sense this is a virtual decomposition, as it becomes very hard to separate organizational culture, or practices from methods. Technology is somewhat easier to separate, though what is done manually in one organization may be automated in another.

2.4.1 Methods

Some methods find their basis in experience. For example, in Leveson's method for designing safety critical systems [Leveson94], the principle 'always fail with the systems off' is derived from various disasters where the failure occurred with the systems on. One learns as much from doing things when they turn out to be wrong as when they turn out to be right.

Some of our methods are the result of theoretical concerns. For example, in the Inscape Environment [Perry89], the underlying principle is that once one has constructed the interface of a code fragment, one need not worry about the internal structure of that fragment. The interfaces have the property of referential transparency, that is, one only needs to know what is reported at the interface boundaries.

A serious problem arises when trying to maintain this principle in the presence of assignment. Assignment is destructive, that is, assignment does not maintain referential transparency. Knowledge may be lost when assignment occurs: Whatever properties the assignee had before the assignment are lost after the assignment. Thus, if multiple assignments are made to the same variable, knowledge that is important is lost if that variable is visible at the code fragment interface.

If multiple assignment is allowed, the fundamental principle upon which Inscape rests cannot be maintained. For example, in the following case some facts are lost about the variable a.

```
a := b;
a := a + c;
a := a * q
```

The first statement does not cause any problems as one must only maintain that no information is lost at the interface boundaries. Here, a assumes a new value that would be visible at the interface. However, with the second and third statements, a assumes a new value and the properties of the previous assignments are lost – and so is the referential transparency that is required by Inscape.

The solution to this problem is provided by a method that requires the use of distinct variables for each assignment. Thus, the previous example should use another variable name for the first and second assignment since it is the value of the third assignment that is to be seen at the interface.

```
v1  := b;
v2  := v1 + c;
a   := v2 * q
```

In this way, referential transparency is preserved: There are no intermediate facts hidden from the interface that might interfere with the propagation of preconditions, postconditions or obligations in the context in which the code fragment interface is used.

Thus methods evolve, not only as a result of experience and of theoretical considerations, but also because of technology and organizations. In any of these cases, their evolution affects how software systems are evolved.

2.4.2 Technology

The tools used in implementing software systems embody fragments of process within them and because of this induce some processes and inhibit others. Because of this fact, it is important that the tools and technology used are congruent with the prescribed processes.

For example, the tools used for compiling and linking C programs require that all names be resolved at linking time. This induces a particular coding and debugging process that is quite different from that possible within the Multics environment [Organick72].

In the UNIX environment, the name resolution requirement means that every name referenced in a program has to have a resolvable reference for the linking process to complete, and hence for the user to be able to debug a program. That means that the program has to be completely coded, or has to have stubs for those parts that have not been completed. Thus, while debugging incomplete programs is possible, it requires extra scaffolding that must be built and ultimately thrown away.

In the Multics environment, because segmentation faults are used to resolve name references, one may incrementally debug incomplete programs as long as the part that does not yet exist is not referenced. This is a much more flexible and easier way to incrementally build and debug programs.

New tools and changes in the environment all cause changes in the processes by which one builds and evolves software and hence may affect the way that the software itself evolves.

2.4.3 Organization

Organizations provide the structure and culture within which processes are executed and software systems are evolved. The organizational culture establishes an implicit bias toward certain classes of processes and modes of work. However, the organizational culture does not remain static, but evolves as well – albeit relatively slowly. This evolution too affects the way systems evolve by changing the implicit biases, and eventually, the processes and products.

Not only do organizations establish an overall structure, they also establish the structure of the projects, the structure of the processes, and, inevitably, the structure of products [HG99]. Given that there is such direct influence on these product structures, it is disturbing that organizations seem to be in such a constant state of flux. This organizational chaos can only have adverse affects on the evolution of the software system.

Someone at IBM stated that 'The structure of OS360 is the structure of IBM' [LB85]. This is not an observation only about IBM but is true of large projects everywhere. (It is also true of the software processes used: The process structure reflects the structure of the organization.) Moreover, as a system ages, inertia sets in and the system can no longer adapt. When this happens, the system and the organization get out of step and the system can no longer adapt to the needs of the organization. This happened with OS360: The system could no longer adapt to the organization and it fractured along geographical lines into VS1 and VS2 for the United States and Europe, respectively [LB85].

Not only does the way an organization evolves affect the way software systems evolve, but also the way that organizations and systems interact has serious consequences for the way that a system may evolve.

2.5 Summary

To understand the evolution of software systems properly, one must look at the dimensions of the context in which these systems evolve: the domains that are relevant to these systems; the experience gained from building, evolving and using these systems; and the processes used in building and evolving these systems. Taking this wholistic view, one gains insight into the sources of evolution not only of the software systems themselves but also of their software evolution processes as well.

The domains needed to build software systems are a fundamental and direct source of system evolution. They are the subject matter of the system. Changes to the domains often require corresponding changes to the software system.

- The real world intrinsically evolves as a result of introducing and evolving the software system. The context of the system in the real world also changes independently.
- The application model of the real world evolves first, because it is inherently unstable (because it must contain a model of itself) and second, because our assumptions and judgments about the real world change over time.
- As the model changes, the specification changes and forces changes in its reification (the operational system).
- While some of the supporting theory may be stable, many of the subdomains have either evolving theory, weak theory or no theory at all (apart from that embodied in the model and specification). Improvements in the supporting theories offer opportunities for changes to the evolving systems.

Experience is also a fundamental source of system evolution, not because of changes in the subject matter, but because of changes it brings to the understanding of the software system and its related domains. This experience provides an evolving basis for judgment.

- Feedback provides insight into the modeling, specification and reification of the operational system. It is a major source of corrections, improvements and enhancements.
- Scientific, statistical and engineering experiments supply focused knowledge about various aspects of the software systems and processes. The resulting insights enable one to improve and enhance the systems.
- The accumulation of knowledge by means of feedback, experimentation, and learning is of little use if it does not evolve the understanding of the system. This evolution of understanding and judgment is a critical element in the evolution of software systems.

Experience is also a major source of process evolution. It provides insight and understanding into the processes – the methods, techniques, tools and technologies – by which systems are built and evolved. These processes offer an indirect source of system evolution: As processes evolve they change the way one thinks about building and evolving software systems. This change in thinking results in changes in the systems themselves – changes in processes bring about a second-order source of system evolution.

- Whether the evolution of the methods and techniques used in building and evolving software systems are based on experience or theory, they change the way one thinks about and evolves those systems. They shape perceptions about the system and about ways in which it may evolve.
- Tools and software development environments embody processes within themselves. As in methods and techniques, they both limit and amplify the way things are done and thus the way software systems are evolved. As tools, methods and techniques evolve, the way they limit and amplify evolves as well.
- Organizations provide the contextual culture and structure for software systems and processes. While one tends to think of them as providing third-order effects on evolution, they do have direct, fundamental and pervasive effects both on the evolution of the systems and on the evolution of the processes.

These three dimensions of evolution provide a wide variety of sources of evolution for software systems. They are interrelated in various ways and interact with each other in a number of surprising ways as well. Not only do they provide direct sources of evolution, but they provide indirect sources as well.

One will be able to effectively understand and manage the evolutions of our systems only when there is a deep understanding of these dimensions, the ways in which they interact with each other and the ways in which they influence and direct system evolution.

2.6 Acknowledgments

This chapter would not have been possible without the foundational work of Professor Manny Lehman. Moreover, much in the current chapter is a result of discussions with Manny in the context of the FEAST project.

References

[AU72] A.V. Aho and J.D. Ullman, *The Theory of Parsing, Translation and Compiling*, Vol. 2, Prentice-Hall, 1972.

[Codd70] E.F. Codd, "A relational model for large shared data banks", *Commun. ACM*, v. 13, n. 6, pp. 337–387, 1970.

[DDH72] O-J. Dahl, E.W. Dijkstra and C.A.R. Hoare, *Structured Programming*, Academic Press, 1972.

[GR93] J. Gray and A. Reuter, *Transaction Processing: Concepts and Techniques*, Morgan Kauffman, 1993.

[Guindon90] R. Guindon, "Designing the Design Process: Exploiting Opportunistic Thoughts", *Human-Computer Interact.*, v. 5, pp. 305–344, 1990.

[HG99] J.D. Herbsleb and R.E. Grinter, "Splitting the Organization and Integrating the Code: Conway's Law Revisited", *21st International Conference on Software Engineering*, Los Angeles, ACM Press, 1999.

[HU79] J.E. Hopcroft and J.D. Ullman, *Introduction to Automata Theory, Languages, and Computation*, Addison-Wesley, 1979.

[HS78] E. Horowitz and S. Sahni, *Fundamentals of Computer Algorithms*, Computer Science Press, 1978.

[Humphrey89] W.S. Humphrey, *Managing the Software Process*, Addison-Wesley, 1989.

[Knuth73] D.E. Knuth, *The Art of Computer Programming: Sorting and Searching*, Vol. 3, Addison-Wesley, 1973.

[LB80] M.M. Lehman and L.A. Belady, "Programs, Life Cycles and Laws of Software Evolution", *Proc. IEEE*, v. 68, p. 9, 1980.

[LB85] M.M. Lehman and L.A. Belady, *Program Evolution. Process of Software Change*, Academic Press, 1985.

[Lehman84] M.M. Lehman, "A Further Model of Coherent Programming Processes", *Proceedings of the Software Process Workshop*, Surrey, UK, 1984.

[Lehman91] M.M. Lehman, "Software Engineering, The Software Process and their Support", *The Software Eng. J.*, v. 6, n. 5, pp. 243–258, 1991.

[Leveson94] N. Leveson, *Safeware: System Safety for Computer-Based Systems*, Addison-Wesley, 1995.

[LPS02] M. Leszak, D.E. Perry and D. Stoll. "Classification and Evaluation of Defects in a Project Retrospective". *J. Syst. Software*, v. 61, 173–187, 2002.

[Organick72] E.I. Organick, *The Multics System: An Examination of its Structure*, Cambridge, MA, MIT Press, 1972.

[Perry89] D.E. Perry, "The Inscape Environment". *Proceedings of the Eleventh International Conference on Software Engineering*, Pittsburgh, PA, IEEE Computer Society Press, 1989.

[PPPVW02] J.E. Perpich, D.E. Perry, A.A. Porter, L.G. Votta and M.W. Wade, "Studies in Code Inspection Interval Reductions in Large-Scale Software Development", *IEEE Trans. Software Eng.*, v. 28, p. 7, 2002.

[PSV94] D.E. Perry, N.A. Staudenmayer and L.G. Votta, "People, Organizations, and Process Improvement", *IEEE Software*, v. 11, p. 4, 1994.

[PQCC80] B.W. Leverett, R.G.G. Cattell, S.O. Hobbs, J.M. Newcomer, A.H. Reiner, B.R. Schatz and W.A. Wulf, "An Overview of the Production-Quality Compiler-Compiler Project", *Computer*, v. 13, n. 8, 38–49, 1980.

[Turski81] W.M. Turski, "Specification as a theory with models in the computer world and in the real world", *Info. Tech. State of the Art Report*, v. 9, p. 6, 1981.

[Votta93] L.G. Votta, "Does Every Inspection Need a Meeting", *Foundations of Software Engineering*, Redondo Beach, CA., *ACM SIGSOFT Software Engineering Notes*, 1993.

3

IT Legacy Systems: Enabling Environments That Reduce the Legacy Problem: A Complexity Perspective

Professor Eve Mitleton-Kelly

This chapter is a revised version of the paper by Mitleton-Kelly E. and Papaefthimiou MC. 2001, Co-Evolution of Diverse Elements Interacting within a Social Ecosystem, in Systems Engineering for Business Process Change, Vol. 2, Edited by Henderson P., Springer-Verlag, ISBN 1-85233-399-5, with kind permission of Springer Science and Business Media.

3.1 Introduction

IT legacy systems are typically large, the cost of maintaining them is very high and they tend to constrain the business from responding fast enough to changes in business strategy, as they are not sufficiently flexible to allow significant modifications. The applications supported by the legacy systems, however, are often vital to the business and to its day-to-day operations. The IT systems cannot therefore be taken down or off line for upgrading without massive disruption and high cost. In addition, upgrading legacy systems is a risky operation as multiple upgrades create a very complicated system with many interdependencies that cannot be readily identified, as documentation tends to be incomplete and those who built and later modified the system are no longer available. One of the risks is that the new system will quickly become another legacy system unable to fully support the constant changes in business strategy or the frequent introduction of new products. Until the underlying reasons for the creation of legacy systems are understood, the cycle will keep repeating itself.

Three key concepts will be introduced – one is *co-evolution* or the reciprocal influence between related entities that results in a change in two or more related entities. The term *entities* is used, as the concept can apply to (a) units of analysis in different disciplines such as species in biology or organisations in the social sciences; (b) interacting departments or groups within the same organisation or (c) different types of related organisations such as suppliers, buyers, customers, etc.

The second concept is that of *feedback* as this is closely related to the co-evolutionary process and in turn to the legacy problem. A deeper understanding of the two concepts will help practitioners make better use of them. One of the insights that will be offered is that feedback is not a simple linear input-process-output mechanism that can adequately be described as positive or negative. When applied to a complex evolving system like a human organisation, feedback becomes a *nonlinear, multi-loop* and *multi-level process*.

The third concept is that of a *social ecosystem*, which includes all the related co-evolving entities such as businesses, governments, financial institutions, regulatory and standards bodies, customers, etc., which are able to influence each other.

The central thesis of this chapter is that *if co-evolution between the business process and IT development is enabled, then the problems associated with legacy systems will be reduced* [Koza & Lewin 1998, Liu *et al.* 2002, Rosenkopf & Tushman 1994, Tromp & Hoffman 2003, Van de Ven & Garud 1994]. Two case studies, one with an international Bank and another with a UK Building Society (BS), will be used to illustrate how co-evolution was facilitated and thus helped reduce legacy problems – but if this process is to continue beyond individual projects, then the organisation needs to create *enabling environments* that will facilitate the reduction of the legacy problem, by identifying both the social and the technical conditions that will help it do so. This chapter emphasises the *relationship* between the business and IT domains by focussing on the social context. Although it discusses some technical issues it does not deal with them in detail.

In the Bank case, for example, the notoriously difficult relationship between the system developers and the business users was enabled and this in turn created an environment, which had a significant impact on the technical development of the system such that it ensured that the project was delivered on time, when the delivery date was critical for the introduction of the common European currency. The Bank case study will be used to illustrate the co-evolutionary and feedback processes. These are just two principles of complex evolving systems, identified by complexity theory.

The BS case study will be used to introduce and illustrate some additional complexity theory principles. When these principles are understood, then businesses can work with them rather than work inadvertently against them and they can be used to create enabling environments.[1]

Before going any further, however, it may be useful to explain briefly what is meant by *complexity theory*. The theory explains the behaviour of systems that (a) have many interacting parts; (b) are able to adapt and co-evolve with a changing environment and

---

[1] Both case studies were part of a 3-year research project led by the Complexity Group at the London School of Economics. This was one of 30 research projects funded by the UK's Engineering and Physical Science Research Council (EPSRC). In 1996, the Council set up a managed research programme entitled Systems Engineering for Business Process Change (SEBPC) with a total fund of £4.5 m. The aim of the programme *was to release the full potential of IT as an enabler of business process change, and to overcome the disabling effects, which the build-up of legacy systems has on such change* [Preface, Henderson 2000].

(c) are able to create 'new order' in the form of new structures, or patterns of behaviour, or properties. Complexity theory applies to the kind of complex systems that demonstrate all three characteristics. Most machine-type systems that have many interacting parts, but are, for example, unable to create new order, would be called 'complicated' rather than 'complex'. All human systems and, consequently, organisations are complex evolving systems [Mitleton-Kelly 2003a describes ten of the principles of complex evolving systems].

The first part of the chapter will explain what is meant by the legacy problem and introduce the three concepts of *feedback, co-evolution* and *social ecosystem*; the second part will describe the two case studies; part three will discuss the socio-technical enabling environments created in the Bank and the BS and some insights will be summarised in the conclusion.

3.2 The Legacy Problem

There are several definitions of IT legacy systems [see papers in Henderson 2000, Henderson 2001; see also www.dur.ac.uk/CSM/SABA/legacy-sig/; Liu *et al.* 2002, Reddy & Reddy 2002, Tromp & Hoffman 2003] and they include the standard definition of 'legacy' as a valuable inheritance as well as the idea that the system is old and obsolete. In this context, the definition used by Tromp & Hoffman (2003) provides a good starting point and supports the findings that will be presented in this chapter.

> 'A legacy system is an operational system that has been designed, implemented and installed in a radically different environment than that imposed by the current IT strategy'.

To bring this definition in line with the argument of the chapter, the following qualification should be added '*and no longer supports the current business strategy*'.

The IT legacy problem is usually associated with old and large systems, written in assembly or an early version of a third-generation language. They have been developed 20 to 30 years ago without anticipating that they would still be running decades later. The architectures and technology used to build the systems were relatively inflexible, and they had not been designed to accommodate such a magnitude of change over an extended period of time. The software systems have been changed extensively, but in an incremental and *ad hoc* manner. This provided the required improvement in functionality in the short term, but at the cost of increased connectivity and interdependence, and with relatively poor system understanding. Moreover, they are associated with high maintenance costs and they have become very difficult and expensive to change to further support the business objectives. When the balance between the technical and business dimension is lost, legacy can be seen as a *gap* between the business needs and the technical capabilities.

Once legacy is seen as that gap, then it is no longer confined to old systems. *New* systems may quickly become 'legacy systems' in the sense that they do not meet the full requirements of the users and are unable to fully support business evolution. This is often the outcome of a lack of understanding and communication between IT professionals and the business IT-users and strategists, or lack of adequate and appropriate feedback, which leads to separate evolutionary paths and to a divergence of interests and hence to differing future directions. In such cases there has been a low rate of co-evolution or interaction leading to reciprocal influence and change, between the business and IT domains.

For legacy problems to be reduced, the IT professionals need to understand the business process, its language, values, direction and future development, if they are going to provide IT systems that support the business. On the other hand, the business users and strategists need to understand the technical potential as well as the limits of the IT systems. Since the individuals who are attracted to the IT and business domains are psychologically and culturally different, this kind of interaction and mutual understanding is neither simple nor easy, and it certainly does not happen as a matter of course. A study carried out by Mitleton-Kelly in 85 organisations, between 1988 and 1992, interviewing over 300 business and IT strategists, indicated that communication, which leads to a deep understanding of the other domain was very rare. When it did occur, it depended on specific individuals taking the initiative. The general interaction between the business and IT domains, however, was limited to occasional formal exchanges when necessary. There was little regular informal interaction and the professionals in each area of operation felt uncomfortable with the other. The two case studies showed that this was not always the case and that with the right enabling environment, co-evolution and feedback between the two sets of strategists was facilitated.

3.2.1 Feedback

In an engineering context, feedback is understood as a mechanism or a loop linking a linear input-process-output system and feedback mechanisms tend to fall into two types: (a) positive (reinforcing or amplifying) feedback and (b) negative (balancing, moderating or dampening) feedback. The former is likely to create change while the latter creates stability and tends to be predictable.

Feedback in human systems, however, cannot be a simple linear process with predictable and determined outputs. Actions and behaviours vary with different individuals, as well as with time and context. When applied to a complex evolving system like a human organisation, feedback becomes a *nonlinear, multi-loop and multi-level process* operating at different scales – at the level of the individual, the group, the organisation, the industry, the economy, etc. [Lehman 1996, Lehman 1997, Rosenkopf & Tushman 1994, Van de Ven & Garud 1994, Bateson 1993, Doyle *et al.* 1992] Feedback in a social system's context will be defined as *influence, which changes potential action and behaviour*.

3.2.2 Co-evolution

Co-evolution in both biological and social systems is taken to mean that *the evolution of one domain is partially dependent on the evolution of the other* [Ehrlich & Raven 1964, Kauffman 1993, 1995a, b, Koza & Lewin 1998, McKelvey 1999a, b, Pianka 1994] *or that one domain changes in the context of the other.* In human systems, co-evolution focuses on the *relationship* between the co-evolving entities and can be defined as the *reciprocal interactions among entities at all levels of analysis* [McKelvey 1999b] *that result in reciprocal change* (the term *entity* is used as a generic term, which can apply at different scales to individuals, teams, organisations, industries, economies etc.; it can also apply to nonhuman artefacts such as IT systems that interact with human users, developers, etc.).

There are two issues to note, one is that co-evolution takes place when related entities influence and change each other (sometimes in very subtle ways – the co-evolutionary process does not necessarily imply large or significant change; when two individuals are in discussion and each begins to see things a little differently as a result of that interaction, co-evolution has taken place). The other point to note is that co-evolution happens at all scales of interaction. It can happen between individuals and teams (e.g. software engineers, IT developers, users, business project managers, strategists, etc.); between individuals and artefacts (IT systems); between departments, organisations, industries, economies, etc. The other issue is that co-evolution can only take place within an ecosystem. (This point will be explored further in Section 3.2.3.)

3.2.3 The Social Ecosystem

In biology an ecosystem is an environment where 'each kind of organism has, as parts of its environment, other organisms of the same kind and of different kinds' that interact [Kauffman 1993 p. 242]. In an organisational context, a *social ecosystem* is the broader social environment that contains all related businesses, within the same and other industries, suppliers, customers and shareholders, as well as the financial, economic, political and legal systems that can have an influence upon and are influenced by each other. Rosenkopf & Tushman (1994) describe the social ecosystem as an 'organisational community' and define it as *'the set of organizations that are stakeholders for a particular technology. Depending on the technology, this set of organizations can include suppliers, manufacturers, user groups, governmental agencies, standards bodies, and professional associations'*. Since each entity needs to evolve in the context of other related entities, co-evolution cannot take place in isolation – it takes place within an ecosystem and it does so at all scales. Within a social context, the notion of 'ecosystem' therefore can apply both within the organisation and to the broader environment.

Hence *a complex co-evolving ecosystem is one of intricate and multiple intertwined interactions and relationships*. It is not just a nested hierarchy of 'levels' but also of multi-directional influences and links, both direct and many-removed. Connectivity and interdependence propagate the effects of actions, decisions and behaviours throughout the ecosystem, but that propagation or influence is not uniform as it depends on the *degree of connectedness*, which in turn affects the quality and type of feedback.

Both biological and social systems are not fully connected but display different degrees of connectedness over time. 'Real (biological) ecosystems are not totally connected. Typically each species interacts with a subset of the total number of other species, hence the system has some extended web structure' [Kauffman 1993, p. 255]. In human ecosystems, the same is true. There are networks of relationships with different degrees of connectedness. The degree of connectedness means the strength of coupling and the dependencies known as *epistatic interactions* – that is, the fitness contribution made by one individual will depend upon related individuals. This is a contextual measure of dependency, of direct or indirect influence that each entity has on those it is related to or is coupled with. Each individual belongs to many groups and different contexts and his/her contribution in each context depends partly on the other individuals within that group and the way they relate to the individual in question. Consider how the same individual can behave in a different way and show a range of characteristics in various contexts – part of the reason is how others within each group influence the behaviour and, consequently, the contribution that each individual member feels able to make. Degree of connectedness, dependency or epistatic interaction may determine the strength of feedback.

Linking the above, it is suggested that *legacy is the outcome of restricted co-evolution and inadequate feedback* between the changing business process and IT development. The *business and IT domains are evolving along two separate evolutionary paths with minimal co-evolution.*

The two domains exist within multiple environments, that is, within business, market and technological environments, which are themselves changing. As these entities interact, they cocreate their co-evolving social ecosystem. However, *weak coupling* such as infrequent interaction and/or lack of understanding and knowledge about the other's domain, lowers the *rate of co-evolution*, and creates legacy systems, which do not support the changing business process.

The Mitleton-Kelly 1988–1992 study showed that the relationship between IT professionals and business strategists or project managers was consistently restrained, and this exacerbated isolated evolution. They only talked to each other when absolutely necessary. The users drew up requirements without understanding what the technology was able to offer; these were often minimal lists of functionality and did not explain the broader business context. Future plans for new products or a change in strategy were not communicated to the developers, as a matter of course. They therefore had to design or modify the IT system with only a very limited view of what was required. There was rarely any open, extended, face-to-face discussion of future plans and requirements and of consequent implications for system design. There was therefore very limited and highly constrained co-evolution.

To understand co-evolution, a distinction needs to be made between adaptation *to* a changing environment and co-evolution *within an ecosystem* [Mitleton-Kelly & Papaefthimiou 2000]. Adaptation to, implies that there is a hard boundary between the system (or the organisation) and its environment. While co-evolution places the system within its ecosystem and assumes flexible boundaries between interrelated elements that reciprocally influence each other. For example, when suppliers become 'partners' or when end-users participate in the design of a new IT system and become part of the design team, the boundaries of identity and relationship change.

The emphasis therefore changes from a simple relationship between the system and its environment to a complex relationship between multiple interacting elements within a social ecosystem, co-evolving *with* each other. In this context, feedback can be seen as those processes that influence change in decisions, actions and behaviours between the multiple differentially coupled entities. In one sense the *feedback loop* becomes a *multi-dimensional spiral* as each change in one entity may trigger a change in a related entity, which in turn may trigger other changes in its coupled entities. Just to complicate matters, this is not a linear causal process in the sense that change A *causes* change B. Many changes, for example, A, D, G, M, etc., may *together* contribute to change B. *The reciprocal influences or feedback processes are neither uniform nor universal. They depend on the degree of connectedness, on epistatic interactions and on time and context.* Furthermore, the consequences of actions and decisions are again not totally determined or fully predictable and there is always a range of possible consequences (or possible futures) arising from each decision or action taken.

3.3 The Two Case Studies

One case study is with an international Bank and the other with a UK Building Society. They were part of a larger research project carried out by the author and colleagues. Data was collected through semi-structured interviews with business users, systems developers, business and IT strategists. Part of the methodology [Mitleton-Kelly 2003b] was to identify and study a *natural experiment*, in the sense that a group of individuals developed a different way of working and relating, which was different from the established working practice, and which could not be supported by the dominant culture of the organisation. (The experiment was undertaken by those involved, it was not 'done to them' by senior managers or researchers.) The dominant culture of the Bank, for example, supported a particular way of relating and working, which had inadvertently contributed to the legacy problem. A different way needed to be found and the UK office created a completely new way. Although certain individuals took particular actions, no one was deliberately *orchestrating* the process. Certain socio-technical conditions were introduced, which encouraged and supported a different type of interaction and this facilitated the co-evolutionary process. In other words, certain individuals in the Bank's UK office initiated the conditions that facilitated the creation of a new enabling environment, which helped ameliorate the legacy problem.

The **Bank** is an international bank, but the case study concentrated on its European operations prior to the introduction of the common European currency, the Euro. The main European system was on two hardware bases. Eleven European countries, with smaller branches, using HP hardware, were serviced from the United States, while the larger branches, with IBM systems were run from the United Kingdom. Originally the IBM system was implemented in seven different countries and it started in the late 1970s, early 1980s, as a branch or country-centric system, referred to as '*a Bank in a box*' and it ran all the local Bank's operations. Since then, the Bank has gone through several phases of restructuring. The first set of changes in the mid-1980s was to regionalise the environment, that is, the hardware and the software were brought into central service centres, and the branches were run remotely. The branch users run their terminals connected over leased lines into one of the service centres. These centres were subsequently centralised in the United Kingdom. This involved two phases: moving the technology and then the branch back-office processing.

These changes were part of a co-evolutionary process, in the sense that, the *organisational restructuring* (a social aspect) *changed the systems' architecture* (a technical aspect) when the Bank went through its various restructuring phases and the architecture in turn affected the ways of working.

The **BS** in the United Kingdom redesigned its IT systems to meet two objectives (a) to enable new insurance products to be designed and marketed within a shorter period of time and (b) to migrate all the old products to the Future Product Framework (FPF) system, which would serve as a single processing engine. Regarding the first objective, it was expected that many problems would be resolved in the release process and testing, and new products would be marketed within a couple of weeks rather than eight weeks. To achieve the second objective, FPF was to be used as a single processor, by using standard building blocks to design a new product. This would enable the organisation to react very quickly to the marketplace.

Although FPF was initially perceived as a solution to legacy, it did not fulfil that aim. On the contrary, it showed signs of becoming another legacy system. Part of the reason was that the patterns of behaviour that had created the old legacy system were being repeated. However, as part of the process of migration and upgrading, several other things happened that had a beneficial effect on the relationship between the business and IT domains and these will be outlined below.

This study is used for three reasons:

(a) Unless patterns of behaviour that create legacy systems are understood and changed, the legacy problem will continue to recur; it is therefore essential to learn from these experiences.
(b) Some conditions were created that did improve the relationship between the two domains; if they are acknowledged and reinforced they will form the basis of an enabling environment.
(c) To introduce some additional principles of complexity within an organisational context.

One of the positive things that happened was when the female IT Manager in the BS started to pick up the telephone on a regular basis to invite her business colleagues to discuss the current and future needs of the organisation. This was quite a revolutionary step, but it worked and the regular feedback sessions not only facilitated the co-evolutionary process and produced better systems but also accelerated the *rate of co-evolution* and increased the speed at which modifications were made.

Before discussing the enabling environments, three types of factors will be described to provide some of the background – they are (a) business and market, (b) organisation and management and (c) technology. The distinction between the three factors is primarily conceptual, in the sense that it offers a framework for understanding the interdependence and interrelationship between them. It is also relevant for recognising and creating the complex socio-technical conditions, which enable co-evolution between the business and IT domains.

3.3.1 Business and Market

In the Bank, *changes in business processes*, products and services had an *impact* on the Bank's *technological infrastructure*. For example, new business development in other geographical areas and changing business objectives often required the development of a new system or enhancements of the existing systems. Other examples include intensifying *competition* and the need to offer *new products* to respond to market forces. Offering new products demanded changes in the existing systems to accommodate new functionality or the development of a new system that had to interface with the existing ones. Further, *changing customer expectations* that demanded sophisticated service, affected the way information was provided by the current software infrastructure. This resulted in the need for building new interfaces to support the information. Furthermore, the economic climate and the market exerted financial pressures that affected the allocation of funds to build or rebuild an application. As a consequence, new applications were often built on old technology or incremental functionality was added onto the existing system, which in turn contributed to the problem of legacy. Another way of looking at these influences is that co-evolution needs to take place at all levels: from the macro-level between the organisation and its social ecosystem (which includes all related businesses, customers, competitors and suppliers as well as the economic and cultural environment) to various micro-levels within the organisation. Furthermore, changes at the organisational macro-level affected the various interrelated micro-levels within the organisation, such as the IT systems.

In the BS, *changes in the strategic focus* of the organisation (whether, for example, the priority lay with insurance products sold directly or through intermediaries or through cross-selling), had important *implications* for the *technological infrastructure*. The *life cycle of some insurance products*, like pensions, also contributed to the legacy problem as they are very long (around 25–30 years). Even if a product is withdrawn from the market, the IT application that supports it cannot be *'switched off'* for a number of years, until all existing policies have reached maturity. This partly explains the existence of many interconnected systems, of different technological characteristics and ages of systems that run in parallel. This interconnection and interdependency of systems again exacerbates the legacy problem.

Changes in legislation have an impact on the business in terms of the products sold, and the systems that support these products have to be adjusted to accommodate the new regulations. These adjustments might range from simple code upgrades to changing the system itself, alterations to other systems that interface with the original system, the development of a new system that will interface with other older systems or all the above. The influence of exogenous institutional factors, like legislation, is also part of the feedback process, which impacts decisions, IT systems and ways of working and also contributes to the legacy problem.

Social co-evolution is dependent on feedback in the form of information and the communication of that information, and in turn influences and may even shape feedback channels of communication.

3.3.2 Organisation and Management

In both case studies, some of the legacy issues were closely linked to the human and the organisational context, such as the delivery of applications. Short cuts and compromises were made to the systems' capabilities and frequently only a part of the original specification was delivered. This resulted in incremental system enhancements and eventually to complicated and problematic applications. Some more specific problems were as follows: (1) The *communication gap* between the developer and user communities further impeded the development process due to the different views and the use of different languages (e.g. IT and business jargon). As a consequence of this poor appreciation of each other's domain, developers did not deliver according to users' expectations. (2) The *lack of skills* to maintain the legacy systems was another consideration. It was difficult and expensive to recruit people who had knowledge of the old systems since current training was focused on the current rather than the older technologies. Furthermore, resistance to change at times prevented some people from moving away from the old technology. Consequently, some new applications did not benefit from the state-of-the-art technologies and the legacy problem was perpetuated. (3) The age of employees as well as exposure to new technology contributed to an individual's attitude towards change, but the attitude of the organisation was also important, as this directly affected the support of *training* and *education* in the workplace. (4) Personal *career agendas* were sometimes in conflict with underlying business needs. Younger employees were keen to use the latest technological tools to improve their CV. This attitude was reinforced by senior managers who committed more time and resources to the development of new systems while ignoring the old legacy systems. As they were often in place for only a short time (e.g. only 2 years in the Bank) they wanted to be associated with introducing 'new sexy technology'. There was not much kudos in being associated with the old legacy systems. *'Obsession with the new technology'* and personal choices in moving on with one's career seemed to override some of the underlying needs of the organisation, such as maintaining and upgrading the old legacy systems that were still essential to the business. (5) *Management discontinuity* further exacerbated the problem. The managers responsible for new initiatives did not as a rule stay in their job long enough to complete a project and to make any real impact and, as a result, projects were often not completed as each new manager wanted to introduce new ideas rather than complete those initiated by his predecessor.

3.3.3 Technology

Some of the issues associated with the technology, in both cases, were as follows: (i) Rapid technological change and the need to keep up with current technology exerted a constant pressure on the management, which had to be offset against the cost of the investment. (ii) The existing technological infrastructure, in combination with the increasing obsolescence of technology failed to meet emerging expectations and to keep up with new business requirements. (iii) Alignment and interfacing between existing and new technology (in terms of new platforms, new hardware, new software and processes) introduced multifarious problems contributing to institutional friction.

3.3.4 Interactions between the Various Elements

In the Bank case study, a high degree of interconnectivity and interdependence between the b*usiness, market, organisational* and *technical* elements created a complex social ecosystem that influenced and impacted both the business process and the IT systems. The co-evolutionary processes supported by feedback influences included the following interactions, which have been simplified for ease of illustration: Changes in the business and the market necessitated changes in products. This in turn meant adjustments to the existing applications. After many repetitions of this process, positive feedback created applications with cumulative incremental enhancements, which exacerbated the legacy problem. Yet each enhancement worked in the short term and created a balance between the business need and its IT support – that is, there was short-term balancing (negative) feedback. In the longer term, however, each short-term adjustment added to the legacy problem. The legacy systems in turn constrained the business from offering new products. This was *a continuous reinforcing process, interspersed with occasional balancing processes.* In other words, there were *multiple feedback processes* 'embedded' within each other. *Co-evolution took place in the sense that each domain* (i.e. IT systems and business process) *changed in the context of the other, and in turn influenced each other.* Coupled interactions and feedback processes, therefore, contributed to the creation of a problem space associated with legacy systems, which constrained the way business could evolve. Yet each attempt to aid business evolution reinforced the legacy problem.

Following are some examples of how interacting elements created the legacy systems problem in the Bank case study. (For a more detailed account of this case study, please see Mitleton-Kelly & Papaefthimiou 2000).

(a) One element arises from increasing interconnectivity and interdependence among the *system components and the applications.* The Bank services *'very high value global corporate clients'*. The basis of that service is that it will provide those customers with the technology infrastructure to support their business. This means that the Bank will often customise or engineer solutions into its systems, and change their coded components, to support individual clients. Over time a layered system infrastructure was created, which was tailored to service many different customers. The interconnectivity and interdependence become so intricately intertwined that a point is reached when *'to undo that complexity is almost insurmountable without going back to the business perspective and understanding where those customers are going and whether they are willing to accept a change in the way that we're working with them which allows us to undo some of the legacy and therefore some of the complexity'* (Bank Senior IT Manager). An important point to note is that emphasis was placed on the *relationship* between the business and its customers and the IT developers that was based on a reciprocal understanding of business direction (related to the future needs of customers) and IT constraints. This kind of relationship, leading to an understanding of each other's domain, helps create the environment that enables co-evolution.

(b) Another element contributing to the operational complexity of the socio-technical system was that *organisational restructuring* (a social aspect) *changed the systems' architecture* (a technical aspect) when the Bank went though its various restructuring phases in the 1980 s and 1990s.

(c) The *identification of ownership of common components* and of the need for upgrading was much more difficult as multiple owners had to be identified and to be persuaded of the benefits, before they would sign off. The technical problems associated with upgrading the systems impacted the organisational issue of ownership and the geographically dispersed organisational structure added to the problem. The multi-ownership issue did not arise with systems that were managed and owned locally in a single country. This example shows how the intricate interrelationship and feedback processes through influence and impact, between technological and organisational factors, create the complex problem space of legacy: A technical problem impacted an organisational issue while organisational changes exacerbated the technical concerns.

(d) Another aspect was that the Bank had made a conscious effort to try and isolate modules of the legacy 'Bank in a box' system and to *create stand-alone components*, which still communicated with it. They were Windows NT-based front-end servers. They had not succeeded in replacing the full set of legacy software and the partial replacements used current technology. In an effort to update the system with new technology (instead of incremental adjustment), it had created new complex interfaces with the old systems.

(e) Another element contributing to the legacy problem was that the maintenance and further development of the IT systems had been centralised within the UK group, which controlled 16 systems on both HP and IBM platforms. Thus, as resources for the maintenance and support were held centrally, *local knowledge* of the branch technology of the system was lost. Hence an organisational issue (centralisation and cost reduction) affected the technology infrastructure, which in turn affected the knowledge base. This may have consequences on the future maintenance of the local systems and on the local business.

The above examples illustrated the complex interactions of diverse geographic, business, organisational and technical elements within a co-evolving social ecosystem.

3.4 The Socio-Technical Enabling Environment

3.4.1 The Bank's Enabling Environment

Despite the above and other problems, the Bank project was completed successfully. One of the main drivers was the exogenous pressure of legal and regulatory requirements imposed by the European Union, which needed to be implemented before the Bank was ready to handle the common European currency. However, although the exogenous pressure was a necessary condition, it was not sufficient for success. Many other conditions needed to be created internally and this section describes some of them, which contributed to a local *socio-technical enabling environment*.

The project introduced new technologies, and because of its high profile was also able to import an international team of technical experts. But what facilitated the technical success were certain social conditions initiated by the project manager in charge of the project. One of the most important aspects was the facilitation of a closer working relationship between the business and information systems professionals. The project manager introduced a regular monthly meeting where all developers, business project managers and operational staff met to update each other on progress. There were two rules: (a) everyone had to make time to attend the meeting and (b) they all used the minimum of jargon and tried to be as intelligible as possible to those not familiar with their specialist field. The first couple of meetings were strained and tense – but once connections and insights started happening about how problems could be resolved or how the technology could be used, or understanding what the business wanted and needed to achieve, the meetings became generative and creative and were welcomed. But what they achieved beyond a 'feel good' atmosphere was that it facilitated feedback and the co-evolutionary process between the developers and the business managers and it accelerated the rate of that co-evolution to a significant degree.

An enabling environment was created that included the following social conditions:

- New procedures introducing regular monthly meetings, which enabled *good networking* and *trust*, as well as a *common language* leading to mutual *understanding*.
- *Autonomy*: the project manager was allowed to introduce the new procedures, without interference.
- A *senior manager supported* the changes, but did not interfere with the process.
- *Stability*: sufficient *continuity* to see the project through, in an environment where constant change of personnel was a given.
- An *interpreter* mediated the dialogue between the domains. This ensured understanding on both sides but also protected the technologists from constant minor changes in requirements.

The monthly meetings, supported by weekly information updates, enabled the technologists and the business and operations professionals to talk together regularly and in a way that was going against established ways of working. In time, the various stakeholders involved in the projects began to identify *cross-dependencies in terms of the business project relationships*, which led to new insights, and new ways of working. Once the conditions were provided, the individuals involved were able to self-organise, to make the necessary decisions and take the appropriate actions. (*Self-organisation* occurs in a social context when a group of individuals decide to undertake a certain task that is not part of their daily routine – they decide on what to do, when and how to do it, without anyone outside the group directing their actions.) This illustrates micro-agent interaction, at the level of individuals and groups, which is neither managed nor controlled from the top. Once the inhibitors were removed and the enablers put in place, new behaviours and ways of working emerged. (*Emergent* properties, patterns, qualities or behaviours are more than the sum of the parts and tend to be unpredictable. It is the nonlinear, nondetermined interactions between the parts or micro-agents that create emergent patterns at the next macro-level.) The monthly sessions improved communication between the different domains by improving understanding, but they also allowed for the *emergence of new ways of working*, and in the process helped the business become fitter or more competitive. The point to note is that new ways of working were not designed or determined in advance. They came into being or emerged when the relationships and interactions changed.

Another important element was the *articulation of business requirements* as an iterative process with regular face-to-face meetings. These meetings were at a senior management level with (a) a vice president who owned the product, was responsible for the profit and loss and determined the business requirements; (b) a senior and experienced business project manager who was a seasoned Banker, with a good knowledge of the Bank, and (c) a senior technology project manager who defined the Information Systems (IS) platform(s) and the technical development of the project. This constant dialogue created a willingness to *communicate* and a level of *trust*, which were essential enablers of co-evolution. These social processes can also be seen as *feedback enabling or facilitating processes*. For example, trust facilitated better communication, which in turn enabled the building of IT systems that facilitated the evolution of the business.

What was achieved took a particular individual, supported by his senior manager, to create the conditions that enabled dialogue, understanding and a good articulation of requirements. He created the initial conditions, to improve the relationship between the domains, but he could not foresee how the process would work or whether it would work. As it happened, it did work and a substantial *network rapport* was established between the domains based on *trust, a common language and mutual understanding*. They worked well together, because the conditions were right and they were prepared to *self-organise* and work in a different way. The new relationships were not designed or even intended. They happened spontaneously in the sense that their emergence was enabled but not stipulated.

The achievement, however, could be a one-off. Unless the new procedures and ways of working become *embedded* in the culture of the organisation, they are likely to dissipate over time. Once the initiator is no longer in place, the danger of dissipation or reversion to the dominant mode of working will assert itself. In this case there has been some embedding and some continuity, but the process is fragile. A new set of organisational changes could destroy it. Part of the embedding is the networking rapport that has been established. But the network rapport is implicit and informal, and is therefore under threat if there are too many and too frequent changes and the Bank's culture is one of constant change in management positions. '*Every two years someone else is in the post so that there is that lack of continuity*'. If the rate and degree of change is too great, then the network will become invalid.

An essential aspect of creating an enabling environment is the conscious appreciation of what is happening, why it is taking place and how it can be facilitated in future. Those particular types of meetings were appropriate to that organisation at a specific time. The generic principle is that improved *communication*, which includes some face-to-face meetings, is an essential element. It builds *relationships*, *networks* and *trust* and a *deeper understanding and knowledge* of other, but closely related, parts of the business. There are organisations like Shell, where building and maintaining one's network within the organisation is recognised as an essential part of one's career plan. The Shell culture acknowledges the importance of networks and actively facilitates their construction. But this is not enough. There are other social and technical conditions that need to be acknowledged and facilitated such as *supporting training and education in new technologies*, while at the same time appreciating the importance of the deep knowledge that IS professionals develop over years working with particular systems, that are old but essential to the business. The loss of knowledge and expertise also applies to *local knowledge* (technical and business) when restructuring and centralisation take place. Once lost, it is very difficult (often impossible) to resurrect, and much time and effort can be wasted in re-learning what has been lost. A degree of continuity may also be necessary. Constant movement of personnel because of restructuring or specific policies, needs to be kept under review and be flexible.

3.4.2 The Building Society and Some Complexity Principles

The emphasis in the Bank study was on the interaction of multiple socio-technical elements at micro- and macro-levels of interaction, focussing on co-evolution and feedback processes. It also used the example of a natural experiment to illustrate how some enabling conditions helped create a new way of working and relating, that was different from the dominant culture. The BS case study will be used to introduce and illustrate some additional principles of complex evolving systems, identified by complexity theory. When these principles are understood then they can be used to create enabling environments.

(a) *'Gurus' as emergent phenomena; operating far-from-equilibrium and exploration of the space of possibilities.* The part functionality and shortcomings of the legacy systems, the continuous changes and enhancements, and the difficulty involved in the process due to lack of proper documentation gave rise to the so-called *system experts* or *gurus*. These people had invaluable system knowledge and expertise and had either a business or a technology background. The 'experts' from the business side, acted as interpreters between the business users and the IT developers by helping to translate business requirements into technical language. This helped to overcome the communication problem between the business users and the IT developers. While the technical gurus had a deep knowledge of the undocumented legacy system and were able to help the new developers navigate its intricacies.

The 'gurus' *emerged* out of necessity. They were not appointed and no one defined their job description. Lack of skills, lack of system knowledge and lack of documentation, exacerbated when IT professionals moved, retired or left the company, acted as a constraint to business evolution. *Constraints* are not always undesirable, as they can force both the individual and the organisation to find a different way of working, which can often be innovative, to overcome the constraint. The organisation therefore had to find a different way of operating by *exploring its space of possibilities* or possible alternatives. Exploration is not always explicit or systematic – it can be intuitive and is often quite creative, particularly when trying to overcome a constraint. It can, however, be restricted if there is a risk-averse or a blame culture that does not encourage experimentation. By definition, when one is trying out different alternatives a few will work and many will not. But to find the ones that work people need to work through some that do not. Exploration therefore carries the risk of failure – but if the alternatives that do not work are seen as part of the exploration process, then employees may be encouraged to try out new, creative procedures that are not the norm. The corollary of this freedom, however, is responsibility. In organisations where this approach has worked, each individual carried and was aware of carrying responsibility for their actions, and whatever new ideas they tried out they could not risk injuring the organisation.

One way of looking at the process is that constraints may push the organisation *far-from-equilibrium*, in the sense that they push it away from the standard way of working, away from the norm. The gurus are not the norm, there is no career path or job description for them and no one could have predicted their emergence. When pushed, far-from-the-norm individuals and organisations are forced to explore alternatives. This exploration may be deliberate or it could be implicit and emergent. However, exploration needs to be enabled and emergent properties need to be recognised and not inhibited. In this case the gurus enabled a different way of working, and helped to overcome certain constraints that could have had a deleterious effect on the development of the business.

(b) *Self-organised informal networks, epistatic interactions and connectedness*. One multi-disciplinary project on legacy systems, in the BS, brought together various experts. They found that they worked well together and could help each other. This was a new departure in established ways of working. Once that project was completed the team was disbanded, but the *informal network* it created, has since been often resurrected, on a self-organised basis. Whenever there is a project related to IT legacy systems, people in the network call each other and try to work on the project together, on an informal basis. Because of their previous experience of working together, they know each other's expertise and can call on those with the necessary knowledge. No manager external to the group dictates or directs these interactions. The individuals within the self-organised group initiate them. This is self-organisation at a micro-scale where individuals take the initiative to talk to others and to carry out tasks they recognise as necessary. With improved communication, results were always good. The enablers here were knowledge of available skills and expertise gained through the initial project. But subsequently, flexibility in allowing self-organised groups to work together helped. However, to create a robust enabling environment, it would be necessary to acknowledge the value of such interactions and actively encourage them. Both the self-organised groups and the gurus are also illustrations of *epistatic interaction*. The contribution of each individual depended on those other individuals he/she worked with, and was enhanced in particular contexts. The quality of contribution or epistatic interaction also depended on the degree of *connectedness*. Networks or webs are not constantly connected [Kauffman 1993, Kauffman 1995a]. Their robustness depends on their ability to re-establish dormant connections, when necessary. But the

quality, density or intensity of the connections, even between the same individuals, varies over time; hence the degree of connectedness is not a constant.
(c) *Legacy as positive feedback and pattern repetition.* The way management viewed the legacy systems, and continuation of the same processes reinforced the legacy systems. The business, organisation and technology processes interacted with each other on established and *repeated patterns* to produce more legacy. Once a pattern of interaction was established, it continued to reinforce itself through a positive feedback process.

Even when the organisation has explored its space of possibilities and introduced new technology, established thinking, ways of working and relating can counteract and reduce the expected advantages. The BS had implemented a new approach to systems development that could reduce time to market for new insurance products, from eight to two weeks. This would enable the organisation to co-evolve quickly with its marketplace. However, despite all the expectations, the mindsets, technology procedures and ways of working, which originally helped create the old legacy systems, were being repeated. The repetitions of patterns of behaviour, as *reinforcing feedback processes*, recreated the legacy problem. In this case, it was important to recognise what was happening and to break the cycle. This process had begun by encouraging the marketing people to build new applications, but going against well-established norms is difficult and needs constant support and acknowledgement. An important initiative had been taken, what was needed was stronger and continuous support as well as recognition of the difference the new procedures made when a new application created a new product quickly in response to market demand.

3.5 Summary and Conclusions

This chapter has examined the nature of IT legacy systems and explored some of the factors that created them. An important insight has been that legacy is not a purely technical issue but a socio-technical one and some of the co-evolutionary and feedback processes that contributed to legacy were described. Another key insight was that in most organisations IT development and the business process tend to interact minimally and the two domains often evolve in isolation from one another. If, however, co-evolution between them were facilitated, the legacy problem might be reduced.

It was suggested that legacy arises from a multiplicity of intricately interrelated and interdependent socio-technical factors which influence and change each other, through multiple, but inadequate feedback processes. Feedback in complex social systems is based on multi-loop, multi-level processes, at many interrelated micro- and macro- levels. Emergence operates at the micro–macro interactions, but self-organisation, far-from-equilibrium conditions, and exploration of the space of possibilities are also operating at cross-entity interactions within a co-evolving social ecosystem. Reinforcing and balancing feedback mechanisms introduce change and stability respectively, and may operate sequentially or in parallel. The feedback loops, which take place at both micro-agent and macro-structure levels, vary in their intensity and influence. They may be imagined as *a plethora of interacting and interconnected micro-feedback-processes whose connectivity and interaction creates emergent macro-feedback-processes and structures.*

The chapter looked at two case studies with severe legacy problems. They each tried to resolve the problem by facilitating new ways of working and relating and by creating an environment that facilitated interaction. Both the Bank and the BS case studies emphasised the importance of *communication, trust* and *understanding* as essential feedback processes facilitating co-evolution between the business and IT domains.

The Bank case study was used to illustrate the interaction of diverse elements and their feedback processes, in terms of influence, within their social ecosystem. The elements chosen were the organisational, market and technological environments and their influence on business evolution and IT development. The case also showed the relationship between micro-agent interaction and macro-level relationships, within a social ecosystem. Finally, some of the conditions that enabled co-evolution were identified, both between the business and IT domains, and among the organisational, market and technological environments. The BS case study was used to illustrate (a) how repeated patterns of behaviour recreate legacy systems and (b) some complexity principles and their contribution to the creation of an enabling environment.

Enabling environments may be transient but can also be made more robust if the underlying principles of how organisations function, as complex social systems are better understood [Mitleton-Kelly 2003a]. For example, providing the conditions for generative interaction and then allowing the individuals and groups involved to work out their own way of working, often creates innovative and more efficient and effective procedures. There needs to be a balance between the prescribed and the emergent to allow space for self-organisation and a culture that encourages a degree of risk taking in the exploration of the space of possibilities; but employees need also to appreciate that they are responsible and they cannot risk the well-being of the organisation.

Most change initiatives try to define or design the new organisational form (of a department or a whole organisation) and its interactions in detail. The logic of enabling environments, on the other hand, argues for providing the social and technical conditions that offer all the necessary support but then allow for emergence and self-organisation. In addition, awareness of the importance of facilitating co-evolution and how its rate can be accelerated could have a significant impact on resolving extremely difficult issues such as the IT legacy problem. Finally, it is essential to appreciate that complexity theory principles do not work in isolation and their interrelationship needs to be understood – for example, co-evolution is dependent on feedback and so is emergence, while connectivity and interdependence are necessary to all of them.

3.6 Acknowledgements

This chapter is based on research enabled by two EPSRC awards under the SEBPC Programme: IT & Computer Science Programme (GR/MO2590).

An earlier version of this chapter has been published as a paper by Mitleton-Kelly & Papaefthimiou 2001. Papaefthimiou coauthored that paper and I am grateful to her for her contribution.

References

Note: An extensive bibliography on complexity is available on http://www.lse.ac.uk/complexity
Bateson R.N. 1993 *'Introduction to Control System Technology'*, Prentice-Hall, Englewood Cliffs, NJ.
Doyle J.C., Francis B.A & Tannenbaum A.R. 1992 *'Feedback Control Theory'*, MacMillan, New York.

Ehrlich P.R. & Raven P.H. 1964 'Butterflies and plants: A study in Co-evolution' *Evolution*, vol. 18, pp. 586–608.

Henderson P. (ed.) 2000 '*Systems Engineering for Business Process Change*', Springer-Verlag, 2000, ISBN-1-85233-222-0.

Henderson P. (ed.) 2001 '*Systems Engineering for Business Process Change*', Vol. 2, Springer Verlag, 2001, ISBN 1-85233-399-5.

Liu K., Sun L. & Bennett K. 2002 "*Co-design of Business and IT Systems*" Introduction by Guest Editors in Information Systems Frontiers 4:3, pp. 251–256, 2002 ABI/INFORM Global.

Kauffman S. 1993 '*The Origins of Order: Self-organisation and Selection in Evolution*', Oxford University Press.

Kauffman S. 1995a '*At Home in the Universe*', Penguin.

Kauffman S. & Macready W. 1995b 'Technological Evolution and Adaptive Organizations' *Complexity*, vol. 1, no. 2, pp. 26–43.

Koza M.P. & Lewin A., 1998 'The Co-evolution of Strategic Alliances' *Org. Sci.*, vol. 9, pp. 255–264.

Lehman M.M. 1996 'Feedback in the Software Evolution Process' in *Information & Software Technology 38*, Elsevier, pp. 681–686.

Lehman M.M. 1997 *Laws of Software Evolution Revisited*, position paper, *EWSPT96*, Oct. 1996, LNCS 1149, Springer-Verlag, 1997, pp. 108–124.

McKelvey B. 1999a 'Self-organization, Complexity Catastrophe, and Microstate Models at the Edge of Chaos', in Baum J.A.C. and McKelvey B. (eds), *Variations in Organization Science: In Honor of Donald T. Campbell*, Thousand Oaks, CA, Sage, pp. 279–307.

McKelvey B. 1999b 'Visionary Leadership vs Distributed Intelligence: Strategy, Microcoevolution, Complexity' in *Proceedings of EIASM Workshop*, Brussels, June 1999.

Mitleton-Kelly E. 1988–1992 study (unpublished) in 85 organisations. EMK interviewed over 300 business and IT strategists looking at the relationship between the two domains. The study was carried out in the UK and the USA – primarily New York and San Francisco.

Mitleton-Kelly E. & Papaefthimiou M-C. 2000 'Co-evolution and an Enabling Environment: A Solution to Legacy?' in Henderson P (ed.) *Systems Engineering for Business Process Change*, Springer-Verlag, ISBN-1-85233-222-0.

Mitleton-Kelly E. & Papaefthimiou M.C. 2001 'Co-Evolution of Diverse Elements Interacting within a Social Ecosystem' in '*Systems Engineering for Business Process Change*', Vol. 2, Henderson P. (ed.) Springer-Verlag, ISBN 1-85233-399-5.

Mitleton-Kelly E. 2003a 'Ten Principles of Complexity & Enabling Infrastructures' in '*Complex Systems & Evolutionary Perspectives of Organisations: The Application of Complexity Theory to Organisations*' Mitleton-Kelly E., selected papers on complexity by 14 international authors, Elsevier, 2003, ISBN 0-08-043957-8.

Mitleton-Kelly E. 2003b 'Complexity Research – Approaches and Methods: The LSE Complexity Group Integrated Methodology' in Keskinen A., Aaltonen M., Mitleton-Kelly E. (eds). "*Organisational Complexity*". Foreword by Stuart Kauffman. Scientific Papers 1/2003, TUTU Publications, Finland Futures Research Centre, Helsinki, 2003.

Pianka E.R. 1994 '*Evolutionary Ecology*', HarperCollins, New York.

Reddy S.B. & Reddy R. 2002 'Competitive agility and the challenge of legacy information systems' *Industrial Management & Data Systems*, vol. 102, no. 1, MCB University Press, pp. 5–16 (12).

Rosenkopf L. & Tushman M.L. 1994 'The Co-Evolution of Technology and Organization' in Baum J.A.C. and Singh J.V. (eds), *Evolutionary Dynamics of Organizations*, Oxford University Press.

Van de Ven A.H. & Garud R. 1994 'The Coevolution of Technical and Institutional Events in the Development of an Innovation' in Baum J.A.C. and Singh J.V. (eds), *Evolutionary Dynamics of Organizations*, New York/Oxford, Oxford University Press.

4

Facets of Software Evolution

Roland T. Mittermeir

This work is based on an earlier work: 'Software Evolution: Let's Sharpen the Terminology before Sharpening (Out-of-Scope) Tools', in International Conference on Software Engineering, Proceedings of the 4th International Workshop on Principles of Software Evolution, 2001, pages 114–121, © ACM, 2001. http://doi.acm.org/10.1145/602461.602485.'

4.1 Introduction

Software and evolution are very general terms. Hence, people use them in different contexts with quite different semantics, with the risk of inconsistent conclusions. To avoid this problem, this chapter focuses on terminology in the area of software evolution. It is intended to motivate other software engineering researchers to precisely define the scope of the problems they are addressing in their research and to help students understand the breadth of the topic.

On the basis of reflections on the nature of software and on aspects of evolution, a categorisation of software is proposed to help practicing software engineers to choose a proper evolution strategy, depending on the nature of both, the system at hand and the change to be performed.

To advance in any discipline requires that one emphasises the role of efficient communication. Interactive speech acts allow the communicating partners to probe directly whether the frame of reference is adequately adjusted so that the terms used in the communication are properly understood. With written communication, one has to be more careful. Notably, when using highly generic terms, speaker and listener take a risk to find themselves, perhaps unknowingly, caught in a homonym trap. Different mental specialisations of the generic term might be so far apart that miscommunication will eventually set in. *Software* and *evolution* are both generic terms. It is, therefore, no wonder that in discussions involving these terms, participants talk at cross purposes, unaware of the fact that they are addressing different problems and proposing different cures.

Sharpening the semantic focus of these terms is the central aim of this chapter. It first discusses the semantic content of the term *software* and considers the various interpretations one might attach to the word *evolution*. After this initial consideration, the term software is mapped to five different levels of a size/complexity spectrum. On the basis of this stratification, approaches to handle evolution are mentioned to exemplify the situation and show approaches to cope with it. The difference in these approaches is due to humans' limitations in information processing. The arguments raised are demonstrated in the context of a sizable software system.

4.2 What is Software?

Answering the question: 'What is software'? should be easy for software professionals. However, an *ad hoc* experiment conducted by Osterweil in preparing a panel for ICSE 2001 [1] showed that even a sample of renowned software engineering researchers could not come up with a common definition for this term. Instead, analogies and relations to other artefacts were voiced.

4.2.1 Software: A Technical Artefact

When introducing new concepts, notably those related to methodology, software scientists resort to analogies with other engineering artefacts. For instance, when arguing that prototyping should become an accepted part of software development methodology, the spectrum of analogies used ranged from assembly line produced items like cars, via complex industrial products like airplanes to strictly custom-specified unique objects, like architect-designed houses [2]. This indicates that the concepts people have in mind when talking about software cover a wide range. A point of consensus might be that software, at least software that is subject to evolution, is a technical artefact created in a human thought process. The opinion, software is executable mathematics, though occasionally voiced, will, as pointed out by Parnas [3], not apply to evolutionary software. But while analogies serve well for demonstrative purposes, they are less adequate as basis for definitions.

When coining a definition for a tangible object, one usually refers to aspects such as the material it is made of, its external appearance, such as shape, colour or size, or to its purpose, that is, the function it is to serve. For software, this does not yield convincing results.

As generally agreed, software has no physical substance. It is immaterial. Thus, it lacks shape and colour. Nevertheless, one talks about the size of software. However, size needs qualification when referring to software. Some people would measure it by Lines Of Code (LOC), others by Kilo Delivered Source Instruction (KDSI) [4–6]. In another context, one might refer to the amount of physical memory consumed on disk or on working-storage. Intellectual complexity might also be an important indicator of size. However, it can only be measured indirectly by referring to the volume of code or documentation or by measures derived from code, such as the cyclomatic number [7].

4.2.2 Software: A Utility

Taking purpose as key criterion, one might consider the overall utility software-based systems serve for end-users or for society at large. This approach fails in so far, as systems serving some end-user need never consist of software alone. They need at least hardware on which this software is to run. Thus, defining software as 'the thing that makes computers behave in some prescribed way' seems to hit a point. This is at least in agreement with several earlier attempts at defining software. It comes close to the utilitarian approach that claims function dominates material [8, 9]. But it is, once again, quite unsatisfactory to define something by just focusing on the relationship between this still undefined something and some other well-defined class of objects. Moreover, focusing exclusively on functionality may lead to contradictions when separating the required functional properties from nonfunctional requirements that must also be met [10]. It will also be totally at odds with established architectural principles claiming that the architecture of the building has to consider amongst other things the construction material to be used. This principle has not only aesthetic merit but it is also of major technical concern for the maintenance process and hence for everything that has to do with evolution. Thus, even when accepting that software is immaterial, one has to look for a positive answer concerning its very nature.

4.2.3 Software: A Text, Reflecting Reality

Focussing on size as measured by LOC or KDSI points to source code's textual representation. But is not design, the intermediate result of an early stage of development, also software? So are binaries, the result of a later development stage![2] The linguistic representation also crosses with the purpose, since it can be changed drastically (e.g. by replacing an algorithm with a more efficient one) without changing the functionality of the software system. Likewise, different compilers will yield different binaries from the same source code. The differences might be due to variations in the optimisation strategies or might result from compiling for different machines. This should raise further questions against the argument that the relationship between machine and observable behaviour is the very nature of software. At least from the source code perspective, it is twice the same product. Looking at binaries, though, two different products and hence different relationships are seen.

A teleological perspective on the software development process might yield an answer though. Sizable software is not built in a single step that takes one from problem statement to executable binaries. It is rather constructed in an iterative process. In transforming the output of one step to that of a following step, information is added and layers of representations of the very same software result. This information initially stems from the problem domain. It is elicited during domain modelling and during requirements engineering. In later steps (design, programming), it rather relates to the solution domain. During compilation and when loading and interacting with the runtime environment, the information is likely to relate to the machine on which this software is to be executed.

While some of the information added in early phases serves only scaffolding purposes and is, therefore, removed in later steps, all information added throughout the process is added on purpose. Hence, taking a teleological perspective, one builds software systems to reflect in the information domain something that happens (or something the client

---

[2] In line with [4, 11] the term *software* is in the sequel not restricted to code only. It encompasses also upstream products of textual or diagrammatical form as well as alternative downstream representations, such as carefully designed test-suites describing the desired behaviour.

wishes to happen) in the real world. Executable software is the ultimate reflection of some reality in a chain of intermediate products reflecting this reality. These intermediate reflections differ in their degree of precision, their granularity, as well as in the extent that they take into account the machine on which the executable software is finally to be run. Considering software as a specifically constrained form of a linguistic expression allows this term to encompass not only binaries but also source code and all upstream products necessary to derive an operational software system from an initial problem statement.

4.2.4 Software is Information

The contents of these intermediate representations are apparently information to be passed to software professionals of the next development stage. To account for the individuals involved in this process, one must leave the communications-theoretic definition of information given by Shannon and Weaver [12] and move towards an interpersonal definition. From this perspective, information does not exist per se but only in relation to a recipient. The information content of a message may then be regarded as the degree to which the data it contains influences the state or behaviour of the recipient of this message. That recipient can be a human or a machine.

The state space of the receiver can be described by a probabilistic measure attached to the individual values it might assume. Thus, the probabilities attached to this state space may change upon receipt of the message. Hence, if the message cannot be interpreted or if the interpreted message does not lead to a change in the receiver's state space, the data contained in the message does not qualify as information from the receiver's subjective perspective. If, on the other hand, the message leads to a state change, the degree of that change characterises the subjective information content of the message.

Conceptualising software as information yields several benefits:

(a) It provides a clue why software is such a complex entity that is not 'soft' at all. It hints at why software is difficult to write and even more difficult to modify. Lehman's funnel-concept [13] not only wants to cure the problem of its being mistakenly perceived as soft by 'hardening' it. It also leads to a materialised separation of concerns. Middleware systems, properly used, come close to this ideal.
(b) It also helps to clarify some limits faced in both, software development and software evolution. With information as defined above, one is shifting the focus from the machine to the humans who have to deal with software systems. This has a direct consequence for tool builders, methodology developers as well as for technical managers.

Identification of software as information raises two issues:

(a) Since programs are also data with the information encoded in it arranged to process other information encoded in some other form (data), the overall relationship represents a tricky recursion.
(b) That recursion will be recognised as even more subtle when one observes that software reflects some reality. In doing so, it reacts with this reality and thus becomes part of it.

The former loop is central to the concept of the von Neuman computer and thus central to the nature of software. It certainly constitutes one of the difficulties encountered when writing software. The second loop has been broadly discussed (e.g. Lehman's *E-type systems* [14] or Yeh's definition of *wicked systems* [15]). Taken together, these loops remind one of the artfully interwoven loops one finds in Bach's fugue or in Escher's drawings as discussed in Hofstadter's book relating recursive structures in mathematics, drawing, and music to computing [16].

Before dwelling on these considerations, the next section focuses on the term *evolution*.

4.3 Evolution

This section describes two issues of importance for evolution of software systems: the phenomenon of evolution and drivers for evolution.

4.3.1 Principles

According to the COBUILD dictionary [17], *evolution* refers to 'a process of gradual change that takes place over many generations' or 'a process of gradual and uninterrupted change and development in a particular situation over a period of time'. Evolution is thus distinct from both, revolution ('a complete, pervasive, usually radical change in something') and complete standstill. The word evolution is also often used in the context of the activity supporting a particular transition in a gradual change process, as, for example, in the phrase 'evolution of a notion or an idea' or, in software engineering, the evolution from assembly to compilable (high-level) languages or from batch to interactive systems. This latter usage occurs sometimes in the context of presenting some methodology (e.g. [18]) or tool (e.g. [19]) conceived to aid the evolution of software.

Studying the phenomena of sustained change, that is, using the term evolution as noun, is less frequent. Amongst this usage, the ground-breaking analysis of the IBM OS 360 by Belady and Lehman [20] as well as Lehman's subsequent work, most recently pursued in the FEAST projects [21], Parnas's ICSE keynote on software aging [3] or Tamai's analysis [22] are to be mentioned as exceptions in the vast literature on software maintenance where the word evolution appears repeatedly.

In studying change processes, software engineers have learned that, even if developers and maintainers are quite often caught by surprise, change does not occur at random. Lehman has shown that only a certain portion of a system changes between releases [23]. Its size remains stable within a rather constant bandwidth. Investigations by Baker and Eick [24] and by Gall *et al.* [25] have shown that the statistically constant change effort is unevenly distributed over modules. The reason for these observations may differ from situation to situation. Sometimes, managerial decision based on adherence to a predictable sequence of releases and employing a relatively constant workforce for system maintenance may be the primary source of the observed behaviour. In the other situations, the different exposure of system components to different change drivers is likely to cause this effect.

The assumption of different change drivers operating at different times is substantiated by the work of Antón and Potts [8]. Studying the evolution of features of a telephone system, they identified a set of specific evolution patterns. Among other results, this study showed that evolution of systems in terms of integration of new features does not progress gradually and linearly. New features tend to be introduced in bursts, followed by withdrawal of some of them (premature or misjudged developments). Such abrupt stepwise (Antón and Potts call them 'saltationist') evolutionary stages are followed by a period of calm, during which the system is stabilised, at least from the point of view of features. Considering Lehman's laws of system evolution [26] helps to interpret some of these results. These laws state that in order to remain alive, systems need to evolve. This necessitates periodic restructuring, that is, work must be applied to restore or improve the systems' internal technical quality. Considering the constant activity law, one must assume that there are periods of feature extension, of feature stabilisation and of internal (mainly architectural) stabilisation.

Relating these observations, two interlinked driving forces for system evolution can be identified as follows:

(a) external market factors (or comparable social phenomena);
(b) internal feedback factors (while of technical nature, they too are influenced by human concerns).

4.3.2 Evolution Drivers

Market factors depend on human decisions. They involve the expectation and anticipation of decisions by other humans. Antón and Potts identified withdrawal periods immediately after substantial feature extensions. This suggests causes beyond mere technical problems. Rather, the social system was not ready to accept the full extent of the change offered. Human acceptance of change via the social system determines to a large extent what kind of new features are introduced at which time and at which level within the system evolution phase identified in [27].

With other systems, it is not the marketplace that drives evolution. Systems that have to keep up with legislative changes fall into this category. However, even in these cases, it is the social system that drives the change. Technical progress, too, is controlled by social processes of market forces as well as by the technology adoption behaviour of society. On a more detailed level, limited capacity of the maintenance/evolution staff determines the extent to which new technology (of whatever kind) is accepted as a driver for changing existing operational software.

From these reflections, the following hypotheses are proposed.

Hypothesis 1:

Human-based considerations are the main external driving factor behind systems (and software) evolution.

Considering software as information structured in a particular form in order to express or implement some reflection of reality leads to:

Hypothesis 2:

Human (and social) limitations in information processing (acquisition, restructuring) limit the extent of software evolution.

From the software producers/maintainers' perspective, this applies to both, evolution stemming from external change drivers, and evolution due to the feedback properties of very large software [28]. The second hypothesis brings size and complexity into play. If software is regarded as structured information, the distinction between size and complexity need not be considered directly. The intellectual reach of the individual user and the intellectual reach that an individual software developer can span will be of primary concern. The literature on programmer productivity and on attempts to provide indicators for planning the duration of a given development or maintenance task (e.g. [4–6]) provide clues as to what this intellectual span might be. The difference between the productivity for writing new code as opposed to maintaining old code [29] points to the fact that an author of new code just has to relate the intermediate result from a previous development step to his or her own ideas, whereas a maintenance programmer has to try to recover the encodings somebody else has made, interpret them and relate them to her or his own ideas.

To bring mere size and complexity to a comparable level, one might resort to Halstead's definition of program volume [30]. As the detailed operationalisation of V and V* can be questioned, this chapter does not delve deeper into Halstead's theory. Nevertheless, the broad brush notion of these concepts capture the basis on which rest the ensuing considerations.

4.4 Strata of Software-Size and Complexity

The categorisation of software into different strata, which possibly follow different evolutionary patterns, will be defined by the number of people being involved with developing or maintaining the respective entity. Although this is a rather coarse measure, it is directly observable. Knowing that the number of people to be productively employed in solving a given software development task can be varied only within certain limits [31] adds sufficient credibility to this measure as long as one may assume that, for good engineering reasons, the real observable exemplars are of about the size and complexity to be handled by an adequately skilled person or by an adequately composed group of software engineers.

For the sake of differentiating strata of software evolution the following categories are proposed:

- *module*,
- *design unit*,
- *architecture*,
- *system*,
- *system-of-systems*.

Readers might note that these categories do not define a linear order. Notably, architecture is a sidestep on a size dimension one might conceptualise between module and system-of-systems. However, the abundant work on software architecture and not least the arguments raised in [27] justify to distinguish at the system level between the system in its entirety and those engineering key decisions and 'load bearing walls' [32] that define its architecture. On the basis of Hypothesis 2 proposed above, these five categories are characterised as follows:

4.4.1 Module

A module is a unit of work produced or maintained by an individual programmer. Thus, the information content of a module is within the limits of this programmer's intellectual span. Therefore, evolution on the module level need not be a smooth process at all. If some external technological change requires a module to be changed, this change may be radical. The module may even be replaced by a completely new one. The only (evolutionary) requirement is that the new module adheres to the interfaces of the environment it is to be placed into.

The feasibility of module replacement as evolution strategy does not only follow from the established teachings on information hiding. It is also a strategy in development-with-reuse [33] and got new impetus from COTS-based development [34].

One should note that both development-with-reuse and COTS-based development might yield good arguments that neither size nor any other complexity metric is used directly in the definition of the *module* given above. If, for whatever reason, the developer feels sufficiently at home with the component to integrate it in her/his software and if maintenance could be done in a way that this component is not opened up by the maintainer but rather replaced in its entirety by another component satisfying the new specification, the definition given above is satisfied for this particular environment.

Perceived independently though, this component might be classified as subsystem or even as a system on its own. A classical example of software that is a complex system on its own but can be seen in a particular system-context just as a module is a database management system. Given clean interfaces, it is quite feasible that a single individual replaces the currently used relational DBMS by the relational DBMS of another vendor, even if both DBMS' are highly complex systems on their own, developed by large structured groups. It is possible to perceive this software just as a module in the context of an application system, since relational theory in conjunction with the respective DBMS's description allow the maintenance programmer to abstract from most of the details contained in these software entities. The information that needs to be kept mentally active at a time is sufficiently small for a single individual to cope with. This example can be extended to other situations, where a COTS-based developer does not need to see all the details. Sufficient information can be presented at a higher level of abstraction to trust that the component serves the functionality and role needed. The particular representational form of this information is of secondary concern as long as it allows for a trustworthy and concise specification.

4.4.2 Design Unit

The term *design unit* was introduced in the context of work on software reusability to denote an entity more complex than a module, but falling short of the properties of a system or of a fully operational subsystem [35]. *While a design unit might not have all the closure properties one assumes when referring to a subsystem, it is a component big enough to warrant some kind of formal design, but small enough that this design can follow a single mastermind.*

Thus, a design unit is a component consisting of several interacting subcomponents (modules, classes, procedures) that interact among themselves to achieve a common purpose in the context of a system. This description does neither focus on a particular representational form nor on a particular stage in the development process. The component constituting a design unit can be represented in the form of code as well as in the form of a formal design with all associated additional documentation and test-suits. But while the closure properties of a module (e.g. encapsulation of a distinct portion of the state space controlled by the system) make modules suitable candidates as reusable software components, this requirement is not necessarily given for a design unit. It might be a complex object and thus reusable, but it might also be just a data-flow connected portion in the afferent or efferent part of a conventional system [36, 37]. There might be a specific small, single-minded team responsible for maintaining this part and for evolving it according to change requests against the system, even if this part is neither general enough nor sufficiently self-contained to qualify as reusable component. The design effort needed for such components is justified for either one of the following two reasons:

- The design unit is developed by a team and this team needs a documented design to allocate work-packages and to define interfaces.
- The component is developed by a single individual who needs an extensive period of time. Then, formal design is needed by this person in order to stick to his or her own interface agreements, agreements that might otherwise be challenged by fading memory.

In short, documented design is needed as a communication device (information), because on the code level, the volume of a design unit would exceed an individual's intellectual span. On the more abstract and, therefore, more compact design level though, a single individual can oversee the various decisions that this design incorporates.

With design units, one should refrain from unconstrained revolutionary modification since the unit is too big for an individual to change it. However, evolutionary bursts might be observed because in a concerted effort, a group will still be able to perform arbitrarily radical changes. These 'arbitrarily radical changes' will be limited by the design unit's environment. Within limits of arbitration, one might either radically change the design units internals but keep its interface to the rest of the system more or less unchanged (that is interface changes are limited to the changes directly driven by internal modifications) or the designer's intellectual capability might be distributed adequately among changes to be coordinated with others and changes under the design owner's independent authority.

4.4.3 Architecture

With architecture, one refers to the system's skeletal structure, that is to its 'load bearing walls' [32, 38]. This definition does not depend on a specific architectural phase in the development process [39] nor on some specific language or notation [40]. Whether this architecture is described in terms of some modern architectural description language or whether it is only implicit, to be potentially recovered by some re-architecting venture, is relatively unimportant for this discussion. *Architecture* here refers to key structural properties observable in the actual system. These structural properties, however neat or ugly they might be, are present in any system at any time. They matter to the extent that many subordinate decisions depend on the particular nature of such 'load bearing walls'. It has to be understood, though, that architecture does not need to be explicitly present (with physical artefacts one would say 'materialised') in code. Software development seen as a stepwise decision process (c.f. [31]) requires decisions that have scaffolding purpose only. Their effects might remain only implicit in the final system. Perry and Wolf require that architectural descriptions also contain rationale among the central aspects [32]. This is to ensure that information of structural importance for the overall system is not forgotten, even if it remains only implicit in the final code.

With software like with houses, you do not remove or arbitrarily modify a load-bearing wall without either taking precautions for everything resting on this wall or being severely punished by breakdowns or costly repair operations thereafter. Hence, architectures remain relatively stable over a long period of time and evolution. If architectural changes take place, they will be rather in the form of extensions. As a consequence, hybrid structures, comparable to what can be seen in many European churches, may result. There, generations of builders have made extensions, some of them being rather square to the initial architect's plans. However, even when parts are torn down and replaced by newer realisations, the original mastermind and thus the basic style used in the initial construction will remain noticeable over centuries. With software systems, the centuries considered as yardstick for physical buildings might pass in quick motion during decades or even during biennia. All other aspects of the analogy remain valid though.

Therefore, normal architectural changes will be evolutionary. Over time, some spikes of activity will result, though, when somebody decides to rearchitect the system. However, such evolutionary spikes do not occur too often during a system's lifetime. The degree of aging [3] due to regular maintenance operations will largely determine whether and when such evolutionary spikes will happen in a system's architecture. Thus, within limits, technical arguments will be the key driver for architectural evolution.

4.4.4 System

System, in this context, refers not just to a skeleton but to the complete (delivered and operational) software in its entirety with all kind of documentation shipped with this system or kept somewhere else to support future maintenance operations or related questions. This entirety obviously consists of lower granularity entities (design units, modules). However, because of the diseconomies of scale in software engineering, systems need to be discussed separately. Moreover, the system is not only the unit produced by an organisation, it is also the unit of presenting a product to the customers. Hence, on this level the customers' ability to absorb changes will be the delimiting factor for system-level changes. This suggests a pattern like the one observed by Antón and Potts on the feature level. However, before reaching a conclusion too quickly, the structure of the user base has to be considered.

A telephonic system has a large community of users with every user requesting more or less the same service. Hence, to model thousands of users by one single representative seems to be legitimate. In corporate environments though, one is usually confronted with different user groups sharing needs within the group but renouncing common needs on all other users. In this case, one can assume intellectual limits of users to serve as limiting factors for evolutionary speed only if the different user groups can be considered as largely interdependent. Thus, the flow (and nature) of user-driven change requests depends on the organisational environment of the system. Seen in conjunction with Lehman's 'constant effort'–law [26], the actually observable evolution strategy results from an interaction between the relatively constant workforce of system maintenance and the more erratically arriving change requests from users or their representatives.

4.4.5 System-of-Systems

The concept of *systems-of-systems* was introduced in Zemel and Rossak's definition of mega-systems [41, 42]. They identified a *system-of-systems* as *a particular form of a conglomerate mega-system*. Such huge agglomerations are suitable for reflecting on evolution and evolvability at instances where complete systems are to be integrated.

Integration of highly complex systems happens usually in the context of mergers and acquisitions when already relatively huge information systems need to be integrated. This definitely causes a very particular challenge. The challenge is not only due to difficulties in the integration of software per se; the challenge also involves integrating the data repositories accumulated at the organisation(s) in question as well. Thus, a distinction between software proper and the data processed by this software becomes at least at this level of complexity and size inadequate when system consolidation is aimed for. This gives further evidence to the information-based definition of software proposed earlier. In such a consolidation process and in any evolution process to be followed thereafter, not only will convincing system technicians be the limiting factor. It might be as difficult to convince application experts who used the system for years that a now feature, proposed by somebody outside of their peer group, is a valuable feature indeed. At least initially, they might rather consider it a bug, prohibiting them to continue operations with some workaround they might have discovered in the mean time.

Thus, at least at this stratum, Lehman's dictum [43] that, once a system exceeds a certain size, it is no longer the product manager who controls system evolution finds its justification. He proposed that it is rather feedback forces of system evolution that are controlling the product manager. Evolution finds its limitation by the extent a system's (social) environment is ready to tolerate (and on the same token to create) change.[3] These considerations call for a change in the yardstick. What was initially introduced as the intellectual span of an individual now becomes the intellectual span of an organisation or society. This will be larger than an individual's span, but by all means far less than the sum of the spans of the individuals concerned. Results such as those of Fischer, pointing out that individual users apply only a very limited amount of features presented by very complex systems, can be used as an argument in support of a distinction between the change requests voiced by a user community and change tolerance accepted by individual users [44].

This is not the place to speculate on a precise metric of such a combined span. It is fair to assume, however, that it is indirectly bound by the information processing capacity of the individuals concerned. Therefore, the closer the environment of such a system-of-systems has interlinked itself, the lesser is its capacity to tolerate big leaps in system evolution.

4.4.6 Discussion

When focusing on large entities, a distinction between the system in its entirety and those aspects of the system one might consider to be its backbone has been proposed. Again,

---

[3] This sentence must not be misread: It does not say that evolution and evolution processes are independent of managerial decisions. On the contrary, one has to acknowledge that actual evolution of the class of systems the term software evolution has originally been coined for, evolve in two interacting and mutually reinforcing cycles: evolution of the requirements concerning this system and evolution of the technical implementation of the software system itself. Since these cycles are interacting, neither of them can be fully externally controlled by product managers or technical managers. Managers can, however, by defining the organisation of the processes they are responsible for, considerably influence the evolution process. Thus, organisations have certainly the role of an intervening variable in the evolution process. In his keynote at IWPSE 2001 in Vienna, Lehman even referred to organisation as driving factor [28].

this distinction does not refer to a specific representational form. The distinction between the system's architecture and the system's final realisation in the form of executable code seems warranted, though, at least for the reason that changing X lines of code is (should be!) quite a different activity, if this causes a modification in the application's surface structure or if the modification addresses the system's architectural core.

Organisationally, an entity is at the system stratum if it exceeds the size and complexity to be reliably handled by an individual group. Thus, the system- and architecture stratum refer to something that needs a levelled organisation for building and maintaining it (c.f. the definition of 'large program' as one requiring 'an organisation of at least two levels of management for its development or maintenance' in [45]). However, to distinguish it from systems-of-systems, a system's high-level conceptualisation might still follow a single masterminded plan. The importance of such a plan and the mastermind behind it influence the nature of system evolution [27]. As long as the mastermind behind the development can control changes and additions to an already operational product such that the system's initial architecture is preserved, the system is in an offensive evolution stage. Once this person controlling development and progressive evolution has left, the system enters a rather defensive servicing stage. The servicing stage continues until system support finally comes to a halt and the system is phased out, possibly replaced and closed down.

Not least with reference to the above statements does it seem necessary to state that scientific discussion of evolution, notably the empirical work of Lehman, started with entities in mind that are referred to here as systems. However, over the years people used the word evolution to refer simply to the phenomenon of enduring change, disregarding the size or nature of the software artefact. Hence, this chapter also discusses these smaller granules for which the laws of software evolution were originally not defined and where they will not apply to their full extent.

On the system-of-systems stratum one has to recognise though that the usual viewpoint – reality is given and the software- and information system has to be a more or less a faithful reflection of this reality – changes. Of course, the relationship between software and the reality it reflects has to be carefully maintained always. But with big systems, notably with systems-of-systems, the potential of prescriptive power will change. Whenever it is easier to change the organisation (the real world reflected in a software system) than changing the system, the organisation might follow what the software system prescribes. If this is unacceptable, either the software system has to die (thus, something of a revolutionary nature will take place in the software) or even the organisation might perish because of its inability to co-evolve with its environment.

4.5 Approaches to (*R*-)evolve

As argued in the previous paragraph, the nature of evolution depends on the nature of evolution drivers. These, in turn, depend on the scale of the artefact under consideration. Arriving from these general considerations to concrete hints for ways to cope with evolution, one has to consider other factors too. Some of them are environmental, such as the volatility of requirements. While the considerations mentioned in the above paragraph put constraints on this volatility, volatility can still vary within a considerable bandwidth. This has to be taken care of. Other factors are system-immanent.

The most important among the system-immanent factors is whether software is changed off-line or in a running system.

(a) In most situations, software is changed and tested off-line. Only after it has been tested on the development machine with specially prepared test data, will it be transferred to the hardware environment where real user data is processed. To ensure consistency, this roll-out is made at a time when the operational system can be brought to a brief temporary halt. Then it is reinitialised with its previous (possibly transformed or adjusted) state. In this case, the evolution of the software in the proper sense of this word (i.e. change of the shell encapsulating the data describing relevant parts of the reality reflected) happens in a situation somehow resembling an artificial laboratory situation. Therefore, one might refer to it as *in vitro* evolution.

(b) In contrast to this comparatively keen situation, certain systems, notably real-time systems, cannot be brought to a complete halt when switching to a new version. Evolution of such a system has to take place during operation where not only the software proper changes but also the data this software operates on has to be changed in sync. This case has to be handled with much more care, since it is obviously more complex and the proper evolutionary steps cannot be tested off-line [46]. To contrast this situation from the one described in (a), one might call it *in vivo* evolution.

In order not to lose track, the rest of the chapter will abstract from these considerations and concentrate on the five categories presented in the previous section. Without attempting to achieve completeness, some strategies to cope with evolution are mentioned for demonstration purposes.

4.5.1 Changes in Modules

On the module stratum, clean interfaces and adherence to classical design principles will make modules robust against evolution in other parts of the system. Information hiding and, more general, design for reuse will be adequate strategies. With design for reuse or design for component-based development, planning for the possibility of revolutionary change by completely replacing a module with another one is specifically highlighted.

Thus, the overall design of the system has to be in such a way that with individual components, even revolutionary change cannot radically shake the system. Thus, the strategy to cope with evolution is not inward directed, considering the component itself. It rather considers the relationship between the component and its software-technical environment. Thus, strong cohesion and consequently minimal coupling have to be interpreted such that the individual module provides single-minded semantics and has a clear interface. Obviously, object-orientation provides an important set of concepts supporting this goal.

However, not only reuse or object-orientation are to be considered in this context. Developments in the realm of high-level programming languages also matter in this respect. On a keystroke-level, changing a symbol is always just of unitary nature in a textual representation. In terms of informational content, the complexity of the change will depend on the complexity of the semantics attached to this symbol. In terms of intellectual span, finally, one has to consider how well understood the abstraction attached to this symbol (set of symbols) is, to assess whether the textually observable change causes high or low intellectual effort. As evidence for this claim, one might refer either to Halstead's work or to the various language calibrated conversion tables from function points [47] or modified versions of this concept to either line of code or to effort [5].

4.5.2 Modifying Design Units

With design units, precautions for evolution have to be such that change requests from the design level can be easily accounted for at the implementation level. From this stratum onwards, one has to consider that change needs to be propagated from the complex stratum down to lower (closer to implementation) levels. Thus, what might be bursts of evolution for a design unit might be revolutionary change for some of the modules constituting the respective design unit. Hence, loose coupling of the individual components is one key strategy, state separation is another one. Thus, classical design wisdom leading finally to strategies recommended as design for reuse [33] will serve as a basis for economical evolvability. Further, at this level, one should already consider something like volatility management, that is, a well-defined strategy of how to allocate those parts of the system that are most likely to change repeatedly over the system's lifetime. This issue is too tricky and too domain dependent as to give a general recommendation. Single-minded components versus encapsulation of volatility laden aspects might be conflicting design strategies that can only be resolved considering a more global perspective on the design space.

4.5.3 Evolution on the Architectural Level

On the architecture stratum, the distinction between components and connectors (with connectors being special purpose communication components) can at first be seen as the distinction between living rooms and working rooms versus hallways and walls. With the walls, a further distinction has to be made. They can be either load-bearing walls of the system or they might just highlight and assure separation of concern, being software analogues to easily movable Japanese screens. This distinction has to be consciously made and clearly documented. Thus, design for volatility, a side consideration at the level of design units, becomes a major concern in architectural design.

One can witness this design for volatility on the architecture level also when considering the discussions in the intersection of research on software architecture with research on product lines [48]. With the definition of a product line, the system structure is basically partitioned into those parts that are robust with respect to varying user populations and those parts where substantial variations between different subdomains of a common application domain occur. Thus, the homogeneity of the user population (application subdomain) is considered as a factor limiting the volatility and, therefore, the need and speed of evolution. A good product line architecture will consider partitioning of the overall market. When each instance of the product line is targeted towards a homogeneous subdomain of this market, product evolution can be controlled more easily. Thus, market segmentation determines product segmentation. The argument that establishing product lines yields a high reuse potential for the (sub)systems has been put forward in Northrop's keynote to ICSE 01 [49].

4.5.4 System-Level Evolution

At the system level, one has to consider again that a software system is the realisation of reflections, charted coarsely at more abstract levels during initial steps of the development process. These high-level descriptions are progressively refined and augmented with implementation-relevant information till development reaches the fine granular, detailed level of executable code. Thus, what is charted on a high level in such a way that some highly skilled individual(s) can intellectually capture an all-encompassing perspective, exceeds this span when all items are represented at an executable level. Hence, various evolution support strategies can be followed. These strategies, however, will be only supplementary to the strategies mentioned on the design unit and on the architecture level.

Given that the system is small enough, using frameworks can be mentioned as a strategy. Frameworks yield some standardisation, a standardisation that will bear on the lower-level components. Thus, frameworks and patterns might be considered as matching pairs. But while patterns are a rather scale-independent concept, there will be limits of the size of systems, where frameworks can provide an adequate answer.

Another low-level idea that scales up after generalisation and re-transformation is parameterisation. Parameterisation is more powerful than its routine use for parameters in the data space. Procedural parameterisation does scale up to a certain degree, if adequate instrumentation assures security walls comparable to those that a strong type system establishes for conventional parameterisation. Attempts reported in [50] and [51] are initial steps in a direction that might be termed meta-parameterisation.

4.5.5 Evolution of Systems-of-Systems

On the system-of-systems stratum, one can observe that change is of a dual nature. To some extent, these large entities will be constantly subjected to gradual change. Individual change drivers will be mainly related to individual systems contained in this conglomerate. Therefore, strategies of confinement are important. However, radical changes within the reality these systems are reflecting, will come seemingly at random points in time. Mergers and acquisitions might be considered as examples of such radical changes in the real world. Accepting this duality, one has to also accept that it will be insufficient to allocate evolution support only within the system. One has to take care of evolvability on a more general, that is, on a strategic level to prepare these mega-systems for eventual radical changes.

Standardisation might be the strongest mechanism in this context. It can be conceived as a strategy to allow modular, that is, revolutionary evolution behaviour of components even if their internal complexity is beyond the grasp of an individual. However, standardisation is not and cannot be on the scale of mega-systems. Hence, loose and indirect coupling of those parts that lend themselves at least to some extent to standardisation might be the other key strategy to be followed in preparing mega-systems for changes happening in reality. Notably for changes that cannot be accommodated by small incremental steps within the system, this might be a worthwhile strategy. However, this advice contains a certain contradiction in itself. On the one hand, mega-systems are so big that their mere size prohibits radical change. On the other hand, they are so big that certain changes, whatever the architecture of the system might be, will be very big too. Perhaps the point where this drive for evolution and blockage against evolution overlap will eventually define the limit of growth for mega-systems.

On a smaller scale, the phenomenon that the system defines reality and not vice versa happens already when organisations put complex ERP-systems into operation. Such systems do not provide standardisation in the strict sense of this term. The reverse effects these systems have as change drivers seem interesting though, since the naïve statement that software has to keep up with reality does no longer apply. In this context, one is reminded that what seems as external change driver on first glance might not only have sources independent from the software system under consideration. Feedback loops are operational, such that a software system, once fielded in an environment causes changes in this environment, which lead to changes in the requirements to be covered by the respective system [14].

4.6 An Example

In this section, we discuss the aforementioned issues through an example: the evolution of the SESAM/AMEISE system, a teaching and research environment to practice software project management [52]. SESAM[4] simulates software development according to a process model comprising continuous as well as discrete process elements. It constitutes the core of the AMEISE system[5] [53] developed by a consortium of three Austrian universities. Taken together, SESAM/AMEISE's lifetime extends over 15 years.

In the sequel, a selection of evolutionary aspects of this system is discussed along the strata defined in Section 4.4 Placing interesting changes to the system into historical and organisational background should highlight the evolutionary aspect and show the broad picture. But software evolution, perceived to be continuous from a long-term perspective, happens in discrete steps of releases or updates to a configuration [54]. Thus, any single-step perspective will necessarily lead to the impression that the instance discussed just amounts to a more or less complex maintenance operation. The narrower the focus of observation becomes, the more this criticism applies.

4.6.1 A System-of-Systems?

Considering its size of roughly 150,000 LOC, SESAM/AMEISE certainly does not qualify as a system-of-systems. However, the fact that the development has been distributed over different groups (two in the same city at different institutions, the remaining about a one-day train ride apart) with different backgrounds (Ada versus Java development environments) and two different chief-engineers certainly determined the trail of evolution. For example, the original developers would certainly have implemented AMEISE's multi-user support in the SESAM-core. The AMEISE-group avoided touching this Ada-core as much as it could. At the expense of performance, it achieved multi-user functionality by saving the sizable state space of individual users and reloading it into the wrapped SESAM-core. This costly operation was justified by both, lack of Ada-experts and by the need to keep the various instances of the state space in a persistent database, for various user support features they built.

Likewise, requirement modifications were made in the light of system properties. An AMEISE needs statement called for developing 'simpler models to allow using the system in introductory classes'. This would require empirical work and revalidation of such small-scale models[6]. As it was unclear whether the associated costs are warranted by didactical gains, it was decided to implement support features that allow instructors to vary the

---

[4] SESAM (Software Engineering Simulated by Animated Models) can be obtained via //www.informatik.uni-stuttgart.de/se/research/sesam/index_e.html.

[5] The extensions and modifications made in the AMEISE project (A Media Education Initiative for Software Engineering) can be perused at//ameise.uni-klu.ac.at. AMEISE has been funded by bm:bwk under NML-1/77.

[6] The current process model has been defined and validated for developments in the range of 200 to 1000 adjusted function points (AFPs). It consists of about 25,000 LOC in a proprietary language.

complexity of the assignment by varying the magnitude of support mechanisms provided to students.

While trade-offs of risky requirements against safe flexibility can be made at any stratum, they are most likely to happen in complex system or development situations. The example also represents cases where evolving requirements leave the range foreseen at system conception. Instead of linearly extending the range of some parameters, system designers open other avenues by providing features that recapture requirements within the range the system has originally been designed for.

4.6.2 System-Level Changes

The SESAM history started in 1990 at the University of Stuttgart. Initially, a Smalltalk-80/Visual Works 2.0 prototype helped to shape the basic ideas of teaching software project management by a quantitative simulation system. In 1997, a complete re-implementation in Ada95 has been undertaken under the direction of the original chief architect, comprising currently over 75 KLOC. In 2001, a consortium of Austrian universities decided to build its AMEISE tool for SE-project management following the concepts of SESAM and building directly upon SESAM. Among other aspects, AMEISE should provide a new user interface, group support and various features deemed interesting for didactical reasons. Currently, AMEISE's extensions encompass 72 KLOC Java code.

Building on top of SESAM allowed AMEISE to become already operational in spring 2002. Since then, it has been substantially extended till, eventually, limits were reached that required to shift effort from feature extension to internal purification of the system.

In AMEISE, multi-user functionality was needed. Some further new requirements were as follows:

- Students should be able to operate AMEISE without direct instructor supervision.
- AMEISE should become operational via a web interface.
- Support for student- and class management should be provided.

This led to reconsiderations at the architecture level and required a clear distinction between the legacy system and the new one.

A client-server architecture with a completely new student interface, a newly built instructor interface, a data repository and some load-balancing device had to be built. On the other hand, the SESAM-user interface had to be untangled from the system. Because of the ingenuity of the original design, this could be carried out in a straightforward manner. However, as call-backs were handled differently from straight inputs, some cutting and gluing was necessary. Likewise, changes in the dictionary of SESAM's pseudonatural language interface became necessary.

For consistency reasons AMEISE features its own graphical user interface as well as SESAM's traditional textual user-interface, relying heavily on call-backs. Performance monitoring has shown that providing for those call-backs is quite costly and user supervision demonstrated that the textual user-interface is hardly ever used. Sacrificing the textual interface will reduce communication complexity. This allows for scrapping a sizable portion of interface code and structural improvements within the client. Hence, it will be a forthcoming step in system-level evolution.

4.6.3 Architectural Decisions

Architecture can be discussed on several levels. On the domain-level, SESAM provides a clear separation into

- the *model*, containing all entities (persons, documents, activities) relevant in a software development project, and rules establishing qualitative and quantitative relationships among them;
- the *simulator*, executing commands of the user acting as project manager, and
- the *interface(s)* for students and for instructors operating the system.

This separation proved helpful in early prototyping and remained stable for the single-user architecture of SESAM as well as for the multi-user AMEISE system.

Technically, AMEISE followed its own architectural decisions, which can be seen from two perspectives:

- A *client-server architecture*, allows k independent clients (each one on its own machine) to connect via one (or more) load-balancing components to n wrapped SESAM cores (on n machines) cooperating with one database server. This architecture fully exploits SESAM's simulation and modelling functionality while being free in terms of hardware-base and AMEISE's group support features. Further, it provides flexibility concerning performance aspects.
- A *data model* has been designed as semantic architectural backbone. While required for student and class management, it had become the focal point for functional system evolution. Besides the wrapped SESAM cores and the load balancer, it is the only logically central feature. Its main sections, class management, user management, model management, support-features management, and user-run management allow individual AMEISE features to keep relatively tight and clean interfaces and to be (with few exceptions) memory less. So far, the data model became the key evolution facilitator.

Up to now, these architectural decisions have withstood the proof of concept by requests for several extensions of support features during AMEISE's two years of operation. Most of these extensions were feature extensions. Multi-lingual support for German and English could also be easily integrated. Handling French as a third language caused ripples though. To allow for handling of accents, constraints in the parser had to be weakened.

4.6.4 Design Units

Design units, as defined in Section 4.4.2 are relatively closed portions of a system, big enough to require a team effort to develop them. Thus, they require some documented design. In AMEISE, the database, the load balancer, and the user-client are such units. Various administrative clients or monitoring devices might also be seen as software design units. Design units that rather have the character of data are the simulation model (a set of several hundred rules), the dictionary and the explanation component with its specific aid tables. Among those, the SESAM-core as well as the simulation model are under the strict authority of the group in Stuttgart. The user-client contains modules developed by two different sites in Klagenfurt. For post-development work, it has been placed under the control of the Technikum Klagenfurt. The rest of the AMEISE system is under the responsibility of the Klagenfurt University. The dictionary plays a special role, as it is a cornerstone between model, user interface and explanation component. Hence, dictionary modifications require consensus among all partners and utmost care in version control.

From an evolution perspective, the client might be of particular interest. Its internal architecture is a simple façade-like structure [55]. Its only interface to the rest of the system is via the load balancer. Its components though, encompassing the GUI-based user-interface, the textual user-interface, and graphical user-interfaces subordinate to various explanatory components are rather complex. Functional evolution of the system is of course always reflected in the client. Its structure allowed for easy integration of these extensions though.

Like the original SESAM user-interface, the client is stateless. However, to accommodate the full functionality of the pseudonatural language legacy interface, a number of bookkeeping operations are necessary to resolve ambiguities by call-backs. The graphical user-interface allows sending only complete and syntactically correct commands. Hence, dropping the communication intensive textual interface will allow structural improvements also in several other user-related client components. After these forthcoming structural cleanups, only the 'friendly peer', an agent observing the last user actions in a window of limited depth, keeps local memory. It remains to be seen how much its communication protocol with the database at start-up and shut-down can be further streamlined within the overall protocol simplification.

The explanation component was specifically designed to allow for continuous evolution. To accommodate changes in or replacements of simulation models, its design follows the interpreter pattern [56] in a two-level recursive manner. On the basis of the current user state, it constructs a set of SQL queries into tables monitoring the user's actions and into specific aid tables. The results of these queries are used to construct another SQL query. Out of these results, the message displayed to the user is composed. This general principle allows experts of a different kind (instructor, model-builder) to build new or change existing explanations of model effects by just modifying some database entries and by letting the system worry that the individual changes are properly reflected on the user-interface . This design decision is in line with the overall AMEISE architecture of having the database as the evolutionary backbone of the system. It allowed shifting design-unit (or even system level) evolution to the level of strictly confined modular changes. This has also implications on the organisational level. While such changes definitely involve client, server, and model (i.e. organisationally three teams), this specific decision is one aspect that allows passing the maintenance responsibility for the client to one team only, though the modules it contains were built by two distinct teams. As long as changes of the explanation component, be it corrective maintenance or be it extensions in explanatory power, stayed within the given (textual and graphical) syntactical framework, the concept kept up with the requirements. Accommodating French, though, necessitated levying the restriction that the dictionary's parser accepts only strict ASCII code.

The database schema itself is also considered as a design unit. As a component of architectural significance, it has been designed by a group of three with a single mastermind and was heavily reviewed before being implemented. Considering the individual relations as modules it has been heavily revised on the module level since. Apart from actually implementing the multi-lingual aspects which where architecturally foreseen though, the changes required so far were confined to only few interrelated tables each. Because of the logical centrality of the database, its proper versioning needs to be done with utmost care.

To summarise, the specific aspects mentioned rest on the basis of organisational and technical decisions that allowed not only letting the system grow in the direction originally foreseen, but also to accommodate requirements originally not anticipated. Examples of those are the French version as well as various requirements resulting from users and from developers. An example, where user and developer requirements could be accommodated by a common feature was the user requirement to allow students to outsource certain development tasks and the developer's need to develop a test-bed for performance tests. The 'external software house'–feature satisfies both. Reaping such benefits is possible only when change management from requirements onwards till feature integration allows planning. One might term this *evolution control*.

In terms of evolution control, the explanation component's history is worth considering. Nothing comparable was foreseen in SESAM. AMEISE introduced the concept and adopted the design mentioned above. As this proved useful, a tool was developed that generates the database entries from higher-level descriptions. But there is still no direct coupling to the model driving simulations. Hence, on the very long term agenda is the development of a component that allows creating the chunked SQL-scripts and explanatory hints of the explanation component directly from the rules defined in the model or concurrently with the definition of these rules. This will raise consistency and ease development of new applications. But the respective decision has to be taken at the architecture level.

4.6.5 Modules

Module evolution took place in various forms so far. In most cases evolution involved incremental changes in both, requirements and implementation. To highlight the discussion of Sections 4.4.1 and 4.5.1, three exemplary cases are mentioned though.

- *Behaviour preserving revolutionary change*: The SESAM Tcl/Tk user interface had been completely replaced by a Java interface initially. This allowed to experiment with the initial version of a simple client-server architecture consisting of wrapped SESAM-core, simple DB-structure for state dismemberment, load balancer and simple user interface. Later, this simple textual interface had been replaced by a client system, hosting this interface and various prototypes of support features. This eventually evolved to the current client architecture hosting various components that are on the module or the design-unit level. Thus, user functionality was fully preserved throughout various versions of the system while technically this functionality was provided by three completely different generations of components.
- *Technical revolution with evolutionary behaviour*: The transition from the Tcl/Tk user-interface to the Java Interface was certainly a revolutionary change. Replacing the textual user-interface by an interface based on selection from dynamically created menus could also be considered revolutionary on a technical level. However, for consistency reasons, the textual interface remains available and the composed text is visible to the user. Both modules[7] reside currently in the user-client and either one can be

---

[7] The textual user-interface and the graphical user-interface are modules in the sense of Section 4.4.1 as they can be overseen by a single individual. In object-oriented terminology, they might be called packages consisting of several classes.

selected by means of a pull-down menu. Hence, from a user's perspective, the change was just evolutionary.
- *Revolutionary behaviour change by technical evolution*: Contrary to these changes, development of a new model (e.g. a maintenance model) might seem to be a radical change from the user's perspective. Technically though, it required just some new entries in the dictionary module (evolution), new versions of some tables in the specific aid portion of the database and of course a completely new model with new rules and new quantitative parameters. The remainder of the system is sufficiently parametric to cope with these changes though.

4.6.6 Discussion

The SESAM/AMEISE system has evolved over 15 years. With currently about 150 KLOC programs, integrated components such as a DBMS, and an application model comprising 24 KLOC it is beyond the size a single individual can oversee completely. As a living system, it is still growing. Because of legacy concerns, several evolutionary decisions might not qualify as standard textbook material. Had the AMEISE-consortium produced a SESAM-3 system from scratch, quite a number of decisions would probably have been taken in a more appealing way. However, this was not the situation. The AMEISE team was more than happy to build its extensions on an already sizable legacy system. In (re-)defining the architecture of the system, AMEISE designers had to consider that emerging design units and modules are small enough to be completed in term projects of groups of students or within MA-theses of individual students. Further, design units had to be small enough to be overseen by a single supervisor. Therefore, decisions were taken in the light of available staffing, available competence and given organisational dispersion.

As with extensions to physical buildings, architectural and design decisions had to be made carefully considering legacy decisions. Likewise, when new things were added, one had to consider how to interface the old with the new. Interfacing between the old and the new involves turning down parts of the existing construction and rebuilding them in a new style and it implies compromises and respect for organisational and intellectual constraints. This applies equally to evolving a successful software system as it does to a valuable ancient mansion.

4.7 Summary

The chapter departs from the perspective that software is always a reflection of some reality and as such it rests on the statement that software, in its substance and in its effects, is structured information. On this basis, a bridge is established between evolution and human's information processing capability or evolution and society's information processing capability respectively. Building on these assumptions, a stratification of software according to the information processing capability of individuals, groups and organisations is given. The strata described are at the levels of system-of-systems, system, architecture, design unit and module.

The discussion of concepts and tools supporting evolution at these levels shows that it will be futile to aim for the ideal overall evolution support strategy. On the contrary, a spectrum of evolution support mechanisms, each mechanism adequately scoped, will be needed to solve the problem at a given level of system size or system complexity.

References

[1] L. Osterweil (Panel Chair). Determining the impact of software engineering research upon practice; *23rd International Conference on Software Engineering*, Toronto, May 2001. IEEE-CS and ACM: 697.

[2] S.L. Squires, M. Branstad, M. Zelkowitz (eds.) Special issue on rapid prototyping. *Working Papers from the ACM SIGSOFT Rapid Prototyping Workshop*, ACM Software Engineering Notes, Vol. 7(5): Columbia, MD, 1982.

[3] D.L. Parnas. Software aging. In *Proceedings, 16th International Conference on Software Engineering*, Sorrento, Italy, May 1994. IEEE-CS and ACM: 279–287.

[4] B.W. Boehm. *Software Engineering Economics*, Prentice Hall Inc., Englewood Cliffs, 1981.

[5] B.W. Boehm, C. Abts, A. Brown, S. Chulani, B. Clark, E. Horowitz, R. Madachy, D. Relfer and B. Steece. *Software Cost Estimation with COCOMO II*, Prentice Hall PTR, 2000.

[6] N.E. Fenton and S.L. Pfleeger. *Software Metrics: A Rigorous & Practical Approach*, 2nd ed, International Thomson Computer Press, 1997.

[7] T.J. McCabe. A complexity measure. *IEEE Trans. Softw. Eng.*, 1976, vol. SE-2(4): 308–320.

[8] A.I. Antón and C. Potts 2001, Functional paleontology: System evolution as the user sees it, In *Proceedings, 23rd International Conference on Software Engineering, IEEE-CS and ACM*, Toronto, Ontario, May 421–430.

[9] M. Jackson. The world and the machine. In *Proceedings, 17th International Conference on Software Engineering*, Seattle, April 1995, IEEE-CS and ACM: 283–292.

[10] G. Kotonya and I. Sommerville. *Requirements Engineering: Processes and Techniques*, John Wiley & Sons, 1998.

[11] R.T. Mittermeir, A. Bollin, H. Pozewaunig and D. Rauner-Reithmayer. Goal-Driven combination of software comprehension approaches for component based development. In *Proceedings SSR '01, Symposium on Software Reusability*, Toronto, May 2001. ACM/SIGSOFT: 95–102.

[12] C. Shannon and W. Weaver. *The Mathematical Theory of Communication*. 8th ed, Urbana, 1959.

[13] M.M. Lehman. The funnel: A software unit or function channel. Technical Report 29, Imperial College, 1977.

[14] M.M. Lehman. Program evolution, programming process, programming support. In W. Sammer and H. Morgenbrod, (eds). *Programmierumgebung und Compiler (Sonderdruck zu)*, Vol. 18a. German Chapter of the ACM, Teubner Verlag, 1984.

[15] R.T. Yeh. System development as a wicked problem. *Int. J. Softw. Eng. Knowl. Eng.*, 1991, 1(2): 117–130.

[16] D.R. Hofstadter. *Gödel, Escher, Bach: An Eternal Golden Braid*, Basic Books, New York, 1979.

[17] Collins COBUILD. *English Language Dictionary*, Collins, 1991.

[18] R.T. Mittermeir. Semantic nets for modeling the requirements of evolvable systems – an example. In J. Hawgood (ed.) *Evolutionary Information Systems*. IFIP TC-8; North-Holland Publishers, 1982, 193–216.

[19] H. Pirker, R.T. Mittermeir and D. Rauner-Reithmayer. Service channels – purpose and tradeoffs. In *Proceedings 22nd Computer Software & Applications Conference*. IEEE-CS Press, August 1998; 204–211.

[20] L. Belady and M.M. Lehman. A model of large program development. *IBM Syst. J.*, 1976, 15(1): 225–252.

[21] M.M. Lehman and P. Wernick. System dynamic models of software evolution processes. In B. Balzer et al. (eds.) *International Workshop on Principles of Software Evolution*, JSST, Kyoto, Japan, 1998, 6–10.

[22] T. Tamai and T. Nakatani. An empirical study of object evolution processes. In B. Balzer et al., (eds). *International Workshop on Principles of Software Evolution*, JSST, Kyoto, Japan, 1998, 33–37.

[23] M.M. Lehman and L.A. Belady. *Program evolution: Processes of Software Change*, Academic Press, London, 1985.

[24] M.J. Baker and S.G. Eick Visualizing software systems. In *Proceedings, 16th International Conference on Software Engineering, IEEE-CS and ACM*, 1994, 59–67.

[25] H. Gall, M. Jazayeri and C. Riva. Visualizing software release histories: The use of color and third dimension. In *Proceedings International Conference on Software Maintenance*, Oxford, September 1999. IEEE-CS press: 99–108.

[26] M.M. Lehman. Programs, life cycles and laws of software evolution. *Proc. IEEE*, 1980, 68(9): 1060–1076.

[27] K.H. Bennett and V.T. Rajlich. Software maintenance and evolution: A roadmap. In A. Finkelstein (ed.) *The Future of Software Engineering 2000*, ACM press, 2000, 73–87.

[28] M.M. Lehman and J.F. Ramil. Evolution in software and related areas. In T. Tamai, M. Aoyama, K. Bennett, (eds.), *Proceedings 4th International Workshop on Principles of Software Evolution IWPSE 2001*, 2001, ACM SIGSOFT: Vienna, Austria, 1–16.

[29] W.S. Humphrey. *A Discipline for Software Engineering*, Addison-Wesley Publ, 1995.
[30] M. Halstead. *Elements of Software Science*. Elsevier North Holland, 1977.
[31] L. Putnam. A general empirical solution to the macro software sizing and estimating problem. *IEEE Trans. Softw. Eng.*, 1978, SE-4(4): 345–361.
[32] D.E. Perry and A.L. Wolf. Foundations for the study of software architectures. *ACM SigSoft Softw. Eng. Notes*, 1992, 17(4): 40–52.
[33] L. Dusink and P.A.V. Hall (eds). *Software Re-use, Utrecht 1989. BCS Workshops in Computing*, Springer-Verlag, 1991.
[34] G.T. Heineman and W.T. Councill (eds.) *Component-based Software Engineering: Putting the Pieces Together*, Addison Wesley, 2001.
[35] R.T. Mittermeir and W. Rossak. Reusability. In P.A. Ng and R.T. Yeh (eds.) *Modern Software Engineering: Foundations and Current Perspectives*. Van Nostrand Reinhold, 1990, 205–235.
[36] W. Stevens, G. Myers and L. Constantine. Structured design. *IBM Syst. J.*, 1974, 13(2): 115–139.
[37] E. Yourdon. *Modern Structured Analysis*, Yourdon/Prentice Hall, 1989.
[38] D.E. Perry. Software architecture: Leverage for system/program comprehension. In *Proceedings 9th International Workshop on Program Comprehension*. IEEE-CS Press, May 2001: 123.
[39] D.M. Weiss and F.J. van der Linden. Development process. In F. van der Linden (ed.) *Development and Evolution of Software Architectures for Product Families*, LNCS 1429, Springer, 1998, 170–171.
[40] D.E. Perry and J. Kramer. Architectural description. In F. van der Linden, (ed.) *Development and Evolution of Software Architectures for Product Families*, LNCS 1429, Springer, 1998, 49–51.
[41] W. Rossak and V. Kirova. A development process for systems-of-systems. In *Software Systems in Engineering*, ASME, 1995, volume PD-Vol. 67: 195–198.
[42] T. Zemel and W. Rossak. Mega-systems – the issue of advanced systems development. In *Proceedings 2nd International Conference on Systems Integration*, IEEE-CS Press, June 1992; 548–555.
[43] M.M. Lehman. Software system maintenance and evolution in an era of reuse, cots, and component-based systems. In keynote delivered at ICSM, Oxford, GB, 1999.
[44] G. Fischer. Human-computer interaction software: Lessons learned, Challenges attached. *IEEE Softw.*, 1989, 6(1): 44–52.
[45] M.M. Lehman. Laws of program evolution – rules and tools for programming management. In *Why Software Projects Fail, Infotech State of the Art Conference*, pages 11/1 – 11/25, April Pergamon Press, 1978, and Chapter 12 in [23].
[46] H.P. Siy and D.E. Perry. Challenges in evolving a large scale software product. In B. Balzer *et al.* (eds). *International Workshop on Principles of Software Evolution*, JSST, 1998, 29–32.
[47] A.J. Albrecht and J. Gaffney. Software function, source lines of code and development effort prediction. *IEEE Trans. Softw. Eng.*, 1983, SE-9(6): 639–648.
[48] J.-M. DeBaud and K. Schmid. A systematic approach to derive the scope of software product lines. In *Proceedings, 21st International Conference on Software Engineering*, Los Angeles, CA, May 1999, IEEE-CS and ACM: 34–44.
[49] L.M. Northrop. Reuse that pays. In *Proceedings, 23rd International Conference on Software Engineering*, Toronto, Ontario, May 2001. IEEE-CS and ACM; 667.
[50] R.T. Mittermeir and L.G. Wüfl. Greedy reuse: Architectural considerations for extending the reusability of components. In *Proceedings 8th SEKE*, KSI, 1996: 434–441.
[51] M. Rakic and N. Medvidovic. Increasing the confidence in off-the-shelf components: A software connector-based approach. In *Proceedings Symposium on Software Reusability*, ACM Press, 2001; 11–18.
[52] A. Drappa and J. Ludewig. Simulation in software engineering training. In *Proceedings, 23rd International Conference on Software Engineering*, IEEE-CS and ACM, Toronto, Ontario, May 2001: 199–208.
[53] R.T. Mittermeir, E. Hochmüller, A. Bollin, S. Jäger and M. Nusser. AMEISE – A media education initiative for software engineering: concepts, the environment and initial experiences. In M.E. Auer and U. Auer, (eds). *Proceedings International Workshop ICL – Interactive Computer Aided Learning*, Villach, 2003, ISBN 3-89958-029-X.
[54] R.T. Mittermeir. Software evolution: a distant perspective; *Proceedings 6th International Workshop on Principles of Software Evolution*, IWPSE '03, IEEE-CS Press, Vienna, Austria, 2003: 105–112.
[55] E. Gamma, R. Helm, R. Johnson and J. Vlissides. *Design Patterns*, Addison-Wesley, 1995.
[56] M. Shaw and D. Garlan. *Software Architecture: Perspectives on an Emerging Discipline*, Prentice-Hall, 1996.

5

Evolution in Software Systems: Foundations of the SPE Classification Scheme

Stephen Cook, Rachel Harrison, Meir M. Lehman and Paul Wernick

This chapter was originally published as Evolution in Software Systems: Foundations of the SPE Classification Scheme by Stephen Cook, Rachel Harrison, Meir M. Lehman, Paul Wernick. Journal of Software Maintenance and Evolution: Research and Practice, Volume 18, Issue 1, 1–35. Copyright John Wiley and Sons, Ltd., reproduced by permission.

5.1 Introduction

The primary aim of this work is to contribute to the development of the theory of software evolution by re-examining and clarifying Lehman's SPE taxonomy of evolving software systems. The SPE classification scheme has had mixed fortunes since it was first proposed in 1980. The E (Evolving) category, which includes most software systems, has been influential and has become widely accepted. In contrast, the S (Specified) and P (Problem) categories have not been studied in detail, and the taxonomy's rationale has received little attention. It has been known from empirical studies, for example, (Lawrence 1982; Godfrey and Tu 2000; Cook *et al.* 2001; Siebel *et al.* 2003), that software systems are not uniform in their patterns of evolution. However, studies of such differences have made little use of either theory-based classifications such as SPE, or classifications based on observed properties of systems such as development process, application domain and so on. The juxtaposition of these developments raises some interesting questions. Do the same general principles of evolution apply to all software systems? Can the 'Laws of Software Evolution', which were based on empirical data obtained from E-type systems, be modified or extended to apply more generally, or even universally? What would constitute a sound basis for classifying evolving software systems?

To answer these questions, it seems reasonable to start from the existing SPE scheme, given the success of its E category and the absence of strong competitors. This work begins the process of re-examining SPE by describing recent progress in the following inter-related areas. We explain how the theory of software evolution can be related to generic theories of evolution. We also show how software evolution theory provides a bridge between the technological concerns of software engineering and the philosophical concepts of hermeneutics and paradigm. Our proposed unification of these concepts provides a better understanding of why the use of software systems in the real world leads to uncertain outcomes. This material is then used to propose a refined definition and rationale for the SPE categories, referred to as $SPE+$. Thus this work is focussed on establishing the conceptual basis of $SPE+$, as a necessary precursor to empirical studies of the classification of evolving software systems.

It will be apparent that the scope of this work is rather broad and touches on topics that may be unfamiliar to some readers. Some of the material may seem, at least initially, rather distant from the usual concerns of software engineering. Nevertheless, this work is based on the position that the effects of software evolution cannot be managed successfully unless a better understanding of software evolution becomes an integral part of the software engineering paradigm. The evolution of software systems cannot be fully understood solely in terms of the operations of computers and programs. To achieve a more complete understanding of software evolution, one requires some knowledge of developments and discoveries that have been made in various branches of philosophy and in the study of generic theories of evolution. To assist readers who may wish to explore these issues in greater depth, the bibliography is both longer and broader than usual.

The work is organised in the following way. Section 5.2 introduces background material and concepts. Section 5.2.1 discusses the concept of evolution in the context of software systems. The original SPE scheme is summarised in Section 5.2.1.4. Section 5.2.2 explains the related concepts of stakeholder, architecture and global software process. Section 5.2.3 introduces concepts from the hermeneutic tradition in philosophy and from the philosophy of science. Section 5.2.4 applies these concepts to the process of requirements analysis. Section 5.3 explains the details of SPE+ and shows how the definitions of the categories are based on the concepts described in Section 5.2. Finally, Section 5.4 discusses the impact of these proposals on the theory of software evolution and suggests some worthwhile directions for future research.

5.2 Background and Related Work

5.2.1 Software Evolution

This section discusses the concept of evolution in software systems. Sections 5.2.1.1 and 5.2.1.2 show how generic concepts of evolution, particularly Dawkins' concept of replicator, can be applied to software. Section 5.2.1.3 returns to the specific characteristics of software evolution with a brief summary of 'Lehman's Laws'. Section 5.2.1.4 summarises the original formulation of the SPE taxonomy.

5.2.1.1 What is Evolution?

Evolution is an elusive term to define. Common sense and dictionary definitions imply that it refers to 'a gradual process of change and development'. This leaves plenty of room for interpretation. For example, users and administrators of databases could have different ideas about what kinds of change qualify as 'evolution' in a database. To the users of a database, evolution might mean that the uses of the database system or the semantics of its data have changed over time. On the other hand, database administrators might consider such changes to be within the normal use of the system. They might use the term 'evolution' to refer to changes in the definition of a database's schema or the features of its Database Management System (DBMS), while the system's users might be unaware of such changes or unconcerned about them.

Evolution can also be defined in ways that are independent of subjective viewpoints. A 'top–down' approach describes the generalised character of evolutionary processes. For example, at a recent workshop[1], Lehman proposed the following very general statement, defining evolution as

> 'a ... process of discrete, progressive, change over time in the characteristics, attributes, [or] properties of some material or abstract, natural or artificial, entity or system or of a sequence of these [changes]'.

This definition captures important characteristics of evolution in many situations, including software systems. It is applicable to both natural and artificial systems, and to abstractions such as ideas. It provides a very general, universal definition of evolution that can be specialised for particular domains, such as software, natural languages and genes.

An alternative, complementary approach works in the opposite direction, that is, 'bottom–up'. Such definitions focus on identifying the minimum starting conditions for evolution. For example, Dawkins (Dawkins 1999) defines evolution as 'the external and visible manifestation of the differential survival of alternative replicators'. Blackmore (Blackmore 1999) paraphrases this as

> 'if there is a replicator that makes imperfect copies of itself only some of which survive, then evolution simply *must* happen'. [emphasis in original]

A *replicator*, as defined by Dawkins (Dawkins 1999), is anything that can be copied. Genes are replicators and so are many other things. In a software context, replicators include fragments of source code, complete programs, designs, design patterns, algorithms, operating manuals, policy statements and so on. Copies of replicators may be 'imperfect', in the sense of 'variant' or 'with alterations'. This may happen accidentally, as in the case of random mutations in genes. Alterations to replicators may also happen through deliberate actions, as when a programmer adapts the source code of a program or replaces the algorithm or design pattern that is used in it.

At least in the software domain, the 'top–down' and 'bottom–up' definitions of evolution described above are consistent with each other. Whenever a process involving a software system satisfies Lehman's 'top–down' definition, there will be differential survival among the replicators within the system, that is, this kind of change in a software system always involves adding, deleting or changing one or more replicators. Similarly, from the 'bottom–up' perspective, whenever a process of differential survival among a

---

[1] 'Software Evolution and Evolutionary Computation Symposium' (EPSRC Network on Evolvability in Biology and Software Systems), Hatfield, UK, 7–8 February 2002. http://homepages.feis.herts.ac.uk/~nehaniv/EN/seec/program.html.

collection of software replicators is sustained for a sufficient length of time, it will produce system effects that satisfy the 'top–down' definition of evolution.

5.2.1.2 A Replicator Perspective on Software Evolution

This section explores the replicator concept in more detail by illustrating some of its applications to the software domain.

In Dawkins' model, replicators travel around in *vehicles*. A vehicle can be

> 'any relatively discrete entity ... which houses replicators, and which can be regarded as a machine programmed to preserve and propagate the replicators that ride inside it' (Dawkins 1999).

Genes, for example, travel around in living things, which tend to preserve and propagate them, often in very complex and elaborate ways. Software-related replicators travel around in software itself, and also in books, websites, system documents and the brains of programmers and software engineers.[2]

Evolution 'takes off' as a process when at least some replicators are *germ-line*, rather than *dead end*, but only some of their vehicles survive long enough to propagate the replicators that are travelling in them. A germ-line replicator is 'a replicator that is potentially the ancestor of an indefinitely long line of descendent replicators' (Dawkins 1999), whereas the dead-end category lack this capability. Dawkins uses the metaphor that evolution occurs when replicators aspire to immortality[3] but some fail to achieve it sooner than others.

The approach of Dawkins and his colleagues and successors to the definition of evolution is explicitly Darwinian but their concepts are not defined in exclusively biological terms. Blackmore (Blackmore 1999) and Plotkin (Plotkin 1994), for example, show how this approach can be applied in nongenetic domains. The use of Darwinian concepts in theories of *generic* evolution is particularly interesting and relevant to the software domain. Previous attempts to make direct analogies between evolution of living things and in software systems have often been unsatisfactory. Establishing a relationship between the theories and concepts of software evolution and generic evolution seems more promising.

For example, the concepts of germ-line and dead-end replicator can be applied to software. All replicators that travel in open-source software are germ-line. This is because each copy of an open-source program can spawn new lines of indefinitely long descent for the replicators that it hosts. In principle, *every* copy of an open-source program could do this independently, but most do not. The situation with proprietary software products is more complex and the replicator concept can be used to explain this. The replicators in the design, source code, and so on are, in general, germ-line only within the relevant development community. They can be reused, possibly with alterations, in subsequent

---

[2] This implies that the replicators found in software could be treated as a class of 'meme' (Dawkins 1976). Blackmore (Blackmore 1999) briefly mentions the possibility of developing memetic explanations for software evolution.

[3] The concept of immortality has been applied to software by Edwards and Millea (Edwards and Millea 2002).

releases of the product or be copied into other vehicles, for example, programs, Unified Modeling Language (UML) diagrams, Computer-Assisted Software Engineering (CASE) repositories. However, those replicators that get copied into each *end-use* copy of a proprietary product are effectively dead end. They cannot become ancestors of descendent replicators without unlicensed reverse engineering. In the absence of cooperation from the product's owner, this process may be difficult, unreliable and exposed to the risk of sanctions.

However, if a proprietary product has been conceived, designed and implemented as a reusable and adaptable component, it can become a germ-line replicator in its own right, even if none of its source code is available as a replicator. When a piece of software is reused as a component, it takes on a replicator role and it uses the systems in which it has been incorporated as its vehicle. The component may get adapted if its interface permits this, or it may be discarded as its host system evolves.[4] Meanwhile, the component will continue to play the vehicle role for its own 'payload' of replicators.

The concepts of generic evolution that have been developed by Dawkins, Plotkin, Blackmore and others provide a framework for understanding the features of evolution that are common to different domains, including software. They also provide a vocabulary for discussing the distinctive features of software evolution. For example, because software can be structured in hierarchical, recursive and reflective ways, many software artefacts can act as either replicator or vehicle or play both roles simultaneously. This can be contrasted with biological systems, where, in general, an entity may be either a replicator (for example, a gene) or a vehicle (for example, an organism), but not both at the same time.

Nested replicator-vehicle relationships in software can be very simple or arbitrarily complex. A relatively simple example is found in the pipe-and-filter (Buschmann *et al.* 1996) architectural style. Each filter is a vehicle for a collection of replicators – source code, algorithms, design patterns and so on – and also behaves as a replicator that can be copied from one pipeline to another. More complex examples of nested replicator-vehicle relationships can be found in, for example, the use of application frameworks (Roberts and Johnson 1998) to guide the evolution of a software system. Relatively simple kinds of similar relationships are also found in other engineering structures. For example, Alexander (Alexander *et al.* 1977) describes the hierarchical arrangement of reusable design patterns, that is, replicators, that are involved in designing the 'built environment'. However, some complex arrangements of replicators and vehicles, such as those found in reflective meta-programming, are only possible in software systems.

5.2.1.3 Theories of Software Evolution

The concept of software evolution can be traced back to Lehman's 1969 study (Lehman 1985b) of the programming process within IBM. He identified several long-term trends in software systems that seemed to be independent of the intentions of any of a system's stakeholders (see Section 5.2.2.1), for example, programmers, project managers, marketing departments, user organisations. These trends included tendencies for programs to steadily increase in size and complexity and to become progressively harder

---

[4] This phenomenon has also been investigated by Lehman and Ramil (Lehman and Ramil 1998).

to adapt. Initially, Lehman and Belady called these phenomena 'program growth dynamics' but later they coined the term *software evolution* (Belady and Lehman 1972). Since then, a growing body of research and experience has confirmed many of their original insights and contributed new information, hypotheses and investigative techniques. Lehman and Ramil (Lehman and Ramil 2003) provide a convenient summary of the principal advances.

It is helpful to distinguish two broad approaches to the study of software evolution:

explanatory: concerned with understanding causes, processes and effects

This approach attempts to achieve a holistic view and considers, for example, the impact of software evolution on the effectiveness of organisations and the planning of organisational change.

process improvement: concerned with the development of better methods and tools

This approach addresses such questions as 'How should software engineering activities such as design, maintenance (Kitchenham *et al.* 1999; Chapin *et al.* 2001), refactoring (Fowler *et al.* 1999), re-engineering and so on be used to manage the effects of software evolution'?

Lehman *et al.* (Lehman *et al.* 2000) have described these complementary strands as the *What?* and *How?* of software evolution. The distinction is important because of the tendency in software engineering practice to over-emphasise short-term 'fixes' for fundamental problems. To surmount the limitations of *ad hoc* solutions, it is essential to develop process improvement techniques that are robust. This requires a sound understanding of the phenomena that the techniques address. The research described in this work falls in the 'explanatory' category.

Laws of Software Evolution
Lehman's 'Laws of Software Evolution' are a major contribution to identifying the causes and processes of this complex phenomenon. The eight laws that have been discovered so far are summarised in Table 5.1, adapted from Lehman *et al.* (Lehman *et al.* 1997). They describe a set of general principles for the evolution of E-type (see Section 5.2.1.4) software systems.

Lehman's use of the term 'law' in the context of software evolution has sometimes been misunderstood. Unlike some laws found in sciences such as physics, Lehman's laws do not specify precise invariant mathematical relationships between directly observable quantities, and were never intended to. Their purpose is to capture knowledge about the common features of frequently observed behaviour in evolving software systems. As this knowledge deepens and becomes more detailed and reliable, it is likely that future versions of the laws may be expressed in more precisely quantified terms.

Thus *law* is being used by Lehman in the same sense that social scientists use the term to describe general principles that are believed to apply to some class of social situation 'other things being equal, which they rarely are'. For example, Say's Law[5] in economics

---
[5] Say's Law can be expressed informally as 'supply creates its own demand'. Economists, for example, (Heimann 1945), have discussed different interpretations and applications of this general principle.

Table 5.1 Laws of software evolution, adapted from (Lehman *et al.* 1997)

	Name	Brief description
I	Continuing Change (1974)	E-type systems must be continually adapted else they become progressively less satisfactory
II	Increasing Complexity (1974)	As an E-type system evolves, its complexity increases unless work is done to maintain or reduce it
III	Self Regulation (1974)	The evolution process of E-type systems is self regulating, with a distribution of product and process measures over time that is close to normal
IV	Conservation of Organisational Stability (1980)	The average effective global activity rate in an evolving E-type system is invariant over a product's lifetime
V	Conservation of Familiarity (1980)	During the active life of an evolving E-type system, the average content of successive releases is invariant
VI	Continuing Growth (1980)	The functional content of an E-type system must be continually increased to maintain user satisfaction with the system over its lifetime
VII	Declining Quality (1996)	Stakeholders will perceive an E-type system to have declining quality unless it is rigorously maintained and adapted to its changing operational environment
VIII	Feedback System (1974–1996)	The evolution processes in E-type systems constitute multi-level, multi-loop, multi-agent feedback systems and must be treated as such to achieve significant improvement over any reasonable baseline

describes a general principle about the relationship between demand and supply, which may need to be modified when it is applied to particular situations. Since the theory of software evolution is similarly describing social situations that are extremely variable in practice, this use of the term 'law' is appropriate.

5.2.1.4 The SPE Classification Scheme

Lehman devised his SPE taxonomy (Lehman 1980) to explain why programs vary in their evolutionary characteristics. He realised that, from the perspective of software evolution, there is a fundamental distinction between programs written to satisfy a fixed and pre-existing specification, and programs developed to satisfy some need in the real world.

This insight was refined into the three types described by the SPE taxonomy. The 'specification-based' programs became the S (for Specification) type and the 'real-world' programs inspired the E (for Evolving) type. A third type, P for Problem, was also identified. However, early studies of P-type programs suggested that, in practice, they always satisfied the definition of either S-type or E-type. Thus, in his subsequent work Lehman ignored type P. A major contribution of this work is to provide a revised definition and description of the P category that is both conceptually sound and relevant to software engineering practice.

The notion of E-type software has achieved widespread acceptance. It has informed all of Lehman's subsequent work and has been accepted by many other researchers in software evolution. However, the S and P categories and the rationale of the taxonomy have received less attention.

Type S – Programs with the following characteristics belong to type S:

- all the program properties, functional and nonfunctional, that matter to its stakeholders have been *completely* defined in a specification, which in practice will be expressed in a formal language, and
- the *only* criterion of the program's acceptability to its stakeholders is satisfaction of the specification (Lehman 1985a).

These properties define conditions in which software evolution does not occur.

Once an S-type program satisfies its specification, and hence its stakeholders, it can be put to use. There is no good reason for changing it subsequently. The program cannot be improved since, by definition, it already completely satisfies its acceptance criteria. On the other hand, any change to the program exposes it to the risk that it will no longer satisfy its specification and will have to be repaired. So, *any* change to the program will waste resources.

If a specification is changed, then, in general, it will be necessary to amend any program derived from it, to restore stakeholders' satisfaction with the program. However, the definition of type S precludes this because the completeness property implies that the specification and any programs derived from it are conceptually static. If the *text* of an S-type specification Z – which by definition is complete – is reused in a different specification Y, then Y is conceptually a *new* specification. It follows that Y must be implemented by a *new* program, although in practice this may well involve copying some replicators from previous programs. Conversely, if stakeholders treat a specification X' as an *evolution* of an earlier specification X, then regardless of whether the text of X was reused in X', it follows that X was incomplete and therefore not S-type.

The effect of these conditions is that S-type programs are rare in the real world. Although many programs are intended to satisfy formal specifications, this is insufficient to qualify them as S-type and, in general, they will evolve in the manner of E-type or P-type programs. In practice, a 'frozen' specification rarely leads to a satisfactory system. This is because stakeholders' satisfaction with a software system often depends on issues that are very difficult to specify completely without some experience of using the system, for example:

- programs are rarely used in isolation but need to be compatible with other software, for example, an operating system, and a hardware platform;
- many nonfunctional properties, for example, usability, depend on assessments that are subjective or situation-specific;
- when writing the specification, stakeholders may have included incorrect assumptions or omitted important assumptions about the application domain or the operating environment of the system.

Nevertheless, despite being rarely observed, the S category is conceptually important because it defines conditions under which software evolution does not occur. The fact that these conditions are rarely satisfied has implications for the 'global software process' (see Section 5.2.2.3) of almost all software systems. It is also important because many approaches that attempt to increase the formality of software engineering *implicitly* assume that the system will not evolve, that is, S-type conditions are tacitly assumed. Such approaches ignore the temporal dimension and their formalisms do not provide any means of representing the possible evolution of a system. For example, the Acme (Garlan *et al.* 2000) Architecture Description Language (ADL) (Medvidovic and Taylor 2000) has no constructs to represent the situation where a system's architecture could be different at times t_0 and t_1. Given that the IEEE definition of architecture refers explicitly to 'evolution' (see Section 5.2.2.2), it is important to be aware of this limitation in Acme and similar ADLs. The existence of the S category within SPE makes it easier to uncover these assumptions.

Type P – In Lehman's original treatment of SPE, type P was derived from the observation that designing a *useful*, problem-solving program generally requires compromises between stakeholders' goals. For example, trade-offs may be made between design elegance and the need to produce practical results. In many cases, the inputs and outputs of a program can only be accurate to some level of precision, rather than correct in terms of a formal proof as type S requires. This issue potentially arises in every numerical problem, other than arithmetic with integers and rational numbers. However, Lehman did not identify any *necessary* characteristics of P-type programs and this contributed to his perception that the category was redundant. Section 5.3.2 proposes a revised definition that provides a justification for the category and gives it a vital role in SPE+.

Type E – Programs that depend on or interact with the real world belong to type E. They include programs that 'mechanise a human or societal activity' (Lehman 1980), or make assumptions about the real world, or interact with the real world by providing or requiring services. In general, such programs must be adapted to match any changes in the real world that affect whether the program satisfies its stakeholders' objectives. Since the real world is dynamic, an E-type program must in practice be continually adapted to remain faithful to its application domain, compatible with its operating environment, and relevant to its stakeholders' goals (van Lamsweerde 2001) and expectations. Situations that include E-type programs can become very complex. This happens because

> 'the installation of the program together with its associated system ... changes the very nature of the problem to be solved. *The program has become a part of the world it models*, it is *embedded* [and executed] in it. Conceptually at least the program as a model contains elements that model itself, the consequences of its execution' (Lehman 1980).

An important consequence is that evolution processes in E-type software systems are subject to positive feedback loops. In particular, the introduction of a new or improved system may produce unexpected side effects rather than restore equilibrium. That is to say, regardless of whether a system change satisfies the requirements of any stakeholder, introducing the change may create or expose issues that must be addressed by making further changes to the system. For example, a system change may stimulate some stakeholders to revise their ideas about the problem that they want the system to address, or the service that the system provides, or the way that the system achieves its results. Chatters *et al.* (Chatters *et al.* 2000) describe a simulation of this process.

The stakeholders who experience the, possibly unexpected, impacts of system changes may be the same stakeholders who originally requested the change or other stakeholders. In either case, earlier compromises between the concerns of different stakeholders may be disrupted in unpredictable ways by 'improvements' to the system. Consequently, the dynamic behaviour of the global software process (see Section 5.2.2.3) for an E-type system will be complex, difficult to predict and sometimes counter-intuitive (Chatters *et al.* 2000).

5.2.2 Stakeholders, Architecture and Software Evolution
5.2.2.1 Stakeholders and Software Systems

Software systems vary considerably in the complexity of the roles that are involved in their development and subsequent use. At one extreme is the solitary programmer who writes a program solely for personal use. At the opposite extreme, many different individuals, groups and organisations can be involved in and affected by a software system over its lifetime. Their objectives, viewpoints and concerns will often differ and tend to reflect their role – for example, customer, user, architect, programmer – in relation to the system.

The concept of *stakeholder* is useful for capturing the active, directed character of roles in systems. It is borrowed from management theory, where a stakeholder is

> 'any individual or group who can affect or is affected by the actions, decisions, policies, practices or goals of the organization' (Freeman 1984).

In the context of software architecture, IEEE defines a *system stakeholder* as

> 'an individual, team, or organization (or classes thereof) with interests in, or concerns relative to, a system' (IEEE Computer Society 2000).

Although different stakeholders may agree about the objectives of a system, they will usually have different concerns about it. In the context of software systems, IEEE defines *concerns* as

> 'those interests which pertain to the system's development, its operation or any other aspects that are critical or otherwise important to one or more stakeholders' (IEEE Computer Society 2000).

For example, users tend to have concerns about a system's functionality and usability, whereas customers may be more concerned about costs of ownership, and software engineers are likely to be concerned about maintainability and evolvability.

Stakeholders' concerns are an important driver in the definition of *architectural viewpoints*. The same IEEE standard defines a viewpoint as follows:

'A specification of the conventions for constructing and using a view. A pattern or template from which to develop individual views by establishing the purposes and audience for a view and the techniques for its creation and analysis' (IEEE Computer Society 2000).

So a stakeholder who has concerns about, say, system evolvability, may define or reuse an existing viewpoint that abstracts the features of the evolvability quality, which are deemed to be important and explains how they should be observed and represented. The viewpoint may then be used to generate evolvability *views* of specific systems.

The concepts of concerns and viewpoints help to explain why different stakeholders may see apparently contradictory views of the same system, as in the example described in Section 5.2.1.1. Some apparent discrepancies can be resolved by distinguishing carefully between the system in itself and a particular stakeholder's partial view of and knowledge about the system. However, some proposed definitions of software evolution implicitly entangle these two aspects. For example, Chapin *et al.* have proposed a comprehensive taxonomy of software maintenance and evolution that defines software evolution in terms of 'customer-experienced functionality or properties [of software]' (Chapin *et al.* 2001).

Nevertheless, differences between stakeholders' views cannot always be reconciled by references to objective facts. Because stakeholders differ in their concerns and viewpoints, they legitimately interpret the world in different ways, which may not be obviously commensurable.[6] The hermeneutics tradition in philosophy studies the process of interpretation. Some of its conclusions are discussed in Section 5.2.3 and applied to the requirements analysis process in Section 5.2.4

5.2.2.2 Evolution and System Architecture

This section considers the relationship between the concepts of architecture and evolution. In the context of software systems, IEEE Standard 1471-2000 provides a definition of architecture that explicitly refers to evolution:

'The fundamental organization of a system embodied in its components, their relationships to each other, and to the environment, and the principles guiding its design and evolution' (IEEE Computer Society 2000).

Thus every system has architectural properties, which may be deliberate or accidental. In either case, they crystallise assumptions about the expected evolution of the system. However, the evolution that actually occurs may not be what the designers of a system's architecture were expecting at the time when architectural choices were made. Whenever a system's architecture incorporates assumptions about the real world that no longer hold and the discrepancy cannot be overlooked, then the system's stakeholders may be faced with either replacing or re-architecting the system. If a software system models a real-world domain, there will always be a risk that this situation could arise.

Real-world domains have, in general, an unbounded number of properties. For example, the properties of the 'retailing' domain cannot be listed exhaustively. Consequently,

---

[6] The concept of commensurability has also been used by Kuhn (Section 5.2.3.3) to discuss the difficulties that can arise when comparing paradigms.

modelling such domains in a finite software system involves an unbounded number of assumptions. Many, perhaps even the overwhelming majority, of these assumptions will be irrelevant to a particular software system at any moment. However, over time the relevance and accuracy of real-world assumptions will change in unpredictable ways. In many cases, even stakeholders who are domain experts cannot fully justify their assumptions about a domain and are obliged to infer from their past experience, which may not be a reliable predictor of the future. In other cases, stakeholders are simply unaware of assumptions that they have made. Consequently, many software systems have properties that are effectively hidden because they are not currently referenced by any concerns of that system's stakeholders. Some of these hidden properties may be architectural, that is, they are part of the 'fundamental organisation' of the system and therefore cannot be changed easily.

The relationship between architecture and evolution has also been explored in architecture's original domain, the 'built environment'. Alexander's work on the role of design patterns (Alexander *et al.* 1977) in architecture has been influential in many domains, including software engineering (Gamma *et al.* 1995). One of his themes is that the architectural process, including the use of patterns, should support the gradual, piecemeal evolution of the built environment so that it becomes increasingly congruent with the changing ways in which people want to use buildings (Alexander 1979), as opposed to more rigid approaches to design in which people have to adapt to the preconceptions of an architect. These ideas have also been explored by Brand, who identified a number of different temporal patterns in the co-evolution of buildings and their uses (Brand 1994).

Architectural concerns in software systems can be described in various ways (Shaw and Garlan 1996). From a software evolution perspective, Zachman's (Zachman 1987; Sowa and Zachman 1992) taxonomy of architecture viewpoints is useful. He identified five levels of abstraction and six categories of concern in architectural descriptions. Their product gives a matrix of 30 viewpoints, which Zachman proposed as atomic components that could be combined into more complex, stakeholder-specific viewpoints. Zachman's levels of abstraction are summarised in Table 5.2, where they are illustrated by viewpoints based on data-oriented concerns.[7] The viewpoints use different models to describe the information that is relevant to stakeholders' concerns at each level of architectural abstraction.

The two most abstract levels, Contextual and Conceptual, share the property that they are primarily concerned with application domain–dependent information, that is, concerns at these levels can only be fully understood in relation to the application of the system to some real-world problem. Conversely, the two least abstract levels, Physical and Components, are largely context-free with respect to application domains. An example from the Physical level is that a relational database product can be used in a wide range of application domains and its properties, for example, locking strategy, index structure, are derived from the domain of database technology, not from any specific application domain.

5.2.2.3 Stakeholders, System Evolution and the Global Software Process

Traditionally, software development methodologies have concentrated on two roles that people can play in the software process, 'user' and 'developer'. One of the benefits of

---

[7] Zachman's taxonomy also includes Function, Network, People, Time and Motivation categories of concerns.

Table 5.2 Levels of abstraction in architectural descriptions (after Zachman), as applied to data concerns

Contextual: planner's viewpoints, concerned with a system's scope and relationship to other systems and policies
Example: develop a business analysis or scenario that explains why some category of information is important to a system's stakeholders

Conceptual: owner's viewpoints, concerned with a system's fitness-for-purpose in relation to some social or business process
Example: describe the organisational roles, entities, relationships and rules that are involved in creating, updating and using a particular kind of information

Logical: designer's viewpoints, concerned with the specification of the computational entities, relationships, processes, algorithms and so on, and with resolving design constraints independently of any particular implementation language or product
Example: define a logical data schema that specifies entities, attributes and constraints in terms of some computational data model, for example, relational, object-oriented, deductive

Physical: builder's viewpoints, concerned with resolving construction constraints and with the impact of the engineering properties of specific technologies on a system
Example: define tables, indexes, procedures etc. in terms of a specific data manipulation language, for example, a proprietary dialect of SQL

Components: assembler's viewpoints, concerned with the physical production and assembly of a system's components
Example: construct a schedule of machine and file addresses where the database components will be located

---

software evolution research has been to broaden this perspective. The term *global software process* (Lehman and Kahen 2000) has been proposed to refer to a *holistic* concept of the organisational processes, roles and forces that affect the evolution of software systems. In this context, the term 'global' does not necessarily imply 'worldwide'; the *geographical* extent of a global software process could be very small.

The actors in a global software process include the stakeholders who can make decisions that cause the system to evolve, those who carry out the changes and those who are affected by its evolution. Although the power to *implement* changes to a software system might be confined to professional IT staff, decisions about its semantics and policies are usually more diffused. For example, the stakeholders of most business-related software systems will include a variety of governmental and other regulatory bodies whose decisions may invalidate a system's assumptions and thus cause it to either evolve or become less useful (Lehman and Ramil 2001).

Previous work by Lehman *et al.*, for example, (Lehman *et al.* 1997; Chatters *et al.* 2000), has identified the complex role of feedback in software evolution processes. Where a software system solves problems or provides services in the real world, stakeholders usually need feedback from different parts of the global software process to help them refine their requirements for the system. The scenario that is familiar to every software developer is that stakeholders' ideas may change while the system is being designed and built. To a greater or lesser extent, this risk can be mitigated by various methodologies for iterative and incremental software development. However, stakeholders' ideas can also change as a consequence of using the software, or of observing its effects on the real world, or in response to any other events in the world. These effects are much harder to predict but may be more influential in determining stakeholders' overall satisfaction with a system.

Ideally, the evolution of large-scale software systems should be managed through a defined process, sometimes referred to as IT governance.[8] In practice, software evolution also happens in unplanned ways. Consider a situation where the users of a subsystem decide to change their use of a data field, for example, changing the basis for calculating depreciation values in an accounting system. If the revised use is consistent with the field's syntax and functions, then the change may be *functionally* transparent to other subsystems that share this data but still have a significant *semantic* effect on stakeholders who need to *use* the data, but may not have been involved in the change decision or even be aware of it.

Management information systems and data warehouses that import data from loosely coupled tributary systems are particularly vulnerable to this kind of rippling evolution. Creators and distributors of information are often unaware of how semantic changes could affect indirect consumers of the information. Similarly, consumers may be unaware of semantic changes in the information that they use until discrepancies or inconsistencies come to their attention. This kind of 'misunderstanding' arises very easily, even within a single organisation, when information collected for one purpose, for example, maintaining an asset register and depreciation accounts, is reused for a secondary purpose, for example, project management. Mergers and acquisitions between organisations often create similar difficulties.

5.2.3 Hermeneutics and Software Evolution

We now explore the philosophical foundations of the theory of software evolution, particularly the hermeneutics tradition in philosophy and Kuhn's extended concept of *paradigm* in the philosophy of science. This apparent digression from software engineering provides concepts that will be used in Sections 5.3.2.1 to 5.3.2.4 to justify SPE+.

5.2.3.1 Software Systems and the Interpretation Problem

It is possible to design and use software in an entirely abstract way that merely manipulates mathematical and logical expressions. However, for a software system to do something useful in the real world, its inputs, algorithms and outputs must be assigned additional meanings by relating them to the real world.

In simple scenarios, for example, using a pocket calculator, the meaning of each computation is known only to the machine's user and is not represented *within* the machine. However, most software derives its power, usefulness and complexity from more complicated scenarios where the real-world application of computations is represented within the software to a greater or lesser extent. Furthermore, when a software system is used as a control system, then it not only holds a representation of part of the real world but is also an active participant whose operations directly change the real world. Such uses of software systems involve several interpretative processes:

---

[8] See, for example, the IT Governance Institute http://www.itgi.org/.

1. The requirements of the software must be formulated, based on some prior understanding of the problem that it will solve or the knowledge domain that it will model.
2. The requirements must be understood, related to relevant technologies and implemented in a system.
3. The results of using the software system must be understood and related to the relevant aspects of the real world.

The interpretation problem becomes even more complex when feedback loops arise from the use of a system (Kahen *et al.* 1999; Lehman and Kahen 2000). Such feedback may change the knowledge or invalidate the assumptions that had supported previous interpretations. Thus, interpretative processes continually introduce uncertainty into E- and P-type software systems, during both their initial development and their subsequent evolution. The philosophical tradition that is most relevant to understanding the interpretation process is hermeneutics, which is discussed in the following section.

5.2.3.2 Hermeneutics, Language and Dialogue

The central concern of hermeneutics is interpretation: how do readers and listeners discover meanings in texts, utterances and similar acts of communication? Habermas has defined hermeneutics as

> 'the art of understanding the meaning of linguistic communication and, in the case of disrupted communication, of making it understandable' (Habermas 1986).

Although the origins of hermeneutics can be traced back to ancient Greece, the modern study of hermeneutics is usually attributed to the work of Friedrich Schleiermacher (1768–1834) and Wilhelm Dilthey (1833–1911). Their approaches tended to be positivist, that is, they assumed that each text had a single, correct meaning that could be extracted reliably by following the right method. Mallery *et al.* (Mallery *et al.* 1990) refer to this tradition as *methodological hermeneutics*.

However, since the work of Heidegger and his successors, particularly Gadamer and Habermas, it is generally accepted that, at least in principle, multiple interpretations of a text are always possible because both the author and the reader contribute their unique experience and perspective to the interpretative process. Mallery *et al.* (Mallery *et al.* 1990) refer to this tradition as *phenomenological hermeneutics*. Philosophers within this tradition continue to disagree about the extent of readers' grasp of the potential complexity of hermeneutic processes. There are significant methodological problems in assessing a reader's awareness of (a) his/her subjectivity in reading a text, (b) the author's subjectivity in writing the text, and (c) any interactions between their subjectivities. Habermas and others have stressed the role of dialogue in helping both participants, the sender and the receiver, become aware of their own and the other's assumptions.

The insights of hermeneutics help to explain some of the strengths and limitations of formal languages for specifying requirements. Languages such as Ross's Structured Analysis (Ross 1977) made important advances in understanding the linguistic basis of stakeholders' requirements and encouraged the recognition of different stakeholders' viewpoints. However, when applied to the real world, such languages must still rely on shared assumptions that cannot be enumerated exhaustively. They may also risk over-abstracting from statements that are authentic but resist formalisation, for example, fuzzy but important concepts such as 'user-friendly'.

Thus, a hermeneutic perspective implies that some expectations of formal specification have been over-ambitious. In hermeneutic terms, some advocates of formal languages appear to have overlooked the insight that the interpretation of a text also depends on context – the situations in which language is used – and pragmatics (Mallery *et al.* 1990) – the meaning inferred from using a sign or symbol in a context – as well as on syntax, grammar and semantics. Some more recent contributions to the formalisation of requirements, for example, Goguen's Algebraic Semiotics (Goguen 1999), have tried to avoid these traps by advocating the use of formality to assist reasoning about social situations (Goguen 2004), rather than to eliminate uncertainty in interpretation.

In practice, there are some domains where a methodological hermeneutics can often produce effective results, and the complexities of phenomenological approaches can therefore be set aside. These domains have been studied by Kuhn. They are characteristic of well-established scientific disciplines, such as chemistry and electricity, but they can also be found on a smaller scale as isolated pockets in many other domains. Kuhn used the terms *paradigm* and *normal science* to express his concept of what makes these domains different from, say, astrology. Kuhn's contribution is described in the following section and its relevance to SPE+ is explained in Section 5.2.4.

5.2.3.3 Kuhn's Theory of 'Normal Science'

Kuhn's approach (Kuhn 1970) to the question of how scientific knowledge develops is helpful for understanding evolution in software systems. His primary concern was to explain a pattern of knowledge development that seemed characteristic of sciences such as chemistry and the various disciplines within logic and mathematics. This pattern consists of successive periods of what Kuhn called *normal science* that each take place within a particular framework or *paradigm*. A paradigm, in this context, is

> 'the general theoretical assumptions and laws and the techniques for their application that the members of a particular scientific community adopt' (Chalmers 1999).

This use of the term paradigm is more specific than its everyday meaning, and in Kuhn's theory it became an elaborate concept with several related senses.

Kuhn's core concept of the paradigm was that during conditions of 'normal science', a discipline has a single, accepted body of knowledge that is taught to practitioners, that defines their research programme and guides their methodology. Analogously, from a requirements analysis perspective, a paradigm also defines the conceptual framework or theory that must be modelled by, and can be taken for granted by, software systems that model knowledge in the domain of that paradigm.

Kuhn also identified that the process of 'normal science' within a discipline is occasionally disrupted by episodes of crisis that fundamentally change the way in which the discipline is defined and practised. Sometimes the crisis takes the form of a 'scientific revolution' in which the previously accepted paradigm is overthrown and replaced by a new one. Kuhn's examples include the demise of alchemy and its replacement by modern chemistry. Some crises have a more limited scope, resulting in the partial replacement of a paradigm. When such upheavals occur in the processes of 'normal science', corresponding changes must be made in software systems that depend on the affected paradigm.

Characteristics of Paradigms

A major contribution of this work is to argue that there is a correspondence between Kuhn's concept of paradigm and the *P* category in SPE+. This section describes the relevant aspects of Kuhn's work and draws attention to Masterman's important contribution to the clarification of Kuhn's concepts. The relationship with SPE+ is explained later, in Section 5.3.2.2.

When Kuhn was developing his theory of 'normal science', he needed to name his innovative concept that describes the distinctive, unifying character of a scientific discipline. He chose to use the term *paradigm* and to extend its everyday meaning. This has sometimes led to misunderstandings about the nature of Kuhn's concept, and subsequently Kuhn regretted (Kuhn 2000) that he had not chosen a more distinctive name for it. However, by then the extended meaning of paradigm had become widespread and it has continued to be used by both scientists and philosophers of science.

Masterman (Masterman 1970) identified three distinct but related senses or aspects of paradigm in Kuhn's work. They are summarised here from Masterman's descriptions, and illustrated with examples from object-oriented software engineering.

Construct aspect – a technique, instrument, language or model that is used to solve puzzles. This is the most concrete sense of paradigm in Kuhn's work and the closest to the everyday meaning of the term. *Example*: the UML enables software designers to 'specify, visualize and document models of software systems, including their structure and design'[9] in a standardised way using object-oriented concepts.

Sociological aspect – the processes and organisations that are used by the experts in a discipline to sustain a consensus on its guiding principles and to systematically teach them to new entrants. Masterman identified the sociological sense of paradigm as Kuhn's most innovative contribution to understanding the scientific process. *Example*: the object-oriented software community organises journals and conferences, for example, ECOOP, OOPSLA, that perform important sociological functions. For example, the peer review process tends to encourage innovation provided that it appears constructive within the existing paradigm. It protects the community's core values, knowledge and achievements by expecting scholarly contributions to acknowledge and build on relevant prior work.

Metaphysical aspect – a partial world view or theory that identifies a discipline and provides it with a distinctive conceptual framework. The metaphysical sense of paradigm includes not only the explicit, formalised, theory of a discipline but also its assumptions, which often seem so obvious, at least to its practitioners, that they are taken for granted. *Example*: Fowler (Fowler 1997) discusses some of the differences between the assumptions that are implicit in object-oriented design notations and those of other methodologies that are needed to understand business entities and relationships.

Paradigm Formation Processes

Masterman observed that, historically, scientific paradigms usually originate from the Construct sense, described above. Someone discovers a way of solving a problem that

---

[9] 'Introduction to OMG's Unified Modeling Language (UML)', http://www.omg.org/getting-started/what_is_uml.htm.

was previously intractable, or not even recognised as a problem. The discovery does not 'fit' into existing paradigms but it opens up new opportunities for doing 'normal science' and consequently wins adherents. For example, the Copernican revolution in cosmology can be traced to two kinds of constructs. First, Copernicus and Kepler discovered that astronomical calculations could be simplified by assuming, respectively, a sun-centred universe and elliptical planetary orbits. Both assumptions contradicted the existing paradigm for cosmology and, initially, could only be justified on the grounds that they worked. Second, the invention of the telescope enabled Galileo to make observations, for example, of Jupiter's satellites, that also did not fit into the existing paradigm.

When a new paradigm emerges in this way, it initially justifies itself by its practical success in solving puzzles, particularly those that the previous paradigm could not solve or did not recognise. In the early stages of a paradigm's development, its theoretical basis is often weak or even nonexistent – it works as a technique but its advocates cannot adequately explain why this is so. Over time, the processes of 'normal science' may elaborate the paradigm by developing it in the metaphysical sense, and institutionalise the paradigm by creating organisations that sustain it in the sociological sense. In the case of the Copernican revolution in cosmology, Newton's laws of motion provided its metaphysical basis until they were superceded by the concepts of Einstein's theory of general relativity. An example of the sociological sense of paradigm is the foundation of the Royal Observatory, Greenwich by Charles II in 1675.

One of the effects of these processes is that paradigms tend to develop a stable, hierarchical structure. The paradigm's practitioners gradually identify the ideas that provide the foundations of their discipline, and usually they try to express these ideas in the form of laws and principles. Lakatos (Lakatos 1970) examined this aspect of the natural sciences. He found hierarchical structures of knowledge that were broadly divisible into a 'hard core' of fundamental theories and principles, and a 'protective belt' of progressively less certain and revisable knowledge and observations that depends on the hard core. The processes of 'normal science' produce continual incremental changes within the protective belt of a paradigm. Simultaneously, the sociological role of the paradigm prevents fundamental change within the hard core unless the case for it is overwhelming, resulting in a Kuhnian 'scientific revolution'. Similarly, Kuhn observed that the processes of 'normal science' in disciplines with mature, successful paradigms tend to constrain the evolution of the paradigm to incremental changes that fill in gaps rather than overturn previous results.

The processes of paradigm formation are not inevitable and need not proceed uniformly in every knowledge domain. In some domains, one or more of the three senses of paradigm remain unfulfilled or there are competing candidates. In this work, such domains are said to be *nonparadigmatic* in terms of Kuhn's and Masterman's criteria. For example, the domain of astrology has neither a governing body that sets standards and trains new entrants, nor an overarching consensus on what constitutes 'good practice'.

Masterman also described a transitional category between nonparadigms and paradigms, referred to in this work as *emerging paradigms*. During the process of paradigm formation, a domain may present competing alternatives for its techniques, metaphysical assumptions and social organisation. This diversity may lead to the development of distinctive, and often competing, 'schools' within a domain, for example, the various approaches to psychotherapy.

In this work, the term *pre-paradigmatic* will be used to refer collectively to nonparadigmatic and emerging paradigm domains. In Section 5.3.2.1, it will be argued that there is a correspondence between pre-paradigmatic domains and the E category in SPE+.

5.2.4 Requirements Analysis, Paradigms and Hermeneutics

We now consider how the concepts of hermeneutics and paradigm apply to the requirements analysis process. General considerations that apply to all real-world software, that is, E-type and P-type systems, are described below. There are also significant differences, depending on whether the application domain is paradigmatic or pre-paradigmatic. These issues are discussed in two subsections.

Ideas that inform stakeholders' requirements for a software system can be drawn from various sources. For example, they can be derived from paradigms, in Kuhn's extended sense of that term, and from various kinds of pre-paradigmatic knowledge, including 'common sense' and *ad hoc* notions. In practice, stakeholders often express their goals, assumptions and requirements in the form of scenarios and exemplars. Consequently, an analyst must use a discovery process to find the *underlying* theories and assumptions. An analyst's aim should be to achieve a sufficient understanding of the viewpoints that different stakeholders have implicitly adopted. In other words, the theories that stakeholders hold about the real-world domain of a system have to be inferred from the partial information that is available at the time that the analysis is carried out.

The interpretation of stakeholders' theories involves an unbounded set of assumptions that are made by both analysts and stakeholders. Assumptions about software systems arise from the abstraction, reification and bounding processes that are essential to reduce the unbounded number of properties of any real-world domain to a bounded set of requirements that can be implemented in a system.

Some assumptions may be known from the start of the requirements analysis process, and others may be discovered during it. Using requirements engineering techniques[10] should improve the discovery rate but an unbounded number of implicit, unrecognised assumptions will always remain. The subset of assumptions that stakeholders are aware of will tend to change continually over the lifetime of a system. Of course, many assumptions are, at least initially, irrelevant to the development and use of the system. However, as the world changes, some previously irrelevant assumptions may become relevant and some that were previously valid may become invalid. All assumptions are potentially a source of unexpected program behaviour. This may occur either when an assumption fails, or when an assumption that had already failed becomes relevant to the program because of some other change. Either case may lead to unacceptable or incorrect results from the program.

5.2.4.1 Requirements Analysis in Paradigmatic Domains

In paradigmatic domains, an analyst can validly use methodological hermeneutics. In such domains, requirements analysis must consider both the resources provided by the paradigm, and the statements made by stakeholders from their various perspectives. Depending on a paradigm's stage of development, it may provide constructs, theories, assumptions, organisations, and so on that an analyst can mine for domain knowledge

---

[10] Lamsweerde (van Lamsweerde 2001) provides an interesting summary from the viewpoint of goal analysis.

that is relevant to a software system. This knowledge can be used by an analyst in several ways as follows:

- to derive a baseline model of the domain that a system's stakeholders may wish to extend;
- to validate stakeholders' descriptions of the domain;
- to identify stakeholders' theories that are idiosyncratic with respect to the accepted paradigm for the domain.

That is to say, the requirements analysis process *within* a paradigm can and should use the particular methodological hermeneutics defined by that paradigm.

This approach is most effective in the kinds of scientific domain that Kuhn studied but it is not restricted to the natural sciences. It can be applied validly in other domains that share Kuhn's descriptions of the 'normal science' mode of inquiry and conform to Masterman's three roles of paradigms. For example, Wernick (Wernick 1996) and Wernick and Hall (Wernick and Hall 2004) examined whether the software engineering discipline is paradigmatic in Kuhn's terms.

However, outside the natural sciences, paradigms that are well formed in the Kuhn–Masterman sense usually have a very restricted scope and are difficult to compose into the larger bodies of knowledge and theory that characterise sciences such as chemistry and biology. Nonscientific disciplines are more likely to have one or more paradigmatic 'islands'. For example, natural languages use many different alphabets and writing systems. They have evolved through complex cultural, rather than scientific, processes. Nevertheless, the Unicode standard attempts to solve a specific problem – encoding different natural languages in software – by creating a framework that mimics many features of a scientific paradigm. The Unicode 'paradigm' includes problem-solving constructs, an organisation that manages the Unicode standard, and a set of concepts for understanding its domain. It is, however, an isolated paradigm-in-the-small compared to, say, the role of the Periodic Table in chemistry.

The scope of a particular software system need not coincide with a single paradigm. Consequently, in practice, the requirements of many scientific and most nonscientific software systems refer to multiple paradigms and also to pre-paradigmatic knowledge. Nevertheless, analysts can consider using the paradigm concept to modularise requirements and should be aware that different hermeneutics are appropriate within a Kuhnian paradigm and in the absence of such paradigms.

5.2.4.2 Requirements Analysis in Pre-paradigmatic Domains

In pre-paradigmatic domains, requirements analysis must rely primarily on phenomenological hermeneutics. In such domains, the kinds of resource that can be used within a methodological hermeneutics are less extensive, or less reliable as sources of domain knowledge, or they may not exist. In pre-paradigmatic domains, the process of discovering the relationship between the real world, the description of a problem, and a software model of the problem must rely primarily, and sometimes wholly, on skilful interpretation of stakeholders' statements. That is to say, an analyst must use *phenomenological hermeneutics* and *dialogue* to discover what stakeholders 'really' mean.

Similarly, stakeholders of systems in pre-paradigmatic domains must also rely on these processes if they wish to assess whether an analyst has reached a sufficient understanding of the domain to produce an adequate software model of it. The phenomenological aspect of this process is that the participants should 'adopt a stance of critical self-understanding' (Mallery *et al.* 1990) that recognises that everyone brings their own subjectivity, assumptions and concerns to the dialogue.

Mallery *et al.* (Mallery *et al.* 1990) draw attention to Ricoeur's (Ricoeur 1971) distinction between *discourse* and *dialogue,* which is relevant in this context. For Ricoeur, discourse is a more detached, impersonal process that occurs when an interpreter engages with a text, for example, an analyst tries to understand a published standard. Dialogue is more interactive and more clearly related to a specific situation. In the context of requirements analysis, dialogue includes the possibility of negotiation between the speaker and the interpreter, and also allows for case-based justifications.

5.3 SPE+

5.3.1 Introduction

This section describes the proposed refinement of the SPE categories and shows how they can be defined in terms of the key concepts that were introduced in Section 5.2, namely, *replicator, hermeneutics* and *paradigm.*

SPE+ includes several significant innovations over earlier presentations of SPE:

- SPE+ asserts explicitly that the E category represents the default case for the evolution of software systems.
- SPE+ defines the P and S categories as special cases that arise from certain kinds of stakeholders' requirements.
- SPE+ replaces the ambiguous definition of the P category in SPE with a definition of P-type systems that is derived from Kuhn's concept of 'normal science' and the Kuhn-Masterman concept of paradigm. To recognise this change, 'P' stands for *Paradigm-based* in SPE+.
- The definitions and descriptions of the categories in SPE+ are derived not only from the domain of software engineering but also from relevant philosophical traditions and theories of generalised evolution.

Nevertheless, SPE+ retains the spirit of the original definitions of the S, P and E categories and does not conflict with the earlier work. The effect of the SPE+ refinements is to make some of the implicit aspects of the original descriptions explicit and more specific.

5.3.2 The SPE+ Taxonomy

5.3.2.1 E category – 'Evolving'

Defining Characteristics of E-Type Systems

In SPE+, the default case of evolution in software systems is represented by the E category. Unless there are exceptional circumstances, which are described later under the P and S categories, a software system will tend to evolve continually during its productive lifetime. Conversely, E-type systems that do not evolve for some exceptional reason, for example, resource shortages, inflexible architecture, will tend to become progressively less useful. Lehman summarised this relationship in 'Law I of Software Evolution – Continuing Change' (Lehman *et al*. 1997). The tendency for E-type systems to continually evolve has implications for a system's stakeholders, its architecture and its global software process.

The distinguishing characteristics of the SPE+ categories can also be described from perspectives that are not centred on engineering concerns. So, in terms of Kuhn's paradigm concept (see Section 5.2.3.3), the distinguishing feature of the E category is that each system's requirements are wholly or partially drawn from one or more *pre-paradigmatic* domains. That is to say, if a set of requirements has dependencies on knowledge from domains that are not paradigmatic in the sense described by Kuhn and Masterman (see Section 5.2.3.3), then any system that implements those requirements will be E-type.

Section 5.2.4.2 identified an equivalence between pre-paradigmatic domains and the use of phenomenological hermeneutics to analyse stakeholders' requirements. It follows that the process of developing a conceptual model for an E-type system involves making judgements within an iterative, interpretative process. This process necessarily uses phenomenological hermeneutics and dialogue, both between stakeholders to resolve any conflicting requirements, and between stakeholders and the analyst to reach a shared understanding.

The discipline of software engineering provides an analyst with general guidance and techniques, for example, Parnas's information hiding principles (Parnas *et al*. 1985), but they can only be used effectively in conjunction with detailed knowledge of the domain. That is to say, mathematical and engineering techniques can help an analyst to work systematically but they cannot be substituted for hermeneutic interpretation of domain knowledge that must usually be gained through dialogue with domain experts and other stakeholders. Some of the analyst's tools and methods may be paradigmatic *within* software engineering (Wernick 1996; Wernick and Hall 2004), but their application to a pre-paradigmatic domain cannot completely eliminate choice from the analysis process or uncertainty from its conclusions. This implies that there are limits on the application of formal methods to E-type systems.

E-Type Systems and the Behaviour of Replicators
The SPE+ categories can also be understood in terms of the concepts of replicators and vehicles (see Section 5.2.1.1). Every evolving software system can be seen as a vehicle for a collection of replicators that have *differential* survival rates. That is to say, the replicators within an evolving system vary in their success rates for getting copied into the next release or into another system or artifact, and for avoiding being discarded. However, each replicator does not necessarily behave independently in this situation. The survival chances of a replicator often depend partially on the survival of its 'neighbours' because, in practice, replicators in software tend to be copied or discarded in related groups. An analogy is the phenomenon of 'gene linkage' (Dawkins 1999) that is found in living things.

Many of the linkages between replicators found in software follow from the requirements of the system. For example, in a learning management system, a concept of *assessment credit* may depend on a concept of *course*. Thus, the survival chances of the 'assessment-credit-concept' replicator have become linked with those of the 'course-concept' replicator. If the 'assessment-credit-concept' replicator gets copied somewhere, it is very likely that the 'course-concept' replicator will travel with it. Linkages can also arise because a particular combination of replicators does something that is useful in a domain-independent way, for example, the various useful combinations of design patterns that have been identified by Gamma *et al.* (Gamma *et al.* 1995). Some of these combinations, for example, patterns relevant to software frameworks (Johnson 1992), have been proposed as 'pattern languages' (Alexander *et al.* 1977), increasing the chances that their constituent replicators will get copied as a group.

The distribution of replicator linkages, in terms of their number, size, strength and other properties, will vary between systems. At one extreme, *all* the replicators in a system can be tightly bound in a single linkage that is copied or discarded as a unit; it will be seen later that this is characteristic of S-type systems. At the opposite extreme, each replicator's chance of survival is independent of every other replicator.

The distributions of replicator linkages that can be found in E-type systems are likely to be very diverse. The dominant characteristics of E-type systems – multiple pre-paradigmatic domains, unstable environment, feedback from system use to evolving requirements – tend to increase divergence in the survival rates of replicators. Conversely, in the absence of the control exerted by a paradigmatic domain, it is very unlikely that all or most of the replicators will be strongly linked together as far as their survival chances are concerned. Thus, it is more likely in an E-type system that there will be a large number of small groups of linked replicators and that many of the linkages will be relatively weak and transient. The linkages are more likely to depend on the requirements and design choices of each system, and less likely to depend on paradigms and externally defined standards. Thus the evolution of an E-type system, considered in terms of the outcome of the differential survival of the replicators that it hosts, is likely to have a high number of degrees of freedom. This is because there will usually be many possibilities for the survival rates of its replicators to differ from each other.

The replicator-based perspective described above is consistent with the Laws of Software Evolution (Table 5.1 in Section 5.2.1.3). An E-type system must be continually adapted to maintain stakeholder satisfaction (Laws I, VI). Each adaptation provides opportunities for 'indigenous' replicators to get copied into the next release, and for 'migrant' replicators to enter the system. It also presents threats of ejection to indigenous replicators, as a result of refactoring or rationalisation (Law II). However, the turnover in a system's population of replicators is constrained (Laws III, V), and the capacity of a system to absorb new replicators is also limited (Laws II, IV). Therefore, there will be competition between replicators for survival and hence differential survival rates.

Uncertainty in E-Type Systems
The characteristics of pre-paradigmatic domains, and the unavoidable use of phenomenological hermeneutics to analyse the requirements of E-type systems, contribute to uncertainty in the global software process of E-type systems. This is part of Lehman's 'Software Uncertainty Principle':

> 'In the real world, the outcome of software system operation is inherently uncertain with the precise area of uncertainty also not knowable' (Lehman 1990).

Lehman (Lehman 1990) identified three primary sources of uncertainty in the results of programs; one of these sources, 'Pragmatic' uncertainty, arises because E-type systems are 'finite models of an unbounded, effectively infinite universe of discourse, and one can never be certain that one has identified all necessary assumptions' (Lehman 1990).

This is equivalent to saying that to understand the relationship between an E-type system and its domain requires phenomenological hermeneutics.

Implications for Global Software Processes
From the viewpoints of its stakeholders, an E-type system often appears to be in or to approach a state of continual change (Law I of Software Evolution). An E-type system's evolution is affected by both organisational and engineering processes, which sometimes appear to act independently, sometimes harmoniously, and sometimes opposing each other. These processes are themselves affected by the interpretations, decisions and actions that stakeholders make from time to time. For example:

- stakeholders in E-type systems can define and redefine problems without referring to the constraints of an accepted paradigm;
- stakeholders' requirements for the scope of a system are more open to reinterpretation and revision when there is no accepted paradigm to provide reference cases.

The global software process is also affected by the environment in which E-type systems operate, which changes continually in both predictable and unexpected ways.

Consequently, the global software process of an E-type system usually exhibits several levels of feedback, for example:

- When a system is brought into use, stakeholders may experience feedback about inconsistencies between their theory of the problem and its models in both the system and the real world. They may also notice unexpected discrepancies between the software model and the real world.
- The assumptions about and approximations of the real world in the software model may have become less acceptable to stakeholders since the time when the system was planned because the real world has been changed in several ways by the system development process itself:
  - The real world now includes a new or revised software system.
  - The domains in which the system operates have changed as a consequence of designing, building, installing and operating the system.
  - Any change in the use of the system tends to produce side effects in the interactions between stakeholders and other real-world entities outside the software system.

    For example, if a form in a business process is made available in an electronic format, this may reduce clerical errors because the electronic form can actively check for some kinds of error. However, it may also raise issues about other aspects of the business process, such as automated routing of forms and paperless authorisation procedures.
  - Nonfunctional aspects of the system may interact with entities and processes in the system's environment.

    For example, stakeholders may require the security aspect of a system to conform to externally defined standards and processes which evolve according to their own dynamics. Thus many e-commerce systems have required adaptations, not only to

fix their own security loopholes but also to take account of external changes, for example, in the on-line payment systems that they collaborate with, in the practices required by their bankers and credit agencies, and in regulatory frameworks. Many of these changes are themselves responses to the spread of on-line shopping and its side effects, such as new opportunities for fraud.

In pre-paradigmatic domains, the stakeholders of a software system can respond to feedback by adjusting their theory, and subsequently the system, in *ad hoc* ways to fit their revised perceptions. Conversely, in paradigmatic domains the processes of 'normal science' create strong pressures to protect core theories and to resist adjustments that merely accommodate anomalous observations (see Section 5.2.3.3).

Architectural Implications
The uncertainty that is associated with E-type systems has architectural implications. In general, E-type systems must be expected to evolve, and it therefore becomes very important for stakeholders to consider whether a system is likely to be adaptable to changing circumstances. In many cases, the architecture of an E-type system will be an important factor in maintaining stakeholders' satisfaction with the system. This is because one of the roles played by a system's architecture is to define which system properties are adaptable and which are fixed (see Section 5.2.2.2).

For any particular adaptation to a system, the properties to be changed and preserved may be specified at various levels of architectural abstraction, and the ownership of the specifications may cut across organisational boundaries. An example of a Contextual (see Table 5.2 in Section 5.2.2.2) level requirement is the identification and protection of the critical success factors for a software system, for example, that the system conforms to a particular interface. In the genealogical domain, for example, software products are often judged by the quality of their support for the GEnealogical Data COMmunication (GEDCOM)[11] *de facto* standard for data interchange. The specification of this interface evolves with its own dynamics, which is influenced by many stakeholders, who include both suppliers and users of genealogical software products. The interface is specified at the Logical and Physical levels using BNF syntax. However, at the Conceptual level, the meaning of the various data types is described informally. At the Component level, the relevant program code in a conforming product might be distributed over several modules. Thus, a stakeholder in an E-type software system often needs to track the co-evolution of several specifications and objectives that are expressed in different languages and at different levels of abstraction.

It might appear that ideal E-type systems would be designed with 'separation of concerns' (Parnas 1972; Parnas *et al.* 1985) at multiple levels of architectural abstraction, and with explicit links between related requirements at different levels of abstraction. However, in practice, system designers and architects will usually find that trade-offs and compromises are unavoidable. Some stakeholder concerns, notably security and performance, tend to cut across all other concerns. Highly elaborate separation of concerns may make a system difficult to understand. The technique of aspect-oriented design has been proposed (Ossher and Tarr 2001) to mitigate these problems. Nevertheless, E-type

---

[11] GEDCOM Standard 5.5 has been published at various, often ephemeral, websites including http://homepages.rootsweb.com/~pmcbride/gedcom/55gctoc.htm

systems always contain the possibility that an assumption, either consciously made or unexamined, will become invalid. Theories of software evolution imply that there are no perfect solutions to these issues.

5.3.2.2 P and S Categories: Common Features

The P and S categories of software systems are special cases where stakeholders have made explicit policy decisions that affect the kinds of evolution that can occur in the system. The effect is to reduce, or even remove, the influence of some sources of evolution that are found in E-type systems. The particular decisions that lead to the creation and perpetuation of P- and S-type systems are explained in Sections 5.3.2.3 and 5.3.2.4 respectively.

The decisions that define P- and S-type systems have to be made and enforced explicitly by stakeholders. If the decisions are implicit or the conditions arise accidentally, then it is much less likely that they will be complied with consistently over a system's lifetime. They must also be policy decisions. In terms of Zachman's taxonomy (Table 5.2 in Section 5.2.2.2), the stakeholders of P- and S-type systems have identified a strategic requirement, that is, at Zachman's 'Contextual' level, to restrict the possible evolution of a system. Otherwise, it is likely that the decision will be neglected, or traded-off against other concerns, or made irrelevant by events, which would produce an E-type system.

In practice, the strategic decisions that characterise P- and S-type systems also have to be embedded in both a system's architecture and its global software process. Otherwise the system is likely to become progressively more like an archetypal E-type system. Some of the implications are considered in more detail below.

5.3.2.3 P Category – 'Paradigm-Based'

Defining Characteristics of P-Type Systems
The previous section distinguished P- and S-type systems from E-type systems by their association with strategic decisions that restrict the possible evolution of a system. The additional property that distinguishes a P-type system from the S category is that the satisfaction of its stakeholders depends on the system *maintaining* consistency with a single paradigm over the system's lifetime. An example of a large-scale system that is based on a single paradigm is the Virgo (Hellemans and Mukerjee 2004) simulation of the evolution of the universe. In this case, the relevant paradigm is the laws of physics as they apply on a cosmological scale. The success of Virgo depends both on the accuracy of its results, compared to astronomers' observations, and on its consistency with gravitational theory.

This kind of dependency can also be made on an *external* standard that is treated as a paradigm by the system's stakeholders. For example, during the 1990s, British Telecommunications plc operated a software system (Homan 1999) in its telephone exchanges that provided an interface between analogue subscriber line switches, which conformed to a written specification, and its digital network, which implemented an international standard. The success of the system depended on its conformance to these specifications, which played the role of a paradigm in this context.

Thus, the evolution of a P-type system is constrained by the strategic decision of its stakeholders to keep the system consistent with a paradigm. This constraint will be experienced in two ways. It will prevent some kinds of change that might otherwise have occurred. It may also induce change, either when the paradigm is updated or when opportunities arise, for example, through technological change, to improve the system's consistency with its paradigm.

Stakeholders of systems in paradigmatic domains are more constrained than stakeholders of E-type systems in changing their theory of any *specific* problem within that domain. A paradigmatic domain provides an overarching conceptual framework that has a significant degree of internal coherence and discipline and is shared with other experts in that field of knowledge. Consequently, the task of understanding how to model a *particular* problem can use the methodological hermeneutics that the paradigm defines. The discipline's paradigm defines both a general model for the problems that are within its scope, and techniques for applying the generic model to a specific case. The paradigm also restrains stakeholders from making piecemeal or arbitrary adjustments to either their 'local' theory or its software model, if this would reduce the credibility of the system within the paradigm's community. The importance of this distinction between E-type and P-type systems is not undermined by the fact that paradigms themselves evolve in limited ways (see Section 5.2.3.3).

Thus for a P-type system, the domain's paradigm pre-defines a complex structure of assumptions, theories and techniques that are already familiar to many of the system's stakeholders. This has effects on the feedback loops within the global software process, particularly from the use of a software system back to its requirements (Chatters *et al.* 2000). In the case of P-type systems, this loop is indirect and mediated through the processes of scientific discovery, peer review and so on. That is to say, using a P-type system can only change the paradigm that defines the system's concepts if use of the system leads to the acceptance of new scientific knowledge into the same paradigm. The closer the concept lies to the paradigm's 'hard core', the less likely it is that the paradigm's community will decide to change it.

Replicator Behaviour in P-Type Systems

The dependence of P-type systems on paradigmatic domains can also be expressed in terms of replicator behaviour. It produces a situation where the domain-specific replicators in a software system have their survival chances yoked together by depending on a paradigmatic domain. Furthermore, replicators that are domain-independent will also find that their survival chances are influenced by the extent to which they help the system conform to the paradigm. Thus the differential survival of replicators in a P-type system tends to be dominated by a single persistent source of evolutionary pressure, whereas an E-type system would usually have multiple, possibly competing, evolutionary pressures that might change over time.

P-Type Systems and Software Reuse

The characteristics of the P category give it a strong association with software reusability. Many design techniques for promoting software reuse can be understood in SPE+ terms as attempting to disentangle coherent P-type components from each other and from E-type noise. The pattern catalogues in, for example, (Gamma *et al.* 1995; Buschmann *et al.* 1996) provide repertoires of reusable P-type solutions to software design problems. They are largely independent of specific implementation languages and application domains. Fowler's use of analysis patterns (Fowler 1997) implicitly abstracts P-type information elements from the complexity and incidental detail of real-world, E-type, domains. Edwards et al. (Edwards and Millea 2000, 2002) proposed a similar approach to the design of 'immortal' software.

Simon's work (Simon 1969) on evolution in both natural and artificial systems implies that reusing components should tend to reduce the costs of system evolution. P-type components at any level of architectural abstraction can play the role of Simon's *stable intermediate forms*. Simon used this term to refer to subsystems that can be used as building blocks or components, that is, they can be used and reused in the evolution of more complex, but possibly less stable, systems, including E-type systems.

Many systems constructed from P-type components will also have the quality that Simon called *nearly decomposable* (Simon 1969), that is, interactions between the system's subsystems are weak but not necessarily negligible. Consequently, nearly decomposable systems tend to have more predictable behaviour at both the subsystem and aggregate levels, and over different timescales. This can be contrasted with E-type systems, where it is common to find that changing a subsystem tends to cause ripples of consequent changes.

5.3.2.4 S Category – 'Specification-Based'

Defining Characteristics of S-Type Systems

The E and P categories in SPE+ define two idealised types of evolving systems. Real-world software systems can be expected to conform to these types to a greater or lesser extent. The S category is somewhat different. As explained in Section 5.2.1.4, the S category defines the conditions in which software evolution does not occur. These conditions are very restrictive and, in practice, few fully conforming S-type systems are found.

The condition that is necessary to prevent the occurrence of software evolution is that the *sole* criterion of stakeholder satisfaction with a software system is its correctness with respect to a *finalised* specification. If stakeholders care about any property of the system that has not been completely specified, then it is likely that the system will evolve for the reasons explained in previous sections, and the system will therefore be P- or E-type. In particular, if stakeholders care about a system's relevance to the real world, then the system will not be S-type.

The centrality of specifications to the S category implies that S-type systems are more likely to be based on paradigmatic domains, particularly mathematics and logic. Nevertheless, in principle, the specification of an S-type system can be drawn from any or no domain. The essential property of an S-type system is that, once the specification of its requirements has been decided, the specification must be divorced from any paradigm or theory that it was derived from and must be treated as axiomatic. That is to say, any future evolution in a 'parent' paradigm cannot be allowed to affect the specification, which must be self-sufficient and the only criterion for judging the system. To restate points made earlier in the context of E- and P-type systems, if a system's specification retains dependencies on any paradigm, then the system cannot be S-type. If the dependency is a strategic decision by stakeholders, then the system can be P-type, otherwise it will be E-type, and its evolution will be subject to the appropriate dynamics.

Architecture and Design in S-Type Systems

Further limitations on the practicality of S-type systems arise from the relationships among program size, complexity and design. In practice, as Dijkstra (Dahl *et al.* 1972) observed, design trade-offs cannot be ignored. As a program increases in size and/or complexity, it becomes more difficult to prove its correctness unless the designer has structured the program to facilitate the relevant kinds of proof. Hence, in practice, a stakeholder requirement for correctness also implies design choices that will permit correctness to be demonstrated.

Replicators in S-Type Systems

The replicators that are found in S-type systems include functions and algorithms, and also more abstract artifacts such as the design styles and patterns alluded to by Dijkstra. By definition, an S-type system does not evolve. Therefore, *differential* survival of replicators does not occur within an S-type system but it can occur within *collections* of formally specified systems, which may include S-type systems. Replicators can be copied from one formally specified system to another as part of the process of writing a new program, which could be S-type. When replicators are copied between formally specified systems, this produces the effect that Dijkstra called a 'system family' (Dahl *et al.* 1972), in which a collection of similar programs share a common abstract specification but differ in their concrete specifications.

5.3.3 Validation of SPE+

As far as the authors are aware, the available evidence is consistent with SPE+ and illustrative examples have been mentioned where appropriate. However, this is insufficient to make a compelling argument and more extensive and rigorous tests are required to establish whether SPE+ is valid.

SPE+ should be used to infer hypotheses and models about possible differences in the observed evolution of E- and P-type systems. Section 5.3.2 makes many allusions to the impacts on stakeholders, global software processes, system architecture, and so on, which can be expected when software systems evolve. We are already conducting further research in this area by investigating whether E-type and P-type modules can be identified within systems, and if so, whether they exhibit differences predicted by SPE+. For example, the current research of three of the authors (Cook, Harrison and Wernick) is focussed on a case study of an industrial-scale telecommunications system. It is desirable that similar tests should also be carried out under controlled, laboratory conditions where this is feasible.

The validity of SPE+ can also be considered in a broader sense, by considering its implications for various kinds of software processes, the *How?* of software evolution. The following paragraphs illustrate this by sketching some issues that could be explored using SPE+.

5.3.3.1 SPE+ and Stakeholder Policy Decisions

Lehman's initial exposition of SPE emphasised the importance of user satisfaction in the dynamics of software evolution. SPE+ reinforces this by identifying stakeholders' strategic decisions as the critical factor in creating and perpetuating P- and S-type systems.

This should encourage further research into the global software process and its relationship to policies and practices in IT governance.

5.3.3.2 SPE+ and Open-Source Software

Section 5.2.1.1 showed that the concept of replicator can be used to identify theoretical differences in the evolutionary potential of open-source and proprietary software products. Previous empirical research, for example, (Godfrey and Tu 2000), has suggested that open-source software processes may exhibit variations from the classic form of Lehman's Laws. These lines of research have yet to be coordinated with SPE+. So it remains an open question whether an observed difference in evolutionary behaviour between software systems should be attributed to the following:

- The open/closed character of the software process, or
- The SPE+ category of the product, or
- A combined effect of the categories of the process and the product, or
- Other factors.

Such research would help to establish the relative importance of the SPE+ category in determining the likely evolution of a software system.

5.3.3.3 SPE+, Design Patterns and Software Reuse

An implication of SPE+ is that E- and P-type systems have different architectural properties and thus may be suited to different kinds of design patterns. P-type components appear to be good candidates to fulfil the role in evolving systems that Simon called *stable intermediate forms* (Simon 1969) (see Section 5.3.2.3). Conversely, designing E-type components to have lower evolution costs will usually be more challenging. Their association with pre-paradigmatic domains increases the probability of changes to their architectural properties at the 'Conceptual' and 'Contextual' levels, which makes them less suitable candidates for stable intermediate forms. Andrade *et al.* (Andrade and Fiadeiro 2001) have suggested that design patterns based on concepts of coordination and superposition may be effective for separating volatile business rules from 'immortal' (Edwards and Millea 2000, 2002) properties in E-type systems. Concepts of aspect-oriented design (Noda and Kishi 1999) are also relevant.

5.3.3.4 SPE+, Agile Methods and Architectural Concerns

Alternatively, there may be a case for designing some E-type components to be cheaply disposable, rather than modifiable. The higher rate of churn in the design of Web interfaces, compared to their underlying information sources, appears to illustrate this. However, this approach may increase the risk that architectural principles and other strategic stakeholder decisions will be neglected. One of the challenges facing the advocates of both 'agile methods' and 'enterprise architecture' is how to reconcile their conflicting concerns in conditions of great uncertainty and rapid change for software systems. SPE+ provides a set of concepts and definitions within which these ideas can be investigated.

5.4 Conclusions and Future Research

This work is primarily concerned with refining the metaphysical aspect of the emerging paradigm of software evolution, to use the terminology of Section 5.2.3.3. We have described a set of concepts, drawn from software engineering and other domains, which provide the foundations for understanding what software evolution is. We have demonstrated the value of this conceptual framework by using it to propose refinements to the SPE taxonomy of evolving software systems.

The revised form of the SPE taxonomy, presented here as SPE+, addresses some perceived weaknesses and ambiguities in the original formulation. SPE+ provides a basis for classifying evolving software systems that demonstrate a unification of concepts drawn from software engineering, from generic theories of evolution, from the hermeneutic tradition in philosophy, and from Kuhn's concepts of paradigm and 'normal science'. The strongest aspect of the original SPE taxonomy, namely, its insights into evolution in E-type systems, has been retained and is entirely consistent with the refinements of the P and S categories in SPE+.

The focus in this work is on theory-building. It needs to be complemented by more empirical approaches. In particular, it is important that further work should be done to develop testable models and hypotheses from the conceptual definitions and descriptions of the E and P categories. An important test of the validity and relevance of SPE+ will be whether it leads to different predictions for the evolution of E- and P-type systems and whether these differences are observable, both under laboratory conditions and in industrial-scale software systems. This work is currently in progress within our own research groups and we hope that other teams will also feel encouraged to explore the implications of SPE+ and to test its validity.

The theoretical developments described in this work indicate that there is a continuing need for empirical studies of evolution in industrial-scale software systems. The diversity of software systems and software processes means that an extensive corpus of studies is required both to test conjectures and to suggest further refinements to theories. For example, the Feedback, Evolution And Software Technology (FEAST) projects carried out pioneering work in this area but a limitation of those studies was that they concentrated on software development processes that were derived essentially from Royce's waterfall (Royce 1970) methodology. The theory of software evolution, including SPE+, predicts that its effects will also be found in software systems that have been developed using other approaches, for example, iterative/incremental (Larman and Basili 2003), open source (DiBona *et al.* 1999) and agile (Beck 1999). Valuable work has begun in these areas, for example, Godfrey's study (Godfrey and Tu 2000) of evolution in open-source software, but much more is needed. An important research aim should be to establish more precisely which phenomena of software evolution are universal, and which vary according to parameters such as the development method, the application domain, and so on.

Such studies can take various forms. For example, case studies of well-documented, long-lived systems are valuable because they can provide opportunities to observe and measure a wide range of properties of a system, its global software process and its relationship to its application domain. There is also a role for studies that emphasise breadth rather than depth. For example, a collection of software system histories could be analysed using techniques such as case-based reasoning (Gebhardt *et al.* 1997). In contrast, classical experimental designs involving control groups and statistically reliable sample sizes, present formidable difficulties in this research area. Given the practical difficulties of conducting nontrivial experiments in software evolution, this work is likely to require collaborative efforts. Empirical research in software evolution could be an interesting application area for a 'semantic grid' approach.

The concept of software evolution is gradually becoming accepted. The work reported here contributes to that process by showing that the theory of software evolution is capable of further development. In particular, this work uses SPE+ to show how the theory of software evolution can be integrated with other aspects of software engineering and with wider philosophical concerns.

The theory of software evolution also has implications for the practice, management and planning (Lehman and Ramil 2001) of software development and adaptation. In particular, as software becomes ubiquitous, it will become increasingly important to be aware of the various assumptions – which may be inconsistent, out-of-date or simply wrong – that have been incorporated into software, and hence into products, processes and services that human society relies on. That is to say, as software becomes pervasive in everyday life, so too will the effects of software evolution. Unless we improve our understanding of its underlying processes, we are likely to be surprised by its emergent effects.

By balancing detailed investigations with broader perspectives, researchers into software evolution can help colleagues and IT practitioners to understand what software evolution is, why it happens, how it can be planned and managed, and how systems can be designed with evolution in mind – in short, how the benefits of software evolution might be realised and how its risks can be mitigated.

Glossary

ADL	Architecture Description Language
CASE	Computer-Assisted Software Engineering
COTS	Commercial Off-The-Shelf
DBMS	Database Management System
FEAST	Feedback, Evolution And Software Technology
	http://www.cs.mdx.ac.uk/staffpages/mml/feast1/index.html
Semantic grid:	a generic, easy-to-use infrastructure for e-science
	http://www.semanticgrid.org/
UML	Unified Modeling Language
Unicode:	the universal character encoding standard used for representation of text for computer processing, http://www.unicode.org/

5.5 Acknowledgements

The work of Stephen Cook and Rachel Harrison was supported by the UK Engineering and Physical Science Research Council (grant no. GR/N01859) and the University of Reading.

The work of Paul Wernick was supported by the University of Hertfordshire.

Earlier work by Lehman and his colleagues was variously supported by the European Office of the US Army and by the UK Engineering and Physical Science Research Council.

The authors gratefully acknowledge the many helpful and incisive comments on draft versions of this work that they have received from colleagues and anonymous reviewers.

References

Alexander, C. 1979. *The Timeless Way of Building*. New York: Oxford University Press.

Alexander, C., Ishikawa, S. and Silverstein, M. 1977. *A Pattern Language: Towns, Buildings, Construction*. New York: Oxford University Press.

Andrade, L.F. and Fiadeiro, J.L. 2001. Coordination: the evolutionary dimension. In: Pree, W. ed. *Proceedings 38th International Conference on Technology of Object-Oriented Languages and Systems (TOOLS 38): Components for Mobile Computing*, Zurich, Switzerland; New York, NY: Prentice Hall, pp. 136–147.

Beck, K. 1999. *Extreme Programming Explained: Embrace Change*. Reading, MA: Addison Wesley.

Belady, L.A. and Lehman, M.M. 1972. An introduction to program growth dynamics. In: Freiburger, W. ed. *Statistical Computer Performance Evaluation*. New York: Academic Press, pp. 503–511.

Blackmore, S.J. 1999. *The Meme Machine*. Oxford: OUP.

Brand, S. 1994. *How Buildings Learn: What Happens After They're Built*. New York: Viking Penguin.

Buschmann, F., Meunier, R., Rohnert, H., Sommerlad, P. and Stal, M. 1996. *Pattern-Oriented Software Architecture: A System of Patterns*. Chichester, UK: John Wiley.

Chalmers, A.F. 1999. *What is this Thing Called Science?* Buckingham, UK: Open University Press.

Chapin, N., Hale, J.E., Khan, K.M., Ramil, J.F. and Tan, W.-G. 2001. Types of software evolution and software maintenance. *Journal of Software Maintenance and Evolution: Research and Practice*, vol. 13, no. 1, pp. 3–30.

Chatters, B.W., Lehman, M.M., Ramil, J.F. and Wernick, P. 2000. Modelling a software evolution process: a long-term case study. *Journal of Software Process: Improvement and Practice*, vol. 5, no. 2–3, pp. 95–102.

Cook, S., Ji, H. and Harrison, R. 2001. Dynamic and static views of software evolution. In: *Proceedings of the IEEE International Conference on Software Maintenance (ICSM 2001): Systems and Software Evolution in the Era of the Internet*, Florence, Italy, 7–9 November 2001. Los Alamitos, CA: IEEE Computer Society Press, pp. 592–601.

Dahl, O.-J., Dijkstra, E.W. and Hoare, C.A.R. 1972. *Structured Programming*. London: Academic Press.

Dawkins, R. 1976. *The Selfish Gene*. Oxford: OUP.

Dawkins, R. 1999. *The Extended Phenotype: The Long Reach of the Gene*. Oxford: OUP.

DiBona, C., Ockman, S. and Stone, M. eds. 1999. *Open Sources: Voices of the Open Source Revolution*. Sebastopol, CA: O'Reilly.

Edwards, J. and Millea, T. 2000. Genotypes, phenotypes, word processors and financial IT systems: common elements in software evolution. In: Bennett, K. ed. *Proceedings of the Two Day Workshop on Software and Business Co-Evolution (SOCE'2000)*, London, UK, 12–13 July 2000. Durham, UK: University of Durham.

Edwards, J.M. and Millea, T.A. 2002. Cheating death (better software evolution). In: Henderson, P. ed. *Systems Engineering for Business Process Change: New Directions*. London: Springer-Verlag, pp. 81–93.

Fowler, M. 1997. *Analysis Patterns: Reusable Object Models*. Boston, MA: Addison-Wesley.

Fowler, M., Beck, K., Brant, J., Opdyke, W. and Roberts, D. 1999. *Refactoring: Improving the Design of Existing Code*. Harlow, UK: Addison-Wesley.

Freeman, R.E. 1984. *Strategic Management: A Stakeholder Approach*. Boston, MA: Pitman.

Gamma, E., Helm, R., Johnson, R. and Vlissides, J. 1995. *Design Patterns: Elements of Reusable Object-Oriented Software*. Boston, MA: Addison-Wesley.

Garlan, D., Monroe, R.T. and Wile, D. 2000. Acme: architectural description of component-based systems. In: Leavens, G.T. and Sitaraman, M. eds. *Foundations of Component-Based Systems*, chapter 3, Cambridge, UK: CUP, pp. 47–68.

Gebhardt, F., Vob, A., Grather, W. and Schmidt-Belz, B. 1997. *Reasoning with Complex Cases*. Boston, MA: Kluwer Academic.

Godfrey, M.W. and Tu, Q. 2000. Evolution in open source software: a case study. In: Werner, B. ed. *Proceedings of International Conference Software Maintenance (ICSM'00)*, San Jose, CA, 11–14 October 2000. Los Alamitos, CA: IEEE Computer Society, pp. 131–142.

Goguen, J.A. 1999. An introduction to algebraic semiotics, with application to user interface design. In: Nehaniv, C.L. ed. *Computation for Metaphors, Analogy and Agents*. Berlin, Germany: Springer-Verlag, pp. 242–291.

Goguen, J.A. 2004. Semiotics, compassion and value-centered design. In: Liu, K. ed. *Virtual, Distributed and Flexible Organisations: Studies in Organisational Semiotics*, Reading, UK, 11–12 July 2003. Dordrecht, Netherlands: Kluwer Academic, pp. 3–14.

Habermas, J. 1986. On hermeneutics' claim to universality. In: Mueller-Vollmer, K. ed. *The Hermeneutics Reader: Texts of the German Tradition from the Enlightenment to the Present.* Oxford, UK: Basil Blackwell, pp. 294–319.

Heimann, E. 1945. *History of Economic Doctrines: An Introduction to Economic Theory.* New York: OUP.

Hellemans, A. and Mukerjee, M. 2004. Computing the cosmos. *IEEE Spectrum*, vol. 41, no. 8, pp. 22–28.

Homan, D. 1999 10 years of software maintenance or crawling through the mire. *Position Paper Presented at The Workshop on Empirical Studies of Software Maintenance (WESS99)*, Oxford, UK. Available online from: http://dec.bmth.ac.uk/ESERG/WESS99/homan.ps [Accessed 23 November 2004].

IEEE Computer Society. 2000. *IEEE Recommended Practice for Architectural Description of Software-Intensive Systems.* New York: IEEE Computer Society.

Johnson, R.E. 1992. Documenting frameworks using patterns. In: Paepcke, A. ed. *Proceedings of the Conference on Object Oriented Programming Systems, Languages and Applications (OOPSLA'92)/*, Vancouver, BC, Canada, 18–22 October 1992. New York: ACM Press, pp. 63–76.

Kahen, G., Lehman, M.M. and Ramil, J.F. 1999. *Empirical Studies of the Global Software Process – the Impact of Feedback. Workshop on Empirical Studies of Software Maintenance (WESS'99)*, Oxford, UK. Available online from: http://www.cs.mdx.ac.uk/staffpages/mml/feast2/papers/pdf/622.pdf [Accessed 10 January 2005].

Kitchenham, B.A., Travassos, G.H., von Mayrhauser, A., Niessink, F., Schneidewind, N.F., Singer, J., Takada, S., Vehvilainen, R. and Yang, H. 1999. Towards an ontology of software maintenance. *Journal of Software Maintenance: Research and Practice*, vol. 11, no. 6, pp. 365–389.

Kuhn, T.S. 1970. *The Structure of Scientific Revolutions.* Chicago, IL: University of Chicago Press.

Kuhn, T.S. 2000. *The Road Since Structure: Philosophical Essays, 1970–1993, With an Autobiographical Interview.* Chicago, IL: University of Chicago Press.

Lakatos, I. 1970. Falsification and the methodology of scientific research programmes. In: Lakatos, I. and Musgrave, A. eds. *Criticism and the Growth of Knowledge: Proceedings of the International Colloquium in the Philosophy of Science*, London, UK, 11–17 July 1965, vol. 4. Cambridge, UK: CUP, pp. 91–195.

van Lamsweerde, A. 2001. Goal-oriented requirements engineering: a guided tour. In: *Proceedings 5th IEEE International Symposium on Requirements Engineering (RE'01)*, Toronto, Canada, 27–31 August 2001. Washington, DC: IEEE Computer Society, pp. 249–263.

Larman, C. and Basili, V.R. 2003. Iterative and incremental development: a brief history. *Computer*, vol. 36, no. 6, pp. 47–56.

Lawrence, M.J. 1982. An examination of evolution dynamics. In: *Proceedings of the 6th International Conference on Software Engineering*, Tokyo, Japan, 13–16 September 1982. New York, NY: IEEE Computer Society, pp. 188–196.

Lehman, M.M. 1980. Programs, life cycles, and laws of software evolution. *Proceedings of the IEEE*, vol. 68, no. 9, pp. 1060–1076.

Lehman, M.M. 1985a. The environment of program development and maintenance programs, programming and programming support. In: Lehman, M.M. and Belady, L.A. eds. *Program Evolution: Processes of Software Change*, chapter 20. London: Academic Press, pp. 451–468.

Lehman, M.M. 1985b. The programming process. In: Lehman, M.M. and Belady, L.A. eds. *Program Evolution: Processes of Software Change*, chapter 3. London: Academic Press, pp. 39–83.

Lehman, M.M. 1990. Uncertainty in computer application. *Communications of the ACM*, vol. 33, no. 5, pp. 584–586.

Lehman, M.M. and Belady, L.A. (eds.) 1985. *Program Evolution: Processes of Software Change.* London: Academic Press.

Lehman, M.M. and Kahen, G. 2000. A brief review of feedback dimensions in the global software process. In: Ramil, J.F. ed. *FEAST 2000 Workshop: Feedback and Evolution in Software and Business Processes*, London, UK, 10–12 July 2000. London, UK: Imperial College of Science, Technology and Medicine, pp. 44–49.

Lehman, M.M. and Ramil, J.F. 1998. *Implications of Laws of Software Evolution on Continuing Successful Use of COTS Software.* London, UK: Imperial College of Science, Technology and Medicine.

Lehman, M.M. and Ramil, J.F. 2001. Rules and tools for software evolution planning and management. *Annals of Software Engineering*, vol. 11, no. 1, pp. 15–44.

Lehman, M.M. and Ramil, J.F. 2003. Software evolution – background, theory, practice. *Information Processing Letters*, vol. 88, no. 1–2, pp. 33–44.

Lehman, M.M., Ramil, J.F., Wernick, P.D., Perry, D.E. and Turski, W.M. 1997. Metrics and laws of software evolution – the nineties view. In: *Proceedings of 4th International. Symposium on Software Metrics (Metrics 97)*, Albuquerque, NM, 5–7 November 1997. Los Alamitos, CA: IEEE Computer Society, pp. 20–32.

Lehman, M.M., Ramil, J.F. and Kahen, G. 2000. Evolution as a noun and evolution as a verb. In: Bennett, K. ed. *Proceedings of the Two Day Workshop on Software and Business Co-Evolution (SOCE'2000)*, London, UK, 12–13 July 2000. Durham, UK: University of Durham.

Mallery, J.C., Hurwitz, R. and Duffy, G. 1990. Hermeneutics. In: Shapiro, S.C. ed. *The Encyclopedia of Artificial Intelligence*, vol. 1. New York: John Wiley, pp. 362–376.

Masterman, M. 1970. The nature of a paradigm. In: Lakatos, I. and Musgrave, A. eds. *Criticism and the Growth of Knowledge: Proceedings of the International Colloquium in the Philosophy of Science*, London, UK, 11–17 July 1965, vol. 4. Cambridge, UK: CUP, pp. 59–89.

Medvidovic, N. and Taylor, R.N. 2000. A classification and comparison framework for software architecture description languages. *IEEE Transactions on Software Engineering*, vol. 26, no. 1, pp. 70–93.

Noda, N. and Kishi, T. 1999. On aspect-oriented design: an approach to designing quality attributes. In: *Proc. Sixth Asia Pacific Software Engineering Conference (APSEC'99)*, Takamatsu, Japan, 7–10 December 1999. Los Alamitos, CA: IEEE Computer Society, pp. 230–237.

Ossher, H. and Tarr, P. 2001. Using multidimensional separation of concerns to (re)shape evolving software. *Communications of the ACM*, vol. 44, no. 10, pp. 43–50.

Parnas, D.L. 1972. On the criteria to be used in decomposing systems into modules. *Communications of the ACM*, vol. 15, no. 12, pp. 1053–1058.

Parnas, D.L., Clements, P.C. and Weiss, D.M. 1985. The modular structure of complex systems. *IEEE Transactions on Software Engineering*, vol. 11, no. 3, pp. 259–266.

Plotkin, H.C. 1994. *Darwin Machines and the Nature of Knowledge: Concerning Adaptations, Instinct and the Evolution of Intelligence*. London, UK: Penguin.

Ricoeur, P. 1971. The model of text: meaningful action considered as text. *Social Research*, vol. 38, pp. 529–562.

Roberts, D. and Johnson, R. 1998. Patterns for evolving frameworks. In: Martin, R.C., Riehle, D. and Buschmann, F. eds. *Pattern Languages of Program Design 3*. Reading, MA: Addison-Wesley, pp. 471–486.

Ross, D.T. 1977. Structured Analysis (SA): a language for communicating ideas. *IEEE Transactions on Software Engineering*, vol. 3, no. 1, pp. 16–34.

Royce, W.W. 1970 Managing the development of large software systems: concepts and techniques. *WESCON Technical Papers*, vol. 14, no. A/1, pp. 1–9.

Shaw, M. and Garlan, D. 1996. *Software Architecture: Perspectives on an Emerging Discipline*. Upper Saddle River, NJ: Prentice-Hall.

Siebel, N.T., Cook, S., Satpathy, M. and Rodríguez, D. 2003. Latitudinal and longitudinal process diversity. *Journal of Software Maintenance and Evolution: Research and Practice*, vol. 15, no. 1, pp. 9–25.

Simon, H.A. 1969. *The Sciences of the Artificial*. Cambridge, MA: M.I.T. Press.

Sowa, J.F. and Zachman, J.A. 1992. Extending and formalizing the framework for information systems architecture. *IBM Systems Journal*, vol. 31, no. 3, pp. 590–616.

Wernick, P. 1996. *A belief system model for software development: a framework by analogy*. Ph.D., Thesis. University College London.

Wernick, P. and Hall, T. 2004. Can Thomas Kuhn's paradigms help us understand software engineering? *European Journal of Information Systems*, vol. 13, no. 3, pp. 235–243.

Zachman, J.A. 1987. A framework for information systems architecture. *IBM Systems Journal*, vol. 26, no. 3, pp. 276–292.

6

A Simple Model of Software System Evolutionary Growth

Władysław M. Turski

In analyses of software system growth (evolution), it is of interest to relate the actual (observed) growth to an idealised pattern generated from a simple, manageable dynamic model of software system evolution. The interest in and the value of such studies derive from several sources. First, of course, one may wish to *validate* the model itself, i.e. to check if the growth patterns it generates sufficiently closely resemble actual system evolution, and therefore could be used, for instance, for prediction of its future evolutionary behaviour, a property very valuable to responsible project management. Alternatively, if a trustworthy model already exists, one may wish to examine the differences between the actual and model patterns, aiming to discover whether an actual system evolves 'as it should' or not, and, in the latter case, perhaps to identify causes of anomalous behaviour. There is yet another reason for model building: One may wish to construct a *causal* theory of software system evolution, i.e. to provide a calculable answer to the problem *why growing software systems display the observed pattern*? The present chapter is motivated primarily by the last concern.

There are at least two ways to build a calculable model. We may take the observational data and try to fit (interpolate) them with a suitable polynomial (or a more sophisticated function) of one or more variables, using regression analysis (or more advanced statistical techniques) to determine which of the variables are independent, and estimate how good is the fit we obtained. Alternatively we may *postulate* that the system evolutionary growth is driven by one or more causes, provide a relationship (a function, perhaps) between this cause and a measure of the system growth, and then check if the growth pattern generated by the postulated 'mechanism' resembles what is observed in reality. The charm of the second approach is most easily appreciated when the postulated models are intellectually simple and cheap to calculate with: We can easily verify if a proposed causal relationship

---

Software Evolution and Feedback: Theory and Practice   Nazim H. Madhavji, Juan C. Fernández-Ramil and Dewayne E. Perry
© 2006 John Wiley & Sons, Ltd

holds and thus get a better idea of what makes the software evolution tick. In this chapter, we shall mix these two approaches: We shall start with a straightforward interpolation and then will explore (some) consequences of a simple postulative model that is derived from a generalisation of what the interpolation provided.

The raw data on which a system growth analysis is based usually include a series of system size measurements; often, these are the *total number of modules* or the *total number of lines of code*. When dealing with large software systems, the latter appear less informative as a measure than the former: System evolution is driven more by changes in functionality than by low-level tinkering with code; system functionality changes, in turn, are reflected in added, removed or otherwise handled (cf. [1]) modules. For the time being we assume, as did Lehman in his early studies, that *system size is measured by the number of modules* it contains.

Data on system evolution must also include some means of relating the series of size measurements to a 'time' coordinate. For the time being, we assume that this coordinate is expressed in *Release Sequence Numbers* (RSN). Such an approach has two advantages: The system is precisely defined exactly at times of releases (by the released medium), and the release intervals correspond to well-defined units in the system life history.

Hence, we concentrate on system evolution as described by a series of pairs (release sequence number, total number of modules).

A typical set of data[1] is presented in Table 6.1. Note that the actual system size can grow, decrease or stay nearly constant from one release to another.

In order to select an appropriate interpolation formula, following the fourth of Lehman's original Laws of System Evolution, we assume that the incremental effort spent on each release remains roughly constant throughout the system evolution[2]. Let E be a measure of this effort. Assume further that the incremental growth of the system size, Δ_i, is entirely due to the effort E spent on release i. To relate Δ_i and E we need to take into account the size of the release i, s_i, which acts here rather like mass in a dynamic system or capacitance in an electrical one. Intuitively, the larger s_i, the greater the resistance to

Table 6.1 Data

RSN	Size	RSN	Size	RSN	Size
1	977	8	1800	15	2151
2	1344	9	1595	16	2091
3	1390	10	1897	17	2095
4	1226	11	1832	18	2101
5	1246	12	1897	19	2312
6	1492	13	1902	20	2167
7	1581	14	2087	21	2315

(© 1996 IEEE. Reproduced by permission of IEEE)

---

[1] These data were obtained from an actual financial transaction software and are reproduced here courtesy of the development organisation.

[2] 'During the active life of a program, the global activity rate in the associated programming project is statistically invariant' [1, p. 412].

change, the smaller Δ_i will result from exerting the same effort E. Thus, the first relation that comes to one's mind is $\Delta_i = E/s_i$.

This relation, however, does not take into account the growth of system *complexity* concomitant with its enlargement. Considering that we measure the system size in number of modules, we may assume – naturally, only as a first approximation, but all considerations here are of this nature – that the complexity is expressed by the number of intermodular interaction patterns. This being roughly proportional to the square of the number of modules, another relation $\Delta_i = E/s_i^2$ to work with is obtained. As we need to refer to this relation quite frequently in the sequel, we give it the name of *the inverse square law* (cf. [2]).

Assuming the validity of this law we get

$$s_1 = s_1$$
$$s_2 = s_1 + E/s_1^2$$
$$s_3 = s_2 + E/s_2^2$$
$$\ldots$$

which can be easily rewritten as

$$s_1 = s_1$$
$$s_2 = s_1 + E/s_1^2$$
$$s_3 = s_2 + E/s_2^2 = s_1 + E(1/s_1^2 + 1/s_2^2)$$
$$\ldots$$

Each of these equations (except the first one) can be resolved for 'its' value of E, yielding

$$E_1 = \frac{s_2 - s_1}{1/s_1^2}$$

$$E_2 = \frac{s_3 - s_1}{1/s_1^2 + 1/s_2^2}$$
$$\ldots$$

where the right-hand sides contain data on releases only. Now we can calculate the average of the obtained values, in the case of data contained in the table $\overline{E} = \left(\sum_{i=1}^{20} E_i\right)/20$, and consider it as the average effort per release. This should be a good numeric approximation to the Lehman's 'statistically invariant' effort throughout the system evolution (we do not enter here the somewhat confusing issue of units in which this 'effort' is measured, a decision that should become clearer in the sequel).

Using $\overline{E}$ we may plot the system evolution according to the inverse square law

$$s_1 = s_1$$
$$s_2 = s_1 + \overline{E}/s_1^2$$
$$s_3 = s_2 + \overline{E}/s_2^2$$
$$\ldots$$

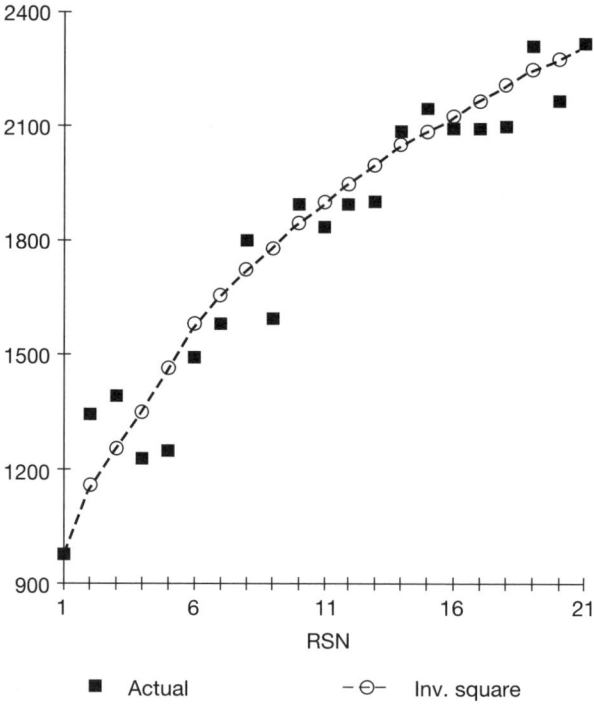

Figure 6.1 Number of modules as a function of RSN

In Figure 6.1, we present the actual (solid squares) and calculated (circles) sizes for the considered system.

The average deviation for the calculated system size is -30.6 ± 106.5. Figure 6.2 presents the plot of deviations as a function of RSN. Note that the deviations follow a pattern ('ripples') similar to that exhibited by traces of negative feedback controlled systems, where a deviation from a set course is overcompensated leading to a deviation of the opposite sign etc. (which explains the large variance). However, no satisfactory simple mechanism capable of reproducing the ripples[3] has been found (see Chapter 17).

The simple inverse square model has been successfully fitted to evolution data on several other systems (cf. [3, 4]).

A further interesting feature of this model is its surprisingly good *predictive power*. For the plots in Figures 6.1 and 6.2, we used value of $\overline{E}$ (our only 'free' parameter!) calculated from *all* available data on 21 releases. Assume now that only the first n releases are available. We can apply the described calculational procedure, obtain $\overline{E}_n$ (i.e. the average from the first n releases) and, using this value, predict sizes of releases $n+1, n+2, \ldots$. Then, when actual releases $n+1, n+2, \ldots$ become available, we can calculate the deviations 'predicted − actual', find an average deviation and its mean error.

---

[3] Note the difference between wavelike ripples and one-off *bumps* in the calculated curve resulting from the inverse square law adjustments for more data (a bump at release 5 in Figure 6.1).

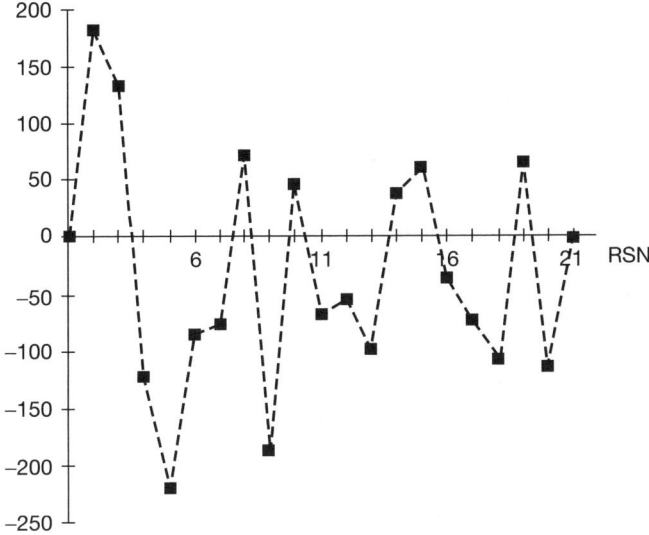

Figure 6.2 Differences in 'actual – calculated' size

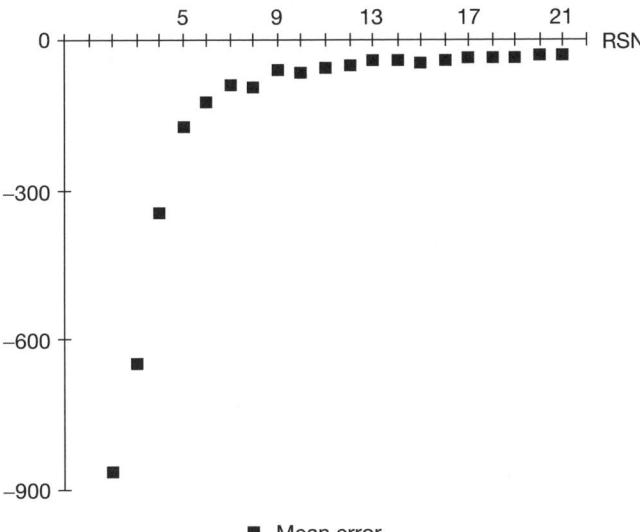

Figure 6.3 Mean error of predictions

Repeating this process for ever larger n, we can check how quickly (or slowly) the consecutive average deviations tend to the value obtained for $n = 21$. In Figure 6.3, we present the results of such experiments for $n = 2, 3, \ldots$ It can be seen that as few as five or six releases are sufficient to provide predictions for the size of the remaining ones that are off target by rather less than 10%. Using data from the first half of the observed evolution period is enough to obtain predictions that are off target by no more than a few percent, at least for the releases available for this study.

This rather remarkable property of the inverse square model is perhaps its most useful one. If the model fits the evolution of a particular system (or, to put it differently: if a particular system is of the kind for which the inverse square law is an appropriate model), then as soon as the data on the first few releases are available, one may quite accurately predict the sizes of subsequent releases.

The inverse square law may be generalised (cf. [5]) by replacing the set of *difference* equations by a *differential* one for which a closed-form solution may be obtained.

We assume the growth of software system size (S) to be governed by a dynamics, in which the rate of growth is *inversely proportional* to the system complexity, i.e. $dS/dt = k/C$. In general, the system complexity, C and the coefficient k may be regarded as functions of time. Whether and how the coefficient k is related to the previously considered average effort $\overline{E}$ is intentionally left unspecified. Two simplifying assumptions are now made as follows:

(i) The coefficient k remains constant throughout system evolutionary growth or, at least, over a significant stretch of time. In the latter case the entire evolution period will consist of a small number (two or three perhaps) of intervals, each with its own constant value of k. This chapter is limited to considering system evolution during an interval characterised by a constant value of k.

(ii) $C \sim S^2$, i.e. it is assumed that system complexity is proportional to the square of the number of modules in the system. This assumption is justified by a simple reasoning given above.

With these assumptions, we can integrate the rate of growth equation and get $S = a\sqrt[3]{t} + b$, with a and b as suitable constants. Above (and in the note [2]), with a and b determined from historic data, the system evolution was plotted for 'pseudo-time', the independent variable expressed in uniform inter-release intervals, which was justified by the fact that the data on system size were available exactly for the release instants. If we plot the cubic root curve against *uniform* independent variable (calendar time) and mark on the t axis the release instants, the shape of the plot remains, of course, unchanged. However, if we rescale (nonuniformly) the t axis, so that the inter-release intervals are of the *same length*, and calculate the system size for each *correct* release instant (of the calendar time), we get a sequence of points that lie *off* the smooth cubic root curve.

In Figure 6.4, the (uniformly spaced) inter-release instants are calculated according to the formula: $t_i = t_{i-1} + r + 1$, where r is a random variable uniformly distributed over (0, 1) so that the inter-release intervals vary randomly between 1 and 2 units of the uniform time. For each release instant, the system size is calculated from the formula $S_i = \sqrt[3]{t_i}$, i.e. we assume $b = 0$ and $a = 1$ (note that b is the initial system size, here taken to be 0, and a is just a vertical scaling factor). In Figure 6.4, the results of the calculations are shown as discrete points; the continuous cubic root curve, which would have resulted *if the inter-release intervals were actually equal*, is shown for comparison. It can be seen that the points – representing a 'simulated' evolution of a system size in case of unequal inter-release intervals – follow the characteristic 'ripple' pattern (see Figure 6.1), noted in plots of real system evolutions in note [2] and papers [3, 4]. Thus,

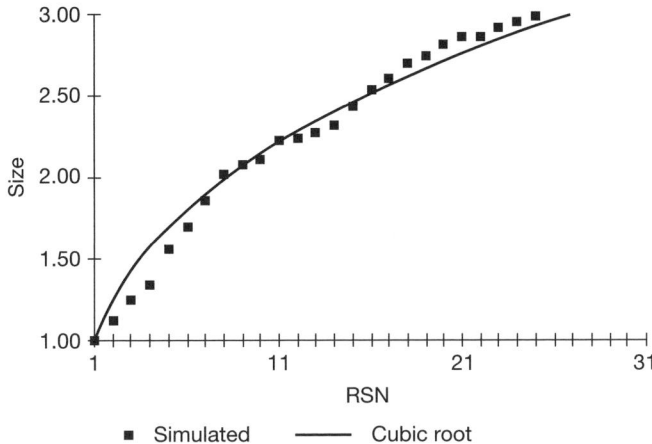

Figure 6.4 Effects of unequal release intervals. (© 2002 IEEE. Reproduced by permission of IEEE)

the somewhat puzzling phenomenon of 'ripples' *may* need no further explanation beyond attributing it to the variations in the inter-release intervals that almost inevitably occur in the actual system evolution.

The exercise in building a manageable, simplified model of software system evolution may be extended in several ways. I believe that a valuable insight may be gained from studying very simple, 'back-of-an-envelope' models that exhibit *causal* rather than statistics-based *correlational* relationships. Such models, albeit purely mental, help understand why certain observed phenomena constitute intrinsic aspects of software system evolutionary growth rather than being incidental.

As an example of such a model, consider a system represented by a sphere of volume S. The radius of this sphere, $\rho = \sqrt[3]{(3S/4\pi)} \approx 0.62 S^{1/3}$, is a slowly growing function of time: $\rho \sim t^{1/9}$. The modules constituting the surface layer of the sphere may be considered as *easy to modify*, whereas the remaining modules, the 'core', are *hard to modify*. The number of the former modules can be approximated by $M = 4\pi\rho^2$, and their relative frequency $M/S = (4\pi\rho^2)/\left(\frac{4}{3}\pi\rho^3\right) \sim \rho^{-1} \sim t^{-1/9}$ is proportional to a decreasing function of time which asymptotically tends to 0; correspondingly, the relative frequency of the hard to modify modules, H/S, asymptotically tends to 1.

Figure 6.5 shows the trends of relative frequencies of modules of these two categories plotted for a period corresponding to 3000 units of the independent variable (e.g. days), i.e. for a period corresponding to some 30 releases separated, on the average, by 100 units. The need to change over to equally spaced release instants is now less clear than before. Relative frequencies, i.e. approximations to probabilities, are most useful in answering questions of the following kind: 'When a system module is picked at random, is it likely to be "easy" to modify?' Such questions pertain to activities *between* rather than *at* release instants.

Plots of the Figure 6.5 confirm the widely shared belief (and experience) that the older the system, the more likely it becomes that a randomly chosen module is hard to modify.

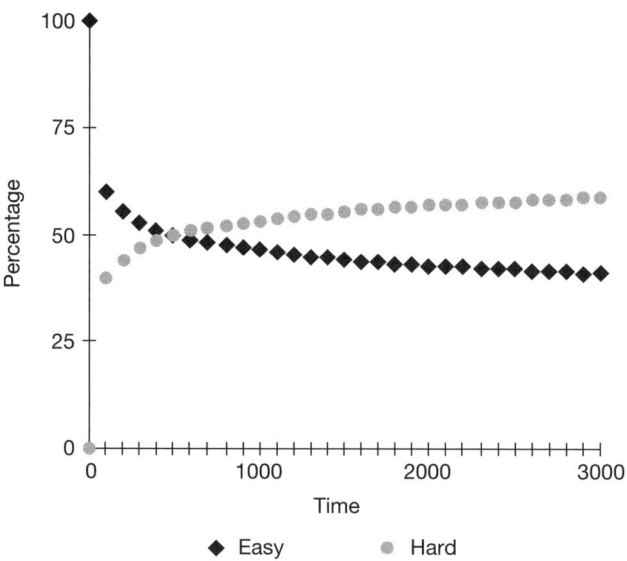

Figure 6.5 Easy and hard modules – trends. (© 2002 IEEE. Reproduced by permission of IEEE)

The spherical model, with all its crudity, provides a means to quantify this belief. The specific values of various parameters (here chosen for clarity of presentation) determine the curvatures of the plots and the position of their intersection point; their trends, however, remain the same.

More sophisticated models can, of course, be proposed and constructed. These could, for example, take into consideration various module-clustering principles that lead to system heterogeneity and to a more structured distribution of 'easy' and 'hard' modules.

For instance, consider a fictitious example of a software system of the kind that follows the $S \sim t^{-3}$ growth pattern (see Figure 6.6) and assume it has a spherical distribution of easy (to handle), i.e. surface, and hard (to handle), i.e. core, modules.

The initial growth of the system is marked in Figure 6.6 by solid circles. As the system grows, the percentage of easy modules falls; c.f. solid circles in Figure 6.7. When the proportion of easy modules falls below 50%, the project management decides to put further development into a separate subsystem, of a similar kind and module-distribution characteristic as the original system. The solid diamonds in Figures 6.6 and 6.7 represent this phase.

As expected, the proportion of easy modules instantly increases (see solid diamonds in Figure 6.7). Note, however, that because the freshly created subsystem is 'young', its growth follows the steepest part of the inverse cubic root curve.

The rules used in plotting the solid diamond parts of plots in the figures were as follows:

- For simplicity, the interaction between the two subsystems (and thus the added complexity) is ignored.
- In Figure 6.6, it is assumed that the growth of the old part is stopped as soon as the decision to start the new subsystem is taken, and the growth of the latter follows the formula $S \sim t^{-3}$ with t counted from the same instant.

A Simple Model of Software System Evolutionary Growth

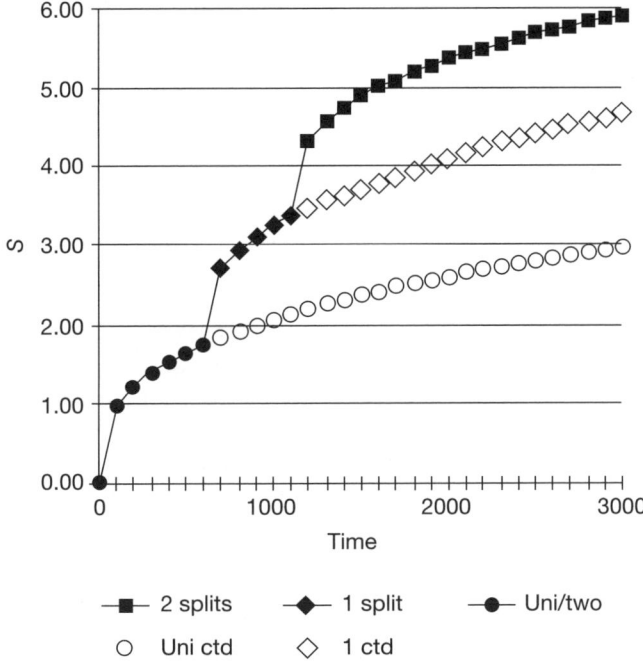

Figure 6.6 Total system size

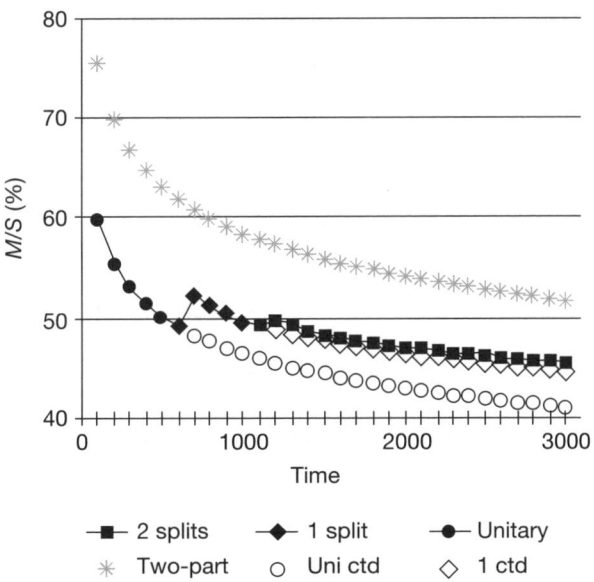

Figure 6.7 Percentage of easy modules

- In Figure 6.7, the percentage of easy modules is a weighted average of percentages of easy modules in both subsystems, i.e.

$$\frac{M_{\text{joint}}}{S_{\text{joint}}} = \frac{S_{\text{new}}\frac{M_{\text{old}}}{S_{\text{old}}} + S_{\text{old}}\frac{M_{\text{new}}}{S_{\text{new}}}}{S_{\text{old}} + S_{\text{new}}}.$$

- Although, for expressiveness, the M/S notation is being used, the actual plots are obtained from the simplified formulae $M/S = 4\pi r^2 / \frac{4}{3}\pi r^3 \sim r^{-1} \sim t^{-9}$ (hence the fractions above were not simplified).

It can be noted that, although the expected improvement in the percentage of easy modules does indeed occur, it is quite slight, and their ratio soon drops again below 50%. The project management decides to reapply the remedy, and a third subsystem is started, represented by solid squares in Figures 6.6 and 6.7. The rules for obtaining the final phase of the plots are the same as before, with obvious modifications. Observe that improvement in terms of the percentage of easy modules is now quite negligible, whereas the penalty (in rapid growth of the total system size) is quite heavy.

The solid line in Figure 6.6 represents the 'continuous' growth of the total system size. Note that without the knowledge of the underlying history, the plot of the system size growth appears to consist of three roughly 'parallel' sections. This kind of growth curve has been observed in actual system histories [6, 7] and could have been used as an argument against applicability of the $S \sim t^{-3}$ rule. It is, of course, not being claimed that whenever the evolutionary size growth of a software system exhibits the 'layered' pattern of the solid curve in Figure 6.6, the underlying cause is *actually* the mechanism just described. As with the 'ripple' phenomenon before, the only claim now being made is that no more sophisticated mechanism is needed to explain the observations and – therefore – unless there is compelling *additional* (independent) evidence suggesting such a mechanism, one can rely on a simple explanation such as that given above.

It is highly illuminating to contrast the system history just described with another, that which would have resulted if the decision to build the system from two (roughly) equal subsystems were taken *ab initio*. The total size would have followed the line of circles (solid and hollow) in Figure 6.6 because at *all times* the total would have consisted of two equal halves of the unitary system. As to the proportion of easy modules, that can be easily computed. Let ρ denote the radius of a subsystem and σ its size (i.e. volume), then for the 'half systems' we have $\frac{\rho}{r} = \left(\frac{\sigma}{S}\right)^{1/3} = \left(\frac{1}{2}\right)^{1/3}$, whence $1/\rho = 2^{1/3}/r \approx 1.26/r$, and the percentage of easy modules (marked by stars in Figure 6.7) would have been consistently at least 25% higher than the best for the development in which the subsystems are split off 'as needed'. If the system was designed to consist of n equal subsystems, the improvement would be $n^{1/3}$, but, of course, with n larger than 3 or 4, one could not possibly neglect interaction between the subsystems and the substantial increase in complexity thus generated.

A further lesson that can be learned from this example relates to the feedback effects in software evolution. A growth-related phenomenon, the percentage of easy-to-modify modules, responds to control decisions (such as 'let us start a fresh subsystem') in a *highly nonlinear* fashion. Thus, the sooner such a decision is taken, the greater is its long-term effects. It seems that nothing can beat a proper initial design; an ounce of forethought is better than a pound of on-the-fly fiddling.

References

[1] Lehman M.M. and Belady L.A.: *Program Evolution – Process of Software Change*, Academic Press, 1985.
[2] Turski W.M.: Reference model for smooth growth of software systems. *IEEE Trans. Softw. Eng.*, **22**(8), 1996, pp. 599–600.
[3] Lehman M.M., Ramil J.F., Wernick P.D., Peny D.F. and Turski W.M.: Metrics and laws of software evolution – the nineties view. *Proceedings Fourth International Software Metrics Symposium, Metrics '97*, Albuquerque, NM, 1997, pp. 20–32.
[4] Lehman M.M., Perry D.E. and Ramil J.F.: On evidence supporting the FEAST hypothesis and the laws of software evolution. *Proceedings Fifth International Software Metrics Symposium, Metrics '98*, Bethesda, MD, 1998, pp. 84–88.
[5] Turski W.M.: Reference model for smooth growth of software systems revisited. *IEEE Trans. Softw. Eng.*, **28**(8), 2002, pp. 814–815.
[6] Lehman M.M., Perry D.E. and Ramil J.F.: Implications of evolution metrics on software maintenance, *Proceedings International Conference Software Maintenance (ICSM'98)*, Bethesda, MD, 1998, pp. 208–217.
[7] Rajlich V.T. and Bennett K.H.: A staged model for the software life cycle, *Computer*, **33**(7), 2000, pp. 66–71.

7

Statistical Modelling of Software Evolution Processes

Tetsuo Tamai and Takako Nakatani

Based on "Process of Software Evolution" by Tetsuo Tamai which appeared on Proceedings of the First International Symposium on Cyber Worlds (CW2002), (c) 2002 IEEE.

7.1 Introduction

Software changes and the speed of change are accelerating. The phenomenon of software change can be expressed in many ways, that is, 'software ages', 'software is maintained' and 'software evolves'. The phrase 'software ages' connotes becoming obsolete [Parnas 1994], although software does not decay or wear out as physical devices. It gets old because the internal structure of software degrades because of the impact of repeated maintenance and because of lack of adaptation of the software to changes in the environment.

So, software is maintained and thereby it ages. The term 'maintenance' is borrowed from conventional engineering disciplines like mechanical and electrical engineering but software maintenance is quite peculiar. Software does not wear out, thus there is no need for 'maintaining' it in order to preserve its original functions. Software maintenance generally includes defect removal (debugging) as well as functional enhancement, while these activities are not considered part of 'maintenance' in other engineering domains.

In general, the phrase 'software evolves' denotes the same phenomenon as 'software is maintained', but it sounds more positive. Another difference is that the verb 'evolve' is used intransitively as opposed to the verb 'maintain', which is used transitively. The former suggests an approach of observing and analysing software evolution objectively, while the latter invariably makes us conscious that software is an artifact and the activity of maintenance is conducted by humans.

Naturally, the concept of software evolution has been influenced by Darwinian evolution. The pioneering work by Belady and Lehman [Belady 1976, Lehman 1985] started by the study of empirical data of OS/360's took its own perspective. This work led to the identification of several 'laws' that characterise software evolution. The work of Lehman and his collaborators focused on the study of the evolution of a system over versions of releases. Tamai and Torimitsu [Tamai 1992] examined evolution processes of application systems, especially focusing on system replacement strategies. In biological terms, their work treated evolution processes of not just a single generation but over multiple generations.

The above two works were concerned with evolution at the system level. Again, in biological terms, this approach has been similar to evolution study at the species level or to the level of individual organisms. Current software systems, however, are composed of relatively independent objects or components. For such systems, evolution at the object or component level may have the same or even greater significance. Component instances of the same class may live within multiple systems concurrently and may keep on living after the death of the system they belonged to, migrating into another system. There is a large population of components living and evolving in the world, many of which are interacting and moving through the Internet. Using an analogy to biology, the component level evolution can be compared to the gene level evolution, whereas the system level is compared to the species level evolution [Dawkins 1976].

The essence of Darwinian evolution can be abstracted to the two key factors: replication and natural selection. Process possessing these factors can be regarded as evolution, be it natural or artificial. Thus, R. Dawkins coined the term *meme* as a counterpart of *gene* for interpreting the concept dissemination in social phenomena. According to Dawkins, a meme is a unit of cultural replication, for example, tunes, ideas, catchphrases, fashions, ways of building pots or of building arches. Many followed in extending this idea of meme, including S. Blackmore [Blackmore 1999]. Evolution of software components obviously shares the characteristics of meme base evolution.

Many different approaches need to be employed to study software evolution. In general, they fall into two categories, as indicated in Lehman *et al.* [Lehman 2000]: those who see evolution as a noun and focus on 'the what and the why' of the phenomenon on the one hand and those who see evolution as a verb and address 'the how' of software evolution on the other. These two categories are illustrated, respectively, by studies that

- observe evolution processes and find patterns or laws governing software evolution, an example of addressing the what and the why questions;
- design computational models or languages that support development of evolvable software, an example of addressing the how question.

This chapter is concerned with the 'what and why' approach. The objective is to analyse evolution patterns of objects or components and build statistical models. If sound models are successfully constructed, it will be beneficial not only by providing a basis for understanding real evolution process but also by supporting software engineers and managers in their decision making concerned with long-term software evolution processes. This can help towards the achievement of a software evolution environment that is compatible with such models.

The structure of this chapter is as follows. Section 2 introduces an approach and the overview of a set of initial case studies. In section 3, the evolution patterns identified through those case studies are presented. In section 4, attention is focused on statistical models that fit and interpret software evolution data, applying them to a large-scale software system evolution process. In the final section, the lessons learned from the study are discussed, together with an indication of future research directions.

7.2 Approach

7.2.1 Measurement

Analysis should start with measurement. The problem is what to measure. Simple metrics such as the number of classes, number of methods and number of lines of source code are commonly used. A suite of metrics was advocated by Chidamber and Kemerer's [Chidamber 1994] supplemented with additional indices. Similar sets of metrics can be found in the literature [Lorenz 1994]. Each of such metrics represents one-dimensional data distributing over a set of classes or a set of methods. When the number of classes and methods of a system gets larger, the volume of data for even a single metric correspondingly gets larger. Handling multiple sets of those data makes it hard to identify the general characteristics of the system.

One way of dealing with such voluminous data is to use visual representations like scattered diagrams or histograms. They help us intuitively grasp the characteristics of the target software and the behaviour of an attribute over time, and the shape of the trend visually illustrates its evolution process.

While graphs are convenient for intuitive understanding, they are not directly amenable to analytical reasoning. Thus, the approach of summarising data by taking the mean – or weighted mean – the variance and other statistics is usually practised. However, summary statistics like the mean and the variance are useful for the normal distribution but it is not assured that those data we are interested in follow the normal distribution. On the contrary, as will be shown later in this chapter, it is not the case and hence the mean and variance are too simplistic to reflect the observed structure of distributions.

The idea is to treat data distributions by fitting appropriate statistical distribution models. If a good distribution model is found, observed software data can be characterised by a small set of parameters that determine the model and much deeper interpretation can be given to the structure of the data.

7.2.2 Case Studies

At the first stage of this research, an empirical approach was taken, that is, through conducting case studies. The following three cases were chosen for the study.

1. **Heat Exchange Simulation System**
   - *Description*: A system to simulate heat flow and temperature distribution within a system composed of various heat devices.
   - *No. of versions*: Four
   - *Development period*: 8 months
   - *No. of programmers*: One
   - *Language*: Visual Smalltalk
   - *Size*: 52 classes in Version 4
2. **Cash Receipts Transaction Management System**
   - *Description*: A system that manages money paid in by customers by matching payments to invoices. This system has been used in a service company.

- *No. of versions*: Four
- *Development period*: 8 months
- *No. of programmers*: One
- *Language*: Visual Smalltalk
- *Size*: 62 classes in Version 4

3. **Securities Management System**
   - *Description*: A system to store information on securities owned by a company and support investment decisions. Data items stored by the system include face value, purchasing price, interest and redemption.
   - *No. of versions*: 14
   - *Development period*: 3 months
   - *No. of programmers*: Four
   - *Language*: Visual Smalltalk
   - *Size*: 133 classes in Version 14

For each case study, data on four or more versions of the system were available. The meaning of 'version' is different for the first two systems and the third. In the first two systems, each version was delivered to its customer and the customer returned feedback and new requirements for the next version. However, for the third system, a version corresponds to a snapshot of the system being developed at a certain checkpoint during the development phase. At each checkpoint, the current design was evaluated and, if necessary, redesigned. All these systems are rather small but are nevertheless intended for practical real world use, with the first two being actually now used.

7.2.3 Metrics

A set of metrics was defined and the series of version data of the three systems were measured. The metrics were classified into three layers: system, class and method. Measured data include the number of classes or the depth of the class tree for the system layer, the number of methods, instance variables and subclasses for the class and the number of lines of code for the method. The number of lines is counted by the number of carriage return's (CR) in the text after automatic formatting, thus including comment and blank lines. Aggregated or averaged measures of a lower layer can also become measures for an upper layer; for example, the total or average number of lines of code over methods is a metric for a class.

No effort was made to add totally new kinds of metrics to the stock of metrics for object-oriented systems. What should be new in this approach is the way data are collected and analysed:

- Data were measured through a sequence of versions as time-series data and were analysed in that way.
- With regard to basic statistics, the concern was not only with means and variances but also with their distribution shapes.

7.3 Observed Evolution Patterns

Quantitative analysis using the above metrics was reinforced by qualitative analysis of tracing class structure and other semantic property changes. Project documents were also surveyed and interviews to the developers of the systems were conducted. All these results were consolidated in the efforts to relate the users' requirements change and the developers' design intention change to the system and object evolution processes.

The major observations can be summarised into the following four points [Nakatani 1997].

- Fundamental statistics and distribution shapes are relatively stable over time.
- On the other hand, some peculiar sample points with exceptionally large values exist. They may imply the existence of either some design anomalies or exceptional design decisions.
- Many of measured values display a growing trend over versions but the growth rate is not homogeneous; sometimes, it increases rapidly and then it slows. These periods of discontinuous change often indicate the occurrence of architectural level change.
- There appear to exist a unique metric that characterises class trees.

The above four points are discussed in detail in the following subsections.

7.3.1 Stable Statistic Model

Some folklore data are known in terms of object system size. A. Aoki, who has developed one million lines of code in his long career as a Smalltalk programmer [Aoki 1996], once said that in all systems or libraries he developed the average number of methods per class is 20, the average number of lines per method is 10 and thus the average number of lines per class is 200. Moreover, these values are also stable at the same level even for standard libraries supplied by vendors or other organisations.

Interestingly, the measurement done in these case studies presented here also confirmed this observation. Table 7.1 shows some basic statistics that are consistent with the above observation. Those values are roughly the same over time (versions) and over systems.

Figures 7.1 and 7.2 show typical histograms of size data. It can be seen that not only the mean values are about the same among different versions or systems but also the distribution has a common shape. All graphs appear to imply that there exists a common statistical model that explains these distributions.

At first glance, the Poisson distribution model would appear to fit. However, some trial fitting soon revealed that the Poisson distribution is not a good fit. The geometric distribution model was also tried but it did not fit well either. Then, the focus was shifted

Table 7.1 Basic statistics of heat exchange simulation system

Number of methods per class				
Version	1	2	3	4
Mean	15.1	19.4	19.7	18.3
Std. dev.	10.3	16.5	19.4	19.9
Number of lines per method				
Version	1	2	3	4
Mean	8.1	8.5	9.1	9.4
Std. dev.	10.8	16.0	19.5	21.5

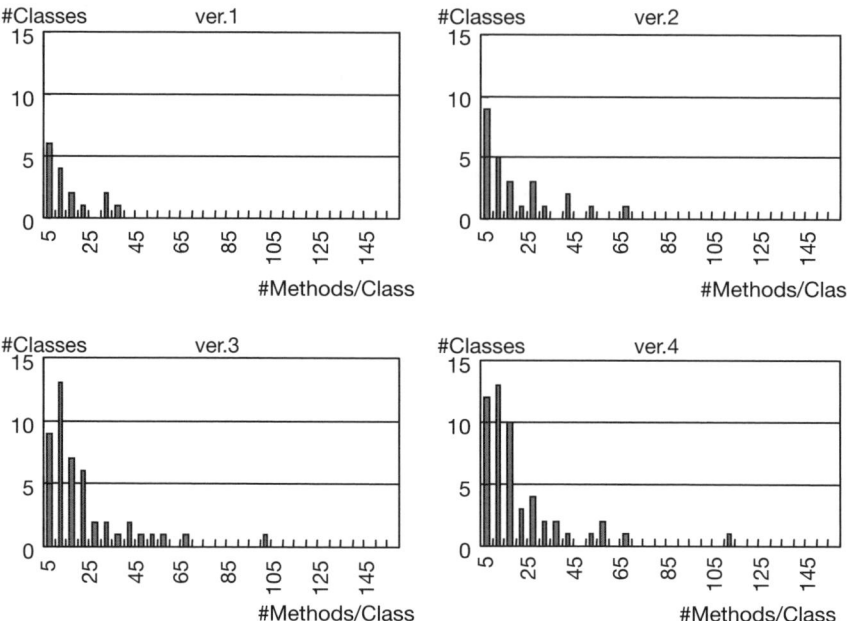

Figure 7.1 Histograms of number of methods per class in the heat exchange simulation system

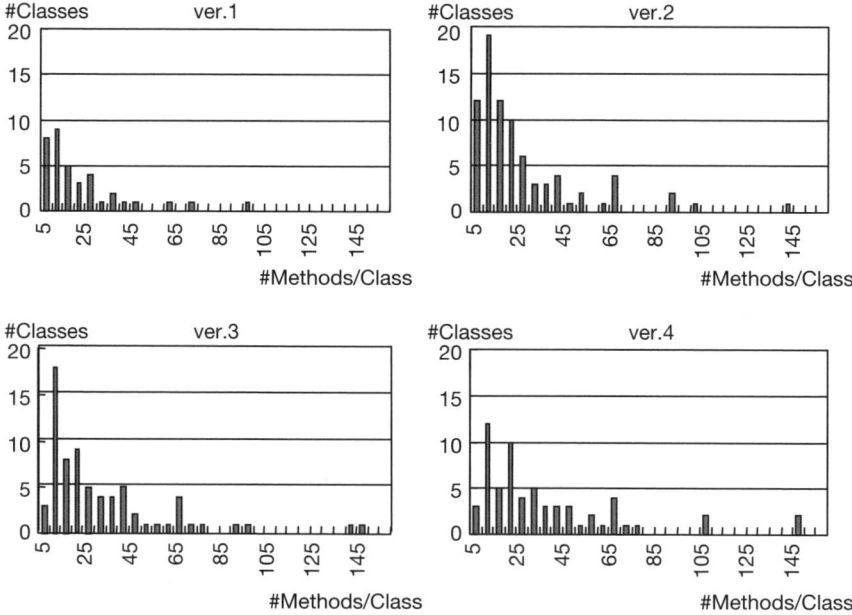

Figure 7.2 Histograms of number of methods per class in the cash receipts transaction management system for the four versions studied

to the negative binomial distribution, which provided much better results. The reasons the negative binomial distribution is preferred are as follows.

- Its variance is larger than that of the Poisson distribution for an equal mean value. It is expected to fit better to the distributions like Figure 7.1 and 7.2 that have long right tails.
- The negative binomial distribution originally has the meaning of *length*, because it is derived as representing the distribution of the Bernoulli trial length when a certain event S occurs exactly a fixed number of times [Feller 1968]. Thus, this type of distribution can provide an interpretation for explaining the code length distribution. This is further elaborated later in this chapter.

Figure 7.3 shows the curve fitting of the negative distribution model to the Cash Receipts Transaction system LOC data. The fitting looks good but when the Pearson's test of goodness of fit is applied, it did not pass the test of 5% reliability level.

To refine the model application, the set of classes were decomposed into subsets, each corresponding to a class tree. As will be shown in the next section, classes belonging to the same class tree generally share some common properties, which distinguish them from classes of other class trees. Thus, it is expected that the model fitting applied to each set of classes belonging to a tree may give better results than when the model is applied to the distribution of all classes of the whole system. Actually, when tests were applied to the subset of classes in the same class tree, it turned out that the hypothesis that the negative binomial distribution model fits could not be rejected at the 5% level χ^2 test for most of the trees of the three case study systems.

We will come back to this negative binomial distribution model in the later sections.

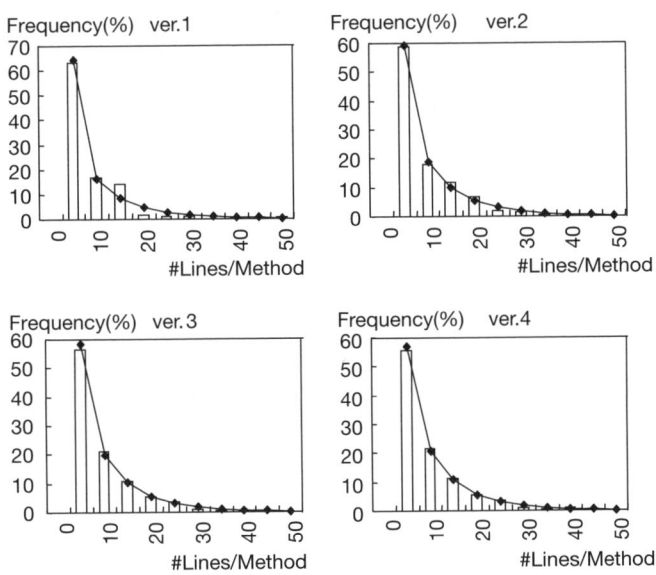

Figure 7.3 Fitting of negative binomial distribution model to number of lines per method distribution for the four versions of the cash receipts transaction management system

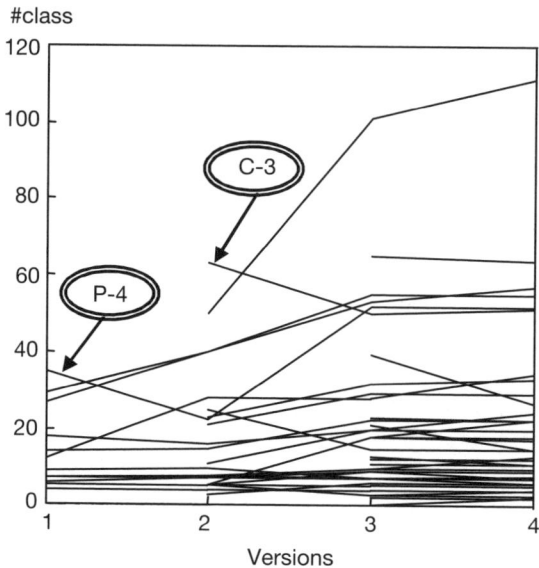

Figure 7.4 Traces of class size for the heat simulation system

7.3.2 Exceptional Data

As Figures 7.1 and 7.2 show, one or two exceptionally large classes are observed that lie far out of the distribution range of the other classes. Moreover, they tend to increase their size even more as the system evolves. A closer look into the contents of those classes reveals they are main controller type classes, and one of the causes of their such disproportionate growth appears to be 'quick and dirty' style functional enhancement activities.

By interviewing the developer, it was found that these huge classes were identical to those that had been listed up by the developer himself as candidates to be redesigned. It implies that the evolution metrics may detect some design anomaly or potential classes worth considering refactoring. At the same time, some refactoring efforts seem to have actually taken place. Figure 7.4 shows traces of the number-of-methods data for each class of the heat simulation system.

The size of the largest class 'P-4' in Version 1 reduces its size in Version 2 and the largest class 'C-3' in Version 2 also reduces its size in Version 3. While the largest in Version 3 keeps growing, the second largest of Version 3 slightly shrinks itself in Version 4. The way the classes P-4 and C-3 were structurally transformed can be observed in Figure 7.5 Both classes went through a drastic change, where their superclasses were replaced during the revision process. These changes clearly indicate conscious refactoring efforts by the developer and it was confirmed in the interview.

7.3.3 Discontinuous Change

In the case of the heat simulation system, the size of the whole system is nearly doubled between Version 1 and 2 and also doubled between Version 2 and 3. However, the

Statistical Modelling of Software Evolution Processes 151

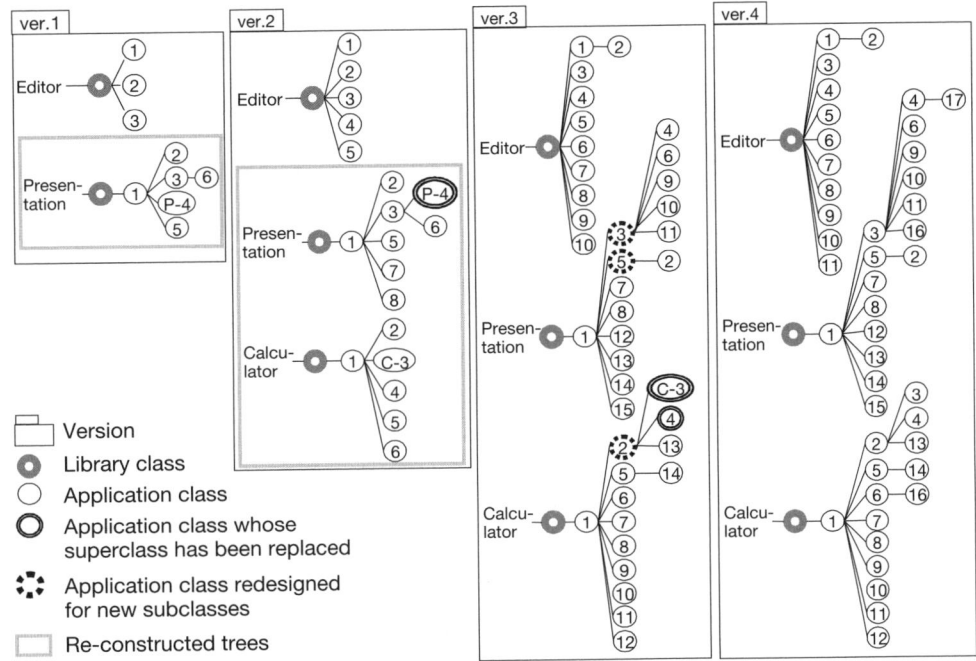

Figure 7.5 Evolution of class trees of the heat simulation system

change in size between Version 3 and 4 is not so drastic. Such difference in growth rate can be observed in the other systems. As the release intervals are roughly uniform in most of the cases, this cannot be simply explained by changes in the release intervals.

A large increase in size often reflects an important design decision made at the architecture level. For example, as Figure 7.5 shows, one of the two major class trees in Version 1 is divided into two in Version 2, which actually corresponds to an architectural change deliberately made by the developer. However, a large increase in size does not always correspond to an architectural change. For example, although the number of classes and the lines of code were doubled between Version 2 and 3, the basic tree structure did not change, which means that the change was not at the architecture level but at lower levels, with functions being massively extended to handle new kinds of heat devices.

7.3.4 Class Tree Characteristics

As expected, the number of lines and the number of methods per class have a strong correlation. In fact, when statistical testing was conducted, the significance of the correlation between the number of lines and the number of methods of a class was validated for each of the three systems.

The scattered diagram of these two variables over the classes of the Heat Exchange Simulation System is illustrated at the top-left of Figure 7.6. A conspicuous pattern of this diagram is the emergence of multiple lines. Actually, each of these lines corresponds

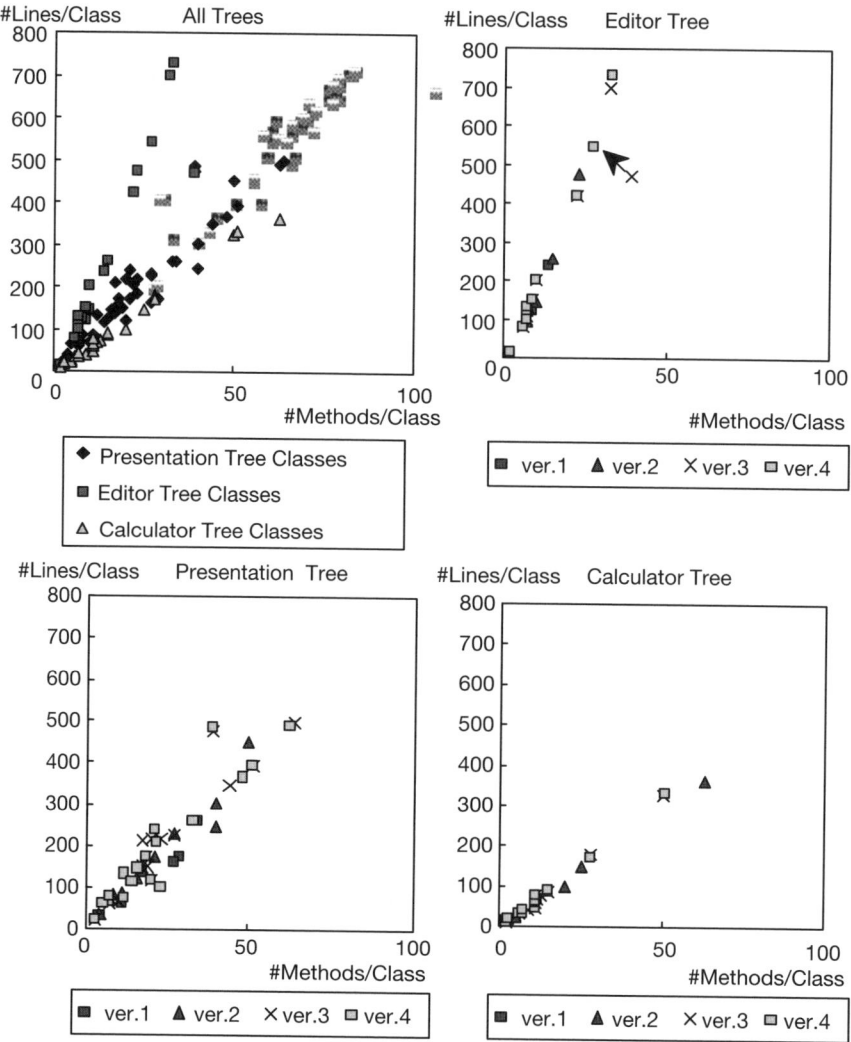

Figure 7.6 Scattered diagrams of number of lines versus number of methods per class for the heat exchange simulation system

to a set of classes that belong to the same class tree, as the other three diagrams in the figure show. These are three major class trees: the Editor Tree, the Presentation Tree and the Calculator Tree, which are also illustrated in Figure 7.5.

The most peculiar phenomenon can be observed in the diagram of Editor Tree (top-right). Here, the arrow represents a move of one class from Version 3 to Version 4. The class had an exceptional value for the ratio 'Number of Lines/Number of Methods' in Version 3 but it regressed to the 'normal' value in Version 4. This phenomenon suggests that the characteristic value of 'Number of Lines/Number of Methods' or the regression coefficient between the two metrics for each class tree has a strong constraining power.

To explore the significance of these class tree characteristics, we set up three hypothesis and conducted their statistical testing. The hypothesis and the results were as follows.

- The regression coefficients between different class trees are different.
  This hypothesis was supported by the outcome of the statistical test, which rejected the null hypothesis of equality between two coefficients of different trees in all the three systems.
- The regression coefficient of a class tree is stable over evolution.
  This was supported by the fact that the null hypothesis of equality between two coefficients of different versions could not be rejected.
- The regression coefficient of a class tree is stable over different programmers.
  In the data examined in this research, there was only one case where classes of a single tree were divided into two and developed by different programmers. Data of that case were tested and the result showed that the difference between the works of the two programmers was not statistically significant.

These findings suggest that there exist some kind of design criteria for each class tree that designers implicitly assume. Monitoring this metric will give good feedback to the designers, particularly if deviations from the linear behaviour could be related to low-quality, high-complex code.

7.4 Distribution Model

7.4.1 Negative Binomial Distribution

For a long time, program size data, typically the number of lines of code per module, have been collected as the most fundamental measures. Histograms of those data have been frequently drawn but strangely, no discussions seem to have been made so far whether such distributions obey some statistical models or not.

As examples in Figure 7.2 show, size data of object classes and methods have common features like

- the histogram is asymmetrical with the peak at the left of the histogram;
- the position of the mean is to the right of the peak and to the left of the centre of the x-axis range;
- the right side of the distribution shape has a long trailing skirt.

As seen in Section 3.1, the negative binomial model was found to fit surprisingly well to measured data in many cases. So far, there have been a few studies that employed the negative binomial model for software analysis, for example, fitting the distribution of program complexity [Mayer 1989] and defects found in classes [Succi 2003], but there seems to be no work that has applied the model to program size distribution data.

The negative binomial distribution is defined as follows. Consider a series of trials conducted in order to observe whether an event S occurs or not. Assume that trials are mutually independent and the probability p of occurring S is constant over time. Trials fulfilling these properties are called *Bernoulli trials*. Assuming that x is the number of trials to be required to have exactly k times of S event occurrence, the probability function of x is given by

$$p(x) = \binom{x-1}{k-1} p^k (1-p)^{x-k}. \tag{1}$$

This stochastic distribution of x is called the *negative binomial distribution*. The model is determined by two parameters, p and k.

The expected value of x that obeys the negative binomial distribution is given by

$$E(x) = k/p, \tag{2}$$

and its variance is

$$V(x) = k(1-p)/p^2. \tag{3}$$

Given a set of sample data that is hypothesised to obey the negative binomial distribution, the parameter estimators $\hat{p}$ and $\hat{k}$ are given by

$$\hat{p} = \bar{x}/(s^2 + \bar{x}), \tag{4}$$

and

$$\hat{k} = \bar{x}^2/(s^2 + \bar{x}), \tag{5}$$

respectively, where $\bar{x}$ is the mean of the data and s^2 is the unbiased estimated variance [McCullagh 1989].

Significance of the negative binomial distribution is large not only because of its goodness of fit but also because of a plausible interpretation of the model that reflects software development process. The process determining the length of code may be interpreted as a stochastic process as follows. Suppose the programming activity of a programmer is being observed by a third person. To the observer's eyes, the programming looks like repetitive random selections of statements (lines) or methods. When a defined number (corresponding to the parameter k) of statements or methods that have specific properties are chosen, it will complete a method (or a class). The probability (corresponding to the parameter p) that a randomly chosen statement/method has this property is constant.

The specific set of statements (or methods) that contribute to the method (or class) completion is determined by conventions, styles or constraints derived from the programming language, the application domain and the development environment. The simplest example is a constraint determined by the language syntax such that the first statement after the procedure declaration should be **begin** (or {) and the last should be the corresponding **end** (or }). In this case, the first statement is fixed and cannot be regarded as a 'random' selection but the 'random' selection of **end** terminates the trials.

Of course, this interpretation does not precisely reflect the reality. For example, if begin-end pairs can be nested, the judgement whether each statement belongs to the specific pool or not cannot be independent. In the first place, the programming activity itself is far from a random process. However, if we abstract away all the concrete factors, including conventions, styles and constraints that determine the program size and reduce them to a binary property whether the unit (statement or method) contributes to decreasing the distance to the end of the program or not, and if the process is viewed from outside, ignoring the highly sophisticated mental activity of programming, this model may give a viable interpretation.

In this interpretation, the larger k means that the programmer has to choose more statements/methods from a specific pool that are required by conventions, styles and constraints and the larger p means that the programmer has to choose them more often compared to nonconstrained statements/methods. So, it can be said in general that when software design and/or programming is more free, that is, when it allows more room for programmers' decisions, k and p tend to be small and when the process is more patterned or disciplined, the parameters become larger.

7.4.2 Evolution of Model Parameters

Since the pair of p and k determines the model, it contains richer information than the mean and the variance. The statistical structure of a large data set can be represented by a point in the two dimensional space of (p, k), opening a way of conveniently handling a series of version data, each of which comprises a large amount of data.

Figure 7.7 plots these estimated parameter values for class trees of the Heat Exchange Simulation System, where arrows indicate directions of version advancement. Similar graphs are given for the Cash Receipt Transaction Management System in Figure 7.8 and for the Securities Management System in Figure 7.9.

These graphs suggest the following points.

- There exists a strong linear correlation between the two parameters. A line can be drawn to fit the points that go through the origin of the coordinates, indicating a relation of

$$k = mp, \qquad (6)$$

where m is a constant coefficient.

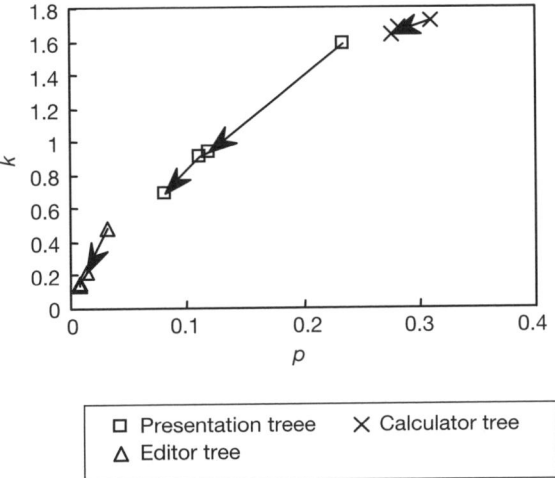

Figure 7.7 Trace of parameters (p, k) for the heat simulation system

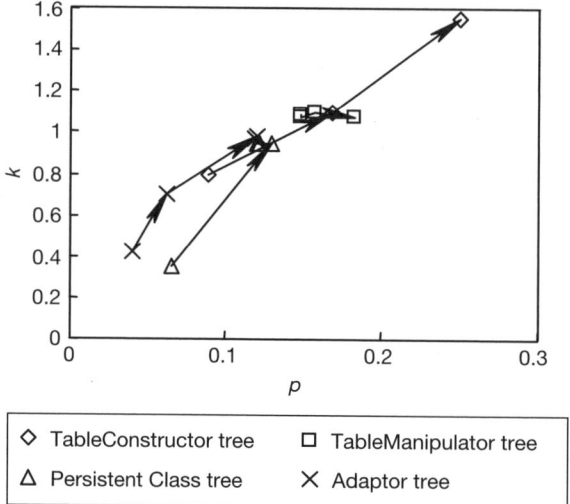

Figure 7.8 Trace of parameters (p, k) for the cash management system

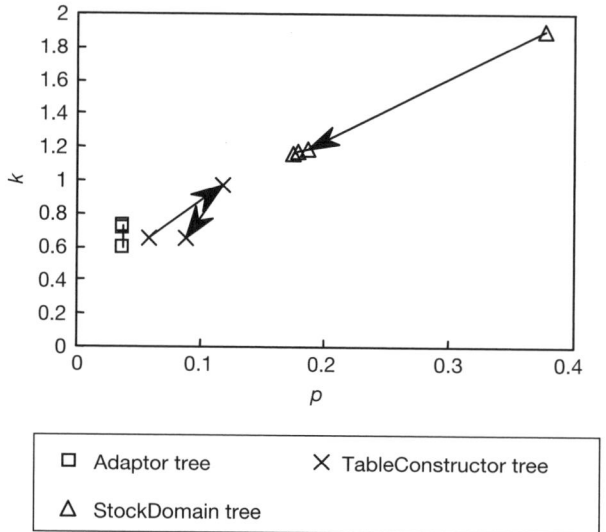

Figure 7.9 Trace of parameters (p, k) for the securities system

Recalling equation (2), $E(x) = k/p, m$ corresponds to the expected value of x, which means that the average of method length is constant over versions.
- As the result of the above linear relation, when the value of k gets larger, also the value of p gets larger and when the former gets smaller, so does the latter. The larger k and p may be interpreted as more patterned coding, stronger convention or uniformly organised programs and the smaller k and p may imply more room for programming decisions.

- As seen by the arrow direction, k and p are getting smaller as the version proceeds in the Heat Simulation System, getting larger in the Cash Management System and not conclusive in the Securities System. On the basis of the implication of larger/smaller values of k and p stated above, these trends seem to explain the fact that the Heat Simulation System took the process of adding new modules according to the users' requirements change, while the Cash Management System followed the process of restructuring the system by the software designer. In fact, it was found through the interview to the software developers as well as the inspection of the class structures that such design intentions really existed.

7.4.3 Larger Case Study

As a larger case study, a system of graphic library, Jun, was chosen that has been developed and evolved over five years, producing 360 versions [Aoki 2005, Aoki 2001]. It is written in Smalltalk and all version data are preserved.

Nineteen major released versions were selected from Version 93 to Version 206. Version 93 was the first one that was released to the public as an open source program. Version 206 was the latest one whose data were available at the time of the study. The development period of these versions was over 14 months. During this period, the size of the system roughly doubled; the number of classes enlarged from 195 to 390, the number of methods from 4532 to 7708, and the lines of code from 25,542 to 47,736.

The negative binomial distribution model was applied to five major class trees of all 19 versions. Figure 7.10 shows one example of method size distribution of classes in a tree named *Geometry* and fitting of the negative binomial distribution. Goodness of fit was statistically validated [Nakatani 2001].

Figure 7.11 shows the change of the parameters p and k for the model applied to Geometry Tree over 19 versions. Figure 7.12 draws the same transition in the two-dimensional (p, k) plane.

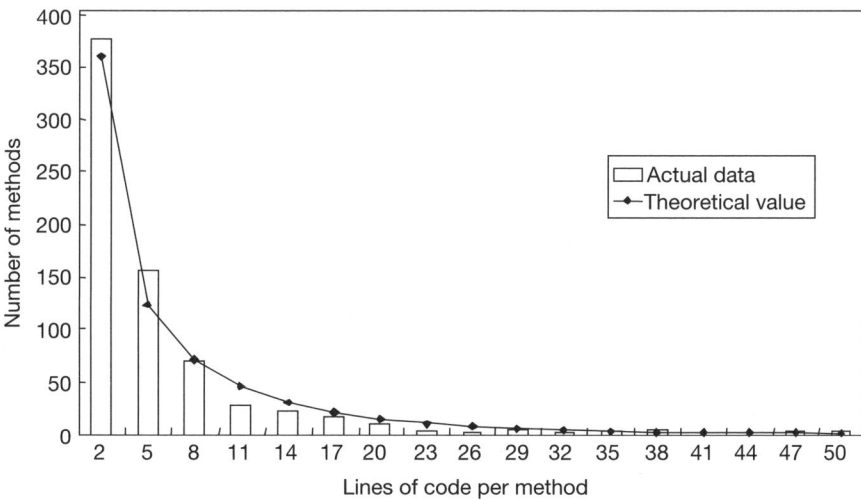

Figure 7.10 Fitting the negative binomial distribution to classes of geometry tree

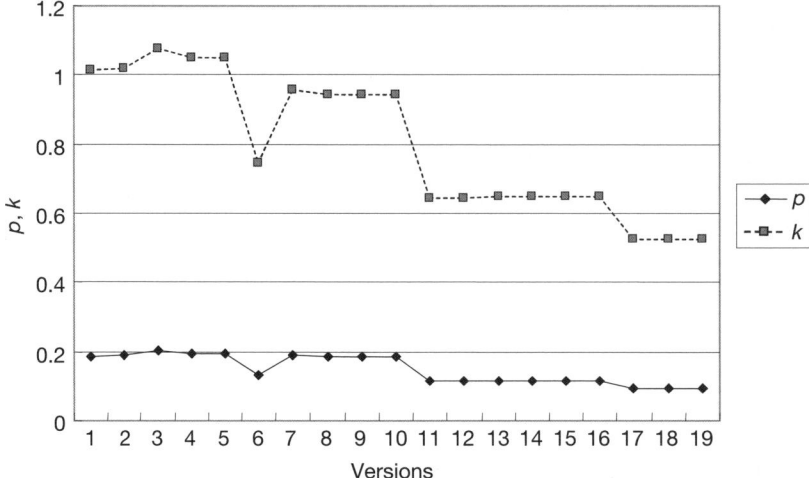

Figure 7.11 Change of p and k over time

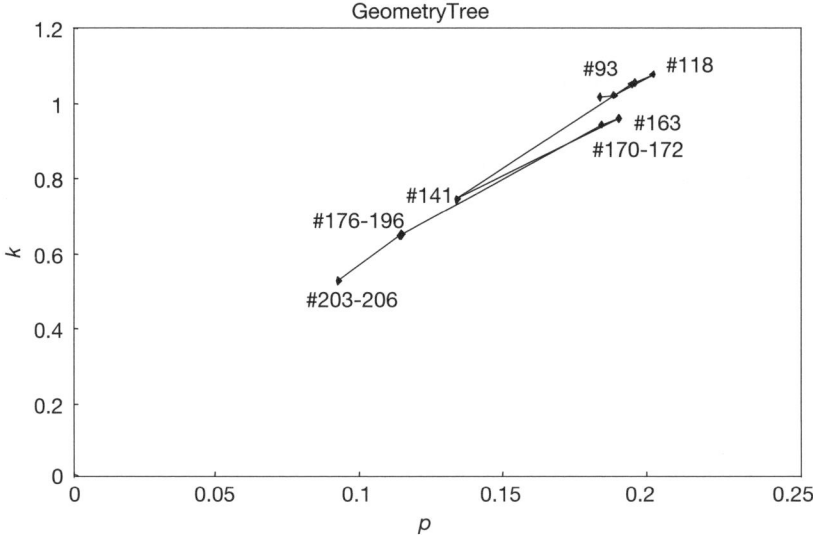

Figure 7.12 Trace of p and k in (p, k) plane

As observed in the previous cases, p and k have clear linear relation. It can be more clearly shown when mp and k are plotted instead of p and k, where m is an estimated mean value, as shown in Figure 7.13.

The second observation is that four relatively stable levels of p and k are discerned in the range of versions 1 to 5, 7 to 10, 11 to 16, and 17 to 19. There are three big jumps downward at 5 to 6, 10 to 11, and 16 to 17 and two big jumps upward at 2 to 3 and 6 to 7.

During this period, the size of the system in terms of the number of classes, methods and lines of code is monotonically increasing. On the other hand (p, k) level is generally

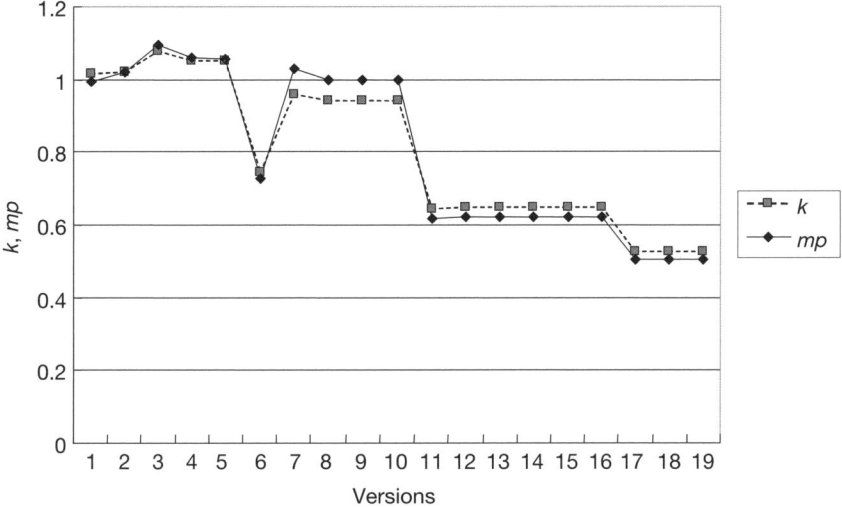

Figure 7.13 Change of mp and k over time

decreasing but the move is not monotonous as seen in the upward changes of 2 to 3 and 6 to 7. As discussed in the previous section, the period of upward (p, k) move can be regarded as the time for refactoring and downward move as function enhancement. Thus, while the general trend is (p, k) decreasing according to function enhancement, the activities of refactoring appear alternately. Such design intention of the software developer was also confirmed by the interview as well as the class structure inspection.

7.5 Discussions

Using the distribution model and its interpretation, insights to the system evolution process were obtained visually as well as logically. It can be argued that the stability of the average size could have been observed directly by just calculating the mean of the measured data. It is also true that increase and decrease of (p, k) roughly (but not always) correspond to decrease and increase of the variance. But since the parameters p and k not only determine the mean and variance but also the distribution shape itself, they give much richer information, especially valuable for tracing the chronological system change pattern. For example, suppose some points in the real observed data are found to lie far out of this distribution model, and then analysis can be made to explore the reasons. Also, the value of k may be interpreted in terms of concrete programming conventions and constraints by collecting more data covering different programming styles and relate them with the parameter k.

How can these results be exploited? So far, past version data have been analysed in this research. But if systems are monitored in real time through evolution processes, the observation can be feedbacked to development engineers. If a gap is found between the intention of designers/programmers and the observed phenomena, it would give them a chance to reconsider their activities. Also, various kinds of anomaly may be depicted by monitoring, visualising and analysing data as the examples of Sections 3.2, 3.3, and 3.4 show.

The parameters p and k show the same linear relation in all systems analysed so far but their values themselves differ by systems and by class trees in the same system. To explore what determines this difference besides the loose or strict design/programming constraints remains the future work.

References

[Aoki 2005] A. Aoki. *Jun for Smalltalk: A 3D graphic multi-media library that supports topology and geometry*. http://www.sra.co.jp/people/aoki/Jun/ 2005.

[Aoki 1996] A. Aoki. *Smalltalk Textbook*. http://www.sra.co.jp/people/aoki/SmalltalkTextbook/index.html 1996.

[Aoki 2001] A. Aoki, K. Hayashi, K. Kishida, K. Nakakoji, Y. Nishinaka, B. Reeves, A. Takashima and Y. Yamamoto. A case study of the evolution of Jun: an object-oriented open-source 3D multimedia library. In *International Conference on Software Engineering (ICSE'01)*, pp. 524–533, Toronto, Canada, 2001.

[Belady 1976] L.A. Belady and M.M. Lehman. A model of large program development. *IBM Syst. J.*, 15(3): 225–252, 1976.

[Blackmore 1999] S.J. Blackmore. *The Meme Machine*. Oxford University Press, 1999.

[Chidamber 1994] S.R. Chidamber and C.F. Kemerer. A metrics suite for object oriented design. *IEEE Trans. Softw. Eng.*, 20(6): 476–493, 1994.

[Dawkins 1976] R. Dawkins. *The Selfish Gene*. Oxford University Press, 1976.

[Feller 1968] W. Feller. *An Introduction to Probability Theory and its Applications*. 3rd ed., Wiley, New York, 1968.

[Lehman 1985] M.M. Lehman and L.A. Belady. *Program Evolution: Processes of Software Change*. Academic Press, 1985.

[Lorenz 1994] M. Lorenz and J. Kidd. *Object-Oriented Software Metrics*. Prentice-Hall, 1994.

[Lehman 2000] M.M. Lehman, J.F. Ramil and G. Kahen. Evolution as a noun and evolution as a verb. In *SOCE 2000 Workshop on Software and Organization Co-evolution*. Imperial College, London, 2000.

[Mayer 1989] A. Mayer and A. Sykes. A probability model for analysing complexity metrics data. *Softw. Eng. J.*, pp. 254–258, 1989.

[McCullagh 1989] P. McCullagh and J.A. Nelder. *Generalized Linear Models*. 2nd ed., Chapman and Hall, London, 1989.

[Nakatani 2001] T. Nakatani. Quantitative observations on object evolution. In *International Workshop on Principles of Software Evolution (IWPSE'01)*, pp. 154–157, Vienna, Austria, 2001.

[Nakatani 1997] T. Nakatani, T. Tamai, A. Tomoeda and H. Matsuda. Towards constructing a class evolution model. In *Asia-Pacific Software Engineering Conference*, pp. 131–138, Hong Kong, 1997.

[Parnas 1994] D. Parnas. Software aging. In *16th International Conference on Software Engineering*, pp. 279–287, Sorrento, Italy, 1994.

[Succi 2003] G. Succi, W. Pedrycz, M. Stefanovic and J. Miller. Practical assessment of the models for identification of defect-prone classes on object-oriented commercial systems using design metrics. *J. Syst. & Softw.*, 65(1): 1–12, 2003.

[Tamai 1992] T. Tamai and Y. Torimitsu. Software lifetime and its evolution process over generations. In *Proceedings Conference on Soft-ware Maintenance – 1992*, pp. 63–69, Orlando, Florida, 1992.

8

Software Requirements Changes Due to External Factors

Vic Nanda and Nazim H. Madhavji

Based on "The Impact of Environmental Evolution on Requirements Changes" by Nanda, V. and Madhavji, N.H., which appeared in the Proceedings of the IEEE International Conference on Software Maintenance, October 2002, Montreal, pp. 452–461. (c) 2002 IEEE.

8.1 Introduction

A vast class of software, termed E-type by Lehman, is subject to continual evolutionary changes [1, 2]. E-type systems are systems that address an application in the real-world. They solve problems that cannot be completely specified for all possible uses of the system. As Lehman pointed out, E-type systems are in a feedback loop relation with their operational domain, that is, their environment. Why? The installation of a version of the system can induce changes in the environment that could lead to new and changed requirements that, in turn, could lead to new version of the software system, and so on. Other sources of change are exogenous to the software. An E-type software system would generally need to be evolved because of new and changed functional and nonfunctional requirements that, if not satisfied, could pose threat to the fitness of the system in its operational environment. We define evolution as all the work needed to keep a reasonable degree of fitness of the software system in its environment. Ultimately, such fitness can be measured by the degree of satisfaction of the software stakeholders.

The threat to a system's fitness can arise from factors *internal* or *external* to the software system. Internal factors include degradation of the system's quality attributes [3], which manifests as increasing difficulty to understand and change the code, increasing response time to implement changes, decreasing usability of the user interface, and others. External factors include changes in what we call the *environment*[1] of the system. For example, the

---

[1] An *environment* may be defined as the entities and their conditions external to the software system that affect the development, evolution and fitness of the software. For a given software product (or system), its

customer need for *interoperability* or the need for an *integrated solution* could lead to poor fitness of the system if those evolving the software fail to implement these requirements. In general, recognition of poor fitness to the environment will result in requirements changes (and, consequently, in the need for further evolution of the software).

The majority of empirical studies of software evolution have focused on the study of how certain internal attributes evolve, such as the size of the code. There is a need for studies that address the evolution of requirements triggered by external factors. External factors can be quite challenging to address by those managing the evolution of a software system because they tend to be outside their control.

This chapter focuses on *external* factors affecting system fitness. Specifically, it describes how changes in the environment of a software system can drive changes in software requirements that, in turn, can result in software evolution. The authors describe a four-year case study to assess the impact of environmental changes on an innovative software system, called the *Congruence Evaluation System* (*CES*) [4], along with an instrument used to perform the case study. Because of the dynamics in the system's environment, the environment was evolving rather rapidly, which, in turn, dictated the stability of the system in its environment.

The primary motivation behind studying the impact of external factors on software evolution was to uncover how, at different times, evolving external factors could possibly affect the system's requirements and, in turn, the fitness of the system. In many cases, with such an explicit understanding, timely corrective-action can be taken, provided there is a will and the necessary resources, to increase, or at least *maintain*, the fitness of the system in the target environment.

Note that the notion of fitness of a system in the target environment applies to *all* E-type software systems, which represent the vast majority of systems developed and evolved in the software industry. It is as important for systems developed for mass usage as it is for systems developed for specific customers. Thus, the ideas from this case study should find wide application (as is, or after some tailoring) in the software industry. For example, software companies competing in the same market sector frequently seek to upstage each other by being the first to offer a significant new product offering or enhancements to a current product offering. For this and similar purposes, an organisation's ability to be in the forefront of *detecting changes* in an existing product's environment or *recognising emerging need* for a new product is clearly important.

8.1.1 Organisation of This Chapter

The next section describes the case study, and includes overview of the CES system; CES context and key events in the four-year period of the case study; strategy for the original implementation of CES; analysis of CES capabilities and the problems that beset it; and finally, the impact of environmental changes on the CES requirements. Section 8.3 lists the lessons learnt and concludes the chapter.

---

environment includes, but is not limited to, the users and their purpose when using the product in the real-world, business processes in which the product is being (or to be) used, domain theories and concepts implemented in the system, risks of external origin, interoperability considerations with other systems in the environment of the product, customer requirements, industry specifications, underlying platforms and standards applicable to the product.

8.2 Congruence Evaluation System (CES): A Case Study

Congruence Evaluation System was a proof-of-concept system developed by a research organisation over two years with three person-years of effort, from concept understanding to system validation [4]. While this system served excellently for the basic purpose of proof of concept, it failed to evolve as a cohesive part of a collective suite of tools being built concurrently in the organisation. CES was thus scrapped. Particularly, the reason was that its *environment* – a suite of tools and the goal and rationale behind these tools – had evolved so much so that by the time CES was built it was hopelessly inadequate in satisfying the *emerging requirement* that the disparate yet complementary tools increasingly work together in an integrated tool-set; it was an *external* source of threat that brought on the demise of the CES system.

Emerging tools and components in the environment of CES included a system for eliciting process models, a system for generalising product and process models, a system for tailoring models, a common interface to these systems, and a common (object-oriented) database through which all the described tools would interact with each other. These tools were being implemented on a Unix platform. The CES system, on the other hand, did not use object-oriented database, it had a nongraphical user interface and was implemented in FoxPro on the MS-DOS platform. For more details on the core issue of congruence evaluation, and how it serves to assess process quality, the reader is referred to [4].

8.2.1 CES Context and Key Events

The original CES implementation began in Sept 1992 and it took two years to build. From Sept 1994 until Feb 1995, the capabilities and limitations of the original CES were analysed, along with the impact of environmental evolution (during the period of system development) on the system requirements (details appear in Sections 8.2.4 and 8.2.5). The analysis concluded that in order to effectively address the limitations of the implementation, and to satisfy the newly identified requirements due to environmental evolution, CES would have to be re-implemented from scratch. Therefore, in Feb. 1995, CES was scrapped and work began on re-implementing it, reusing concepts and algorithms, as appropriate, from the original CES. The new CES took approximately one year with one person-year of effort to build. The size of the new system was approximately 20K LOC in C and the underlying platform was X/MOTIF. It provided all the services of the original CES system, but was designed to be highly customisable, was user-friendly (the command line interface of the old system was replaced with a graphical user interface), and was fully compatible with the suite of other tools in the environment.

8.2.2 Contribution, Relevance and Applicability of This Case Study

From this experience, however, emerges the following key question, which is explored in this chapter:

'How do changes in the environment drive software evolution'?

This question is important because it deals with the difficult issue of requirements engineering in an evolving environment, which experience suggests is often overlooked at the start of implementation of a new software system. Contributions to this answer would increase our collective experience, currently thin on this particular question, and can be used to better plan and evolve software systems.

The type of software environment studied is typical in research organisations, such as corporate R&D departments where tools or systems in a suite are being developed concurrently. In this respect, lessons learnt from this case study may be readily transferable to these contexts. In addition, in many rapidly growing commercial environments (e.g. those developing tools for Internet services), one can find concurrent development, which start out as isolated, often unrelated, systems and are subsequently gradually integrated to attain evolving business goals. With care, the lessons learnt from this case study may also be applicable in these contexts.

Take note, however, that the effort expended in the initial development of the system described in this case study is relatively modest compared to projects of many person-year effort in the industry. Thus, though the essence of this case study investigation might trigger other such investigations, *as-is* comparisons of specific factors and their impact on requirements with corresponding situations in large projects would be naïve. That said, large projects are not monolithic and are indeed composed of smaller projects, subsystems and components – many of which have comparable development effort to CES – and so the lessons learnt may possibly apply at these sublevels in a fairly direct way and, with care, may be scaled up to larger projects.

8.2.3 CES: Background and Implementation Strategy

Congruence Evaluation System was an *E-type* system, in Lehman's classification of systems [2]. This system was aimed to assist process designers and managers in the evaluation of process model congruence, and allowed for process model customisation (to optimise process model congruence) [4]. *Congruence* is a measure of how fit a process model is in the given development environment. CES is based on the premise that higher the congruence measure of a process model, better the effectiveness of a process that follows the model. CES was developed after analysing data gathered during a field study [5] to determine the relationship between a process model and the process context characteristics with respect to process performance. The system was validated to ensure that the congruence measure and process model customisation had empirical relevance.

When CES was implemented, the prime focus of the design strategy was on demonstrating (within the shortest time possible and within the limited budget) the concept of congruence and the validity of the congruence method. The *environmental* requirements were implicit at that time and were not considered explicitly (though not deliberately) in the design of CES. This is in direct contrast to the approach in its re-implementation, where the prime concern was one of evolvability of the system in the environment while retaining its validity.

The design strategy for CES was thus to employ the programming language and the development platform most familiar to the developer. It was essentially a *prototyping approach* to empirically understand the underlying theory of congruence and process fitness [6]. Because it was the first implementation of such a system, the requirements were not clearly specified, and thus the developer was expected to follow an *exploratory* approach. This implied that the development process followed was *evolutionary*.

During the initial development of CES, the usual software development concerns for user 'customisability', 'user-friendliness' and future 'evolvability' did not form part of the design strategy. While these are critical issues, they were all superseded by the prime focus of demonstrating the proof of concept as fast as possible and within the limited research budget. In addition, the concern for 'integration' with the *then existing* (and *evolving*) environment (initially consisting of only one other tool and, later, a suite of tools) was nonexistent because the other tool appeared to be completely unrelated (which in subsequent years turned out to be untrue because of the evolution of the suite of tools). Also, the overall state of the environment (of the collective suite of tools being developed concurrently) was not clear at the outset. Thus, the 'survivability' goal for CES emerged as a prime concern only once CES had successfully been demonstrated as a proof of concept.

8.2.4 Analysis of CES Capabilities

In September 1994, work began on analysing the strengths and weaknesses of the original CES. Requirements satisfied by the system (old requirements) were identified by the research team leader and associates, and new requirements formulated, *a priori*, on the basis of observed limitations (these are presented in the first two columns of Table 8.1). It should be noted that the old requirements were not documented explicitly except in the form of project notes and a document equivalent to a technical white paper. Therefore, CES was assessed by using the quality criteria listed by Boehm *et al.* [3], which were further augmented as necessary.

8.2.4.1 Analysis Method

A 15-question instrument to assess system deficiencies and change in requirements (see Appendix A) was used for conducting the survey amongst the relevant team members in the organisation. There were eight survey respondents. The team members worked as a cohesive research group and often conducted collaborative research. The instrument used a semantic differential 7-point scale[2] [7] for each question. The survey required the respondents to include their 'confidence level' in giving the response and the rationale for the response[3]. Subsequently, responses with a confidence level of *less* than 6 ('Quite high') were excluded[4] from data analysis, while the median of all responses with a confidence level of 6 or higher was considered for system assessment purposes. The high level of confidence in the responses meant that there was significant collective confidence in the findings from the case study.

---

[2] Scale: 1–Extremely low; 2–Quite low; 3–Slightly low; 4–Medium; 5–Slightly high; 6–Quite high; 7–Extremely high. This generic scale shown above had to be customised for *each* question in the instrument.

[3] The scale used to record the 'confidence level' was similar to the one used to record the question response.

[4] Out of the total 120 responses from 8 respondents, 14 responses (11.67%) were of confidence level less than 6 or were 'Don't Know' responses that were eliminated from the analysis of survey results.

8.2.4.2 Analysis Results

The analysis results of the data gathered during this survey are shown in Figure 8.1. Basically, there were two types of questions that were asked to those participating in the survey:

(a) Type 1: *What were the purposes served by CES?*
This helped in identifying the system requirements (hereafter, the set: 'R1') *satisfied* by the system. The set R1 is listed in Table 8.1. This set also includes functional and nonfunctional requirements (R1.1 to R1.6) that were derived from the system description in the white paper.

(b) Type 2: *What were the deficiencies of CES at the time of completion of the system (Sept 1994)?*
This helped in identifying the system requirements that were *not satisfied* by the system, and which thus matured[5] into new requirements for the re-implementation of the system (hereafter, the set: 'R2'). This set is listed in Table 8.1 as R2.1 to R2.9, spread over different requirement types.

The following subsections describe the findings from the survey.

Type 1: Purposes Served by CES

Figure 8.1 shows that CES was assessed as 'Quite high' for the criteria of system 'conciseness', 'consistency', 'validity' and 'reliability'. The key requirements for CES were to have an easily understandable system that was reliable, valid and concise. The system was also regarded by the respondents as highly 'consistent' in its operation, which concurs with the ease of system understanding. Clearly, the system was driven by certain key requirements that *had* to be met. The system performance based on these key issues was thus highly satisfactory. Figure 8.1 also shows that the system ranked[6] as only 'Slightly high' for the criteria of 'completeness' and 'efficiency'. All these requirements (which were to be satisfied by CES when it was built) can be regarded as belonging to the requirement set: 'R1', the old requirements for the system.

Type 2: Deficiencies of CES Upon Completion

These requirements (set 'R1') are further categorised into *system-specific requirements* and *environment-specific requirements*. Figure 8.1 shows that the system-specific requirement 'customisability' (A12) was moderately met by the system. The system was regarded as 'Slightly low' in 'maintainability' (A6), that is, documentation support for future maintenance activities (corrective, adaptive or perfective), and 'Quite low' in 'user-friendliness' (A8) owing to the lack of on-line help, and in 'portability' (A13) because the system's implementation in FoxPro on MS-DOS rendered it unportable to Unix.

The system was evaluated as 'Extremely low' in satisfying the system-specific requirements 'security' (A4) and 'structuredness' (A10), and the environment-specific requirements 'integrability' (A14) and 'survivability' (A15). There were no significant system

---

[5] A requirement is considered to be 'mature' when it reaches a point of sufficient definition and completeness such that it can be effectively and unambiguously articulated for implementation in a product, and any questions seeking clarification regarding the requirement can be adequately answered by the requirement author.

[6] Note that the detailed rationale for the ranking in the form of free-text comments from the respondents providing justification for their responses was also gathered in the survey. However, these are not included in the chapter as it is not considered to be of general interest or necessary for understanding the chapter.

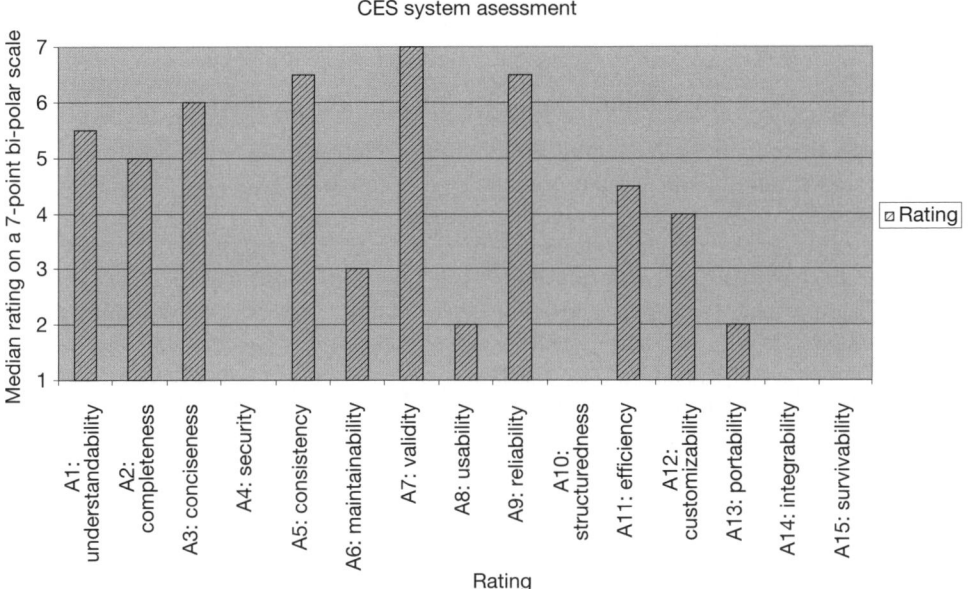

Figure 8.1 CES system assessment in September 1994. (Scale: 1–Extremely low; 2–Quite low; 3–Slightly low; 4–Medium; 5–Slightly high; 6–Quite high; 7–Extremely high)

security features when it was implemented and the system was not modular. In addition, because the system was completely stand-alone, its 'integrability' with other tools in the environment was low. Also, the system was not 'robust' enough to survive changes in the environment, which was evident from the fact that it failed to fit in the new environment, which had resulted from its continuous evolution during the course of the development of the system. The new requirements (R2.1 to R2.9 in the set R2) that emerged for the re-implementation are shown in Table 8.1.

Here, it is interesting to note that the new environment-specific requirements ('portability', 'integrability' and 'survivability' in Figure 8.1) were more devastating to CES than the new system-specific requirements (all 'other' requirements in Figure 8.1). That is, while some of the new system-specific requirements could have been satisfied, albeit with some effort, *all the new environment-specific requirements required that the system be re-implemented.*

8.2.5 The Impact of Environmental Evolution

This section examines the evolution of the development environment during the course of initial system implementation (Sept 1992 to Sept 1994) and then during the re-implementation (Sept 1994 to March 1996). This is essential because, as will be demonstrated in Section 8.2.5.4, the changes in the development environment have a profound effect on the requirements of the systems housed in that environment. Therefore, the requirements for CES changed not only because of the new requirement set R2 (denoting deficiencies in the original implementation), but also because of new requirements that were introduced as a result of the environmental evolution (the set R3 representing the period Sept 1992 to Sept 1994, and the set R4 representing the period Sept 1994 to March 1996).

8.2.5.1 Environmental Evolution from Sept 1992 to March 1996

The analysis method for determining the environmental changes was similar to the one adopted for determining the system deficiencies (Section 8.2.4). The criteria that were used to assess the environmental evolution can be categorised into three clusters: questions pertaining to environment goals, questions pertaining to the predictors of environmental change, and other miscellaneous questions. The questions were derived from the interviews with other team members and from the literature [1, 8, 9], and the questionnaire was piloted prior to use. All these questions were included in a 17-question[7] *Instrument to Assess Environmental Evolution*[8], to assess the environmental evolution from Sept 1992 to Sept 1994, and again from Sept 1994 to March 1996 (see Appendix B)[9]. The 1992 data was gathered through the instrument (Appendix B) but applied in 1994, not in 1992, however, asking the respondents to answer on the basis of the state of the environment in 1992. The 1992 data was assessed by the researcher conducting the survey to be generally consistent with the documentary evidence from that time – of the group's projects and results, open-ended interviews with lead researchers at that time, software systems that existed in the group's environment at that time. The 1994 and 1996 data were gathered in the respective years.

Majority of the questions included in Appendix B contain the keywords 'realisation of the goal'. This is because goals are widely recognised as important precursors to product requirements. Recently, Anton and Potts [12], with the aid of the Goal-Based Requirements Analysis Method (GBRAM), have studied the use of goals to surface requirements for the redesign of existing or legacy systems. The GBRAM method involves the timely posing of systematic questions to uncover new requirements and improve current requirements as early as possible.

8.2.5.2 Analysis Results: Sept 1992 to Sept 1994

The analysis results of the data gathered during this survey are shown in Figure 8.2. The three adjacent bars correspond to the three separate environment assessments corresponding to Sept 1992, Sept 1994, and March 1996. A missing bar shows a one (1) rating on the 7-point scale. Each set of bars corresponds to a specific question in the instrument; there are 17 questions (see Appendix B). Clearly, in Sept 1992, there was a very low realisation (almost negligible!) of the environment goals (Questions B1–9), predictors of environment change (Questions B10–12), and other environment-related issues (Questions B13–17).

Interestingly, this low realisation of the predictors of environmental change explains why the environmental changes had such a devastating effect on CES, since the environmental changes were totally unexpected. When CES was implemented (Sept 1992 to

---

[7] The questions are labelled from B1 to B17 (see Appendix B).

[8] For readers who desire to develop such an instrument and, generally, incorporate empirical methods in their investigation, we recommend [10] and [11].

[9] Out of the total 408 responses from 8 respondents, 65 responses (15.93%) were of confidence level less than 6 or they were 'Don't Know' responses, which were eliminated from the analysis of survey results.

Software Requirements Changes Due to External Factors

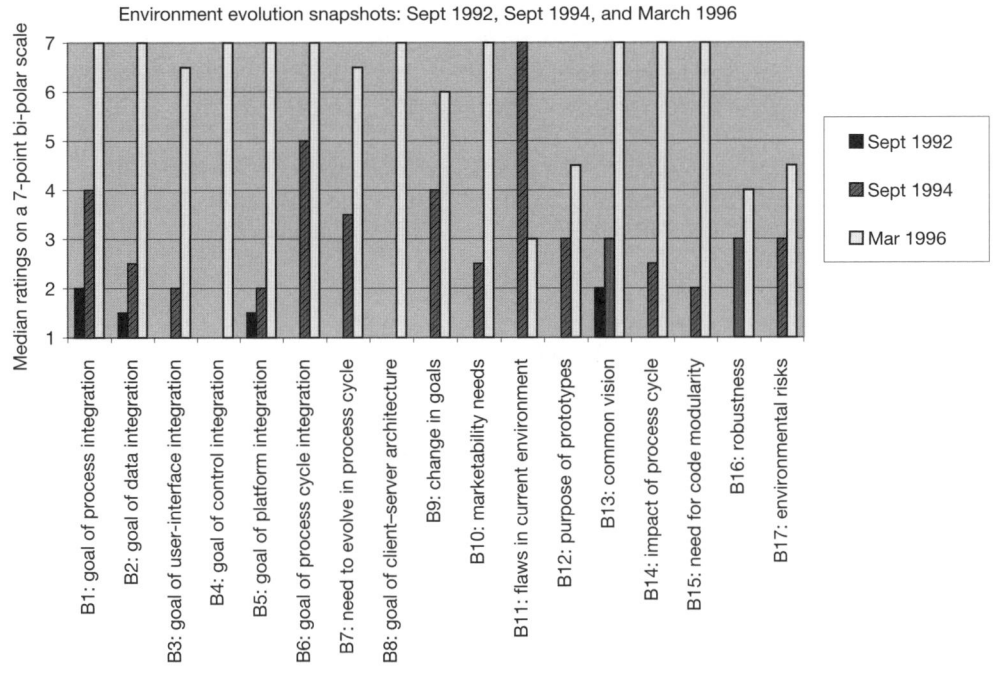

Figure 8.2 Environment evolution snapshots: Sept 1992, Sept 1994, and March 1996. (Scale: 1–Extremely low; 2–Quite low; 3–Slightly low; 4–Medium; 5–Slightly high; 6–Quite high; 7–Extremely high)

Sept 1994), there was substantial ignorance on the part of the developers of the evolution of the environment and thus the survivability of the system. That is also revealed by the extremely poor response to the realisation of a likely serious impact of environmental changes on the prototype systems housed in the environment (Question B17). The original developer of CES also believed that it would be possible to enhance the system in some way and blend it with the other tools, although strategies were not clear at that time.

That the environment had a weak impact on the development activities (in Sept 1992) is evident from the fact that there was a low realisation of the existence of a common vision (Question B13, Figure 8.2) for the entire team. It may also be noted that while most of the respondents to the survey did not know (in Sept 1992) of the existence of this 'common vision', only the chief architect of all the tools had begun to realise how the environment could drive the development activities of the entire group.

At the time of system completion in Sept 1994, the environment had changed dramatically with an increased realisation (generally, 'Quite low' or 'Slightly low') of most of the criteria mentioned in the questionnaire (see Figure 8.2). This growing realisation was observed in the responses both from all the team members and the chief architect. In fact, the trend of increased awareness of the chief architect – of environment-related issues – was even more pronounced at this time (the chief architect's responses on average recorded an increase in realisation by four scale points from Sept 1992 to Sept 1994!).

Now, the highest awareness was of the fact that there were flaws (or limitations) in the existing operational environment that could cause it to evolve in the future (see Question B11). Also, the respondents believed that there was a 'Slightly high' realisation about integrating CES in the environment (see Question B6).

In Sept 1994, there was a 'Moderate' realisation of the goal of having an integrated tool-kit comprising of the prototype systems being developed (Question B1); the goal of evolving CES in the environment (Question B7); and, the change of focus from 'software process concepts and methods' to 'software process concepts, methods *and tools*' (Question B9).

The realisation of the goal of *data*, *user-interface* and *platform* integration of the tools varied from 'Slightly low' to 'Quite low' (Questions B2, B3, and B5 respectively). Also, now there was an emerging realisation of a common vision for the team (Question B13). The Questions B12, B14, B15, B16 and B17 dealt with more subtle issues relating to the 'analysis' of the software systems housed in the environment. The 'Quite low' to 'Slightly low' realisation of these environmental issues (in Sept 1994) clearly showed a modest increase in the awareness (since Sept 1992) of the impact of the environment on the software systems housed in it.

The lowest realisation at this time (Sept 1994) was regarding the issues of *control* integration for all the prototype systems and also a distributed, client–server architecture (Questions B4 and B8). These were questions that required a good understanding and realisation of data, user-interface and platform integration as a prerequisite. However, the realisation for these prerequisites was itself poor, thus contributing to an 'extremely low' realisation in response to Questions B4 and B8.

In summary, there was a considerable shift in virtually all aspects of the environment by September 1994, compared to the environment in September 1992.

8.2.5.3 Analysis Results: Sept 1994 to March 1996

Figure 8.2 also shows that there was a marked change in the environment from Sept 1994 to March 1996. It was observed that, on average, realisation of the various environmental characteristics increased by approximately three scale points, which is quite substantial on the 7-point semantic differential scale used.

Figure 8.2 shows that 13 out of the 17 criteria recorded a response of 'Quite high' to 'Extremely high' realisation in March 1996. However, even at the time of completion of the re-implemented system, awareness of certain environmental issues was only 'Moderate'. These were the issues pertaining to whether the researchers realised that the existing prototypes were 'throwaway' or 'evolutionary' prototypes (Question B12), awareness of the 'robustness' of the prototype systems to survive changes in the environment (Question B16), and realisation that environmental changes could seriously affect the prototype systems housed in it (Question B17). Interestingly, all these questions had the same underlying reasoning to explain the response: The researchers *believed* that they are developing reasonably 'robust' systems that can survive changes in the environment in the near future; however, they *could not claim* with conviction that they had thoroughly understood the environmental changes in the present or in the future. Therefore, the responses depicted a 'cautious optimism' about the survivability of the prototype systems in the future. Also, the realisation in response to Question B11 fell from a high of

'Extremely high' (in Sept 1994) to 'Slightly low' (in March 1996). This was the only environmental issue that recorded a fall in realisation from the response in Sept 1994. Again, it only reconfirmed the fact that all the team members, to the best of their knowledge, could not foresee any major changes in the environment in the future and thus all their present development activities were driven by this observation.

8.2.5.4 Requirements Changes Due to Environmental Evolution

From the above description, one can observe the steady increase (from Sept 1992 to March 1996) of awareness in the entire team of the environmental issues. Depicting the environmental changes as in Figure 8.2 makes it explicit how new requirements emerge because of an evolving environment. Specifically, one can identify the new requirements, set R3, which emerged after the environment assessment in Sept 1994, and the set R4 that emerged after the assessment in March 1996.

First, however, it should be noted that not all the growing awareness of the criteria listed in the questionnaire (see Appendix B) would necessarily result in new requirements. This is because the increased awareness of certain environmental characteristics is still not concrete enough to be molded into formal requirements. This is the case with the assessment in Sept 1994 (see Figure 8.2), which resulted in only three new requirements (set R3: R3.1 to R3.3). On the other hand, with the assessment in March 1996, new requirements (set R4: R4.1 to R4.4) were generated because of maturation of the understanding of environmental changes.

With respect to the set R3 generated in Sept 1994, the realisation of the goal of having an integrated tool-kit (Question B1) implied that no system in the environment should be stand-alone. This question (which is closely tied to Question B6[10] and, in part, to Questions B10, B13 and B14) led to the new requirement R3.2. The increased awareness of the goal of evolving CES in the environment (Question B7) led to the new requirement R3.3. In fact, the growing awareness in response to Questions B11, B12, B16 and B17 (see Figure 8.2) also contributed to the decision that the system be re-implemented in a 'flexible' way.

Similarly, with respect to the set R4, four new requirements arose in March 1996 and all these were specific to the details of establishing an integrated tool-kit. For example, the realisation of the goal pertaining to 'data integration' (Question B2) led to the new requirement R4.1. The realisation of the goal of 'user-interface' integration (Question B3) led to the new requirement R4.4.

One should note, however, that the set R3 had a *devastating* impact on CES. Basically, the system had to be re-implemented, whereas the set R4 would induce *evolutionary* changes to the re-implemented system. Revisiting Lehman's laws, we see that the emergence of the sets R3 and R4 supports the *seventh law* of software evolution – Declining Quality: '*Unless rigorously adapted to take into account changes in the operational environment, the quality of an E-type system will appear to decline as it is evolved*' [2].

The severity of the requirements changes such as the sets R3 and R4 can approach 100% enhancements, according to Jones [13], due to major architectural or platform changes.

---

[10] Note that in Sept 1992 (see Figure 8.2), the realisation of the goal of integration (Question B6) was nonexistent.

Also, Mittermeir's analysis of the impact of evolution in the strata of 'system-of-systems' (integrated set of systems or programs) states that a radical change, such as the integration of complex systems, throws up challenges due to problems pertaining to software and data repository integration (see Chapter 4). He cautions that such radical changes cannot be accommodated by small incremental evolution of the systems. Instead, he advocates that an organisation having such a system-of-systems prepares itself for such radical changes by loose coupling of parts of the systems that lend themselves to standardisation.

The above description, then, explains how system requirements can emerge (or *germinate*) in response to an evolving environment. Both the bar charts (Figures 8.1 and 8.2) form a strong rationale[11] for the requirements that are generated at a given point in time. Looking at the environment at the three time stamps of Sept 1992, Sept 1994, and March 1996, we can observe how the requirements have changed from the original set R1.

Thus, the requirement set for the re-implemented system (in Sept 1994 to March 1996), R_{re-imp}, is defined as

$$R_{re-imp} = (R1 \cup R2 \cup R3) \backslash R_{deleted}$$

where
- R1: the requirement set for the original CES (R1.1 to R1.13)
- R2: the new requirement set for CES re-implementation due to deficiencies in the original CES (R2.1 to R2.9)
- R3: the new requirement set for CES re-implementation due to environmental changes from Sept 1992 to Sept 1994 (R3.1 to R3.3)
- $R_{deleted}$: the requirements for the original CES that were not needed for the re-implementation

The requirement set after completion of the re-implemented system (March 1996), R_{post_re-imp}, is defined as

$$R_{post\_re-imp} = R_{re-imp} \cup R4$$

where
- R4 : the new requirement set for future revisions to CES due to environmental changes from Sept 1994 to March 1996 (R4.1 to R4.4)

The purpose of these equations is to show, in a succinct form, how the requirements have evolved over time. Perhaps, such documentation could be helpful in the maintenance of system requirements in an organisation.

Note: The re-implemented system has not as yet been assessed and therefore some additional requirements are expected because of system deficiencies for future release of the system.

Table 8.1 shows the change in system requirements from Sept 1992 to March 1996. The requirements included functional, nonfunctional and quality requirements. A requirement belonging, say, to the set R1 is identified as R1.x where x is an integer $>= 1$.

Table 8.1 shows how the requirements for CES changed from Sept 1992 to March 1996. These changes were primarily due to the fact that when the system was first implemented,

---

[11] Documentation such as Figures 8.1 and 8.2 with specific links to the sets R3 and R4 can help answer some of the fundamental issues in requirements traceability, for example, the very reason for the existence of a requirement.

Table 8.1 Requirements changes for CES

Requirement set: R1 [September 1992]	Requirement set: R2 [September 1994 – February 1995]	Requirement set: R3 [September 1994 – February 1995]	Requirement set: R4 [March 1996]
R1.1: The system should facilitate the evaluation of process model fitness, based on the model/context attributes and their relationships	R2.1: The system must be programmed on the Sun OS	R3.1: The system must be so programmed that the 'software functionality' is separated from 'integration mechanisms' so as to enable easier 'tool integration'	R4.1: The system should be 'data integrated' with the other prototype systems
R1.2: The system must display the 'Trouble Spot List' for the process model and context attributes that exhibit poor fitness	R2.2: The system must be programmed in C++/MOTIF programming language	R3.2: The system must be integrable with the process cycle tool-kit	R4.2: The system should be 'control integrated' (as appropriate) with the other prototype systems
R1.3: The system should assist in designing process models, i.e. given process context characteristics, it should identify the fitness of the different values of each process model attribute	R2.3: The system must be user-programmable. i.e. it must allow the user to change the data stored in the database	R3.3: The system must be survivable (for a reasonable duration) in environment changes[1]	R4.3: The system should run as a client in a distributed client–server architecture
R1.4: The system must employ the congruence evaluation and design assistance algorithms as developed during the congruence evaluation method study	R2.4: The system must be well documented to assist in future maintenance		R4.4: The system should be 'user-interface integrated' with the other prototype systems

(continued overleaf)

Table 8.1 (*continued*)

Requirement set: R1 [September 1992]	Requirement set: R2 [September 1994 – February 1995]	Requirement set: R3 [September 1994 – February 1995]	Requirement set: R4 [March 1996]
R1.5: The system must be programmed on the MS-DOS operating system (OS)	R2.5: The system should be user-friendly and there should be 'help menus' throughout the system screens		
R1.6: The system must be programmed in FoxPro programming language	R2.6: The system should be programmed in a structured language so as to aid in 'intrinsic' understandability of the system and system maintenance		
R1.7: The system must be easily understandable in its operation	R2.7: The system should be portable to other UNIX OS with minor changes, e.g. LINUX		
R1.8: The system must be reliable in its operation (must repeatedly produce correct results)	R2.8[2]: The system must be integrable with the process cycle tool-kit		
R1.9: The system must concisely display information in screens without sacrificing understandability	R2.9[3]: The system must be survivable (for a reasonable duration) in environment changes		

Software Requirements Changes Due to External Factors

R1.10: The system must exhibit consistent terminology, symbols, concepts and notations in its operation

R1.11: The system must provide all the key features in the domain of process fitness (to the best of knowledge of the researchers)

R1.12: The system must be efficient in its operation without a waste of resources (e.g. CPU time, memory requirements, etc.)

R1.13: The system must be validated to ensure that the congruence measures produced by the tool indeed characterise congruence

[1] Note that it was emphasised to the survey respondents that these were reasonable changes in the environment (such as a further refinement or slight modification of user need), and not radical and/or unprecedented changes that could render the system to be unusable.
[2] same as R3.2.
[3] same as R3.3.

the concept of process model congruence was highly original and it was not possible to decide all the tool features at that time, and, in addition, the application domain was also unclear. Lientz and Swanson's early observations [14] are thus relevant in this situation: that requirements change continually, often from experience gained from the use of systems and in response to organisational change (which can here be equated to environmental change). As many as 9 of the 16 new requirements (specifically, requirements R2.8, 2.9, R3.1 to R3.3, R4.1 to R4.4) were introduced because of environmental changes or environment-related issues. Clearly, environmental changes have a major impact in determining system requirements.

8.2.6 Threats to Validity

In any empirical study, there can be one or more threats to the validity of the research results. It is important to identify possible threats and to ensure that they do not negate the findings of the study. In the described case study, there were several possible threats, in the main: the type and size of the system being investigated; instrument validity; data quality; data analysis and interpretation, and researcher bias.

By industrial scale, the 20KLOC CES system is not a large software system. However, not all software systems are large; for example, embedded software systems in devices and appliances are often of comparable size. Also, with a thrust toward component integration as a way to quickly build a large software system, the size of the CES system is comparable to that of many software components used in such systems. In this sense, the results of our case study can be interpreted, with caution, in these contexts. Beyond this, however, there is an overall and an important message from the case study – that of determining key environment variables and monitoring them in a timely fashion so as to make requirements changes as early as possible in order to keep the system current. This message is universally applicable to any E-type system. Thus, the value of the case study in this respect is fundamentally that of motivating others dealing with E-type systems to empirically examine their systems and to take appropriate action.

The design of the instruments used in the case study is rooted in sound procedures for empirical research (see, for example, [10] and [11]). Content and face validity are satisfied through domain knowledge in the field of software maintenance and evolution, congruence evaluation, group's software systems, and generally in software engineering, and, where appropriate, repeated cycles of reviews were conducted to ensure that concepts were appropriately represented in the instruments.

Data quality was ensured by having confidence level indicator in the responses as well as rationale for the responses. Where clarifications were warranted, these were diligently carried out through iterations with the respondents concerned. Also, as described in the study, low confidence data was eliminated from analysis. In the main, therefore, there was considerable focus on the quality of the data gathered so as to support quality results. Likewise, data analysis and interpretation involved sharing the results with the respondents so as to assess the existence of any concerns with the findings.

Finally, researcher bias was avoided by involving others in the group, as appropriate, throughout the investigation. This meant that data came from the collective knowledge of the group and not the researcher alone. Thus, such an open process would highlight any biases and would be dealt with through reviews and iterations.

8.3 Lessons Learnt and Conclusions

After reflecting on the described case study, the following set of lessons learnt emerged.

1. That it is possible to monitor environmental changes explicitly (using an instrument such as that in Appendix B), and repeatedly, at different points in time during a system's evolution. However, we do not believe that there is a standard timeframe for the frequency of assessments for all types of systems. This depends on factors such as volatility of the requirements, market competition for product success, management commitment and others.
2. That it is possible to link such environmental changes to specific new requirements (see Section 8.2.5). This is not quite the practice in industry today nor, to our knowledge, has it been attempted by other researchers previously.
3. While known from literature [1] that the requirements for a system stem not only from system-specific deficiencies but also from changes in the environment, it was observed that these environmental changes may not necessarily translate into new system requirements unless the changes are 'mature' enough (see Section 8.2.5.4).

These lessons suggest a circumspective analysis of the kind of criteria identified in Appendix B, at various points in time and as a system grows. Lesson 1 (on the use of an explicit instrument) puts a valuable tool in the hands of practitioners in the industry and researchers in academia to continually monitor changes in the environment of their software systems. Lesson 2 (on the link between environment changes and new requirements) helps the practitioners in identifying new requirements (due to environmental changes) at an early stage so that actions can be taken as soon as possible (if at all) to ensure system survivability. This particular lesson therefore adds to the baseline scientific knowledge on adaptive maintenance [15]. Also, the record of environmental changes, the time stamps of these changes, and their relationships to particular new requirements can form a documented rationale for the existence of these new requirements. This aids in requirements management through simplified traceability [16]. Lesson 3 (on mature changes) adds to the baseline scientific knowledge in the requirements engineering field. In particular, knowing the details of requirements 'germination' could help the developers or users in assessing system stability in a given changing environment.

Besides the aforementioned lessons, this chapter gives some empirical support for Lehman's seventh law of software evolution [2], which deals with changes in the operational environment and its impact on the quality of an evolving system. This is an important step in the progress of the field of software evolution because until now this law has neither been empirically supported nor refuted.

References

[1] M.M. Lehman and L.A. Belady (eds.) *Program Evolution: Processes of Software Change*, Academic Press: London, 1985.
[2] M.M. Lehman and J.F. Ramil, "Rules and tools for software evolution planning and management", *Ann. Softw. Eng.*, 11: 15–44, 2001, To appear in this volume.
[3] B.W. Boehm, J.R. Brown, H. Kaspar, M. Lipow, G.J. MacLeod and M.J. Merritt. *Characteristics of Software Quality, TRW Series of Software Technology*, North Holland Publishing, 1978.

[4] G. Perez, K.E. Emam and N.H. Madhavji, "A system for evaluating the congruence of software process models", *Proceedings of the 4th International Conference on Software Process*, Brighton, UK, 1996, pp. 49–62.

[5] K.E. Emam and N.H. Madhavji, "A field study of requirements engineering practices in information systems development", *Proceedings of the Second IEEE International Symposium on Requirements Engineering*, York, England, pp. 68–80, 1995.

[6] W. Fry and D.A. Smith, "Congruence, contingency, and theory building", *Acad. Manage. Rev.*, 12(1): 117–132, 1987.

[7] C. Osgood, G. Suci and P. Tannenbaum, *The Measurement of Meaning*, University of Illinois Press, 1967.

[8] A.I. Wasserman, "Tool integration in software engineering environments, *International Workshop on Environments*, Chinon, France, 1989.

[9] D.P. Chattopadhyaya. *Environment Evolution and Values*, South Asian Publishers: New Delhi, 1982.

[10] C. Marshall and G.B. Rossman, *Designing Qualitative Research*, 3rd Ed, Sage Publications: Thousand Oaks, 1999.

[11] N.E. Fenton and S.L. Pfleeger, *Software Metrics – A Rigorous & Practical Approach*, International Thomson Publishing Inc.: London, 1997.

[12] A. Anton and C. Potts, "The use of goals to surface requirements for evolving systems", *International Conference on Software Engineering (ICSE '98)*, Kyoto, Japan, pp. 157–166, 1998.

[13] C. Jones, *Applied Software Measurement*, 2nd Ed, McGraw Hill: New York, 1996.

[14] B.P. Lientz and E.B. Swanson. *Software Maintenance Management*, Addison-Wesley: Reading, MA, 1980.

[15] E.B. Swanson, "The dimensions of maintenance", In *Proceedings of the 2nd International Conference on Software Engineering*. IEEE Computer Society Press: Los Alamitos, CA, 1976; 492–497.

[16] B. Ramesh and M. Jarke, "Toward reference models for requirements traceability", *IEEE Trans. Softw. Eng.*, 27(1): 58–93, 2001.

Appendix A: An Instrument to Assess System Deficiencies[12]

A1. **Understandability:** Is the system easily understandable[13]? (i.e. Is the purpose of the system clear? Is the system operation easy to comprehend? Exclude system design and implementation issues here.)

A2. **Completeness:** Does the system provide all the key features necessary in the domain of process fitness?

A3. **Conciseness:** Is the system concise (i.e. there is no 'excess' information in user screens or in the system as a whole) without sacrificing understandability?

A4. **Security:** Can you damage the process model/context values and relationships and does the system warn you of such inadvertent actions?

A5. **Consistency:** Does the system exhibit consistent terminology, symbols, notations and concepts in its operation?

A6. **Maintainability:** Has adequate documentation of the system been provided to assist in future maintenance (corrective, adaptive or perfective)?

A7. **Validity:** Has the system been validated with respect to the underlying concept of congruence (i.e. the congruence measures produced by the tool indeed characterise congruence)?

A8. **Usability:** Is the system user-friendly? (e.g. are the displays simple to understand; does the system have 'help' menus?)

---

[12] For better compatibility with the answering scale used, the questions must have included at the beginning 'To what extent...' and not as 'yes/no' questions. However, it is believed that the respondents correctly understood the meaning of the question and of the scale.

[13] This question refers to the understandability of the operation of the system from the point of view of the user.

A9. **Reliability:** Is the system reliable? (i.e. does it repeatedly produce correct results?)
A10. **Structuredness:** Has the system been developed with a high degree of structuredness (for instance, using a highly structured language like C++ and/or structured design methods)?
A11. **Efficiency:** Does the system fulfill its purpose without a waste of resources (for instance, CPU time, memory requirements)?
A12. **Customisability:** Is the system user-programmable (i.e. is it possible to customise data stored in the database, for instance, can the user add or delete existing process model attributes; can the user change the process model- context relationship values?)?
A13. **Portability:** Is the system portable to other platforms (say, UNIX)?
A14. **Integrability:** Is the system stand-alone or must it be executed as part of the process cycle tool-kit?
A15. **Survivability:** Is the system 'robust' enough to survive any changes[14] in the environment?

Appendix B: An Instrument to Assess Environment Evolution

B1. Was there realisation of the goal of having a process cycle tool-kit (i.e. 'process integration', all tools to be used to support a software development process)?
B2. Was there realisation of the goal of having 'data integration' for all the tools in the process cycle environment (i.e. data is shared among different tools, e.g. by using a shared repository)?
B3. Was there realisation of the goal of having 'user-interface integration' for all the tools in the process cycle environment (i.e. all the tools can be invoked from a common user interface)?
B4. Was there realisation of the goal of having 'control integration' for some or all the tools in the process cycle environment (i.e. a tool can be invoked through another tool)?
B5. Was there realisation of the goal of having 'platform integration' for all tools in the process cycle environment (i.e. all tools run on the same or compatible operating system so as to allow 'interoperability')?
B6. Was there realisation of the goal of integrating the CES system, in particular, in the process cycle environment?
B7. Was there realisation of the goal of evolving the CES system in the process cycle environment?
B8. Was there realisation of the goal of having a distributed, client–server architecture in the process cycle environment?
B9. Was there realisation of change of goals (for the entire team) from focus on 'software process concepts and methods' to 'software process concepts, methods and tools'?
B10. Was there realisation that software organisations will be more interested in a 'fully integrated' (all types of integration) tool-kit than in isolated tools?
B11. Was there realisation of the existence of 'flaws' in the existing environment, which could cause the environment to evolve in the future (i.e. could it have been predicted

---

[14] Strictly speaking, there is no system that can survive 'any changes in the environment'. However, the question expressed in this way (in combination with the scale) seems to have served well the purposes of the survey.

at any given time that there would be an imminent change in the environment in the future)?

B12. Was there realisation that existing prototypes were 'throw-away' prototypes rather than 'evolutionary' prototypes?

B13. Did a 'common vision' for the entire team (guided by the process cycle) exist?

B14. Was there realisation of the impact of the concept of process cycle on actual software development activities?

B15. Was there realisation about the prioritisation on separating code dealing with 'software functionality' from code dealing with 'integration mechanisms' (i.e. standards to facilitate different types of integration. e.g. MOTIF as a standard to support user-interface integration)?

B16. Were the existing software systems 'robust' enough to survive any changes in the environment (this is analogous to Darwinian concept of 'Survival of the fittest'!)?

B17. Was there realisation that any changes in the laboratory environment could seriously affect the prototype systems housed in the environment (i.e. realisation that the systems were not immune to changes in the environment)?

9

Understanding Open Source Software Evolution

Walt Scacchi

9.1 Introduction

This chapter examines the evolution of open source software and how their evolutionary patterns compare to prior studies of software evolution of proprietary (or closed source) software. Free or open source software (F/OSS) development focuses attention to systems like the GNU/Linux operating system, Apache Web server, and Mozilla Web browser, though there are now thousands of F/OSS projects under way. As these systems are being ever more widely used, questions regarding their evolution are of considerable interest.

This chapter is organized around four themes. First, it presents a brief survey of empirical studies of software evolution. As the majority of published studies of this kind are associated with the development of the laws of software evolution due to Lehman and colleagues, the kinds of findings they provide are described. Additionally, a sample of other empirical studies of software evolution are provided as well, in order to round out what is presently known about software evolution, at least in terms of studies of closed source software systems developed within centralized software development centers.

Second, it presents selected data and evidence that has begun to appear that characterizes change and evolution patterns associated with the evolution of F/OSS. Along the way, attention shifts to an analysis of where, how and why the evolution of F/OSS does or does not conform to prior empirical studies, models or theories of software evolution. Without revealing too much at this point, it is fair to say that there are patterns of data from studies of F/OSS that are not fully explained by prior studies of software evolution, as presently stated.

Third, it presents a brief review of models and theories of evolution from domains outside of software. This will help facilitate understanding of some of the challenges and alternative historical groundings that might be used to shape our collective understanding of how to think more broadly about software evolution, as well as the significance of theorizing about it.

The fourth and last section addresses whether it is necessary to reconsider the models, laws and theory and how they can be modified and supplemented to better account for the observations and findings emerging in studies of new software development processes and environments, such as those associated with the development of F/OSS. Prior models of software evolution were developed on the basis of careful study of conventional, closed source software system that evolve within industrial settings. Studies of F/OSS examine systems that typically are evolved outside of industrial settings, though some F/OSS systems are used in industrial settings, even though they are evolved in nonindustrial environments. However, it is appropriate to consider how to update and revise the models, laws and theory of software evolution to better account for both open and closed source software system being evolved inside or outside of industrial settings.

As such, the remainder of this chapter progresses through each of these themes in the order presented here.

9.2 Empirical Studies of Software Evolution

To understand the state of the art in the development of a theory of software evolution, and whether and how it might be extended, it is necessary to identify and describe what empirical studies of software evolution have been reported.

9.2.1 Studies of the Laws of Software Evolution

The most prominent studies of software evolution have been directed by M.M. Lehman and colleagues over a 30-year period dating back to the mid-1970s. The studies have given rise to eight laws of software evolution, as formulated and refined by Lehman and colleagues [Lehman 1980, Lehman 2001]. These laws are the result of careful and challenging empirical studies of the evolution of large-scale software systems found in a variety of corporate-based settings. These laws seek to consistently account for observed phenomena regarding the evolution of software releases, systems and E-Type applications, as defined by Lehman and colleagues. The laws and theory can be formulated in a manner suitable for independent test and validation, or refutation [Lakatos 1976, Popper 1963], but this requires making assumptions about details that are not explicitly stated in the laws. Thus, there are many challenges in how such empirical testing of these laws should be performed (e.g. how many or what kinds of software systems constitute an adequate or theoretically motivated sample space for comparative study), what the consequences for refutation may be (rejection or reformulation of the laws/theory), and whether or how the laws and theory might be refined and improved if new or contradictory phenomena appear [cf. Glaser and Strauss 1976, Yin 1994].

The published studies by Lehman and colleagues provide data from evolution of releases primarily from five software systems: Two operating systems (IBM OS 360, ICL VME Kernel), one financial system (Logica FW), two versions of a large real-time telecommunications system, and one defense system (Matra BAE Dynamics). Other studies have also been conducted and found to yield consistent growth models, but their results are not widely available. The data is summarized as a set of growth curves, as described in Perry and Ramil [2004]. In plotting these growth curves as graphs, the X-axis denotes the sequence number of the software release that was analyzed, while the Y-axis denotes the growth of the size of the system (e.g. measured in the number of modules) after the first release. The graphs suggest that during its evolution (or maintenance process), a system tracks a growth curve that can be approximated either as linear or inverse-square model [Turski 1996]. Thus, these data/curves explicate conformity to the first six laws, in that they suggest continual adaptation via incremental growth, system complexity controls the growth rate in a constant/bounded (linear or inverse-square) manner. The last two laws addressing quality and feedback systems cannot be directly observed within the data, but may conform to observations made by Lehman and colleagues about these systems. Therefore, this data set and the diversity of data substantiate and support the laws.

However, it is unclear whether such a data set is a representative sample of different kinds/types of software systems, or whether the laws can be interpreted as providing theoretical guidance for what kinds/types of software systems to study. It may be apparent that the majority of systems are large or very large software systems developed and maintained in large corporate settings, that the customers for such systems are also likely to be large enterprises (i.e. they are not intended as software for a personal or hand-held computer). In addition, some of the software systems or associated data that were examined in the studies by Lehman and colleagues are confidential, and thus are not open for public inspection, or independent examination and assessment. Subsequently, students and other scholars cannot readily access these systems or data for further study.[1]

9.2.2 Other Empirical Studies of Software Evolution

Many other empirical studies have been conducted and published. Here, attention is directed to a sample of these studies in which non-open source software systems were being investigated. This is mainly intended to see if other studies of software evolution conform to, refute or otherwise extend and refine the laws and theory of software evolution.

Bendifallah and Scacchi [1987] present qualitative data and analysis of two comparative case studies, revealing that similar kinds of software systems in similar kinds of organizational settings have different evolutionary trajectories. They report the differences can be explained by how system maintainers and end-users deal with local contingencies in their workplace and career opportunities in the course of maintaining their software systems.

Tamai and Torimitsu [1992] present data and observations from a survey study of mainframe software system applications across product generations. Among other things, they report that software lifetime in their survey is on average about 10 years, the variance in application lifetime is 6.2, and that small software applications tend to have a shorter life on average. They also report that applications that constitute what they call *administration systems* (e.g. back-office applications) live longer than *business supporting* (i.e. mission-critical) systems, and that application systems that replace previous generation systems grow by more than a factor of 2 compared to their predecessors. Last, they report that some companies follow policies that set the predicted lifetime of an application system at the time of initial release, and use this information in scheduling migration to next generation systems.

---

[1] Early data from Lehman's studies can be found in one of his books [Lehman and Belady 1985]. Unfortunately, the *unavailability* of empirical data from software measurements studies is in general all too common an occurrence. However, studies of F/OSS may indicate a different future lies ahead regarding public data availability [cf. Koch and Schneider 2000, Robles-Martinez *et al.* 2003].

Cusumano and Yoffie [1999] present results from case studies at Microsoft and Netscape, indicating strong reliance on incremental release of alpha and beta versions to customers as business strategy for improving evolution of system features that meet evolving user requirements. They show that user satisfaction can improve and be driven by shortening the time interval between releases. They also find that unstable releases (e.g. alpha and beta versions) will be released to users as a way to enable them to participate in the decentralized testing and remote quality assurance, and thus affecting software evolution. Their study does not confirm or refute the laws of software evolution, but they introduce a new dynamic into software evolution by making the release activity an independent output variable rather than an input variable.

Gall *et al.* [1997] provide data and observations based on software product release histories from a study of a large telecommunications switching system. The growth of this system over twenty releases conforms to the general trends found in the data of Lehman and colleagues. However, they report that though global system evolution follows the trend and thus conforms to the laws, individual subsystems and modules do not. Instead, they sometimes exhibit significant upward or downward fluctuation in their size across almost all releases. Eick *et al.* [2001] also provide data demonstrating that source code decays unless effort and resources are allocated to prevent and maintain the system throughout the later stages of its deployment, and that the decay can be observed to rise and fall in different subsystems and modules across releases.

Kemerer and Slaughter [1999] provide a systematic set of data, analyses and comparison with prior studies, revealing that problems in software maintenance can be attributed to a lack of knowledge of the maintenance process, and of the cause and effect relationships between software maintenance practices and outcomes. However, they do observe that their data may be associated with the growth of system complexity and other outcomes over time, which they attribute to the laws observed by Lehman and colleagues.

Perry *et al.* [2001] report findings from an observational case study of the development of large telecommunications systems that indicates extensive parallel changes being made between software system releases. This notion of parallel changes that may interact and thus confound software maintenance activities is not accounted for in an explicit way by the laws of software evolution. Thus, it does introduce yet another organizational factor that may affect software evolution.

With the exception of Cusumano and Yoffie [1999], these studies either conform to or suggest extensions to the laws and theory of software evolution. Thus, these conditions may point to the need for either revisions to the laws or alternative theories of software evolution that may or may not depend on such laws.

9.3 Evolutionary Patterns in Open Source Software

F/OSS development has appeared and disseminated throughout the world of software technology, mostly in the last ten years. This coincides with the spread, adoption and routine use of the Internet and World Wide Web as a global technical system. This infrastructure supports widespread access to previously remote information and software assets, as well as the ability for decentralized communities of like-minded people to find and communicate with one another. This is a world that differs in many ways from traditional software engineering, where it is common to assume centralized software development locales, development work and administrative authority that controls and manages the resources and schedules for software development and maintenance. Thus, to better understand whether or how patterns of software evolution in the technical and social regime of F/OSS conform to or differ from prior studies or models of software evolution, it is appropriate to start with an identification of the types of entities for F/OSS evolution, then follow with an examination of empirical studies, data and analyses of F/OSS evolution patterns.

9.3.1 Types of Entities for Studying F/OSS Evolution

The scheme of objects types that are suitable to address in studies of software evolution has been identified in the studies by Lehman and colleagues over the years [cf. Lehman 1980, Lehman 2002]. The primary types of entities are software releases, systems, applications, development processes and process models. Accordingly, each of these can be cast in terms of F/OSS as follows.

F/OSS Releases – Large F/OSS systems continue to grow over time and across releases. This suggests consistency with the sixth law of software evolution. Both stable and unstable F/OSS release product versions are being globally distributed in practice. Periodic alpha, beta, candidate and stable releases are made available to users at their discretion, as are unstable nightly F/OSS build versions released for developers actively contributing software updates to a given release. F/OSS releases for multiple platforms are generally synchronized and distributed at the same time, though may vary when new platforms are added (in parallel). F/OSS releases thus evolve within a nontraditional process cycle between full stable releases. F/OSS releases are also named with hierarchical release numbering schemes, sometimes with three or four levels of nested numbering to connote stable versus unstable releases to different audiences. However, the vast majority of F/OSS systems, primarily those for small- and medium-size F/OSS systems, do not continue to grow or thrive, perhaps because the software is not intensively or widely used [Capiluppi et al. 2003].

F/OSS Systems – F/OSS systems or programs evolve from first statement of an application concept or a change required to an existing system released and installed as an operational program text with its documentation. F/OSS systems may be small (<5K SLOC[2]), medium (5K-100K SLOC), large (100K-1000K SLOC) or very large systems (>1M SLOC), with large and very large systems being the fewest in number, but the most widely known. Most large or very large F/OSS systems or programs may exist in related but distinct versions/releases intended for different application platforms (e.g. MS Windows, Solaris, GNU/Linux, Mac OS X). Many F/OSS are structured as distributed systems, systems configured using scripts (e.g. using Perl, Python, or Tcl), middleware, or as modules that plug-in to hosts/servers (e.g. Apache and Mozilla both support independently developed plug-in modules). Additionally, some F/OSS are dynamically linked systems configured at run-time, when developed in a programming language like Java or others enabling remote service/method invocation.

F/OSS Applications – A much greater diversity and population of F/OSS applications are being investigated for evolution patterns. Those examined in-depth so far include

---

[2] Source Lines of Code, where 50 SLOC represents the equivalent of one printed page of source code, single spaced.

the Linux Kernel, Debian Linux distributions[3], Mono, Apache Web server, Mozilla Web browser, Berkeley DB, GNOME user interface desktop, PostgreSQL database management systems (DBMS) and about a dozen others[4]. Studies of F/OSS application populations, taxonomy and population demographics for hundreds to upwards of 40K F/OSS systems have appeared [Madey et al. 2002].

F/OSS Process – F/OSS is developed, deployed and maintained according to some software process. It is, however, unclear whether F/OSS processes, as portrayed in popular literature [DiBona et al. 1999], are intended only to be viewed as a monolithic process, just the top-level of a decomposable process, or whether specific software engineering activities have distinct processes that may also evolve, either independently or jointly. Furthermore, a small number of recent studies have begun to observe, describe and compare F/OSS development processes with those traditional to software engineering [Reis and Fortes 2002, Mockus et al. 2002, Scacchi 2002a, b, Scacchi 2004] that point to differences in the activities and organization of the F/OSS process. In addition, F/OSS activities surrounding software releases may have their own distinct process [Erenkrantz 2003, Jensen and Scacchi 2003] that may not reflect the activities involved in the release of closed source systems examined in the preceding section.

Models of F/OSS Process – Existing models of software development processes [Scacchi 2002b] do not explicitly account for F/OSS development activities or work practices [cf. Scacchi 2002a, c, Jensen and Scacchi 2005]. Thus, it is unclear whether models of software evolution processes that characterize closed source software systems developed within a centralized administrative authority can account for the decentralized, community-oriented evolution of F/OSS.

Overall, evolving software systems may be packaged and released in either open source or closed source forms. The packaging and release processes and technical system infrastructure may at times differ or be the same, depending on the software system application and development host (e.g. a website for open source, a corporate portal for closed source). But the decentralized community-oriented technological regime and infrastructure of F/OSS appears different than the world of the centralized corporate-centered regime and infrastructure of the closed source systems that have been examined as the basis of the laws of software evolution. Nonetheless, the laws of software evolution seem to apply, at least at a very high level in accounting for the evolution of F/OSS.

9.3.2 Patterns in Open Source Software Evolution Studies

Attention is now directed to examples of studies where F/OSS systems are being investigated, with the focus on how their results can be compared with those of Lehman and colleagues.

Godfrey and Tu [2000] provide data on the size and growth of the Linux Kernel (>2M SLOC) from 1994 to 1999, and find the growth rate to be superlinear (i.e. greater than

---

[3] A GNU/Linux distribution includes not only the Kernel but also hundreds/thousands of utilities and end-user applications. Distributions are typically the unit of installation when one acquires GNU/Linux, while the Linux Kernel is considered the core of the distribution. However, many F/OSS applications are developed for operating systems other than Linux (e.g. Microsoft Windows), thus assuming little/no coupling to the Linux Kernel.

[4] Smith, Capiluppi and Ramil [2004] have published preliminary results from an ongoing comparative study of 26 OSS systems and applications. Such studies begin to suggest that future studies of software evolution will focus attention to F/OSS for a variety of reasons.

linear), as portrayed in Figures 9.1 through 9.3. They also find similar patterns in F/OSS for the Vim text editor. Schach *et al.* [2002] report on the result of an in-depth study of the evolution of the Linux Kernel across 96 releases [cf. Godfrey and Tu 2000], indicating that module coupling (or interconnection) has been growing at an exponential (superlinear) rate. Their data are displayed in Figure 9.4. They predict that unless effort to alter this situation is undertaken, the Linux Kernel will become unmaintainable over time. Koch and Schneider [2000] studied the GNOME user interface desktop (>2M SLOC) and provided data that shows growth in the size of the source code base across releases increases in a superlinear manner as the number of software developers contributing code to the GNOME code base grows. Data from their study is plotted in Figure 9.5.

Robles-Martinez *et al.* [2003] report in their study of Mono (a F/OSS implementation of Microsoft's .NET services, libraries and interfaces), their measurements indicate superlinear growth rate in the code size and the number of code updates that are committed within the code base. They also report a similar growth pattern in the number of people contributing source code to the emerging Mono system over a 2–3 year period. According to Gonzalez-Barahona *et al.* [2001], their measurements indicate that as of mid-2001, the Debian GNU/Linux 2.2 distribution had grown to more than 55M SLOC, and has since exceeded 100M SLOC in the Debian 3.0 distribution. O'Mahony [2003] presents data from her study of the Debian GNU/Linux distribution from releases spanning 0.01 in 1993 through 3.0 in late 2002 that show growth of the size of the distribution rises at a superlinear rate over the past five years. Last, Gonzalez-Barahona *et al.* [2004] also provide data on the growth of the Apache project community and number of modules, revealing once again, a superlinear growth pattern over the five-year period (1999–2004) covered in their data.

In contrast, Godfrey and Tu [2000] find linear growth in Fetchmail, X-Windows, and Gcc (the GNU compiler collection), and sublinear growth in Pine (email client). Such trends are clearly different from the previous set of F/OSS systems.

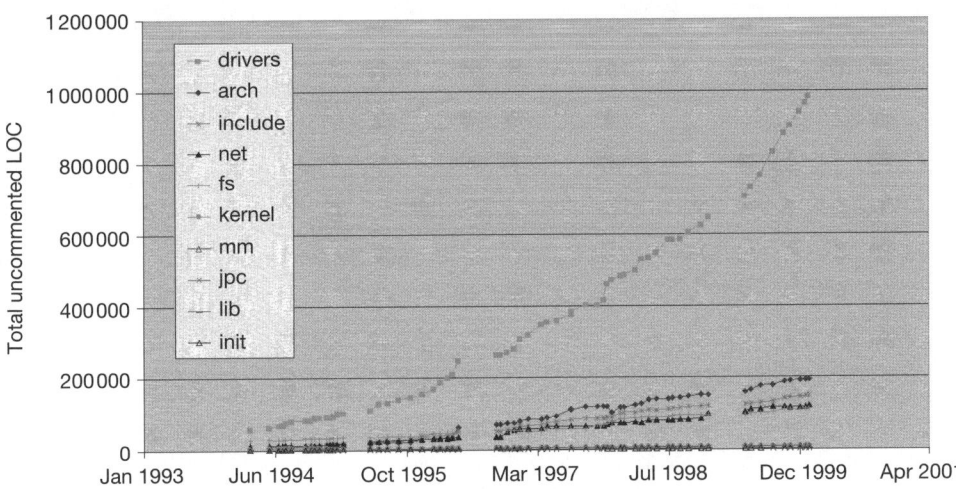

Figure 9.1 Data revealing the size and growth of major subsystems in the Linux Kernel during 1994–1999 [Source: Godfrey and Tu 2000]

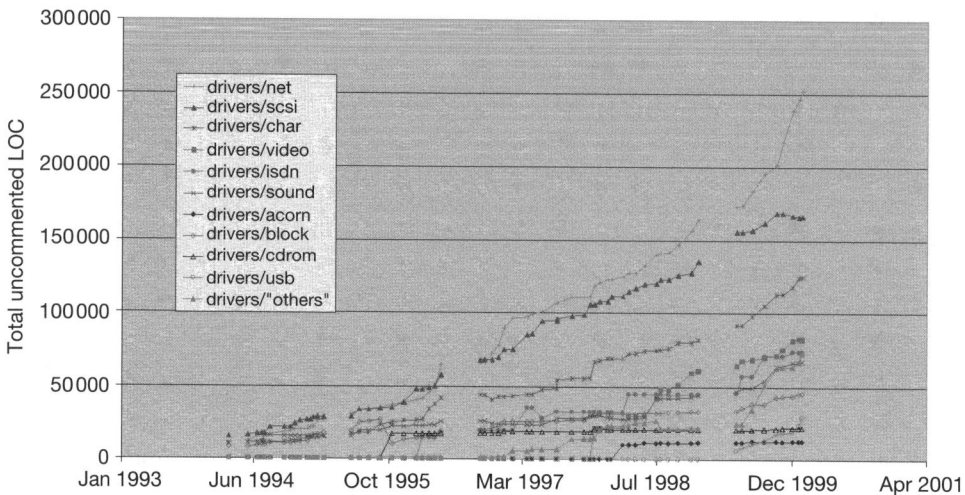

Figure 9.2 Data revealing the size and growth of device drivers in the Linux Kernel during 1994–1999 [Source: Godfrey and Tu 2000]

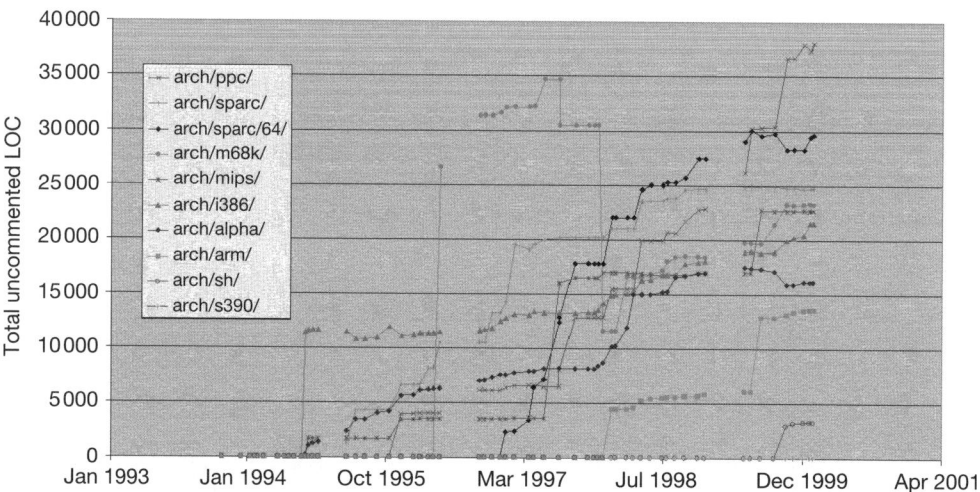

Figure 9.3 Data revealing the size and growth of the Linux Kernel for different computer platform architectures during 1994–1999 [Source: Godfrey and Tu 2000]

Why is there such a high growth rate for some F/OSS systems like the Linux Kernel, Vim, GNOME, Mono, the Debian GNU/Linux distribution, and the Apache project, but not for other F/OSS? Godfrey and Tu [2000] report in the case of the Linux Kernel that (a) much of the source code relates to device drivers, as seen in Figure 9.2, (b) much of the code is orthogonal and intended for different platforms, as suggested in Figure 9.3, and (c) contributions to the code base are open to anyone who makes the requisite effort. In addition, Godfrey and Tu observe (d) Linux Kernel source code configurations (or

Understanding Open Source Software Evolution

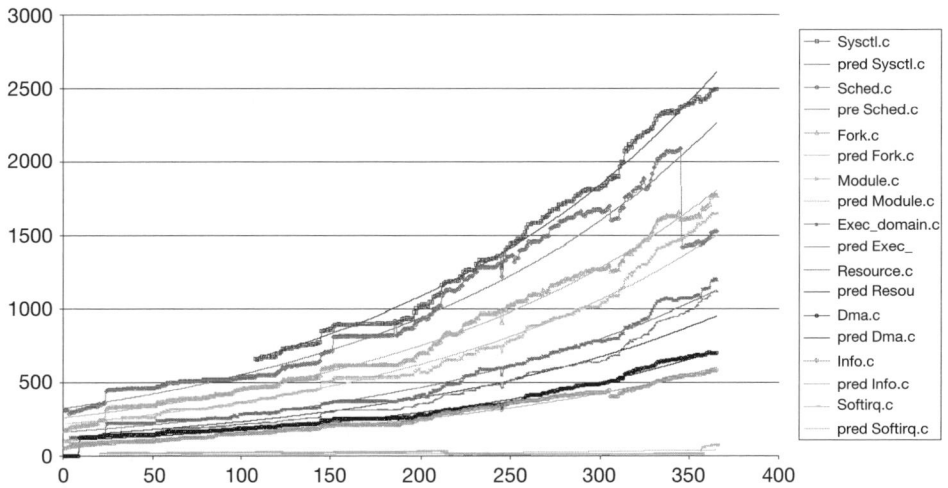

Figure 9.4 Measured (discrete points) versus predicted (smooth curves) of common coupling of source code modules in the Linux Kernel across releases [Source: Schach *et al.* 2002]

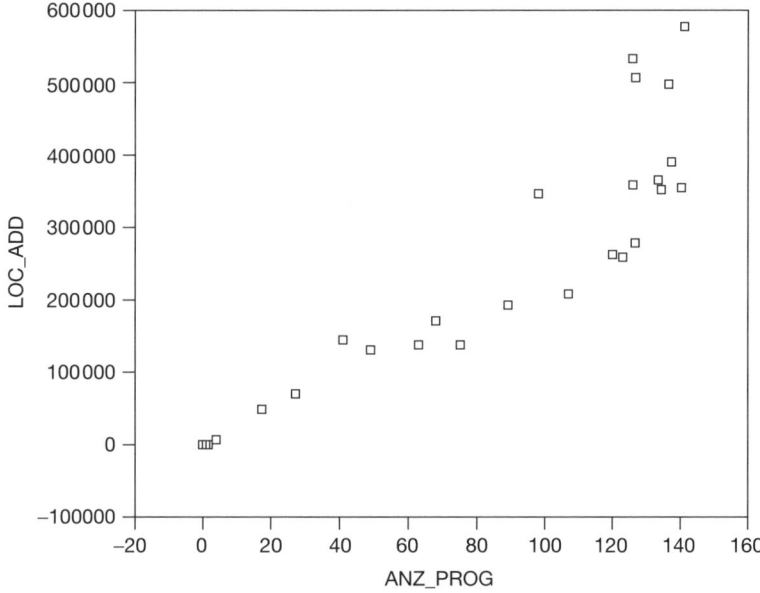

Figure 9.5 Growth of the lines of source code added as the number of software developers contributing code to the GNOME user interface grows [Source: Koch and Schneider 2000]

'builds') are specific to a hardware platform or architecture (see Figure 9.3), and use as little of 15% of the total Linux Kernel source code base. It is possible but uncertain whether these conditions also apply to GNOME, Vim, Mono and the Apache project, since they may have source code configurations that are specific to different operating systems

(Linux, BSD, Windows or Mac OS/X). However, it is unclear why they would or would not apply to Fetchmail, X-Windows, Gcc and Pine. Perhaps, it might be because the latter systems are generally older and may have originally been developed in an earlier (pre-Web) technological regime. Elsewhere, Cook *et al.* [2000] in their comparison study of the closed source Logica FW system, and the F/OSS Berkeley DB system, find that growth across releases is not uniformly distributed, but concentrated in different system modules across releases. A similar result may be seen in the data in Figure 9.3, from Godfrey and Tu [2000].

Nakakoji *et al.* [2002] report findings from a comparative case study of four F/OSS systems, the Linux Kernel, Postgres DBMS, GNU Wingnut and Jun (a 3D graphics library). They provide data indicating that these systems exhibit different evolutionary patterns of splitting and merging their overall system architectures across releases, as shown in Figure 9.6. Thus, it appears that it is necessary to understand both the *age* and *architectural patterns* of subsystems and modules within and across software releases, whether in closed source or open source systems, in order to better understand how a system is evolving [Godfrey and Lee 2000]. This observation is also implicated by earlier studies [Tamai and Torimitsu 1992, Gall *et al.* 1997, Eick *et al.* 2001, Perry *et al.* 2001].

Hunt and Johnson [2002] report discovery of a Pareto distribution in the size of the number of developers participating in F/OSS projects, from a sample population of >30 K projects found on the SourceForge Web portal.[5] Their results indicate that the vast majority of F/OSS projects have only one developer, while a small percentage have larger, ongoing team membership. Madey *et al.* [2002], in an independent study similar to Hunt and Johnson, find that a power law distribution characterizes the size of F/OSSD projects

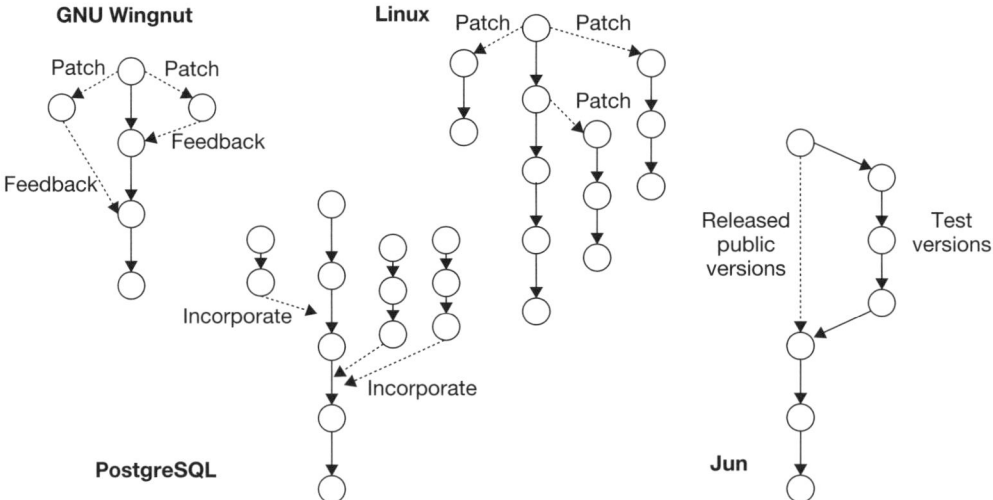

Figure 9.6 Patterns of software system evolution forking and joining across releases (nodes in each graph) for four different F/OSS systems [Source: Nakakoji *et al.* 2002]

---

[5] The SourceForge Web portal can be found at www.sourceforge.net. As of January 2006, there are 110K F/OSS projects registered at this specific F/OSS project portal. Other F/OSS Web portals like www.freshmeat.org and www.savannah.org include other projects, though there is some overlap across these three portals.

across a population of some 40K F/OSS projects at SourceForge. Independently, Hars and Ou [2002] report a similar trend, finding that more than 60% of F/OSS developers in their survey reported participating in 2–10 other F/OSS development projects. Capiluppi *et al.* [2003] also draw from a sample of 400 F/OSSD projects posted on SourceForge. They find that the vast majority of systems in their sample are either small- or medium-size systems, and only a minor fraction is large. Only the large F/OSS systems tend to have development teams with more than a single developer. Their results might also be compared with those of Tamai and Torimitsu [1992], thereby substantiating that small F/OSS systems have a much shorter life than large F/OSS systems. Overall, this suggests that results from studies that characterize large F/OSS efforts are not representative of the majority of F/OSS projects.

Di Penta *et al.* [2002] provide results from a case study focused on the refactoring of a large F/OSS application, a geographical information system called *GRASS*, which operates on a small hand-held computer. Their effort was aimed at software miniaturization, reducing code duplications, eliminating unused files, and restructuring system libraries and reorganizing them into shared (i.e. dynamically linked) libraries. This form of software evolution and architectural refactoring has not been reported in, or accounted for by, the laws of software evolution. For example, miniaturization and refactoring will reduce the size of the software application, as well as potentially reducing redundancies and code decay, thereby improving software quality. Elsewhere, Scacchi [2002c] reports results from a case study of the GNUenterprise project that find that the emerging F/OSS E-Commerce application system being developed is growing through merger with other independently developed F/OSS systems, none of which was designed or envisioned as a target for merger or component subsystem. Scacchi labels this discontinuous growth of F/OSS system size and functionality, *architectural bricolage*. This bricolage may account for the discontinuities that can be seen in the growth trends displayed in Figure 9.3.

Mockus *et al.* [2002] in a comparative case study of Apache Web server (<100K SLOC) and Mozilla Web browser (>2M SLOC), find that it appears easier to maintain the quality of system features for a F/OSS across releases compared to closed source commercial telecommunications systems of similar proportions. They also find evidence suggesting large F/OSS development projects must attain a core developer team size of 10–15 developers for its evolution to be sustained. This might thus be recognized as an indicator for *a critical mass in the number of core developers* that once achieved enables a high rate of growth and sustained viability. Whether and how long such growth can be sustained, however, is unclear, as the number of core developers changes over time.

[Scacchi *et al.* 2002a, c, Elliott and Scacchi 2005, Jensen and Scacchi 2005] provide results from comparative case studies of F/OSS projects within different communities. They find and explicitly model how F/OSS requirements and release processes differ from those expected in conventional software engineering practices. They also find that evolving F/OSS depends on co-evolution of developer community, community support software, and software informalisms as documentation and communication media. Nakakoji *et al.* [2002] also report that the four F/OSS systems they investigated co-evolve with the communities of developers who maintain them. Finally, Gonzalez-Barahona *et al.* [2004] provide a detailed data set that visualizes the growth of the developer community over a five-year period corresponding to growth in the number of modules incorporated in the Apache project.

von Hippel and Katz [2002] report results of studies that reveal some end-users in F/OSS projects become developers, and most F/OSS developers are end-users of the systems they develop, thereby enabling the co-evolution of the system and user-developer community. This observation of developers as users is also independently reported in other studies as well [Mockus *et al.* 2002, Scacchi 2002a, Nakakoji *et al.* 2002]. Last, much like Hars and Ou [2002], Madey *et al.* [2002] report finding that some F/OSS developers, whom they designate as *linchpin developers*, participate in multiple projects. These linchpin developers effectively create social networks that interlink F/OSS projects and enable the systems interlinked in these social networks to also share source code or subsystems. A sample from their data appears in Figure 9.7.

However, across the set of studies starting above with Mockus *et al.* [2002], there are no equivalent observations or laws reported in prior studies of closed source software evolution that account for these data and evolutionary patterns addressing team and community structures. Clearly, such a result does not imply that the observed conditions or patterns do not occur in the evolution of closed source software. Instead, it reveals that other variables and patterns previously not addressed in prior empirical studies may be significant factors contributing to software evolution.

Last, in a recent study comparing open versus closed source software development products, Paulson *et al.* [2004] find that overall evolutionary growth of both types of software are comparable and consistent with the laws of software evolution, for the systems they examined. Specifically, in modeling and visualizing the growth of the systems in their studies, as displayed in Figure 9.8, their research design employs linear approximations to depict system growth trends over time. Thus, it is not possible to tell from

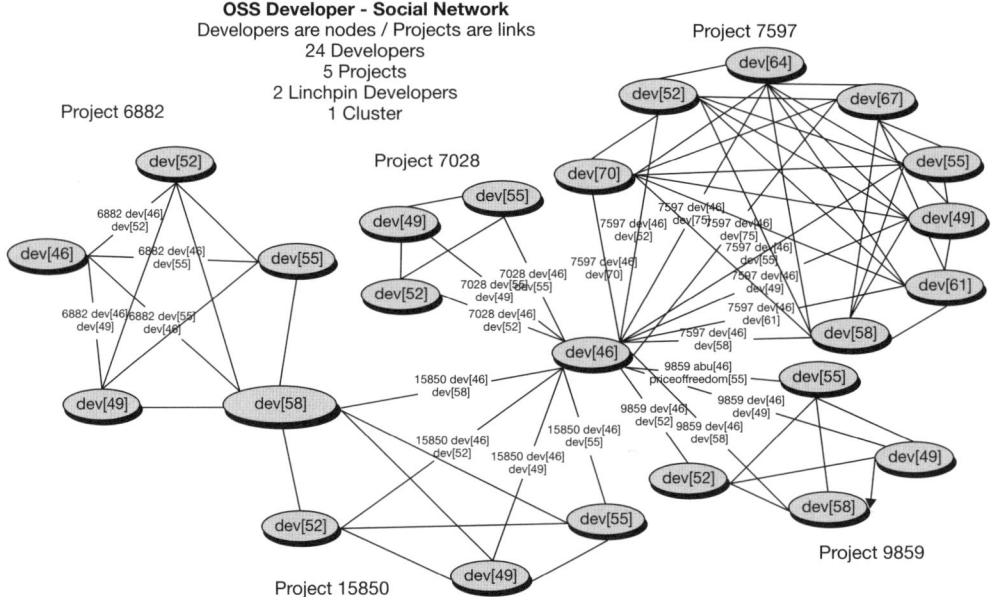

Figure 9.7 A social network of F/OSS developers that interlinks five different projects through two linchpin developers, dev[46] and dev[58] [Source: Madey, Freeh and Tynan 2002]

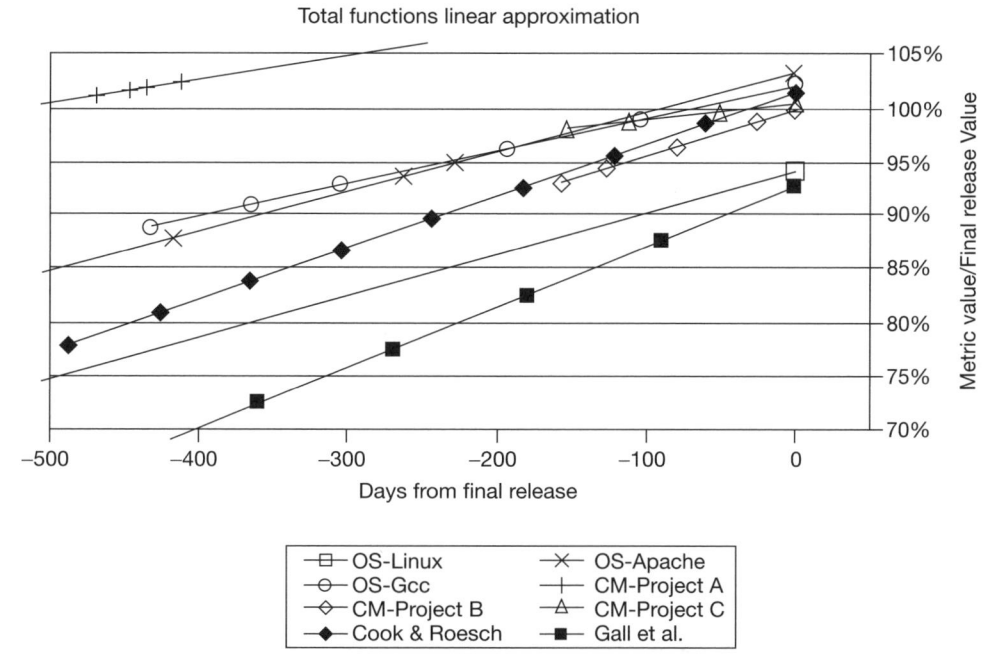

Figure 9.8 Linear approximations of the growth of a sample of open and closed source software systems [Source: Paulson, Succi, and Eberlein 2004]

their results if these approximations 'linearize' the inverse-square growth curves reported by Lehman and colleagues or the exponential curves of the kind shown in Figures 9.1 through 9.5, or the nonlinear growth shown in Figure 9.6. However, they do plot a growth curve for the Linux, as seen in Figure 9.8, which may suggest their linear approximation in this instance flattens the exponential growth pattern for Linux seen in Figures 9.1 through 9. 5.

Overall, in evolving large F/OSS, it seems that it may be necessary for a critical mass of developers to come together to anchor the broader community of users, developers and user-developers to their shared system. This critical mass and community will co-evolve with the architectural patterns that are manifest across unstable and stable F/OSS system releases as they age over time. Subsequently, older F/OSS systems that may have emerged before the F/OSS gained widespread recognition as a social movement and cultural meme may have a lower rate of architectural and system release co-evolution. Furthermore, it may well be the situation that for large F/OSS systems/releases to evolve at a superlinear rate, this may be possible only when their development community has critical mass, is open to ongoing growth, and that the focal F/OSS systems entail internal architectures with orthogonal features, subsystems, or modules, as well as external system release architectures that span multiple deployment platforms.

Last, it appears that the evolutionary patterns of F/OSS systems reveal that overall system size and architecture can increase or decrease in a discontinuous manner, because of bricolage-style system mergers, or to miniaturization and refactoring. Clearly, the laws of software evolution as presently stated, and based primarily on the study of large closed source systems, do not account for, nor anticipate, the potential for superlinear growth in software system size that can be sustained in the presence of satisfied developer-user communities who collectively assure the quality of these systems over time.

9.4 Evolution Models and Theories

As a first step, it is desirable to provide a definition of evolution that is satisfied by examples that cover different scientific and technological disciplines. Lehman and Ramil [2004] provide an appropriate definition for software evolution. In the definition that follows, an attempt has been made to address properties applicable in a general sense. Individual disciplines may have additional properties not identified here. Accordingly, evolution is a process of progressive change and cyclic adaptation over time in terms of the attributes, behavioral properties and relational configuration of some material, abstract, natural or artificial entity or system. Such a definition accommodates both 'evolutionistic' models that draw attention to stages and direction of developmental progress, and 'evolutionary' models that focus attention to mechanisms, forces or impinging constraints that give rise to evolution [cf. King and Kraemer 1984].

Theories of biological evolution have been the subject of scientific inquiry and speculation for centuries, with Charles Darwin's *Origin of Species* (1859) being the most widely known and cited theory. Darwin's theoretical analysis was based in part on his field studies of animal species on the Galapagos archipelago. His theory began a century of scientific debate that included religious and moral substance undertones [Bowler 1989]. It led to the emergence of concepts such as *developmental biology* that examines the role of genetics, reproductive (natural) selection, co-evolution (among co-located species) and adaptation to ecological circumstances shaping the lives of organisms. In contrast, *evolutionary biology* accounts for the influence of genetics, reproduction, lineage, speciation and population growth and diffusion shaping the long-term or transgenerational lives of species of organisms. The concepts of developmental versus evolutionary biology help draw attention to two alternative ways to view the evolution of a system, one focusing on a system's life cycle, the other on changes manifest across generations of related systems. In addition, the concept of biological *systematics* further helps draw attention to the 'progress', direction, or (punctuated) equilibrium of evolution based on associating the developmental properties (e.g. agency, efficiency and scope) of living organisms with those found in the fossil and geological record [Nitecki 1988, Gould 2002].

Culture, language and economy, which arise from the social actions and interactions of people, may evolve in ways similar or different from that in the natural science of biology. Culture, for example, may rely on the development, diffusion and assimilation of *memes* (i.e. concepts, compelling ideas or cultural 'genes') that embody recurring social practices, situations, beliefs or myths that can be shared, communicated or otherwise transported as a basis for their evolution [Gabora 1997]. Despite differences, 'open source' and 'free software' are examples of related memes. Thus, rather than conjecturing physical (biological) conditions or circumstances, cultural evolution relies on social actions and narrative records that relate to physical conditions and circumstances that enable the ongoing evolution of diverse cultures and cultural experiences. Language evolution [Christiansen and Kirby 2003] seems to share and span ideas from culture and biology with respect to efforts that associate language learning, perception and semiotics with neurological mechanisms and human population dynamics. Elsewhere, topics like *competition, resource scarcity, population concentration/density, legitimacy* and *organizational ecologies* appear as factors shaping the evolution of markets, organizations and economies, at least at a macro level [Hannan and Carroll 1992, Nelson and Winter 1982, Saviotti and Mani 1995]. Beyond this, the evolution of culture, language and economy are being explored experimentally using computational approaches [e.g. Gabora 2000]. Overall, this tiny sample of work draws attention to associations more closely aligned to evolutionary biology, rather than to developmental biology.

The evolution of modern technology has also become the subject of systematic inquiry. For example, in Abernathy's [1978] study of the American automobile industry, he finds that the *technical system* for developing and manufacturing automobiles associates product design and process design within a *productive unit* (i.e. the manufacturing systems within a physical factory or production organization). Each depends on the other, so that changes in one, such as the introduction of new techniques into a productive unit, are propagated into both product design and production process layout/workflow. King and Kraemer [1984] provide similar findings in their analysis of the evolution of computing systems in organizational settings. Hughes [1987] in his historical study of the technical system of electrification draws attention to the role of the *infrastructure* of electrical production and distribution as spanning not just equipment, mechanisms (e.g. power generators, substations), cabling and power outlets but also the *alignment* of producers, retailers and consumers of devices/products together with the processes that depend on electrification for their operation. Meyer and Utterback [1993] were among the first to recognize that productive units and technical systems of production and consumption were increasingly organized around *product lines* that accommodate a diversity of product life cycles centered around the *dominant design* [Utterback 1994] or product architecture that dominates current retail markets.

From an economic perspective, Nelson and Winter [1982] independently termed the overall scheme that associates and aligns products, processes, productive units with producers, retailers and consumers, a *technological regime*. Last, though the development, use and maintenance of software is strongly dependent on computer hardware, there are now studies that examine how different kinds of computer hardware components exhibit evolutionary patterns across technological generations or regimes [e.g. Victor and Ausubel 2002, van den Ende and Kemp 1999]. The evolution of technology through technological regimes that depend on product features, development processes, infrastructure and productive units seems immediately relevant to understanding the evolution of software systems and technologies.

Software programs, systems, applications, processes and productive units continue to develop over time. For example, there is a plethora of software innovations in the form of new tools, techniques, concepts or applications, which continue to emerge as more people experience modern computing technology and technical systems. These innovations give rise to unexpected or unanticipated forms of software development and maintenance, as, for example, software systems that are dynamically linked at run-time instead of compile-time [Mens *et al.* 2003, Kniesel *et al.* 2002]. Software innovations are diffused into a population of evermore diverse settings and technical systems via technology transfer and system migration. Software processes are subject to ongoing experience, learning, improvement and refinement, though there is debate about how to most effectively and efficiently realize and assimilate such process improvements [Conradi and Fuggetta 2002, Beecham *et al.* 2003]. Software systems are also subject to cultural forces [Elliott and Scacchi 2005], narrative and informal documentation [Scacchi 2002a] and economic conditions [Boehm 1981] within the productive units or work settings that affect how these systems will be developed and maintained. These forces can give rise to similar kinds of systems in similar settings evolving at different rates along different trajectories [Bendifallah and Scacchi 1987]. This suggests that software systems are developed and evolved within particular organizational and informational ecologies [cf. Nardi and O'Day 1999], as well as situated within a technical system of production and larger overall technological regime.

Overall, this brief review of evolutionary theory across a sample of disciplines raises an awareness of the following issues. First, in studying software evolution, it is necessary to clarify whether, in fact, attention is directed at matters more closely aligned to development of a given system throughout its life, or with the evolution of software technologies across generations that are disseminated across multiple populations. It appears that much of what are labeled as studies of 'software evolution' are more typically studies of patterns of development of specific systems, rather than patterns of evolution across different systems within one or multiple product lines (or species), at least as compared to work in biological evolution. However, the laws and theory of software evolution articulated by Lehman and associates depend on empirical findings that examine a variety of software systems in different application domains, execution environments, size of system, organization and company marketing the system, as their basis for identifying mechanisms and conditions that affect software evolution.

Second, when considering the subject of software evolution at a macro level, it appears that there are no easily found or widely cited studies that examine issues of memes, competition, resource scarcity, population concentration/density, legitimacy and organizational ecology as forces that shape or impinge on software systems or software technology. The study of software evolution is still in its infancy. In general, existing theory of the development or evolution of software does not yet have a substantial cultural, language or economic basis. Studies, analyses and insights from these arenas are yet to appear, and thus need to be explored.

Last, conventional closed source software systems developed within centralized corporate productive units and open source software systems developed within globally decentralized settings without corporate locale represent alternative technological regimes. Each represents a different technical system of production, distribution/retailing, consumption, differentiated product lines, dominant product designs and more. Similarly, software development methods based on object-oriented design and coding, agile development and extreme programming entail some form of alternative technological regime. Concepts from theories of technological evolution and observations on patterns of software development and maintenance can be used to help shape an understanding of how software evolves. Additional work is required to compare and contrast evolutionary behavior under different software development regimes. The present discussion concentrates on the socio-technical regime of open source software development.

9.5 Do We Need New or Revised Models, Laws or Theories for Open Source Software Evolution?

At this point, it is reasonable to ask about whether prior studies, models or laws adequately account for the evolution of F/OSS systems, at least according to the studies and data presented above. For example, other studies of software evolution do not provide a suitable account for the sometimes superlinear, sometimes sublinear growth curves reported in studies and figures of F/OSS presented above. Beyond this, data trends and patterns accounting for the evolution of F/OSS in some cases conform, and in other cases it is unclear whether or how different F/OSS conform to the laws of software evolution. As such, refining or reformulating them to account for the data at hand is beyond the scope of this chapter. However, it is possible to consider the underlying ontologies for software evolution to rethink what kinds of theory or models of software evolution may further help in understanding, reasoning about, and explaining the evolution of both closed and open source software systems.

9.5.1 Embracing the Feedback Control Systems Ontology

Feedback and feedback systems appear to be a central part of the conceptual foundation of the laws and theory of software evolution developed by Lehman and colleagues. So why not refine these laws in a way that more fully embraces feedback control theory in articulating the laws so that they can address the evolution of F/OSS? The system dynamics modeling and simulation approach has been widely used to study software project management [Abdel-Hamid and Madnick 1991] and various types of software processes. However, the approach can also be used to model and simulate feedback control systems expressed as a system of differential equations [Bateson 1993, Doyle *et al.* 1992]. Combining the laws of software evolution with modeling concepts from system dynamics and feedback control systems should be possible with an eye toward the interests of the audience for whom the laws are intended to serve. For example, executives and senior managers responsible for large software development centers want to know where to make strategic investments and how to better allocate their software development staff, schedules and related resources. Software developers may want to know what kinds of tools and techniques to use to make their software evolution efforts faster, better and cheaper. Scholars of software evolution theory want to know what kinds of data to collect, what types and sizes of systems to study, what types of criteria to use in designing theoretically motivated samples of software systems under study, and what tests to apply to verify, refine or refute the laws or theory at hand. In terms of feedback control systems, there is need to identify where sensors should be placed in a software productive unit to collect different types of software change data, and to what or whom they should provide their feedback.

Similarly, there is need to identify where feedback control loops are to be placed, where their begin and end points are to be located, what functionality is located within each loop, and what decision function determines whether a loop iterates or exits. It is also necessary to identify what roles people and software tools play in the regulation or control of the feedback system, or what feedback they produce, use or consume along the way. Managers, developers and scholars want to know how different types of feedback get employed to regulate and control the centralized corporate or decentralized open source productive unit that develops and maintains software systems of different size, type, age and application setting.

Recent efforts by Lehman et al. [2001], for example, have begun to employ system dynamics modeling techniques and simulation tools to demonstrate and iteratively refine an operational model of software evolution that embodies the existing laws. Their model seems able to reproduce via simulation the evolutionary data trends that conform to the laws of software evolution. More recently, Ramil and colleagues [Smith et al. 2004] examine and qualitatively simulate F/OSS evolution data for 26 systems they have studied. Their data and analyses from this latest study confirm and incorporate further refinements to the laws of software evolution, though they also find some puzzling trends that are not well explained by the laws. However, the trends reported in their data appear to differ from many of the studies prior to those published before 2000 that gave rise to the laws of software evolution. But the stage is set for how to proceed in pursuing the ontological foundation of the laws and theory of software evolution.

On the other hand, if the theory of feedback control systems becomes too complicated or too rigid of an ontological framework for describing and explaining software evolution, then alternative ontological frameworks may be employed to further such study.

9.5.2 Alternative Ontologies for F/OSS Evolution

One observation from studying the evolution of technical systems is that the technologies and techniques for developing and maintaining F/OSS constitute a distinct technological regime. This regime for F/OSS is not anticipated or adequately covered by other studies of software evolution. The same may also be true of emerging technologies like component-based software systems and those with dynamically composed run-time architectures. Thus, it seems that any ontology for software evolution should account for the emergence, deployment and consequences of use for new tools, techniques and concepts for software development, as well as the productive units, technical system infrastructure, and technological regime in which they are situated.

A second observation from the study of the evolution of F/OSS is that different types of software system evolve at substantially different rates – some superlinear, some constant, some sublinear, some not at all. Small software systems may not evolve or thrive for very long, nor will they be assimilated into larger systems, unless merged with other systems whose developers can form a critical mass sufficient to co-evolve with the composite system and productive unit. Drawing from biological evolutionary theory, it may be that software evolution theory requires or will benefit from *taxonomic analyses* to describe, classify and name different types of software systems or architectural morphologies, thus refactoring the conceptual space for software system evolution. Similarly, it may benefit from *phylogenetic analyses* that reconstruct the evolutionary histories of different types of software systems, whether as open source and closed source implementations. Last, it suggests that a science of *software systematics* is needed to encourage study of the kinds and diversity of software programs, components, systems and application domains, as well as relationships among them, across populations of development projects within different technological regimes over time. This would enable comparative study of contemporary software systems with their ancestral lineage, as well as to those found within the software fossil record (e.g. those software systems developed starting in the 1940s onward for mainframe computers, and those developed starting in the 1970s for personal computers). Finally, this could all be done in ways that enable free/open source computational modeling of such a framework for software evolution.

A third observation from the emergence and evolution of F/OSS is that the beliefs, narratives and memes play a role in facilitating the adoption, deployment, use and evolution of F/OSS. Their role may be more significant than the cultural and language constructs that accompanied the earlier technological regime of centralized, closed source software development that primarily developed systems for deployment in corporate settings. Similarly, relatively new software language constructs for scripting, plug-in modules, and extensible software architectures have been popularized in the regime of F/OSS. But these constructs may also have enabled new forms of architectural evolution and bricolage, thereby accelerating the growth rate of large F/OSS in a manner incommensurate to that seen in the world of mainframe software systems, an earlier technological regime. Finally, large and popular F/OSS systems are being extended and evolved to accommodate end-users and developers whose native language or ethnic legacy is not English based. The internationalization or localization of F/OSS systems, while neither necessarily adding nor subtracting functionality, does create value in the global community by making these systems more accessible to a larger audience of prospective end-users, developers, reviewers and debuggers. These software extensions add to the bulk of F/OSS code release size in probably orthogonal ways, but may or may not represent antiregressive work [cf. Lehman *et al.* 2001].

A fourth observation from the evolution of F/OSS is that they have emerged within a technological regime where competitive market forces and organizational ecologies surrounding closed source software systems may have effectively served to stimulate the growth and diffusion of F/OSS project populations. Furthermore, it may be the case that these circumstances are co-evolving with the relative growth/demise of open versus closed source software product offerings, and the communities of developers who support them. Other studies of software evolution make little/no statement about the effects of market forces, competition, organizational ecology, co-evolution, or the spread of software project populations as contributing factors affecting how software systems may evolve. Yet many of the largest F/OSS systems are pitted directly against commercially available, closed source alternatives. These F/OSS systems typically compete against those developed within centrally controlled and resource managed software development centers. Thus, it seems appropriate to address how co-evolutionary market forces surround and situate the centralized or decentralized organizational ecologies that develop and maintain large software systems in order to better understand how they evolve.

A last observation from a view of F/OSS as a socio-technical world is that the evolution of F/OSS system is situated within distinct web of organizational, technological, historical and geographic contexts. However, feedback control systems typically do not account for organizational productive units or their historical circumstances. Similarly, there is no accounting for the motivations, beliefs or cultural values of software developers who may prefer software systems to be developed in a manner that is free and open, so as to enable subsequent study, learning, reinvention, modification and redistribution. But as seen above, these are plausible variables that can contribute to the evolution of F/OSS, and thus further study is required to understand when, where and how they might influence how particular F/OSS systems may evolve.

9.6 Conclusions

The laws and theory of software evolution proposed by Lehman and colleagues are recognized as a major contribution to the field of software engineering and the discipline of computer science. These laws have been generally found to provide a plausible explanation for how software systems evolve throughout their life. They have been explored empirically over a period of more than 30 years, so their persistence is a noteworthy accomplishment. Developing laws and theory of software evolution relying on empirically grounded studies is a long-term endeavor that poses many challenges in research method, theoretical sampling of systems to study, theory construction and ongoing theory testing, refutation and refinement. However, it may prove to be an endeavor that gives rise to new ways and means for conceptualizing evolutionary processes in other domains of study.

As the technology, process and practice of software development and maintenance has evolved, particularly in the past ten years and with the advent of large numbers of free/open source software development projects, it has become clear that the existing models of software evolution based on empirical studies of closed source systems prior to 2000 may be breaking down, at least from results of the many empirical studies of F/OSS reviewed in this chapter. The models and prior studies do not address and therefore do not provide a rich or deep characterization of the evolution of F/OSS systems. Prior models of software evolution were formulated in the context of software development and maintenance processes and work practices that were based in centralized, corporate software development centers that built large closed source system applications with few competitive offerings for use by large enterprises. Large F/OSS systems, on the other hand, are developed and maintained in globally decentralized settings that collectively denote a loosely coupled community of developers/users who generally lack the administrative authority, resource constraints and schedules found in centrally controlled software centers. These F/OSS systems are typically competing alternatives to closed source commercial software product offerings. Subsequently, it may be better to consider whether the primary evolutionary dynamic associated with F/OSS is reinvention, renovation or revitalization of established software systems or applications that have proved to be useful, but now merit redevelopment, refinement and new extensions or extension mechanisms [Scacchi 2004]. Similarly, as large F/OSS are sometimes observed to exhibit sustained superlinear or exponential growth, can such rates of growth go on unabated, or will the concurrent growth of system complexity eventually change the shape of the growth curve to something more like an 'S' curve, with exponential growth in the early stages, followed by inverse-square growth in the later stages [cf. Lehman and Ramil 2002]? Further study of such matters is clearly needed.

There is a growing base of data, evidence and findings from multiple studies of F/OSS systems that indicate F/OSS systems co-evolve with their user-developer communities, so that growth and evolution of each depends on the other. Co-evolution results of this kind are not yet reported for closed source systems, and it is unclear that such results will be found. In short, prior models of software evolution were developed within and apply to systems maintained and used in a corporate world and technological regime that differs from the socio-technical communities, global information infrastructure, and technological regime that embeds open source software.

It appears that we need a more articulate explication and refinement of models of software evolution if they are to account for the evolution of F/OSS systems. One way this might be done is to embrace and extend reliance of the ontology of feedback control systems theory. This would entail identifying the types, operations, behaviors and interconnection of mechanisms that embody and realize a complex, multilevel, multiloop, and multiagent feedback system. Building computational models and simulations of such a system (or family of systems) could be a significant contribution. Otherwise, alternative evolutionary ontologies might be adopted, individually or in some explicit hybrid combination form. The choice of which ontology to use will suggest the types of entities, flows, mechanisms and controls for software evolution should be modeled, measured, improved and refined according to some conceptual or theoretically motivated framework. Otherwise, use of alternative ontologies may accommodate new models of theories of software evolution that do not rely on high-level, abstract or overgeneralized models, but instead may result in theories or models of smaller and more precise scope that better account for the complex, socio-technical ecological niches where software systems evolve in practice, as well as for the type and history of the system in such context.

Theories of software evolution should be empirically grounded. They should be formulated or modeled in ways in which they can be subject to tests of refutation or refinement. The tests in turn should examine comparative data sets that are theoretically motivated, rather than motivated by the convenience of data at hand that may have been collected and conceived for other more modest purposes. There should be theories that address software evolution within, as well as, across generations of software technology or technological regimes. Laws and theories of software evolution should have a computational rendering so that their source code, internal representation and external behavior can be observed, shared, studied, modified and redistributed. They should be free (as in *libre*) and open source. These models should then also be suitable for simulation, analysis, visualization, prototyping and enactment [Scacchi 2002b, Scacchi and Mi 1997]. By doing this, the software engineering and computer science community can make a new contribution in the form of reusable assets that can be adopted and tailored for use in other domains of evolution theorizing.

The future of research in software evolution must include the technological regime of F/OSS as a major element. This will be an increasingly practical choice for empirical study of individual systems, groups of systems of common type, and of larger regional or global populations of systems. This is due in part to the public availability of the source code and related assets on the Web for individual versions/releases of hundreds of application systems, as well as data about their development processes, community participants, tools in use, and settings of development work. Not that collecting or accessing this data is without its demands for time, skill, effort and therefore cost, but that useful and interesting data can be accessed and shared without the barriers to entry and corporate disclosure constraints of intellectual property claims or trade secrets. It seems unlikely that the software engineering community will get open access to the source code, bug report databases, release histories or other 'property or secrets' of closed source systems that are in widespread use (e.g. Microsoft Windows operating systems, Internet Explorer, Word, Outlook, Office, Oracle DBMS or SAP R/3) in ways that can be shared and studied without corporate trade secrets, nondisclosure agreements and publication constraints. In contrast, it is possible today to empirically study the ongoing evolution of the GNU/Linux operating systems (Kernel or alternative distributions), the Mozilla Web browser, Open Office, SAP DB, Apache project or GNUenterprise, which together with their respective technically and socially networked communities, have publicly accessible Web portals and software assets that can be shared, studied and redistributed to support research into models, laws and theory of software evolution. The future of research in software evolution should be free, open and constructive since it will likely take a community of investigators to help make substantial progress in developing, refining, sharing and publishing models, laws and theories of software evolution.

9.7 Acknowledgements

The research described in this report is supported by grants from the National Science Foundation #ITR-0083075, #ITR-0205679, #ITR-0205724 and #ITR-0350754. No endorsement implied. Mark Ackerman at the University of Michigan Ann Arbor; Les Gasser at the University of Illinois, Urbana-Champaign; John Noll at Santa Clara University; Margaret Elliott, Mark Bergman, Chris Jensen and Xiaobin Li at the UCI Institute for Software Research; and Julia Watson at The Ohio State University are also collaborators on the research project from which this article was derived. Finally, Manny Lehman, Nazim Madhavji and Juan Ramil provided many helpful comments, suggestions and clarifications on earlier versions of this chapter.

References

W.J. Abernathy, *The Productivity Dilemma: Roadblock to Innovation in the Automobile Industry*, John Hopkins University Press, 1978.

T. Abdel-Hamid and S.E. Madnick, *Software Project Dynamics: An Integrated Approach*. Prentice Hall Software Series, New Jersey, 1991.

R.N. Bateson, *Introduction to Control System Technology*, Prentice-Hall, Englewood Cliffs, NJ, 1993.

S. Beecham, T. Hall and A. Rainer, Software process improvement problems in twelve software companies: an empirical analysis, *Empir. Softw. Eng.*, 8(1), 7–42, 2003.

S. Bendifallah and W. Scacchi, Understanding software maintenance work, *IEEE Trans. Softw. Eng.*, 13(3), 311–323, 1987;. Reprinted in D. Longstreet (ed.), *Tutorial on Software Maintenance and Computers*, IEEE Computer Society, 1990.

B.E. Boehm, *Software Engineering Economics*, Prentice-Hall, 1981.

P.J. Bowler, *Evolution: The History of an Idea* (Revised Edition), University of California Press, Berkeley, CA, 1989.

A. Capiluppi, P. Lago and M. Morisio, Characteristics of open source projects, *Proceedings of 7th European Conference on Software Maintenance and Reengineering*, Benevento, Italy, March 2003.

M. Christiansen and S. Kirby (eds.), *Language Evolution: The States of the Art*, Oxford University Press, 2003.

R. Conradi and A. Fuggetta, Improving software process improvement, *IEEE Softw.*, 19(4), 92–99, 2002.

S. Cook, H. Ji and R. Harrison, *Software Evolution and Software Evolvability*, unpublished manuscript, University of Reading, Reading, UK, 2000.

K. Crowston, H. Annabi and J. Howison, Defining open source software project success, *Proceedings of International Conference Information Systems (ICIS 2003)*, Seattle, WA, 327–340, December, 2003.

M.A. Cusumano and D.B. Yoffie, Software development on internet time, *Computer*, 32(10), 60–70, 1999.

C. DiBona, S. Ockman and M. Stone, *Open Sources: Voices from the Open Source Revolution*, O'Reilly Press, Sebastopol, CA, 1999.

M. Di Penta, M. Neteler, G. Antonio and E. Merlo, Knowledge-based library refactoring for an open source project, *Proceedings of IEEE Working Conference Reverse Engineering*, Richmond VA, October 2002.

J.C. Doyle, B.A Francis and A.R. Tannenbaum, *Feedback Control Theory*, Macmillan, New York, 1992.

J. Erenkrantz, Release management within open source projects, *Proceedings of 3rd Workshop on Open Source Software Engineering, 25th International Conference Software Engineering*, Portland, OR, May 2003.

S.G. Eick, T.L. Graves, A.F. Karr, J.S. Marron and A. Mockus, Does code decay? assessing the evidence from change management data, *IEEE Trans. Softw. Eng.*, 27(1), 1–12, 2001.

M. Elliott and W. Scacchi, Free software development: cooperation and conflict in a virtual organizational culture, in S. Koch (ed.), *Free/Open Source Software Development*, Idea Press, Hershey, PA, 151–172, 2005.

L. Gabora, The origin and evolution of culture and creativity, *J. Memet. – Evol. Models Inf. Transm.*, 1(1), 1–28, 1997, http://jom-emit.cfpm.org/vol1/gabora_l.html.

L. Gabora, The beer can theory of creativity, in P. Bentley and D. Corne (eds.) *Creative Evolutionary Systems*, Morgan Kaufman, 2000.

H. Gall, M. Jazayeri, R. Klösch and G. Trausmuth, Software evolution observations based on product release history, *Proceedings of 1997 International Conference on Software Maintenance (ICSM'97)*, Bari, IT, October 1997.

B. Glaser and A. Strauss, *The Discovery of Grounded Theory: Strategies for Qualitative Research*, Aldine Publishing, Chicago, IL, 1976.

M.W. Godfrey and E.H.S. Lee, Secrets from the monster: extracting Mozilla's software architecture, *Proceedings of Second International Symposium Constructing Software Engineering Tools (CoSET-00)*, Limerick, Ireland, June 2000.

M.W. Godfrey and Q. Tu, Evolution in open source software: a case study, *Proceedings of 2000 International Conference on Software Maintenance (ICSM-00)*, San Jose, CA, October 2000.

J.M Gonzalez-Barahona, L. Lopez and G. Robles, Community structure of modules in the Apache project, *Proceedings of 4th Workshop on Open Source Software Engineering*, Edinburgh, Scotland, May 2004.

J.M Gonzalez-Barahona, M.A. Ortuno Perez, P. de las Heras Quiros, J. Centeno Gonzalez and V. Matellan Olivera, Counting potatoes: the size of debian 2.2, *Upgrade Mag.*, II(6), 60–66, 2001.

S.J. Gould, *The Structure of Evolutionary Theory*, Harvard University Press, Cambridge, MA, 2002.

M.T. Hannan and G.R. Carroll, *Dynamics of Organizational Populations: Density, Legitimation and Competition*, Oxford University Press, New York, 1992.

A. Hars and S. Ou, Working for free? Motivations for participating in open-source software projects, *Intern. J. Electron. Commer.*, 6(3), 25–39, 2002.

T.J. Hughes, The evolution of large technological systems, in W. Bijker, T. Hughes and T. Pinch (eds.), *The Social Construction of Technological Systems*, MIT Press, Cambridge, MA, 51–82, 1987.

F. Hunt and P. Johnson, On the Pareto distribution of sourceforge projects, in C. Gacek and B. Arief (eds.), *Proceedings of Open Source Software Development Workshop*, 122–129, Newcastle, UK, February 2002.

C. Jensen and W. Scacchi, Simulating an automated approach to discovery and modeling of open source software development processes, *Proceedings 4th Software Process Simulation and Modeling Workshop (ProSim'03)*, Portland, OR, May 2003.

C. Jensen and W. Scacchi, Process modeling across the web information infrastructure, *Software Process–Improvement and Practice*, 10(3), 255–272, July–September 2005.

J.L. King and K.L. Kraemer, Evolution and organizational information systems: an assessment of Nolan's stage model, *Commun. ACM*, 27(5), 466–475, 1984.

C.F. Kemerer and S. Slaughter, An empirical approach to studying software evolution, *IEEE Trans. Softw. Eng.*, 25(4), 493–505, 1999.

G. Kniesel, J. Noppen, T. Mens and J. Buckley, *WS 9. The First International Workshop on Unanticipated Software Evolution*, Workshop Report, Malaga, Spain, June 2002. http://joint.org/use2002/ecoopWsReport USE2002.pdf.

S. Koch and G. Schneider, Results from software engineering research into open source development projects using public data, *Diskussionspapiere zum Tätigkeitsfeld Informationsverarbeitung und Informationswirtschaft*, H.R. Hansen and W.H. Janko (Hrsg.), Nr. 22, Wirtschaftsuniversität Wien, 2000.

I. Lakatos, *Proofs and Refutations: The Logic of Mathematical Discovery*, Cambridge University Press, Cambridge, UK, 1976.

M.M. Lehman, Programs, life cycles, and laws of software evolution, *Proc. IEEE*, 68, 1060–1078, 1980.

M.M. Lehman, Rules and tools for software evolution planning and management, in J. Ramil (ed.), *Proceedings of FEAST 2000*, Imperial College of Science and Technology, London, 53–68, 2000; Also appears with

J.F. Ramil in an expanded version as Rules and tools for software evolution management, in *Ann. Softw. Eng.*, 11, 16–44, 2001..

M.M. Lehman, Software evolution, in J. Marciniak (ed.), *Encyclopedia of Software Engineering*, 2nd Ed, John Wiley and Sons Inc., New York, 1507–1513, 2002; Also see Software evolution and software evolution processes, *Ann. Softw. Eng.*, 12, 275–309, 2002.

M.M. Lehman and L.A. Belady, *Program Evolution – Processes of Software Change*, Academic Press, London, 1985.

M.M. Lehman and J.F. Ramil, An approach to a theory of software evolution, *Proceedings 2001 International Workshop on Principles of Software Evolution*, ACM Press, New York, 70–74, 2001.

M.M. Lehman and J.F. Ramil, An overview of some lessons learnt in FEAST, *Proceedings of Eighth Workshop on Empirical Studies of Software Maintenance (WESS'02)*, Montreal, CA, 2002.

M.M. Lehman and J.F. Ramil, *Software Evolution*, in this volume, 2004.

M.M. Lehman, J.F. Ramil and G. Kahen, *A Paradigm for the Behavioural Modelling of Software Processes using System Dynamics*, technical report, Department of Computing, Imperial College, London, September 2001.

M.M. Lehman, J.F. Ramil, P.D. Wernick, D.E. Perry and W. Turski, Metrics and laws of software evolution – the nineties view, *Proceedings of 4th International Symposium on Software Metrics*, 20–32, Albuquerque, NM, November 1997.

G. Madey, V. Freeh and R. Tynan, The open source software development phenomenon: an analysis based on social network theory. *Proceedings of Americas Conference on Information Systems (AMCIS2002)*. 1806–1813, Dallas, TX, 2002.

T. Mens, J. Buckley, M. Zenger and A. Rashid, Towards a taxonomy of software evolution, *Second International Workshop on Unanticipated Software Evolution*, Warsaw, Poland, April 2003. http://joint.org/use2003/Papers/18500066.pdf.

M.H. Meyer and J.M. Utterback, The product family and the dynamics of core capability, *Sloan Manage. Rev.*, 34(3), 29–47, Spring 1993.

A. Mockus, R.T. Fielding and J. Herbsleb, Two case studies of open source software development: apache and mozilla, *ACM Trans. Softw. Eng. Methodol.*, 11(3), 309–346, 2002.

K. Nakakoji, Y. Yamamoto, Y. Nishinaka, K. Kishida and Y. Ye, Evolution patterns of open-source software systems and communities, *Proceedings of 2002 International Workshop Principles of Software Evolution*, ACM Press, Orlando, FL, 76–85, 2002.

B. Nardi and V. O'Day, *Information Ecologies: Using Technology with Heart*, MIT Press, Cambridge, MA, 1999.

R.R. Nelson and S.G. Winter, *An Evolutionary Theory of Economic Change*, Belknap Press, Cambridge, MA, 1982.

M.H. Nitecki (ed.), *Evolutionary Progress*, University of Chicago Press, Chicago, IL, 1988.

S. O'Mahony, Developing community software in a commodity world, in M. Fisher and G. Downey (eds.), *Frontiers of capital: Ethnographic Reflections on the New Economy*, Social Science Research Council, Duke University Press, Durham, NC, 2006.

J.W. Paulson, G. Succi and A. Eberlein, An empirical study of open-source and closed-source software products, *IEEE Trans. Softw. Eng.*, 30(4), 246–256, 2004.

D.E. Perry and J.F. Ramil, *Empirical Studies of Software Evolution*, in this volume, 2004.

D.E. Perry, H.P. Siy and L.G. Votta, Parallel changes in large-scale software development: an observational case study, *ACM Trans. Softw. Eng. Methodol.*, 10(3), 308–337, 2001.

K.R. Popper, *Conjectures and Refutations*, Routledge & Kagen, 1963.

C.R. Reis and R.P.M. Fortes, An overview of the software engineering process and tools in the Mozilla project, *Proceedings of Workshop on Open Source Software Development*, 155–175, Newcastle, UK, February 2002.

G. Robles-Martinez, J.M. Gonzalez-Barahona, J. Centeno Gonzalez, V. Matellan Olivera and L. Rodero Merino, Studying the evolution of libre software projects using publicly available data, *Proceedings of 3rd Workshop on Open Source Software Engineering*, Portland, OR, 2003.

P.P. Saviotti and G.S. Mani, Competition, variety and technological evolution: a replicator dynamics model, *J. Evol. Econ.*, 5(4), 369–392, 1995.

W. Scacchi, Understanding the requirements for developing open source software systems, *IEE Proc. – Softw.*, 149(1), 24–39, 2002a.

W. Scacchi, Process models for software engineering, in J. Marciniak(ed.), *Encyclopedia of Software Engineering*, 2nd Ed, John Wiley and Sons Inc., New York 993–1005, 2002b.

W. Scacchi, *Open EC/B: A Case Study in Electronic Commerce and Open Source Software Development*, technical report, Institute for Software Research, July 2002c.

W. Scacchi, Free/Open source software development in the game community, *IEEE Softw.*, 21(1), 59–67, 2004.

W. Scacchi and P. Mi, Process life cycle engineering: approach and support environment, *Intern. J. Intell. Syst. Account. Finance, Manage.*, 6, 83–107, 1997.

S.R. Schach, B. Jin, D.R. Wright, G.Z. Heller and A.J. Offutt, Maintainability of the linux kernel, *IEE Proc. – Softw.*, 149(1), 18–23, 2002.

N. Smith, A. Capiluppi and J.F. Ramil, Qualitative analysis and simulation of open source software evolution, *Proceedings of 5th Software Process Simulation and Modeling Workshop (ProSim'04)*, Edinburgh, Scotland, UK, May 2004.

T. Tamai and Y. Torimitsu, Software lifetime and its evolution process over generations, *Proceedings of Conference in Software Maintenance*, Orlando, FL, 63–69, November 1992.

W. Turski, Reference model for smooth growth of software systems, *IEEE Trans. Softw. Eng.*, 22(8), 599–600, 1996.

J.M. Utterback, *Mastering the Dynamics of Innovation: how Companies can Seize Opportunities in the Face of Technological Change*, Harvard Business School Press, 1994.

N.M. Victor and J.H. Ausubel, DRAMs as model organisms for study of technological evolution, *Technol. Forecast. Soc. Change*, 69(3), 243–262, 2002.

J. van den Ende and R. Kemp, Technological transformations in history: how the computer regime grew out of existing computing regimes, *Res. Policy*, 28, 833–851, 1999.

E. von Hippel and R. Katz, Shifting innovation to users via toolkits, *Manage. Sci.*, 48(7), 821–833, 2002.

R. Yin, *Case Study Research: Design and Methods*, 2nd Ed, Sage Publications, Newbury Park, CA, 1994.

10

Structural Analysis of Open Source Systems

Andrea Capiluppi[1], Maurizio Morisio and Juan C. Fernández-Ramil

Based on "Structural analysis of Open Source Systems" by Andrea Capiluppi, Maurizio Morisio, Juan F. Ramil which appeared on "Ricerca ed impresa: Conoscenza e produzione per la società dell'Informazione", AICA 2004, XLII Congresso Annuale, Benevento, Italy, 28–30 Sept 2004.

10.1 Introduction

The long-term evolution software systems that are actively used in real-world domains and environments[2] is an interesting topic of empirical study. Such study can lead to insights and useful lessons both for researchers and practitioners. While systems not actively used, or prototypes, can be the subject of analysis, the conclusions derived from their study are limited in their applicability to real-world applications and domains. The empirical studies of real-world software processes and products are necessarily circumscribed to the kind of artefacts that an investigator may be able to obtain and measure: Proprietary systems are in general difficult to be studied, since the public disclosure of data reflecting those systems is forbidden in the vast majority of the cases.

In the work reported in this chapter, we have used metrics derived from a number of Open Source Software (OSS) systems in order to study the characteristics of their long-term evolution, and, in particular, how their folder structure evolves. The naming of the files that contain the code generally follows a folder structure and we have found this an interesting attribute of study, which reveals some aspects of the evolving structure of

---

[1] The work reported here was done while Andrea Capiluppi was a PhD candidate at the Politecnico of Torino.
[2] This class of systems has been termed *type E* by Lehman, to indicate that they must be evolved as their operational domain changes in order to maintain the satisfaction of its stakeholders [Lehman and Belady, 1985]. See Chapter 1.

the code. Choosing OSS systems for studying software evolution is an advantage since important amounts of data concerning software products and processes is available in freely accessible forms on the Internet such as mailing lists, releases and configuration management repositories.

In this chapter, we study OSS systems from the point of view of their structural evolution. This involves the study of their enhancement, adaptation and, if it happens, their restructuring. One of the goals of our research has been to understand how OSS projects evolve with regard to source code structure. Given the importance of the software architecture and the software code structure, we are particularly interested in identifying patterns in the evolution of software code structure and what are the structural characteristics of successfully evolved software systems. In this work, one of our aims is to consider folder structures as a specific view of a system's architecture. The long-term aim of this type of study is to provide empirically based architectural guidelines for achieving software that is likely to evolve successfully. This is, of course, a long-term goal and the present study is just a very preliminary exploration.

Our dataset is composed of 25 OSS systems, which we observed in a discrete-time perspective, that is, studying each publicly available release. The dataset globally represents 992 releases, the data points in this study. In general, we were interested in observing source code structure and its changes, to learn from long-lived OSS systems what types of structural patterns emerge, what structural changes are more frequently brought to the source code, and also to seek for patterns in the evolutionary trends. Given that code structure and in general system architecture can be visualised using a variety of means, we focus on one of the simplest possible approaches: the observation of the *source folder structure*. By *folder*, we mean any directory in the code repository, which contains source files.

10.2 Related Work

Empirical studies on software development gained momentum after the pioneering work of Lehman and his collaborators on the study of the evolution of the proprietary operating system OS/360 [Lehman, 1969, Belady and Lehman, 1976]. The initial study observed some 20 releases of OS/360. The results that emerged from that investigation, and subsequent studies of other proprietary commercial software [Lehman, 1974, 1980, Lehman and Belady, 1985, Lehman *et al.*, 1997, Lehman *et al.*, 1998], include the *Software Production Enterprises (SPE)* program classification and a set of laws of software evolution. The findings made in the seventies and eighties were refined and supplemented in the *F*eedback, *E*volution *A*nd *S*oftware *T*echnology FEAST projects [Lehman *et al.*, 1998, Lehman and Ramil, 2005a].

Other groups have also studied the software evolution phenomenon. For example, Kemerer and Slaughter [1999] looked at the evolution of two proprietary systems using two approaches: one based on the time series analysis, and the other based on a technique called *sequence analysis*. This and other studies (e.g. [Barry *et al.*, 2003]) identified and categorised software evolution patterns in IT systems. Eick *et al.*, found some evidence of code decay when studying data representing 15 years of the evolution of very large telephone switch software [Eick *et al.*, 2001].

During the last few years, it has been realised that OSS systems have an advantage over commercial ones when it comes to availability of data. This has facilitated a number of independent studies since initial research involving the Apache web server and Mozilla browser [Mockus *et al.*, 2002].

OSS evolution studies include those which examined single OSS projects [German, 2003, Koch and Schneider, 2000, Aoki *et al.*, 2001, González-Barahona *et al.*, 2001, Stamelos *et al.*, 2002, Godfrey and Tu, 2000], and those which involved several systems [Capiluppi *et al.*, 2003, Capiluppi, 2003].

Even though the vast majority of OSS evolution studies are based on direct trend visualisation and curve fitting, simulation-based modelling to study OSS evolution has been recently proposed through both quantitative [Antoniades *et al.*, 2003] and qualitative [Smith *et al.*, 2004] methods.

The work illustrated in this chapter explores the study of the folder structures and their evolution, a new dimension not covered in any of the above studies. In doing so, this work aims at improving the understanding of OSS evolution by looking at the structure, an important but not previously considered factor.

10.3 Rationale

When investigating code structure of various OSS systems, one may encounter different patterns of modifications. If we consider code structure from the perspective of file naming, code organisation and storage (one example is depicted in Figure 10.1), it is possible to visualise elementary components (source files, source folders) as composing a tree, with the root of the tree being represented by the parent folder. When analysing software evolution in a tree-perspective, one distinguishes two dimensions:

1. *vertical growth*, that is, creating a sub-branch in an existing branch (upper part of Figure 10.1),
2. *horizontal growth*, that is, adding a new branch over an existing branch (lower part of Figure 10.1).

If we consider Figure 10.1 from a tree-perspective, we may also state that any vertical growth adds depth in code structure, that is, a new level has been added under an existing level. The upper part of Figure 10.1 shows that creation of folder F3 has introduced a

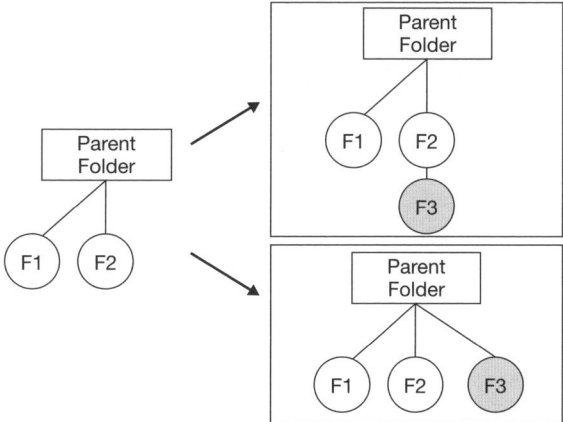

Figure 10.1 Two possible modifications to the folder structure in which code is stored

new level under a current level, which is composed of F1 and F2. Alternatively, as shown in the lower part of Figure 10.1, F3 can be added at the same level of F1 and F2, that is, without adding a new level.

The initial focus for the research reported here is based on Figure 10.1, and on the common assumption that evolution in software systems is generally implemented in an incremental fashion. Our aim is to understand if source code trees have a common pattern of growth, and if (and how) those patterns have an impact on the evolvability of the systems. If a common evolutionary pattern appears more frequently than other patterns in the empirical observations, the next question would be: Why such a pattern occurs and whether it can be linked to other characteristics of the software and its related domains. Moreover, the empirical study of structural evolution may help us to identify, and even predict, when and how structural changes occur and whether this can be related to transitions between phases [Rajlich and Bennett, 2000, Nakakoji *et al.*, 2002] in the evolution of a software system.

This investigation of code structure evolution in OSS requires one to address the following research questions:

- How does the source tree evolve over real time or releases?
- How does the depth of the source tree relate to code size?
- How does the code structure evolution relate to the rate of functional growth and change of a system?
- What common patterns emerge in source tree growth, given the horizontal and vertical perspective introduced in Figure 10.1 and in the above discussion?
- How could one, by visualizing the evolving code structure, distinguish functional enhancement and adaptation activities, usually the predominant effort during the evolution of source code, from other activities such as refactoring and restructuring[3]?

10.4 Approach

The approach followed in this study involved the steps listed below. The steps are not applied in a fully sequential manner, since some steps provide feedback to other steps.

1. *Projects selection*: As reported in a previous work [Capiluppi *et al.*, 2003], we have created a database with empirical data representing over 400 OSS systems, randomly selected from a popular OSS repository[4]. Initially, we classified these systems based on a number of process and product characteristics. In general, when one is studying patterns in software evolution, one could argue that the smaller the size of the system, the less likely it is that the system will display recognisable patterns in evolutionary behaviour. The evolution of a small system can be more easily driven by the decisions and actions of a small group of developers. On the other side, larger systems with larger number of developers and users are more likely to exhibit an *evolution dynamics* that is not under the control of a single individual, but the resultant of the interactions between groups of people who interact through complex feedback loops subject to information amplification, distortion and delay [Lehman and Belady, 1985,

---

[3] All software process activities, such as restructuring and refactoring, which are aimed at reducing the complexity of a software artefact without changing user-observed characteristics of the software were termed *anti-regressive* by Lehman. [Lehman, 1974]

[4] http://freshmeat.net (as of Sept 2005).

Lehman and Ramil, 2005a]. We argue that these larger systems are more likely to display repetitive and identifiable evolutionary patterns. In the present study of structural evolution we decided to focus primarily on the larger systems, but without excluding some smaller systems whose datasets are particularly complete. The larger systems are also likely to involve the more complex and richer functionalities and code structures, hence their relevance. Even though we are aware that the definition of 'large' can be arbitrary, for the present study, we define as such those systems whose size is 100 thousand lines of source code (KLOCs) or above. Furthermore, in order to achieve a more representative sample, we selected from the dataset eight somehow smaller systems, but with datasets particularly complete: For these eight smaller systems, we believe, all the releases in the system's evolution were publicly available for investigation. In total, the sample for the present study includes 25 OSS systems, which is what we could investigate within the time and the resources available. Some characteristics of these systems are listed in the appendix.

2. *Attribute definition and metrics derivation*: Since our focus is on measuring systems' evolution, we collected a set of metrics that include system's size, an indicator that is generally accepted as a surrogate of the functional power of the system and an important cost factor in systems developed by paid personnel[5] [Boehm, 1981]. Section 10.5 provides a description of this and other attributes.

3. *Parsing tools*: Automatic data extraction is key in systems' evolution analysis. In this study, we used off-the-shelf, freely available utilities (e.g. [Goenka, 2004]) for counting lines of code (LOCs). In addition, we built our own scripts for parsing source trees (these tools are available to anyone who wishes to replicate this study). Next, we used the *dot* graphic tool [Ellson *et al.*, 2006] for extracting source folder trees out of the extracted data, and, finally a practical extraction and report language (PERL) script to quantify the number of changes made in between subsequent releases.

4. *Data analysis and pattern recognition*: As in previous studies, basic plots and visualisations were used as a means to identify recurring patterns.

5. *Interpretation*: In addition to observing patterns, it is useful to formulate possible explanations for them. These can be based on the various *theories* of software evolution reflected in the existing literature (e.g. [Rajlich and Bennett, 2000, Nakakoji *et al.*, 2002]), new observations by the authors and insights provided by the documentation of the software, which is available on the Internet (see Chapter 16).

10.5 Attributes Studied

10.5.1 Source Code Size

The majority of studies on the evolution of software systems so far have involved one type or another of source code size metrics [Lehman and Belady, 1985], even though there are exceptions in which other data sources are used [e.g. Anton and Potts, 2001]. In this study, we measured source code size in three different forms as follows:

1. *LOCs*: The total amount of lines of code, which we usually counted through off-the-shelf utilities (*wc-l*, for instance).

---

[5] The identification of the determinants factors of the effort required in OSS development and evolution remains an open question but it is very likely that size will also play a role, as it does in systems developed by paid developers.

2. *SLOCs* (*source lines of code*): The total amount of SLOCs, that is, the number of LOCs remaining after blank lines and comments have been purged.
3. *KBs*: The size of a source file in kilo bytes.

10.5.2 Code Structure
10.5.2.1 Code Components

Research has been done aiming at correlating various structural evolutionary metrics to fault and failure discovery rates [Nikora and Munson, 2003], [Barry et al., 2003] based on the view that evolutionary characteristics may be directly related to a few common evolution attributes measured at the file or module level. This chapter focuses at a coarse level of granularity by measuring attributes of the whole system. For example, we deal with code structure in three different forms as follows:

1. *Source files*: All files that contain source code (e.g. '*.c')
2. *Source folders*: Directories containing at least one source file.
3. *Folder levels*: Each level in the code structure where topologically folders may be placed.

Files, folders and levels together form a structure that could be represented as a tree. Such a tree can provide some insight into the evolving architecture of the system, particularly when other architectural views are not available and are difficult to recover [e.g. Di Lucca et al., 2000].

10.5.2.2 Folders and Levels

We use the term *encapsulated* to refer to a folder that is contained inside another one. Each additional encapsulation leads to an increase in the depth of the source file structure; the number of encapsulations can be related to a depth-attribute, which we call *level*. This metric represents the distance from the top to the bottom of the tree (called *root*). Our interest is therefore to analyse the characteristics of the levels of folder structures, to observe maximum depth, the size of each level, patterns of change, and break points in the evolution of source folder trees.

10.5.3 Modification Types

Classifications of maintenance and evolution activities have been proposed over the years, for example, [Kemerer and Slaughter, 1999], [Chapin et al., 2001]. In this study we identified which files were added, modified or deleted between two subsequent releases, as briefly described in the following:

1. *Source additions*, calculated as the set of source files added in between two subsequent releases.[6]

---

[6] In the absence of distinct releases, and a Concurrent Version System (CVS) repository, the same approach may be used, comparing the same system in two different moments in time, separated by one week, one month and so on.

2. *Changed files*, calculated as the set of files modified in between two subsequent releases. File deletions may or may not be considered depending on whether information about these is available. For this study, we have not taken into account any file deletions if they occurred.
3. *Number of touched files* (or files handled [Lehman and Belady, 1985]), calculated as the cardinality of the union of the set of added files and the set of changed files during a particular release interval (the time between two consecutive releases). The percentage of touched files at release (or time period) j is calculated as the number of files touched at release (or period) 'j', divided by the total number of files present at '$j - 1$' the previous release (or period).

10.6 Evolution of Code Structure

When we observed the evolution of the folder structure, we recognised some recurring patterns. In a first attempt to categorising these patterns, we were able to identify basically three main cases. Here we briefly describe all of them, while in the next sections we discuss in some detail three software systems that are illustrative of each of these three types. Before discussing the types, we need to briefly introduce the notion of *articulated source tree*. By articulated source tree we mean a tree that consists of at least two or more levels, which in turn implies the presence of at least one sub-branch in the source folder structure. The three structural patterns that emerged are the following:

1. *Horizontally expanding*: A first pattern is characterised by the early presence of an articulated source tree at the first release available for study. The articulated tree continues to exist during the subsequent releases; no vertical growth is observed (or the number of levels does not grow), but there is horizontal growth in the existing levels. We observed this pattern in 10 out of 25 analysed projects.
2. *Vertically shrinking*: A second pattern is characterised by an initial articulated source tree that evolves into a source tree with a smaller number of levels. This vertical shrinking is not accompanied in general with horizontal shrinking: in other words, some levels get lost in the evolution of the source tree (vertical dimension), but we do not observe a decrease of the number of source folders (horizontal dimension) for the remaining levels. We observed this pattern in 4 out of 25 projects.
3. *Vertically expanding*: A third recognised evolution pattern starts with a simple tree structure which then evolves adding at least one level. We observed this in 11 out of 25 projects. In the majority of the cases, the pattern followed is a vertical expansion from an early articulated source tree. However, there are 3 systems from this set of 11 whose first observation was a simple source tree (consisting of 1 level only), which in turn evolved into an articulated one.

It is worth noting that a horizontally shrinking pattern did not emerge in any of the systems studied. That pattern simply did not exist in the dataset.

10.6.1 Horizontally Expanding

The first evolutionary pattern that we have identified is based on a structure whose vertical dimension remains constant over the entire observed evolution of the application: We observe, in general, a horizontal growth of new branches and leaves, but there's no growth in the vertical dimension, that is, the maximum depth keeps the same value. In some specific cases, new vertical levels were added in the evolution of the system, but then they were discarded in latter releases (e.g. the Grace system). In the following subsections, we will analyse a subset of the systems that display this first pattern, and we indicate some background information on their evolution in order to better understand and interpret the observed behaviours.

ARLA

The ARLA project made available its first public release[7] in February 1998, and its most recent release is labelled 0.35.12 (February 2003)[8]. Thirty-five major releases were developed. Sixty-two total releases are available on the Internet, which include 27 minor releases. ARLA project's main goal was to achieve similar functionality as the IBM AFS file system. It is likely that ARLA has currently achieved even more functionality than AFS. Its application domain is distributed file systems management, a domain in which a lot of knowledge is available and is openly shared. In this respect, this system is similar to flagships OSS successes (such as Linux or Apache). In ARLA's evolution, there have been two basic ways of enhancing and evolving the system: adding common features for the system (e.g. supporting of specific network protocols), and adding ports so that the system supports different configurations.

Observing its folders make-up, as measured by the number of files per folder level (Figure 10.2), we observe that the majority of the source code files have been located at Levels 2 and 3. Level 4 experienced a sudden mid-life increase at around release 25, accompanied by a sudden decrease at Level 3. Several new folders were added on Level 4. Other folders were moved to Level 4 from other parts of the system such as Level 3.

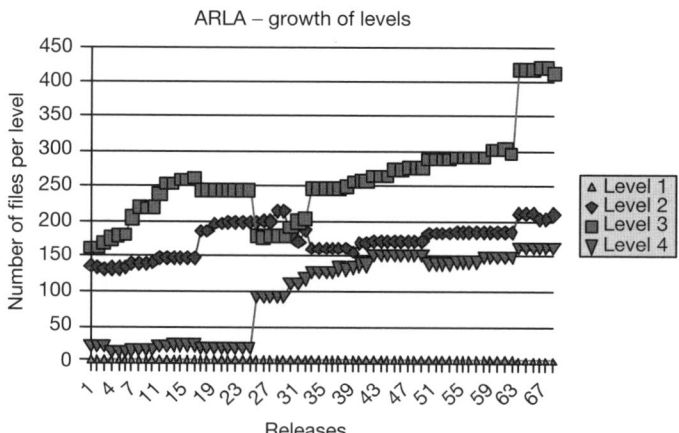

Figure 10.2 Number of files in each folder tree level for the ARLA system

---

[7] For some of the systems studied, the first release available for study is not the actual first release, but a later one. For this reason, in the figures and text that follow, the term release should be read *release sequence number*.

[8] There have been additional releases after the study reported in this chapter was completed.

Structural Analysis of Open Source Systems 215

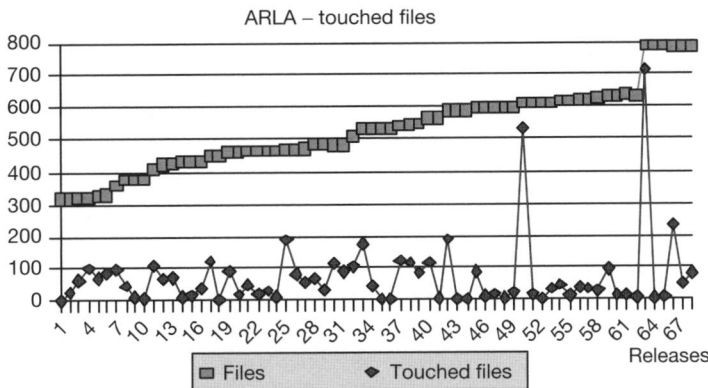

Figure 10.3 ARLA evolutionary trends: total size and files touched per release

In Figure 10.3, we observe the trend of the evolution of ARLA as depicted by the total number of source files and total number of touched files, both attributes plotted over releases. The growth trend can be interpreted as two segments of positive but decaying growth rate with a mid-life growth regeneration point at about release 32. The trend presents similarities with those observed in commercial systems [Lehman *et al.*, 1997, Lehman and Ramil, 2005a, Ramil and Smith, 2002]. The increase in the number of files at Level 4 and other folder changes at around release 30 in Figure 10.2 suggests that the regeneration in growth rate observed in Figure 10.3 is immediately preceded by some restructuring of the system.

In Figure 10.3 the number of files touched per release presents one major peak at release 50 (95% or so of the size of the system at the previous release was touched), while all other peaks of file touched do not surpass 60%. With the exception of the outlier around release 50, one can observe a predominantly decreasing trend with a superimposed oscillation in this attribute. The peaks correspond to the major releases. In the case of the ARLA system, the decreasing growth rate in the last third of its evolution history can be interpreted as a transition into a 'servicing stage', a period in which only essential changes to keep the system operational are made, [Rajlich and Bennett, 2000, Nakakoji *et al.*, 2002], as revealed by the declining evolution rate, suggested by the decreasing trend in the proportion of files touched. More recent releases of ARLA suggest that the system entered again into a phase of functional growth (right part of Figure 10.3). This in turn, suggests the need for some revision of Bennett and Rajlich's model for the OSS domain, since their model did not consider this type of transitions between 'service' and functional growth (what Bennett and Rajlich call 'evolution' stage).

10.6.2 Vertically Shrinking

The second evolutionary pattern observed is that of a structure that becomes less articulated as the system is evolved. This means that some branches are pruned from the source tree, so that the global amount of vertical levels is lower than the initial observations. As we did for the first pattern, we will show below evolutionary trends of an open source system that displays this pattern.

Gwydion-Dylan

Gwydion-Dylan is an object-oriented compiler supporting rapid applications development, and aiming to become a complete development environment. We observe 21 subsequent releases for this system, but they do not represent its whole life cycle, since its earlier evolution is not available for study, neither in the form of releases, nor in CVS storing. The available releases reflect 4 cycles of major releases, spanning over 1673 days.

We observe in Figure 10.4 that the first available data point is composed of 7 nested levels. It is likely that these have been accomplished through a previous series of releases for which we do not have data.

The folder structure of the most recently observed release is composed of only 5 levels. The evolution of source folders and files grow proportionally with the evolution of code (on its earliest stage: 64 source folders and 607 source files; on its latest stage 137 source folders and 1147 source files). A mid-life restructuring of the system is clearly observable in Figure 10.4 after release 11, which can explain the recovery of functional growth experimented by the system during the last half of the observed sequence of releases (Figure 10.5). The behaviour of the proportion of files touched for this system is displayed in Figure 10.5.

10.6.3 Vertically Expanding

The third evolutionary pattern is based on a structure that expands during the observed evolution of the application: this means that new branches are added in one or more sections of the tree, and new vertical levels appear. Besides, horizontal levels may be added, but we observed that there is not a clear relation between the growth in the two dimensions.

A case study is analysed in the following sections, and additional information, beside size and structure, is provided in order to gain insights on the observed pattern.

Vovida SIP Stack

Vovida is the system that has experienced one of the largest delta sizes (13 KLOC to 650 KLOC) in the dataset, when one considers the growth from the first to the most recent available release. Vovida is an open source application that implements the SIP (Session Initiation Protocol) stack protocol, for multimedia sessions. It is a particularly

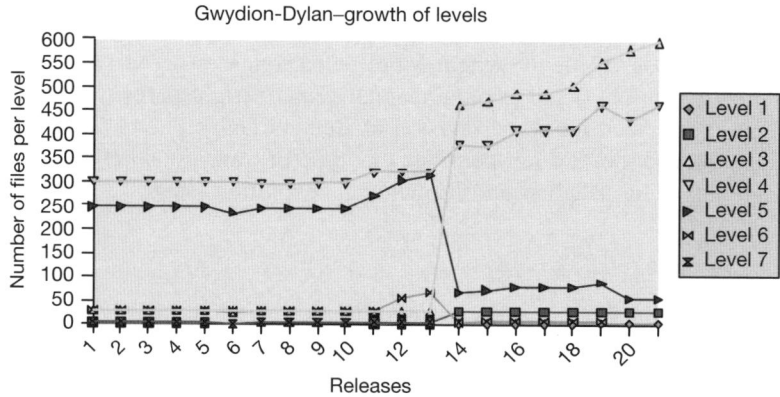

Figure 10.4 Number of files per level for Gwydion-Dylan

Structural Analysis of Open Source Systems

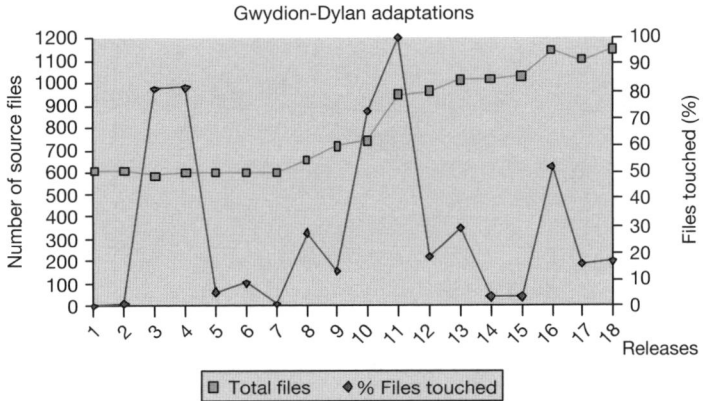

Figure 10.5 Files touched over releases for the Gwydion-Dylan

interesting application from the point of view of levels growth: We have been able to access the entire lifetime of this system, and it evolved through nesting several levels (from a single level in first release, to 8 levels in the latest available; see Figure 10.6).

In Figure 10.6, we can observe that starting with Level 1, next Level 2 and so on, all levels as well as new source files and folders were started to grow at different releases. The evolutionary trends suggest that a massive amount of evolution effort has been made in this application, in order to add new features and functionality.

As part of this large amount of effort in code additions, we observed that the source adaptation trend displays peaks with high values, suggesting again a high evolution rate (Figure 10.7). The rapid evolution rate of this system can be linked to a dynamic and growing community of developers interested in this type of application.

Despite the brief presentation given above of three systems illustrating the three different structural evolution modes observed, the visualisations suggest that folder tree metrics such as the size of the levels in the folder structure can provide further insights. For example, drastic changes in folder tree metrics suggest the presence of restructuring phases in the evolution of a system, which, in turn, can provide an explanation for the

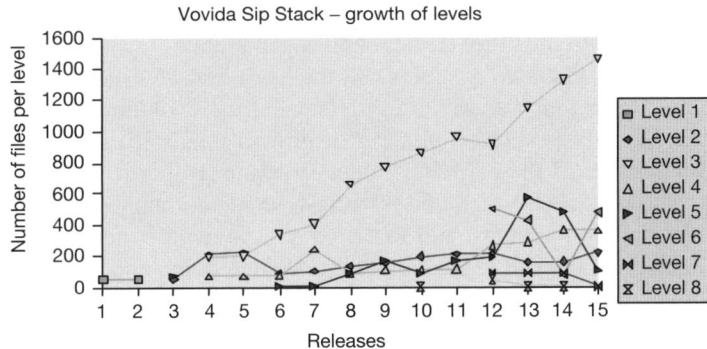

Figure 10.6 Number of files per level for the VOVIDA system

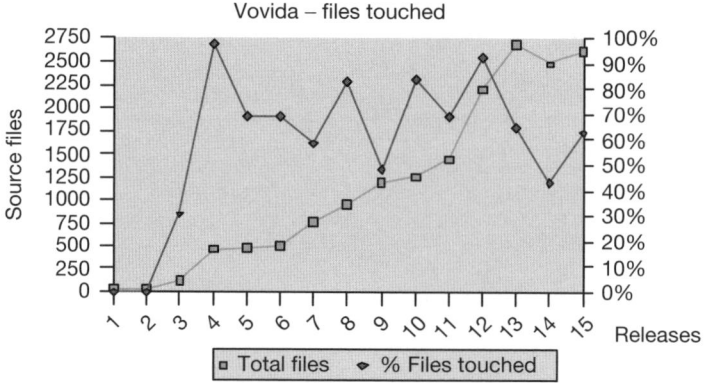

Figure 10.7 VOVIDA evolutionary trends: total size and files touched per release

recovery in growth rates observed in some of the systems. The relation between changes in the folder structure and files touched is not so clear at the moment.

The brief analysis presented above is only introductory and clearly more work is needed to relate these OSS observations to observations made in other studies of open source (e.g. [Scacchi, 2005]) and of proprietary systems (e.g. Lehman's Laws of Software Evolution [Lehman and Ramil, 2005a]). We also need further work to be done in order to better understand the evolutionary trends of the systems studied and the implications of the observed patterns for software development and management. The final sections of this chapter present a summary of our findings and topics for further work.

10.7 Summary

In this chapter, we have analysed the evolution of 25 OSS systems, possibly one of the largest datasets in a study of this kind. The systems studied are of different size ranging from 700 LOCs to 700 KLOCs and represent a diverse set of application domains. Seventeen out of 25 can be considered large systems given that their size at the most recently observed release is greater than 100 KLOCs.

These systems are a subset taken from a version history database of OSS systems that we have collected for our research. The systems in this database were randomly extracted from a popular software repository dedicated to open source. In this particular study we have sought to identify interesting patterns in the evolution of these systems, with focus on the source code. Our aim was to better understand the evolution of OSS systems and to relate traditional analysis such as plotting of growth trends [e.g. Lehman and Belady, 1985] with visualisation of the evolving folder structure. In particular, we are interested in topological patterns, that is when and how new source components are added, how do they relate to existing components, and to the existing overall structure. In this work, we define a *source file* as each single file containing source code, and *source folder* as each directory containing at least one source file.

The first pattern is based on an invariant code structure on the vertical dimension: we observed this pattern in 10 systems out of 25 analysed. Deepening the analysis of these 10 systems, we realised that in three of them the system has already been subject to evolution work before its first public release: a core group was in charge of developing the system before it became publicly available. This can explain why the system has a structure that is vertically stable at the first available release. Moreover, we observed a higher growth rate in some cases and slower in others. Next, we tried to identify why this was so, looking at details of the development process aspects without having a definitive answer. At the moment, we hypothesise that higher growth rate evolution trends will emerge for the systems which have a stable and flexible architecture and in which it was easier for potential contributors to become so, that is, where more effort and feedback was available (the ARLA system is a typical example of a system in which it is easier to become a contributor because of the provision of templates to the development of new port, for example).

The second recognisable pattern is when the vertical dimension (depth) grows. We had initially expected this as the predominant pattern emerging from our analysis, but we found the pattern on only 10 systems out of 25. What is more, several of these underwent some shrinks and expansions in the depth of the code tree, as well.

10.8 Current and Future Work

In this chapter, we have illustrated an approach for studying the evolution of software systems, which is mainly focused on a particular level of granularity: the structural level as reflected by the source folder structure. Similar to biological entities, software systems may be studied at other levels: the global level (its size), the level of its structure (its folder tree representation), the components level (its files and folders) and the subcomponent level (its functions, when dealing with procedural languages, or classes, when analysing object-oriented languages). Further work has been done and is still in progress in visualising these levels which together provide a rich description of the evolution of a system [Capiluppi and Ramil, 2004a]: multiple levels of granularity help to discover stages of evolution, similar to the ones described in [Rajlich and Bennett, 2000], as well as to highlight discrepancies among visualisations, as for instance, when stages observed at one level of granularity do not correspond to stages in other levels.

In future studies, we plan to relate the source folder view of software structural evolution and other structural views (for example, obtained through what is called *design recovery* [e.g. Di Lucca *et al.*, 2000]) with factors such as size and type of application, effort subsumed by the evolution work and the type of software process model being used. Further work needs to be devoted to identify which parts of the code show higher complexity than others and how this relates to the changes in the architecture of the system, as reflected by the folder structure. We have started some work in identifying which parts of the system are both highly complex and at the same time are subject to the higher evolutionary pressures [Capiluppi and Ramil, 2004]. We need to extend this work to cover the relationship between complexity at the file and function levels and the changes in the system's architecture as reflected by the evolving folder structure.

In our future work, we plan to continue the search for identifiable patterns of structural evolution and their interpretation. One of the challenges is to be able to interpret the patterns in terms of characteristics of the application domain, the process and programming methodologies. We plan to relate these to other system characteristics (like, for instance, the application domain of the software system). As in the past [Lehman and Belady,

1985], if further evolutionary patterns can be found and satisfactorily interpreted, they can provide guidelines to software developers with regard to good software evolution practice. However, the extent to which the results of the empirical study of the evolution of OSS systems can be applied in proprietary domains, and vice versa, remains to be investigated.

No matter what type of domain a software system belongs to, its empirical study can be useful in order to identify correlations between key evolutionary attributes, find recurring patterns, assess whether the system has evolved successfully and, in this way, eventually predict and even control how certain software systems are likely to evolve. However, much work is still required before achieving these aims.

10.9 Acknowledgements

Andrea Capiluppi acknowledges financial support from The Open University, UK. Juan C. Fernández-Ramil is grateful to the UK EPSRC for financial support via grant GR/S90782/01, CRESTES project, 2004/5.

References

Goenka V., "Extract Source Code Comment (XSCC)", A tool for extraction source lines of code, available online at http://members.tripod.com/vgoenka/unixscripts/xscc.html (as of January 2006).

Anton A., and Potts C., "Functional Paleontology: System Evolution as the User Sees It", *Proceedings of 23rd ICSE*, Toronto, Canada, 12–19 May 2001, pp. 421–430.

Antoniades P., Samoladas I., Stamelos I., and Bleris G.L., "Dynamical simulation Models of the Open Source Development Process". *Free/Open Source Software Development*, in S. Koch (ed.), Idea Group, Inc, 2003.

Aoki A., Hayashi K., Kishida K., Nakakoji K., Nishinaka Y., Reeves B., Takashima A., and Yamamoto Y., "A Case Study of the Evolution of Jun: an Object-Oriented Open-Source 3D Multimedia Library", *Proceedings of 23rd International Conference on Software Engineering, ICSE 23*, Toronto, Canada, 12–19 May 2001, pp. 524–533.

Barry E.J., Kemerer C.F., and Slaughter S.A., "On the Uniformity of Software Evolution Patterns", *Proceedings of ICSE 25*, Portland, Oregon, 3–10 May 2003, pp. 106–113.

Belady L.A, and Lehman M.M., "A Model of Large Program Development", *IBM Systems Journal*, vol. 15, no. 1, 1976, pp. 225–252.

Boehm B.W., *Software Engineering Economics*, Prentice Hall, Englewood Cliffs, NJ, 1981.

Capiluppi A., "Models for the Evolution of OSS Projects", *Proceedings of the 7th International Conference on Software Maintenance, ICSM*, Amsterdam, The Netherlands, 22–26 September 2003, pp. 65–74.

Capiluppi A., Lago P., and Morisio M. "Characteristics of Open Source Projects", *Proceedings of the 7th European Conference on Software Maintenance and Reengineering, CSMR*, 26–28 March 2003, pp. 317–327.

Capiluppi A., Morisio M., and Ramil J.F., "Folder Structure Evolution in Open Source Software", *Proceedings of the 10th International Software Metrics Symposium, METRICS 2004*, Chicago, IL, 14–16 September 2004, pp. 2–13.

Capiluppi A., and Ramil J.F., "Multi-Level Empirical Studies: An Approach Focused on Open Source Software", late breaking paper, (METRICS 2004), 14–16 September 2004a. http://swmetrics.mockus.us/metrics2004/lbp/Metrics2004_LBP.html (as of September 2004).

Capiluppi A., and Ramil J.F., "Change Rate and Complexity in Software Evolution", *Proceedings of the Ninth IEEE Workshop on Empirical Studies of Software Maintenance (WESS 2004)*, Chicago, IL, 17 September 2004.

Chapin N., Hale J.E., Khan K.M., Ramil J.F., and Tan W.G., "Types of Software Evolution and Software Maintenance", *Journal of Software Maintenance and Evolution: Research and Practice*, vol. 13, no. 1, 2001, pp. 1–30.

Di Lucca G.A., Fasolino A.R., and de Carlini U., "Recovering Class Diagrams from Data Intensive Legacy Systems", *Proceedings of ICSM 2000*, San Jose, CA, 11–14 October 2000, pp. 52–63.

Eick S.G., Karr A.F., and Marron J.S., "Does Code Decay? Assessing the Evidence from Change Management Data", *IEEE Transactions on Software Engineering*, vol. 27, no. 1, 2001, pp. 1–12.

German D., "Using Software Trails to Rebuild the Evolution of Software", *International Workshop on Evolution of Large-scale Industrial Software Applications (ELISA)*, Amsterdam, The Netherlands, 23 September 2003, http://prog.vub.ac.be/FFSE/Workshops/ELISA-Workshop.html, (as of Sept. 2003).

Godfrey M., and Tu Q., "Evolution in Open Source Software: A Case Study", *Proceedings of 2000 ICSM*, San Jose, CA, 11–14 October 2000, pp. 131–142.

González-Barahona J.M., Ortuño-Pérez M.A., de las Heras-Quirós P., Centeno-González J., and Matellán-Olivera V., "Counting Potatoes: The Size of Debian 2.2", *Upgrade Magazine*, vol. 2, no. 6, 2001, pp. 60–66, http://people.debian.org/~jgb/debian-counting/counting-potatoes-0.2/(as of June 2004).

Ellson J., Gansner E.R., and Koutsofios E., North S.C., and Woodhull G., "Graphviz and Dynagraph – Static and Dynamic Graph Drawing Tools", available online at http://www.research.att.com/sw/tools/graphviz/ (as of January 2006).

Kemerer C.F., and Slaughter S., "An Empirical Approach to Studying Software Evolution", *IEEE Transactions on Software Engineering*, vol. 25, no. 4, 1999, pp. 493–509.

Koch S., and Schneider G., "Results from Software Engineering Research into Open Source Development Projects Using Public Data", in *Zum Tätigkeitsfeld Informationsverarbeitung und Informationswirtschaft*, Hansen H.R., und Janko W.H. (eds.), Nr. 22, Wirtschaftsuniversität, Wien, Austria, 2000.

Lehman M.M., *"The Programming Process"*, IBM Res. Rep. RC 2722, December 1969, p. 46. Also as Chapter 3 in Lehman M.M., and Belady L.A. *Program Evolution: Processes of Software Change*, Academic Press, London, 1985.

Lehman M.M., "Programs, Cities, Students, Limits to Growth?", *Inaugural Lecture, Imperial College of Science and Technology Inaugural Lecture Series, vol. 9*, 1970, 1974, pp. 211–229. Also in Gries D. (ed.), *Programming Methodology*, Springer-Verlag, 1978, pp. 42–62. Reprinted as Chapter 7 in Lehman M.M., and Belady L.A. *Program Evolution: Processes of Software Change*, Academic Press, London, 1985.

Lehman M.M., "Programs, Life Cycles, and Laws of Software Evolution", *Proceedings of the IEEE Special Issue on Software Engineering*, vol. 68, no. 9, 1980, pp. 1060–1076.

Lehman M.M., and Belady L.A. (eds.), *Program Evolution – Processes of Software Change*, Academic Press, London, 1985.

Lehman M.M., Perry D.E., and Ramil J.F., "Implications of Evolution Metrics on Software Maintenance", *Proceedings of the 1998 ICSM 98*, Bethesda, MD, November 1998, pp. 208–217.

Lehman M.M., Ramil J.F., Wernick P.D., Perry D.E., and Turski W.M., *"Metrics and Laws of Software Evolution The Nineties View"*, *Proceedings of Fourth International Software Metrics Symposium, METRICS '97*, Albuquerque, NM, 1997, pp. 20–32.

Mockus A., Fielding R.T., and Herbsleb J.D., "Two Case Studies of Open Source Development: Apache and Mozilla", *ACM Transactions on Software Engineering and Methodology*, vol. 11, no. 3, 2002, pp. 309–346.

Nakakoji K., Yamamoto Y., Nishinaka Y., Kishida K., and Ye Y., "Evolution Patterns of Open-Source Software Systems and Communities", *Proceedings of International Workshop on Principles of Software Evolution (IWPSE 2002)*, Orlando, FL, 19–20 May 2002, pp. 76–85.

Nikora A.P., and Munson J.C., "Understanding the Nature of Software Evolution", *Proceedings of ICSM*, Amsterdam, The Netherlands, 22–26 September 2003, pp. 83–93.

Rajlich V.T., and Bennett K.H., "A Staged Model for the Software Life Cycle", *IEEE Computer*, vol. 33, no. 7, 2000, pp. 66–71.

Ramil J.F., and Smith N., "Qualitative Simulation of Models of Software Evolution", *Journal of Software Process: Improvement and Practice*, vol. 7, 2002, pp. 95–112.

Scacchi W., *"Understanding Free/Open Source Software Evolution"*, 2005, in this volume.

Shankland S., *"Linux Kernel Release Falls Behind Schedule"*, 2000, available on-line at http://news.com.com/2100-1001-240061.html?legacy=cnetandtag=st.ne.1002.thed.1003-200-1808165 (as of June 2004).

Smith N., Capiluppi A., and Ramil J.F., 2004, "Qualitative Analysis and Simulation of Open Source Software Evolution", *Proceedings of the 5th International Workshop on Software Process Simulation and Modeling*, 24–25 May 2004, pp. 103–112.

Stamelos I., Angelis L., Oikonomou A., and Bleris G.L., "Code Quality Analysis in Open-Source Software Development", *Information Systems Journal*, 2nd Special Issue on OS Software, vol. 12, no. (1), 2002, pp. 43–60.

The Scheme programming language, project available at http://www.swiss.ai.mit.edu/projects/scheme/ (as of June 2004).

Appendix

Table 10.A1 Various characteristics, such as size and length of evolution represented by the data for the 25 OSS systems studied

	Files ini	Folders ini	Files fin	Folders fin	KBs ini	KBs fin	LOCs ini	LOCs fin	SLOCs ini	SLOCs fin	Depth ini	Depth fin	Time interval (days)
Arla	321	31	658	69	1,831	4,091	63,663	162,218	40,009	108,838	4	4	1,820
Ganymede	473	28	478	28	5,455	5,646	221,893	229,110	123,093	126,955	6	6	558
Gwydion-Dylan	607	64	1,147	137	6,606	11,012	213,688	348,644	151,145	252,997	6	5	1,673
Ghemical	586	12	555	12	6,426	6,716	217,463	226,769	171,998	180,159	4	4	454
Gimpprint	7	1	136	14	305	2,206	11,156	80,567	9,172	61,895	1	3	1,304
Gist	778	27	1,067	37	4,098	4,519	172,111	190,933	126,987	131,401	5	4	1,436
Grace	91	4	310	14	2,025	4,428	73,691	157,919	63,423	113,668	2	2	2,730
Htdig	136	16	511	24	441	3,926	21,300	153,722	14,529	102,621	3	5	2,451
Imlib	27	4	36	4	2,631	2,692	52,651	55,839	50,300	53,163	2	2	1,277
Ksi	259	19	191	14	2,933	2,708	111,288	100,157	81,681	75,561	4	4	860
Lcrzo	19	3	235	9	197	3,658	6,409	109,323	4,955	70,517	1	6	1,435
Linuxconf	586	46	1,347	117	2,475	6,104	103,498	239,223	82,810	191,594	4	4	2,028
Mit-scheme	1,511	31	1,946	51	17,127	21,941	545,093	704,864	467,151	614,141	3	5	3,430
Motion	2	1	28	1	7	160	239	6,836	204	5,901	2	2	1,281
Mutt	120	2	201	6	1,131	2,391	48,640	96,415	37,477	70,171	2	3	2,032
Nicestep	44	4	140	17	1,173	2,414	33,990	74,441	27,555	59,729	1	2	1,168
Parted	52	6	122	16	417	1,354	16,911	51,907	12,431	38,720	3	3	1,405
Pliant	227	37	641	94	1,255	4,270	36,347	116,947	28,868	101,363	3	5	1,845
Quakeforge	396	17	696	58	3,815	5,696	172,946	233,534	123,234	175,377	5	5	1,268
Rblcheck	1	1	7	5	2	19	104	772	68	447	1	3	1,493
Rrdtool	113	10	153	26	1,926	3,025	86,138	128,211	68,695	102,298	3	4	1,634
Siagoffice	42	5	322	18	356	3,618	15,386	137,504	13,743	108,254	2	2	2,594
Vovida SIP Stack	49	1	2,618	135	13,307	19,809	13,307	665,749	7,406	398,938	1	6	1,309
Weasel	16	1	36	2	142	511	4,449	17,591	2,629	11,924	1	2	834
Xfce	207	12	450	69	1,323	8,450	46,808	277,423	35,317	225,736	2	3	1,662

NOTES:
- In the table header, 'ini' indicates size measured at the first publicly available release, 'fin' indicates size measured at the last publicly available release.
- Columns 2 to 13 represent various size measures
- Column 14 represents the length of the period studied for each software, measured as the interval between the first and the latest available releases available at the time in which this study was conducted (early 2004).

11

A Study of Software Evolution at Different Levels of Granularity

Elizabeth Burd

11.1 Introduction

The business environment is constantly changing, continually impacted, amongst many other factors, by global competition. The successful operation of a business lies to a large degree in its ability to meet ever-changing business environments and demands. All components of the business system have to react – people, business processes, organisational structure, hardware, software, data and others. They are all important in their own right. But the software that reflects business processes is probably one of the most expensive parts of the system to change. Software that is created to meet business needs is likely to become vital to the organisation that uses it rapidly. But what happens when those needs change? The software has to change too in order to accommodate those new demands. At this point, the process of system maintenance and evolution starts. Some authors have suggested that software maintenance and evolution subsume 70% of all system life cycle cost [Tracz88]. This figure can be even greater for long-lived applications, whose operational lifetime spans several years, even decades.

Though the implementation of requirement changes can be one of the most significant software maintenance drivers, there are many others. There might, for example, be a need for performance improvement, correction of identified errors, and adaptation to a new computing environment, improving comprehension of the system. Four different maintenance categories are identified, defined and discussed here [Lientz80]:

Perfective maintenance – this involves improving functionality of software, as, for example, in response to user's defined changes.

Corrective maintenance – this process involves the fixing of errors that have been identified within the software.

Adaptive maintenance – this process involves the alteration of the software due to changes within the software environment.

Preventative maintenance – this involves updating the software in order to improve upon its future maintainability without changing its current functionality, termed *anti-regressive* activity by Lehman [Lehman74]. More recently, the term *refactoring* has been proposed to refer to this type of activity [Fowler99].

Surveys by Lientz and Swanson [Lientz80, 81] suggested that 50% of the total maintenance cost can be attributed to perfective maintenance, 25% for adaptive, 21% for corrective and only four percent for preventive maintenance. A recent survey [Schach2004] suggests that on average corrective maintenance may subsume more work than what was found by Lientz and Swanson. However, the emphasis here is not in the precise figures but in the relatively small percentage of maintenance cost that is attributed to preventative maintenance. Such small portion is not a reflection on its importance, but it is as a consequence of pressures that maintenance teams are placed under. Preventative maintenance offers significant improvements in the simplicity of conducting maintenance interventions in the long term. However, preventative maintenance brings little to no immediate benefits and hence such changes are not high on the priority list of maintenance managers [Lehman74].

As a result of the neglect of preventive maintenance and ageing factors such as those to be discussed, systems age [Parnas94] and become ever more difficult to maintain. Systems become older, larger, and they lose their initial structure, become even more complex and less comprehensible. Added functionality and code implementing it are more or less orthogonal to existing function and structure but must communicate with an ever increasing volume of code [Turski2002]. Hence, such systems become what are often referred to as *legacy systems*. It has been estimated that, as a result, time spent in understanding such systems accounts for between 50 and 90% of the overall time of maintenance [Standish84].

Organisations must continually make decisions how to deal with their ageing software assets in order to sustain market competitiveness. The easiest way to solve the problem would seem simply to get rid of all old software. Not only the high cost but also the potentially long implementation delay and the substantial risk involved prevent the redevelopment of the legacy systems. In most cases, those systems are the only valid, but encapsulated, source of tacit business knowledge. After years of maintenance and evolution, the systems become more and more unreliable but represent the only accurate description of the implemented functionality. All this hinders or even prevents the undertaking of green field development of replacement systems.

A very important aspect for success of maintenance is the attitude towards the process. Despite its cost implications, software maintenance is generally perceived as having a low profile within software organisations. Often, management places little emphasis on maintenance-related activities. Moreover, in most cases changes have to be made so often and under such tight time pressure that there is no possibility to make them in an orderly manner by, for example, preserving the original system structure, avoiding repetition of code and constraining the impact of change. Changes are made in the simplest and quickest way. Unfortunately, however, changes that are simple to make do not necessarily prevent an increase in the current level of complexity of the code. Frequently, the reverse is true; the level of complexity is significantly increased. It is clear that to keep a software system maintainable for longer, more effort than usually applied is needed for preventive maintenance, evolutionary change where its purpose is not solely the satisfaction of a new business demand but it also promotes the improvement of the existing implementation.

Clearly, there needs to be a change in strategy to achieve reliable long-term software maintenance. The maintenance strategy that applies changes in the simplest possible way and neglects anti-regressive activity, that is, preventative maintenance, implies that over time legacy properties become common place; systems become ever more difficult to maintain and may well become unmaintainable. It is undeniable that difficult changes designed to enhance future maintainability are more difficult to justify to management both because they absorb more resources, funds and scarce expertise, and because stakeholders demand that changes be implemented as quickly as possible. To help managers justify such changes, it is important that the process is adequately studied in this context and that the relevant data is collected. The goal must be to provide support for managers in their justification of the long-term cost effectiveness of process changes that show no immediate return but extend the maintainable life of the system and have the potential to significantly reduce future maintenance costs. The data should also help them demonstrate the short-sighted consequences of currently common approaches and ensure that appropriate resources are devoted to the maintenance of all critical software applications, allowing preventative maintenance strategies to be adopted.

Thus, the focus of this chapter is to help provide maintenance managers with the resources to be able to justify preventative maintenance strategies. Thus, the aim of this work is to identify how legacy tendencies occur within software and to investigate approaches for their removal and ultimate prevention. The following section identifies some of the related work in the field of empirical studies of software evolution. Section 11.3 proposes the study of software evolution at three levels:

1. tracking the high level trends;
2. identifying modular structure of code such as removal and deletion of functions; and finally
3. tracking changes to the data.

Case study results are presented for each of the three levels. On the basis of the findings from the case studies some recommendations are made within Section 11.4. These recommendations are related, where applicable, to other studies of evolution. Finally, some conclusions are drawn in Section 11.5.

11.2 Existing Studies of Software Evolution

In 1999, Smith published a book entitled 'Designing Maintainable Software' [Smith99]. The book is based on both theoretical reasoning and his observation how maintainers undergo problem solving. Within the book he provides much helpful advice for a maintainer regarding cognitive structures, the meaning derived from naming conventions and the use of truncation. Though the book does not mention the concept of evolution, it is successful software evolvability that is surely its main objective. While this book is an excellent starting point for the achievement of an understanding of many of the problems of maintenance, it is still necessary to achieve full understanding of the process of software change over time if evolution is to be successfully controlled.

Lehman and his collaborators have conducted research into software evolution at the system level over a period of 30 years. The results of this work have provided high level descriptions of how software systems are likely to evolve. Their observations come from many large case studies they have conducted. The studies have resulted in what are known as the *Lehman Laws of Evolution* [Lehman74, 85, 97, 2004]. The set of laws as presently stated are given in the Table 11.1. These were initially stated in the 1970s [Lehman74] but have been periodically revised [e.g. Lehman97] as increasing insight and understanding have been achieved. They reflect general observations about software system evolution and the attributes of the evolution process and its product. They and the other results also lead to proposals as to how management of the process could be improved [Lehman2001]. The second law, for example, addresses the issue of complexity. Following the first law that states that real world programs must continually be evolved, and that otherwise their usefulness decreases, the second law states that as such a program changes, its complexity reflecting deteriorating structure increases unless work is performed to maintain or reduce it. Law five, termed as *conservation of familiarity*, highlights the phenomenon of safe incremental growth that such systems display. If this growth rate is exceeded, quality and usage problems and time and cost overruns are likely to happen. Together, these laws provide information upon which a high level maintenance strategy can be based, but other factors related, for example, to the nature of the changes to be invoked may have to be considered, for instance, when partial redevelopment is proposed to reduce legacy properties and improve future maintainability.

Eick [Eick2001] has identified a number of potential causes of code decay, which include inappropriate architecture, violations of the original design, imprecise requirements, time pressure, inadequate programming tools, an unsupportive organisational environment, programmer variability and inadequate change processes. Further to this, he has also identified a number of risk factors. These risk factors include issues relating to size, age, complexity, organisational turnover, the volume of requirements the system satisfies and the experience level of the developers. These risk factors differ from the causes raised but do, he believes, raise the likelihood of code decay. Rajlich [Rajlich2000] raises issues from the point of view of future change iterations. He states that software development lays two important foundations. These are the software team expertise and the system architecture. With regard to the system architecture, it is identified that the selection of architecture could either aid or hinder changes made through evolution. Thus, while both Rajlich and Eick agree on the major risk factors, according to Rajlich, the ability of an organisation to be able to successfully perform software change is determined not only by the type of previous changes made but also by decisions made during the initial software development. This would seem to highlight that preventative maintenance strategies are best performed on code developed to be supportive of evolution.

Many of the ageing causes or risk factors raised by Eick also highlight the impact of external influences of the evolution process. When studying software change, it must be recognised that many of the changes occurring within software are due to changes within the external environment within which the software is embedded [Lehman85] and which that software supports. Nanda *et al.* [Nanda2002] have investigated the complex interactions between a business environment and its supporting software. These investigations

Table 11.1 Most recent statements of the Laws of Software Evolution [Source: Lehman2004]

No.	Brief name	Law
I 1974	Continuing Change	An E-type system must be continually adapted else it becomes progressively less satisfactory in use, more difficult to evolve
II 1974	Increasing Complexity	As an E-type system is evolved, its complexity increases unless work is done to maintain or reduce it
III 1974	Self Regulation	Global E-type system evolution is feedback regulated
IV 1978	Conservation of Organisational Stability	The work rate of an organisation evolving an E-type software system tends to be constant over the operational lifetime of that system or segments of that lifetime
V 1978	Conservation of Familiarity	In general, incremental growth (growth rate trend) of E-type systems constrained by need to maintain familiarity
VI 1991	Continuing Growth	The functional capability of E-type systems must be continually enhanced to maintain user satisfaction over system lifetime
VII 1996	Declining Quality	Unless rigorously adapted and evolved to take into account changes in the operational environment, the quality of an E-type system will appear to be declining
VIII 1971, 1996	Feedback System (Recognised 1971, formulated 1996)	E-type evolution processes are multi-level, multi-loop, multi-agent feedback systems

have resulted in a way of monitoring environmental change and how this impacts on change requests to business software. This is an important contribution to the collection of data supporting the change process that, as was stated above, is of great importance to support evolution.

Parnas [Parnas94] identifies that software ageing is inevitable. He states that our ability to design for change depends on our ability to predict the future. He believes that such predictions are inevitably approximate and imperfect. Thus, making changes that violate the originally defined assumptions will be inevitable, and this justifies the need for prevention. He proposes a number of actions that software engineers need to take. These include:

- Aiming to reduce architecture deterioration. He proposes the introduction or recreation of structure whenever changes are made. He recommends that careful reviewing must ensure that each change is consistent with the intent of the original design.
- Upgrading the quality of the documentation continually. He states that this is essential to ensure that future changes are successfully implemented. Such an approach should be part of the change evaluation process as a means of ensuring that design consistency is maintained.

It seems that a common theme of the issues raised by the researchers is based on the importance of maintaining good system architectures. Within this chapter, investigations are carried out at the function level to study architecture and its relation to the overall evolutionary process and to investigate how preventative maintenance can be justified and best used to keep software so that it can be easily modified.

11.3 Case Study Approach

One approach to the investigation of change strategy is to examine successive versions of software applications and to identify the changes that have occurred as a result of the maintenance. In general, this requires a historical study of past changes. One begins with the earliest version of the software for which records are available and then follows, records, structures and analyses the subsequent evolutionary changes that have been implemented over the lifetime of the software. Unfortunately, since the benefits of evolutionary studies of software have yet to establish their significance and benefit within industry, the need to retain past versions and data regarding the environmental circumstances of changes is not generally foreseen. While the author has found very few applications with a record of versions over the entire lifetime of the software product, she has been successful in collecting a great number of systems and system versions on which to base the analysis.

A study of any code changes that are required can then be used to judge the success of the maintenance strategy. In this way, it is possible to later investigate the suitability of the performed restructuring on the code structure. Furthermore, from the accumulated data it is also possible to investigate potential benefits that code restructuring (one form of preventative maintenance) would have had on the future of the software if it had been applied earlier in the change process. While changes made in the past cannot guarantee the suitability of the restructuring approach, it does give an overall indication of its robustness.

The approach adopted by the author is to take successive versions of a software application and to investigate the changes that are occurring. Depending on the general data available regarding the environment of the changes, additional information (such as change logs and or change request forms) may or may not be used. Where possible, the case study is performed using as much information as possible to supplement the overall process. A number of different approaches are adopted, but the fundamental approach analyses changes to the general code structure and to the addition or removal of calls and data items.

The current approach has concentrated on gaining an understanding of the process of evolution at three main levels that are typified by properties such as those indicated:

- *Level 1 – the system level*: it involves the intensity and frequency at which modifications are made to the application in general and the parts of the software affected.
- *Level 2 – the function level*: this level is reflected by the changes in the calling of procedures including additions, deletions and movement of procedures within the call hierarchy.
- *Level 3 – the data level*: this level is represented by changes in data usage (including additions, deletions and movement of data items across procedures).

Broadly speaking, the levels constitute three levels of granularity. The following subsections indicate the research contributions that have been made at these three levels. Although for the sake of brevity, only one example is given to demonstrate each principle or result identified, other case studies conducted across different domains and development languages have revealed similar examples to those presented below [Burd2000c, Burd99c].

For the purpose of this study, four different applications have been analysed. Three of these code samples are from industrial software and one application is the open source GNU software. Half of the industrial applications are commercial retail applications, the remaining two represent operating system and compiler technology. The applications are written in a variety of languages including C, COBOL and an in-house development language. Each of the applications has a long revision history. For each application, a number of successive versions of the software have been analysed ranging from 4 to 30 versions. The version histories only represent a snapshot of their life; sample data is unavailable from the earliest versions of each of the applications. Thus, this chapter uses the term 'Sample Version' to represent this snapshot. In total, approximately 5 million lines of code have been analysed. Table 11.2 summarises these descriptions.

None of the companies involved had a formally defined approach towards preventative maintenance but two of the companies in particular rated maintenance highly and acknowledged that they were constantly seeking ways in which to improve the maintainability of their software. For the GNU software, contacting the current maintainers (the maintainer for 13 of the versions analysed) identified that an *ad hoc* strategy of preventative maintenance was employed, only when time permitted.

Since this analysis involves a number of different programming languages and each of these different languages uses different terms, this chapter seeks to reconcile these terms for clarity. The chapter uses the term 'procedural unit' to refer to the concept of function within the C language and SECTIONs within COBOL. In addition, the term 'call' is used to describe what are also termed *calls* within the C language but PERFORMs within COBOL. The data analysis uses the term 'data item', which refers to each data set manipulated within each application.

This analysis process uses *reverse engineering* as a mechanism to identify the maintainability trends of the software applications under analysis. A reverse engineering process seeks to provide an abstraction of the source code in a form that promotes understanding. It does not make changes to the system but supports the process of understanding as to how these changes should be made and thereby provides a potential to support later *reengineering*.

The approach adopted within this chapter is to represent the 'system's components' at a procedural unit level and the interrelationships between these components by data items. This chapter therefore compares data and procedural changes across versions of each application as a means of investigating the process of increasing (or decreasing) software data complexity.

Table 11.2 Software applications studied – Size is that of the most recent version available for study

	Domain	Language	Number of versions	Approx. size in lines of code
Application 1	Retail	In-house	8	10,000
GCC Application	Compiler	C	Up to 30	300,000
Application 3	Operating system	C	4	20,000
Application 4	Retail	COBOL	4	40,000

The approach in the analysis process was as follows:

1. The *calling structure* of each version was analysed and comparisons were made as to the changes that had been made across versions. All modifications were recorded including the addition, or deletion of procedural units and the addition, or deletion of existing calls within a specific procedural unit.
2. The data usage within each procedural unit was analysed, and changes made to the data usage across versions were recorded. In particular, the addition of new data items or removal of existing data items was recorded.

In order to gain an indication of the effect of different maintenance strategies the four different applications are compared. In addition to this, the maintenance managers of the companies providing the software have been interviewed in order to assess their understanding of the applications' current state with regard to maintenance.

During maintenance, there are often many ways in which a change can be performed. For instance, some changes may be more quickly made through the duplication of code when a change avoiding such an approach is likely to be more complex and time consuming. Current time pressures placed on maintainers will often mean that the first of these options is selected. This case study is performed in order to investigate the frequency of poor maintenance strategies being adopted and to investigate the consequence over time to the software of any undesirable modifications being made.

The results that have been identified from carrying out this process are given in the following section.

11.4 Results

11.4.1 The System Level

To gain a deeper understanding of software evolution at the system level, it is interesting to study a software application as a whole and to investigate how applications change over time. For large applications, this requires one to study the system at a high level of abstraction. Lehman and colleagues have studied this particular area in detail as described elsewhere in this volume. Hence, this level will be considered only in outline here, and this chapter provides more detail and focuses more on the other two, less studied, levels.

Within Figure 11.1, an application is represented at the file level. This represented application is the Gnu C compiler (GCC). In Figure 11.1, each column represents a version of the software. This figure represents the sequential release of 30 versions from the first release of version 2. Moving from left to right, the age of the software increases. Each row represents a different file within the application. Figure 11.1 highlights where changes have been made to one or more of the system files. Those files, which are changed within a specific version, are shaded. Those files, which remain unchanged within a version, are left unshaded. Files that are later added to the system are represented as a change for that version.

Figure 11.1 has been sorted on the basis of the number of changes. Those files that are most frequently changed are at the top of the diagram. Those files changed least frequently are shown towards the bottom. From the diagram, it is possible to see a number of characteristics of changes. Those changes with columns most heavily shaded represent major changes within the software. Those columns with only a few changes may, for instance, represent the result of small defect corrections.

It is interesting to see how most of the changes are made to relatively few of the files, especially, when the major software changes are discounted. Specifically, 30 or 40 files seem to be changed in each software version. It is therefore likely to be these files that are in most need of preventative maintenance as these either represent the core procedural units of the application or they are hard to understand and therefore are a frequent source of misunderstandings and so often require defect fixes. Currently, investigation into these issues is an area of continued research.

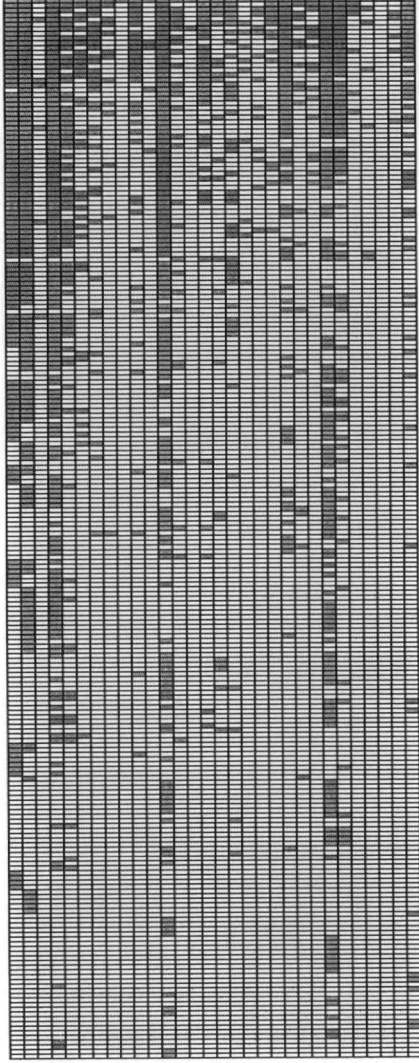

Figure 11.1 Versions for the GCC Application

Other applications that have been studied have shown similar trends although for most applications that have been analysed, it has not been possible to investigate change over so many versions owing to the unavailability of the source code versions. What remains consistent is that for each application a core set of files can be identified as those that are most likely to change.

Eick *et al.* [Eick2001] suggest that one way by which evidence of decay can be identified is to look at temporal behaviour and changes. Turski [Turski2002] also makes a reference to the importance of this criterion. Figure 11.2 shows the changes and temporal measures for the GCC application.

Figure 11.2 shows the number of changes and the time to make these changes. A high number of changes should represent large commitments in time, whereas the minor changes should represent much shorter time commitments. Applications not showing this trend may indicate the presence of legacy properties. For instance, a resulting small modification to a software application that has taken a long time to perform may indicate the need to spend considerable time performing program comprehension. This is particularly likely to be the case when one observes that increasingly greater time commitments need to be allocated per change as the age of the application increases.

From the graph within Figure 11.2, it seems that within the early versions of this application the time commitments are proportionally less than the number of changes. For instance, Sample Versions 2 to 8 on Figure 11.2 show this trend. For the later versions, larger time commitments seem to be necessary. For instance, with changes 26 and

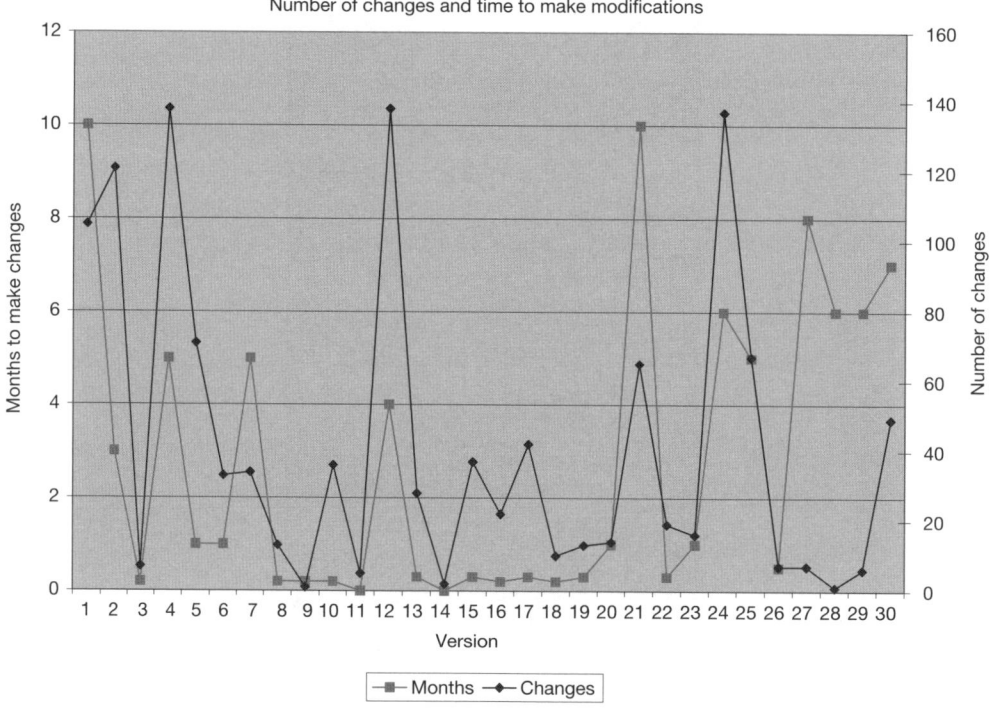

Figure 11.2 Changes to the GCC application and time to make them

onwards the months required for making the required changes are proportionally greater. When compared across the lifetime of the software, a definite increase in time commitments per change can be seen. This may therefore imply that the software is developing legacy tendencies.

Other research conducted at the system level is concerned with the gradual but consistent increase in size of source code, changes in the number of comments and in the number of functions [Wohlin99, Burd99a]. These additional studies seem to be consistent with the findings of Lehman and his colleagues. In addition, Wohlin [Wohlin99] identified that metrics need to be collected to enable full control of evolution. Turski [Turski2002] identified the need to consider various code grouping policies and their relation to issues of varying levels of module complexity within an application. Such an approach is similar to that adopted by Godfrey [Godfrey2000] in their studies of the Linux operating system. While investigating system growth they arrived at the conclusion that the modular structure of the code and the integratedness of the application are major contributors in the growth rate of the application. These research findings, therefore, would seem to point to the need to study the process of change at different levels by comparing different modules within the system in order to be able to identify the specific ageing trends of an application accurately. The advantage of such an approach would be the ability to make recommendations of the need for preventative maintenance for specific modules.

11.4.2 Level 2, The Function Level

Research at this level has concentrated on the evolution of the calling structure of code and to a lesser extent the control structure. Work at this level reveals more about the changes in complexity of individual source code modules and highlights the results and implications of specific change requests in a detailed manner. Such results are essential to fully understand the effects, detrimental or otherwise, of software evolution as a whole and how the change process will affect the future changes required. Specifically, with studies at this level of granularity, it is possible to gain an understanding of the evolution process from the point of view of changes to the comprehensibility of a source code module. It is this change in comprehensibility that will directly affect the future maintainability of the module under investigation.

Studies by Burd and Munro have identified some of the effects of software change [Burd99a, Burd99b, Burd99c, Burd2000b, Burd2000c] relating to the calling structure of the application and how this alters during the lifetime of a software application. Their studies have shown how the modular structure of the code changes. Within Figure 11.3 a call structure change is represented. This is a commercial COBOL application referred to as Application 4 in Table 11.2. The representation of the software on the left of the diagram shows a single module from an early version of the software. The figure shows that three modules result from the single module because of the evolution process. The cause of this splitting process is due to the addition of new functions to the module. In the case of Figure 11.3, these new units are represented as the shaded nodes. The result of the process of evolution shows, as identified by [Parnas94], that since such addition of functionality is inevitable, then if change processes are to support the changing needs of the business, there is a need for existing modules to be designed to allow them to split over time. Furthermore, this splitting process needs to be formalised so that splits occur at appropriate places and the structure of the application is redesigned to accommodate

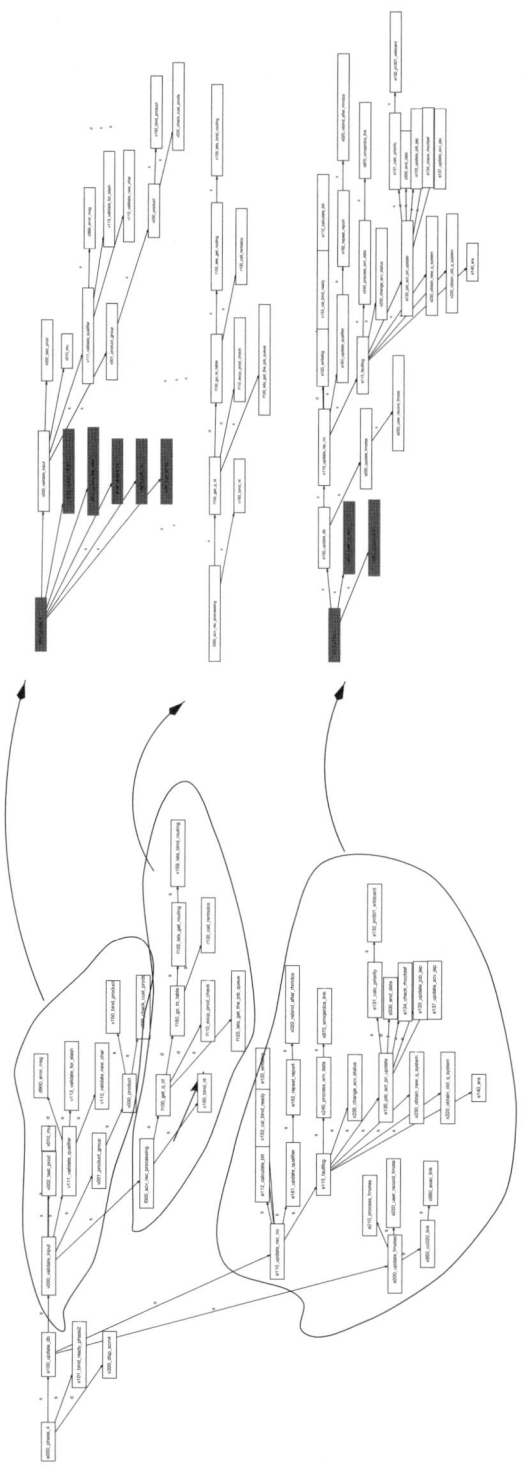

Figure 11.3 Changes in calling structure

such changes. Failure to take account of this need is likely, over time, to be detrimental to the comprehensibility of the application.

Further studies into this phenomenon have indicated that it may be possible to predict the likely places where additional functionality will be added. From studies, it has been identified that where splitting of the modules occurs, it occurs in a specific location of the tree structure. Specifically, this usually occurs, when the module is represented as a tree based on dominance relations [Burd2000d], at a position in the tree where there are a number of branches occurring from a node (i.e. the node has a high fan-out to other nodes). In terms of the calling structure, this equates to a function that calls many other functions. Examples of likely candidate locations for the module splitting are highlighted with arrows within Figure 11.4.

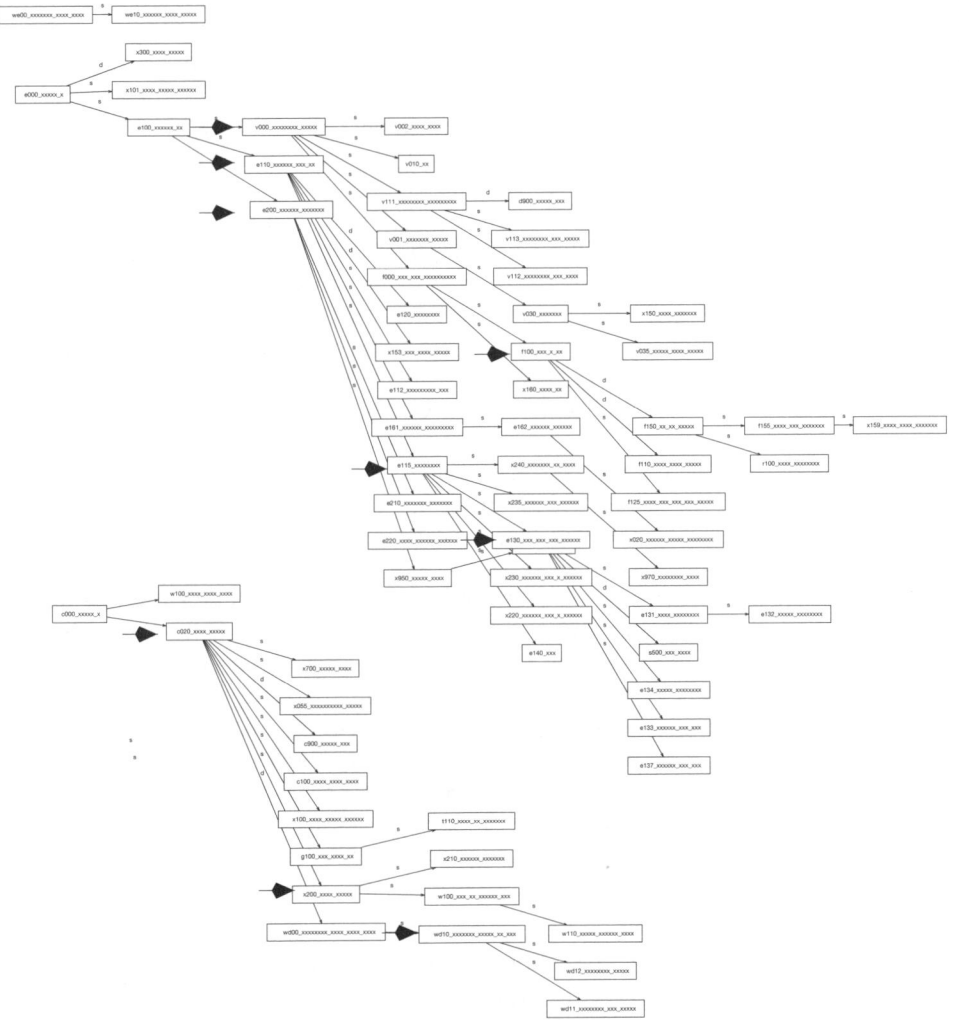

Figure 11.4 Potential portions of dominance tree where splitting is possible

With this knowledge, precautions can be taken in the identified areas to enhance comprehensibility, thus increasing potential adaptability. The benefit of this is that the focus of preventative maintenance can be usefully conducted in more detail than at the file level as highlighted in Level 1. This kind of revelation regarding the evolution of software applications can be used to direct the software development process. Furthermore, it assists the knowledge of the cost benefit process for change management by indicating areas where localised redevelopment may enhance adaptability and thereby reduce some of the legacy properties of software.

Examples of the splitting process have also been identified within applications written in C. However, other interesting properties have also been found within the C applications. In particular, this is the feature of increasing depth of the call structure over time. In general, it has been found that the COBOL applications studied had a greater call depth than the C applications. In most cases, the increase is by approximately two levels.

The call graph depth is an important evolutionary feature owing to the effect that call depth has on the comprehensibility of code. The greater the call depth the more difficult the task is as it will place a greater strain on the maintainer short-term memory. Call depths that are increasing, especially to a level greater than the capacity of short-term memory, are thus representative of worrying evolutionary trends. This feature is similar to Eick's [Eick2001] concept of 'bloated' code.

One example of the process of increasing call depth to software over time is the addition of a new call. An example from the GCC Application is shown in Figure 11.5, where a new call is placed between the two nodes to the graph on the left. The result of the addition of the call is shown in the graph to the right of Figure 11.5, which shows an increased depth of the call structure in the later version of the software. These studies at the calling structure level, once again seem to show an increase in comprehension complexity as a result of the process of software change and hence the possible emergence of legacy properties.

Antoniol *et al.* have conducted further, similar studies at the function level. These studies have recorded changes in class hierarchies within object oriented C++ code [Antoniol99]. Some of the problems that have been identified within these studies are concerned with how the changes are recorded. For instance, when procedural units are added, additional calls must be used to make use of the new functionality that has been inserted. When gross counts are made of additions/deletions of calls, the inclusion of new procedures can distort the results. For this reason, it is also necessary to record why the new calls have been added. The level at which it is necessary to record information (the granularity issue) and precisely what information should be recorded are still issues requiring further study. Therefore, the process of documentation alignment with system change is vital for evolutionary changes to be reviewed. A proper documentation will enable software engineers to trace the environmental pressures that could have triggered a particular change and, hence, they will be able to better understand it.

11.4.3 Level 3, The Data Level

Burd and Davey have also conducted some studies at Level 3 [Davey2000, Burd2000c]. Specifically, these studies have focussed on changes in data usage across versions of a single software module. The results of the findings have been varied, but some of these, which are more revealing about the process of software evolution, are described here.

A Study of Software Evolution at Different Levels of Granularity

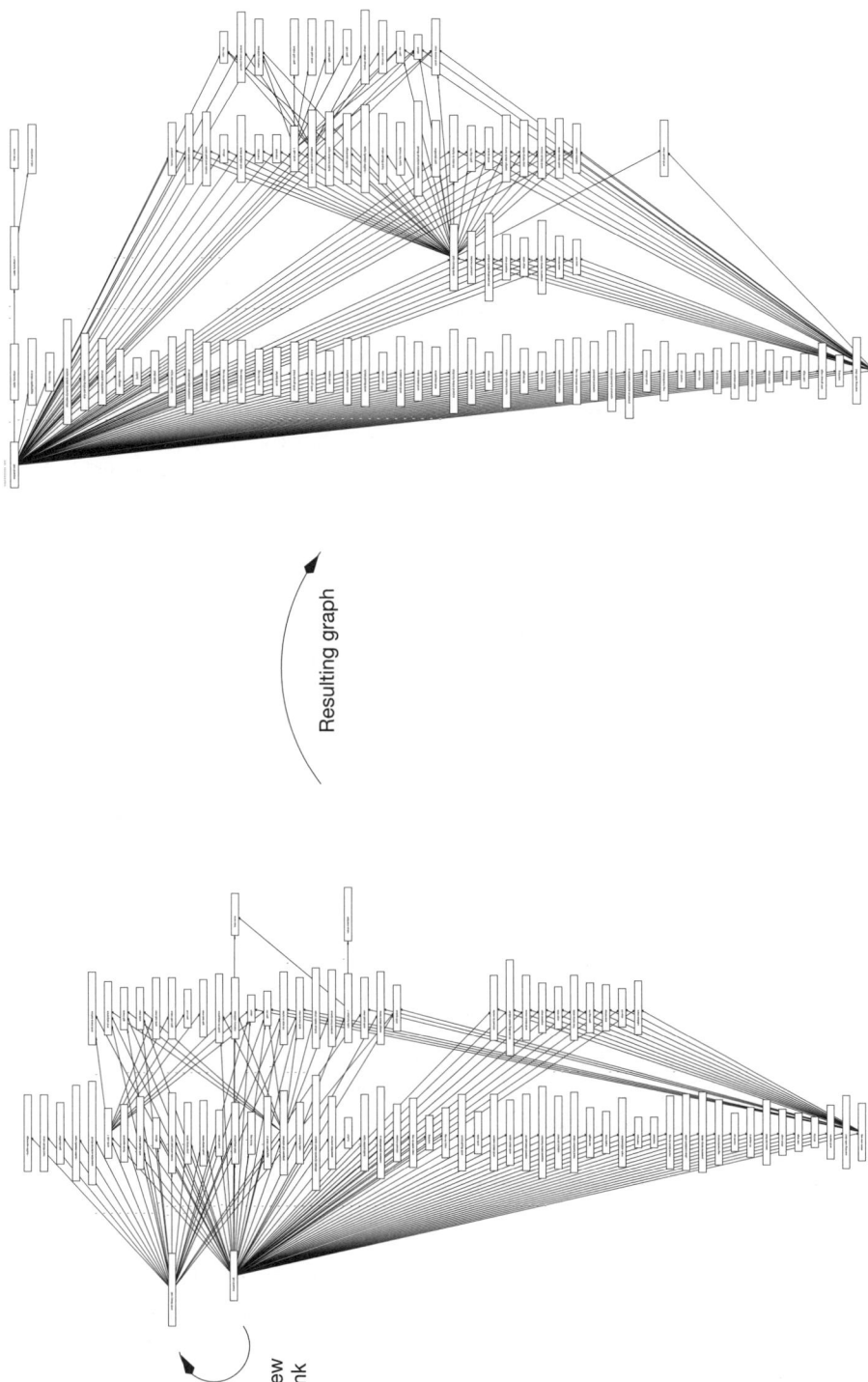

Figure 11.5 Addition of a new call and resulting increase in calling structure

Details at this level are harder to obtain owing to the variety of document sources that must be available and the sheer volume of information that must be collated.

The first of these results is the process of de-localisation of data due to the continued change process. Within Figure 11.6 a COBOL module from Application 4 is represented. The rectangles represent the SECTION within the software module. The figure identifies the change in the usage of a single data item. Where a particular SECTION uses the data item the SECTION is shaded. It can be seen from Figure 11.6 that initially the data item is local to one SECTION but over time (moving left to right) the data item is introduced into 1/3 of the SECTIONs of the software module. Because of the nature of COBOL, for which all data items are global, the consequence of the distribution of these data items is considerably more problematic than for other languages.

The consequence of this to comprehension and change of COBOL applications is great; change ripple effects will be greatly increased, as will the amount of information that maintainers need to comprehend in order to gain an understanding of the change [Burd2000a]. Of course, this is less problematic for other languages, but overall this is a major consequence to maintenance costs due to the large quantity of applications being actively evolved, which remain within the COBOL language domain.

While a single data item is presented in the example above and an argument is made with regard to the increase in complexity of the application owing to the ripple effects, what must be considered is that this figure only represents a single data item. The results of the case studies have identified that the duplication of data items is a general trend within the application and that many data items in an application will receive similar treatment. The consequence of the replication of a single data item as shown in the above text is serious. However, the situation in terms of the software complexity is, in fact, far worse.

Figure 11.7 shows an example from the COBOL code where this general process of increasing data complexity can be identified with many data items becoming de-localised. The figure shows the changes that are occurring within the data usage for each SECTION. Comparisons are made between the data items within a specific SECTION in the earliest version of the software and compared with the data usage of the identical SECTION, but in a later version of the software. As stated above, within the COBOL application all data items are global, thus usages of the same data item within a number of SECTIONs mean that each one must be consulted when a change is applied. The graph in Figure 11.8 shows an overall change in the number of SECTIONs for all data items.

Within Figure 11.7, half of the graph shows data items that are in fewer SECTIONs (those to the left and labelled 'Removal of data items'), whereas the other half of the graph represents the addition of data items. For instance, it can be seen that from the left-hand side, 5 data items have been removed from 4 SECTIONs. Thus, in this case the complexity of the relationships between SECTIONs can be said to be decreasing for these specific data items. However, most of the changes appear in the right-hand side of the graph that relates to the addition of data items. It can be seen on the right-hand side that over 20 data items have been added to another SECTION, but in addition 6 data items have been added to more than 10 SECTIONs. Thus, the graph shows a definite increase in relative data complexity of Application 4 owing to the addition of data items.

Littman [Littman86] identified that the only realistic way of gaining an understanding of an application under maintenance is to adopt what he refers to as an 'As needed strategy'.

A Study of Software Evolution at Different Levels of Granularity

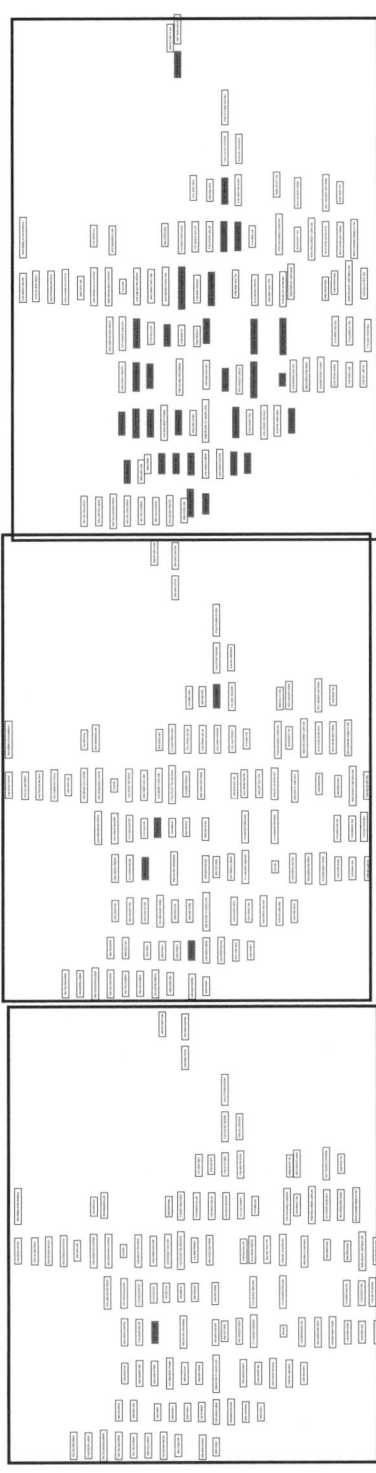

Figure 11.6 Changes to a local data item over time

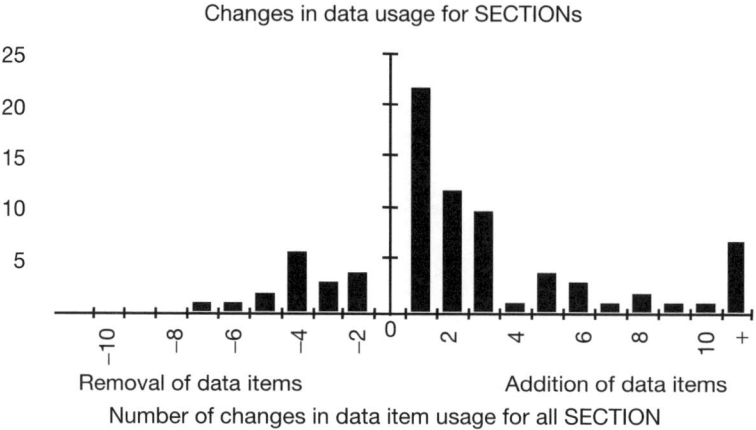

Figure 11.7 Showing the changes in localisation and de-localisation of data

This strategy involves a situation where only a localised understanding of the area to be modified is gained prior to the commencement of maintenance. Littman states that other approaches are unrealistic, for instance, understanding the full application, owing to the size of applications under maintenance today. This partial understanding for de-localised COBOL application may lead to problems during maintenance when unforeseen effects may result from locations within the code which were not considered, as for instance, where previous changes and additions of data items have resulted in an increasing data de-localisation.

Other increases in complexity, at least partly resulting from this phenomenon have also been identified. One of these is an increased complexity in the data interface between subsystems within a software module. An example of this finding is shown within Figure 11.8 of Application 4.

In Figure 11.8, the shaded squares represent sub-systems and the text boxes represent data items. This figure represents the clear interface of data and sub-systems within the initial version of the software (to the left) but shows how this structure is corrupted owing to the evolution process. This is an example where changes have not been made in a way to preserve the system architecture.

Davey, [Davey2000] studying data clustering in Application 3, also found evidence of the data structure being corrupted because of maintenance. Furthermore, he also found evidence of this process being undone when new maintainers were given the task of performing preventative maintenance. From interviewing the managers of the company, it was clear that these expert maintainers have specifically been brought in to deal with the perceived inflexibility of the system to change. This result had major implications on the comprehensibility and future adaptability of the software module. These results are also highlighted within Figure 11.9.

Despite the relatively little amount of work that has been conducted in this area, these results would seem to imply that it is critical that this area is studied further. This work has shown examples where complexity of the software dramatically increases over time.

A Study of Software Evolution at Different Levels of Granularity 241

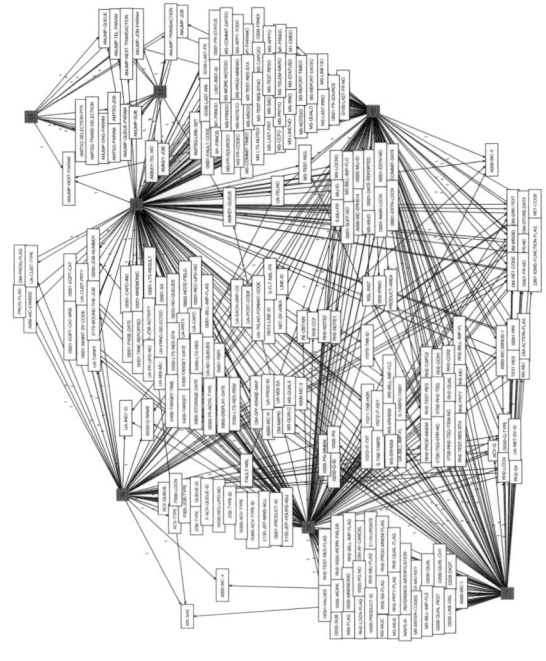

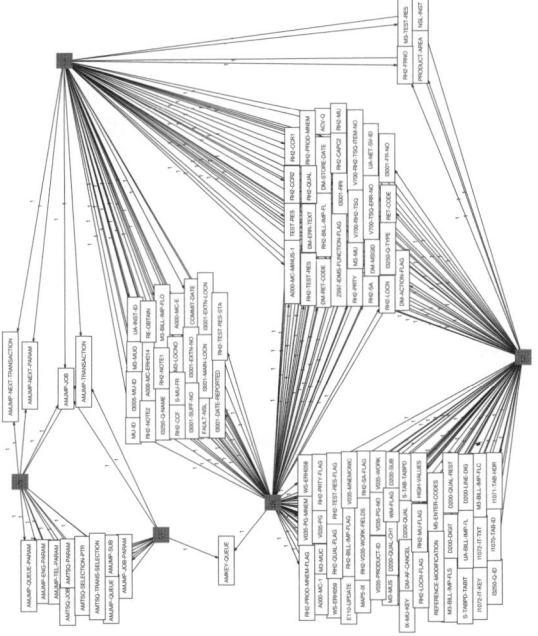

Figure 11.8 Overlap of data usage between sub-systems

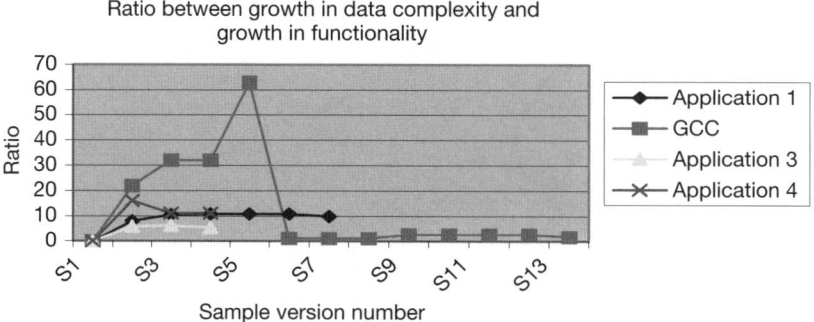

Figure 11.9 Comparing the results of analysis of Levels 2 and 3

11.4.4 Comparing Levels

In order to gain an even greater understanding of the different maintenance trends of applications, the results of call and data analysis can be compared and then related to the evolution of the application as a whole. The approach adopted is to compare the proportion of data items modified and function call changes within each of the applications for each available version. Thus, to compare the results of the analysis of Level 2 and Level 3 it is necessary to relate this to what implications this will have for Level 1.

In order to gain an understanding of the overall changes in complexity of an application, analysis is performed of the changes in data items used within the application. This is then compared to the changes in new procedural units added and modifications to the numbers of calls made within the application to these procedural units. The analysis performed uses a simple metric of the total addition of data items minus the total data items deleted. A similar calculation is made for new functionality and calls to these procedural units. Figure 11.9 shows the results of comparing the proportion of changes to the gross data item change with that of the calls. Studies by Burd and Munro [Burd2000a] have highlighted the fact that there appears to be a tendency for maintainers to preserve the original structure of the architecture of the procedural unit's call structure to the detriment of the code in terms of significantly increasing the complexity of the application's data manipulation. Using the above metric, an indication of this problem would be highlighted by a significant increase in data representation compared to a relative small increase in the addition of new functionality and calls to that functionality. In terms of the application, this most likely represents the fitting of new functionality into the existing procedural units, for instance, increasing the use of control flow statements such as conditional statements. The likely consequence of this action is to widely disperse the new functionality (to maintain the existing structure). Over time the consequence that this has to maintenance is that because of the distributed nature of changes they will take longer to carry out and will be more complex to perform. On this basis, it can be assumed that an application suffering these properties is likely to be subject to an increase in legacy properties. The results of this analysis process are shown within Figure 11.9. The figure does not represent each application from creation as not all data sets have been retained by their owners, and thus sequential sample releases are shown. Thus, the sample number used here does not necessarily refer to actual version numbers of that software. The graph can be interpreted that steep raises for an application highlight potential increase in the legacy properties. Likewise, significant falls are representative of major positive changes to an application. For instance, they may highlight that during the last maintenance intervention, a significant amount of preventative maintenance work was performed. On this basis, a levelling off of an application would indicate that its complexity levels were under the control of the maintenance team.

The graph within Figure 11.9 represents the proportion of data items modified per call change for each of the four applications. The most important features of the graph are the rises and falls of the data/function proportions. This graph would seem to indicate that between Sample Version S1 and S6 (the GCC application) there is a considerably higher proportion of data per call additions than was necessary with changes made to the later versions. A very steep rise (i.e. S4–S5) for this application may indicate that the application was quickly gaining legacy properties during this time. Interestingly, this is followed by a steep fall (i.e. S5 – S6). This would seem to indicate that at this point a preventative maintenance approach had been adopted.

For the other applications represented within Figure 11.9, slight falls within the later sample versions of the software's evolution can be observed. For instance, this phenomenon can be seen within Application 1 and Application 3. From the above graph, it can be observed that the GCC application promotes a steep rise between Sample Version S1 and Sample Version S5. Likewise, the same observation can be made with Application 4 between Sample Version S1 and S2. However, similar to the GCC application each of these applications shows what would appear to be an eventual regaining of control over the application's evolution.

In order to verify the above observation, further investigation needed to be conducted, involving contact with the maintenance teams of these applications, to investigate whether these interpretations matched those of the applications' maintainers. When interviewing the maintainers, no indication of the results of this analysis process was revealed until their interpretations of the lifetime of the software were obtained. The investigation concentrated on areas where significant increases in perceived complexity have been reduced and where any legacy features were seemingly brought under control. The results of this investigation revealed that at each of the points where preventative maintenance appeared, it seemed to have 'turned around' the application. That is, a significant event in the lifetime of the application had occurred.

The company responsible for Application 1 reported that there had been a change in the maintenance team and that the application had been given to the control of one of their best teams. Application 2 was reported to have been involved in a significant remodularisation review by a number of independent maintenance experts and their recommendations were taken into account with each new release. For Application 3 at sample version point 2, there had been a change in ownership and further, in order to make required changes to the application, the software had been restructured. Finally, for the GCC application, it was reported that housekeeping work has been performed for sample release 7. From the descriptions given above of the lifetime of the software, it can be seen that in each case some form of preventative maintenance work has been performed, and thus this metric used would seem to be an indicator of legacy properties and their removal.

The above analysis, which shows some of the interactions between Levels 2 and 3, also raises some interesting points relating to Level 1. From the strategies adopted by the companies involved, it was observed that often they knew that there were problems and that their applications were gaining legacy properties, but in all cases they seemed to have little data to back their assumptions. Although they did perform preventative maintenance eventually, in most cases this was left out until the perception that the problems were significant. This seems to identify that the study of evolutionary trend of software is essential to give companies the data to justify their preventative maintenance changes and to ensure that these changes are made at an optimal time for the software and company concerned.

This work would seem to indicate that the complexity of a software application could increase very quickly over only a few releases. This would therefore seem to be consistent with conclusions that legacy properties are not restricted to 'old' software. On the positive side, this work does indicate that highly skilled maintainers do have the potential to significantly turn-around an application by removing its legacy features.

11.5 General Recommendations

From conducting this analysis process, a number of factors for successful maintenance have been identified. These factors form initial recommendations that the author aims to extend within later studies. However, in order that industry can see the benefits of such research, it is necessary to make some early recommendations. In summary, these are the following:

- *Study entire applications* – by studying the entire changes that occur to files within the application, a more specific investigation can be made as to what type and where preventative maintenance should be applied in the system, so that it is more likely to benefit the future of the application. This recommendation is also supported by the research of Godfrey [Godfrey00] who found that change and growth to components within an application were not evenly distributed between all sub-system constituents.
- *Data seems to be less well understood than calling structure* – when making changes to software applications, it seems that frequently the data is modified in a less than optimal way. Thus, when marking a change, it seems that the call structure is maintained to the expense of the architecture of the data. More effort should be applied when making a change to ensure that wherever possible data cohesion is not adversely affected. Representing data cluster changes is one way of highlighting and evaluating such a problem.
- *Fewer software releases tend to lead to slower increases in data complexity* – when frequent change releases are made, this is often followed by a series of corrective changes. The risks of degrading the system architecture using frequent releases will be higher than when a number of changes are considered at a time. The latter strategy encourages an optimal solution for the set of requests. Thus, a maintenance strategy that tends to batch change requests and issue releases at set periodic time-scales has the opportunity to develop a more considered overall maintenance change and to optimise and integrate the design with an entire set of requests. This observation is strongly supported by Lehman's fifth law of 'conservation of familiarity' [Lehman97].
- *Best people should be assigned to maintenance* – this research has highlighted that when some of the best programmers were assigned to the maintenance tasks, the overall quality of the code tended to improve. This may result in a complete reversal of the standard evolutionary path of software under maintenance where often a steady increase in software data complexity is identifiable.

- *Preventative maintenance needs to be a continuous theme* – preventative maintenance is not something that can be performed once and then forgotten, rather it must either be a task that is carried out in detail at specific time periods or more appropriately as a continuing theme. It is clear from the interviews with maintainers that when preventative maintenance strategies were adopted as standard practice, a more stable system resulted. For instance, Figure 11.7 shows examples of systems seemingly brought back under control when preventative maintenance was adopted.
- *Plan for maintenance* – as highlighted by Lehman [Lehman74] and Parnas [Parnas94], modifications are always needed for software. The results presented in this chapter support the view of Parnas [Parnas94] that if the structure of code is organised in a way that makes it easier to maintain, then maintenance can be less costly over the long term.

The author intends to conduct additional work in this area to try to gain further insights into properties of specific maintenance changes and how these changes affect the evolution of software applications. From this, it is hoped that other insights into appropriate strategies for maintenance providers will emerge and solutions can be adopted for incorporating a realistic and cost-effective plan for maintenance within the software lifecycle.

11.6 Conclusions

This chapter has taken a unique view of software evolution by providing viewpoints at three levels of granularity. It has demonstrated the importance of focusing on preventative maintenance and to justify this with examples from each of the levels. This will allow managers to consider the cost/benefits of their proposed actions, such as, for instance, to evaluate maintenance options of differing levels of financial commitment. Furthermore, at Level 1 this work has shown empirical evidence for many existing studies of software evolution including the Lehman's laws of software evolution. For some of these laws-specific issues have been shown at the lower levels (e.g. at the code level). This is important in order to be able to convince software maintainers, those directly responsible for software evolution, about the consequences of certain implementation strategies.

Within Section 11.5, some recommendations are made as to how evolution strategies should be modified to be more supportive of software evolution. Informal evaluation of the work has allowed the assessment of the quality of the maintainer as well as rough estimates of the difficulties associated with the selection of some maintenance changes. These have currently been verified on an informal basis, mainly through interview, by management teams associated with the industrial case studies.

One important conclusion that can be drawn from this work is that managers of software application often realise that they are dealing with legacy systems and that some staff have the capability of dealing with the software in such a way that these problems can be reduced. Performing preventative maintenance will have cost implications to companies and often the payback of performing these preventative changes is a long-term one. While managers seem to identify their problematic software, what they are not able to do is to empirically justify their beliefs and to show the cost/benefit of making modifications. Thus, the collection of data and the continued study of evolutionary trends of software are essential to ensure that preventative maintenance can become a standard part of software developers' maintenance and evolution strategy.

Thus, continued work into the empirical study of software change processes will be conducted with the intention of ultimately composing a metrics for accurate prediction of the maintainability of software systems. It is hoped that through this work, in time, it will be used to evaluate a number of maintenance proposals and to show the likely consequences of these changes, for instance, to see the long-term affects specific maintenance strategies will have on the maintainability of applications. Thus, this work has the potential to reduce the long-term costs of maintenance while also highlighting the financial benefits and time-scales of preventative maintenance strategies.

References

[Antoniol99] Antoniol G., Canfora G. & De Lucia A., 'Maintaining traceability during object oriented software evolution: a case study', *International Conference on Software Maintenance ICSM'99*, Oxford, UK, 30th Aug – 3rd Sept, IEEE Press, 1999, pp. 211–219.

[Burd99a] Burd E.L. & Munro M., 'Characterizing the process of software change', published in the *Proceedings of the Workshop on Principles of Software Change and Evolution: SCE'1999, ICSE 1999*, California, LA, USA, 16th – 22nd May, 1999.

[Burd99b] Burd E.L. & Munro M., 'Using evolution to evaluate reverse engineering technologies', published within *The Proceedings of the Empirical Studies on Software Development and Evolution; ESSDE'99, ICSE 1999*, California, LA, USA, 16th – 22nd May, 1999.

[Burd99c] Burd E.L. & Munro M., 'Evaluating the evolution of C applications', published within *International Workshop on the Process of Software Evolution*, Japan, 1999, pp. 1–5.

[Burd2000a] Burd E.L. & Munro M., 'Supporting program comprehension using dominance trees', (Invited Paper) published within the Special Issue on *Softw. Maint. Ann. Softw. Eng.*, vol. 9, 2000, pp. 193–213.

[Burd2000b] Burd E.L. Bradley S. & Davey J., 'Studying the process of software change: an analysis of software evolution', *Proceedings of the International Working Conference on Reverse Engineering, WCRE'2000*, Brisbane, Australia, 23–25th Nov. 2000, pp. 232–239.

[Burd2000c] Burd E.L. & Munro M., 'Using evolution to evaluate reverse engineering technologies: mapping the process of software change' Published within the special issue on *The Empi. Stud. Softw. Develop. Evol. J. Softw. Syst.*, vol. 53, no. 1, 2000, pp. 43–51.

[Burd2000d] Burd E.L., *'A Method for Remodularising Legacy Software'*, Ph.D. Thesis University of Durham, 2000.

[Davey2000] Davey J. & Burd E.L., 'Evaluating the suitability of data clustering for software remodularisation', *Proceedings of the International Working Conference on Reverse Engineering, WCRE'2000*, Brisbane, Australia, 23 – 25th Nov. 2000, pp. 268–276.

[Eick2001] Eick S., Graves T., Karr A., Marron J. & Mockus A., 'Does code decay? Assessing the evidence from change management data', *IEEE Trans. Softw. Eng.*, vol. 27, no. 1, 2001, pp. 1–12.

[Fowler99] Fowler M., *'Refactoring: Improving the Design of Existing Code'*, Addison-Wesley Longman, NY, p. 461.

[Godfrey2000] Godfrey M. & Tu Q., 'Evolution in open source software: a case study', *Proceedings of the International Workshop on Software Engineering*, IEEE Press, Limerick Ireland, 2000.

[Lehman74] Lehman M.M., 'Programs, cities, students, limits to growth?' Inaugural Lecture, in *Imperial College of Science and Technology Inaugural Lecture Series*, Vol. 9, 1974, 211–229; Also in Gries D (ed.), *Programming Methodology*, Springer-Verlag, 1978, 42–62. Reprinted as Chapter 7 in Lehman M.M. and Belady L.A. *Program Evolution: Processes of Software Change*. Academic Press, 1985.

[Lehman85] Lehman M.M. & Belady L (eds.), *'Program Evolution – Processes of Software Change'*, Academic Press, London, 1985.

[Lehman97] Lehman M.M., Ramil J.F., Wernick P.D., Perry D.E. & Turski W.M., 'Metrics and laws of software evolution – the nineties view', *Symposium on Software Metrics*, Nov. 1997, IEEE Press.

[Lehman2001] Lehman M.M. & Ramil J.F., 'Rules and tools for software evolution planning and management', *Ann. Softw. Eng.*, vol. 11, special issue on Software Management, 2001, pp. 15–44.

[Lehman2004] Lehman M.M., *'Initial Development of a Theory of Software Evolution'*, invited seminar, TUV, Munich, 19 January, 2004.
[Lientz80] Lientz B.P. & Swanson E.B., *'Software Maintenance Management'*, Addison Wesley, 1980.
[Lientz81] Lientz B.P. & Swanson E.B., 'Problems in application software maintenance', *Comm. ACM*, vol. 24, no. 11, pp. 763–769.
[Littman86] Littman D., Pinto J., Letrovsky S. & Soloway E., 'Mental models and software maintenance', *Empirical Studies of Programmers*, Albex, Norwood, NJ, 1986.
[Nanda2002] Nanda V. & Madhavji N., 'The impact of environmental evolution on requirements Changes', *International Conference on Software Maintenance*, IEEE Press, Montreal, Canada, 3 – 6th Oct, 2002, pp. 452–461.
[Parnas94] Parnas D., 'Software aging', *16th International Conference on Software Evolution*, May 16–21, Sorrento, Italy, 1994, pp. 279–287.
[Rajlich2000] Rajlich V. & Bennett K., 'A staged model for the software lifecycle', *IEEE Comput.*, vol. 33, no. 7, 2000, pp. 66–71.
[Schach2004] Schach S.R., Jin B., Yu L., Heller G.Z. & Offutt J., 'Determining the distribution of maintenance categories: survey versus measurement', *Empir. Softw. Eng.*, vol. 8, no. 4, 2003, pp. 351–365.
[Smith99] Smith D., *'Designing Maintainable Software'*, Springer-Verlag, 0-387-98783-5, 1999.
[Standish84] Standish T.A., 'An essay on software reuse', *IEEE Trans. Softw. Eng.*, vol. 10, no. 5, 1984, pp. 494–497.
[Tracz88] Tracz W., 'Software reuse myths', *ACM SIGSOFT Softw. Eng. Notes*, vol. 13, no. 1, 1988, pp. 18–22.
[Turski2002] Turski W., 'The reference model for smooth growth of system software revisited', *Trans. Softw. Eng.*, vol. 28, no. 8, 2002, pp. 814–815, re-printed in this volume.
[Wohlin99] Wohlin C. & Ohlsson M.C., 'Reading between the lines; an archival study of software from nine releases', *Proceedings of Software Change and Evolution 99, ICSE Workshop*, California, LA, USA, 16th – 22nd May 1999.

12

The Role of Ripple Effect in Software Evolution

Sue Black

12.1 Introduction

The concept of 'ripple effect' in software has an intuitive appeal. Imagine a stone being thrown into a pond; it makes a sound as it enters the water and causes ripples to move outward towards the edge of the pond. It is reasonably easy to transfer this image to source code. The stone entering the water is now a hypothetical change to the source code of a program, and the effect of that change ripples across the source code via data flow. Now imagine that several stones are thrown into the pond at the same time; there will, firstly, be a ripple from each stone and, secondly, other actions created when ripples from individual stones meet each other. The integrated measurement of the individual ripples from each stone and the interaction between the ripples give quite a good idea of the amount of change happening in the pond. The same applies to source code; the individual ripples from each module of code and the interactions between the modules give an idea of the complexity of a program. Those modules that cause more ripples (when bigger stones are thrown into the pond) can also be highlighted if required.

Lehman's laws of software evolution were initially formulated after studying many releases of the IBM OS 360 in the seventies. The change that occurred to the operating system over time was documented and analysed, and from this the laws of software evolution were born. The current set of laws [LEH01] are now accepted as fundamental to the teaching and understanding of software engineering.

Systems are not expected to stay the same over many versions; change is not necessarily a bad thing. Obviously, if there were no changes at all there would be no improvement or continued satisfaction with the system. What is interesting is measuring what changes are occurring and where they are occurring. This is the sort of information that the ripple effect can provide. Measuring ripple effect can provide knowledge about the system as

---

Software Evolution and Feedback: Theory and Practice   Nazim H. Madhavji, Juan C. Fernández-Ramil and Dewayne E. Perry
© 2006 John Wiley & Sons, Ltd

a whole through its evolution: (i) how much its complexity has increased or decreased since the previous version; (ii) how complex individual parts of a system are in relation to other parts of the system; and (iii) to look at the effect that a new module has on the complexity of a system as a whole when it is added. As ripple effect is primarily concerned with change and the effects of that change, it is extremely relevant in the area of software evolution.

Measurement of ripple effect forms part of another area of fundamental importance to software engineering, that of software measurement. Software measurement as a software engineering discipline has been around now for some thirty years [ZUS98]. Its purpose is to provide data which can be used either for assessment of the system in terms of complexity, good structure, and so on, or prediction of, for example, the total cost of a system during the software life cycle. Typically, it is used for assessment either during the initial development of software, or during maintenance of software at a later date. A full description of software measurement and its use are given in [FEN96].

Typically 70% [BEN90] of software development budgets are spent on software maintenance. Thus, measures or tools which can speed up the rate at which changes can be made, or facilitate better-informed decisions on code changes, can make an important contribution. All types of maintenance involve making changes to source code or its documentation; ripple effect can show what the effect of that change will be on the rest of the program or system. Software maintenance is difficult because it is not always clear where modifications will have to be made to code or what the impact of any type of change to code may have across a whole system. The ripple effect measure has been acknowledged as helpful during software maintenance and as such has been included as part of several software maintenance process models that are described here. The usefulness of metrics and models in software maintenance and evolution is described in [CHA00].

In summary, this chapter begins with an introduction to ripple effect and its role in software engineering and maintenance. Impact analysis is described in Section 12.2, and examples of impact analysis are given along with tools used to compute impacts. In Section 12.3, software maintenance is defined, and ripple effect measurement is placed within the context of software maintenance models. In Section 12.4, the background to ripple effect is described in detail, its computation explained, and a brief description given of the tool that has been developed to compute ripple effect for C code. The main focus of this chapter then follows in Section 12.5 namely, a discussion of the rules and practical implications of the laws of software evolution [LEH01] and how they can be addressed using ripple effect measures to provide useful information for future software evolution planning and management. Conclusions from this study form Section 12.6 and ideas for further work end the chapter in Section 12.7.

12.2 Impact Analysis

Most software undergoes some change during its lifetime, and upgrades to software are common as are changes made to amend or adjust the functionality of a piece of software. For example, the software used within mobile phones is upgraded over time to make sure that customers' expectations are met and that particular brands of mobile phones can maintain or gain competitive advantage. Software change impact analysis estimates what will be affected in software if a change is made. This information can then be used for planning, making and tracing the effects of changes before the changes are implemented. Typical examples of impact analysis include [BOH96]:

- using cross referenced listings to identify other parts of a program, which contain references to a given variable or procedure;
- using program slicing [WEI84] to determine the program subset that can affect the value of a given variable;
- browsing a program by opening and closing related files;
- using traceability relationships to identify software artefacts associated with a change;
- using configuration management systems to track and find changes;
- consulting designs and specifications to determine the scope of a change.

A typical impact analysis cycle is as follows: a user, programmer or analyst submits a change for approval, which, when it is approved, will be passed to the programmer who will conduct an impact analysis study to scope out the change and plan its implementation. The software requirements, design, source code and test documentation will be examined to determine the software artefacts involved in the change. The set of impacts currently known can be used to determine an initial set of impacts and the path of impact traced through until the ripples stop and there is no more impact. The final set of artefacts affected by the impact can then be determined.

To trace the effects of change to software there are many methods and tools available. Tools available can be split into two main categories: [BOH96] those used for dependency analysis and those used for traceability analysis. Dependency analysis focuses on impact information captured from source code, for example, data-flow analysis, control-flow analysis and test-coverage analysis. REST, the tool described in this chapter, uses data-flow analysis to track changes across a program. The starting points for hypothetical impacts are found, their impact via data flow on other variables within the program are computed, and then a ripple effect measure is given for individual modules on other modules within a program given, along with a ripple effect measure for the program as a whole.

Traceability analysis identifies affected software artefacts using their traceability relationships and usually represents this information in a graph structure. Alicia (Automated life cycle analysis system) [BOH96] is an example of a traceability-based impact analysis system. It is intended to support the whole software development life cycle by analysing change in the context of development work products. Its three main traceability capabilities are as follows:

- it describes the change and lets the user select the traceability starting point;
- it marks the impacted objects in the project database;
- it lets the user visually traverse and browse the project database.

Impact analysis can be used during software development or maintenance to give programmers and others information about software systems. This chapter is concerned specifically with software maintenance; the next section gives an introduction to maintenance in the context of impact analysis.

12.3 Software Maintenance and Software Maintenance Models

Unlike traditional engineering projects that usually deliver a static finished product that matches the original specification, software systems change over time through several different versions/releases and therefore need to be maintained. The high proportion of the software development budget that can be spent on maintenance highlights the importance of maintenance as part of the software life cycle. Software maintenance was originally classified by Swanson in 1976 into three types [SWA76]:

- *corrective maintenance*: to address processing, performance or implementation failure;
- *adaptive maintenance*: to address change in the data or processing environments;
- *perfective maintenance*: to address processing efficiency, performance enhancement and maintainability.

The classification was redefined by the IEEE glossary [IEE90] in 1990 to also include a fourth type:

- *preventive maintenance*: to address activities aimed at increasing the system's maintainability.

The IEEE redefinition causes some confusion because maintainability is included under both preventive and perfective maintenance. A discussion on the exact definition of preventive maintenance is given in [KAT00], and a fuller description of the definition of software maintenance is given in [BLA01b].

In general, maintenance involves making changes to source code. Ripple effect can show how great the effect of a change will be on the rest of the program or system. It can highlight modules with high ripple effect as possible problem modules, which may be especially useful in preventive maintenance. It can show the impact in terms of increased ripple effect during perfective and adaptive maintenance where the functionality of a program is being modified or its environment has changed.

During corrective maintenance, it may be helpful to look at the ripple effect of the changed program and its modules before and after a change to ascertain whether the change has increased, or perhaps decreased, the stability of the program. Ripple effect along with many other metrics is not the answer to all maintenance problems, but when used as part of a suite of metrics it can give maintainers useful information to make their task easier. Several software maintenance models have been proposed in the past. Boehm's model [BOE87] consists of three major phases: understanding the software, modifying the software and revalidating the software. These are fundamental activities of the software maintenance process. With Yau's model, a methodology for software maintenance [YAU80], impact analysis is introduced into the life cycle. The model consists of four phases, and includes analysis and monitoring of the impact of change at phase three accounting for ripple effect (see Figure 12.1). The aims of the model are to assist in achieving cost-effective software maintenance and the development of easily maintainable software.

The Pfleeger and Bohner model: Structured Analysis and Design Technique (SADT) Diagram of software maintenance activities (see Figure 12.2) [PFL90] has six phases, the main difference from Yau's model being that it includes analyse software change impact

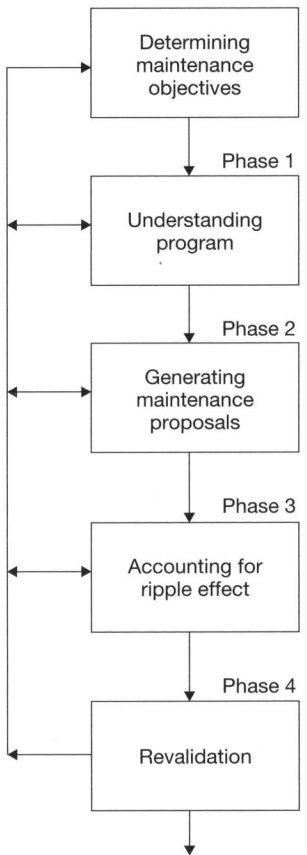

Figure 12.1 A methodology for software maintenance [YAU80]. © 1980 IEEE. Reproduced by permission of IEEE

at phase two, that is, much earlier in the life cycle. The feedback paths in the SADT model indicate attributes that must be measured; the results are then assessed by management before the next activity is undertaken. The metrics act as a controlling mechanism in the progression from existing system and change requests to new system.

Bennett and Rajlich introduced the staged model of the software life cycle in 2000 [RAJ00] which proposes five stages:

- Initial development – the first functioning version of the system is developed
- Evolution – the engineers extend the capabilities and functionality of the system to meet the needs of its users, possibly in major ways
- Servicing – the software is subjected to minor defect repairs and very simple changes in function
- Phase out – no more servicing is undertaken, and the owners seek to generate revenue from the use for as long as possible
- Close down – the software is withdrawn from the market, and any users directed to a replacement system if this exists.

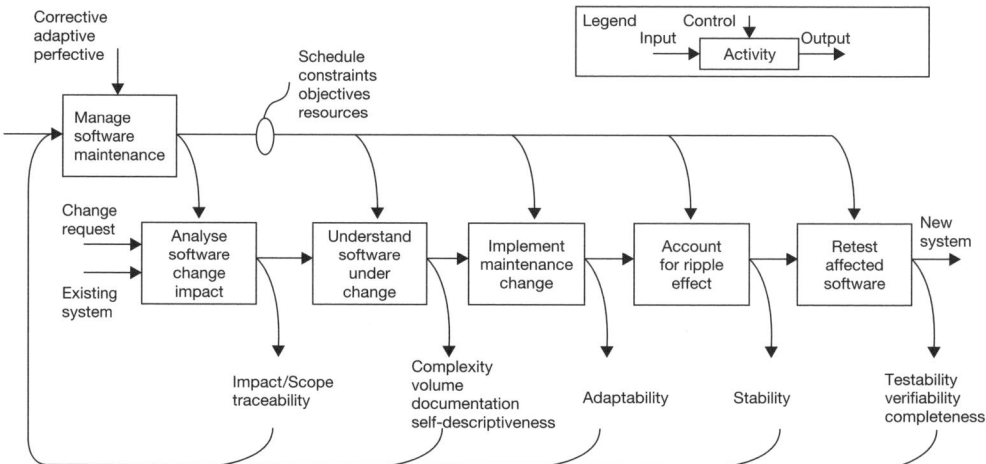

Figure 12.2 SADT diagram of software maintenance activities [PFL90]. © 1990 IEEE. Reproduced by permission of IEEE

The authors contend that 'maintenance' is not a single uniform phase but comprises several distinct phases each with a different technical and business perspective. In this model impact analysis, the use of the ripple effect metric would take place during phases one and two: initial and evolution. It can be seen that impact analysis and ripple effect measurement have over time moved closer to the beginning of software maintenance models, which confirms the importance of measuring for impact within a system at an early stage.

12.4 Background on the Ripple Effect

The term *ripple effect* was first used in a paper by Haney [HAN72] to describe the way that a change in one module would necessitate a change in any other module. He used a technique called *module connection analysis* which applied matrix algebra to estimate the total number of changes needed to stabilise a system. Myers [MYE80] used matrices to quantify matrix independence; a complete dependence matrix was formulated describing dependencies between modules within a system and then used to predict the stability of the system. Soong [SOO77] used the joint probability of connection, a measure which looked at the probability that certain elements within a system were connected to other elements within the same system, to produce a program stability measure. All of the aforementioned methods use matrices to measure the probability of a change to a variable or module affecting another variable or module. Yau and Collofello's ripple effect [YAU78] uses ideas from Haney, Myers and Soong's work, but their ripple effect measure is not a measure of probability.

When Yau and Collofello first proposed their ripple effect analysis technique in 1978 [YAU78], they saw it as a complexity measure which could be used during software maintenance to evaluate and compare various program modifications to source code. Computation of ripple effect involved using error flow analysis where all program variable definitions involved in an initial modification represented primary error sources from which inconsistency could propagate to other program areas. Propagation continued until no new error sources were created. An algorithm for computing design stability was presented in [YAU85], which facilitated computation of stability based solely on design information. It was proposed that a design stability measure would be more useful than previous stability measures because it could be used at a much earlier stage in the software life cycle, before any code was produced, thus potentially saving time and money.

The ripple effect research as described in this chapter builds on the previous work described above. The basis of the approach taken has been to completely reformulate the ripple effect calculation using matrix arithmetic. In addition to making the calculation more explicit, the reformulation reveals how the algorithm's structure can be broken down into separate parts. By focusing on the derivation of one particular matrix, Z_m, an approximation may be made, greatly simplifying the calculation which is important for automatic ripple effect computation. The explicit details and validation of the approximated calculation are described in [BLA01c]. The next section describes the ripple effect algorithm and its computation without the approximation for the purpose of simplicity.

12.4.1 Computation of the Ripple Effect

The computation of ripple effect is based on the effect that a change to a single variable will have on the rest of a program. Given the three lines of code contained in Module m_1, shown in Figure 12.3, a change to the value of b in (1) will affect the value of a in (1), which will propagate to a in (2). In (2), a will affect d which will then propagate to d in (3). Propagation of change from one line of code to another within a module is called *intramodule change propagation*. Matrix V_m represents the starting points for intramodule change propagation through a module. The conditions for this to occur are as follows:

(a) a variable being defined is in an assignment statement;
(b) a variable being assigned a value which is read as input;

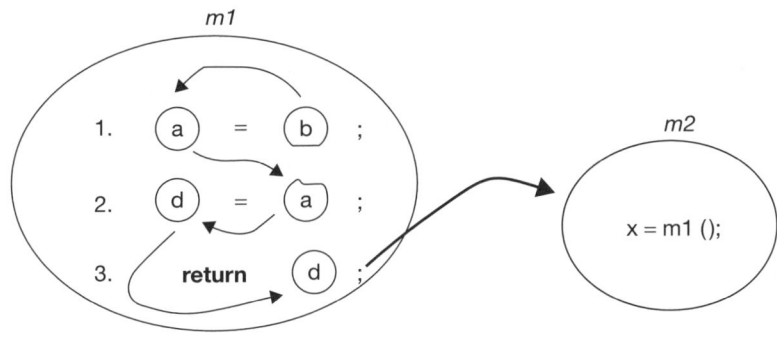

Figure 12.3 Intramodule and intermodule change propagation

(c) a variable is an input parameter to a module;
(d) a variable is an output parameter from a called *module*;
(e) a variable is global.

Each variable definition is uniquely defined in V_m, thus if the same variable is defined twice within a module then V_m contains a unique entry for each definition. In matrix V_m, variable occurrences that satisfy any of the above conditions are denoted by '1' and those which do not by '0'. Matrix V_{m1} for the code in the example (where a is global) is therefore

$$V_{m1} = \begin{pmatrix} a_1^d & b_1^u & d_2^d & a_2^u & d_3^u \\ 1 & 0 & 1 & 1 & 0 \end{pmatrix}$$

where, the notation x_i^d (respectively, x_i^u) denotes a *definition* (respectively, *use*) of variable x at line i. Note that a_2^u is considered a definition because it is global and therefore could be a starting point for propagation. A 0–1 matrix Z_m can be produced to show which variables' values will propagate to other variables within module m. The rows and columns of Z_m represent each individual occurrence of a variable. Propagation is shown from row i to column j. For example, the propagation from a in line 2 to d in line 2 is shown at row 4 column 3 and not at row 3 column 4. Thus, the code in Figure 12.3 produces the following matrix:

$$Z_{m1} = \begin{array}{c} \\ a_1^d \\ d_1^u \\ d_2^d \\ a_2^u \\ d_3^u \end{array} \begin{pmatrix} a_1^d & d_1^u & d_2^d & a_2^u & d_3^u \\ 1 & 0 & 1 & 1 & 1 \\ 1 & 1 & 1 & 1 & 1 \\ 0 & 0 & 1 & 0 & 1 \\ 0 & 0 & 1 & 1 & 1 \\ 0 & 0 & 0 & 0 & 1 \end{pmatrix}$$

Z_m is reflexive and transitive: Every variable occurrence is assumed to propagate to itself, and if v_1 propagates to v_2 and v_2 propagates to v_3 then v_1 also propagates to v_3. Z_m, therefore, represents the transitive closure of variables within module m. In graph theory, term Z_m represents the reachability matrix of some graph.

Propagation from one module to another is called *intermodule change propagation*. This can occur when a variable is:

(a) global;
(b) an input parameter to a called *module*;
(c) an output parameter.

Looking at the code in Figure 12.3, it can be seen that d clearly propagates to any module calling m_1. If a is global, then its occurrence on the left-hand-side could cause propagation to any module using a. Suppose that the above code constituting module m_1 is called by a module m_2, that a is global and modules m_2 and m_3 use a. The (i, j)th entry is 1 if variable i propagates to module j. The propagation of these variables can be represented using a further 0–1 matrix X_{m1}:

$$X_{m1} = \begin{array}{c} \\ a_1^d \\ d_1^u \\ d_2^d \\ a_2^u \\ d_3^u \end{array} \begin{pmatrix} m_1 & m_2 & m_3 \\ 0 & 1 & 1 \\ 0 & 0 & 0 \\ 0 & 0 & 0 \\ 0 & 0 & 0 \\ 0 & 0 & 1 \end{pmatrix}$$

Note that there is no propagation for any variable occurrence to m_1 that is, column 1 is all zeros because intermodule change propagation involves flow of program change across a module boundary. The intermodule change propagation of all variable occurrences in m_1 is the Boolean product of Z_{m1} and X_{m1}:

$$Z_{m1} X_{m1} = \begin{pmatrix} 1 & 0 & 1 & 1 & 1 \\ 1 & 1 & 1 & 1 & 1 \\ 0 & 0 & 1 & 0 & 1 \\ 0 & 0 & 1 & 1 & 1 \\ 0 & 0 & 0 & 0 & 1 \end{pmatrix} \begin{pmatrix} 0 & 1 & 1 \\ 0 & 0 & 0 \\ 0 & 0 & 0 \\ 0 & 0 & 0 \\ 0 & 0 & 1 \end{pmatrix} = \begin{pmatrix} 0 & 1 & 1 \\ 0 & 1 & 1 \\ 0 & 0 & 1 \\ 0 & 0 & 1 \\ 0 & 0 & 0 \end{pmatrix}$$

The product of Z_{m1} and X_{m1} shows which module's variables in module m_1 have propagated to. For example, the '1' in row 2, column 3 of $Z_{m1} X_{m1}$ denotes propagation from b_1^u to m_3, and the '0' in row 3, column 2 denotes that there is no propagation from d_2^d to m_2. Column 1 is all zeros because m_1 is not seen to propagate to itself. Matrix $Z_{m1} X_{m1}$ is different to matrix X_{m1} because it takes into account all paths of intramodule change propagation through m_1, which X_{m1} does not.

The product of V_{m1} and $Z_{m1} X_{m1}$ shows how many variable definitions may propagate to each module from module m_1:

$$V_{m1} Z_{m1} X_{m1} = (10110) \begin{pmatrix} 0 & 1 & 1 \\ 0 & 0 & 0 \\ 0 & 0 & 0 \\ 0 & 0 & 0 \\ 0 & 0 & 1 \end{pmatrix} = (013)$$

In this instance, it can be seen from matrix $V_{m1} Z_{m1} X_{m1}$ that there are 0 propagations to module m_1, 1 to module m_2 and 3 to m_3. A complexity measure is factored into the computation so that the complexity of modification of a variable definition is taken into account; the more complex the module, the more complicated it is to change it. Matrix C, a $1 * m$ matrix represents McCabe's cyclomatic complexity [MCC76] for the modules in the code (the values for m_2 and m_3 have been chosen at random as the code is not complete):

$$C = \begin{array}{c} m_1 \\ m_2 \\ m_3 \end{array} \begin{pmatrix} 1 \\ 1 \\ 1 \end{pmatrix}$$

The product of $V_{m1} Z_{m1} X_{m1}$ and C is:

$$V_{m1} Z_{m1} X_{m1} C = (013) \begin{pmatrix} 1 \\ 1 \\ 1 \end{pmatrix} = 4$$

This number represents the complexity-weighted total variable definition propagation for module m_1. Dividing by the number of variable definitions (so that the ripple effect measure takes into account the number of starting points for propagation) in module m_1, that is, $|V_{m1}|$ the mean complexity-weighted variable definition propagation per variable definition in module m_1 is produced. In simpler terms, this means the average ripple effect measure for the module taking into account the number of starting points and the complexity of the module.

In this example, $|V_{m1}| = 3$, that is, the number of starting points for ripple in module m_1 is 3. The ripple effect for module m_1 is defined to be $4/3 = 1.33$ and the Ripple Effect for the Program as a whole (REP) is:

$$\text{REP} = \frac{1}{n} \sum_{m=1}^{n} \frac{Vm \cdot Zm \cdot Xm \cdot C}{|Vm|}$$

where m = module and n = number of modules.

12.4.2 The REST Software Tool

Computing the ripple effect for a small program manually may take several hours, computing ripple effect for a large program manually may take weeks. Accuracy is also critical, manual computation of ripple effect measures could be erroneous. Even when automated, computation of ripple effect can be time consuming. Yau and Chang [YAU84] give an example of a two thousand line Pascal program's ripple effect taking thirteen hours of CPU time to compute. As that particular research was carried out in 1984 the computation time should be put into context; PC processors have dramatically improved their speed and capability since then.

The tool REST (Ripple Effect and Stability Tool) [BLA01a] has been developed, which computes ripple effect measures automatically but which uses an approximation of intramodule change propagation. Previous attempts at computing ripple effect have suffered from slow computation times, therefore, when implementing REST the decision was made not to take control flow into account within source code modules [BLA01c]. Automation of ripple effect can take two forms: (a) the computation of ripple effect measure for a given program or (b) the tracing of ripple effect on variables through a program or system. Tracing of ripple effect through a program starts with one variable occurrence in a particular module and traces the impact of that variable upon other variables until the impact terminates. Tools have been developed for both of these categories of ripple effect; REST falls under the first category, that is, it computes the ripple effect measure. Other tools which produce a ripple effect measure include a prototype tool for ripple effect analysis of Pascal programs [HSI82] which consist of three subsystems: an intramodule error flow analyser, an intermodule error flow analyser and a logical ripple effect identification subsystem. The developers could not identify primary error sources automatically, thus some user input was required. Another tool which produces a ripple effect measure was produced by Chang [CHA84]. It does not consider intramodule information for computing ripple effect and is thus presented as a design level ripple effect tool. The approach of getting feedback at design level meant that steps could be taken to make programs more stable, or highlight specific problems from an early stage. But there is a tradeoff in that the information gained is not as accurate as information derived from code level measurement.

Tools that trace ripple effect through a system include Data-centered program understanding tool environment (DPUTE) developed by Joiner *et al*. [JOI93], which uses ripple effect analysis along with dependence analysis and program slicing. DPUTE can be used during software maintenance of COBOL systems to enhance program understanding and to facilitate restructuring and reengineering of programs. Program slicing [WEI84] is used to compute intramodule change propagation. SEMIT [COL87] is a ripple effect analysis tool which is based on both semantic and syntactic information. It creates a syntax and semantics database for software, which directly links the program's semantic information with its syntax. All possible ripple effect paths are identified by SEMIT, interaction with an expert maintainer is then needed to define which are the more probable paths. ChAT is a tool which traces ripple effect for object-oriented programs [LEE00] and is implemented in C++ and Java. It comprises three components: parser, analyser and viewer. Users specify changes that they want to make to a program, then ChAT calculates the impact of the change and displays the affected classes.

REST runs on MS DOS and comprises four separate software modules: *Parser*, *Listfuns*, *Funmat* and *Ripple*, as detailed in Figure 12.4. The three modules involved in the actual calculation of ripple effect: *Listfuns*, *Funmat* and *Ripple* took approximately 1-person-year to build, and in total comprise 3000 lines of code. The *Parser* was developed separately, firstly as part of the X-RAY tool [BLA99], and then adapted for use with the other three modules in REST. X-RAY is a tool which analyses program structure.

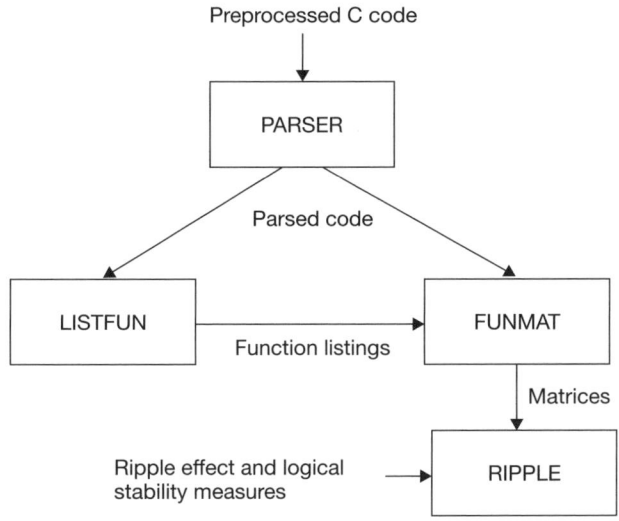

Figure 12.4 Components of the REST software

The initial aim of REST was to produce ripple effect measures as an addition to British Telecommunication's (BT) comprehensive suite of measurement tools, the Code Measurement Toolkit (CMT). The CMT [HAL97] is an integrated environment for the code analysis and maintainability assessment of C and COBOL code. It was developed after BT carried out an analysis of their software, the result of which indicated that it should be possible to predict with 70–80% accuracy as to which source code files in a system are likely to require changing. The CMT also uses X-RAY and QUALMS [BAC90], a tool which produces control-flow graphs and related software measures.

12.5 Links Between Ripple Effect and the Laws of Software Evolution

There is a strong link between the laws of software evolution and ripple effect measurement. The FEAST hypothesis is that to achieve process improvement global dynamics must be taken into account. Investigation of potential changes and the evaluation of alternatives are critical, with the focus of the implementation being on those changes most likely to prove beneficial in terms of the organisation goals. Change is the basis of the computation of the ripple effect measure and its computation can provide information for the evaluation of alternative plans of action. Using ripple effect either to track changes through a program/system or to give an actual measure of the stability of a module/program/system can provide vital information which is fundamental to the practical implications of the laws and the ensuing rules. A case study was carried out [BLA01c] using a mutation testing software tool. The results of the case study are not relevant to this chapter but some information about the different versions of the tool can be used as an example of system evolution. The tool evolved through four versions, the first two written in C and the second two in C++ but fundamentally still C programs. Table 12.1 details the programs and their related data.

It can be seen that as the number of modules and lines of code (LOC) increased the ripple effect increased also. When two modules of code were deleted between the third and fourth versions, the ripple effect decreased also. Unfortunately, these measures were produced after the tool had been fully implemented, so it was not possible to give any constructive feedback to the author. In general, the information, resultant from the computation of the ripple effect, measures for each module of each version and for each version as a whole can be used so that the effects of a given variable or module can be traced over time or multiple releases. This information can be useful to help make

Table 12.1 Description of four versions of the mutation testing software tool

Program	Ripple effect	Modules	LOC
allas1	17.3	20	425
allas2	19.1	27	477
allas3	21.8	44	725
allas4	21.1	42	659

Table 12.2 Laws of software evolution and how the ripple effect is relevant

Law of software evolution	How ripple effect is relevant
1. Continuing Change	Compare versions of program/system
	Highlight complex modules
	Measure stability over time
	Highlight areas ripe for restructuring
2. Growing Complexity	Determine which modules need maintenance
	Measure growing complexity
3. Self Regulation	Helps measure rate of change of system
	Helps look at patterns/trends of behaviour
	Determine the state of the system
4. Conservation of Organisational Stability	Not relevant
5. Conservation of Familiarity	Provide system change data
6. Continuing Growth	Measure impact of new modules on a system
	Help determine which modules to use in a new version
7. Declining Quality	Highlight areas of increasing complexity
	Determine which modules need maintenance
	Measure stability over time
8. Feedback System	Provide feedback on stability/complexity of system

evolutionary decisions about software systems in terms of making future predictions of system quality and in management planning.

Table 12.2 and the sub-sections below examine the laws of software evolution, their practical implications and rules for software evolution planning and management [LEH01], and discuss how the ripple effect measure can be used to provide relevant information.

12.5.1 First Law – Continuing Change

Lehman's First Law of software evolution is the law of continuing change – E-type systems must be regularly adapted else they become progressively less satisfactory in use. Its practical implementation is the unending maintenance that has been the experience of computer users since the start of serious computer applications. Looking at the practical implications of the First Law in detail, it can be seen that it involves looking at why a particular implementation design or algorithm is being used. This can be related to the use of ripple effect and logical stability measurement as these measures can be used to compare versions of programs or systems to ascertain which contains the least ripple effect, that is, which is the most stable. This measurement data can then be used along with other information in making this decision and recorded as part of the decision making process and the subsequent documentation. Another practical implication of the First Law is that there must be a conscious effort to control and reduce complexity and its growth as changes are made to the system and its interfaces. Ripple effect measurement is an obvious candidate in the control of this implication as it can highlight modules, which may cause problems because of their complexity or the ripple effect that they might have if they were changed. The impact of changes to particular modules can be monitored for each version of a system during its evolution and compared with previous/successive measurements for those modules to make sure that the system is not becoming excessively complex. If it is found that particular modules are becoming excessively complex or producing an increasing impact on other modules, steps can be taken to address this. If ripple effect analysis is applied at a system level, the complexity/stability of the system as a whole and its interfaces can be measured.

The safe rate of change of a system per release is constrained by the system dynamics and the fact that the magnitude of change in a release increases in complexity at a greater than linear rate is another practical implication of the First Law. One way of measuring the rate of change is by looking at the system stability as previously described over several versions or releases. As complexity increases at a greater than linear rate [TUR96], it is critical to keep the ramifications of any changes in terms of the increase in complexity to a minimum. Thus, it is critical to keep looking at and measuring the stability of a system. Owing to continuing change it may be necessary to have a release that focuses on structural clean up. For this purpose, ripple effect measures can be used to highlight areas, which are most in need of attention. It is noted in [LEH01] that FEAST 1 and earlier incremental growth models suggest that an excessive number of changes in a release have an adverse impact on release schedule quality. If ripple effect measures are computed at module, program and system level throughout the system's development and during its evolution the impact of all changes can be measured and recorded. Those changes that are determined to be the most detrimental to a system's quality can then be reviewed and their implementation discussed and possibly changed.

Validation of the change to a system needs to address the change itself in terms of interaction with the rest of the system and impact of the remainder of the system. This can obviously be facilitated by use of ripple effect measurement. Ripple effect can measure impact of modules on other modules and programs on other programs within a system through the effect of hypothetical or real changes to a system. It can also be used to track changes through a system to highlight and identify the actual areas of a system that are affected by a particular change. Determination of the number of additions and changes to requirements that are needed to assist the evolution release planning can be beneficial. It can highlight areas that are ripe for restructuring because of high fault rates or high functional volatility. Ripple effect can be used to highlight areas ripe for restructuring and can thus complement other information relating to the determination of the number of additions and changes to requirements. The REST tool, as it is, currently is not able to produce all of this information, but, theoretically, the information could easily be produced using a more sophisticated ripple effect/impact analysis tool.

12.5.2 Second Law – Growing Complexity

Lehman's Second Law is that of growing complexity. Complexity increases unless work is done to maintain or reduce it. The number of potential connections and interactions between modules, objects and so on is proportional to the square of the number of elements involved; thus, the potential for error increases with n^2. A system over time becomes increasingly remote from its initial design concepts and architecture; this can cause a decline in the quality of the system. Complexity control is highlighted as possibly making the difference between the survival or demise of a system. Control of system complexity can be facilitated using ripple effect as part of a comprehensive suite of measures. As there are different types of complexity, for example, structural and algorithmic, different types of complexity measures will need to be part of the suite. The ripple effect measure is based on the connections and interactions between modules and as such its use is completely appropriate for this rule.

Complexity measurement is needed to determine when anti-regressive activity should be initiated. The level of effort also needs to be determined accurately else the system may decline. A strategy needs to be formulated which highlights the amount of effort that should be put in and where. Ripple effect can be used to determine which modules need to be maintained, and if measurements are taken across a system over all versions, the optimum time for anti-regressive activity and the level of effort needed can be determined. This information can then be used in the formulation of the strategy.

12.5.3 Third Law – Self Regulation

Lehman's Third Law is that of self-regulation that is, there are similar gross trends in system growth patterns in which complexity growth is a constraining factor. These patterns are apparent at different levels of abstraction of the system and appear to include a natural 'ripple' that reflects the action of the stabilising mechanisms. Measurement needs to be applied to determine rates of change, patterns and trends, and baselines need to be established.

Lehman has determined three scenarios, which classify systems as follows: safe, risky or unsafe. Ripple effect used, as mentioned earlier, as part of a suite of metrics looking at the complexity of the system across all versions/releases will provide invaluable information, particularly regarding rates of change, and possibly also patterns and trends. It can be used to set baselines for system growth, changes across the entire system, units changed and so on. Ripple effect can also be used following the determination of the state that a system is in, at any given time. Ripple effect can be used if systems are unsafe to highlight which modules in particular are candidates for anti-regressive work such as restructuring.

12.5.4 Fourth Law – Conservation of Organisational Stability

The Fourth Law is conservation of organisational stability; the activity rate remains constant over time unless feedback mechanisms are appropriately adjusted. There are no rules for this law, thus discussion of the applicability of ripple effect measures is inappropriate.

12.5.5 Fifth Law – Conservation of Familiarity

Lehman's Fifth Law is the conservation of familiarity. The incremental growth of systems tends to decline over time; clean up and restructuring, inevitably, must follow. Growth and change data need to be collected and modelled to determine system evolution trends, and automatic tools for the collection of this information need to be developed. Once the model parameters have stabilised, models should provide estimates of change per release, and these should then be updated for each subsequent release. Use of ripple effect measurement in response to rules for the Fifth Law is highly appropriate. System change data, which needs to be collected, should be provided by a suite of metrics including the ripple effect as discussed previously. This can be used to provide the estimates of change per release mentioned above. An automatic tool for the computation of ripple effect measures for C code, REST, (see Section 12.4.2) has already been produced. Further work is now underway to increase the number of languages that REST can provide ripple effect measures for and to make REST more robust. Future work is discussed in more detail in Section 12.7.

12.5.6 Sixth Law – Continuing Growth

Lehman's Sixth Law of continuing growth concerns the continual increase of functional capability of systems over their lifetime. The rule appropriate to this law concerns the penetration from additions to a system into the original system and the control of any effect this may have. Ripple effect measures can be used to show the impact that the new modules have on the old system and steps then taken to minimise any negative influence. If the effect of a new module on a system is shown to be minimal then it may be fully included in many new releases/versions. If its effect is to add a major amount of complexity to the system then its inclusion in the next release can be discussed with respect to the strategy formulated as part of the implications and rules of the Second Law. If there is a choice between two or more modules to be included in the next release/version then ripple effect measures can be used to look at the impact that all of the modules would have on the system. A decision can then be made as to which module, perhaps the one with a balance of the least ripple effect and highest functionality, should be chosen to become part of the system.

12.5.7 Seventh Law – Declining Quality

Lehman's Seventh Law of declining quality concerns the adaptation of systems to take into account changes in the operational environment thus preventing a decline in quality. Rules for this law suggest that practices that reduce complexity or limit its growth should be pursued. Design changes and additions to the system should be in accordance with established principles to limit unwanted interactions between code sections. Resources should be devoted to complexity reduction of all types ensuring future changeability, and system attributes should be monitored to predict the need for maintenance. All these areas can benefit from ripple effect measurement. Interactions between code sections are exactly what the ripple effect looks at. As mentioned in the previous section, if any changes are being made to a system, the potential ripple effect that change may have on other parts of the system can be assessed prior to its finalisation. This ties in with devoting resources to complexity reduction; if ripple effect is computed for each release/version then information will be available for analysis in terms of reducing complexity from version to version. Those modules, which have been shown in past versions to be extremely complex, can be analysed with respect to the way they increase the complexity of the system as a whole. Lessons may then be learnt regarding how to make future versions more changeable.

12.5.8 Eighth Law – Feedback System

Lehman's Eighth Law is the key law which underlies the behaviour encapsulated by the other seven laws. Feedback constrains the way that process constituents interact with one another and will modify their individual, local and collective global behaviour. If feedback is not taken into account, unexpected and even counter-intuitive results must be expected. Thus, for sound software process planning, management and improvement feedback must be taken into account. One of the rules for this law states that models should be developed which include all activities that feed back information and that may be used to direct, change or control the process. Again ripple effect used as part of a suite of metrics may be used to provide this type of information and thus form part of the feedback system.

12.6 Conclusions

The use of the ripple effect as part of a suite of metrics to provide feedback for the strategic maintenance of a system during its evolution has been discussed in this chapter. Software maintenance consumes a large portion of software maintenance budgets; thus its management and application are critical. The ripple effect measure has been previously identified as valid and necessary within several software maintenance models, particularly the SADT model and methodology for software maintenance described in Section 12.3. Maintenance is difficult because it is not always clear where modifications will have to be made to code or what the impact of any type of change to code may have across a whole system. Ripple effect measurement can show the effect of a change on the rest of the program or system. It can highlight modules with high ripple effect as possible problem modules and show impact in terms of increased ripple effect where the functionality of a program is being modified or its environment has changed.

The computation of ripple effect has been briefly explained and described as a basis for the discussion on its use in addressing the practical implications and rules for software evolution planning and management. It has been found to be appropriate for almost all of the laws of software evolution. As part of a suite of metrics looking at the complexity of systems, it can be used to address the decline of systems over time by providing change data that facilitates the optimal modelling of system trends. Because feedback constrains the way that process constituents interact with one another, it needs to be taken into account or else unexpected results may be expected. Software process planning, management and improvement must therefore take feedback into account and models developed which include all activities that may be used to direct, change or control the process. Again, ripple effect used as part of a suite of metrics may be used to provide this type of information and therefore form part of the feedback system.

Because change is fundamental to software evolution and computation of the ripple effect measure is based upon the change to a variable and its effect upon a module, program or system, the two are intrinsically linked. Many of the practical implications and rules from Lehman's paper [LEH01] which have formed the basis of the discussion in this chapter involve change, complexity and its management. Program stability and complexity need to be measured as part of the evolutionary process providing feedback on the system and how it is changing. They can be used to provide baseline measures for comparison throughout the system's lifetime. The measures can be computed for each version or release of the system providing valuable information for analysis and thus providing feedback for future maintenance of the system.

A rule connected to the Second Law, that of growing complexity, suggests that a maintenance strategy needs to be formulated. The strategy will need to include the determination of the level of effort needed in various parts of the system, for optimisation of maintenance resources. If too much effort is spent in maintaining the wrong area system it may lead to decline. As part of this strategy, measurement of ripple effect and logical stability must be included. The stability of the system needs to be measured with regard to making sure that the continuing change, growing complexity and declining quality are kept in check. Ripple effect measurement is invaluable in this context as it can be used to track changes to source code through a system. The ramifications in terms of any additions or changes to a system can be tracked to see exactly which source code is affected by any change or addition. It can also be used to give a measure of the amount of change that those additions or changes may have on the system. This can be computed at module, program or system level thus providing useful feedback at several levels of abstraction.

12.7 Further Work

Further work on the applicability of ripple effect measurement for software evolution planning and management clearly needs to be carried out. This chapter is merely a first look at the connections between the laws of software evolution and ripple effect measures.

For REST to be used to compute ripple effect as part of a suite of metrics for industrial code some, further work needs to be carried out. Facilitation of ripple effect computation for other programming languages besides C is already either at the planning stage or underway [BLA00], [BLA01d]. The robustness of REST also needs to be addressed. Several enhancements need to be made which are mainly concerned with size and parsing of target source code before REST can be used in an industrial context.

12.8 Acknowledgements

The author would like to thank Professor Nazim Madhavji for bringing the work of the FEAST project and its links with ripple effect measurement to her attention and for his patience.

REST was built as part of a project partially funded by British Telecommunications (BT) laboratories.

References

[BAC90] R. Bache and L. Leelasena, *'QUALMS – User Ide'*, CSSE/QUG/DOC/'OwUG/1.0a, Centre for Systems and Software Engineering, South Bank University, London SE1 OAA, UK, 1990.

[BEN90] K.H. Bennett, 'An introduction to software maintenance', *Information and Software Technology*, **12** (1990), no. 4, 257–64.

[BLA99] S. Black and J.D. Wigg, 'X-RAY: a multilanguage, industrial strength tool', *9th International Workshop on Software Measurement* 1999, Montreal, Canada, 36–42.

[BLA00] S. Black and F.H. Clark, Measuring the ripple effect of Pascal programs, In Dumke R. and Abran A. (Eds.), *'New Approaches in Software Measurement'*, Springer-Verlag, Berlin, Heidelberg, Germany, 2001, 161–171.

[BLA01a] S. Black, 'Automating ripple effect measurement', *5th World Multiconference on Systemics, Cybernetics and Informatics* 2001, Orlando, Florida, 22–25th July.

[BLA01b] S. Black, 'Computing ripple effect for software maintenance', *Journal of Software Maintenance and Evolution: Research and Practice*, **13** (2001), 263–279.

[BLA01c] S. Black, *Computation of ripple effect measures for software*, PhD thesis, SCISM, South Bank University, London, United Kingdom, September 2001, 123.
[BLA01d] S. Black and P. Rosner, 'Measuring ripple effect for the object-oriented paradigm', Technical Report SBU-CISM-01-12, South Bank University, 2001.
[BOE87] B. Boehm, 'Software engineering', *IEEE Transactions on Computers*, **12** (1987), 1226–1242.
[BOH96] S.A. Bohner and R.S. Arnold, *'Software Change Impact Analysis'*, IEEE Computer Society Press, Los Alamitos, CA, 1996.
[CHA00] N. Chapin, 'Usefulness of metrics and models in software maintenance and evolution', *IEEE Conference on Software Maintenance* 2000, San Jose, CA, WESS position paper.
[CHA84] S.C. Chang, *A unified and efficient approach for logical ripple effect analysis*, PhD thesis, Department of EECS, Northwestern University, Evanston, IL, June 1984, 94.
[COL87] J.S. Collofello and D.A. Wennergrund, 'Ripple effect based on semantic information', *Proceedings AFIPS Joint Computer Conference*, **56** (1987), 675–682.
[FEA00] FEAST, 'http://www.doc.ic.ac.uk/~mml/f2000/program.html', 23/07/04.
[FEN96] N. Fenton and S.L. Pfleeger, *'Software Metrics: A Rigorous and Practical Approach'*, Chapman & Hall, London, United Kingdom, 1996.
[HAL97] R. Hall and S. Lineham, 'Using metrics to improve software maintenance', *BT Technology Journal*, **15** (1997), no. 3, 123–129.
[HAN72] F.M. Haney, 'Module connection analysis- a tool for scheduling of software debugging activities', *Proceedings Fall Joint Computer Conference*, 1972, 173–179.
[HSI82] C.C. Hsieh, *An approach to logical ripple effect analysis for software maintenance*, PhD thesis, Department of EECS, Northwestern University, Evanston, IL, June 1982, 206.
[IEE83] IEEE, *'Standard glossary of software engineering terminology'*, ANSI/IEEE Standard 729, 1983.
[IEE90] IEEE, *'Standard Glossary of Engineering Terminology'*, Institute of Electrical and Electronic Engineers, New York, 1990.
[JOI93] J.K. Joiner and W.T. Tsai, 'Ripple effect analysis, program slicing and dependence analysis', Technical Report TR 93-84, University of Minnesota, 1993.
[KAT00] M. Katjko-Matsson, N. Chapin and R. Vehvilainen, 'Panel 2: Preventive maintenance! do we know what it is?', *Proceedings International Conference on Software Engineering* 2000, Limerick, Ireland, 11–19.
[LEE00] M. Lee, A.J. Offutt and R.T. Alexander, 'Algorithmic analysis of the impacts of changes to object-oriented software', *Proceedings of the 34th International Conference on Technology of Object-Oriented Languages and Systems 2000, TOOLS 34*, 30 July-4 August 2000, 61–70.
[LEH94] M.M. Lehman, Software evolution, In Marciniak J.J. (Ed.), *'Encyclopedia of Software Engineering'*, John Wiley, New York, 1994, 1202–1208.
[LEH01] M.M. Lehman and J.F. Ramil, 'Rules and tools for software evolution planning and management', *Annals of Software Engineering special issue on Software Management*, **11** (2001), 15–44.
[MCC76] T.J. McCabe, 'A complexity measure', *IEEE Transactions on Software Engineering*, **2** (1976), no. 4, 308–320.
[MYE80] G.J. Myers, *'A Model of Program Stability'*, Van Nostrand Reinhold Company, 1980, 137–155, Chapter 10.
[PFL90] S.L. Pfleeger and S.A. Bohner, 'A framework for software maintenance metrics', *IEEE Conference on Software Maintenance* 1990, San Diego, CA, 320–327.
[RAJ00] V. Rajlich and K. Bennett, 'A staged model for the software lifecycle', *IEEE Computer*, **33** July (2000), no. 7, 66–71.
[SOO77] N.L. Soong, 'A program stability measure', *Proceedings 1977 Annual ACM Conference* 1977, Boulder, CO, 163–173.
[SWA76] E.B. Swanson, 'The dimensions of maintenance', *Proceedings 2nd International Conference on Software Engineering* 1976, San Francisco, CA, 492–497.
[TUR96] W.M. Turski, 'Reference model for smooth growth of software systems', *IEEE Transactions on Software Engineering*, **22** (1996), no. 8, 599–600.
[WEI84] M. Weiser, 'Program slicing', *IEEE Transactions on Software Engineering*, **10** July (1984), 352–357.
[YAU78] S.S. Yau, J.S. Collofello and T.M. McGregor, 'Ripple effect analysis of software maintenance', *Proceedings COMPSAC '78* 1978, Chicago, Illinois, 60–65.
[YAU80] S.S. Yau and J.S. Collofello, 'Some stability measures for software maintenance', *IEEE Transactions on Software Engineering*, **SE-6** (1980), no. 6, 545–552.

[YAU84] S.-S. Yau and S.C. Chang, 'Estimating logical stability in software maintenance', *Proceedings COMPSAC '84* 1984, Chicago, IL, 109–119.
[YAU85] S.-S. Yau and S.C. Chang, 'Design stability measures for software maintenance', *IEEE Transactions on Software Engineering*, **SE-11** (1985), no. 9, 849–856.
[ZUS98] H. Zuse, In Dumke R. and Abran A. (Eds.), *'Software Measurement: Research and Practice'*, Deutscher Universitats Verlag, Wiesbaden, Germany, 1998, 3–37.

13

The Impact of Software-Architecture Compliance on System Evolution

R. Mark Greenwood, Ken Mayes, Wykeen Seet, Brian C. Warboys,
Dharini Balasubramaniam, Graham Kirby, Ron Morrison and Aled Sage

13.1 Introduction

Businesses need software systems that support their ability to evolve in response to their rapidly changing environment. Legacy systems that limit a business's adaptability are seen as significant problems. In this context large successful software systems are developed in an evolutionary manner. The business use of systems provides requirements that feedback into their further development. Research in this context has highlighted flexible architectures as a key technology in ensuring that software systems provide the adaptability required by businesses [1, 2].

Lehman *et al.* have researched software evolution for approximately two decades [3–5] and provided strong arguments for taking a systemic viewpoint and looking at software development as a multi-loop feedback system. In [5] Lehman argues that more attention should be paid to feedback phenomena and to identifying and understanding feedback loops.

The identification of flexible architectures as a key indicator of the capability of a software system to support an evolving business suggests that one possible feedback loop could be based on software architecture. If there is such a feedback loop, what can be measured to help understand and predict the influence of software architecture?

The aim of this chapter is to argue that the evolutionary development of a software system can be influenced by the compliance, or goodness of fit, if its software architecture [6]. Compliant architectures can be tailored dynamically to fit the needs of particular applications. Compliance thus provides an approach to understanding the feedback effects of software architecture. The notion of compliance focuses on the relationship between a software system being developed or evolved, and system functions, such as concurrency control, scheduling, address space management and recovery management. These system functions are often provided by components, e.g. languages, operating systems and libraries, over which the developers have little or no control [7]. Where compliance is good, the system functions match the application requirements to an acceptable level. Where compliance is poor, the system functions provided are inadequate for the requirements and additional code is required to bridge the gap between the functions provided and the application's requirements. Note that this involves taking a systemic viewpoint: considering not just the application architecture but the overall system architecture, including the operating system, run-time libraries and middleware, upon which the application depends.

One way to do this is to consider the operating system, programming language, run-time environment, etc., as a set of system support components that provide the system functions. The application architecture defines requirements for system functions. These requirements can be expressed in terms of policies: e.g. the application's required scheduling policy. The architecture of the underlying system components provides a set of mechanisms through which the system functions are provided to the application. An example of poor compliance is an application that finds it necessary to do its own memory management or scheduling because its specific policy requirements are not satisfied by the architecture of the underlying system components.

This chapter will illustrate compliance by providing details of the 'goodness of fit' between an application's scheduling requirements and the scheduling mechanisms provided by the system support components. Scheduling is chosen as a system function to illustrate the general issues of compliance, in particular, the relationship between compliance and system evolution.

13.2 Evolution and Compliance

The usefulness of software systems is determined by their effect on the environment in which they are used. In most situations this environment is not static: The goals that businesses are trying to achieve are subject to continual revision and re-negotiation. If software does not change to keep up with business changes, then the business loses efficiency and the perceived value of the software decreases. In addition, it is important for businesses to exploit technological advances to remain competitive. It has long been recognised that the full business effects of introducing, or changing, a software system are emergent; they cannot be predicted in advance. This important mutual relationship between businesses and software can be viewed as co-evolution [8]: Business changes create pressures on the software to evolve, and at the same time software changes create pressures on the business to evolve.

The influence and importance of software architecture has grown as more and more software is assembled from disparate components rather than being developed from scratch. An appropriate architecture is seen as essential to understanding a software system and discussing the appropriateness of design decisions. The requirement to support the evolution of software, in response to both predicted and unexpected requirements, blurs the distinction between initial design and development and subsequent 'evolutionary' design and development.

In the context of an evolving software system, the compliance of the underlying system architecture to the user requirements can be many-faceted. Scheduling, concurrency control, address space management, and recovery management are all functions where applications typically exploit facilities provided by the underlying system architecture [7]. If the degree of compliance is poor, then it typically has both a direct and indirect effect on system evolution. If the mechanisms provided by the underlying system architecture embed policies that are not those required by the application (e.g. for scheduling or address space (including memory) management), then there is duplication and potential conflict. A direct effect is that the overall system is harder to understand. This reduces the evolutionary change that can be achieved with a given amount of effort. An indirect effect is that the effective behaviour of the system is difficult to predict. With poor compliance it is hard to know whether a request for an improved Quality of Service (QoS) can be met. Even when possible, it is difficult to predict the effort required and potential future side effects.

System functions are typically associated with QoS type requirements. Can the system provide a better response time? Will moving to a faster machine enable the system to support an expected increase in users? For a successful system these QoS requirements will evolve as the system is used. An application's compliance will therefore change as it is evolved. The monitoring of compliance during evolutionary development involves the explicit management of at least one feedback loop. It requires some measurement of the behaviour of the system and some model of the required behaviour to compare with the observed values. An ideal situation is one where increased knowledge of the application is used to improve the fit between application requirements and system functions.

13.3 A Generic Scheduling Problem

In this chapter, scheduling is chosen as a system function to illustrate the general issues of compliance. The development of the ProcessWeb system [9] is used as a concrete example. However, this is just a particular example of the problem of aligning the scheduling requirements of an application and the scheduling system functions available.

The generic problem, of which ProcessWeb is a specific example, can be summarised as follows. Consider a client server system where the server manages a pool of long-running computations on behalf of multiple users. Each user's client may have a view of multiple computations and can initiate new computations. The lifetime of the computations is orthogonal to the user client sessions, so clients can re-connect to existing computations. Conversely, each computation may have to deal with multiple users, and potentially the computations may interact with one another. There are many systems with these characteristics: workflow enactment systems, software process support systems, multi-user problem solving environments, and web servers providing access to long-running 'stateful' services.

From a scheduling perspective a key problem is how to provide the appropriate responsiveness to users. As the computations are long running, users require information on the current status, and different users may need different views. As user clients may connect, disconnect and re-connect from the server, the workload in updating the connected users is difficult to estimate.

The server implementation will have to manage many logical threads: at least one logical thread for each long-running computation and others for handling users and their views of the computations. The server's run-time environment will provide mechanisms for handling and scheduling logical threads, and deal with the mapping of these onto the operating system. The operating system will deal with mapping its threads onto the hardware. In compliance terms, the key issue is what facilities are available to tailor these scheduling mechanisms to the required application level scheduling policy.

13.3.1 A ProcessWeb Example

The overall system architecture of ProcessWeb has logical threads that have to be mapped onto the scheduling mechanisms provided by its system support components. ProcessWeb is a multi-user system that provides process support through the execution of process models [10]. It conforms to the general scheme outlined above. The core of the system is a server with a layered architecture (see Figure 13.1). The operating system provides a set of mechanisms, its application program interface (API), at the lowest level. The next layer uses these mechanisms and provides a process management language (PML) engine, or virtual machine. PML is an object-based, concurrent language with orthogonal persistence. The mechanisms provided by the PML virtual machine are the pre-defined classes of PML. The top layer consists of the PML application code.

The PML language is based on components, called *roles*, linked by interactions. A role has some similarities to an object in that it encapsulates both code and data. Every role, however, has its own thread of control. Roles operate in a peer-to-peer fashion: One role can send a message to another role but the receiving role is in full control of when to read the messages it has been sent and what to do with them. Interactions are buffered asynchronous channels that form the connectors through which messages are sent from role to role.

The ProcessWeb server executes multiple process models on behalf of its multiple users, who use standard web browsers as their clients. Each model typically includes a set of communicating 'computational' PML roles (CT in Figure 13.1), and a set of 'viewing' PML roles (VT in Figure 13.1) that provide users with their view of the current model state, and provide a channel for handling input from users.

The policy for scheduling PML roles is built into the virtual machine. A scheduler maintains a queue of active roles and selects one of these in a round-robin manner. The

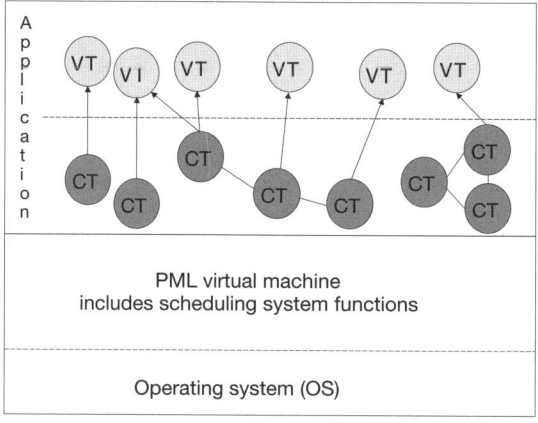

Figure 13.1 Layered architecture of ProcessWeb

role either runs until it reaches a waiting state or until it is timed out, whichever is the shorter. A role reaches a waiting state when there is no more computation that it can perform until there is a message available in an interaction. A role is returned to the end of the queue of active roles when an appropriate message arrives.

The PML application has control over the number of roles created and how they are linked through interactions. All roles are considered equal by the scheduler. However, from the application viewpoint (see Figure 13.1) not all roles are equal. Viewing roles have a natural unit of execution: handling a message. These roles typically spend most of their time in the waiting state. They become active when a message arrives, and return to the waiting state once the message has been handled. Other roles are computationally intensive and spend the majority of their lifetime in the active state.

13.3.2 Programming Around Poor Compliance

The fact that the scheduling policy is built into the PML virtual machine is a classic symptom of where poor compliance can impact system evolution. If the encapsulated policy matches the application needs, then compliance is still good. However, there are no mechanisms for the application developer to communicate additional knowledge about the nature of the application for the scheduler to exploit. If the encapsulated policy does not match the application needs, then overall observed application behaviour is inadequate. Application developers work around the problem by introducing additional code to achieve the desired effects.

One example that occurred during the evolutionary development of ProcessWeb involved interim status messages from computationally intensive roles. The problem observed was that these messages were not delivered promptly to users. Users received a few status messages and then, on completion of the intensive computation, many status messages in rapid succession. As the status messages were to inform users of progress, this was not the desired behaviour.

This problem was reported and the developers decided to evolve the system. The solution involved introducing a 'blocking' interaction, a specialised connector. The only way in PML to reduce the priority of a role is to make it wait for a message from an interaction. After sending the status message, the computational role would wait for a resume message on a 'blocking' interaction. The viewing role would send the resume message.

Here, observing the behaviour of the system identified a mismatch between the policy required by the ProcessWeb application and the mechanisms provided by the PML virtual machine. The virtual machine mechanisms encapsulate a policy of round-robin scheduling based on the assumption that all roles are equal. The feedback and evolution described above are typical of a system with a poor degree of compliance. Because the developers have limited control over the system policy, in this case scheduling, its influence is not fully recognised. (For example, in response to a problem, developers may experiment with a number of implementation alternatives until an acceptable result is obtained.)

13.4 Compliance Through Configuration

Many systems are developed through the assembly of components. Some of these components are brought in, and their development is outside the control of the system developers. To provide flexibility, components may be configurable, in which case the compliance of an application depends upon finding the best values for configuration parameters.

For scheduling, one configuration parameter can be the time slice threshold that determines the maximum time that the scheduler will allocate to an application thread. If this time slice threshold is large, then the scheduling becomes effectively co-operative: Each thread runs until it reaches a natural waiting state and voluntarily gives up control. The disadvantage of this is that responsiveness can suffer. If the time slice threshold is small, then the system cycles through its threads much quicker but the system has much more scheduling to do. The disadvantage of this is that efficiency can suffer. There is the additional overhead of calling the scheduler more frequently.

In 1997, there was a major revision of the PML abstract machine to improve its performance. This led to an evolution of ProcessWeb as it was moved to the revised virtual machine. The scheduling algorithm was now configurable. An administration interface to the PML abstract machine allowed the threshold that controls when a role is timed out to be set. This scheduler threshold is the maximum number of instructions that a role is allowed to execute before being forced to give up control. It is expressed in thousands of PML abstract machine instructions[1], with the default being 25. Given this, one compliance question is how to find the value for this scheduler time slice threshold that gives the best fit with ProcessWeb as a PML application.

A small experiment was undertaken to investigate the effect of this scheduler threshold. The experiment was designed as a simple busy ProcessWeb system, as it is when the system is busy that the scheduler has the most impact in terms of system responsiveness.

As part of the administration interface for the PML abstract machine there is access to monitoring information from which the following can be identified:

- *% roles timed out* is the percentage of roles, given control by the scheduler, that reach the end of their time slice rather than giving up control voluntarily.
- *Scheduler time* is the working time; it includes the time that the roles are running and the time spent in the scheduler itself.

The overall results are shown in Table 13.1, with more detail in Table 13.2. The scheduler threshold was varied and a fixed amount of work was undertaken. For each of the 'scheduler threshold' values the run was repeated with the times varying by less than 2 seconds (less than 1%).

Table 13.1 Varying the scheduler timeout threshold

Scheduler threshold	Roles timed out (%)	Scheduler time (seconds)
5	76	1,033
25	50	979
125	48	952
625	40	942

---

[1] Abstract machine instructions were chosen in preference to absolute time since these represent work done and are not affected by waiting for IO, or the PML abstract machine being suspended to allow another machine process to run.

The general trend of the results is as expected. As the scheduler threshold increases, a smaller proportion of roles are timed out. This means that a correspondingly larger proportion reach a state where they voluntarily give up control because it is a sensible point to do so in application terms. In looking for an appropriate scheduler threshold some guidance based on knowledge of the application is useful. One rule of thumb is that only computationally intensive roles should time out. Viewing roles, which handle a message as their natural unit of execution, should normally not time out. In this experiment the ratio of computational to viewing roles was 50:50, and the computational roles were programmed to occasionally give up control. Based on this, if the percentage of roles timed out is greater than 50%, reducing the scheduler threshold further will not improve responsiveness as some of the viewing roles are being timed out.

When assembling a system from configurable components, finding the best fit between the application and its underlying system architecture involves finding the best values for configurable parameters. It is unlikely that this can be done based on a purely analytical approach and some feedback from measuring the system behaviour is essential. Clearly, as the application evolves, including when it is ported to use new system support components (in this case revisions of the PML virtual machine or operating system), the goodness of fit between them can be monitored.

13.4.1 Trade-offs in Configuration

In Section 13.2 it was identified that compliance can be many-faceted. Often applications exploit several facilities provided by the underlying system architecture. There can be interactions between these. For example, the scheduling algorithm might affect garbage collection.

For a system that manages long-running computations there is often an interaction between scheduling and recovery management. The focus of scheduling is on sharing resources appropriately between users and completing their computations as efficiently as possible. The focus of recovery management is on regularly recording a consistent state on a reliable storage medium. The overall effect is that the processing resource is divided between 'doing the work' and 'mitigating the effect of failures'. The recovery management policy may constrain the sensible values of scheduling configuration parameters as threads have to relinquish control often enough for the recovery management mechanisms to do their job. Likewise the scheduling policy may change the number and nature of the computations, which the recovery management mechanisms must store on a reliable medium.

In Section 13.4 the identification of the appropriate scheduler time slice threshold was based on an understanding of the application and observation of the scheduler time. To understand the full effect of this scheduling configuration parameter, it is necessary to understand the application and other system functions that interact with scheduling and to observe all contributions to the overall time taken by the system.

In the PML virtual machine, the scheduler time is the total time that the roles are executing and the time spent in the scheduler itself. However, the overall time taken to perform a task involves both the scheduler time and the commit time. The commit time comes from the recovery management mechanism that is built into the PML abstract machine.

The PML abstract machine is designed to be highly resilient: Messages between the PML abstract machine and other systems should be reliable, and it should recover with minimum losses in the event of machine failure. To achieve this it checkpoints its computation either every time it sends or receives a message, or every minute if there are no messages. This means that the PML abstract machine does not present separate mechanisms for scheduling and recovery management but encapsulates a policy combining these two.

The full results from the simple ProcessWeb experiment are shown in Table 13.2 (an extended version of Table 13.1 with additional information related to recovery management). The *% roles timed out* and *scheduler time* are as described in Section 13.4. The others are:

- *Roles scheduled* indicate the total number of times that any role is given control by the scheduler; a higher number indicates a larger scheduling overhead.
- *Roles timed out* is the number of roles that reached the end of their time slice.
- *Commit time* is the time that the system spends checkpointing its current state to a persistent store.
- *Total active time* is the overall time spent by the system; it is the sum of the scheduler time, the commit time, and a small amount of time dealing with input and output messages.
- *Store size* and *store growth* relate to the system's persistent store.

Table 13.2 shows that as the scheduler threshold increases, the underlying persistent store grows much more quickly. This means that there is a corresponding increase in the time spent writing data out to the store. In this experiment a larger scheduler threshold leads to more data being committed to the persistent store: data that is produced by one role and has to be stored until another consumes it. The overall effect is that the flexibility offered by the scheduler threshold parameter is limited by its interaction with the recovery management policy, over which the ProcessWeb application has no control.

This example illustrates that configurable parameters can be used to improve compliance between an application and its system support components. However, overall it is a restricted set of the application's policy requirements that can be expressed in terms of the available parameters. (Setting the scheduler threshold gives considerable flexibility

Table 13.2 ProcessWeb experiment of scheduler timeout threshold including commit time

Scheduler threshold (1,000 instructions)	5	25	125	625	3,125	15,625
Roles scheduled	4,220,059	1,292,048	264,044	60,042	20,044	12,082
Roles timed out	3,210,016	642,005	126,000	24,000	4,000	0
% roles timed out (%)	76	50	48	40	20	0
Scheduler time (roles working)	1,033	979	952	942	935	932
Commit time	42	45	48	57	87	155
Total active time (seconds)	1,077	1,027	1,002	1,001	1,025	1,091
Final store size (Mb)	180.2	180.1	180.0	181.9	188.1	205.4
Store growth (Mb)	8.4	8.3	8.2	10.1	16.3	33.6

but does not support changing the basic algorithm, say, to allow priority scheduling.) In addition, the interaction between various configuration choices is difficult to predict. The net effect is that the flexibility offered by such configuration facilities is often little exploited in practice.

13.5 Exploiting an Analytical Model

Where the system architecture is flexible there is the problem of how to identify a good fit for an application. There is a feedback loop with observations of the application behaviour providing additional information that can be used to further guide the search for an acceptable fit. The examples in the previous sections illustrate how some understanding of the application and the underlying system components can be exploited in interpreting the behaviour observed. The issue can be approached as a feedback control problem. What is needed is some model that captures the expected relationship between a configurable parameter and some observable behaviour. The model can then be used to guide the search for the most appropriate parameter setting.

The analytical model can be used to calculate expected values. These can be compared with the actual values from monitoring the application. If there is an acceptable correspondence between the expected and observed values, then the analytical model can be used to guide changes in the configuration parameters. If the difference between the expected value from the analytical model and the observed value indicate that the model is no longer accurate, then it may be possible to re-calibrate or revise the model, using recently monitored values and user input [11].

13.5.1 A First Analytical Model for ProcessWeb

For ProcessWeb an initial model might be that the total active time is the sum of two factors: scheduler time, which decreases as the scheduler time slice threshold increases, and commit time, which increases as the scheduler time slice threshold increases.

Experimental results, such as those above, can be used to calibrate an analytical model. This experiment involved a fixed workload and measured commit time corresponding to several scheduler threshold values (Table 13.2 above). A formula for estimating commit time can be obtained by curve fitting.[2]

Scheduler threshold	Estimated commit time	Observed commit time
th	$0.9\mathbf{th}^{1/2} + 40$	
5	42	42
25	44	45
125	50	48
625	62	57
3,125	90	87
15,625	152	155

---

[2] It is important to remember that the calibration points in the analytic model are points in a multi-dimensional space. In calibration, the assumption is that the relationship between the points is uniform (not necessarily always linear).

This gives us a formula that models the relationship between scheduler threshold (**th**) and commit time.

$$\text{commit time} = s\ \mathbf{th}^{1/2} + t\ (s \text{ and } t \text{ are constants})$$

When working with ProcessWeb and a different workload, initial observations could be used to generate estimates for the constants s and t. Using the same method, a formula for estimating the scheduler time can be obtained.

$$\text{scheduler time} = v\ \mathbf{th}^{-1/3} + w\ (v \text{ and } w \text{ are constants})$$

This can roughly be thought of as a fixed time (w) for the work to be done by the roles and a scheduling overhead that increases the more often the scheduler is called (i.e. the lower the scheduler threshold).

Scheduler threshold	Estimated scheduler time	Observed scheduler time
th	$170/(\mathbf{th}^{1/3}) + 924$	
5	1,023	1,033
25	982	979
125	958	952
625	944	942
3,125	936	935
15,625	931	932

These two parts can clearly be combined to give an overall formula relating the scheduler threshold to overall active time.

The value of developing an analytical model is not just in being able to predict system behaviour and exploit effectively any flexibility offered by the underlying system architecture. The analytic model also increases understanding of the system by highlighting phase changes: areas where a previously insignificant factor starts to have an influence on the system. In the example recorded in Table 13.2 it appears that the persistent store growth can be considered as an unchanging aspect of the system behaviour, until the scheduling threshold gets to somewhere between 125 and 625.

13.6 Discussion

An E-type system [3] becomes part of the world it models. Its validity depends upon human assessment of its effectiveness rather than its correctness with regard to a specification. It is continually adapted in response to user feedback to avoid it becoming progressively less satisfactory (Lehman's First Law, Continuing Change [5]). In many cases sources of dissatisfaction are not observable until the system is used (Uncertainty Principle [4]). The evolutionary development of any E-type system can be influenced by the compliance, or goodness of fit, of its underlying system architecture.

This chapter has taken a particular system function, scheduling, and illustrated the observations required to measure compliance of the underlying system architecture to the needs of a specific application. Such measurements can be used to configure components to improve compliance, and to improve understanding of the system-wide effect of changes.

Where there is limited compliance, a policy is imposed, its effects are observed, and the system is evolved to work around problems. New code is introduced that adds complexity and embeds assumptions about the policy.

This illustrates that the evolution of an E-type system is not independent of the underlying system architecture. There are situations where poor compliance gives rise to dissatisfaction, and thus prompts system evolution. These can be especially difficult to track down as the observed fault (e.g. intermittent poor response, insufficient memory errors) often gives little guidance.

In some systems there is architectural flexibility through the composition of configurable components. This means that although a policy is imposed, some tuning to the application requirements is possible through the configuration parameters. As the system is used, the effects of different configuration parameters can be measured. This feedback is used to evolve the policy. The flexibility achievable through such configuration parameters may not be sufficient for all application requirements. Typically this produces a system where the degree of compliance is variable. It is good so long as the application fits within the flexibility requirements predicted and built into the system architecture, but poor if the application's requirements are outside this envelope.

A highly compliant system has a simpler feedback cycle because this restriction is removed. The key is that the architecture of the underlying system components provides mechanisms, and these can be combined with application specific knowledge to yield a policy that is tailored to the application requirements [12]. The effects of this can be observed and a revised policy produced to address changing requirements.

An important aspect is that the feedback loop is explicitly recognised. Developers are faced with two key questions (adapted from Reference 7). First, how to discover what the system is doing? Second, how to structure the overall system architecture to utilise that knowledge?

There are considerable similarities between this and the use of an architecture model to facilitate dynamic self-adapting software systems [1]. In both cases there is a need for explicit system monitoring and a model of the system itself is required to exploit the monitoring information.

In [13] compliance refers to the notion of selecting one or more middleware platforms that are suitable, based on an application's architecture. The context is the initial design and development of a software system exploiting off-the-shelf middleware components. Like this chapter, it recognises the impact of the 'goodness of fit' between application requirements and the mechanisms provided by underlying components. However, the initial design and development context means that it does not investigate the relationship between compliance and evolution.

In the context of system evolution, the notion of compliant architecture makes developers continually address the issue of whether the system functions are appropriate, given what is known about the system's use. To achieve a high degree of compliance requires that developers have access to the policies that they may wish to change. This contrasts with the common situation where there is duplication because one system component has to include additional code to transform what is supplied into the policy that is needed.

There is a tension between a compliant architecture and reuse of components. Components that are reused in several systems usually evolve in response to the combined feedback from all. They often encapsulate policies to achieve a simple interface, which makes reuse easier, but yields an architecture that is less likely to be compliant to the needs of a specific system.

Observing over several years the evolution of systems, including ProcessWeb, and research in developing highly compliant systems [6, 7] supports the conjecture that compliance also affects the characteristics of software evolution. A system with a compliant architecture will evolve differently since more of its feedback loops will be explicit and actively managed. In this context, how to measure a compliant architecture and its influence is a key research challenge.

13.7 Acknowledgements

Research supported by UK EPSRC Grants GR/M88938 and GR/M88945. Thanks are also due to efforts and patience of the anonymous reviewers whose comments on various drafts led to substantial improvements.

References

[1] Cheng S.-W., Garlan D., Schmerl B., Steenkiste P. and Hu N., Software architecture-based adaption for grid computing, in *11th IEEE Conference of High Performance Distributed Computing (HDPC'02)*, Edinburgh, Scotland, July 2002.

[2] Henderson P. (Ed.), *Systems Engineering for Business Process Change*, Springer, London, 2000.

[3] Lehman M.M. and Belady L.A., *Software Evolution – Processes of Software Change*, Academic Press, London, 1985.

[4] Lehman M.M., Software engineering, the software process and their support, in *Softw. Eng. J.*, vol. 6, no. 5., 1991, 243–258.

[5] Lehman M.M., Laws of software evolution revisited, in Montangero C. (Ed.), *Fifth European Workshop in Software Process Technology (EWSPT'96)*, Nancy, France, Oct. 1996, in *Lecture Notes in Computer Science*, Vol. 1149, 1996, 108–124.

[6] Morrison R., Balasubramaniam, D., Greenwood R.M., Kirby G.N.C., Mayes K., Munro D.S. and Warboys B.C. An approach to compliance in software architectures, in *IEE Computing & Control Engineering Journal*, Special Issue on Informatics vol. 11, no. 4, 2000, 195–200.

[7] Morrison R., Balasubramaniam D., Greenwood R.M., Kirby G.N.C., Mayes K., Munro D.S. and Warboys B.C. A compliant persistent architecture, in *Software Practice and Experience*, vol. 30, no. 4, 2000, 363–386.

[8] Mitleton-Kelly, E. and Papaefthimiou, M.-C. Co-evolution of diverse elements interacting within a social ecosystem, in Henderson P. (Ed.), *Systems Engineering for Business Process Change: New Directions*, Springer, London, 2002, 253–273.

[9] Process Web, http://processweb.cs.man.ac.uk/ [Accessed 16 January 2006].

[10] Warboys B.C., Kawalek P., Robertson I. and Greenwood R.M., *Business Information Systems: a Process Approach*, McGraw-Hill, UK, 1999.

[11] Sage A.I., Kirby G.N.C. and Morrison R. ACT: a tool for performance driven evolution of distributed applications, in *Proceedings: Working Conference on Complex and Dynamic Systems Architecture*, 2001, Brisbane, Australia.

[12] Seet W. and Warboys B.C., A compliant environment for enacting evolvable process models. in Oquendo F. (Ed.), *Ninth European Workshop in Software Process Technology (EWSPT'03)*, Helsinki, Finland, Sept. 2003, in *Lecture Notes in Computer Science*, vol. 2876, 2003, 154–163.

[13] Medvidovic, N. On the role of middleware in architecture-based software development, in *Proceedings 14th International Conference on Software Engineering and Knowledge Engineering (SEKE'02)*, Ischia, Italy, July 2002, 299–306.

14

Comparison of Three Evaluation Methods for Object-Oriented Framework Evolution

Michael Mattsson

Based on "Observations on the Evolution of an Industrial OO Framework" by Michael Mattsson, Jan Bosch which appeared on icsm, p. 139. 15th IEEE International Conference on Software Maintenance (ICSM'99). (c) 1999 IEEE.

14.1 Introduction

An object-oriented framework is a set of classes that embodies an abstract design for solutions to a family of related problems. The important abstractions in the framework are the abstract classes and their way of collaboration. Since the main intention is to capture a common design for a set of similar applications (or subsystem domains), an object-oriented framework is a reusable asset that forms the basis for developing applications in the domains served.

Early examples of the object-oriented framework concept can be found in the Smalltalk environment, for example, [1] and at Apple Inc. [2]. The Smalltalk-80 user interface framework, Model-View-Controller (MVC), was perhaps the first widely used framework. Apple Inc. developed the MacApp user interface framework that was designed for supporting the implementation of applications on the Macintosh computers. Now, object-oriented frameworks have developed into more common technology in object-oriented software development [3, 4] and the framework concept has been used in many different domains, for example, Graphical User Interfaces (GUIs) [5], fire alarm systems [6], measurement systems [7] and telecommunication [8]. Well-known examples of object-oriented frameworks from the domain of GUIs are Java AWT [9], Microsoft Foundation Classes (MFC) [10] and ET++ [5]. Examples of proprietary object-oriented frameworks are the ones developed by UIQ Technology [11]. The UIQ frameworks form the basis for the user interface source code for the Sony Ericsson P800/900 mobile phones and similar phones, having a pen-based GUI and using the Symbian operating system. The majority of the frameworks are proprietary and are not available outside UIQ.

The increased use of object-oriented frameworks is due to the fact that it bears the promise of large-scale reuse and reduced development effort. A study by Rösel [12] indicates increased reuse and reduced development effort. Mattsson [13] reports a quantitative relationship between effort spent on framework development and effort spent on application development using the framework (normally referred to as *framework instantiation*). The data says that the average effort of developing an application based on the framework is less than 2.0% of the effort for developing the framework. The data is based on 31 instantiations of one large framework. There is also a study by Moser and Nierstrasz [14] that reports increased productivity of the developers when using object-oriented frameworks.

As with all software, frameworks tend to evolve, leading to new versions, owing to the incorporation of new or changed requirements, better domain understanding, experiences and fault corrections. Once a framework has been deployed, new versions of the framework will cause maintenance costs for the applications built with the framework. This since a new framework version with major changes (e.g. added functionality or corrections) makes it necessary that the framework-based applications must be upgraded with the new version to incorporate the new functionality. The total cost for this upgrading effort of the applications is depending on the total number of applications, that is, the number of framework instantiations shipped.

This, in combination with the high costs of developing and evolving an object-oriented framework, indicates the importance of understanding and characterizing framework evolution. In this chapter the evolution of a proprietary framework (four consecutive versions), where each version had a development cost between 10,000 to 20,000 person hours and where the size increased from 233 to 598 C++ classes, is reported.

One of the main objectives in managing object-oriented software development is to have controlled and predictable evolution of the framework's functionality and costs (both the development and framework instantiation costs). This requires that there must exist methods assisting and providing management with information about the framework and its evolution. Key management issues of interest include the following:

- *Identification of change prone modules*: Management may decide to proactively maintain the framework to simplify the incorporation of future requirements. In that case, it is important to know which modules exhibit a high degree of change between framework versions and which modules do not. The evolution-prone modules are likely candidates for restructuring. The information about where likely changes occur may reduce the cost of redesigning the framework. A study by Lindvall and Sandahl [15] shows that software engineers without automated support can only identify a subset (<50%) of future changes and they cannot provide the complete view of change. Thus, a more objective method for identifying structural shortcomings in an object-oriented framework will provide more reliable input for maintenance effort estimations.
- *Framework deployment*: Assessment of a framework to decide if it can be released for regular product development in the organization or placed on the commercial market. This assessment is necessary to avoid the shipping of frameworks that do not

fulfil their functional and quality requirements and, consequently, any unnecessary maintenance and release costs. The assessment data can in some cases, if publicly available, be used by potential customers for evaluating and selecting a framework from several alternatives; for instance, if the assessment covers aspects such as reliability and robustness for its users.

- *Change impact analysis*: This is concerned with assessing the impact of changes both on the next framework version and the applications built using the current version. It would be possible for management to use the assessment results for predictions of maintenance effort for both the framework development and the framework instantiations.
- *Benchmarking*: Empirical information collected from the assessments of successful frameworks can be valuable in guiding the development and evolution of new frameworks and can be used to develop criteria for framework classification, for example, benchmarking, in terms of structural stability or other framework maturity aspects [16]. This is desirable since it is difficult and expensive to develop and maintain object-oriented frameworks and empirical data is a valuable input to the cost and effort estimation activities. Currently, little information is available concerning the cost and/or benefits associated with the development and use of framework technology. Empirical information about the distribution of effort in framework development, evolution and instantiation would help in allocating specialists and other personnel to these tasks.
- *Requirements management*: Framework assessment can be used to select the criteria for deciding when to incorporate a new requirement during framework instantiation or not in the next version of the framework. In addition, it supports decisions on the incorporation of new features in the framework, since the impact is made explicit. A primary apparent strategy for an organization is to incorporate the requirements for the different instantiations into the next version of the framework. However, some of the instantiations could have been difficult and expensive to perform and are stretching the limits of the framework and should not have an impact on the next framework version.

This chapter presents the following:

(i) three methods that identify and characterize framework evolution;
(ii) an assessment of these methods against the aforementioned issues; and
(iii) a discussion of the methods, particularly, difficulty in their usage, need for tool support, and their advantages and disadvantages.

The three methods are as follows:

- *Evolution identification using historical information*: This method is used for identifying and characterizing the framework's proneness-to-change, its subsystem and their modules. On the basis of historical information obtained from the framework versions, it is possible to make statements about the framework's evolution in terms of size, growth rate and change rate. The statements about the evolution of the framework, its subsystems or subsystem modules can be made from one version to the next or by considering a set of successive versions. Thus, the purpose of the method is to identify the parts of the framework prone to change.
- *Stability assessment*: This is a metrics-based assessment method for assessing structural and behavioural stability of a framework. The notion of structural and behavioural

stability is viewed as the dual property of evolution. Through collection of a set of architectural and class level metrics together with the calculation of some aggregated metrics, the obtained metric values are used for the assessment of the framework together with a set of framework stability indicators. Each framework stability indicator is used for deciding if the current framework version is stable or not with respect to the metrics dealt with by the indicator. Thus, the purpose of the method is to decide how structurally and behaviourally stable a framework is in terms of framework stability indicator fulfilment.

- *Distribution of development effort*: This method is based on an analysis of the effort consumed during the development of the framework. Effort data is collected per developed framework version and development phase, and effort-per-phase and version in terms relative to the total effort expended per framework version is calculated. The result is presented and a qualitative analysis of what caused the changes in relative effort consumption for the framework versions is carried out. Normally, the application of the method is simple since effort data is often collected and stored in the developing organization's time reporting system. The main purpose of the method is to characterize and analyse the relative distribution of effort per development phase and version for a framework and the relation between framework development effort and framework instantiation effort.

The described three methods have been applied on four consecutive versions of the same framework, the Billing GateWay (BGW) framework, a proprietary object-oriented framework in the telecommunication domain, which makes it possible to assess them with respect to the aforementioned issues. The application and detailed results of the evolution identification using historical information method can be found in [17]. The results of applying the stability assessment method can be found in [18, 19]. In these stability assessment studies, the MFC [10] and Borland's Object Windows Library (OWL) [20] frameworks have been assessed too. Both MFC and OWL are addressing the GUI domain. In this chapter, the MFC framework will be discussed only briefly and the OWL framework not at all. The results from applying the distribution of development effort method on the BGW framework can be found in [13].

This chapter focuses on describing the three methods and comparing them with respect to their suitability for the management issues that were discussed earlier. Consequently, only some major results from the application of the methods are provided here.

The main contribution of this chapter is that it presents a qualitative assessment of three methods for evaluating object-oriented framework evolution, which have all been applied on industrial frameworks, with respect to the identified management issues; that is, identification of change-prone modules, framework deployment, change impact analysis, benchmarking and requirements management.

The remainder of the chapter is organized as follows. Framework terminology and the studied BGW framework are presented in Section 14.2. The three methods and some results from the application of the methods, as well as a short discussion about each method, are described in Section 14.3. In Section 14.4, the comparison of the methods is presented. Related work is found in Section 14.5 and the chapter is concluded in Section 14.6.

14.2 Object-oriented Frameworks

Object-oriented frameworks are reusable designs of all or part of software systems. A framework is defined by a set of abstract classes and the way instances (objects) of those classes collaborate [21]. The development cost of frameworks is high and thus efforts need to be made to reduce these costs. They must provide enough features to be usable and hooks supporting features that are likely to change. Roberts and Johnson [21] describe the typical maturation path an object-oriented framework takes below:

(i) *White-box framework*: A white-box framework relies on the inheritance mechanism as the primary instantiation technique. The instantiations of a concept are easily made through creating a subclass of an appropriate abstract class. A disadvantage of white-box frameworks is that one has to know about internal class details and that the creation of new subclasses requires programming.

(ii) *Black-box framework*: A black-box framework differs from a white-box framework in that the primary instantiation technique is composition. Thus, a black-box framework allows one to combine the objects into applications and one does not need to know internal details of the objects. The use of composition to create applications implies that programming of individual objects is avoided and it is possible to allow the compositions to vary at run time. Often the initial design of a framework is a white-box framework, whereas subsequent versions evolve into a black-box framework.

(iii) *Visual builder*: To evolve to the visual builder stage, the framework must be a black-box framework. A black-box framework makes it possible to develop an application by connecting objects of existing classes. An application consists of different parts. First, a script is used that connects the objects of the framework and then activates them. The other part is the behaviour of the individual objects, which is provided by the black-box framework. Thus, framework instantiation in the black-box case is mainly a script that is similar for all applications based on the framework. On the basis of this, one can develop a separate graphical program, that is, a visual builder that allows the framework user to specify the objects to be included in the application as well as their interconnection. The visual builder generates the code for the application from the specification. The addition of a visual builder to the framework provides a user-friendly graphical interface, which makes it possible for domain experts to develop the applications by manipulating images on the screen.

(iv) *Language tools*: A visual builder framework creates complex composite objects. The compositions created in the visual builder framework need to be inspected and debugged. A visual builder framework basically defines a graphical domain-specific programming language. Thus, in this maturation stage, one can create specific language tools for the framework that support inspection and debugging of the composite objects.

14.2.1 The Studied Frameworks

This section describes the BGW framework, which has been used as a major study subject to investigate the three methods. The other two frameworks studied, MFC and OWL, are not described here because they capture a rather well-known domain, GUIs. For a more detailed description of these two frameworks the reader is referred to [10] and [20], respectively.

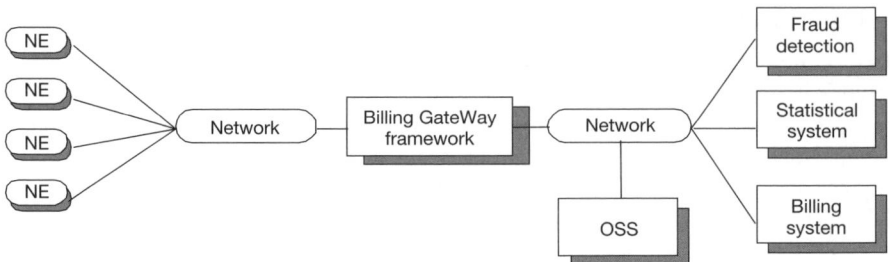

Figure 14.1 The context of the BGW framework

The BGW framework is a major part of the BGW product developed by Ericsson Software Technology, and provides functionality for billing data mediation between network elements (NEs), that is, switches, billing systems or other post-processing systems (PPSs) for mobile telecommunication. The framework collects call information from mobile switches (more generically NEs), processes the call information and mediates it to billing processing systems. Figure 14.1 presents the context of the BGW framework graphically. The driving quality requirements in this domain are reliability, availability, portability, call records throughput and maintainability. The framework is a visual builder framework (black-box plus a graphical interface), that is, the framework provides a number of pre-defined objects for application configuration.

The four consecutive versions studied of the BGW framework, have all been at the visual builder stage, for example, a black-box framework with associated graphical instantiation interface and code generation functionality. Successively, from the second version of the BGW framework, a few specific language tools have been developed.

The BGW framework is instantiated through a graphical configuration window. The application developer (framework user) selects different types of entities and associated operations to be performed, which should constitute the instantiated application. For example, it is possible to select NEs (e.g. a mobile switch), PPSs and different kinds of processing such as filtering and formatting. Each of these entities has during the configuration/instantiation to be specified in more detail, through the use of entity-specific menus. When all entities have been specified, the application to be developed based on the framework is specified, and it is possible to generate the application. The specification data is divided to appropriate classes and objects and the application is generated

To provide an understanding of the evolution of BGW framework, the major requirements for the four framework versions are briefly discussed since they have an impact on the structure and functionality of the framework.

Requirements version 1.0: Develop an architecture that supported the identified variable and stable parts of the domain. For this requirement, the organization could rely on its experience gained from a previously developed application in the same domain.

Requirements version 2.0: Increase flexibility and robustness in the framework. This was achieved through refinement of some of the design concepts, improved encapsulation and the identification of minor domain-specific libraries that provide generalized and abstract routines for data handling and formatting.

Requirements version 3.0: Facilitate 'hot billing'. Hot billing makes it possible to collect call data records from NEs and distribute them to PPSs (such as billing systems) within seconds of call completion. Thus, hot billing facilitates invoicing of services tailored to specific customer needs, such as real-time billing and phone rental. This requirement caused major changes of the data processing in the system.

Requirements version 4.0: Porting the BGW framework to new operating platforms and to facilitate advanced data processing such as call data record matching and rating. Matching makes it simple to collect data from different nodes in the system's network at different times, thereby simplifying the charging of services with more than one call data record such as distance related charging.

14.3 Methods and Results

In this section, three methods for evaluating object-oriented framework evolution together with major results achieved when applying the methods are presented. For a more detailed presentation of the results of applying the methods, the reader is referred to [17] for the evolution identification using historical information method, the stability assessment method is found in [18] and [19] and distribution of development effort method in [13].

14.3.1 Evolution Identification Using Historical Information

14.3.1.1 Method Description

The evolution identification method for identifying and characterizing the proneness-to-change of an object-oriented framework, its subsystems and the modules is an adaptation of an approach proposed by Gall *et al.* [22]. The focus of the study was on software evolution by tracking the release history of a system. Their system comprises about 10 million lines of code and was structurally divided into a number of subsystems where each subsystem was further divided into modules and each module consisted of a number of programs. On the basis of historical information about the programs, subsystems and so on, Gall *et al.* investigated the change rate, growth rate and size of the software (and its parts) using the *version numbering* of the programs as the fundamental studied units. Their study comprised 20 releases of the software systems.

This approach is adapted to better suit smaller, object-oriented, systems (200–600 classes). The adaptation includes a decomposition of the object-oriented framework into subsystems and modules. Modules are composed of classes, not programs as in the study by Gall *et al.* This means that calculations of change and growth rates are made in terms of classes as the studied units. Changed classes are identified by a *change in the number of public operations* in the class interface. The rationale for this is that a change in the public interface represents an addition of the functionality that a class offers to the rest of the system (or a division of existing functionality into two or more public operations). Changes to the private part of a class interface are mostly related to perfective changes such as performance improvements. Data about the following framework properties is collected according to the adaptation of the original method:

- The *size* of each framework, subsystem or module is defined as the number of classes it contains. The notion of classes is used to measure size instead of lines of source

code. This is because it is easier to collect necessary information on the detailed design level compared to the source code level.
- The *change rate* is the percentage of classes in a particular framework, subsystem or module that changed from one version to the next (i.e. a change in number of public operations). To compute the change rate, two versions are required for comparison. The relative number of changed classes represents the change rate.
- The *growth rate* is defined as the percentage of classes in a particular framework, subsystem or module that have been added or deleted from one version to the next. To compute the growth rate, two versions are compared and the numbers of added and deleted classes are counted. The relative number of new classes (i.e. the difference between added and removed classes) represents the growth rate.

On the basis of the information extracted from different framework versions, it is possible to make statements about a framework's evolution related to the following:

1. the complete framework;
2. the subsystems of the framework; and
3. the modules of particular subsystems identified for further studies.

The method comprises the following steps:

1. Calculate, for all releases, the change and growth rate for the complete framework.
2. Calculate, for all releases, the change and growth rate for each of the subsystems.
3. For those subsystems that exhibit high growth and change rates calculate, for all releases, the change and growth rates for the modules.
4. Those modules that exhibit high change and growth rates are identified as likely candidates for restructuring.

14.3.1.2 Results

This section presents results from the application of the method on the BGW framework. The results describe observations on framework, subsystem and module level of the framework.

Framework-level observations. Figure 14.2 shows the number of classes that were added in each version (i.e. added minus removed classes). For example, the figure shows that at version 2.0 more than 120 classes were added to the system. A general observation is that the *number of added classes is decreasing* with newer versions of the framework. This can be taken as an indication that the framework is becoming more mature, that is, achieving a structural stability.

Figure 14.3 compares the change and growth rates for each version of the BGW framework. In general, the change rate is higher than the growth rate. The growth rate is decreasing with successive versions of the framework, from about 40% in version 2.0 down to about 15% in version 4.0. This *decrease in growth rate* is another indication of the framework's structural stability.

The change rate is increasing in version 4.0 and is not following the trend for version 2.0 and 3.0. One reason for this may be a change with *architectural impact*, that is,

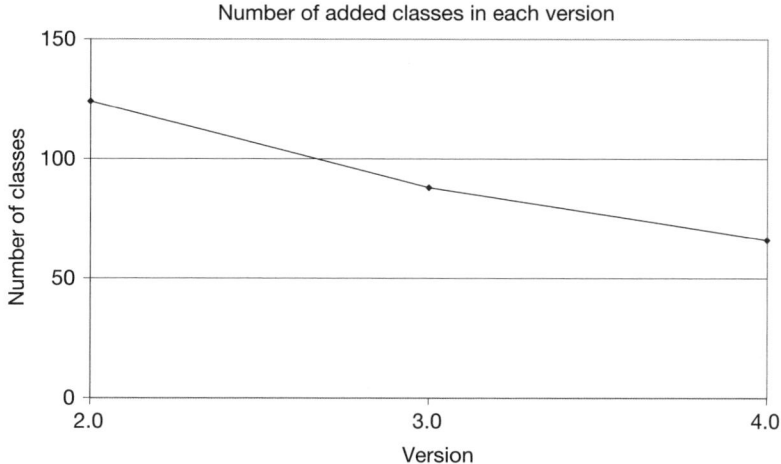

Figure 14.2 Number of added classes in each version

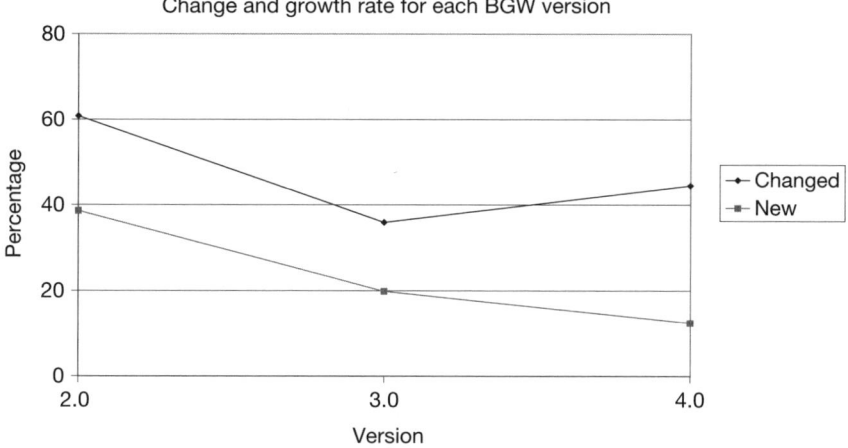

Figure 14.3 Change and growth rates for each BGW version

a change affecting entities throughout the whole system. In the BGW framework, the change with architectural impact was the introduction of hot billing. This requirement caused a conversion from file-based data representation (containing several megabytes) to block-based data representation (containing several tens of kilobytes). This change had an architectural impact and caused changes in many parts of the system.

The observations on the framework levels indicate that the framework evolves in a satisfactory fashion. This since the growth rate is decreasing and the change rate is at an acceptable level. However, the observations are only valid on the framework level, and it may be the case that the subsystems do not behave in the same way.

Table 14.1 Change and growth rates of BGW subsystems

Subsystem	Change rate (%)	Growth rate (%)	Relative size (%)
Subsystem A (graphical user interface)	51	191	34
Subsystem B (server and communication)	64	153	24
Subsystem C (coding/decoding and handling of call data records)	92	191	37
Subsystem D (initialisation, tools etc.)	75	700	5

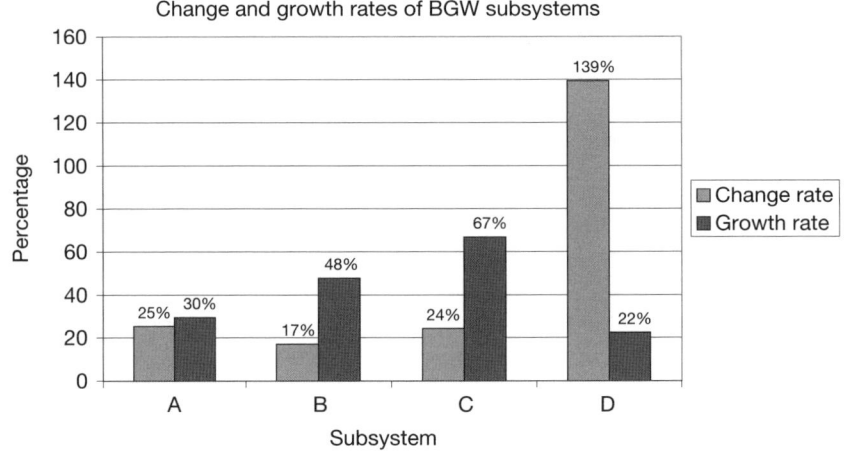

Figure 14.4 Change and growth rates of BGW subsystems

The evolution of subsystems. The previous section discussed the evolution of the whole framework but are the subsystems evolving in the same manner?

Table 14.1 and Figure 14.4 present the change and growth rates for the four subsystems. The rates are based on changes between version 1.0 and version 4.0. Subsystems A and C have a growth rate of 191% each. The relative sizes of the whole system are 34% for subsystem A and 37% for subsystem C, respectively. Thus, both are candidates for further study but since subsystem A represents the GUI part of the system and consists, to a very high degree, of automatically generated GUI classes, it is not a representative subsystem. Subsystem D exhibits the highest growth rate, 700%, but since subsystem D only comprises 5% of the total system size in version 4.0 the subsystem is of minor interest.

Considering the change rate, it is obvious that subsystem C has undergone major changes between version 1.0 and version 4.0 since it has a change rate of 92%. It may also be of interest to investigate subsystem B since its change rate, 64%, is higher than the change rates for the whole framework. Subsystem C represents a major part of the system, 37% of the classes, and is a candidate for further investigations on module level.

Applying the same kind of reasoning regarding change and growth rates shows that subsystem B also needs further investigation due to high change rate. The reader is referred to [17] for a detailed discussion about subsystem B.

To summarize the subsystem level observations, subsystem C needs further investigation due to its high growth and change rates and subsystem B due to its relatively high change rate.

The evolution of subsystem C. Subsystem C exhibits the highest growth and change rates among the subsystems. These facts make the subsystem a likely candidate for restructuring and/or re-engineering activities. Will the modules in subsystem C possess the same evolution characteristics as the whole subsystem or will they behave differently?

Subsystem C consists of five modules, C1 to C5. Figure 14.5 shows that module C3 and C4 are large modules and that they both have had a large increase of the number of added classes. In addition, modules C1, C2 and C5 have been relatively stable in size but a minor increase can be observed for module C1.

Regarding the growth and change rates for the modules in subsystem C; these are presented in Figure 14.6. Module C4 has a high growth rate, 306%, and it represents 25% of the subsystem. Through discussions with the software engineers, it was clarified that the reason for the high growth rate is that the module is responsible for coding and decoding the call data records that exist in a number of formats. Thus, the high growth rate is the result of an increasing number of formats supported by the BGW framework, that is, module C4 handles a number of different call data record formats that results in a set of classes whose objects are used as parameters in the framework. This is, probably, a characteristic observation of framework evolution for a black-box (or visual builder) framework since they rely on composition of objects.

Module C5 has the highest growth rate, 460%, but is the smallest module in the subsystem. All modules except Module C5 exhibit high change rates. A reason for the

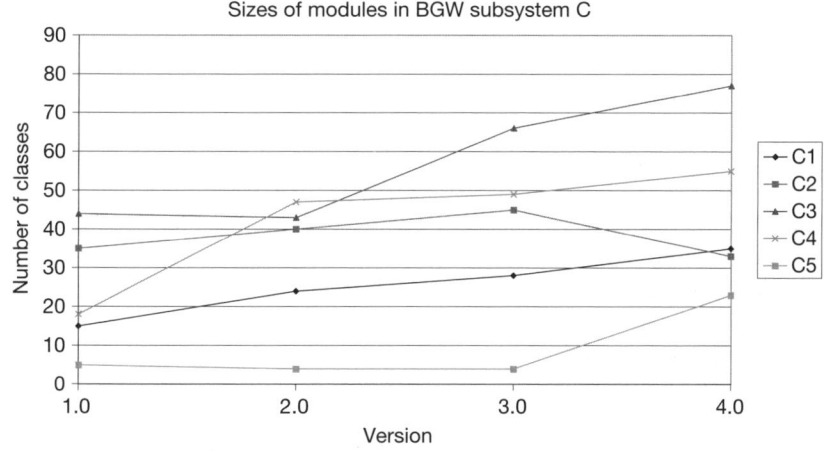

Figure 14.5 Size of modules in BGW subsystem C

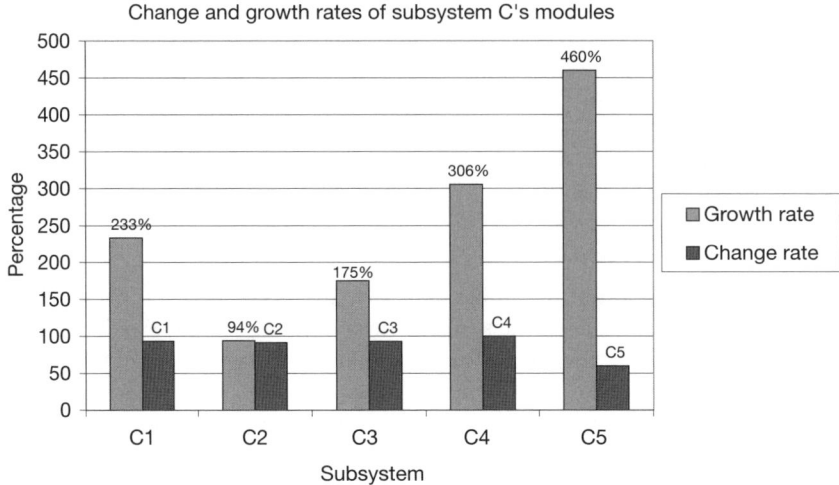

Figure 14.6 Module change and growth rates of BGW subsystem C

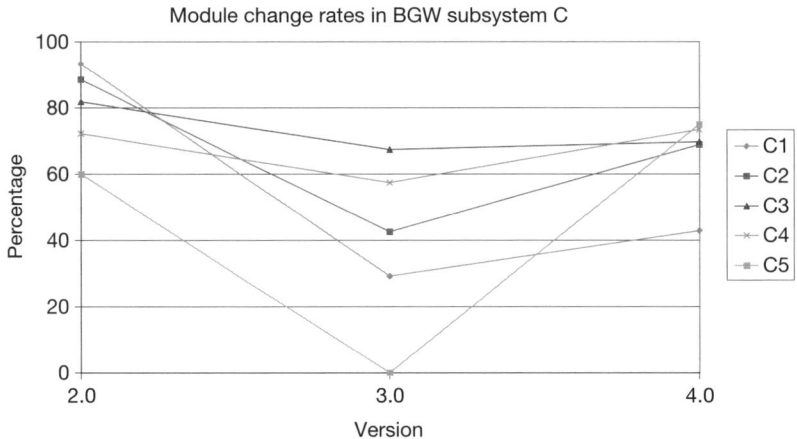

Figure 14.7 Module change rates in BGW subsystem C

relative low change rate for module C5 is that it captures the encapsulation of some software packages that do not require any design changes.

In Figure 14.7, it is shown that the change rates for the modules in subsystem C are increasing from version 3.0 to version 4.0. Modules C3 and C4 exhibit the highest change rates throughout all the versions. From this, it can be seen that the change rates for the modules in subsystem C behave in the same way as the system as a whole.

In addition, all modules in subsystem C have high change rates and the two main reasons for this are as follows:

1. A design concept called *Node* has been divided into two concepts, Childnode and ParentNode, to achieve higher maintainability and lower complexity.

2. Another design concept called *Point* has changed from being file-oriented to be transaction-oriented due to the need to provide decreased latency for the Call Data Record (the billing information input) processing. This was necessary to fulfil the requirement of hot billing.

To summarize the findings of subsystem C, changes in all modules exists due to the changes of the two design concepts. These changes have presumably not achieved full effect on the system design. Regarding module C4 and its growth rate, this is viewed as an anticipated kind of evolution due to the nature of black-box frameworks (an increased number of different objects, representing different types of Call Record Data formats, supporting easier composition).

14.3.1.3 Discussion

Observations from using the adapted method are similar to the study by Gall *et al.*, that is, there is a difference in the behaviour of the whole system versus its subsystems. A relatively stable evolution over time is observed at the framework system level, but detailed studies of the subsystems show that subsystems C and B exhibit different characteristics regarding the change and growth rates compared to the system as a whole. These major differences would not have been identified only by an analysis of the entire system. One module in subsystem C is identified as potential subjects for redesign, that is, module C4. In addition, to a lesser extent, module C3 is a likely candidate for redesign. A similar analysis on subsystem B indicates that module B2 is a potential subject for redesign [17].

14.3.2 Stability Assessment

14.3.2.1 Method Description

A method for quantitatively assessing stability of an object-oriented framework was proposed by Bansiya [16]. In this study, the method has been extended with an additional metric, the *relative-extent-of-change* metric, as well as a set of framework stability indicators. The method consists of the following five steps:

1. Identification of change characteristics.
2. Selection of metrics to assess each change category.
3. Data collection.
4. Analysing the change characteristics and computing the normalized-extent-of-change and relative-extent-of-change metrics in the architecture between versions of the framework.
5. Comparing the metrics data against the framework stability indicators.

Identification of change characteristics. When assessing framework stability, one has to select suitable indicators. Bansiya identifies two categories of change characteristics: *architectural* and *individual class* characteristics. The changes of architectural characteristics are related to the *interaction* among classes and the *structuring* of classes in inheritance hierarchies. Characteristics of individual classes are related to the assessment and change of the *structure*, *functionality* and *collaboration* (relationships) of individual classes between versions. The structure of objects is described and detailed by the data declarations in the class declarations. The functional characteristics are related to the object's methods. The parameter and data declarations that use user-defined objects define the collaboration characteristics of a class.

Selection of metrics to assess each change category. Bansiya selected a subset of object-oriented metrics from [23, 24] and the same set of metrics is used in this study, but it is possible to change the metrics to others that could be more appropriate with respect to a particular organizations processes and application domains. In Table 14.2, the nine architectural framework structure and interaction metrics used are described and in Table 14.3 the architectural metrics values for the BGW framework are found. The individual class metrics comprise in total 11 metrics divided into three separate suits and are described in Table 14.4.

Table 14.2 Architectural metrics descriptions

Architectural metrics (structure)	Architectural metrics (interaction)
DSC, design size in classes	ACIS, average number of public methods in all classes
NOH, number of hierarchies	ANA, average number of distinct (parent) classes from which a class inherits information
NSI, number of single inheritance instances	ADCC, average number of distinct classes that a class may collaborate with
NMI, number of multiple inheritance instances	
ADI, average depth of the class inheritance structure	
AWI, average width of the class inheritance structure	

Table 14.3 Architectural metrics data for the BGW framework

Metric	BGW V1	BGW V2	BGW V3	BGW V4
DSC	322	445	535	598
NOH	30	35	40	44
NSI	265	371	434	480
NMI	5	1	1	1
ADI	1.97	2.24	2.09	2.14
AWI	0.73	0.75	0.74	0.73
ANA	2.00	2.25	2.09	2.14
ACIS	15.84	17.58	18.90	18.68
ADCC	3.61	4.07	3.99	3.98
NSI/DSC	0.82	0.83	0.81	0.80

DSC, Design size in classes; NOH, Number of hierarchies; NSI, Number of single inheritance instances; NMI, Number of multiple inheritance instances; ADI, Average depth of the class inheritance structure; AWI, Average width of the class inheritance structure; ANA, Average number of public methods in all classes; ACIS, Average number of public methods in all classes; ADCC, Average number of distinct classes that a class may collaborate with.

Table 14.4 Class metrics descriptions

Structural metrics	Functional metrics	Relational metrics
NOD, the number of attributes.	NOM, count of all the methods defined.	NOA, the number of distinct classes (parents), which a class inherits.
NAD, the number of user-defined objects used as attributes in a class.	NOP, the number of polymorphic methods in a class.	NOC, the number of immediate children (sub classes) of a class.
NRA, the number of pointers and references used as attributes.	NPT, the number of parameter types used in the methods of a class.	DCC, count of the number of classes that a class is directly related to.
CSB, the size of the objects in bytes from the class declaration.	NPM, average of the number of parameters per method in a class.	

Data collection. The data should preferably be collected using the same tool in order to reduce the probability for different interpretations of the metric definitions. For this study, the data has been collected for each version of the different studied frameworks with the QMOOD++ tool [23].

Analyse the changed architectural characteristics. For each of the frameworks and their versions, the collected architectural data are analysed and the normalized- and relative-extent-of-change metrics are calculated.

The *normalized-extent-of-change-metric* is calculated in the following way. The architectural metric values are normalized with respect to the metric's values in the previous version of the framework. The metric values for the first framework version are used as a base for normalization. The normalized metric values are computed by dividing the actual metric values of a version with the metric's value in the previous version for the actual framework. A temporary aggregated metric, *aggregate change*, is then computed by summarizing all the normalized metrics for a framework version. The aggregate change metric is introduced only to make the calculations easier and is set to the number of metrics used for version 1.0 of the framework (in this study the aggregate change metric value is 9).

The normalized-extent-of-change metric is then computed as the difference between the aggregate change metric for the framework version i, V_i, and the first framework version V_1. For example, in the BGW framework, the normalized-extent-of-change metric for version 3.0 is computed as 9,41 (aggregate change metric value for version 3.0) minus 9 (aggregate change metric value for version 1.0) which is 0,41. Thus, the normalized-extent-of-change metric has the value 0,41 for version 3.0 of the BGW framework. See Table 14.5 for the normalized-extent-of-change metrics for the BGW framework.

The normalized-extent-of-change metric is a relative indicator of the framework's architectural stability. A high value of the metric indicates a relative instability of the framework structure, whereas a low value of the normalized-extent-of-change metric indicates greater stability.

Table 14.5 Normalized-extent-of-change metrics for the BGW framework

Metric	BGW V1	BGW V2	BGW V3	BGW V4
DSC	1	1.38	1.20	1.12
NOH	1	1.17	1.14	1.10
NSI	1	1.40	1.17	1.11
NMI	1	0.2	1	1
ADI	1	1.14	0.93	1.02
AWI	1	1.03	0.97	0.99
ANA	1	1.12	0.93	1.02
ACIS	1	1.11	1.08	0.99
ADCC	1	1.13	0.98	1.00
Aggregate change	9	9.68	9.41	9.35
Normalized-extent-of-change	0	0.68	0.41	0.35

DSC, Design size in classes; NOH, Number of hierarchies; NSI, Number of single inheritance instances; NMI, Number of multiple inheritance instances; ADI, Average depth of the class inheritance structure; AWI, Average width of the class inheritance structure; ANA, Average number of public methods in all classes; ACIS, Average number of public methods in all classes; ADCC, Average number of distinct classes that a class may collaborate with.

Before calculating the *relative-extent-of-change metric* it must be decided how to compute the individual class metrics. A defined class metric can be computed in two ways, that is, including or excluding inherited properties. The first approach requires analysing a class and all its ancestors in order to compute the class metrics. Typically, changes made to the internal parts of parent classes in a framework cause a ripple-effect of changes to all descendants of the parent class. Thus, in this study, the class metrics values are counted including the inherited properties. The metric values for each of the 11 class characteristics can be changed between two successive versions. If the value of a particular metric (e.g. number of methods (NOM) changes from one version to the next, this is defined as one unit of change. Since there are 11 characteristics that can be changed for a class, a class can contribute between 0 and 11 units of change. The 11 metric values of each class are compared with the metric values of the class in the preceding version of the framework to compute the total number of units changed for the classes. The *total-extent-of-change* for a framework version is the sum of units changed in all classes between a version and its predecessor. To assess the significance of the total-extent-of-change measure, it is compared with the maximum possible change. The maximum possible change represents the case where all the metrics would have changed values for all classes in a framework version. The relative-extent-of-change metric is computed as the *total-extent-of-change* divided with the maximum possible change. For example, version 1.0 of the BGW framework has 322 classes, which gives a theoretical maximum of 322×11 (number of metrics that can change for a class) $= 3542$ possible changes for the version. The actual number of changes between version 1.0 and version 2.0 of the BGW framework is 932, which represents a $(932/3542) \times 100 = 26.3\%$ change between version 1.0 and 2.0. Thus, the relative-extent-of-change metric is 26.3% for version 2.0 of the BGW framework. The relative-extent-of-change metrics for the BGW framework are found in Table 14.6.

Table 14.6 Number of units changed and the relative-extent-of-change metric data between consecutive versions for the BGW framework

Metric	BGW V1.0/V2.0	BGW V2.0/V3.0	BGW V3.0/V4.0	Total units changed
NOC	19	31	47	97
NOA	47	13	10	70
DCC	89	80	141	310
NOM	148	142	198	488
NOP	105	93	117	315
NPT	77	125	187	389
NPM	147	156	190	493
NOD	78	126	144	348
NAD	69	51	82	202
NRA	76	88	58	222
CSB	77	125	187	389
Actual units changed	932	1,030	1,361	3,323
Maximum units of change	3,542	4,895	5,885	14,322
Relative-extent-of-change	26.3%	21.0%	23.1%	23.2%

NOC, the number of immediate children (sub classes) of a class; NOA, the number of distinct classes (parents), which a class inherits; DCC, count of the number of classes that a class is directly related to; NOM, count of all the methods defined; NOP, the number of polymorphic methods in a class; NPT, the number of parameter types used in the methods of a class; NPM, average of the number of parameters per method in a class; NOD, the number of attributes; NAD, the number of user-defined objects used as attributes in a class; NRA, the number of pointers and references used as attributes; CSB, the size of the objects in bytes from the class declaration.

The relative-extent-of-change metric is in one way similar to the normalized-extent-of-change metric since it intends to capture the stability of the framework. On the other hand, the relative-extent-of-change metric is on another abstraction level since it is composed of a set of finer grained class metrics and is not directly measured on the architectural level of the framework. Thus, the relative-extent-of-change metric gives a possibility to validate the original normalized-extent-of-change metric. Another important difference is that the normalized-extent-of-change metric addresses the framework's architectural structure, that is, it is more focused on capturing the enhancements, for example, addition of features, of the framework. In contrast, the relative-extent-of-change metric analyses the *core* of the framework, that is, it only measures changes in the set of classes that exist in two consecutive versions. This means that the metric better describes how well the domain is captured and understood by the framework developers. The core of a framework version n consists of the classes that exist in two consecutive versions of the framework. A more formal definition is that the core is the set of classes that exist in both version $n-1$ and version n of the framework. That means that the core does not comprise the classes that existed in version $n-1$ and do not exist in version n of the framework. Neither are the classes added to framework version n part of the core. A consequence of this definition is that the core can grow with newer framework versions since it is defined in terms of two consecutive versions and not the first version of the framework. The set of added classes can be seen as representing a wider and better domain understanding captured by framework version n. This means that the core for framework version $n+1$ is expanded with the set of added classes in version n except for those classes that have been removed in version $n+1$ of the framework and is reduced with those classes in the core for version n that do not exist in framework version $n+1$. Thus, a low relative-extent-of-change value indicates good domain coverage and understanding, whereas a high relative-extent-of-change value indicates that the domain is not well understood and important abstractions have not yet been found.

Framework stability indicator analysis. On the basis of the metric data collected, it is now possible to analyse the framework with respect to the stability indicators. These five indicators are based on experiences from applying the original stability assessment method on three different object-oriented frameworks [18, 19]. The five stability indicators are as follows:

Framework stability indicator 1: Stable frameworks tend to have narrow and deeply inherited class hierarchy structures, characterized by high values for the average depth of inheritance (above 2.1) of classes and low values for the average width of inheritance hierarchies (below 0.85).

Framework stability indicator 2: A stable framework has an NSI/DSC ratio (number of single inheritance instances/design size in classes) just above 0.8 if multiple inheritance is seldom used in the framework. That is, the number of subclasses in a stable framework is just above 80%.

Framework stability indicator 3: The normalized ADCC (averaged directly coupled classes) metrics is going towards 1.0 or just below for stable frameworks, that is, the number of relationships between classes is relatively stable and constant throughout all versions of the framework.

Framework stability indicator 4: The normalized-extent-of-change metric is below 0.4 for a stable framework.

Framework stability indicator 5: A stable framework exhibits a relative-extent-of-change value of less than 25%.

A framework is considered to be more stable when more framework stability indicators are fulfilled for a framework version.

14.3.2.2 Results

In this section, framework stability indicator fulfilments for the BGW and MFC frameworks are presented. For a more detailed presentation of the metric results for the MFC framework, the readers are referred to [18].

In Table 14.7, the five framework stability indicators, *Ind. 1 to Ind. 5*, and the versions for the two frameworks are listed. A 'Y' indicates that the framework stability indicator is fulfilled and a 'N' that it is not fulfilled.

The BGW framework fulfils framework stability indicator 1 and 2 for version 2.0 and all except indicator 1 for version 3.0. Version 4.0 of the BGW framework fulfils all the

Table 14.7 Fulfilment of framework stability indicators

BGW	Ind. 1	Ind. 2	Ind. 3	Ind. 4	Ind. 5	MFC	Ind. 1	Ind. 2	Ind. 3	Ind. 4	Ind. 5
Ver 1.0	N	Y	N	N	N	Ver 1.0	N	N	N	N	N
Ver 2.0	Y	Y	N	N	N	Ver 2.0	N	N	N	N	N
Ver 3.0	N	Y	Y	Y	Y	Ver 3.0	N	N	N	N	N
Ver 4.0	Y	Y	Y	Y	Y	Ver 4.0	Y	Y	Y	N	N
						Ver 5.0	Y	Y	Y	Y	Y

indicators. The BGW values for indicator 1 and 2 can be found in Table 14.3. Table 14.5 relates to indicator 3 and 4. The values for indicator 5 are found in Table 14.6.

For the MFC framework the situation is that it fulfils framework stability indicators 1, 2 and 3 for version 4.0. In version 5.0, the additional indicators 4 and 5 are fulfilled as well.

To summarize, the BGW framework fulfils framework stability indicators to a large extent from version 3.0 and the MFC framework from version 4.0.

14.3.2.3 Discussion

Some important differences with the stability assessment method compared to Bansiya's original approach [16] are as follows:

- A set of framework stability indicators have been added, which enable an objective way of deciding if a framework is stable or not.
- An aggregated metric, the relative-extent-of-change metric based on individual class level metrics, which is on a different abstraction level than the original normalized-extent-of-change metric has been added. The introduction of the relative-extent-of-change metric gives a possibility to validate the normalized-extent-of-change metric with it. The results when applying the method shows that the framework stability indicator based on the relative-extent-of-change metric, indicator 4, indicates framework stability for versions 3.0 and 4.0 for the BGW framework and for version 5.0 for the MFC framework. The architectural metric, normalized-extent-of-change, used in framework stability indicator 5 also indicates framework stability for version 3.0 and 4.0 for the BGW framework and for version 5.0 for the MFC framework. Thus, the normalized-extent-of-change metric indicates stability in the same framework version as that of the relative-extent-of-change metric. The conclusion is that the normalized-extent-of-change metric is a good indicator of framework stability.
- The framework stability assessment methods have been applied on three different frameworks, the BGW, MFC and Borlands' OWL frameworks [18, 19], where the latter has not been discussed at all in this chapter.

The original approach has (indirectly) been validated through the application of the (extended) assessment method on the frameworks and the method does not show any particular weaknesses. The same set of metric that was used in the original approach has been used for the different frameworks. There exists a possibility to change the metric set in the assessment procedure but in this study the original set has been used.

Both the BGW and MFC frameworks have reached stability according to the framework stability indicators. This is a sign of robustness for the assessment method since it seems to cope with a number of framework dissimilarities. Four major dissimilarities between the BGW and MFC framework that are invariant to the stability assessment method are as follows:

- The MFC framework is a commercially available white-box object-oriented framework with an anonymous market, whereas the BGW framework is a proprietary framework. A proprietary-owned framework is a more typical study subject since it represents the more common situation in software industry and because the framework-developing organization has to deal with explicit customers and customer requirements rather than distributing the framework to a mass market.
- The BGW framework is a visual builder (based on a black-box) framework, whereas the MFC framework is a white-box. Black-box frameworks generally contain a larger number of classes and inheritance hierarchies than white-box frameworks.
- The range in size between the different frameworks, is measured in number of classes. The original BGW framework (322 classes) was originally 4.5 times larger than the first MFC framework (72 classes). Version 4.0 of the BGW framework (598 classes) is still 2.9 times larger than the fifth version of the MFC framework (233 classes).
- The domains covered by the frameworks are quite different. The MFC framework implements GUI functionality. Compared to most domains, the GUI domain is quite stable in the behaviour it is supposed to provide. The BGW domain is considerably less stable and the developers of the framework have had to incorporate impressive amounts of requirements changes and additions during the evolution of the BGW framework.

14.3.3 Distribution of the Development Effort

14.3.3.1 Method Description

The distribution of the development effort method is essentially an analysis of the effort data for the various development phases and activities involved in developing a framework. The distribution of the development effort method comprises the following activities:

- Assure that the phases and activities for the framework development and instantiation are clearly defined so there is no doubt about what is included or excluded.
- Collect the effort data from the framework development projects.
- Calculate the relative distribution of the framework development effort and the relative distribution of effort for developing the framework and the (different) framework instantiations (i.e. the applications).
- Perform a qualitative analysis of the data to identify trends in the development, causes for the trends and similarities/dissimilarities with previous framework projects.

14.3.3.2 Results

The development process used by the organization that developed the BGW framework as well as the activities that are included in the framework instantiation process are briefly described in this section. The organization's development process used for the framework development comprises the following phases and activities:

- *Pre-study*: The purpose of the pre-study phase is to assess feasibility from technical and commercial viewpoints, on the basis of the expressed and implicit requirements and needs. Activities comprise planning, securing competence, analysis of possible technologies available and an analysis of required effort.
- *Feasibility*: This phase comprises activities such as more detailed planning; the project organization is defined as well as communication/information paths. A risk analysis is performed, quality assurance techniques are defined for the project and implementation proposals are developed.
- *Design*: Architectural design and detailed design are performed in this phase.
- *Implementation*: The design is implemented and revised if necessary. Basic testing on the implemented classes is made. In the BGW framework case, the implementation was done in C++.
- *Test*: Integration test and system test are performed during this phase.
- *Industrialization*: In this phase, the developed software product is installed at a selected customer site. When the product is in operation and has been functioning correctly for a certain duration, the system development is considered finished.
- *Documentation*: This activity comprises the development of user manuals, system reference manuals and the development of course material for the software product.
- *Administration*: The administration activities comprise project management, quality management, configuration management and project meetings performed throughout the project.

The *instantiation process* of the BGW framework is, in this study, an installation and instantiation process. This is due to the fact that the organization makes no distinction with respect to time reporting between the instantiation of the framework and the installation of the instantiated framework. Thus, the effort reported for instantiation of the BGW framework comprises the following activities:

- Installation of necessary hardware at the customer site (done in most of the cases).
- Installation of the BGW software.
- Configuration of the BGW framework for the specific customer. The customers can do the configuration and re-configurations themselves, but most customers prefer the supplier to do the configuration.
- Acceptance Test.

Development effort data. The effort for the development of the BGW framework versions are in the range 10,000 to 20,000 person hours (on the company's request the exact figures are not published). In Table 14.8, the normalized effort data for the four

Table 14.8 Normalized framework development effort data

	V1.0	V2.0	V3.0	V4.0
Normalized effort	1.000	1.266	1.761	1.620

versions are presented. The normalization is made with respect to the number of hours in version 1.0. That means, in a hypothetical example, if the development of version 1.0 took 10,000 hours the development of version 2.0 took 12,660 hours.

The development cost for version 2.0 was approximately 25% higher than in version 1.0. For version 3.0, a major revision of the framework was made at a cost 76% higher than version 1.0. The development of version 4.0 is slightly less expensive than version 3.0, that is, 162% of the cost for version 1.0.

The effort data is collected from the organization's internal time reporting system. Thus, the reliability of the obtained figures is dependent on the accuracy from the software engineers. The effort data reported does not include the time taken for travelling to customer locations.

Relative effort distribution per phase and version. In Table 14.9, the relative distribution of the effort between the different activities is presented. The distribution of effort is per developed version. The analysis and conclusions of the figures are based on interviews with the software engineers involved in the development of the framework versions.

The figures show that the relative effort for the pre-study and feasibility activities is increasing for later versions of the framework. The major reason for this is that new requirements and proposed changes have to be analysed more carefully. The figure 0.0% for feasibility in version 1.0 is explained by the fact that the software engineers all had experiences from the application domain and the technologies to be used. The dip in design and implementation effort in version 2.0 is because no major new functionality was introduced and a large amount of the effort was spent on restructuring the system. The increase in test effort is caused by the increased size of the framework from 233 to 598 classes. The reason for the peak in administration effort for version 2.0 is explained by a higher focus on quality processes. During version 1.0, the organization experienced problems in managing both the development of the framework (a kind of product development) and the instantiations of the framework (a kind of customization project). These problems seem to be common and have been observed by Rösel [12] too. To handle the change from project-based development to product-based development, new processes were introduced and existing processes were improved. The high percentage of industrialization effort in version 1.0 compared to the other three versions is explained by the

Table 14.9 Relative distribution of effort per framework version and phase

Phase	V1.0 (%)	V2.0 (%)	V3.0 (%)	V4.0 (%)
Pre-study	7.6	1.4	5.4	12.8
Feasibility	0.0	7.7	6.3	9.2
Design	12.0	7.9	10.6	12.7
Implementation	29.3	16.3	23.8	18.8
Test	13.8	16.9	19.2	21.6
Administration	23.0	38.9	22.0	17.6
Industrialization	9.6	3.9	3.7	2.5
Documentation	4.7	6.8	8.9	4.6
Total	*100.0*	*100.0*	*100.0*	*100.0*

fact that the software engineers were fully responsible for the ownership of a software product for the first time.

If effort data for administrative activities such as project and quality management, industrialization and documentation are excluded and the pre-study and feasibility activities are combined into an analysis activity, there will only be technical phases left. Focusing on the more technical phases, the distribution of effort data is more comparable for other organizations. The relative distribution of effort data is found in Table 14.10 and Figure 14.8.

Figure 14.8 shows that during the evolution of the BGW framework the emphasis has shifted from implementation to analysis. The implementation effort in version 4.0 is only 25% of the total effort for the technical activities compared to 50% for version 1.0 of the framework. The effort spent on analysis increased from 12% of the total effort to 30% of the total effort. The relative effort spent on design is just below 20% for all four versions. The test effort is around 30% with an exception for version 1.0, where it is lower. A possible explanation for this could be that part of the testing has been performed during the implementation phase.

Table 14.10 Relative distribution of effort per framework version and technical phase

Technical phase	V1.0 (%)	V2.0 (%)	V3.0 (%)	V4.0 (%)
Analysis	12.1	18.1	18.0	29.3
Design	19.1	15.8	16.2	16.9
Implementation	46.7	32.5	36.4	25.1
Test	22.0	33.6	29.4	28.7
Total	*100.0*	*100.0*	*100.0*	*100.0*

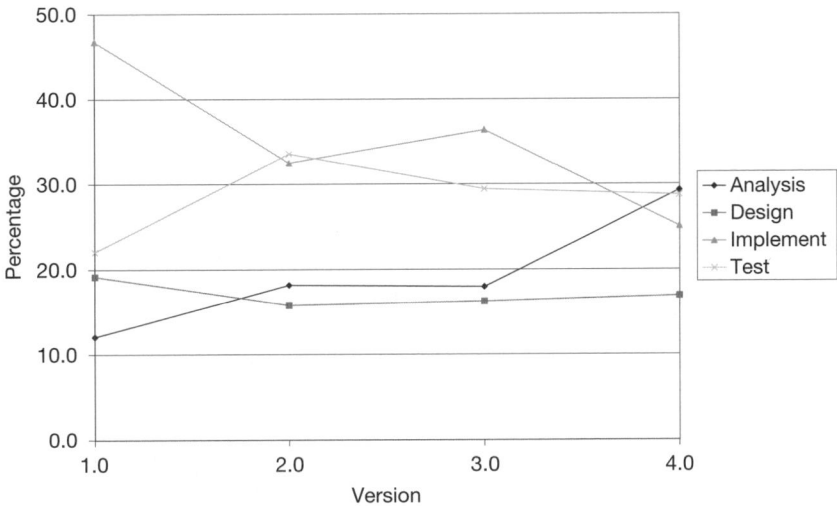

Figure 14.8 Relative effort distribution per framework version and technical phase

Table 14.11 BGW framework instantiation/development effort ratios

Version	# Instantiations	Average	Lower fourth	Median	Upper fourth
1.0	4	1:94	1:72	1:86	1:64
2.0	7	1:42	1:214	1:44	1:33
3.0	20	1:61	1:167	1:81	1:49
Total	31	1:58	1:168	1:75	1:44

The shift of emphasis from implementation and test towards analysis is probably caused by the growing size of the software and the fact that new requirements and proposed changes have to be analysed carefully before being implemented.

Instantiation effort data. In Table 14.11, basic statistics for framework instantiation effort relative to framework development effort is presented. No effort data in person hours is presented due to the company's wish but relative effort data in percentage of the effort needed for developing the framework version is found in [13]. In this section, only the ratios between framework development effort and framework instantiation effort is presented in Table 14.11. For example, version 1 of the BGW framework has been instantiated four times and the average instantiation/development effort ratio is 1:94, meaning that the effort needed for instantiating the 'average application' is only 1.06% of the effort needed for developing the framework versions.

The median effort ratio varies between 1:44 to 1:86 for the different framework versions. The upper fourth ratio varies between 1:33 to 1:64. The last row in Table 14.11 presents the framework instantiation/development ratios for all 31 instantiations. The average framework instantiation/development ratio is 1:58, which means that half of the instantiations required an effort less than 1.8% of the framework development effort. The upper fourth instantiation/development ratio is 1:44, which means that 75% of the instantiations required an effort less than 2.3% of the total development effort.

These figures provide strong evidence supporting the claim that framework technology delivers reduced application development efforts.

14.3.3.3 Discussion

Essentially, the distribution of the development effort method is a qualitative analysis of the effort distribution for the development, with the aim of identifying the reasons and causes for some figures deviating from the estimations or having certain values. One may argue that this analysis should be a part of any project conclusion report. The only difference is that it is more important to perform the analysis when developing a framework since the cost of developing and evolving a framework is higher (since it must be easily reusable) than for a normal software system of comparable size. As mentioned earlier, it is of importance that development phases and activities are well defined so that comparisons with other framework projects are possible. Another issue is to assure that each framework instantiation is viewed as a separate project so that framework instantiation effort is not charged on the development of the next framework version. Otherwise it will be hard, if not impossible, to obtain the framework instantiation/development ratio for the framework.

14.4 Method Comparison

The three evaluation methods presented have been applied to the same framework, that is, the BGW framework, which makes it possible to compare them against each other with respect to the management issues. The management issues discussed are identification of change-prone modules, framework deployment, change impact analysis, benchmarking and requirements management.

In Table 14.12, the three methods are listed together with the five management issues and each table element has one of the following values, *not supported*, *minor support*, *substantial support*, to indicate the degree to which the management issue is supported by each method. The value minor support means that the method partly or/and with minor adaptation will support the management issue to a certain extent.

How each of the methods supports or does not support the management issues are discussed in the following subsections and the section ends with some general comments of each method.

14.4.1 Change-prone Modules

The evolution identification method performs well with respect to identifying change-prone modules. Through systematic application of the method on smaller and smaller parts of the object-oriented framework, the method ends up with a list of change-prone modules (and subsystems). A minor disadvantage with the evolution identification method is that it also identifies modules that have a natural high growth rate and thus are not problematic modules that need to be restructured. An example of this are modules that are responsible for specific framework parameterization aspects, which grows in a natural way with the number of possible parameterization values.

Regarding identification of change-prone modules the stability assessment method gives no support. But a possible approach could be to apply the stability assessment method on subsystems and modules and thereby gain knowledge about change-prone modules.

The distribution of the development effort method does not support identification of change-prone modules. A possible approach could be if effort data is collected per module, but achieving this granularity of effort data collection in practice seems difficult.

Table 14.12 Methods versus management issues

	Change-prone modules	Framework deployment	Change impact analysis	Benchmarking	Requirements management
Evolution identification using historical data	Substantial support	Not supported	Minor support	Minor support	Not supported
Stability assessment	Minor support	Minor support	Substantial support	Substantial support	Not supported
Distribution of development effort	Minor support	Not supported	Minor support	Substantial support	Minor support

14.4.2 Framework Deployment

Since the evolution identification method works with historical data, it does not contribute to the framework deployment aspects that deal with deciding when to release the current framework version under development.

The framework deployment aspect is not directly addressed by the stability assessment method. But if the method is applied more frequently during the iterative development of the framework version, the extent-of-change metrics provide information with respect to whether the framework is becoming more stable or not during the iterations. The other metrics in the stability assessment method also indicate stability or not depending whether the values are deviating from the ones in the framework stability indicators. The observed trends in the metric values give useful information for deciding whether to release the framework version or to iterate the development once again.

A framework deployment decision should not be taken on the basis of effort consumed or other historical effort information but on achieved quality levels of the framework. Thus, the distribution of development effort method does not assist management with the framework deployment decision.

14.4.3 Change Impact Analysis

The evolution identification method assists management with some information when doing a change impact analysis, but since the method uses historical information it will, in most cases, fail in predicting changes for the future version. However, the method identifies modules that are likely candidates for restructuring in the framework.

The result of the stability assessment method gives an indication of how stable the framework version is. Especially the relative- and normalized-extent-of-change metrics provide information of how large an impact the requirements had on the framework structure. If historical trends for the current and other frameworks exist for the metrics, the metric values give a rough indication of the maintenance effort needed. However, this may not be valid for requirements that have architectural impact and thus affect the whole framework. Deviating metrics values from the limit values in the framework stability indicators are indications of evolution that are not desirable and eventually have to be handled explicitly, if time schedule and budgets allow. Thus, the stability assessment method is useful for change impact analysis.

The distribution of the development effort method does not contribute directly to the change impact analysis but if stability assessment is performed on the framework, the effort data may be useful for future effort estimations on change impact analysis based on a stability assessment.

14.4.4 Benchmarking

Regarding the benchmarking aspect, the evolution identification method is able to deliver information for classification and/or characterization of typical evolution-prone module patterns for frameworks. This requires a relatively large number of observed frameworks, their subsystems and modules before typical categories can be established.

The issue of benchmarking is supported by the stability assessment method since it collects a number of metrics and thereby provides empirical information about the evolution of a framework. A historical set of data from previous assessments together with other information will make the prediction of the current framework's evolution more accurate.

Obviously, the distribution of the development effort method provides benchmarking information that can be useful in the development and evolution of new frameworks as well as for the instantiation of these. In a longer perspective, and if it is an organizational objective, the development and the instantiation effort data obtained can provide an empirical foundation for the development of cost models for framework development as well as the investment analysis models.

14.4.5 Requirements Management

The requirements management aspect is not addressed by the evolution identification method and the stability assessment method. Eventually, the stability assessment method will indicate a higher value than expected for any or both of the extent-of-change metrics as a result of incorporating a difficult instantiation requirement.

The distribution of development effort method identifies those instantiations that have been costly to realize. If the organization has adopted the strategy to incorporate the framework instantiation requirements into the next version of the framework, the identification of costly instantiations may point out difficult requirements, which probably should not be incorporated in the next framework version. In that way, the method is useful with respect to the requirements management issue.

14.4.6 Some Comments

This section discusses general aspects such as the difficulty to apply the methods, their need of tool support and experienced advantages and disadvantages of the methods.

The benefit of using the evolution identification method is that it relies on only one simple metric that is easy to collect. The method is simple to apply since it only makes use of class declarations and the number of classes defined. A potential problem is that one must be aware of how to handle the addition of new modules during the framework evolution. Tool support is recommended, but a specialized tool for calculating the growth and change rates and storing the collected data is relatively simple to develop. However, it requires that the organization has a coding standard that prescribes that each class must include a description of which subsystem and module it belongs to.

Tool support is highly recommended for the stability assessment method since a huge amount of data has to be dealt with. In addition, depending on the maturity of the organization the introduction of data collection activities can be relatively costly, but since only product metrics are collected this should be manageable. The stability assessment method as such is fairly simple to apply but it requires that the set of metrics used are clearly defined and consistently interpreted. This consistence must be maintained throughout both framework versions and different frameworks in order to provide comparable data.

The stability assessment method is the most costly to apply, but it offers a number of benefits compared to the other two methods. The metric set used provides a more comprehensive view of the framework compared to the evolution identification method since it addresses five different framework stability aspects. The limits used in the framework stability indicators may be discussed since they may be affected by organizational standards but experiences support that there is a degree of confidence in the limits.

An advantage of the method is the possibility of changing the underlying set of metrics. This is useful if the frameworks developed are adhering to a specific coding standard, a specific technical domain, for example, distributed systems, or any other organizational issue. It is also possible to select a metric set that provides information about inheritance structure changes or to cover the metric used in the evolution identification method. A minor disadvantage of the method is the calculation of the aggregated metrics, especially the class level metrics changes, if no tool support is provided.

In addition, the collected data is a superset of the data required by the evolution identification method. Thus, choosing the stability assessment method automatically facilitates the use of the evolution identification method as well.

The distribution of the development effort method is not difficult or expensive to apply since software development organizations have procedures to collect effort data, often automated. The important thing is to have a clear and well-defined description of the activities in the framework project and that the staff correctly report their time with respect to activities defined. An additional advantage, is that the method may provide support for staffing a framework project with different kind of specialist roles.

14.5 Related Work

The work by Roberts and Johnson [21] present a pattern language that describes typical steps for the evolution of an object-oriented framework. Common steps in the evolution are development of a white-box framework (extensive use of the inheritance mechanism), the transition to a black-box framework (extensive use of composition), development of a library of pluggable objects and so on. These steps give a coarse-grained description of a framework's evolution. However, they do not explicitly address and describe where and how the framework evolves when it has reached a certain state.

Regarding economical aspects of object-oriented framework development and customization only two pieces of work seem to exist. Moser and Nierstrasz [14] discuss the productivity of the framework user. Their study compares the function point approach with their own System Meter approach for estimating framework customization productivity. The idea behind the System Meter approach is to distinguish between the internal and external sizes of objects, and thus to measure only complexity that has a real effect on the size of the system to be implemented, that is, incremental functionality. Their study reports that the effect of framework reuse does not increase the software engineer's productivity using the System Meter approach. Moser and Nierstrasz do not discuss the costs for framework development and customization; nor do the authors discuss the distribution of costs within and between framework versions as in this chapter but they discuss only the productivity aspect.

Rösel [12] is the only reference that presents some quantitative statements about framework development and reuse. Rösel's experience is that the cost of a framework may be 50% of the total cost for the first three applications. Once these three or more applications are implemented, the framework will most likely have paid for itself. He also remarks that to reach this pay-off level, significant commitment and investment is required. Compared to our study, Rösel gives no explicit quantitative support for his claim and the topic is just briefly discussed.

The issue of identification of change-prone modules is discussed by Gall *et al.* [22], where historical information about modules and programs is used as a means to identify structural shortcomings of a large telecommunication switching system. In this chapter, a similar approach is used but on a smaller and object-oriented system, 300 to 600 classes, and historical information about modules and classes are used, which are entities of smaller granularity than in the work of Gall *et al.*

Work by Lindvall and Sandahl [15] shows that software developers are not so good at predicting from a requirements specification how many and which classes will be changed. Their empirical study shows that only between 30 to 40% of the classes actually changed were predicted to be changed by the developers. This can be seen as an argument for using more objective approaches for identifying change-prone and change-prone parts of an object-oriented software system as the one used in our study.

Bansiya [16] and Erni and Lewerentz [25] report work about framework assessments. Bansiya's assessment approach is used as a basis for the assessment approach in this chapter. One difference is that in the presented approach, an additional metric has been added, which has been used for validating one of the original metrics. In addition, a set of framework stability indicators has been added, which can be used for indicating framework stability. The methods presented in this chapter have also been applied on both commercial and proprietary frameworks.

Erni and Lewerentz describe a metrics-based approach that supports incremental development of a framework. By measuring a set of metrics (which requires full source code access), an assessment of the design quality of the framework can be performed. If the metric data is within acceptable limits, the framework is considered to be good enough from a metrics perspective, otherwise another design iteration has to done. The approach is used during the design iterations, before a framework is released and does not consider long-term evolution of a framework, as is the case with the stability assessment method.

14.6 Conclusion

Object-oriented framework technology has become common technology in object-oriented software development. An object-oriented framework is a reusable asset that forms the basis for developing applications in the same domain. As with all software, frameworks tend to evolve. Once the framework has been deployed, new versions of a framework cause high maintenance cost for the products built with the framework. This fact in combination with the high costs of developing and evolving a framework make it important to have controlled and predictable evolution of the framework's functionality and costs.

In this chapter the three methods

- Evolution identification using historical information
- Stability assessment and
- Distribution of development effort

have been discussed and applied to between one to three different frameworks, both in proprietary and commercial domains. The methods provide management with information, which will make it possible to make better and well-informed decisions about the framework's evolution, especially with respect to identification of change-prone modules, framework deployment, change impact analysis, benchmarking and requirements management.

The evolution identification method provides the most support, of the three methods, for the change-prone module identification. The distribution of the effort method supports the benchmarking and requirements management issues. The stability assessment method addresses all issues except requirements management, and it provides most support for benchmarking and change impact analysis.

References

[1] A. Goldberg and D. Robson, *Smalltalk-80: The Language*, Reading, MA, Addison-Wesley, 1989.
[2] Apple Computer Inc., *MacApp II Programmer's Guide*, 1989.
[3] J. Bosch, P. Molin, M. Mattsson and P. Bengtsson, Problems & experiences, in M.E. Fayad, D.C. Schmidt and R.E. Johnson (eds.), *Object-Oriented Application Frameworks*, Wiley & Sons, 1998.
[4] M.E. Fayad, D.C. Schmidt and R.E. Johnson (eds.), *Object-Oriented Application Frameworks: Problems & Perspectives*, John Wiley & Sons Inc., New York, NY, 1999.
[5] E. Gamma, *Object-Oriented Software Development based on ET++: Design Patterns, Class Library, Tools*, (in German), Springer-Verlag, 1992.
[6] P. Molin and L. Ohlsson, Points & deviations – A pattern language for fire alarm systems, *Proceedings of the 3rd International Conference on Pattern Languages for Programming*, Monticello, USA, 1996.
[7] J. Bosch, Design of an object-oriented framework for measurement systems, in M. Fayad, D. Schmidt and R. Johnson (eds.), *Object-Oriented Application Frameworks*, John Wiley, 1998.
[8] H. Huni, R. Johnson and R. Engel, A framework for network protocol software, *Proceedings of the 10th Conference on Object-Oriented Programming Systems, Languages and Applications*, Austin, USA, 1995.
[9] D. Geary, *Graphic Java 1.1: Mastering the AWT*, Prentice Hall, 1997.
[10] G. Shepherd and S. Wingo, *MFC Internals: Inside the MFC Architecture*, Addison-Wesley, 1994.
[11] R. Harrison, *Symbian OS C++ for Mobile Phones*, Symbian Press, 2003.
[12] A. Rösel, Experiences with the evolution of an application family architecture, *Proceedings of the Second International ESPRIT ARES Workshop*, Las Palmas, Spain, pp. 39–48, 1998.
[13] M. Mattsson, Effort distribution in a six year industrial application framework project, *Proceedings of the International Conference on Software Maintenance – 1999*, Oxford, United Kingdom, pp. 326–333, 1999.
[14] S. Moser and O. Nierstrasz, The effect of object-oriented frameworks on developer productivity, *IEEE Comput.*, pp. 45–51, 1996.
[15] M. Lindvall and K. Sandahl, How well do experienced software developers predict software change? *J. Syst. Softw.*, vol. 43 no. 1, 19–27, 1998.
[16] J. Bansiya, Evaluating structural and functional stability, in *Object-Oriented Application Frameworks: Problems & Perspectives*, M.E. Fayad, D.C. Schmidt and R.E. Johnson (eds.), Wiley & Sons, 1998.
[17] M. Mattsson and J. Bosch, Observations on the evolution of an industrial OO framework, *Proceedings of the International Conference on Software Maintenance – 1999*, Oxford, United Kingdom, pp. 139–145, 1999.
[18] M. Mattsson and J. Bosch, Characterizing stability in evolving frameworks, in *Proceedings of the 29th International Conference on Technology of Object- Oriented Languages and Systems*, TOOLS EUROPE '99, Nancy, France, pp. 118–130, June 7–10, 1999.
[19] M. Mattsson and J. Bosch, Stability assessment of evolving industrial object – oriented frameworks, *J. Softw. Maint.: Res. Pract.*, vol. 12, no. 2, pp. 79–102, 2000.
[20] T. Neward, *Core Owl 5.0: Owl Internals for Advanced Programmers*, Manning Publications Company; 1997.
[21] D. Roberts and R. Johnson, Evolving frameworks: A pattern language for developing object-oriented frameworks, *Proceedings of the Third Conference on Pattern Languages and Programming*, Allerton Park, Illinois, 1996.
[22] H. Gall, M. Jazayeri, R.G. Klösch and G. Trausmuth, Software evolution observations based on product release History, *Proceedings of the Conference on Software Maintenance*, Bari, Italy, pp. 160–166, 1997.

[23] J. Bansiya, *A Hierarchical Model for Quality Assessment of Object-Oriented Design*, Ph.D Dissertation, University of Alabama, 1997.
[24] S.R. Chidamber and C.F. Kemerer, A metrics suite for object-oriented design, *IEEE Trans. Softw. Eng.*, Vol. 20, no. 6, pp. 476–493, 1994.
[25] K. Erni and C. Lewerentz, Applying design metrics to object-oriented frameworks, *Proceedings of the Metrics Symposium*, IEEE Computer Society, Washington, DC, 1996.

15

Formal Perspectives on Software Evolution: From Refinement to Retrenchment

Michael Poppleton and Lindsay Groves

15.1 Introduction

Formal methods use mathematical techniques to enhance the quality and dependability of software. System specifications are stated formally using mathematical logic to achieve a level of precision that is not possible with traditional textual and diagrammatic techniques. These specifications can then be validated in various ways, and transformed into more and more detailed designs in such a way that the resulting design is a provably correct implementation of the initial specification. While most work in formal methods has focused on *ab initio* development of a single program from a new specification, researchers are now starting to consider how evolution of such specifications and programs may be formally supported.

This chapter discusses various ways in which formal methods can contribute to the evolutionary development of verifiably correct software. The basic problem to be addressed can be described as follows (see Figure 15.1): Consider an existing specification *Spec*, which is implemented by a program *Prog*, and suppose the specification changes to a new specification *Spec**, similar to *Spec*. How can a new program *Prog** be constructed, which satisfies *Spec**, while exploiting the investment in the original development? This question is central to any kind of evolutionary development, whether the new specification arises from correcting a mistake in the old one, adding new requirements once the system has been completed, adapting a program component to be reused in a different context, or developing a specification for a later release of the system.

If the only artefacts available are the existing specification and program and the new specification, there is little guidance as to how to modify the program to meet the

---

Software Evolution and Feedback: Theory and Practice Nazim H. Madhavji, Juan C. Fernández-Ramil and Dewayne E. Perry
© 2006 John Wiley & Sons, Ltd

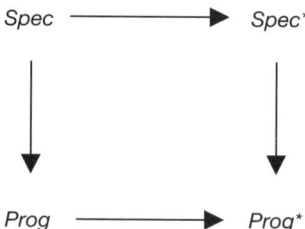

Figure 15.1 The software evolution question

new specification. If some kind of *design history* [1] is available, showing how the existing program meets its specification, this can be used as a basis for determining how a change in the specification should be translated into changes in the implementation. The refinement calculus provides such a design history, in the form of a *derivation*, showing how a specification is transformed into a provably correct implementation. The key questions to be addressed then become how changes to a specification are described and how these changes are then propagated through the derivation of an existing program.

The rest of the chapter is organised as follows. Section 15.2 provides a gentle introduction to the refinement calculus, providing the technical foundation of the chapter and introducing an example used in later sections. Section 15.3 discusses how program modifications can be performed in the refinement calculus by editing a derivation history. Section 15.4 describes a more constructive approach in which the new specification is described by composing a description of the new/modified functionality required with the existing specification, using specification constructors similar to those of the Z schema calculus, and then propagating the change description into the existing program structure to the places where changes are required. Section 15.5 discusses a recent extension of refinement, called *retrenchment*, and its potential contribution to a formal approach to software evolution. Section 15.6 presents some conclusions.

15.2 Program Refinement

The basic idea of program refinement is to start with a specification of the desired system, and to progressively transform this into a program implementing the specification, via a sequence of correctness-preserving transformations. The initial specification is expressed in a rich mathematical language, using abstract data types such as sets, bags and functions, along with powerful operations upon them, to express system requirements, as opposed to the mechanisms by which this behaviour is to be achieved – that is, *what* rather than *how*. This freedom from implementation detail leads to nondeterminism – in every possible system context, the specification includes all behaviours that would be possible in some acceptable implementation.

Specifications and programs are both expressed in a highly expressive, wide-spectrum language, able to express both (possibly nonexecutable) specification constructs and (executable) program constructs. Intermediate steps typically contain a mixture of specification and program constructs; the final program is expressed in an executable subset of the language, called *code*. The sequence of transformations performed, known as a *derivation*, provides a design history showing how the program satisfies its specification, which can be used as a basis for determining how modifications to the specification can be realised as modifications to the program. The refinement approach can be realised in a variety of formalisms, differing in the kind of language used to express specifications and programs, the kinds of transformation that can occur at each development step, and the correctness relation these transformations are required to preserve.

In the *refinement calculus* [2–4], specifications and programs (referred to collectively as *programs*) are expressed in a wide-spectrum language, on the basis of Dijkstra's guarded command language [5, 6],[1] augmented with a number of nonexecutable specification constructs. The most notable of these is the *specification statement*, written w:[*pre, post*], where: the *precondition*, *pre*, describes the assumptions to be made about any state in which the statement is executed; the *postcondition*, *post*, describes the properties that are to be guaranteed in any state in which the statement terminates and the *frame*, w, lists the state variables that may be changed. Thus, w:[*pre, post*] can be thought of as a contract, guaranteeing to establish *post*, changing only variables in w, provided it is only used in situations where *pre* holds initially.

For example, a very simple resource manager can be specified as a module in which the required operations are defined as procedures whose bodies are given as specification statements, as follows:[2]

```
module ResourceManager
  var free: set nat;
  procedure Alloc(result r: nat) is
    r, free:[free ≠ ∅, r ∈ free₀ ∧ free = free₀ - {r} ];
  procedure Free(value r: nat) is
    free:[ r ∉ free, free = free₀ ∪ {r} ];
  initially free = 1 .. MAX
end
```

In this example, *free* is a set of natural numbers, representing available resources, which is initialised to 1 .. *MAX*, for some positive integer constant *MAX*. The variable *free* is local to the module, and persists throughout the entire program execution. There are two operations: *Alloc* allocates a resource from *free*, provided at least one is available; and *Free* returns a resource to *free*, provided it is not in *free* already. In the postconditions of the specification statements, $free_0$ refers to the value of *free* in the state in which the statement is executed, which is the same as *free* in the precondition.

Note that the specification does not say what *Alloc* should do if there is no resource available, or what *Free* should do if asked to release a resource that is already in *free*. Giving *free* ≠ ∅ as the precondition for *Alloc*, explicitly says that the specifier does not care what happens for initial states where this does not hold; and similarly for $r \notin free$ in *Free*. Any client program using this module should ensure that it does not call these operations in states where their preconditions do not hold. Also note that the specification

---

[1] To simplify the presentation, this chapter uses more familiar constructs like those in Modula-2 and Ada, rather than Dijkstra's nondeterministic **if** and **do** commands.

[2] The notation for sets is similar to Z: ∅ is the empty set, #s is the cardinality of set s, – is set subtraction, and 1 .. *MAX* is the set of integers from 1 to *MAX*, inclusive.

of *Alloc* is nondeterministic, since it does not say which resource should be allocated when more than one is available.

A specification, such as that given above, is transformed into an executable program via a sequence of transformations, each preserving the correctness of the previous version. These transformations typically either alter the data structures used, for example, replacing abstract data types such as sets by more concrete ones such as arrays, records and pointers (*data refinement*), or specify details of how the required behaviour is to be obtained, by introducing or modifying algorithmic structure (*operation refinement*), while still conforming to the contract embodied in the initial specification.

In the above example, the first step towards an implementation might be to replace the abstract set variable *free* by a more concrete data structure, say, an array of Booleans:[3]

```
module ResourceManager1
  var b: array [1 .. MAX] of Boolean;
  procedure Alloc(result r: nat) is
    r, b: [true ∈ b[1 .. MAX], r ∈ 1 .. MAX ∧ b₀[r] = true
    ∧ b = b₀[r := false]];
  procedure Free(value r: nat) is
    b:[ b[r] = false, b = b₀ [r := true ]];
  initially (∀i: 1 .. MAX • b [i] = true)
end
```

This data refinement step is valid because the effect of the resulting program is indistinguishable from that of the original. This is justified formally in terms of an *abstraction relationship* showing how the abstract variable (*free*) is related to the concrete one (*b*) – in this case, $free = \{i : 1 .. MAX | b[i] = true\}$, that is, *free* is the set of indices at which *b* is true.

The next step is to implement the bodies of the procedures. *Free* is easy to implement – its body can be replaced by the assignment statement $b[r] := true$, since this has exactly the effect required by the postcondition $b = b_0[r := true]$. Implementing *Alloc* is more complicated, requiring a loop to search for an index at which *b* is *true*. This can be done by initialising *r* to 1 and looking at successive positions in *b* until a *true* value is found, and then setting that element to *false* and returning its position. The required code can be derived from the specification of *Alloc* in six steps, as follows:[4]

(i) The initial specification is split into two statements, one to find a free resource *r*, and one to record that *r* has been allocated. (*Sequence*)

$r, b : [true \in b[1 .. MAX], r \in 1 .. MAX \wedge b_0[r] = true \wedge b = b_0[r := false]]$

becomes

$P :: \quad r : [true \in b[1 .. MAX], r \in 1 .. MAX \wedge b[r] = true];$

$Q :: \quad b : [r \in 1 .. MAX \wedge b[r] = true, r \in 1 .. MAX \wedge b_0[r] = true \wedge b = b_0[r := false]]$

---

[3] $true \in b[m .. n]$ is shorthand for ($\exists i : m .. n \bullet b[i] = true$), and $b_0[r := false]$ is the array value obtained from b_0 by replacing element *r* by *false*.

[4] Introduced specification statements are labelled, $P, Q, \ldots$ for readability. Rule names *Sequence*, *Assignment*, and so on are explained in Section 15.3.

(ii) Anticipating that a loop will be required, specification P is further split into statements that will end up being a loop and its initialisation. The intermediate assertion, $r \in 1 \,..\, MAX \land true \in b[r \,..\, MAX]$, is the intended loop invariant indicating that (since $true$ has not been found yet) the promised $true$ value must be between r and MAX. (*Sequence*)

$P :: \quad r : [true \in b[1 \,..\, MAX], r \in 1 \,..\, MAX \land b[r] = true]$

becomes

$R :: \quad r : [true \in b[1 \,..\, MAX], r \in 1 \,..\, MAX \land true \in b[r \,..\, MAX]];$

$S :: \quad r : [r \in 1 \,..\, MAX \land true \in b[r \,..\, MAX], r \in 1 \,..\, MAX \land b[r] = true]$

(iii) Specification R can be implemented by setting r to 1, since MAX is positive and the precondition ensures that $true \in b[1 \,..\, MAX]$ holds. (*Assignment*)

$R :: \quad r : [true \in b[1 \,..\, MAX], r \in 1 \,..\, MAX \land true \in b[k \,..\, MAX]]$

becomes

$r := 1$

(iv) Specification S requires a loop to search for a suitable value of r. The loop invariant has already been chosen to be $r \in 1 \,..\, MAX \land true \in b[r \,..\, MAX]$. The guard is $b[r] = false$, ensuring that the postcondition holds when the loop terminates. The variant, used to ensure that the loop terminates, is $MAX - r$. (*Repetition*)

$S :: \quad r : [r \in 1 \,..\, MAX \land true \in b[r \,..\, MAX]], r \in 1 \,..\, MAX \land b[r] = true]$

becomes

```
while b[r] = false do
  T:: r : [r ∈ 1 .. MAX ∧ true ∈ b[r .. MAX] ∧ b[r] = false,
       r ∈ 1 .. MAX ∧ true ∈ b[r .. MAX] ∧ r > r₀]
od
```

(v) Specification T can be implemented by incrementing r by one, which ensures that progress is made towards termination (decreasing the variant) and preserves the loop invariant since $r \in 1 \,..\, MAX \land true \in b[r \,..\, MAX] \land b[r] = false$ implies $r + 1 \in 1 \,..\, MAX \land true \in b[r+1 \,..\, MAX]$. (*Assignment*)

$T :: \quad r : [r \in 1 \,..\, MAX \land true \in b[r \,..\, MAX] \land b[r] = false,$
$\qquad\qquad r \in 1 \,..\, MAX \land true \in b[r \,..\, MAX] \land r > r_0]$

becomes

$r := r + 1$

(vi) Finally, specification Q can be implemented by setting $b[r]$ to $false$. (*Assignment*)

$Q :: \quad b : [r \in 1 \,..\, MAX \land b[r] = true,$
$\qquad\qquad r \in 1 \,..\, MAX \land b_0[r] = true \land b = b_0[r := false]]$

becomes

$b[r] := \mathit{false}$

At this stage, the complete module is as follows:

```
module ResourceManager1
  var b: array [1 .. MAX] of Boolean;
  procedure Alloc(result r: nat) is
    r := 1;
    while b[r] = false do r := r + 1 od;
    b[r] := false;
  procedure Free(value r: nat) is
    b[r] := true;
  initially (∀i: 1 .. MAX • b[i] = true)
end
```

The initialisation can be implemented in a similar fashion to *Alloc*, resulting in a loop that sets all the elements of *b* to *true*. The final implementation can then be mechanically coded in an appropriate programming language.

Each step in a successful derivation can be formally justified by appealing to a collection of refinement laws embodying commonly used transformations. Most of these laws support top–down design, by replacing a specification statement by one of the basic programming constructs of the wide-spectrum language. For example:

- *Assignment*: w:[*pre*, *post*] can be replaced by an assignment $x := e$, provided that $x \in e$ and the condition obtained by replacing x by e in *post* and removing zero subscripts holds whenever *pre* holds.
- *Sequence*: w:[*pre*, *post*] can be replaced by the sequential composition w:[*pre*, *mid*]; w:[*mid*, *post*], for any intermediate assertion *mid* not containing w_0.
- *Conditional*: w:[*pre*, *post*] can be replaced by the if statement **if** g **then** w : [*pre* ∧ g, *post*] **else** w : [*pre* ∧ ¬g, *post*] **fi**, for any guard g.
- *Repetition*: w:[*pre*, *post*] can be replaced by the loop **while** g **do** w : [*inv* ∧ g, *inv* ∧ $f < f_0$] **od**, for any guard g, loop invariant *inv* and natural valued variant function f, such that *pre* implies *inv* and *inv* ∧ ¬g implies *post*. The loop invariant and guard are chosen to ensure that the loop will establish the required postcondition; the variant function must reduce on each iteration, but cannot become negative, which ensures that the loop terminates.
- *Local variable*: w:[*pre*, *post*] can be replaced by the block |[**var**x • w[*pre*, *post*]]|, where x does not occur in w, *pre* or *post*.

These laws give rise to *proof obligations* that must be proved to justify the development steps in which they are used. For example, the third step in the above derivation, introducing the assignment $r := 1$, is valid because $\mathit{true} \in b[1 .. MAX]$ implies $1 \in 1 .. MAX \land \mathit{true} \in b[1 .. MAX]$. The latter condition is obtained by substituting 1 for r in the postcondition $r \in 1 .. MAX \land \mathit{true} \in b[k .. MAX]$, and holds because MAX is assumed to be positive.

More generally, program S can be replaced by program T if any client expecting S cannot tell that T has been used instead. This relationship is formalised by saying that 'T refines S', or 'S is refined by T', written $S \sqsubseteq T$, if T establishes any postcondition that S establishes. Refining one specification statement, $w : [pre, post]$, by another, $w' : [pre', post']$, leads to three proof obligations: $w' \subseteq w$, $pre \Rightarrow pre'$ and $\forall w \bullet pre_0 \wedge post' \Rightarrow post$. The last two are similar to the proof obligations for operation refinement in Z [7], and show that a refinement may alter a statement so that it terminates for more initial states (weakening the precondition) or is more deterministic (strengthening the postcondition). Refinement laws, like those listed above, are proved in terms of the semantics of the wide-spectrum language, which is defined in terms of Dijkstra's weakest preconditions [5, 6, 8].

A *derivation* is thus a sequence of specifications, $S_0, S_1, \ldots, S_n$, where S_0 is the initial specification, S_n is the resulting program, and for $i = 1, \ldots, n$, S_{i-1} is refined by S_i. Since refinement is *transitive* (i.e. if $S \sqsubseteq T$ and $T \sqsubseteq U$, then $S \sqsubseteq U$), the result of a sequence of refinement steps is a correct implementation of the initial specification.

The formal definition of refinement suggests that each step should transform the whole program, which would be a very tedious process and would make verifying each step inordinately difficult. Fortunately, as illustrated in the above example, a much simpler approach can be used. Instead of transforming the entire program at each step, an individual component of the program, such as a branch of an **if** statement or the body of a loop or procedure, can be transformed. This works because the program constructors are all *monotonic*, which means that refining such a component of a program gives a refinement of the whole program [9].

Using refinement laws, instead of justifying each refinement step directly in terms of its weakest precondition semantics, also considerably simplifies the refinement process. These laws are proved correct in terms of the weakest precondition semantics, and do not then need to be reproved each time they are used. Many such laws can be proved from the semantics (e.g. see [4]). In practice, most derivations can be done using only about a dozen rules.

A derivation is complete when the final program contains only executable constructs, though it is possible to perform further transformations on an executable program, for example, to improve efficiency. Not all of the specifications that can be expressed in the wide-spectrum language are able to be implemented. In particular, the specification statement: $[P, false]$ must, for any initial state satisfying P, terminate in a state satisfying *false*, which is, of course, impossible. This statement is said to be *infeasible* or *miraculous* (since it violates Dijkstra's *Law of the Excluded Miracle* [5, 6]), and is given the name *magic*. While miracles are not permitted in executable programs (i.e. code), it is useful to allow them in the language, because they simplify the semantic theory and many of the refinement laws,[5] and are sometimes useful within intermediate steps in a derivation [10], in much the same way that complex numbers simplify certain mathematical theories and calculations. More importantly, for practical purposes, their inclusion means that inconsistent requirements can be expressed in the language and the inconsistency identified formally, as infeasibility. Since code is always feasible, it is not necessary to check for

---

[5] In the *Sequence* law it is not necessary to check that the intermediate assertion can be established. If *mid* is *false*, $w:[pre, mid]$; $w:[mid, post]$, is miraculous for initial states satisfying *pre*, and thus refines $w:[pre, post]$, since all programs are refined by *magic*, but cannot be refined to code.

feasibility at every step – if a derivation can be completed, the initial specification and all intermediate versions must have been feasible.[6]

Although tedious when presented and explained in this level of detail, the refinement process mirrors closely the kind of top-down design advocated by authors such as Dijkstra, Gries and Wirth (e.g. [11, 12]), and provides a high level of assurance that the resulting program satisfies the initial specification. Instead of working in terms of the small steps embodied in the basic laws illustrated above, more powerful derived rules can be used, which package several smaller steps. For example, a single derived rule might be used to introduce a counted loop, declaring and initialising a variable to use as a loop counter as well as introducing the actual loop, which would otherwise take about four steps. Importantly, for the purposes of software evolution, program refinement provides a design history that can be used as a basis for effecting modifications to a program. In practice, the most important information contained in a derivation is the abstraction invariants used in data refinement, the intermediate assertions used in introducing sequential compositions, and the loop invariants and variant functions used in introducing loops, since they cannot easily be deduced from the resulting program.

To be practical, program refinement requires sophisticated tool support to assist in selecting and applying refinement rules and derived rules, and in discharging the resulting proof obligations. A refinement tool may also support the use of tactics that embody a piece of programming knowledge, which may produce different code according to the program it is applied to. Such tools have been developed, but are still at the stage of being research prototypes (e.g. [13, 14]).

15.3 Modifying Refinements by Adapting Derivations

The refinement laws discussed above can be thought of as transformation rules that are applied to a component of a program to transform it into a refinement of that component, provided the resulting proof obligations hold. These rules generally require various parameters that dictate just how the transformation is performed, for example, providing variables to be declared or assigned to, guards to be introduced, intermediate assertions to be used, and so on. For example, the derivation for *Alloc* in the above example can be described as a sequence of six rule applications:

(i) Apply *Sequence* to the initial specification, with $r \in 1 \mathrel{..} MAX \land b[r] = true$ as the intermediate assertion. Call the result $P; Q$.[7]
(ii) Apply *Sequence* to P, with $r \in 1 \mathrel{..} MAX \land true \in b[r \mathrel{..} MAX]$ as the intermediate assertion. Call the result $R; S$.
(iii) Apply *Assignment* to R, with $r := 1$ as the assignment.

---

[6] That is, no miraculous statement will ever be executed in a context where its precondition holds.

[7] $P; Q$ is a pattern that is matched with the result of the transformation, in order to provide names for the components that need to be transformed in later steps. For readability, the pattern variables used ($P, Q, \ldots$) correspond to the labels given in the above derivation.

(iv) Apply *Repetition* to S, with $b[r] = \textit{false}$ as the guard, $r \in 1 \mathrel{..} MAX \wedge \textit{true} \in b[r \mathrel{..} MAX]$ as the loop invariant, and $MAX - r$ as the variant function. Call the result **while** G **do** T **od**.
(v) Apply *Assignment* to T, with $r := r + 1$ as the assignment.
(vi) Apply *Assignment* to Q, with $b[r] := \textit{false}$ as the assignment.

This sequence of rule applications, and the associated proof obligations, provides a design history that can be used as a basis for implementing modifications to the program [15]. In general, given the sequence of rules used in deriving a program *Prog*, from its specification *Spec*, and a specification *Spec'* which is similar to *Spec*, it may be possible to construct a new program implementing *Spec'* by applying a similar sequence of rules to *Spec'*. It will not usually be possible to apply exactly the same sequence of rules, because their proof obligations may not hold in the new derivation. But attempting to apply the same sequence of rules will indicate what needs to be changed in order to implement the new specification. This may involve inserting new steps, deleting steps, reordering steps or changing the way that existing steps are applied, for example, changing an intermediate assertion or loop invariant.

As an illustration, suppose the specification given above is modified so that *Alloc* is required to find the *smallest* available resource. In the initial specification, $r \in \textit{free}_0$ becomes $r = \min \textit{free}_0$, and $\textit{true} \notin b_0[1 \mathrel{..} r - 1]$ is added to the postcondition after the data refinement (since $r = \min \{i : 1 \mathrel{..} MAX | b_0[i] = \textit{true}\}$ is equivalent to $b_0[i] = \textit{true} \wedge \textit{true} \notin b_0[1 \mathrel{..} r - 1]$). A similar modification can be made to the subsequent steps, leading to the same program and showing that the existing program happens to already implement the stronger specification. If the specification was instead modified so that *Alloc* was required to find the *largest* available resource, $r \in \textit{free}_0$ would become $r = \max \textit{free}_0$ in the initial specification, and $\textit{true} \notin b[r + 1 \mathrel{..} MAX]$ added after the data refinement. In this case, the implementation would need to be changed more radically; for example, by changing the loop so that it inspects every element of b and updates r every time a true element is found, or changing to a counting down loop. The former requires four additional steps, and minor changes to the existing steps (adding a condition to the loop invariant); the latter uses the same six steps, but with more substantial changes to the parameters used (changing the loop invariant, variant function, initialisation and guard).

Now suppose that the original specification is modified so that *Alloc* also returns the number, n, of resources available. The new specification can be written as follows:

$$r, n, \textit{free} : [\textit{free} \neq \emptyset, r \in \textit{free}_0 \wedge \textit{free} = \textit{free}_0 - \{r\} \wedge n = \#\textit{free}]$$

which, after data refinement, becomes:

$$r, n, b : [\textit{true} \in b[1 \mathrel{..} MAX],$$
$$r \in 1 \mathrel{..} MAX \wedge b_0[r] = \textit{true} \wedge b = b_0[r := \textit{false}] \wedge$$
$$n = \#\{i : 1 \mathrel{..} MAX | b[i] = \textit{true}\}]$$

This modification can be implemented either by computing n in the existing loop, or by introducing a separate loop. The former requires four additional steps, with the original six steps modified to carry the additional conditions pertaining to n; the latter requires nine additional steps to introduce the additional loop, with the original six steps remaining unchanged.

This process of revising derivations is essentially the way that people usually implement modifications to programs developed in the refinement calculus. It is a tedious process to do by hand, because of the need to carry over modifications from one step to another, and rechecking proof obligations to see whether the same modification is required or whether it needs to be varied in same way. Sometimes changes are prompted because proof obligations do not hold in the revised derivation; but sometimes they are prompted by efficiency considerations that are not obvious in the formalism. A refinement tool can record the steps in a derivation in a textual form, as a script or meta-program, which the programmer can edit and re-run in order to implement the required modifications. Alternatively, a refinement tool could be designed to assist in this modification process by identifying a syntactic mapping that will transform the original specification into the new one, and then selectively applying this mapping, updated as necessary, to subsequent steps in the derivation. This approach has been explored in planning, proof and program transformation systems (e.g. see [16]), but not to date in refinement tools.

15.4 A Compositional Approach to Program Modification

An alternative approach to implementing modifications to programs developed in the refinement calculus has recently been proposed [17, 18]. In this approach, instead of just modifying the specification by editing it directly and then comparing it with the original to see how it has changed, modifications to the specification are described by composing the original specification with another specification describing the modified behaviour. The two specifications are combined with a specification operator that combines the two in an appropriate way, similar to the schema operators in Z. Properties of that specification operator are then used to propagate the new requirement into the program derivation to the point(s) where the existing program needs to be changed.

For example, using a program conjunction operator, $\curlywedge$, to combine the effects of two specifications, the first change to *Alloc* discussed above (returning the smallest available resource) can be described as follows:

$$r, \mathit{free} : [\mathit{free} \neq \emptyset, r \in \mathit{free}_0 \wedge \mathit{free} = \mathit{free}_0 - \{r\}] \curlywedge r : [\mathit{free} \neq \emptyset, r = \min \mathit{free}]$$

The second specification captures the added requirement and the conjunction operator $\curlywedge$ says that both postconditions must be established, provided that both preconditions hold, modifying only variables that occur in either or both of the frames. After data refinement, this becomes

$$r, b : [\mathit{true} \in b[1 .. MAX], r \in 1 .. MAX \wedge b_0[r] = \mathit{true} \wedge b = b_0[r := \mathit{false}]] \curlywedge$$

$$r : [\mathit{true} \in b[1 .. MAX], r = \min \{i : 1 .. MAX | b[i] = \mathit{true}\}]$$

Similarly, the second change to *Alloc* discussed above (returning the number of resources available) can be described as follows:

$$r, \mathit{free} : [\mathit{free} \neq \emptyset, r \in \mathit{free}_0 \wedge \mathit{free} = \mathit{free}_0 - \{r\}] \curlywedge n : [\mathit{true}, n = \#\mathit{free}]$$

where, again the second specification captures the added requirement. This is equivalent to the version given in the previous section. After data refinement, this becomes

$r, b : [true \in b[1 .. MAX], r \in 1 .. MAX \wedge b_0[r] = true \wedge b = b_0[r := false]] \curlywedge$
$n : [true, n = \#\{i : 1 .. MAX | b[i] = true\}]$

In both cases, the modified specification is expressed as a conjunction of the old specification and a specification statement expressing the additional requirements. Writing the modified specification in this way makes it much clearer just what the changed behaviour is, and thus easier to see what needs to be changed. In the second example, the *true* precondition makes it clear that this new requirement does not rely on the assumption that *free* is not empty. The combined specification still needs that assumption, however, which is reflected in the requirement that a conjunction of two specifications is required to establish the postconditions of both specifications, modifying variables in the frames of both specifications, only when both preconditions hold.

Laws about program conjunction can now be used to transform the modified specification into a new program, using steps from the existing derivation, possibly modified or supplemented with additional steps, where appropriate. Considering the second modification described above, one option is to immediately eliminate the conjunction and proceed essentially as described in Section 15.3. Alternatively, since there is no interference between the conjoined specifications, the conjunction can be turned into a sequential composition, giving

$r, b : [true \in b[1 .. MAX], r \in 1 .. MAX \wedge b_0[r] = true \wedge b = b_0[r := false]];$
$n : [true, n = \#\{i : 1 .. MAX | b[i] = true\}]$

The two specifications can then be refined independently, the first in the same way as the original development, and the second leading to a second loop (as discussed in Section 15.3).

A more interesting alternative is to push the additional requirement into the original development so that it can be addressed using the existing loop – with the modification to find the smallest available resource, this would be the only sensible approach, since both conjuncts constrain the value of r. The basic strategy is to try to refine the added specification to a program with a similar structure to the existing one, so that the two programs can be merged in a way that respects the semantics of conjunction. Sometimes the original derivation needs to be revised to produce a program whose structure is more suited to the required modification, so in practice the original derivation is repeated, possibly modifying its steps. The new program is constructed in parallel with this, and their structures merged as they are created. This process relies on a rich set of laws for distributing conjunctions over the various program constructs (e.g. a conjunction of **if** statements with the same guard, **if** G **then** S **else** T **fi** $\curlywedge$ **if** G **then** U **else** V **fi**, is equivalent to **if** G **then** $S \curlywedge U$ **else** $T \curlywedge V$ **fi**) and eliminating conjunctions (e.g. turning a conjunction into a sequential composition, where the conjoined programs have disjoint frames).

In the above example, one option is to modify the existing program so that it always inspects all elements of b, since that is required in the added specification, then construct a similar program for the new specification, and merge them. The effect is equivalent to refining the conjunction above to

```
|[ var k •                              |[ var k •
   k := 1;                                 k := 1; n := 0;
   while k ≤ MAX do                        while k ≤ MAX do
     if b[k]=true then r:=k fi;    ⋏         if b[k]=true then n := n+1 fi;
     k := k + 1                              k := k + 1
   od;                                    od
   b[r] := false                       ]|
]|
```

Merging these two programs, then gives

```
|[var k •
  k := 1; n := 0;
  while k ≤ MAX do
    if b[k] = true then r := k; n := n + 1 fi;
    k := k + 1
  od;
  b[r] := false
]|
```

This approach is discussed in detail in [17], which also describes several other operators that can be used to describe other kinds of changes, and laws that can be used to propagate changes into a derivation in the way outlined above. For example, a program disjunction operator can be used to extend the domain of a program, for example, to define the behaviour of *Alloc* when no resources are available. These operators allow a wide range of typical modifications to be described, but undoubtedly do not cover all possible ways in which a specification could be changed.

Unfortunately, there does not appear to be any way to tell from a proposed modification how much an existing program and its derivation would need to be changed. The laws may suggest how a modification might be implemented, but cannot determine exactly what change is required. Any specification change can be implemented in many different ways, some of which will be easy to implement but may be rejected because of the size, structure or efficiency of the resulting program. It will always be preferable in some cases to abandon the existing program and to construct a new program from scratch.

15.5 Retrenchment

As a formal method for verifiable *ab initio* software development, refinement was not originally concerned with the evolution of requirements. The recent advent of more compositional development philosophies, that is, object-orientation and component-based approaches, motivated the definition of correspondingly more compositional forms of refinement, for example, [19, 20]. Although more flexible, and more supportive of agile development processes than previous ones, these forms still did not address the pressing need to support evolving requirements in existing and planned systems. This need has now been addressed: Section 15.2 having introduced Morgan's refinement calculus [4], Sections 15.3 and 15.4 presented some recent proposals for the support of evolutionary processes in conjunction with the calculus.

In this section, a requirements engineering perspective is taken on refinement (discussed in Section 15.5.1 in a relational notation), which links to the question of how software evolution may be supported. Refinement is a powerful formal method for the development of critical software, with a good industrial track record. However, the strong conditions required for its application are also restrictive: In Section 15.5.2 requirements specification scenarios will be identified, which are hard to describe using refinement methods. Addressing some of these limitations motivated the proposal of a generalisation of refinement, called *retrenchment* [21, 22]. Section 15.5.3 introduces retrenchment as a generalisation of refinement. A simple example illustrates the notion, and the increased formal expressiveness that is provided. The requirements perspective suggests that retrenchment may have a contribution to make to the formal support of the software evolution process. As a formal description of the evolved requirement, retrenchment should provide formal support for production of the evolved refinements to code, analogously to the approach of Section 15.4. Section 15.5.4 discusses some recent theoretical results and outlines how retrenchment may in future support software evolution.

15.5.1 Refinement – a Relational Perspective

The simple classical framework of first-order predicate logic (FOPL) will be used to discuss refinement and retrenchment in relational terms. This employs a 'posit-and-prove' style of refinement, in contrast to the calculational style of Morgan's refinement calculus, and is based on a number of classical formalisms, mainly VDM, Z and B [2, 7, 23]. While this increases the notational burden on the reader, it does serve to demonstrate the dominant style of description in model-based formal methods. The real reason, however, is that retrenchment has been developed in this style, and has not yet been expressed in Morgan's calculus.

Whereas Morgan adds structure (by applying refinement laws) to the gap between pre- and postconditions, the posit-and-prove approach starts from an abstract relational model of the specification, and then designs in the structure required to make a correct program, proving the design refinements at each stage. Such proof is from first principles, probably deploying experience from similar, earlier proofs and is usually tool-supported.

Refinement is a relationship between an abstract system model **Abs** and a (more) concrete system model **Conc**. This pair of models may represent any link of interest in a refinement chain. The abstract model has state variable(s) u and a collection of operations **Ops$_A$**. The operation is atomic in this setting – it is the unit of behaviour in the system specification. The operation takes an input, reads and perhaps modifies the state variable, and produces an output. All required behaviour is then specified in terms of the operation compositions that are available in the specification language being used. An operation Op_A in **Ops$_A$** can be described in terms of its transition, or step relation, written $stp_{Op_A}(u, i, u', o)$, between before-state/input pair (u, i) and after-state/output pair (u', o). An initial-state predicate $Init_A(u')$ characterises initial system states u' that satisfy the requirements. Every initial state must satisfy the system *invariant* property, and this invariant must be preserved by every defined operation step from every valid (invariant-satisfying) state.[8] The corresponding concrete model **Conc** is defined in the same way, in terms of state variable v, an operation Op_C in set **Ops$_C$**, its step relation $stp_{OpC}(v, j, v', p)$ between before-state/input pair (v, j) and after-state/output pair (v', p), and initial-state predicate $Init_C(v)$. Loosely speaking, we can link this notation to that of earlier sections as follows: The precondition of Op_A is given by $\exists u', o \bullet stp_{OpA}(u, i, u', o)$, that is, the input/before-state pairs from which it is possible to take a step, and the postcondition is precisely stp_{OpA}.

The usual forward simulation [24] formulation of the refinement of **Abs** by **Conc** follows. Every Op_A in **Ops$_A$** must correspond with exactly one Op_C in **Ops$_C$**, and vice versa. The refinement relationship is expressed in terms of an abstraction relation $G(u, v)$ between the state variables of the two models: For every valid v, this describes the values of u that v represents. There are two conditions that must hold in order that **Conc** be a refinement of **Abs**. The first condition is that every concrete initial state must be witnessed by some abstract initial state through the abstraction relation:

$$Init_C(v') \Rightarrow (\exists u' \bullet Init_A(u') \wedge G(u', v')) \quad (15.1)$$

Relations In_{Op} and Out_{Op} describe how concrete input j (resp. output p) represents abstract input i (resp. output o). In_{Op} and Out_{Op} will simply be the identity relation in the case of no type change in input/output respectively. The second condition is that for every corresponding operation pair Op_A in **Ops$_A$** and Op_C in **Ops$_C$**:

$$In_{Op}(i, j) \wedge G(u, v) \wedge stp_{OpC}(v, j, v', p) \Rightarrow$$
$$\exists u', o \bullet (stp_{OpA}(u, i, u', o) \wedge G(u', v') \wedge Out_{Op}(o, p)) \quad (15.2)$$

That is, starting from before-state/input pair (u, i) represented by (v, j) through In_{Op} and G, every concrete Op_C-step is witnessed by some abstract Op_A-step which establishes representation of (u', o) by (v', p) through G and Out_{Op}. More succinctly we say that Op_C simulates Op_A. That is, Op_C provides a black-box simulation of Op_A in the sense that the (designed) Op_C-step is indistinguishable to the user from its corresponding (user-specified) Op_A-step.

There is an implicit universal quantification at the outer level of these statements: In (Equation 15.2) the condition holds for *all* values of i, j, u, v, v', p that satisfy the antecedent clause of the implication. The nesting of an existential quantification inside gives a significant shape: *Every* valid Op_C-step is witnessed by *some* Op_A-step. That is, there may be many Op_A-steps starting at the (u, i)-pair in question, but only one need be simulated by the Op_C-step. This is refinement's characteristic of reduction of nondeterminism, as the degree of choice in the abstract specification is gradually reduced by addition of algorithmic structure through refinement steps.

By inductive reasoning, there is an implicit quantification in the simulation conditions for refinement: over behaviours. That is, given (Equation 15.1) and (Equation 15.2), any concrete system behaviour (sequence of concrete operations) Op_{C1}; Op_{C2}; ... Op_{Cn} will simulate the corresponding abstract behaviour Op_{A1}; Op_{A2}; ... Op_{An} exactly as per (Equation 15.2).

---

[8] Invariants will not be discussed further in this chapter.

15.5.2 The Need to Generalise Refinement

This section considers three example development scenarios that are difficult to describe satisfactorily with refinement, as motivation for a more general approach. The utility of such a more general approach for software evolution is indicated.

Finiteness

A variation on the simple resource manager example of Section 15.2 will serve both to illustrate refinement and to demonstrate some problems. Given a pool of some existing resources *RSS*, operations are required to record the allocation and deallocation of identified resources from the pool. The design of this example system fragment will be informed by the software engineering principle of separation of concerns [5], which will demonstrate an expressive limitation of refinement.

The most abstract modelling level is concerned only with describing resources, their allocation and deallocation. Separating concerns, questions of finiteness and of structure of each resource are abstracted away. This enables the use of a simple and elegant model using sets and relations (possibly infinite) to describe the system. Finiteness is abstracted away, since it is typical of implementation constraints, which, methodologically, should be specified at a separate stage from basic functional requirements. The state of the abstract model **Abs** is a set of allocated resources *arss*. Initialisation $Init_A$ starts with an empty set. Allocation and deallocation operations have preconditions: $Alloc_A$ may only allocate a resource in the pool not already allocated, and $Dalloc_A$ may only deallocate a resource already allocated.

Although the specification syntax here (a simplification of B syntax [2]) differs from that of earlier sections, there is little semantic difference. The precondition is stated after keyword **pre**, and the operation step is written in 'assignment' style, which has the usual meaning.[9] Initialisation and operations on a single input resource *rs* are defined as

$$Init_A \cong arss := \phi$$

$$Alloc_A(rs) \cong \textbf{pre } rs \in RSS - arss \textbf{ then } arss := arss \cup \{rs\}$$

$$Dalloc_A(rs) \cong \textbf{pre } rs \in arss \textbf{ then } arss := arss - \{rs\} \quad (15.3)$$

The concrete model **Conc** has, correspondingly, allocated resource set *crss*, initialisation $Init_C$, operations $Alloc_C$, $Dalloc_C$. In this model, a finiteness constraint is added: assume that storage space is limited to *cmax* elements. Thus, the total number of concrete resources that can be allocated is limited. The cardinality operator # is used to count the total number of elements in the set. Note that, in the **if**-construct used here, the absence of an **else** clause means 'do nothing; state does not change', that is, '**else** skip'. The abstraction relation G_{AC} from **Conc** to **Abs** is set equality:

$$Init_C \cong crss := \phi$$

$$Alloc_C(rs) \cong \textbf{pre } rs \in RSS - crss \textbf{ if } \#crss < cmax \textbf{ then } crss := crss \cup \{rs\}$$

$$Dalloc_C(rs) \cong \textbf{pre } rs \in crss \textbf{ then } crss := crss - \{rs\}$$

$$G_{AC}(arss, crss) \cong arss = crss \quad (15.4)$$

---

[9] Thus $stp_{Alloc_A}(arss, rs, arss') \cong rs \in RSS - \{arss\} \wedge arss' = arss \cup \{rs\}$. '$\cong$' is read 'is defined to be'.

It is obvious that (Equation 15.1) holds here, and that (Equation 15.2) holds for resource allocation until *cmax* resources have been recorded. After that, *crss* is full (so $Alloc_C$ skips while $Alloc_A$ continues to add new resources) and G_{AC} cannot be re-established. So the refinement only holds as long as the abstract state is as finite as the concrete, otherwise it fails. This is unsatisfactory; an apparent way out is to treat a full *crss* (with *cmax* elements) as an overflow, or exception condition. That is, regard a full *crss* as representing any set *arss* that contains *crss*. The abstraction relation could be redefined as

$$G_{AC}(arss, crss) \cong \text{if } \#crss < cmax \text{ then } crss = arss \text{ else } crss \subseteq arss \qquad (15.5)$$

That way, condition (Equation 15.2) is satisfied, that is, $Alloc_A$ is refined for any number of allocations. However, (Equation 15.5) does not afford a joint refinement of both $Alloc_A$ and $Dalloc_A$, because while $\#arss > cmax$, (Equation 15.5) and thus (Equation 15.2) fail at the first deallocation of an element in *crss*. At this point $\#crss < cmax$, but in general, *crss* is still a proper subset of *arss*.

The only way the refinement designer can fix this is to allow the finiteness constraint to 'percolate up' to the abstract model so that the problem simply does not arise with the simulation conditions (Equation 15.1, Equation 15.2). This is unsatisfactory, since the software engineering principles of separation of concerns and postponing implementation bias until as late as possible are breached; the abstract model is 'polluted' with the lower-level concern of finiteness.

Where are the Requirements?

Albeit simplistic, the example has shown a methodological limitation of refinement. There is mileage in taking the example a little further, in order to show how the reduction of nondeterminism in a refinement step can conceal (from the unwary) the imposition of further constraints on the implementation. Imagine an enrichment of models **Abs** and **Conc** (to **Abs'** and **Conc'** respectively) to allow multiple instances of each allocated resource to be recorded; the mathematical model is a bag[10] rather than a set (for *arss'* and *crss'*), and the allocation/deallocation operations are defined analogously to the unprimed versions of (Equation 15.3, Equation 15.4). This caters for a requirement for provision of many instances of each of a number of resource types, for example, file handles, device drivers and processes in an operating system environment.

Next consider a further, more concrete layer to the design, called **Further'**[11] (subscript F), a data refinement of the finite bag *crss'* by a finite injective sequence *frss'*. Where the abstract bag models **Abs'** and **Conc'** simply count instances of each resource type, **Further'** records each instance allocation ($Alloc'_F$) by appending to the sequence. This gives the designer freedom in choosing how to reduce nondeterminism: The *particular* instance chosen for deallocation is immaterial to the abstract specification, so *any* instance of the input resource can be deallocated. For argument's sake, assume that minimising search time for the input resource is chosen, by specifying $Dalloc'_F$ to deallocate the last instance of *rs* in the sequence. Now observe that this design manifests a certain behavioural property: For a given resource, a deallocation will remove the latest instance allocated. A sequence of deallocations for a given resource will remove instances on a

---

[10] Also called a 'multiset', a variant of a set where each element may have multiple occurrences. In Z, a bag of elements of type X is a partial function of type $X \to NAT$.

[11] For reasons of space the technical details are omitted.

last-in, first-out basis. No such global constraint on behaviour was present in either the intermediate **Conc'** model, or the original specification **Abs'**.

The question arises as to whether this behavioural property was a user requirement or not. If not, there may not be any problem, since **Further'** is simply a case of the designer exercising her freedom of choice in the solution space defined by the specification. On the other hand, it may be that the property inhibits other required behavioural properties; in which case, the abstract specification will need revisiting.

If the property *is* required by the user, it is simply necessary to recognise that the more abstract specification (here, the **Conc'** model, in relation to its concrete counterpart, the **Further'** model) is incomplete in terms of requirements. Thus, whereas classical refinement is usually a black-box process dictating that all requirements are present in the abstract specification, this approach is 'layering in' behavioural requirements through the refinement chain in more of a 'glass box' process. In this scenario the contractual, definitive specification is **Further'** rather than **Conc'**.

From a requirements engineering point of view, what is needed is such a glass box process: a methodology enabling the accumulation of requirements, described in models separated in the refinement chain by separation of concerns, into one contractual, definitive description of all the customer requirements. In the example this works in the refinement of **Conc'** to **Further'**, but the link from **Abs'** down to **Conc'** is broken by not being (usefully) expressible as a refinement. A weaker, more general relation between models is needed, that can resurrect this chain of requirements-accumulating models. Retrenchment [21, 22] is such a relation, which describes the degree to which the lower model refines the upper, and otherwise, exactly what relationship there is between the models. Retrenchment can be interleaved with refinement (C refines B which retrenches A, C retrenches B which refines A, are both valid constructions), and shares the *transitivity* property of refinement (if B retrenches A and C retrenches B then C retrenches A). These properties allow retrenchment and refinement to be interleaved in a layered construction of the contractual requirements specification.

From Requirements Engineering to Evolution

Further examples of the methodological limitations of refinement as applied to requirements engineering can be given, but for reasons of space these limitations will be discussed more briefly. *Feature interaction* [25] is a well-known problem in telephony systems, where the need to provide multi-feature systems is complicated by the fact that features do not in general compose cleanly, and the interaction of features must often be designed for and managed explicitly. For example, the Call Forward (CF) and Incoming Call Screening (ICS) features can interact negatively. Caller X, calling subscriber A, may be forwarded (via A's CF feature) to subscriber B, who has excluded X on his ICS list. Telephony systems are one example of *feature-oriented systems*, constructed from in general noncompositional (functional and nonfunctional) features. Refinement's strong simulation requirement can make it difficult to describe the layering of such noncompositional features into a system specification. For the CF example, an abstract model containing one feature cannot be completely refined by a more concrete model that layers in the second feature, since the requirements of A and B for processing X's call are inconsistent. Some design resolution is required, which will necessarily be inconsistent with either CF or ICS in the case of X.

As shown [26] for telephony feature interaction, the retrenchment method enables the layering of possibly inconsistent requirements with the designed resolution, producing as output the definitive, implementable and contractual specification. This output specification can then be refined to code. The method formally records the relation between this contractual specification, and each of the partial requirements models incorporated at earlier stages. The transitivity property discussed above is the mechanism by which this relation is established. The retrenchment will distinguish between refining and nonrefining behaviours and will be amenable to automated support for formal proof obligations.

The potential utility for the evolution of requirements should now be evident. Evolution cannot be described in terms of refinement because changed behaviour cannot in general simulate legacy behaviour. However, removal from, change to or addition to requirements can be described in terms of the addition of inconsistent (possibly negative) requirements, perhaps in the style of Section 15.4. It will be shown that retrenchment provides a way of describing such evolution of requirements.

15.5.3 Retrenchment: Generalising Refinement

Section 15.5.2 motivated, in terms of some typical system modelling problems, the need to expand, or generalise the applicability of refinement-like methods. Whereas refinement can describe the steps from a contractual specification to an implementation, a retrenchment method is intended to expand the scope of the formal development process to include the requirements capture and reconciliation that will produce the contractual specification. It should describe formally the way in which the specification is built up out of the various, usually conflicting, contributing requirements and implementation constraints. These requirements and constraints should be combinable in a variety of ways (including the use of transitivity) some of which will be refinements, but most will not. A formally documented development, starting with the requirements engineering process, expands the scope of the recorded design history that can be used for effecting evolutionary change, in the style of Section 15.3

The potential applicability of such a more general method to software evolution has been indicated. For the construction of the contractual specification, the intuition is that refinement is too strong, that the exactness of simulation is too exacting, that there is a need to generalise to a more approximate, refinement-like method. A weaker relation, as seen above, might describe an exception, an inconsistency to be resolved through design, or an approximation. One approach is to *strengthen the precondition* over refinement, to allow a finer, more intricate structuring of the relationship between the models. In (Equation 15.3 – Equation 15.4), it may be desirable to describe the refining subdomain of the joint input/before-state space (i, j, u, v) separately from the 'exception' subdomain where no more concrete allocations are allowed. More central to the wish to generalise refinement is the need to *weaken the postcondition*, to allow nonrefining transitions in the two models to be usefully related in the joint after-state/output space. The postcondition abstraction relation can be weakened with a disjunct to allow a looser, nonrefining, approximate notion of representation of abstract by concrete. In the exception subdomain of (Equation 15.3 – Equation 15.4), such a disjunct would relate the incrementing abstract resource set with its concrete approximation, the static concrete resource set.

Retrenchment [27] can be defined in the same terms as (Equation 15.2) above. For initialisation, the same condition (Equation 15.1) as refinement is employed. For operation retrenchment, the simulation condition (Equation 15.2) is generalised using the new terms W (*within* clause) and C (*concession* clause). For every corresponding operation pair Op_A in **Ops**$_A$ and Op_C in **Ops**$_C$:

$$W_{Op}(i, j, u, v) \wedge G(u, v) \wedge stp_{Op_C}(v, j, v', p) \Rightarrow$$
$$\exists u', o \bullet (stp_{Op_A}(u, i, u', o) \wedge ((G(u', v') \wedge Out_{Op}(o, p)) \vee C_{Op}(u, v, u', v', o, p)))$$
(15.6)

To paraphrase the discussion of (Equation 15.2): Starting from before-state/input pair (u, i) represented by (v, j) through W and G, every concrete Op_C-step is witnessed by some abstract Op_A-step, which establishes representation of (u', o) by (v', p) through G and Out_{Op}, otherwise through C.

Compared with (Equation 15.2), the within clause W strengthens the precondition in specifying the subdomain of the joint input/state space where the retrenchment holds. W subsumes the input relation In_{Op} of (Equation 15.2). The within clause allows the description of a more intricate relationship between adjacent levels of abstraction than refinement, insofar as there may be more than one retrenchment relation (defined with more than one application of (Equation 15.6)) over different parts of the joint input/state space. Complementarily, the concession clause C weakens the postcondition: The $\forall - \exists$-quantified operation pair Op_A/Op_C will *either* achieve simulating behaviour $G \wedge Out_{Op}$ or, failing that, will at least achieve C. The concession is thus the minimum level of representation guaranteed by the retrenchment, in the event that simulation cannot be established. This minimum representation can be characterised as one of *exception*, *inconsistency* or *approximation* by considering the previous examples once more.

Notice that every refinement is a retrenchment: Setting $W \equiv In_{Op}$, $C \equiv false$ in (Equation 15.6) reduces to (Equation 15.2), the definition of refinement. A *false* concession guarantees that G is established in the postcondition, that is, simulation is achieved. Thus, retrenchment generalises refinement. At the other extreme, a *true* concession allows *any* concrete operation of the right signature to approximate a given abstract operation. So, methodologically speaking, (i) a strong W denotes a restricted part of the joint input/before-state domain on which a strong retrenchment or refinement statement is to be made, (ii) a weak W indicates a more widely applicable, thus weaker-concession retrenchment, (iii) a strong C indicates an approximation to, or even an exact, refinement and (iv) a weak C indicates a weak approximation or an exception retrenchment.

Recall that in (Equation 15.4) $Alloc_C$ refines $Alloc_A$ on the subdomain where fewer than $cmax$ resources have been allocated; this is described in retrenchment terms as:

$$(W, C) \equiv (\#crss < cmax, false) \tag{15.7a}$$

On the nonrefining subdomain, a complementary retrenchment records the abstract allocation and the corresponding skip operation:

$$(W, C) \equiv (\#crss \geq cmax, crss' = crss \wedge \#arss' = \#arss + 1) \tag{15.7b}$$

The choice of retrenchment (that is, of W and C) is in general a design choice. (Equations 15.7a, 15.7b) can be combined into one retrenchment – a concrete resource *may* be allocated, and an abstract resource *will* be allocated

$$(W, C) \equiv (true, crss' \subseteq crss \land \#arss' = \#arss + 1) \quad (15.7c)$$

(Equation 15.7c) is less incisive than (Equations 15.7a, 15.7b) in not distinguishing the refining and nonrefining behaviours; this distinction can be established in a single retrenchment by the use of a more elaborate concession:

$$(W, C) \equiv (true, \#crss < cmax \Rightarrow arss' = crss' \land$$
$$\#crss \geq cmax \Rightarrow crss' = crss \land \#arss' = \#arss + 1) \quad (15.7d)$$

Retrenchments (Equations 15.7a–15.7d) represent formally documented exceptions, where implementation constraints prevent concrete modelling of idealised requirements, and force design of implementable alternative behaviour.

The obvious criticism of retrenchment is that behavioural simulation (Section 15.5.1) must break down if the abstraction relation G is not guaranteed in the postcondition in (Equation 15.6): the necessary condition to establish the next refinement/retrenchment step has not been re-established. In general this is true, and is the cost of a weaker, more expressive development transformation. Even then, for 'difficult' applications, retrenchment provides the advantage of describing a formal relationship (in principle verifiable by proof tools) between models in the development chain, where refinement cannot offer this. A given application might have specific properties that can be brought to bear to strengthen what the operation can achieve in the postcondition. In (Equation 15.7d), a rich concession structure identifies the conditions under which full simulation can be re-established.

The feature interaction example can be described in retrenchment terms, recording the inconsistency of two feature requirements in adjacent models. The concession clause describes precisely those transitions that are nonrefining, that is, interacting in the way described. Moreover, it has been shown [26] how retrenchment offers a compositional method for the layered specification of feature-oriented systems. The feature interaction example can be described as a chain of two steps: CF, then ICS, then the design resolution of the interaction. The last, or contractual, specification in the chain (with forwarding, screening and interaction-resolving behaviour) is related back to each of the prior models through the respective retrenchments. These retrenchments formally document the extent to which the contractual model approximates the prior models and resolves the inconsistencies.

For applications such as real-to-finite arithmetic [28] and control engineering [29], retrenchment has been shown to afford an *approximate* notion of refinement and simulation, with an *evolving* abstraction relation $G(u, v, \varepsilon)$. Here, the concrete v representation of abstract u is mediated by some error bound ε, itself a function of whatever operation is being performed.

15.5.4 Retrenchment for Software Evolution

Theoretical work applying retrenchment to software evolution is under way. By means of an example this section speculates about the nature of its application, work required to support it, and the possible benefits that should ensue. If the evolution of a set of

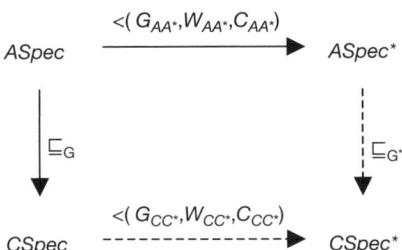

Figure 15.2 Software evolution: a retrenchment view

requirements is described as a retrenchment, then the formal apparatus of retrenchment should be deployable to support the calculation of the evolved refinement chain of those requirements, analogously to Sections 15.3 and 15.4

Consider Figure 15.2. Assume a legacy development, where $ASpec \sqsubseteq CSpec$ (is refined by) is the top of some refinement chain to code, and an evolution of requirements is described as $ASpec < ASpec*$ (is retrenched by). Evolution can then be characterised as a 'square completion' problem comprising the design of three elements: the concrete counterpart $CSpec*$ to the evolved specification $ASpec*$, the evolved refinement $ASpec* \sqsubseteq CSpec*$, and the concrete model retrenchment $CSpec < CSpec*$. The arrow annotations in Figure 15.2 – regarding the arrows as transformations of specifications – give the parameters of these transformations. The square should commute, i.e. the $CSpec*$ produced by $ASpec \rightarrow CSpec \rightarrow CSpec*$ should be the same as, or a refinement of, the $CSpec*$ produced by $ASpec \rightarrow ASpec* \rightarrow CSpec*$. A procedure for completing the commuting square in this way would reuse the design investment in the legacy refinement of $ASpec$ to $CSpec$. Such a procedure would of course be transitive in terms of further evolutions horizontally to (say) $ASpec**$, and so on, and transitive vertically through refinement to code.

The square completion problem, with three unknowns, is highly unconstrained and thus demands various approaches (two have been discussed in Sections 15.3 and 15.4) depending on the particular application and set of evolution constraints at hand. Some structure can be given to the problem by observing that any evolution (addition, deletion or change of requirements) can be described in terms of frame change and weakening/strengthening of precondition/postcondition. The example demonstrates one simple application.

Consider once more a variation on the operation of (Equation 15.3) (here called 'simple' allocation) allowing the allocation of input resource rs to allocated resource set $arss$, regardless of whether rs has previously been allocated or not. A small evolution is designed to be more incisive in dealing with a previously allocated resource rs: such a resource is regarded as suspect, and is thus deleted from $arss$:

$$SimAlloc_A(rs) \cong \mathbf{pre}\ rs \in RSS\ \mathbf{then}\ arss := arss \cup \{rs\} \tag{15.8}$$

$$SimAlloc_A^*(rs) \cong \mathbf{pre}\ rs \in RSS$$
$$\mathbf{if}\ rs \notin arss^*\ \mathbf{then}\ arss^* := arss^* \cup \{rs\}\ \mathbf{else}\ arss^* := arss^* - \{rs\} \tag{15.9}$$

(Equation 15.9) can be described as a retrenchment of (Equation 15.8) in a similar fashion to the retrenchments (Equations 15.7a–15.7d). Abstract/concrete step pairs match for $rs \notin$

arss, and do not otherwise; thus one possible retrenchment design (variables in $SimAlloc^*_A$ are *-superscripted) has within clause *true*, the identity abstraction relation G_{AA^*} and concession

$$C_{AA^*} \cong (rs \notin arss \wedge arss' = arss^{*'}) \vee (rs \in arss \wedge arss' = arss^{*'} \cup \{rs\}) \quad (15.10)$$

There is no frame change in this evolution. It is described as a horizontal (see Figure 15.2) retrenchment relating the identical postcondition regions of *ASpec* and *ASpec** under the precondition constraint $R_A \cong rs \notin arss$, and changed postcondition regions under its negation $\neg R_A$.

$SimAlloc_A$ is refined by $SimAlloc_C$, where the concrete resource allocation is modelled by appending to a sequence. The abstraction relation G relates the two state variables through the sequence range:

$$SimAlloc_C(rs) \cong \mathbf{pre}\ rs \in RSS\ \mathbf{then}\ crss := crss \cap \langle rs \rangle \quad (15.11)$$

$$G(arss, crss) \cong arss = \text{ran}\ crss \quad (15.12)$$

The job at hand is to complete the square of Figure 15.2 with an evolved concrete operation $SimAlloc^*_C$, which refines $SimAlloc^*_A$ and retrenches $SimAlloc_C$. A further constraint is assumed here: The evolution G^* of the abstraction relation G should be either identical or stronger than G. There are of course many possible concrete operation evolutions that satisfy G^*. Guidance in design of $SimAlloc^*_C$, while exploiting the design investment in the legacy refinement of *ASpec* to *CSpec*, is given by composing retrenchment (Equation 15.10) with evolved refinement G^*. This composition (giving the upper-right square traversal) is possible by the transitivity property of retrenchment and the fact that every refinement is expressible as a retrenchment [27]. The composite retrenchment $ASpec < CSpec*$ has parameters

$$G_{AC^*} \cong arss = \text{ran}\ crss^* \qquad W_{AC^*} \cong \text{true}$$

$$C_{AC^*} \cong (rs \notin arss \wedge arss' = \text{ran}\ crss^{*'}) \vee (rs \in arss \wedge \text{ran}\ crss^{*'}$$
$$= arss' - \{rs\}) \quad (15.13)$$

In this simple case, the concrete precondition region where behaviour stays the same is given by:

$$R_C \cong \exists\ arss \bullet (R_A \wedge G) \equiv \exists\ arss \bullet (rs \notin arss \wedge arss = \text{ran}\ crss)$$

$$\equiv rs \notin \text{ran}\ crss$$

Design freedom for $SimAlloc^*_C$ is in choosing whether, for $\neg R_C$ where behaviour must change, to remove *just one* or *all* instances of *rs* from the sequence. Composite retrenchment concession C_{AC^*} (Equation 15.13) shows that in this case *rs* cannot appear in $\mathbf{ran}\ crss^*$:

$SimAlloc^*_C(rs) \cong$

$\quad \mathbf{pre}\ rs \in RSS \quad (15.14)$

$\quad \mathbf{if}\ rs \notin \text{ran}\ crss^*\ \mathbf{then}\ crss^* := crss^* \cap \langle rs \rangle\ \mathbf{else}\ crss^* := \text{rmv}(crss^*, rs)$

where rmv removes all instances of *rs* from the sequence.

In a simple example like this, the square completion can be designed semantically, that is, from an understanding of the transitions entailed by the *stp* relation defining each operation. This approach cannot scale, so further work is required to bridge the gap between such simple intuition and the completion of the square. Rules are needed to calculate the square in practical evolution scenarios, expressed in the specification language of choice, such as Z or B. A starting point is to investigate the nature of square completions that emerge for given simple specification/evolution patterns. As indicated above, evolution of requirements is expressible in terms of change in frame, precondition and postcondition. For a given specification language, it is possible to further decompose addition into some sequence of atomic additions. For example, addition of new case-split processing to a previously static subdomain could be decomposed into a sequence of additions of single cases.

It is anticipated that patterns will emerge for square completion of such simple evolutions, and also for their composition. A link to the compositional approach of Section 15.4 can be seen by expressing this evolution as

$$SimAlloc_A^* \equiv \text{if } R_A \text{ then } S \text{ else } S \oplus \text{ if } \neg R_A \text{ then } T \equiv \text{if } R_A \text{ then } S \text{ else } T$$

$SimAlloc_A$ implicitly does the same thing S both under constraint R_A and its negation. The binary operator $\oplus$ is 'function override': This replaces any transitions satisfying $\neg R_A$ in the precondition in the *stp* relation on the left of $\oplus$, with transitions defined on the right of $\oplus$.

Current work on structuring retrenchments by decomposition [30] will be applicable to evolution. (Equation 15.13) can be decomposed into two retrenchments, within clauses R_A and $\neg R_A$ respectively, each with stronger postconditions (the two disjuncts of C_{AC^*} respectively). Stronger retrenchments will give more incisive analyses and stronger guidance in harvesting legacy design. A theoretical square completion result has been proposed in a recent unpublished work. The result is a very general form of categorical 'pushout' construction, where the procedure generates the canonical (the 'best', in a technical sense) completion of the square, in contrast with the many other possible, theoretical, square completions.

15.6 Conclusions

This chapter has shown how program refinement provides a design history, showing how a program satisfies its specification, and how this can be used as a basis to determine how modifications to the specification can be translated into modifications to the implementation. An approach was described, explaining the usual way in which refinement derivations are modified, by making similar modifications to each step in the derivation, and adding, deleting and reordering steps as necessary. An analysis of a simple example suggests that modifying programs by adding new code requires fewer revisions to the existing derivation steps than equivalent modification adding less code – this is because in the latter case the existing code is doing more work, typically preserving additional properties of the data. This approach is straightforward and effective, but tedious and error prone when applied manually. Some possibilities for tool support were discussed to alleviate these shortcomings.

An alternative approach was then described in which a modification is described by composing the existing specification with a specification of the new/modified behaviour, using operators similar to those of the Z schema calculus. Laws embodying properties of these operators, most notably distribution properties, are then used to merge the new/modified behaviour into the existing program to the places where changes are required. This approach makes it easier to see what changes are required, because the composed specification, and specifications derived from it, are stated separately until such time as they are absorbed into the new program being constructed. There is considerable flexibility in how this approach is applied, and a wide range of implementations of the modified specification can be obtained, according to the laws used. Again, practical application of this approach would require sophisticated tool support, in particular, to allow the programmer to visualise the current state of the development and to explore different sequences of transformations in order to obtain an acceptable implementation.

The chapter then changed perspective to that of the requirements engineer, to provide motivation for the generalisation of the refinement approach. This perspective, and the type of generalisation suggested, were seen to be of value to the support of software evolution. The concept of retrenchment was then presented as a candidate generalisation, and discussion moved from its utility in requirements engineering to its potential support for software evolution.

Retrenchment is clearly a semantic notion, being defined and formalised in terms of a transition-system semantics of the specification models. The refinement-based approaches discussed earlier in the chapter are more syntactic in style, being concerned with formal manipulations of models to achieve the evolutionary changes desired. It is hoped that these syntactic approaches may be integrated in the retrenchment-based framework for software evolution sketched out above.

It has been noted that the retrenchment approach of Section 15.5 extends the refinement-based approaches of Sections 15.3 and 15.4. Retrenchment extends the formally documented refinement-based design history into the requirements engineering process. Thus, the scope of formal documentation that can be edited to develop evolutionary changes as per Section 15.3 is considerably expanded. Section 15.4 proposed compositional mechanisms to describe specification change, and to proliferate such change through the existing refinement chain. In principle retrenchment does the same, from a different perspective. It is therefore anticipated that refinement- and retrenchment-based approaches to software evolution will develop in a complementary, even symbiotic fashion.

References

[1] J. Welsh, "Software is history!", A.W. Roscoe (ed), *A Classical Mind: Essays in Honour of C. A. R. Hoare*, Prentice Hall, pp. 419–429, 1994.
[2] J.-R. Abrial, *The B-Book: Assigning Programs to Meanings*, Cambridge University Press, 1996.
[3] C. Morgan and T. Vickers, *On the Refinement Calculus*, Springer-Verlag, 1993.
[4] C. Morgan, *Programming from Specifications*, (Second edition), Prentice Hall, 1994.
[5] E.W. Dijkstra, "Guarded Commands, Nondeterminacy and Formal Derivation of Programs", *Communications of the ACM*, Vol. 18, pp. 453–457, 1975.
[6] E.W. Dijkstra, *A Discipline of Programming*, Academic Press, 1976.
[7] J.M. Spivey, *The Z Notation: A Reference Manual*, (Second edition), Prentice Hall, 1992.
[8] E.W. Dijkstra and C.S. Scholten, *Predicate Calculus and Program Semantics*, Springer-Verlag, 1990.
[9] R.-J. Back and J. von Wright, *Refinement Calculus: A Systematic Introduction*, Springer-Verlag, 1998.

[10] C.C. Morgan, "Data Refinement by Miracles", *Information Processing Letters*, Vol. 26, pp. 243–247, 1998 (Also in [3]).
[11] E.W. Dijkstra, O.-J. Dahl and C.A.R. Hoare, *Structured Programming*, Academic Press, 1972.
[12] N. Wirth, "Program Development by Stepwise Refinement", *Communications of the ACM*, Vol. 14, pp. 221–227, 1971.
[13] M. Butler, J. Grundy, T. Långbacka, R. Rukššnas and J. von Wright, "The Refinement Calculator: Proof Support for Program Refinement", L. Groves and S. Reeves (eds), *Formal Methods Pacific '97*, Springer-Verlag, pp. 40–61, 1997.
[14] D. Carrington, I. Hayes, R. Nickson, G. Watson and J. Welsh, "A Program Refinement Tool", *Formal Aspects of Computing*, Vol. 10, pp. 97–124, 1998.
[15] L. Groves, "Deriving Programs by Combining and Adapting Refinement Scripts", *Proceedings of 1995 Asia Pacific Software Engineering Conference*, IEEE Computer Society Press, pp. 354–363.
[16] S. Vadera, "Proof by Analogy in Mural", *Formal Aspects of Computing*, Vol. 7, pp. 183–206, 1995.
[17] L. Groves, *Evolutionary Software Development in the Refinement Calculus*, Ph.D. thesis, Victoria University of Wellington, 2000.
[18] L. Groves, "A formal approach to program evolution", *Proceedings of Workshop on Evolutionary Formal Software Development EFSD-02*, Copenhagen, Denmark, July 2002.
[19] J. Derrick and E. Boiten, *Refinement in Z and Object-Z*, Springer, 2001.
[20] A. Mikhajlova and E. Sekerinski, "Class Refinement and Interface Refinement in Object-Oriented Programs", *Proceedings of FME'97:Industrial Applications and Strengthened Foundations of Formal Methods*, Springer, pp. 82–101, 1997.
[21] R. Banach and M. Poppleton, "Retrenchment: An Engineering Variation on Refinement", *Proceedings of B'98: Recent Advances in the Development and Use of the B-Method*, Springer LNCS, Montpellier, France, pp. 129–147, 1998.
[22] M.R Poppleton, *Formal Methods for Continuous Systems: Liberalising Refinement in B*, Ph.D. thesis, University of Manchester, 2001.
[23] C. Jones, *Systematic Software Development using VDM*, Prentice Hall, 1990.
[24] W.-P. de Roever and K. Engelhardt, *Data Refinement: Model-Oriented Proof Methods and their Comparison*, Cambridge University Press, 1998.
[25] M. Calder and E. Magill (eds), *Feature Interactions in Telecommunications and Software Systems VI*, IOS Press, 2000.
[26] R. Banach and M. Poppleton, "Retrenching Partial Requirements into System Definitions: A Simple Feature Interaction Case Study", *Requirements Engineering Journal*, Vol. 8 No. 4, pp. 266–288, 2003.
[27] R. Banach and M. Poppleton, "Sharp Retrenchment, Modulated Refinement and Simulation", *Formal Aspects of Computing*, Vol. 11, pp. 498–540, 1999.
[28] M. Poppleton and R. Banach, "Retrenchment: Extending Refinement for Continuous and Control Systems", *Proceedings of IWFM;00: Irish Workshop on Formal Methods*, Springer Electronic Workshop in Computer Science Series, National University of Ireland, Maynooth, Ireland, 2000.
[29] M. Poppleton and R. Banach, "Controlling Control Systems: An Application of Evolving Retrenchment", *Proceedings of ZB2002: Formal Specification and Development in Z and B*, Springer LNCS, Vol. 2272, pp. 42–61 Grenoble, France, 2002.
[30] M. Poppleton and R. Banach, "Structuring Retrenchments in B by Decomposition", *Proceedings of FME 2003: International Symposium of Formal Methods Europe*, Pisa, Italy, Springer LNCS, Vol. 2805, pp. 814–833, 2003.

16

Background and Approach to Development of a Theory of Software Evolution

Meir M. Lehman and Juan C. Fernández-Ramil

Based on "Towards a Theory of Software Evolution – And its Practical Impact" by M. M. Lehman and J. F. Ramil which appeared as an invited talk, in Proc. ISPSE 2000, Katayama T., Tamai T. and Yonezaki N. (eds.), Kanazawa, Japan, Nov 1–2, IEEE Computer Society Press, Los Alamitos, CA, pp. 2–11. (c) 2000 IEEE.

16.1 Software Evolution

As indicated in the first law of software evolution (Lehman 1974, Lehman and Belady 1985), *E*-type systems, used to solve problems in the real world, must be continually maintained that is, *adapted, extended* and *evolved* if they are to continue to provide satisfactory service (see Chapters 1 and 5). Studies of this phenomenon are spreading rapidly (e.g. Pfleeger 1998, Kemerer and Slaughter 1999, Bennett and Rajlich 2000, Antón and Potts 2001, FEAST 2001, Bauer and Pizka 2003, IWPSE 2005) (see also Chapter 10), stimulated by the universally high cost of software maintenance, many project and software failures and relevant research for over three decades (Lehman 1969, Chong Hok Yuen 1981, Lehman and Belady 1985, FEAST 2001).

Awareness of the need for progress in understanding, planning and controlling software evolution and its achievement are driven by universal experience. The growing use of computers in the home, industry, commerce, government and so on leads to ever greater and more widespread dependence on software and the need for it to remain satisfactory as the *operational domains* in which it operates change and evolve. It is now widely appreciated that as users become evermore sophisticated and dependent on satisfactory

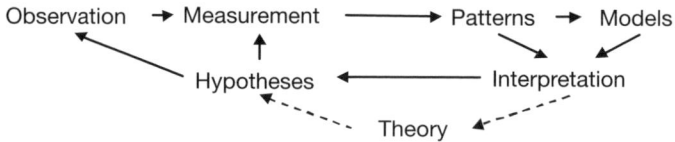

Figure 16.1 The scientific method

operation, the need for timely, reliable, cost-effective evolution of software is growing rapidly.

Changing domains, new needs and opportunities, market forces, advancing technology and so on yield continuing pressure for change, adaptation, extension and replacement. Growing interest in business process improvement, as a result of burgeoning integration of business processes, internationalisation and widespread recognition of organisational dependence on software and the consequent need for business and software co-evolution (e.g. SOCE 2000) has added to the evolutionary pressure.

The observed regularity and predictability of software evolution and growing societal dependence on reliable, effective, evolvable software indicates that a predictable, manageable and effective evolution process is urgently needed. Its development and continuing improvement will be greatly helped by a theoretical framework that describes the evolution phenomenon and yields guidelines for design and improvement of the process, identifying, for example, areas ripe for improvement.

A need for a wider theory of software engineering and the contribution this could make to advancing the technology has been long recognised (e.g. Bennett and Rajlich 2000, Naur and Randell 1968). Its potential is analogous to the role played by theory in the natural sciences (Figure 16.1) where it plays a pivotal role in reaching, integrating, advancing and applying understanding of the phenomena associated within a field. This chapter considers the potential for development of a theory inspired by the Carnap approach applied to current understanding of software evolution.

16.2 Global Views of Evolution

16.2.1 Two Approaches

There are two distinct approaches to the study of software *evolution*. Each accepts the critical importance of maintaining compatibility between a software system, the goals and properties of the application that the system supports, the needs of all levels of its users and the properties of the many domains with which it is concerned and wherein it operates. They also recognise that evolution is implemented in a *process* that disciplines and controls changes to the system and the procedures associated with it. They differ, however, in their primary interpretation of the term *evolution* and in their concerns. Is it to be studied as an *activity* to be implemented, controlled, managed, made more efficient, reliable and responsive or as a *phenomenon*? Both views are valid, relevant and important. Each will gain significantly from advances in the other. But the directions they take and the activities they lead to differ.

The first view, termed *verbal*, seeks the development of improved processes, procedures, methods and tools to plan, implement, manage, support and control the evolution process. It is the *how* of evolution that seeks to develop or improve *activities*, processes, methods and tools to achieve greater effectiveness in terms of factors such as reliability, responsiveness and cost. It is verbal because it focuses on the *activities* relating to implementation and evolution of software.

Success in applying this approach requires identification of developments that may be expected to produce meaningful benefits when implemented and applied. To be really effective it requires full understanding and a disciplined framework to guide identification, choice and pursuit of specific developments. This is indeed true in general for the successful advancement, exploitation and improvement of the characteristics of any phenomenon in a forever-changing world. In the absence of such a framework the verbal approach must rely, instead, on the insight or inspiration of individual researchers and developers. It is essentially *ad hoc*.

The second approach may be termed *nounal*. It regards software and systems evolution as a *phenomenon* to be studied and understood. It seeks increased insight into its causes, impact and characteristics, better *understanding* of the phenomenon. Such understanding must surely strengthen the ability to, for example, inspire, guide and discipline process, method and tool development driving it in directions that yield the highest returns in improvement of the evolution process. It also provides a base and framework for disciplined conception and development of a directed approach to effective software process improvement; the framework referred to in the previous paragraph. In the case of software and computer systems, the results of meaningful studies of the evolution phenomenon taking the nounal approach will surely greatly improve the results to be expected from the verbal approach.

16.2.2 The Verbal Approach

Software evolution studies have, in general, concentrated on the *how* of evolution (e.g. Gilb 1981, IWPSE 2005, WGoSE 2006). This is in response to the spread of computer applications and computers, the increasingly widespread and detailed role they play, the growing cost of maintaining system validity and, above all, the growing dependence of business, government and individuals on the availability and reliability of the computer applications. It expresses the realisation that effective and responsive software evolution is vital in a society evermore dependent on computers. As applications penetrate evermore deeply into the structure and activities of user organisations, as applications and organisations are integrated and inter-operability is required, the interdependence of a business and its software are becoming evermore apparent. As computerisation grows, a business cannot expand more rapidly than it can adapt and evolve its software to cope with changing circumstances that arise as a consequence of growth and expansion. The demands and restrictions that the need for continual software evolutionary adaptation and enhancement places on a business (e.g. SOCE 2000) have added a further dimension on both domains. They must coordinate, synchronise, integrate their evolution and *process improvement*. All this has occurred in a climate of expanding markets, growing competition, advancing technology and growing reliance on software. Effective co-evolution of a business, its parent organisations, organisational processes, the marketplace, computer systems, technology and so on are now of general concern. This sets a potentially high value on any improvement in the ability to cope efficiently, economically and responsively with the need for continual change, results in pressure to concentrate on process, methods and tools. Hence it is on this that software evolution research and development has mainly focussed.

16.2.3 The Nounal Approach

As stated above, the *nounal* view seeks to identify causes, consequences, patterns and characteristic properties of evolution and the means whereby evolution is achieved. Greater *understanding* must improve the chances of identifying, supporting and guiding development of more effective and cost-effective processes, procedures, methods and tools for planning, controlling, implementing, pursuing software evolution. Over the past 35 or so years, this phenomenological approach has advanced to the point where it provides a base and framework to support development of a formal Theory of Software Evolution. Currently, the theory exists as a series of established, but weakly connected, facts. It awaits organisation, establishment of relationships and dependencies and structured organisation into an integrated, coherent whole.

16.2.4 Mutual Support of the Two Views

The reality is that industry must constantly deal with *immediate*, often *urgent*, problems. All enterprises must be concerned with maintaining systems satisfactory in a changing world. Reduction of response time to external change by means of system changes is becoming evermore critical as societal and individual dependence on computers and on software grow. It demands continual system change and process improvement to address new situations and changing needs as they arise. It is true that however clearly and comprehensively the triggers and drivers of evolution (Lehman 1980, 1982, Lehman and Belady 1985, Lehman 1991, 1994, FEAST 2001) and other forces are recognised, it is the discovery of *ways* and *means* to improve the process that brings the ultimate benefit. But this can only be achieved if the phenomenon, the forces that govern successful and reliable computer application, are fully understood. This applies, however, that individual improvements are assessed, measured and evaluated.

It is therefore necessary to support both views. They are complementary (Lehman 2000a) and mutually supportive. Together with the theory they provide solid foundations for continual improvement. To do this effectively requires the exploitation of both approaches to be able to readily exploit windows of opportunity, adapt applications and the systems that implement and support them to changing domain properties and circumstances, to improve those already existing and develop new ones. Each is important, each has potential, and the issue is, surely, only how to divide restricted resources between them.

16.2.5 Process Improvement

In the software engineering context, it is not only computing applications and systems that must change with external circumstances. The *process* of application and software conception, development and evolution must also be improved by developing new or improved process structures, steps, methods and tools in tune with and able to exploit relevant technologies as these and their changing domains of application advance.

The spread of computers, and their penetration into all aspects of human activity have led to this need and to a widespread drive for *software process improvement*. This may be exemplified by the Capability Maturity Model (CMM) (Paulk *et al.* 1993) and Capability Maturity Model Integration (CMMi) (Ahern *et al.* 2001) approaches developed by the Software Engineering Institute. It has also led to a drive for co-evolution with the organisations in which computer applications are directly exploited or with which they interact.

Together, this has resulted in a situation in which changes and additions to software functionality and a need for improved levels of quality, reliability, predictability and responsiveness are now evermore necessary and critical. Significant increases in software productivity, equally significant reduction in levels of software maintenance are also needed as their costs assume an ever increasing proportion of the overall costs of a business or organisation. The need for higher priorities in the study and management of software evolution is clear.

In applying *ad hoc* approaches to identify potential process improvements, an expectation of success in the development and introduction into practice and effective exploitation of what is identified may well be justified. Success depends, however, on the parallel development of technology, valid analysis of potential benefit and the absence of negative side effects. Better understanding of the phenomenon, its nature, causes and consequences will help all these by disciplining the *how* approach to process improvement. It will guide searches for potential means, their evaluation and, if justified, development and increase the likelihood of success and benefit. Better understanding will yield processes that minimise disruption and ensure continuing and responsive satisfaction of stakeholder needs. The need for understanding applies to both the evolution phenomenon and the processes by which it is achieved (see Chapter 1).

16.3 The Case for Theory

The present view of the evolution phenomenon is derived from related but disjointed observations. These must be interpreted and modelled, and their elements analysed, organised, structured and integrated. The resultant insight may then be structured and developed as a model and theory that encapsulate the body of knowledge and understanding including the relationships and dependencies between the elements. Such a theory must discipline, unify and structure the representation, at the elemental and structural level to reflect the phenomenon in its entirety. Given the volume of observations in hand this is attainable, though nontrivial. Its achievement will, in turn, strengthen the process of conceiving, developing and integrating coherent methods and tools, systematic control and improvement of the software process.

The above sets the scene. The remainder of this chapter outlines how one might approach development and formation of a theory of software illustrating this with an informal outline of a potential partial theorem.

Determination of good practice, its transfer into industry and the achievement of willing and widespread acceptance require one to overcome inbred scepticism (Fordham 2000). Managers and practitioners must be convinced of the legitimacy and efficacy of the findings to date, and that they provide data, viewpoints and understanding. It also calls, at the very least, for empirical validation of proposed practice by means of plausible interpretation of observations in terms of the phenomenology, experimentation and case studies. But, in contrast to the extreme empiricist view that 'only observations count', practical systematic progress inevitably benefits from a combination of empirical and theoretical work. As already observed these strengthen and sustain each other.

Once established, a theory will serve several purposes. It should provide well-founded and plausible interpretations of empirical evidence derived from observed phenomena. This should yield reasoned support and understanding of the *why* of good practice and give management and, in practice, give software professionals a high degree of confidence in proposed changes. Such confidence is essential to obtain support for them and to justify their cost. Finally, as it develops, the theory will provide a growing base and framework to inspire and guide continued empirical work to support verification, and extension of results and, hence, provide input to direct and drive further development, theoretical and practical.

Past studies have yielded a body of empirical data that, though incomplete and informal, has advanced understanding of observed behaviour. The FEAST projects (FEAST 2001) have largely confirmed, refined and advanced earlier insights, widened the domain of relevance and potential applicability of the concepts and observations, and strengthened confidence in their validity. The resultant body of empirical knowledge and understanding together with results provided by others (e.g. Kemerer and Slaughter 1999, Bennett and Rajlich 2000, Turski 1981, Turski and Maibaum 1987) has yielded generalisations that are regarded as the foundations of an *observational level* theory (Carnap 1966). Derivation of a theory constitutes significant progress towards development of software technology as a rigorous discipline based on technical and management factors in the context of both system and operational domains properties. Its explanatory powers should provide a base for well-founded and disciplined methods for software development and evolution.

The direct and immediate practical application and value of a theory of software evolution appear clear. Current interest in software architectures (Shaw and Garlan 1996), and pressures for moves to reuse components and COTS-based system structure (Lehman and Ramil 2000b) reflect the increasing human dependence on computers that has led to a search for more reliable, cheaper, more evolvable, higher quality software. Explanatory theory that identifies sources of evolutionary pressures, the nature of the consequent behaviour and stabilising controls and constraints will yield significant progress in the design of evolvable systems. Such theory can help to achieve reliable evolution in timely fashion.

Process improvement, as widely understood and pursued, is improvement of the means whereby software is developed and evolved (maintained). It considers modification or addition of various process areas or activities, technical and managerial, to increase product quality and reliability, productivity and response time while reducing costs. Past approaches to improvement of the process have been largely *ad hoc*. A comprehensive explanatory theory provides a coherent framework that facilitates and directs reasoning about the process, identifies areas that appear to have potential and permits the derivation of qualitative and quantitative management and implementation practice guidelines.

As an example, consider the theory fragment of Section 16.6. This is related to the fact that all *E*-type systems embed an *unbounded assumption* set (Lehman 1989, 1990). This set is injected by the abstraction processes necessary to bound an application and the system implementing it. Abstraction is indeed a key activity in all software development, from problem statement through specification, design and coding to validation and installation. It must retain properties of the application and its domain that can influence the outcome of the behaviour modelled by the software. Other properties, overlooked or considered irrelevant, are excluded. But as the application and operational domains change, the excluded properties not reflected in the system may become relevant. Others not abstracted out, that is, reflected in the system, may no longer be correctly reflected. In either event, the system will no longer be faithful to the application and operational domains in their current state. It cannot be absolutely correct, may be dangerously at fault.

The technology of assumption management provides an outstanding example of potential in software technology so far generally not recognised. Its emergence now is entirely due to better understanding of software evolution, its causes and nature. The fact that assumptions, adopted explicitly or implicitly, have become invalid during the operational life of a software system have been a major factor in system failure the world over (e.g. Finkelstein and Dowell 1996, CERN 1998). As acceptance of this fact spreads, it will lead to major process changes. These will include the provision of methods, techniques and tools to capture, record and regularly review assumptions, those explicitly stated, those implied by others and those implied by omission. Such activity will become an integral part of all software development and maintenance, that is, of *software evolution*. Such is not established practice today even in sensitive areas such as safety critical or business critical systems.

The above is an example of good practice derived from a theory of software evolution. Further guidelines and rules have been identified (Lehman 1978) (see also Chapter 27). Unless shown to be incompatible with the theory, these will be part of, or follow from it, so extending it. Current understanding suggests that most of those already recognised will, directly or after modification, be shown to be consistent with and related to one another, with the relationships systematically derivable and also part of the theory.

Summing up, it must be concluded that a consistent theory can and will make a direct contribution to improvement of the software process, provide a sound rationale for a good software engineering practice.

16.4 Theory Development

Figure 16.2, illustrates an approach to theory development inspired by Carnap's views (e.g. Carnap 1966).

The figure establishes a relationship between two levels, *observational* and the *theoretical*, at which real-world theory may be represented. The first presents the phenomenology and its generalisations, derived, in the case of a theory of software evolution from, for example, systematic study of evolution data from numerous industrial processes and their products (FEAST 2001). These will include, but not be limited to, system and process metrics numerical validation data. Recurrent patterns in such data may be interpretable as reflecting behavioural invariants related to the observed phenomenology. Where they

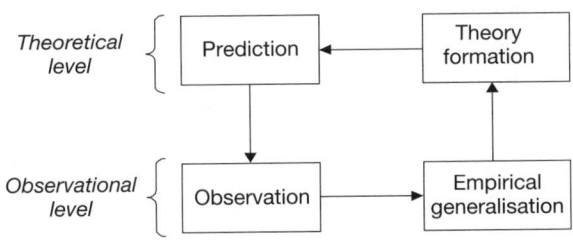

Figure 16.2 Theory formation

are restricted to a subset of systems, they will reflect common domain characteristics of that subset. This would suggest a lower level sub-theory addressing the evolutionary properties of that group. Any theorem or other statement so constrained would be part of the general theory, but include an appropriate qualification defining the class of systems or process domains to which it is applicable.

For example, the Laws of Software Evolution (Lehman 1974, 1978, Lehman and Belady 1985, Lehman *et al.* 1997) (see Chapter 1) derived from the FEAST projects and its forerunners comprise an unstructured, observational theory that are, at least for the moment, restricted to release-based *E*-type systems developed by approaches based on the waterfall model (Royce 1970). The extent to which the resultant theory is applicable to *S*-type (Lehman 1980) (see also Chapters 1 and 5), component and COTS-based systems or to, say, object-oriented, open source or agile processes needs to be assessed. There are empirical results offering a starting point for such assessment (e.g. Kemerer and Slaughter 1999, Godfrey and Tu 2000, Succi *et al.* 2001, Bauer and Pizka 2003) (see also Chapters 9 and 10). But more needs to be done. However, much of the observed behaviour is understood in absolute terms that can, subject to minor qualifications, be shown to be independent of the nature of the software or the process by which it is evolved. In other cases, the statement of the theorem reflecting it includes a qualification. The Principle of Software Uncertainty, for example, is at present only formulated for *E*-type, that is, real-world systems. In any event, the accumulated observations, knowledge and understanding can be assembled into a coherent whole to constitute a general theory. As the theory evolves in extent and detail, observations previously excluded will be addressed in its terms and become part of it, though the theory may need to be modified.

Observations correctly predicted by the theory confirm fundamental insights as well as behavioural invariants in computer application and operation domains, software development and evolution, interacting organisations and systems. Relevant inferences, suitably reformulated, from hypotheses or conclusions previously reached, for example, by Dijkstra (1968), Gilb (1988), Hoare (1969, 1971), Parnas (1972) and Wirth (1971), may also be candidates for the theory.

16.5 A World View

16.5.1 Real-World Program Relationship

The planned approach to the development of a theory of software evolution as in Figure 16.3 involves and links constituents such as *application domains, specifications*, derived *programs* and relationships of *abstraction* and *satisfaction* (Turski 1981, Lehman 1984, Turski and Maibaum 1987). The abstraction relationship implies that both program and the real world are *models* of the specification. Either may, however, have properties not possessed by the other (Turski 1981) though these must not be inconsistent with the specification. As a human creation an E-type program implementing an application in an E-type domain cannot reflect all the unbounded number of properties of that domain. Thus the program is only a partial model of the domains and applications with which it is involved. Nevertheless, an E-type program will be acceptable to its stakeholders as long as it satisfies the intended application in its intended operational domain.

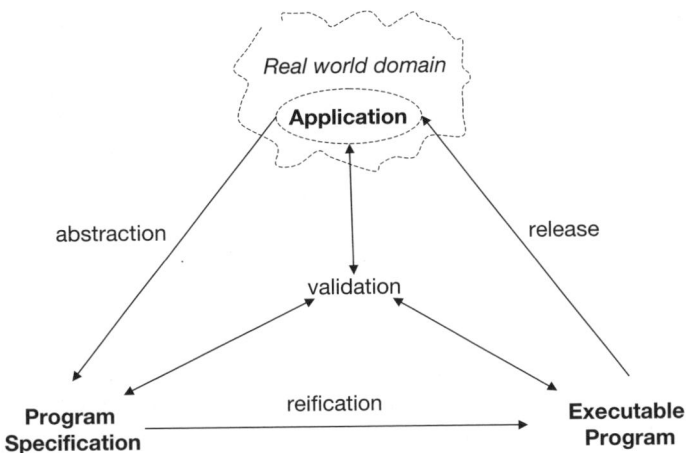

Figure 16.3   The 'Real-World/Specification/Program' relationship

An inconsistency with the real-world operational domain that can affect the computational behaviour indicates an error or omission in the specification. Nevertheless, the results of execution may be *satisfactory*, at least for a while, and applied as required. If, as a consequence or for other reasons, the results of execution are *unsatisfactory* in some sense, so is the program.

Intuitive interpretation of the terms *satisfactory* and *unsatisfactory* provides an insight into criteria for program acceptance. It represents a starting point for the development of formal definitions. But fundamental issues must be resolved before such definitions can be formulated. For example, E-type programs are generally developed for use by many users, individual and organisational. Even a specific installation is likely to have users at several levels. An air traffic control system, for example, will have operators, maintenance staff, programmers and others who interact directly, though in quite different ways, with the installation. Others, for example, controllers, air crew, ground staff, passengers, do not, generally, have such access but will be in communication with the system, directly or via a human intermediary. All will experience the impact of its execution in one way or another. Airlines, their financial officers, fuel suppliers, in-flight caterers and many others will, directly or indirectly, provide information to and receive information from the system. All are *users* in the spirit of the term. All have needs, desires and expectations, conscious or unconscious, and all will have reactions to system behaviour or misbehaviour. Yet each will be sensitive to quite different aspects of that behaviour. Needs and reactions will be based on the nature of their interaction with, dependence on and expectations from the system. What is invalid or unsatisfactory to one will pass unnoticed by another. Formulating a universal definition for what is satisfactory even in only one context is not trivial.

16.5.2 Assumptions

The concept of assumptions was introduced in Section 16.3. When a computer application and the system that realises it are developed, *assumptions* about properties of the problem to be addressed, its operational domains, potential approaches to a solution, the execution systems and so on are continually made or implied. They are unavoidable (Lehman 1989, 1990) and play a vital role in the evolution process. As briefly discussed above, there is, however, no *certainty* about the assumption set reflected in the implementation and this leads to uncertainty in the results of E-type program execution. Though not explicitly shown, assumptions are, in fact, an important constituent of the view of Figure 16.3. They are all pervasive, reflected in every system element; they may be injected knowingly or unknowingly, implicitly or explicitly, by commission or omission and may be valid or invalid. Injection may have occurred during creation of an element, changes to it or during transition from an element to its successor. If valid at the time of injection, those unrelated to or irrelevant in the context of the intended system purpose and foreseeable state of the application domains at times of usage, may not be of immediate concern. But in a dynamic world that is continually changing, there can be no guarantee that the same assumptions will not have unforeseen relevance and impact at a later time.

The practical implications of this may be exemplified by its immediate impact on the statement of requirements, at least for an E-type system. Every such statement must include, in fact, begin with the following two requirements:

1. It must be accepted that the real-world and operational domains are dynamic and always subject to change. Moreover, the development and usage of the system introduce new needs, procedures, ideas, opportunities and so on. Hence any requirement may change, in general or in detail, any one may become obsolete or new ones may arise. Thus, both the requirement set and the application procedures must be kept under constant review and consequent system changes implemented when analysis shows that they are necessary or desirable.
2. For any system other than, perhaps, the one for very short-term use (and even then) changes in requirements implies system changes. Thus the system, its documentation, procedures, domains and so on must be reliably and cost-effectively and often speedily, changeable. The resultant implications on software development and evolution process, on methods, procedures and tools and on the economics of computerisation must be faced. A program must reflect every aspect and property of the operational domains that may affect the validity or usability of the results as they are at each moment of execution (Turski 1981, Lehman 1984). The presence of unknown assumptions and the consequent changes in system requirements and behaviours constitutes a major, as yet largely unrecognised, threat to program validity, a recognised societal challenge.

In the context of assumptions, at least for systems addressing problems or operating in the real world, one further fact should be stated. It is simple to show that the real world and each of its sub-domains are unbounded in the number of its properties. However many one identifies, one can always identify another. The system, soft, hard and human, that implements it is finite, constrained in time, space, knowledge and understanding. Thus at all stages of the conception, specification, design, implementation and so on, one has to ignore an unbounded number of properties. Every property so ignored represents at least one assumption that its rejection is irrelevant to the obtaining of a satisfactory solution to the problem being addressed. Hence, in defining a solution to a specific problem or class of problems, every E-type system, each of its software elements, for example, reflects an unbounded number of assumptions. As applications, users and application domains change, as they must in a dynamic world, some of these assumptions must influence the real-world application addressed. Since they are not reflected in the software, changes to them cannot affect the computation. Thus the system no longer faithfully reflects the application and related activity. The consequences may range from being negligible to disastrous. The fact is the underlying source that leads to the Principle of Software Uncertainty (Lehman 1989, 1990).

16.6 Example

16.6.1 Introduction

The preceding has provided a broad background for the development of a theory of software evolution. The approach to be adopted for such theory formation will be exemplified by providing an empirical outline proof of the Principle of Software Uncertainty. This is of interest not only in its own right but also as an early candidate theorem of the proposed theory. Note also that the phenomenon underlying the principle has much more general ramifications, and it is, in fact, universal. Demonstration and discussion of this are now underway.

In addition to rules of inference, development of a theory requires definitions and axioms. The statements of these and of observations that follow are all tentative. Some of the *observations* are derived from past work. All will have to be made precise, possibly formal, to be satisfactory for theory formation. The set presented has been chosen because it suffices for proof of the Principle of Software Uncertainty. Proofs of other inferences cannot be provided here. If the extended definition set and the resultant theory can be formalised some, at least, of the observations may, be restatable as *axioms*. *Inferences* may become theorems.

The material presented here is only a fragment of the informal theory that already exists or the fuller theory to be developed. In the present context, many details cannot be addressed. Even the term *real world* is not defined. Determination of a meaningful and appropriate definition involves issues whose resolution is closely bound up with the remainder of the developing theory. It would, for example, have to account for the fact that the operational software becomes part of the real word that specifies it, that the system contains an implicit model of itself and that its development, installation and operation change the real world (in its conventional sense) (Lehman 1977, 1984, Lehman and Belady 1985). The real world is truly dynamic, always changing at a rate that is increased by development, installation and use of the system (Lehman and Belady 1985). Other relevant issues are similarly glossed over in this example. Many issues remain to be resolved. Change is inevitable as the work proceeds.

16.6.2 Preliminary Definitions

1. In the computing context, an *application* is a computation to be evaluated or an activity or procedure to be controlled, modelled, monitored and so on.

2. An E-type program is one that is executed in addressing an *application* in the real world or that is part of (embedded in) an E-type system.
3. Such a program is said to be *acceptable* if the solution is perceived to be acceptable (in its everyday meaning) in some defined sense at a stated level of concern.

Note 1: Acceptance of an E-type program implies a belief that its properties provide, for example, a valid, usable and cost-effective solution when that program is executed in the specified domains.

4. In the computing context a program *stakeholder* is any individual, organisation or other grouping that has some interest in or concern about the behaviour, correctness, performance, quality, cost, profitability and so on of that program.
5. A *level of concern* is the minimum or maximum value, as appropriate, of a measure or statement of precision or other measure of quality or other execution attributes considered satisfactory to the stakeholders.
6. In the computing context, the *real world* includes a stated level of acceptability, applications implemented in a program, the domains in which the computation is to be relevant and, when relevant, the activity or procedure pursued.
7. An E-type *specification* of E-type software is an abstraction of an application, a real-world domain and an executable program, which together define the required properties of the program.
8. A program specification is a *theory* of a computer application in its operational domain.
9. The application and its domain are models of the specification (see Figure 16.3).
10. *Specification acceptability* is recognition that, to the required level of concern, it reflects all real world and program properties that are necessary to ensure application acceptability by the stakeholders.
11. A program that addresses an application satisfactorily for *all* instances of the domain required, explicitly or implicitly, by the specification is also a *model* of the *theory* that the specification constitutes.
12. Properties not addressed in an E-type program specification are of *no concern*, that is, they are believed not to influence the outcome of the activity or computation being determined or controlled by the program.
13. An assumption reflected in an E type specification or program is *invalid* if, when a program satisfying the specification is executed, the result is unacceptable for reasons that can be associated with the assumption.

16.6.3 Observations

1. The real world may be partitioned in an unbounded number of ways into domains that, in general, each possesses an unbounded number of properties.
2. The real-world domain from which the specification of an E-type program is abstracted has an unbounded number of properties.
3. The set of properties of the real world undergoes continuing change.
4. The number of *discrete* properties of a specification and of a program is finite.

5. For a program to produce *acceptable* results its procedures, variables, constants, and so on must reflect the properties of all happenings, features, objects and so on that affect real-world behaviour at the level of *concern*.

16.6.4 Inferences

1. The number of *assumptions* reflected in an E-type program about the applications and domains addressed is unbounded.
2. As the real world changes, assumptions reflected in the specification may become invalid and the specification is no longer a valid abstraction of the real world of concern.
3. The number of *distinct* and *stated* behavioural properties of an E-type program is bounded.
4. An E-type program is inherently incomplete in that there exist an unbounded number of real-world properties not explicitly reflected in it.
5. *Corollary 1*: An E-type program reflects an unbounded number of assumptions.
6. If, as a result of changes, a specification is no longer a valid abstraction of the real-world domain of execution, the E-type program that models the specification may be unacceptable.
7. *Corollary 2*: Though an E-type program is a model of a specification of which the real world at the time of execution is also a model, it may be unacceptable.
8. The behaviour of an E-type program when executed is always inherently uncertain, that is, it cannot be guaranteed to be satisfactory (Principle of Software Uncertainty, Lehman 1989, 1990).
9. A property not addressed in the specification of an E-type program implies an assumption that whether or not the domain possesses or the program satisfies that property is of *no concern*.
10. Conversely, a property not reflected in an E-type program implies an assumption that the real-world behaviour or object dependent on or influenced by that property is of no concern.
11. Since the real world is dynamic, its properties are always changing, the Principle of Uncertainty follows.

16.6.5 Guidelines

From these statements, guidelines such as the following may be derived.

Guideline 1. During system evolution, amend the specification, that is, co-evolve it with the system, to ensure that the specification remains a valid abstraction of the real world and that a valid specification-program equivalence, is *maintained*;

Guideline 2. Regularly capture, document, review the validity and impact of assumptions sets underlying specifications and programs and search for newly injected ones.

The above statements express observations and thoughts about software evolution and the properties that the proposed theory might reflect. They are based on years of observation and study and are believed to be rich enough to provide foundations for development of a theory of at least part of the evolution phenomenon. The set is nontrivial despite being only a fragment of the envisaged theory. The latter requires further consideration, detailed development and formalisation where possible.

16.7 The Theory

It is premature to discuss the form the proposed theory might take or to provide more details of its likely content. Though preliminary ideas have been discussed, a formally defined statement of even just the eight laws of software evolution (Lehman 1974, 1978, Lehman and Belady 1985) (see Chapter 1) does not yet exist. Significant structuring of the knowledge and understanding of those elements of software evolution that already exist and of the relationships between them are required before a fuller picture begins to emerge.

Abstraction of insights, interpretations and understanding of evolution as developed over the years, most recently in FEAST (2001), provide a basis and framework for theory formation. It has already yielded foundations and guidelines for further progress in technology improvement. A theory derived from this will be rooted in observed phenomenology, analysis of empirical data, behavioural invariants and its successful and convincing formalisation and extension by theoretical reasoning and a proven set of theorems. The very process of developing the theory will provide major direction for forming and firming the ideas. Its development can and will make a significant contribution to software engineering technology. As an integrated and coherent body of knowledge and understanding, it will also have implications for general business process improvement.

16.8 Organisation of Theory Development

The concepts presented to this point have been maturing for some time based on consistent results obtained in over 30 years of software evolution studies. On that basis and on spreading interest in software evolution the time is ripe for systematic structuring and extension. In the context of software engineering, it represents a pioneering effort in uncharted waters. The development is by no means straightforward and requires widespread exposure and discussion with involvement and contribution of many researchers from the wider field of software engineering, software process, empirical evolution measurement and analysis, formal methods, architecture, practitioners and so on.

As envisaged, a major goal (Lehman 2000b) is the development of a, partially formal, theory of software evolution and the derivation of implications in terms of practical rules, tools and guidelines for software evolution such as those outlined in Section 16.6.5 and in other papers (Lehman 1978) (see also Chapter 27). The rigorous application and expansion of the example presented in the previous section constitutes a start. *Modal action* logic has been suggested as the logic to be used at the theoretical level. A body of codified knowledge to permit initial theory formation, reasoned exploration and refinement already exists. Once initiated, enrichment process would continue in parallel with axiomatic extension by interpretation of the phenomenology to follow the paradigms illustrated in Figures 16.1 and 16.2. This will facilitate reasoned exploration and interpretation of the phenomenon, refinement and extension of the emerging theory and pointers to practical application.

16.9 Goals

As currently visualised, the proposed development includes the following objectives:

1. Develop formal explanatory, observational level, theory of software evolution on the basis of observed behavioural invariants and evolutionary patterns of industrially developed, marketed and maintained systems.
2. Develop theory-level partial theories, in selected formalisms where appropriate.
3. Derive and prove theorems that follow from the theory as they develop.
4. Interpret theorems and validate them against empirical real-world data.
5. Determine the practical implications of such theorems and their potential for exploitation.
6. Fully document and disseminate results of the work to encourage critical examination, refinement of results, extension of the theory and the approach to its development and, above all, wide take up.
7. Explore industrial exploitation and support industrial introduction of the practical implications of theorems.

Progress towards these objectives requires the following activities:

1. Subject to authorisation by the original owners, create a web-based repository of software evolution data and models for wider dissemination, reaction and exploration.
2. Isolate, classify and structure patterns, invariants and other observations to identify potential empirical generalisations.
3. Apply the results of the previous step to identify individual patterns and potential relationships that provide an emerging descriptive theory of behaviour but no interpretation or explanation.
4. Develop models in appropriate form and seek interpretations of the relationships and behaviour.
5. Check models against data other than that used to develop them and if appropriate improve them.
6. Explore models, using techniques from other disciplines, for example, discrete control theory, to the observations and inferences and seek to refine or further develop models.
7. Generate behavioural hypotheses and test against data.
8. Integrate the models in the descriptive theory.
9. Identify sub-models that are candidates for formalisation and develop as appropriate.
10. Subject to authorisation by the respective owners, extend the repository by correction and addition of additional data, models and description.
11. Return to step two.

16.10 Related Work

The need for a theory, formal or otherwise, of the software process as such has been discussed in the literature and in the FEAST group (FEAST 2001) for some time. There are references to the absence of a theoretical basis and framework for software engineering and to the role that such a theory could play. In a recent overview of the field Bennett and Rajlich (2000), for example, state '... A major challenge for the research community is to develop good theoretical understanding and underpinning for maintenance and evolution, which scales to industrial applications...'. However, other than initial thoughts outlined in workshop papers (Lehman 2000c, Lehman and Ramil 2000a) and in a project proposal (Lehman 2000b), there does not appear to be any existing work in the development of a theory of the related and interdependent areas of software process, evolution, process improvement, maintenance and the many other activities that make up the, so called, discipline of software engineering. Mathematical theory that relates to formal representations, *formal methods* (e.g. Turski 1981, Turski and Maibaum 1987) and programming languages do exist and may prove important in supporting the proposed study. At the specialist level, it is strictly symbolic. Descriptive models may be provided for clarification or to assist understanding but do not form part of the models or the science *per se*. Such theory is qualitatively different to that being proposed here. As a phenomenological descriptor, that is more akin to the theories of the physical sciences (Shrager and Langley 1990). But these too largely reflect natural phenomena, where the influence of human intervention is small or absent. Subject to limitations such as quantum mechanical effects, they can be made as precise as experimental technology permits. In software engineering, human creativity, involvement and activity – intellectual and physical – play a major role as do human judgement and decision. Such an area can never be fully formalised (Lehman 1977).

The basis for deductive theory development as epitomised by Euclidean geometry and used for many centuries in mathematics and, implicitly, by application in the physical sciences, is well established. So is the application of formal methods and of the many representations and logics in computer science (e.g. Turski and Maibaum 1987) as illustrated by their many successes. Success in the proposed investigation will benefit from the knowledge, understanding and experience gained in these fields. But it also requires advances that arise from the different situations created by human intellectual involvement, their creativity and the abstract objects that they create, manipulate, change and evolve. It will require the coordinated involvement of an extended multi-disciplinary team with expertise in the many fields involved. It truly represents a grand challenge.

16.11 Final Remarks

It has been observed that the absence of a theory is a genuine obstacle to the advancement of software technology, software process improvement, the mastery of feedback in the software process, and full mastery of software evolution. The first two are already matters of concern and major expenditure, to industry. The others should be. The past and current record in software and software project failures (e.g. Finkelstein and Dowell 1996) support the need for appropriate research in the area. While industry has not yet, in general, homed in on the related problems of software evolution and feedback in the software process, growing research interest in these areas and progress to date as summarised in this book and in this chapter suggest that the time is ripe for a major initiative.

The current research hypothesis is that the software evolution phenomenon, and the associated global process that is determined by the activity of all involved in the evolution process, may be described by a formal theory. This may be so despite the role played by human decision taking (Lehman 1977) and feedback (Belady and Lehman 1972, Lehman 1994) in that process. Because of the FEAST (2001) and earlier studies, it is believed that the established facts indicate that this is so. To address this hypothesis constructively, the main issues that arise relate to the selection of an appropriate axiom set and the application of the logics, methods and modelling techniques, briefly discussed above, to a domain where, it is believed, they have not previously been applied.

A sound theory will provide an answer. A theory that supports, rationalises, integrates and extends evolution studies and, in particular, the rules and guidelines, will contribute towards the creation of confidence in the good practice guides derived from them. Such confidence is required to achieve the advances in software quality; increases in productivity and reductions in response time that are needed in an age with the society relying ever more on the computer and on software in all spheres of activity. The many costly failures of computer projects all over the world are solid evidence that the topics discussed here must receive urgent and widespread attention.

16.12 Acknowledgements

We are grateful to former colleagues at Imperial College, Goel Kahen and Siew F Lim, for their questioning and constructive criticism and their continuing support, and to Tom Maibaum for clarifying current views of theory development. We also thank José Fiadero, Dewayne Perry and Wlad Turski for many discussions and much enlightenment over a long period.

References

References indicated with an "*" were reprinted in Lehman and Belady 1985.

Ahern D., Clouse A. and Turner R. (2001), *CMMI Distilled – An Introduction to Multi-discipline Process Improvement*, SEI Series in Software Engineering, Addison Wesley, Reading, MA.

Antón A. and Potts C. (2001), *Functional Paleontology: System Evolution as the User Sees it, ICSE 23*, Toronto, Canada, 12–19 May, pp. 421–430.

Bauer A. and Pizka M. (2003), The Contribution of Free Software to Software Evolution. *Proceedings of the International Workshop on Principles of Software Evolution (IWPSE)*, Helsinki, Finland, Sept. 2003.

*Belady L.A. and Lehman M.M. (1972), An Introduction to Growth Dynamics, in W. Freiburger (ed.), *Statistical Computer Performance Evaluation*, Academic Press, New York, pp. 503–511.

Bennett K.H. and Rajlich V.T. (2000), Software Maintenance and Evolution: a Roadmap, in A. Finkelstein (ed.), *The Future of Software Engineering, ICSE 2000*, Order Number 592000-1, 4–11 June, ACM Press, Limerick, Ireland, ACM Order Nr. 592000-1, pp. 75–87.

Carnap R. (1966), *Philosophical Foundations of Physics*. Basic Books, New York.

CERN (1998), *The Earth Breathes on LEP and LHC*, CERN Bulletin 09/98, 23 Feb. 1998, http://bulletin.cern.ch/9809/art1/Text_E.html.

Chong Hok Yuen C.K.S. (1981), *Phenomenology of Program Maintenance and Evolution*, PhD thesis, Department of Computing, Imperial College, London, England.

Dijkstra E.W. (1968), GOTO Statement Considered Harmful, Letter to the Editor, *Commun. ACM*, vol. 11, no. 11, Nov. 1968, pp. 147–148.

FEAST (2001) *Feedback, Evolution And Software Technology*, http://www.doc.ic.ac.uk/~mml/feast/ <as of Oct. 2001> See also http://www.cs.mdx.ac.uk/staffpages/mml as of Feb 2004.

Finkelstein A. and Dowell J. (1996), A Comedy of Errors: The London Ambulance Service Case Study, *Proceedings of 8th International Workshop on Software Specification & Design*, IWSSD-8, 22–23 March, Schloss Velen, Germany, pp. 2–4, http://www.cs.ucl.ac.uk/staff/a_finkelstein/papers/lascase.pdf.

Fordham R.G. (2000), Software Development Challenges for the 2000's, in F. Bomarius and M. Oivo (eds.), Keynote Address, *Proceedings of PROFES'2000 2nd International Conference on Product Focused Software Process Improvement*, Oulu, Finland, 20–22 Jun. 2000, LNCS 1840, Springer-Verlag, Berlin, Germany, p. 3.

Gilb T. (1981), Evolutionary Development, *ACM Softw. Eng. Notes*, vol. 6, no. 2, April 1981, p. 17.

Gilb T. (1988), *Principles of Software Engineering Management*, Addison-Wesley, Wokingham, England.

Godfrey M.W. and Tu Q. (2000), *Evolution in Open Source Software: A Case Study*, Proceedings of International Conference on Software Maintenance, ICSM 2000, San Jose, CA, 11–14 Oct. 2000, pp. 131–142.

Hoare C.A.R. (1969), An Axiomatic Basis for Computer Programming, *Commun. ACM*, vol. 12, no. 10, Oct. 1969, pp. 576–583.

Hoare C.A.R. (1971), Proof of a Program FIND, *Commun. ACM*, vol. 14, no. 1, Jan 1971, pp. 39–45.

IWPSE (2005), *Proceedings of International Workshop on Principles of Software Evolution*, Lisbon, Portugal, 5–6 Sept. 2004, IEEE CS Press http://www.rcost.unisannio.it/iwpse2005/html/paper.htm <as of Feb 2006>.

Kemerer C.F. and Slaughter S. (1999), An Empirical Approach to Studying Software Evolution, *IEEE Trans. Softw. Eng.*, vol. 25, no. 4, July/Aug., pp. 493–509.

*Lehman M.M. (1969), *The Programming Process*, IBM Research Report RC2722M, IBM Research Center, Yorktown Heights, New York, Sept. 1969.

*Lehman M.M. (1974), *Programs, Cities, Students – Limits to Growth*, Imperial College *Inaugural Lecture Series, Vol. 9*, 1970–1974, pp. 211–229; also in Gries, 1978.

*Lehman M.M. (1977), Human Thought and Action as an Ingredient of System Behaviour, in R. Duncan and M. Weston Smith (eds.), *Encyclopedia of Ignorance*, Pergamon Press, Oxford, England.

*Lehman M.M. (1978), Laws of Program Evolution-Rules and Tools for Programming Management, *Proceedings of Infotech State of the Art Conference, Why Software Projects Fail*, 9–11 April 1978, London, England, pp. 1V1–1V25.

*Lehman M.M. (1980), Program Life Cycles and Laws of Software Evolution, *Proceedings of IEEE Special Issue on Software Engineering*, Sept. 1980, pp. 1060–1076.

*Lehman M.M. (1982), *Program Evolution*, reprinted as chapter 2 in Lehman M.M. and Belady L.A., *Program Evolution. Process of Software Change*, Academic Press, 1985.

Lehman M.M. (1984), A Further Model of Coherent Programming Process, *Proceedings of the Software Process Workshop*, Egham, Surrey, 6–8 Feb. 1984, IEEE Cat. no. 84 CH 2044–6, pp. 27–35.

Lehman M.M. (1989), Uncertainty in Computer Application and its Control Through the Engineering of Software, *J. Softw. Maint.: Res. Pract.*, vol. 1, no. 1, Sept. 1989, pp. 3–27.

Lehman M.M. (1990), Uncertainty in Computer Application, *Commun. ACM*, vol. 33, no. 5, May 1990, pp. 584–586.

Lehman M.M. (1991), Software Engineering, the Software Process and Their Support, *IEE Softw. Eng. J.*, Special Issue on Software Environments and Factories, vol. 6, no. 5, Sept. 1991, pp. 243–258.

Lehman M.M. (1994), Feedback in the Software Evolution Process Keynote Address, *CSR Eleventh Annual Workshop on Software Evolution: Models and Metrics*, Dublin, 7–9 Sept. 1994, *Workshop Proceedings, Information and Software Technology*, special issue on Software Maintenance, vol. 38, no. 11, 1996, Elsevier, 1996, pp. 681–686.

Lehman M.M., Perry D.E., Ramil J.F., Turski W.M. and Wernick P. (1997), Metrics and Laws of Software Evolution – The Nineties View, *Proceedings of Fourth International Symposium on Software Metrics, Metrics 97*, Albuquerque, NM, 5–7 Nov. 1997, pp. 20–32. Also in K. El Eman and N.H. Madhavji (eds.), *Elements of Software Process Assessment and Improvement*, IEEE CS Press, 1999, pp. 343–368.

Lehman M.M. (2000a), Evolution as a Noun and Evolution as a Verb, *SOCE 2000 Workshop on Software and Organisation Co-evolution*, 12–13 July 2000, Imperial College, London, England.

Lehman M.M. (2000b), *These – Towards a Theory of Software Evolution*, EPSRC Proposal, Case for Support Part 2, Department of Computing ICSTM.

Lehman M.M. (2000c), *Approach to a Theory of Software Process and Software Evolution*, FEAST 2000 Preprints, 10–12 July 2000, Imperial College, London, England.

Lehman M.M. and Belady L.A. (1985), *Program Evolution – Processes of Software Change*, Academic Press, London, England.

Lehman M.M. and Ramil J.F. (2000a), Towards a Theory of Software Evolution – and its Practical Impact, inv. talk, in T. Katayama, T. Tamai and N. Yonezaki (eds.), *Proceedings of the ISPSE 2000*, Kanazawa, Japan, Nov 1–2, IEEE Computer Society Press, Los Alamitos, CA, pp. 2–11.

Lehman M.M. and Ramil J.F. (2000b), Software Evolution in the Age of Component Based Software Engineering, *IEE Proc. Softw.*, special issue on Component Based Software Engineering, vol. 147, no. 6, Dec. 2000, pp. 249–255; earlier version as Technical Report 98/8, Imperial College, London, Jun. 1998.

Lehman M.M. and Ramil J.F. (2001b), An Approach to a Theory of Software Evolution, in T. Tamai, M. Aoyama and K. Bennett (eds). *Proceedings of IWPSE 2001*, IEEE CS Press, Vienna, Sept. 10–11, 2002, pp. 70–74.

Naur P. and Randell B. (1968), *Software Engineering – Report on a Conference Sponsored by the NATO Science Committee*, Scientific Affairs Division, Garmisch, Germany; NATO, Brussels, Belgium, 1969, http://homepages.cs.ncl.ac.uk/brian.randell/NATO/ as of July 2004.

Parnas D. (1972), On the Criteria to be Used in Decomposing Systems into Modules, *Commun. ACM*, vol. 15, Dec. 1972, pp. 1053–1058.

Paulk M.C., Curtis B., Chrissis M.B. and Weber C. (1993), *Capability Maturity Model for Software, Version 1.1*, Technical Report CMU/SEI-93-TR-24, Software Engineering Institute.

Pfleeger S.L. (1998), The Nature of System Change, *IEEE Softw.*, vol. 15, no. 3, May–June 1998, pp. 87–90.

WGoSE (2006), Working Group on Software Evolution, ERCIM, European Research Consortium for Informatics and Mathematics, http://w3.umh.ac.be/evol/ (last accessed in Feb. 2006).

Royce W.W., (1970), *Managing the Development of Large Software Systems*, Proceedings of IEEE Westcon, Los Angeles, CA, August, pp. 1–9.

Shaw M. and Garlan D. (1996), *Software Architecture: Perspectives on an Emerging Discipline*, Prentice Hall.

Shrager J. and Langley P. (eds.) (1990), *Computational Models of Scientific Discovery and Theory Formation*, Morgan Kaufmann Publishers, San Mateo, CA, p. 498.

SOCE (2000), *Proceedings of the Workshop on Software and Organisation Co-evolution*, Imperial College, London, 12–13 July.

Succi G., Paulson J. and Eberlein A. (2001), Preliminary Results from an Empirical Study on the Growth of Open Source and Commercial Software Products, *EDSER-3 Workshop, Co-located with ICSE 2001*, Toronto, Canada, 14–15 May 2001.

Turski W.M. (1981), Specification as a Theory with Models in the Computer World and in the Real World, *Infotech State Art Rep.*, vol. 9, no. 6, pp. 363–377.

Turski W.M. and Maibaum T.S.E. (1987), *The Specification of Computer Programs*, Addison-Wesley, Wokingham, United Kingdom.

Wirth N. (1971), Program Development by Stepwise Refinement, *Commun. ACM*, vol. 14, no. 4, April 1971, pp. 221–222.

Part Two

Feedback

This part of the book covers the chapters with a strong focus on 'feedback'. The abstracts below give an overview of the chapters that follow.

Chapter 17: Difficulties with Feedback Control in Software Processes

Early data on the phenomenology of software system evolution suggest that such evolution involves and is, to some extent, governed by feedback. This feedback may take the form of information fed back to individuals or groups as a form of learning from experience or may take the form of observation and data that are used to control some aspect of the process. This chapter puts the former to one side and concentrates only on feedback to explicit control mechanisms.

Chapter 18: Governing Software Evolution through Policy-oriented Feedback

On the basis of historical data or experience, policies can be specified to help govern the evolution of a software system and its evolution process. In this chapter, we describe how automated support can help detect violation of evolutionary policies, thereby providing feedback to guide software evolution. The two key concepts discussed are a mechanism for detecting policy violations, and a contextual framework for supporting the activities of software evolution.

Chapter 19: Feedback in Requirements Discovery and Specification: A Quality Gateway for Testing Requirements

The testing of software must be accepted as an integral part of building a system. However, if the software is based on inaccurate requirements then, despite well-written code, the software will be unsatisfactory. Instead of limiting our testing to code, one should start testing as soon as work commences on development of product requirements. In order to do this one needs to establish effective feedback connections between all the different classes of stakeholders: developers, testers and business people. This chapter describes a quality gateway that defines agreed entry criteria for the requirements specification. Tests based on these entry criteria are concerned with ensuring that stated requirements are accurate, and do not cause problems by being unsuitable for design and implementation stages later in the project.

The quality gateway described in this process is part of the Volere requirements process. The process has been adopted and applied by many organizations in a wide variety of domains and countries.

Chapter 20: Requirements Risk and Software Reliability

In order to continue to make progress in software measurement as it pertains to reliability, metrics that characterize the risk of making requirements changes must be added to those that emphasize design and code metrics. By doing so one can improve the quality of delivered software, because defects related to problems in requirements specifications will be identified early in the evolution of the software. This chapter provides an approach that can help identify requirements change risk factors, which, in turn, are needed to predict reliability problems. We discuss a case example consisting of 24 Space Shuttle change requests, 19 risk factors and the associated failures and software metrics. The approach can be generalized to other applications with numerical results that would vary according to the application.

Chapter 21: Combining Process Feedback with Discrete Event Simulation Models to Support Software Project Management

Process feedback is an essential part of process change planning and software project management. This chapter discusses on-going work with an industrial partner to integrate feedback from the software development process with a discrete event simulation model to improve predictions of process performance. A flexible metrics repository provides feedback that is used to generate updated simulation model parameters at predefined project milestones. Model predictions using updated parameters and current project data are compared to Outcome Based Control Limits (OBCLs) defined for the project. These predictions enable the program manager to take corrective action as necessary with the simulation model providing feedback and insight on potential performance impacts of the proposed corrective actions. This creates a feedback loop with the process enhancing model predictions supporting project management decisions. An illustrative example using a simulation model and metrics repository that has been applied at a leading software development firm is shown.

Chapter 22: A Feedforward Capability to Improve Software Reestimation

More effective cost estimation models are needed when E-type systems are being developed. This chapter proposes a feature to feed forward the model assumptions and properties in formats and language that match early project experiences. The intention is that this information matching will greatly ease critical early project reestimation of cost and schedule. The operation of a feedforward capability, implemented as part of a cost estimation model, is discussed. Examples are provided to suggest that a feedforward feature would improve project reestimation and risk management.

Chapter 23: Modelling the Feedback Part of the Software Process in Software Resource Estimation

All software processes are driven by feedback from their leaders, users and other stakeholders. However, resource estimation approaches do not take this feedback into account. It is therefore important to consider whether the predictive power of cost estimation approaches will improve if feedback characteristics of the process are explicitly considered as cost factor. The answer is not obvious in the context of *lighter-weight* cost estimation approaches, such as those termed *algorithmic*. This chapter discusses some related current approaches to resource estimation and provides suggestions for empirical investigation of the issue. In particular, it suggests that an explicit cost factor representation for key characteristics of the information feedback structure within the software process may significantly improve algorithmic estimates and that feedback could be the missing link in algorithmic and other cost estimation methods.

Chapter 24: Value-Based Feedback in Software and Information Systems Development

The role of feedback control in software and information system development has traditionally focused on a milestone plan to deliver a pre-specified set of capabilities within a negotiated budget and schedule. One of the most powerful approaches available for controlling traditional software projects is called the *Earned Value system*. However, the Earned Value Management process is generally good for tracking whether a project is meeting its original plan. It becomes difficult to administer if the project plans change rapidly. And more significantly it has absolutely nothing to say about the actual value being earned for the organization by the results of the project. This chapter begins by summarizing a set of four nested feedback and feedforward loops that have been successfully used to scope, estimate, control and improve the predictability and efficiency of software development and evolution. It then proposes an alternative approach for project feedback control. It focuses on the actual stakeholder value likely to be earned by completing the project. And a framework is provided for monitoring and controlling value in terms of a Benefits Realization Approach and business case analysis. An order processing system is used as an example to illustrate the value-based feedback control mechanisms. At the end of this chapter, it presents the conclusions and directions for future research and development.

Chapter 25: Expert Estimation of Software Development Cost: Learning through Feedback

Expert estimation is the most popular software development effort estimation approach. This reliance on expert estimation is understandable considering its flexibility. Surprisingly, several empirical studies report that the amount of estimation experience is not a good predictor of estimation accuracy, even in situations where the experience is believed to be highly relevant, leading us to conclude that there are problems connected with learning from on-the-job estimation experience. This chapter discusses potential reasons for this poor learning from on-the-job experience. On the basis of these reasons, we describe and justify four guidelines for improved learning: (1) Increase the motivation for learning estimation skills, (2) Reduce the impact from estimation- learning biases, (3) Ensure a fit between the estimation process and the type of feedback from past estimation performance and (4) Provide learning situations. These guidelines extend the 'experience factory' framework, a general software experience-learning framework, with estimation-specific learning guidelines. Through an experiment involving software professionals, we demonstrate how a simple change in the estimation process based on the guidelines (2) and (3) made the estimation accuracy feedback significantly more useful for the improvement of estimation performance.

Chapter 26: Self-Adaptive Software: Internalized Feedback

This chapter discusses a revolutionary idea: that the feedback processes of software development and maintenance can be internalized in the running software itself. In the normal development process, programs are produced in one environment, then run in other environments. Users of the application request changes, which are then fed back to the development and maintenance process. Self-adaptive software is software that internalizes monitoring and evaluation functions, and can rapidly, *at runtime,* respond to the need for change. We discuss the dynamic binding roots of Self-Adaptive Software. We also present a description of the technological underpinnings of Self-Adaptive Software, and the sort of applications to which it has been applied.

Chapter 27: Rules and Tools for Software Evolution Planning and Management

On the basis of the Laws of Software Evolution and on further results of the FEAST research projects, this chapter develops and presents some 50 rules for application in software system process planning and management and indicates tools available or that could usefully be developed to support their application. The listing is structured according to the laws that encapsulate the observed phenomena and that lead to the recommendations. Each sub-list is preceded by a textual discussion providing at least some of the reasoning that has led to the recommended procedures. The references direct the interested reader to the literature that records observed behaviours, interpretations, models and metrics obtained from industrially evolved systems, and from which the recommendations were derived.

17

Difficulties with Feedback Control in Software Processes

Meir M. Lehman, Dewayne E. Perry and Wlad Turski

This chapter originally published as an invited talk "Difficulties with Feedback Control in Software Processes" by Meir M. Lehman, Dewayne E. Perry and Wladyslaw M. Turski, Proceedings of the 19th Australasian Computer Science Conference, Melbourne, Australia, 31 Jan.–2 Feb. 1996, pp. 107–115. Copyright ACS, reproduced by permission.

17.1 Introduction

Software development and evolution processes [Osterweil87, Lehman87] have become a significant area of software engineering and software engineering research. Among topics of importance are process formalisms, process support, process assessment, process architecture and process improvement. One of the underlying motivations for the emergence of this relatively new direction in research and practice is the need to move the development and evolution of software systems from a craft venture to an engineering one. An expected consequence of this move is that the methods and techniques by which software systems are built and evolved will be open to scrutiny and evaluation by the community rather than considered to be secrets passed amongst the initiated.

Given that the functionality of systems built (and hence the systems themselves) can be exceedingly complex [Brooks86, Turski86], that the processes used to build and evolve these systems are complex, that the organizational structures that provide their development and operation context are equally complex, and that there is undoubtedly extensive feedback in the processes used and the organization that executes them, it is surprising that feedback and feedback control have [ABD91] been so little investigated in the context of software systems evolution.

Despite the fact that the role and the impact of feedback has received little attention as a research topic, it has long been recognized as a significant factor in software processes.

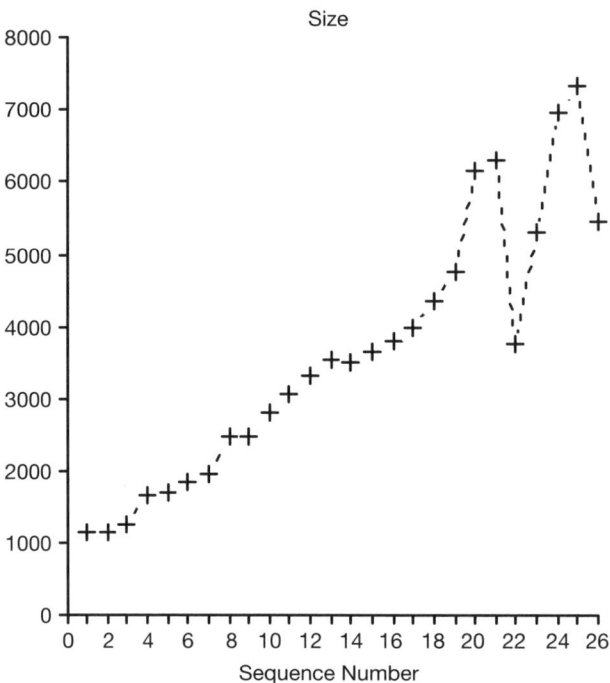

Figure 17.1 Growth (in number of modules) of OS/360 over releases

It was, for example, referred to in passing by several people at the software engineering workshop in Garmisch [NR68] and is also discussed briefly in Lehman's Programming Process report [Lehman69].

Lehman and Belady [BL72, Lehman85] provide one of the earliest examples of feedback control at work in the evolution of OS/360. Figure 17.1 depicts the growth of OS/360 in terms of number of modules over a period of 26 releases. The cyclic pattern evident in the plot from release 1 through release 20 is characteristic of feedback systems. They observed

> ... the ripple is typical of a self stabilizing process with positive and negative feedback loops. From a long-range point of view the rate of system growth is self-regulatory, despite the fact that many different causes control the selection of work implemented in each release, with budgets varying, increasing numbers of users reporting faults or desiring new capability, varying management attitudes towards system enhancement, changing release intervals and improving methods ...

It is in this context of evolutionary software development that we have for some time studied feedback and feedback control, a study for which the FEAST[1] project has provided a formal framework for this past two years [Lehman95, Feast1, Feast2, and Feast3]. This chapter first examines the definitions and nature of feedback and control, and then

---

[1] FEAST stands for Feedback, Evolution And Software Technology.

presents a research manifesto and feedback control model as the initial basis for further investigation. On the basis of this groundwork, the chapter then considers various facets of feedback and control in the context of software evolution processes: what feedback control means in design processes as opposed to production processes; what feedback control means when it leads to a change in processes rather than in their regulation; and finally, the contrast between feedback influence and feedback control in relatively immature processes.

17.2 Feedback and Control

As the term *feedback* is used in a wide variety of contexts, it is worthwhile to take a look at the basic meanings of the word. *Webster's New Collegiate Dictionary* defines 'feedback' as follows:

> **feedback: 1:** the return to the input of a part of the output of a machine, system or process (as for producing changes in an electronic circuit that improve performance or in an automatic control device that provides self-corrective action) **2 a:** the partial reversion of the effects of a process to its source or to a preceding stage **b:** the return to a point of origin of evaluative or corrective information about an action or process <student ~ was solicited to help revise the curriculum> <we welcome ... ~ from our readers – brickbats as well as bouquets – *Johns Hopkins Mag.*> **also:** the information so transmitted

The mere return of information, even if it is *evaluative or corrective*, does not guarantee that it will have any effect. To have an effect, this information must be somehow used, that is, it must produce a change in something. And, while there are a variety of ways in which feedback may have an effect, the interest here is in one specific means of producing such effects, namely, feedback control.

The verb *control* also has two principal (families of) meanings. Quoting again from the *Webster's New Collegiate Dictionary*:

> **1:** to check, test, or verify by evidence or experiments **2a:** to exercise restraining or directing influence over: REGULATE **b:** to have power over: RULE

These two meanings are often used interchangeably in everyday speech. However, when applied to software evolution processes, the activities denoted by 'control – 1' are quite different from those denoted by 'control – 2'.[2] The confusion is amplified (or, perhaps, generated) by the fact that a single person (or a single group) often performs *both* actions, 'control – 1' and 'control – 2' with respect to a productive activity. In addition, it may happen that the same person or group performs 'control – 2' over several activities, particularly when 'control – 2b' is meant.

---

[2] The distinction between 'control – 2a' and 'control – 2b', although important in many contexts, is less fundamental in our considerations as, usually, one has to have power over something if one is to exercise restraining or directing influence over it. With some hesitation one could accept that in the context of software evolution processes 'control – 2a' implies 'control – 2b'.

Nevertheless, a precondition for any sensible approach to a scientific and technological treatment of software evolution processes is that the meanings of 'control' are *disentangled*. From now on, the word *check* will be used for 'control – 1' and *regulate* (or possibly *rule*, if it is needed) for 'control – 2'. Thus *checking* is distinct from *regulating*.

In a disciplined work environment, all productive work actions are checked: **do** *action* **until** *check-successful*. This qualitative function of checking is a part of production, not part of control. It guarantees an established level of completeness or quality of the production.

Regulation, on the other hand, is the control of the production process on the basis of the production results. It is this meaning of control that is used in the combination *feedback control*. The whole idea of applying feedback control to software evolution processes rests on the assumptions that there is a stream of similar production tasks and that regulation of the production processes is required to maintain an ideal production state.

There are at least two factors that effect the maintenance of this ideal production state: instability and random events. It is difficult to deny that software evolution processes are often unstable, or that random events occur in and impact these processes. Thus, many software development processes require feedback control to contain the tendency toward instability and to control the consequences of randomness.

In contrast to checking, regulating may have one of the following effects as a result of evaluating feedback.

- Change the processing, that is, change various parameters that govern the production process.
- Change the process, that is, change the process structure itself rather than the parameters that control the process. There are the following two ways in which this change may be achieved.
    ○ Statically – use an alternative part of the production process.
    ○ Dynamically – change the existing process or create a new process.

17.3 Technology versus Sociology

Given our definitions of feedback and control, there are still a wide variety of feedback control phenomena that are excluded from these investigations. One such general category is that of *learning* as an example of feedback control. In this case, feedback is the information returned to a *person* placed at the point of origin, who absorbs the information and via an act of human learning modifies his or her future behavior, for example, the way this person manages whatever happens to be his or her activity domain.

This interpretation is acceptable for the *sociology* of software evolution processes. It can be a part of a manager's or developer's education: 'thou shalt pay (more) attention to the feedback you are getting'; or even more aggressively: 'thou shalt seek more feedback about the actions you manage'. It can be elaborated by supplying a list of sources from which the feedback is to be considered or sought categorized into 'important', 'vital', and 'irrelevant' classes. Suitable case studies may be conducted, yielding instances of the benefits that accrue when one heeds such feedback and of the disasters that follow when the feedback information is neglected. This, no doubt, can (and will) be a useful part of education and training for both managers and developers.

However, this type of feedback and control cannot easily be interpreted and modeled as a technological view of software evolution processes. The point is that the evaluation and control machinery is all in the human brain. Moreover, even if one accepts that feedback provides the stimulus and basis for learning, one still faces a dilemma: Either one explains what the appropriate reactions are that need to be learned, or one leaves that to intuition or creativity.

In the former case, that is, when it is ultimately known what are the recommended, beneficial, profitable reactions to a particular combination of feedback signals received, then one does have an explicit control machinery ('when you get too many error reports coming from the customers, strengthen the quality control', 'when you are late with delivery, cut down on the most time-consuming activity' etc.).

In the latter case (invoking intuition) such machinery is not readily apparent, but it is hard to see what advice can be given to a manager or developer as the (necessary) second part of the admonition to pay more attention to the feedback. A rational person will almost certainly ask: *'What am I supposed to do when I collect all this information fed back to me? How can I act on it?'* Unless one is prepared to answer 'use your head' or some similarly profound platitude, one is inextricably bound to construct control machinery.

Whatever other kinds of feedback are considered, if they are to be used for improving the software process, they must be turned into explicit control mechanisms (see Chapter 18). Thus, the concentration here is, at least initially, on feedback control as a technological rather than a sociological endeavor.

17.4 Manifesto and Model

As a prelude to these investigations (in the FEAST project), we laid down a manifesto defining project goals, identifying supporting postulates, describing a basic model and enunciating a research hypothesis. One of the advantages of this approach is that the manifesto provides the primary inputs to defining a project and developing a work plan.

There are two general goals for our investigations:

- To produce specific recommendations, guidelines, methods and tools for software evolution process improvement, and
- To contribute to a science of software process and software evolution.

These goals are to be pursued in the context of process systems that satisfy a set of requirements about their structure and composition. That is, the FEAST project is limited to process systems that implement the evolution of software systems and that satisfy the following postulates:

- These systems have rich networks of feedback.
- Some of the feedbacks stabilize characteristics in these systems.
- Some feedbacks are controllable.

The basis for these investigations is a process model of feedback and control. This model consists of a process element (PE) that applies resources (R) to transform inputs

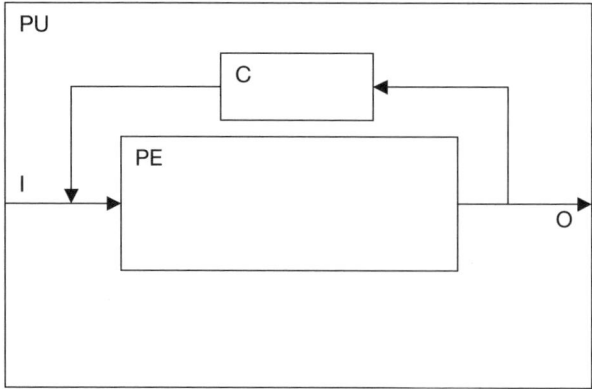

Figure 17.2 A process model unit involving feedback and control

(I) into outputs (O). If one of the destinations of the output is a controller (C), where output is fed back into the process element, we obtain a general controlled feedback loop (as in Figure 17.2). We term this general controlled feedback loop a process unit (PU). Process elements can contain process units.

The hypothesis for this chapter is that *a process or process system that satisfies the postulates above can be usefully decomposed into a manageable number of process units*.

A number of important issues arise in the investigation of this hypothesis using the model we have proposed. The first of these issues is how to model software evolution processes, in particular, what does one model and what is the basic unit of modeling. There are two general approaches one might use: One is to model people and organizations, the other is to model what people and organizations do, that is, their activities. Choosing *people and organizations* would lead to a decomposition similar to an organizational chart of a company. For different projects executed by the same company, the charts need not be identical, even when the projects are concurrent. While these organizational charts are useful for some purposes, they are not useful here.

The goal is, instead, to model the *activities* in software evolution processes. A process element in this model, then, represents an activity performed in evolving a software system. Moreover, this choice represents a focus on the design of the processes and their activities, not their implementation in terms of people, tools, environments and organizations. It should be emphasized that the resulting model may not map readily to a traditional organizational structure, in particular, the control aspects in the model are associated with the elements they control and not with the parts of the organization that may execute them.

The second issue is that of process element decomposition. Given that activities are both the basic building block and the decomposable building block, how does one structure software evolution processes recursively using this model? A process element may be composed of both process elements and process units. It is not necessary that a productive action has feedback control. It may simply be an activity that produces something necessary for the overall product of the evolution processes. The activities may be composed sequentially or in parallel into a larger unit with or without a controller. The internal structure of a process element then may look like a graph with multiple paths starting with the initial input and resulting in the final output. How the decomposition is arrived at and how far the modeling effort is taken, that is, how many levels of recursion one has, is a matter of design choices.

Given that one can recursively decompose the process element of a process unit into a combination of process elements and process units (each with their own controller), the third issue is that of how far a controller can extend its control. Obviously, the controller may affect the parameters that it regulates. These parameters may affect the control of the checking in various process elements (such as how many errors are allowed to be found before rewriting is required) or they may affect the control of the subordinate process units (changing their parameters and thus indirectly changing their range of control). Secondly, the controller may effect a change in the activity structure by selecting a different, but existing path through the process element. And finally, the controller may modify the internal structure of the process element it controls. These may range from simple changes to the process elements and their interconnections to radical redesigns of the entire activity.

A critical question at this point is the extent to which a controller may effect its control – how far into the recursive structure can a controller see? Since it is the intent of this research to keep the model as simple as possible and introduce complexity only when it is clear that one cannot do otherwise, the span of control is limited to only one level of nesting. That does not, however, preclude the controller from establishing changes in the controllers it regulates to cause them to carry out desired changes beyond its limits.

The fourth issue is the form and frequency of the output from the process element that is used as input to the controller. A classical feedback control approach would suggest that the output from the process element is discrete and separated in time by whatever delay exists because of the arrival of input and the time to transform that input into output. For subelements nested deeply in the hierarchy, this time delay may not be significant, but at the top level of a process that evolves a very large software system, the delay may be on the order of months or even years.

In this latter case, the delay means that the controller will be able to effect its regulation only infrequently. In practical terms, however, control is exercised on a much more frequent basis, especially by such organizations as project and process management. Moreover, one can certainly see in the current processes and activities the production of project, process and product information, which can be considered output of a sort – though different from that of the product itself. If one permits this sort of output, one gets something more akin to continuous output that can be assessed and evaluated by the process element controller and used to regulate the process in a more timely manner during, rather than between, the transformation of input to output.

This more continuous stream approach raises a side issue: What determines the extent of visibility of these project, process and product data? We certainly want to avoid an information explosion because that is as poor a data modeling technique as having too many lines of control. In the end, it is the controller that determines what information is needed if its job of regulation is to be effectively performed. Thus, the information output (other than the product itself) is precisely that required by the controller as necessary to properly regulate its process elements and its subelements.

A number of extensions to this model, that may be allowed if one cannot properly model evolution processes without them, suggest themselves at this point.

- Allow a controller to be recursively decomposable into a collection of subunits that together define the controller.
- Allow arbitrary input to the controller where now the only input is that which is produced by the process element and, indirectly, that from the ruling controller.

As with many software engineering analytic tools, the very act of decomposing a process in a particular fashion may yield substantial dividends, quite apart from any benefits that may accrue from applying subsequent steps. A very important kind of dividend is the listing of a regulator's admissible actions and required inputs. Quite likely one will discover how *badly* defined the regulators' prerogatives are, how arbitrarily they are distributed between various regulators, and how little justification there is for allowing some regulators to do things that are just as groundlessly denied to others. If this hunch proves correct, a very concrete improvement to many software evolution processes would be instantly available: the unification of regulators scope under similar (or even more so under identical) stimuli. Translated into shop-floor terms, one would advise giving similar powers to people who control similar activities.

This piece of advice is of course trivial; the difference is that with the decomposition in hand one can flesh out the similar parts of the advice.

The desired result of a fully realized multilevel control model is the identification of controllers, their settings and their predicted results so that the well-regulated processes so modeled reach a steady state, that is, reach a state of stability and predictability.

17.5 Influence versus Control

On the basis of the OS/360 phenomenology [Lehman85] and our model, various process modeling exercises were undertaken to explore the various issues in feedback and control. The general result was a paucity of feedback control examples. The most frequently encountered kind of control is that where control changes or redesigns the controlled process element. Examples of changing process or control element parameters, that is, of regulation in the classical sense, were almost impossible to find. There was, however, anecdotal evidence of several examples of this type of classical regulation. These examples are discussed in the next section.

Despite the difficulty in identifying predictable control mechanisms, it was clear that there is a wide variety of feedback effects, that is, feedback control that is implicit and unpredictable rather than explicit and well defined.

There are a number of reasons for this state of affairs:

- First, the fields of software engineering, in general, and process engineering, in particular, are relatively immature.
- Second, there may well be feedback overload in which the various feedback paths interact in unknown ways and hinder the understanding of individual feedback and control mechanisms.
- Third, process changes as a result of control tend to be step functions, not regulation.

- Fourth, classical feedback control mechanisms are generally applied to production. Their applicability to design processes such as software production and evolution processes have not been widely studied.

17.5.1 Immaturity

As a field, software engineering is relatively young and as a subfield of software engineering, process engineering is very young. One might characterize most software evolution processes as being in the "chitty, chitty, bang, bang" stage, that is, the entire enterprise is just barely held together and all the effort goes just to keep the enterprise afloat. As such, the evolution processes are workable, but only just, and all the time is spent tuning and repairing the enterprise with no resources left for more formal feedback and control mechanisms to be put in place.

While the previous description may be somewhat of a caricature, it is undeniable that there is little theory for software evolution processes, process improvement or even of process systems and their architectures [Perry94, CDP95]. Because of this lack of theory, little is known about what controls are available, and if they are known, virtually nothing is known about what their settings are and what effects they have.

Clearly, research is needed to establish appropriate theories from which necessary control mechanisms can be derived, and experimentation is needed to establish their settings and effects.

17.5.2 Feedback Overload

A basic result in linear control theory may provide an explanation of why there is a lack of readily discernible 'control knobs' in software evolution processes.[3] While these processes are not linear systems, the analogy is a reasonable initial approximation.

If a systems' open-loop transfer function (that is, with no feedback) is A and a fraction of the system output b is fed back (negatively) to the input, then the system's closed-loop transfer function is $A^* = A/(1 + bA)$. Thus, in a system where there is a significant amount of feedback, A^* approaches $1/b$ and the transfer function tends to be merely a function of b more or less independent of A.

While this makes it difficult to find the control knobs in evolution processes, it does have a possible and very interesting side effect: It is possible for intrinsically poor software processes to produce good products because the actual process execution is dominated by the feedback (the set of bs) and not the basic process. This is observed in practice in software development and evolution processes when a high degree of corrective feedback is supplied by, for example, capable and experienced lead developers or project managers.

17.5.3 Step Functions versus Regulation

One of the means of regulation was that of changing or redesigning the controlled processes. It is this category of control that was found most often in these explorations. Almost uniformly, however, these process changes represented step functions rather than control knobs by which a process could be regulated, that is, they change the process

---

[3] This explanation was suggested by Ray Offen, Macquarie University, in an informal discussion about the problems of finding feedback control in software processes.

(often significantly) by improving one or more of its aspects, not by providing a means of regulation.

Watts Humphrey's Personal Software Process (PSP) [Humphrey95] provides one such example. PSP is introduced in a series of steps where each step concentrates on a particular aspect of the personal process. A fundamental part of the process is measurement of key process factors, which provides feedback to the person executing the process. The key to the personal process is *personal defect management* in which the *yield* measure is the most important: Yield is the percentage of defects found and fixed before compilation and testing.

In teaching PSP, the students are given a set of 10 programs that are developed sequentially as different parts of PSP are introduced. Design and code reviews are introduced just prior to Exercise 7. This introduction represents *the* major change in the evolution of PSP from its introduction to a fully fleshed out process. While there is a slight increase in yield between Exercise 1 and Exercise 6, there is a significant jump after the introduction of reviews, causing the average yield to change from about 8% to about 50%, and thus representing a significant process improvement. After that through the end of the exercises, there again is some slight improvement.

This introduction of design and code reviews represents a step function that improves the process; it does not represent a turnable knob that enables one to regulate PSP.

Still, this use of step functions is not so different from what happens in other fields, for example, economics, and one sees progress in these fields from applying principles of feedback control.

17.5.4 Design versus Production

While software production is often considered to be design and implementation, where implementation refers principally to code *production*, a key insight to understanding software development and evolution processes is that the entire design and coding processes are actually design processes; they are not manufacturing or production processes. Code represents simultaneously the lowest level of design and the beginning of construction. Building a software system is like building a new and unique bridge. The notions of control are as difficult to express there as they are in software processes. How does one apply feedback to a creative process?

Where, then, is the production part of software processes? It is in the compilation and linkage of the component parts, that is, in the production of an executable version of the system. This production part is, however, entirely automated and not very interesting from a feedback control standpoint.

As an analogy to software evolution, consider the evolution of a particular brand of automobile. That evolution is not in the production line. For individual instances of cars (the ones we own), evolution takes place in the repair shop. But, evolution of a particular car line takes place in the design laboratory. The governor aspect of control is not applicable at the design level, and feedback at the production level is orthogonal to design and evolution. The controllers are changed for assembly and production as a result of design changes. However, evolution of the product line cannot be explained by *its* controllers, nor reduced to *its* controllers.

This analysis suggests that the manufacturing and production process with all the feedback controllers that go along with it are of little direct interest to studying the software process. Software processes are more related to invention than to production and manufacturing. Phenomenological data (for example, Figure 17.1), however, suggests otherwise, and this is something that requires further investigation.

A first insight indicates that, for example, feedback plays a significant role in the coding and testing part of the processes. One reason for this is that coding and testing are where one is closest to the noncreative aspects of the process. Moreover, at a certain distance of abstraction, one can view the design and coding processes as the transformation of input specifications to output products. It is this latter view, of course, that suggests the utility of feedback control principles.

17.6 Examples of Feedback Control

As mentioned above, the most common kind of feedback control found in these explorations was that which led to changes in the process. Votta and Zajac [VZ95] describe this type of example in their study of design process waivers. In the evolution of their large-scale, real-time system, features are the unit of work. These range in size from several lines of code to multiple thousands of lines of code. The same design process is used for all features. However, for the smaller ones, waivers may be submitted to omit various parts of the process, which while appropriate for large features are inappropriate for smaller ones.

Votta and Zajac acted as the control element of the process and collected a large set of waivers over a period of time. After collecting these waivers (as outputs from the design process), they evaluated the various requests and assessed their merits. The result was a control action to define three separate paths of design dependent on the estimated size of the feature; each class of features would have a design process appropriately scaled to its needs as determined by its size.

In this example, the controller changed the process by introducing several extra paths through the internal process elements and process units that are governed by a size switch. While it is an example of feedback control, the control itself is as creative in its effects as the design process it regulates.

In the search for the more classical regulating control, there is anecdotal evidence of one such control in the use of code reviews. While there is no specific documentation, it is a case that is entirely plausible. The regulation works as follows: If there are too many errors in the code units being produced, extra code reviews are introduced to reduce the number of errors; if time is critical and the number of errors is sufficiently low, code reviews are removed from the process to speed up the process at the expense of an increase in errors.

17.7 Summary

This work during 1995 has been primarily a philosophical or intellectual exploration of the problems of applying feedback control principles to software evolution processes. This exploration has been based on the combined industrial and research experience of the authors and those of the various participants in the FEAST Workshops. As noted in the discussions in the preceding sections, there is phenomenological evidence that classical feedback control is at work in the evolution of software systems and that there is a significant amount of feedback present in these processes. While it is apparent that these various feedback paths have a variety of effects, the explorations reported here have yielded little that can be counted as predictable control. It will require extensive scrutiny and modeling of current industrial processes to determine the actual impact of feedback and control.

Meanwhile, developers continue to build and evolve software systems. They continue to make progress in their understanding of those processes though there is little record of their investigation of feedback paths and its impact.

The agenda of this research is focused on exploiting practical, real-world experience as the basis for understanding and delineating feedback control in software evolution processes: noticing correlations between feedback and effects, finding patterns in feedback phenomena and performing engineering and scientific experimentation to determine both useful control effects and their underlying mechanisms.

This research utilizes a three-pronged approach: collecting and analyzing system evolution phenomena, applying systems dynamics modeling and experimenting with feedback controls.

The phenomenology of system evolution was one of the starting points for this research, a phenomenology of a 1960s operating system. There are questions as to how relevant that phenomenology is today: perhaps it was the result of the specific application, or perhaps the result of the specific environment or organization. However, the authors' intuition is that it is the phenomena of large systems' evolution and independent of the time, application and environment. The very first data on a 1990s system that the authors have just begun to study[4] appears to confirm the earlier observations and support our intuitions.

To understand the complexity of feedback paths, control and their interactions, systems dynamics models will be created of several currently used evolution processes. In this way, the models can be validated with current project data and insights gained into the various feedback phenomena that are at work in building and evolving software systems. Industrial partners are the source of these processes and data.[5]

Insights gained into feedback control phenomena will be confirmed and explored further by means of both engineering and scientific experiments. In this way, the identifiable impact of feedback controls and their range of effects can be determined.

The intent of this research, thus, is to extend the science of software evolution and develop methods, techniques and tools to aid both system evolution and process improvement.

17.8 Acknowledgments

We wish to thank the various participants in the FEAST workshops and our industrial partners for their insights, questions and discussions on the various aspects of feedback and control phenomena.

---

[4] This is a reference to a financial transaction system. A report of this study is presented in Lehman MM, Perry DE, Ramil JF, Turski WM and Wernick P, Metrics and Laws of Software Evolution – The Nineties View, Proc. Fourth Int. Symp. on Software Metrics, Metrics 97, Albuquerque, New Mexico, 5–7 Nov. 97, pp. 20–32.

[5] For results of this investigation, see the FEAST website http://www.doc.ic.ac.uk/~mml/feast/ ≪as of August 2005≫.

References

[ABD91] T. Abdel-Hamid and S.E. Madnick, *Software Project Dynamics – An Integrated Approach*, Prentice Hall, 1991.

[BL72] L.A. Belady and M.M. Lehman, An Introduction to Program Growth Dynamics. *Statistical Computer Performance Evaluation*, Academic Press, 1972, 503–511.

[Brooks86] F.P. Brooks, No Silver Bullet – Essence and Accidents of Software Engineering. *Proceedings of the IFIP Congress 1986*, Elsevier Science Publishers, Dublin, Ireland, 1069–1076 September 1986.

[CDP95] D.C. Carr, A. Dandekar and D.E. Perry, Experiments in Process Interface Descriptions, Visualizations and Analyses. *Software Process Technology: EWSPT'95*, Noordwijkerhout, The Netherlands, 119–137 (April 1995).

[Feast1] *FEAST Project – Preprints: FEAST Workshop I*, Imperial College, London UK, 16–17 June 1994.

[Feast2] *FEAST Project – Preprints: FEAST Workshop II*, Imperial College, London UK, 24–25 October 1994.

[Feast3] *FEAST Project – Preprints: FEAST Workshop III*, Imperial College, London UK, 28 February–1 March 1995.

[Humphrey95] W. Humphrey, *The Power of Personal Data*, Software Engineering Institute, 1995.

[Lehman69] M.M. Lehman, *The Programming Process*. In M.M. Lehman and L. Belady (eds), *Program Evolution – Processes of Software Change*, Academic Press, 39–83, 1969.

[Lehman85] M.M. Lehman and L. Belady (eds), *Program Evolution – Processes of Software Change*, Academic Press, 1985. Available from links at http://w3.umh.ac.be/evol/publication.html <<as of Oct 2005>>.

[Lehman87] M.M. Lehman, Process Models, Process Programs, Programming Support – Invited Response to a Keynote Address by Lee Osterweil. *Proceedings of the 9th International Conference on Software Engineering*, Monterey CA USA 14–16 (March/April, 1987).

[Lehman95] M.M. Lehman. Software Process Improvement – The Way Forward. *Proceedings CAiSE 95*, LNCS, Springer Verlag, 1–11 (June 1995).

[NR68] P. Nauer and B. Randall (eds), Software Engineering – Report on a Conference, Sponsored by the NATO Science Committee. *Scientific Affairs Division*, NATO, Brussels, Garmisch, 1968. Available online at http://homepages.cs.ncl.ac.uk/brian.randell/NATO/

[Osterweil87] L.J. Osterweil, Software Processes are Software Too, *Proceedings of the 9th International Conference on Software Engineering*, Monterey CA USA, 2–13 (March/April 1987).

[Perry94] Dewayne E. Perry, *Issues in Process Architecture*. Proceedings of the 9th International Software Process Workshop, Airlie VA, 138–140 (October 1994).

[Turski86] W.M. Turski, And No Philosophers Stone Either. *Proceedings of the IFIP Congress 1986*, Elsevier Science Publishers, Dublin, Ireland, 1077–1080 (September 1986).

[VZ95] L.G. Votta and M.L. Zajac, Design Process Improvement Case Study Using Process Waiver Data. *Software Engineering – ESEC'95*, Sitges, Spain, 44–58 (September 1995).

18

Governing Software Evolution through Policy-oriented Feedback

Nazim H. Madhavji and Josée Tassé

Based on "Policy-guided Software Evolution" by Madhavji, N.H and Turgeon, J. Proceedings of the IEEE International Conference on Software Maintenance, September 2003, Amsterdam, pp. 75–82. (c) 2003 IEEE.

18.1 Introduction

It is well recognised that a software system is increasingly more difficult to evolve over time unless appropriate measures are taken. While there are standards (e.g. IEEE 1219 and ISO/IEC 14764) and empirical results in the area of software evolution – such as Lehman's laws [Lehman and Ramil, 2001], evolution patterns of objects in object-oriented systems [Tamai and Nakatani, 1998], the impact of developmental characteristics on maintenance effort [Ramanujan *et al.*, 2000], the impact of the changing environment on software requirements [Nanda and Madhavji, 2002], and many others – today the software engineering community cannot claim that it has software evolution challenges under control.

In this chapter, therefore, we describe an approach that can help in monitoring an evolving software system, or its evolution process, against stipulated policies so that any feedback obtained can be used to improve the software system or its process. The two parts of our approach are

- a *policy-checking mechanism* to detect violations of evolutionary policies and
- a *contextual framework* to support activities of evolving a software system beyond the next release.

This is akin to building a wall of bricks where, from time to time, the builder 'stands back' to assess the progress made and to project the future direction of the wall before laying down the next set of bricks (In this analogy, a brick represents a release, and the wall, a mosaic of releases.).

The policy-checking mechanism requires two key inputs:

- a model (or part thereof) of the product or the process in question (e.g. software architecture decomposition or a data flow diagram) – as an entity-relationship structure (ERD)[1] and
- a formally codified evolutionary policy (e.g. the desirable size-growth limit for the next release) – in first-order logic[2].

It then analyses whether the model satisfies the requirements specified in the policy, yielding, as output, feedback information that managers and developers can analyse to make project decisions.

While the policy-checking mechanism, by itself, has potentially wider applicability (e.g. in checking the conformance of run-time communications between agents in distributed systems[3]), it is unlikely to be adequate without an appropriate 'contextual framework' that helps project staff produce the needed inputs and evolutionary policies, triggers the checking mechanism, and provides guidance on how to use the generated outputs of the policy-checking mechanism.

We have thus developed an overarching framework consisting of three key complementary and interacting components:

- 'new-release development' where the policy-checking mechanism is used in the development of the next release;
- 'across-releases analysis and knowledge-base' where previous releases of the system in question are analysed, projections are made, and knowledge of this is stored – for the development of the next release and
- 'across-products analysis and knowledge-base' where multiple products are analysed, projections are made, and knowledge of this is stored – to make corporate-level decisions on product strategy.

Together, the policy-checking mechanism and the framework provide an approach for managing software evolution. Customisation of this overall approach is also possible, for example, where there is only one system to manage.

The benefit of our approach is that, depending on the specifics of the implemented policies and the kinds of analyses that are made, it would help in: sustaining the quality of a software system as it evolves, reducing evolutionary costs, and improving evolutionary processes.

The rest of this chapter first demonstrates the policy-checking mechanism, followed by a description of the contextual framework. This is followed by some details on implementation and on technological support. We then describe the validity of our approach, related work and conclusions.

---

[1] ERD was our choice when we started the precursor work on elicitation, in 1995 [Turgeon and Madhavji, 1996]. Currently, we are extending our approach to other data models, for example, UML.

[2] First-order logic was chosen for its flexibility and expressiveness, and because it had already been used successfully in [Behm and Teorey, 1993] for specifying business rules on ERD models.

[3] As can be seen in the IEEE International Workshops on Policies for Distributed Systems and Networks (2004 and 2005).

18.2 The Policy-Checking Mechanism

Here, we give two example uses of the policy-checking mechanism. The policies used are derived from third-party empirical work ([Lehman and Ramil, 2001] and [Mattsson and Bosch, 1999]), explained below, and the examples deal with pertinent issues in software evolution, such as incremental growth of a system and re-engineering change-prone modules. For the interested reader, two other third-party examples (on regression test coverage and on consistency between code and documentation) can be accessed from our website http://www.csd.uwo.ca/~nazim/ex.pdf[4].

18.2.1 Controlling System Growth

Over the years, Lehman and his colleagues have observed patterns of incremental growth in large software systems. This, together with the observation that software process performance is constrained by feedback-based system dynamics, led to Lehman's *third law* of software evolution, which states that: '*... system evolution processes are self regulating*', because of feedback mechanisms present in the software process [Lehman and Ramil, 2001]. From these findings they suggest that, assuming the mean of the incremental growth of previous releases is m and their standard deviation is s, a new-release increment is

- *safe* when its incremental growth $\leq m$;
- *risky* when $m <$ incremental growth $< m + 2s$; and
- *unsafe* when incremental growth $\geq m + 2s$.

Similar rules may also result from applying other techniques, for example, *time-series* analysis, as used in [Antoniol *et al.*, 2001].

Let us now consider a 50 K C++ lines of code (LOC) software system (called V-elicit[5]) that has undergone six versions (or internal releases) since 1994. For the purpose of this example, we assume that we are at the moment in time when the sixth version, V6, is under development. Figure 18.1 shows the functional decomposition of the system at this moment in time. This functional decomposition shows that a new component, called '*View Merging*' (version V1), is to be developed (of estimated size 7670 LOC) and it

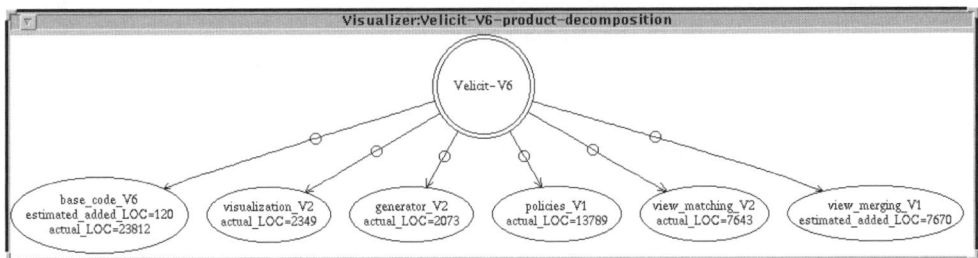

Figure 18.1 Functional decomposition of version 6 of the V-elicit system

---

[4] Last access on 01/02/2006.

[5] V-elicit is a system for eliciting models of products and processes using view-based techniques [Tassé and Madhavji, 2001].

Table 18.1 Previous five versions of V-elicit

Version no.	Size in LOC
V1	23,812
V2	26,161
V3	28,234
V4	42,023
V5	49,666

requires minor changes to the 'base code' (whose estimated increase in size for version V6 is 120 LOC) so as to integrate the new component into the system.

Table 18.1 shows the actual sizes of V-elicit over releases, the average *incremental growth* of which is 6464 LOC. Following the incremental growth rule given in [Lehman and Ramil, 2001], this can now be used to control the growth of version V6 in order to 'prevent' *instability*[6] in subsequent releases and delays in the implementation of further releases.

A policy can thus be specified (in first-order logic), to ensure that the sum of the estimated added LOC over all components does not exceed the mean incremental growth, plus a percentage of error on this upper bound (for example, $+10\%$[7], which, say, is historically used in the projects), for the new release:

Policy 1:
$$\sum_{c \in \{components\}} c.estimated\_added\_LOC \leq 6464 * 1.1$$

The result of verifying the product model (Figure 18.1) against Policy 1 is shown in Figure 18.2. The upper-left window in the figure describes the policy chosen: its name, a formal specification and then an informal description. The upper-right window shows the model being checked (see Figure 18.1), in a text format. Finally, the lower window shows the actual result of policy checking: 'False' means that the policy is *not* satisfied because the estimated size growth of 7790 is beyond the calculated upper bound of 7110.

A decision thus needs to be made to: (i) either take the risk of implementing a largish version, or (ii) decompose the new component to be added into appropriate subparts, which could be implemented as a series of versions. Such decisions have implications for

---

[6] According to Lehman [Lehman and Ramil, 2001]: 'Stability, as sought by management, means *planned* and *controlled* change, not constancy. Managers, including software managers, in general, abhor surprises or unexpected changes. They all desire, for example, constant workloads and increases in productivity; software managers, a steady decline in defects; senior management, a decline in costs and growth in profit and, for example, market share and sales'.

[7] Note that the 10% error margin is only one of the options. [Lehman and Ramil, 2001] suggest 'mean + standard deviation' (which would be 11,979 LOC). However, whatever option is chosen should have an *empirical* validity in the evolving software concerned and in the organisation evolving it. Such empirical validity can be achieved ideally from the study of historical data of the same system and determining the rules, by observing whether larger release increments have been problematic: in terms, for example, of the difficulty in integrating the new code to the existing code base, the error rate, difficulty of acceptance by users who had to learn many new functions and so on.

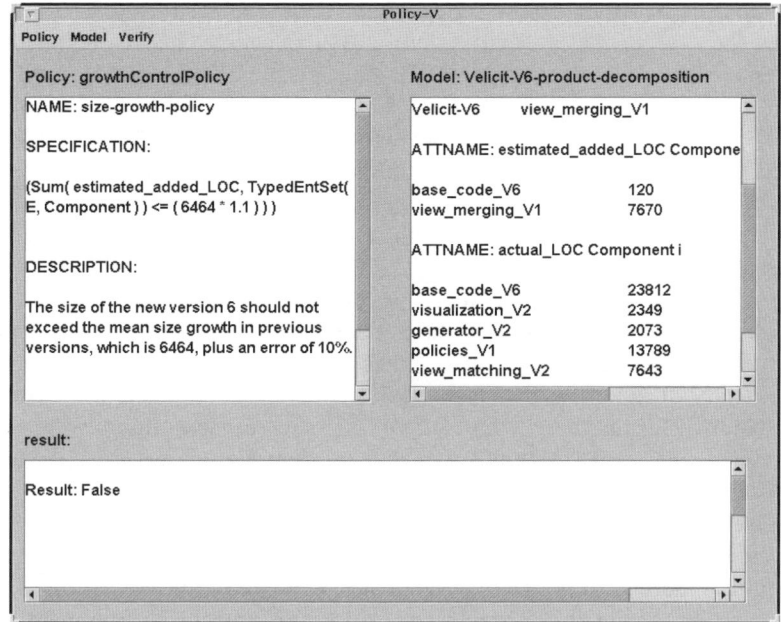

Figure 18.2 Checking the estimated incremental growth against its policy

how the software system would evolve in the future. The largish version, for example, could result in increased system degradation; whereas, the serial versions would permit controlled growth of the system with potentially slower degradation.

Note that Policy 1 could also be specified to automatically compute the mean growth so as not to 'hard-wire' the number '6464'. This would require, as input, the product model decompositions (as in Figure 18.1) of all the (or selected) previous versions.

18.2.2 Re-engineering Change-Prone Modules

In [Mattsson and Bosch, 1999], an approach is proposed to identify those modules of a system that require re-engineering. Proactively maintaining the software (an object-oriented framework in their case) by restructuring the change-prone modules could 'simplify the incorporation of future requirements'. In their approach, the change-prone modules from past releases are identified based on their size, change rate and growth rate.

Once it has been decided which modules or components have to be re-engineered during the development of a particular version, one issue is to ensure that all of the identified modules do go through such an effort. Such verification can be done on a process model, using the following policy:

Policy 2:

$\forall c \in \{p \in \text{TypedEntSet}("Component") \mid p.name \in <list\ of\ components>\}\bullet$

$\quad \exists\ r(a,m,t) \in \text{TypedRelSet}("activity\ consumes\ component")\bullet$

$\qquad a.name = "re\text{-}engineering"$

in which the part <list of components> has to be replaced by the actual list. For example, in the case of the V-elicit system used in Section 18.2.1, one such list could be {"view_matching_V1", "generator_V2"}. The meaning of this policy is that for each component in the list provided, there should be an activity 're-engineering' consuming it.

A process model can then be checked against this policy. The model can either represent the planned process before its enactment (with the policy-checking mechanism used to ensure the plan is complete), or represent the process as it has been performed up to the time when the model was elicited (the policy checking acting as a process monitoring tool in this case).

As an example, Figure 18.3 shows a process model representing the planned process for the development of the sixth version of the V-elicit system. For simplicity, it contains only the high-level activities to be performed: 'make_changes', 're-engineering', and 'testing'. More specifically, it identifies that the 'view_matching' component will need to be re-engineered (moving from version 1 to 2). As one can see here, this plan is not correct: the 'generator' component (version 2, which was identified above for re-engineering) is mistakenly left out from the re-engineering effort (i.e. this component is not an input to the 're-engineering' activity box in Figure 18.3). Such mistakes do happen when building prescriptive models in the planning phase, even in moderate sized projects. This is why it is quite important to verify the planned process (prescriptive model) – against the prescribed policies – prior to its execution, in order to prevent development (and hence evolution) errors.

Figure 18.4 shows the result of verifying the plan against the described policy results in the listing of violations, that is, those components that were supposed to be re-engineered but have not been included in the plan. Note that, in essence, this is an *automated* plan inspection, which is much preferable to hand-checking the plans as carried out (if at that!) in practice today. Its value is particularly felt in large or complex systems, when

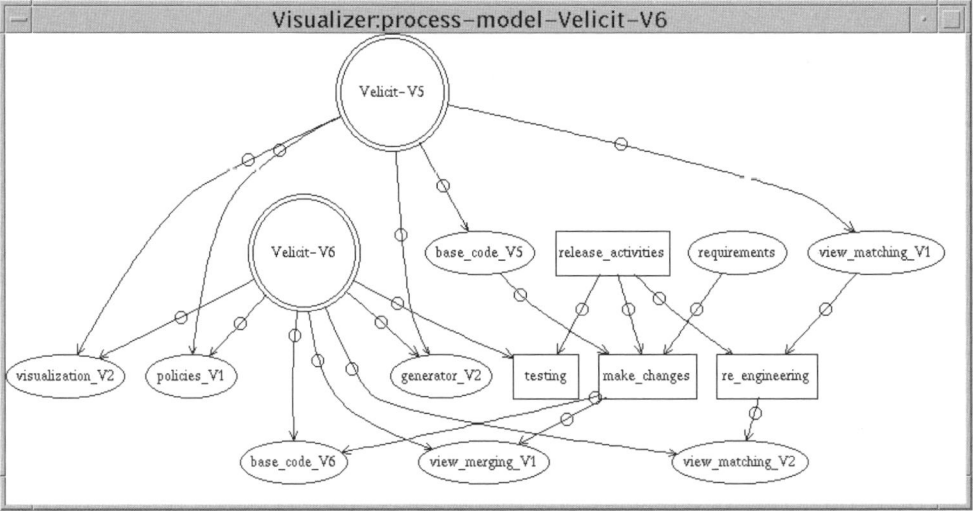

Figure 18.3 Overall process model for the development of the sixth version of V-elicit

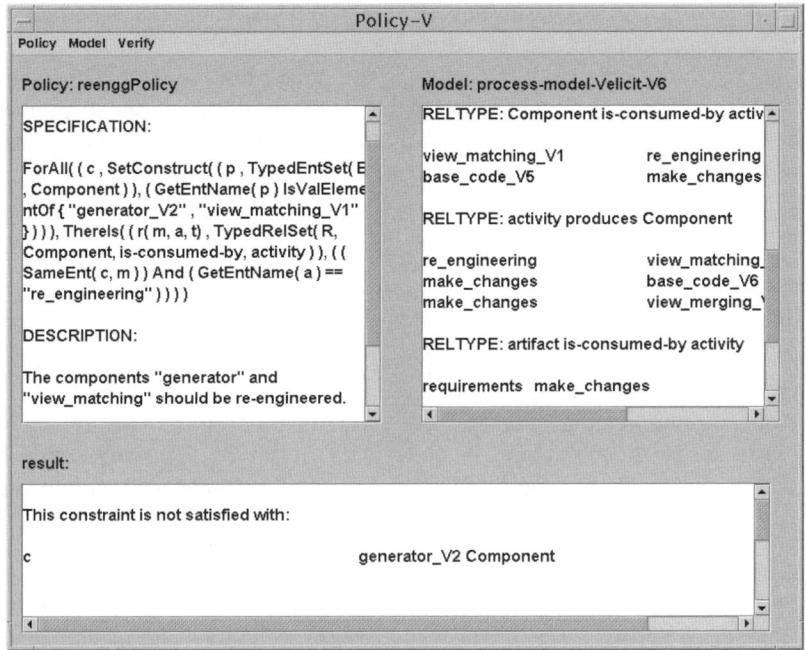

Figure 18.4 Result of the verification that the proper modules have been re-engineered as planned

many individuals are involved in the project, when quality is at stake and when time is at a premium.

It should be noted that this policy could easily be modified to detect automatically which components should be re-engineered. For example, one may want to enforce that components having a change rate higher than a certain level should be re-engineered after a given period of time. Such an assumption can be formally defined and incorporated in the policy above, replacing the fixed list of components.

18.2.3 Discussion

The described two examples, while simple, are illustrative in the basic use of the policy-checking mechanism, which should be separated from its two input 'parameters' (*policy* and the *model* to be checked). This is because the 'relevance' of the outcome (not to be confused with the 'accuracy' of the result) from the policy-checker is directly dependent on the quality of the two input parameters (and not on the policy-checker itself, which we can assume to be correctly implemented), just as much as the relevance of the outcome of executing a computer program is directly dependent on the quality of the program (possibly with its data) and not on the compiler/run-time system.

The policy-checking mechanism can also be used for controlling product evolution over multiple releases. For example, in [Marshall, 1994], the problem of migrating from a centralised system to a client-server architecture is described, which can be carried out gradually over several releases. A policy could thus be specified to ensure a gradual transition to the new architecture by limiting the number of separate servers and clients to be implemented in particular subsequent releases. This is akin to 'standing back' and planning in the wall metaphor described earlier.

Thus, what we have achieved by developing the policy-checker is a shift in complexity from the 'problem' domain (i.e. how to ensure that policy infractions in product design or processes do not go undetected) to the 'solution' domain (i.e. how to determine useful policies, models and data; how to manage these software artefacts; and how to institutionalise the policy-checker in a practical environment.). The solution domain is represented as a contextual framework, described in the next section.

18.3 The Contextual Framework

The framework embodies the described policy-checker in the day-to-day development of a new release, the different types of staff-roles involved in the release development, and numerous communication and feedback links. In this section, we first describe our vision of how a new release could be developed, followed by a subsection on roles, communication and feedback, and finally we describe the framework architecture.

18.3.1 New-Release Development

Figure 18.5 depicts key activities and related entities involved in policy checking during the development of a new release. The key purpose of these is to ensure that the new release is being developed according to the software evolution goals of the product over a period of time.

The activity (depicted by a box) *Verify* checks the *models* of the system or process concerned against the policies (as described in Section 18.2). The verification results are analysed and feedback is provided to the appropriate stakeholders for improvement of the models (and policies[8]) that, eventually, could lead to product or process changes.

Two inputs are necessary for the Verify box:

- a product or process model and
- related policies.

For the first input, a product model can be obtained from system documentation or, in its absence, can be elicited or reverse-engineered. If the model is that of a process then a *descriptive* model can be elicited [Tassé and Madhavji, 2001], and a *prescriptive* model can be either a modified descriptive model or developed anew – considering such inputs in its design as:

- feedback from verification,
- adopted policies,
- product information, and
- external knowledge (as analyses results from previous releases of this product and from other projects).

---

[8] We recognise that the framework has important implications for policy changes (i.e. the meta-level) but because the focus here is software primarily, the policy-centred work (including the management of a set of policies) is outside the scope of this chapter.

Governing Software Evolution through Policy-oriented Feedback

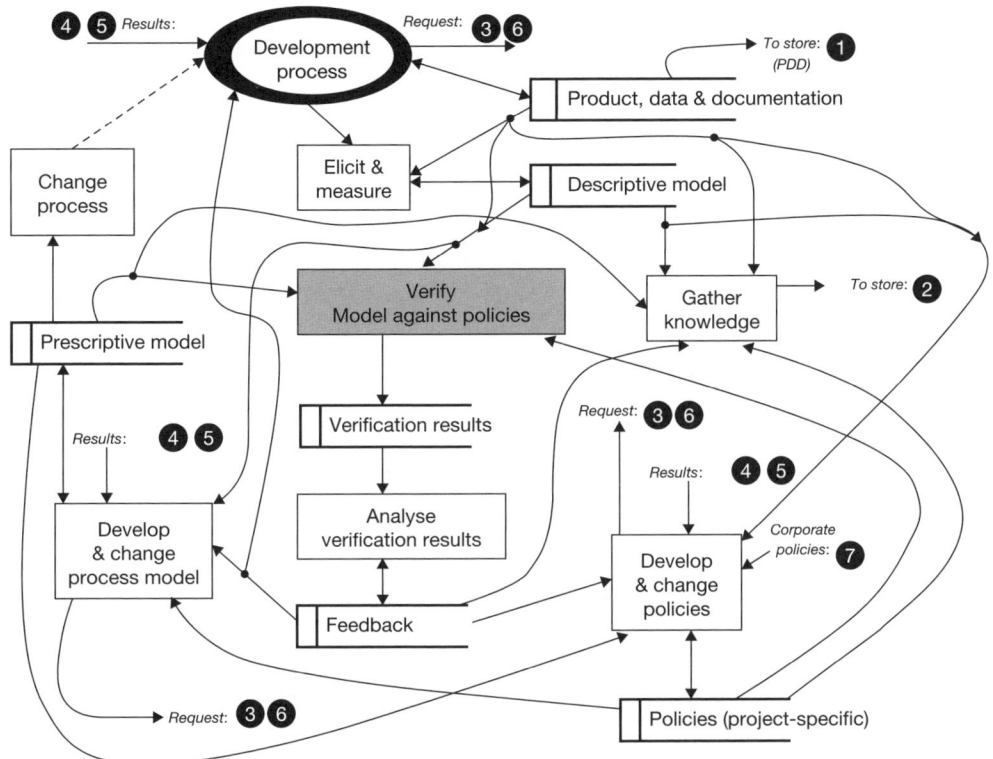

Figure 18.5 New-release development

For the second input, the policies adopted in the project are developed from information obtained from various sources, such as:

- verification feedback,
- project performance data,
- prescriptive and descriptive models,
- external knowledge,
- corporate-level policies,
- and, of course, expert judgement.

The ellipse at the top of Figure 18.5 represents the enacted new-release development process, which results in product descriptions and project data.

That said, this component (Figure 18.5) should not operate in isolation, in much the same way a bricklayer would not generally operate without respecting a grander plan for wall design. This is why this component interfaces with other components of the framework (Figure 18.6) via links 3 and 6, 4 and 5, and 7 in Figure 18.5, which provide information pertaining to the evolution of the next release under development.

It is in this set of activities, release after release, that the grip over *system evolution variables* of the product (such as system complexity over time, architectural integrity over

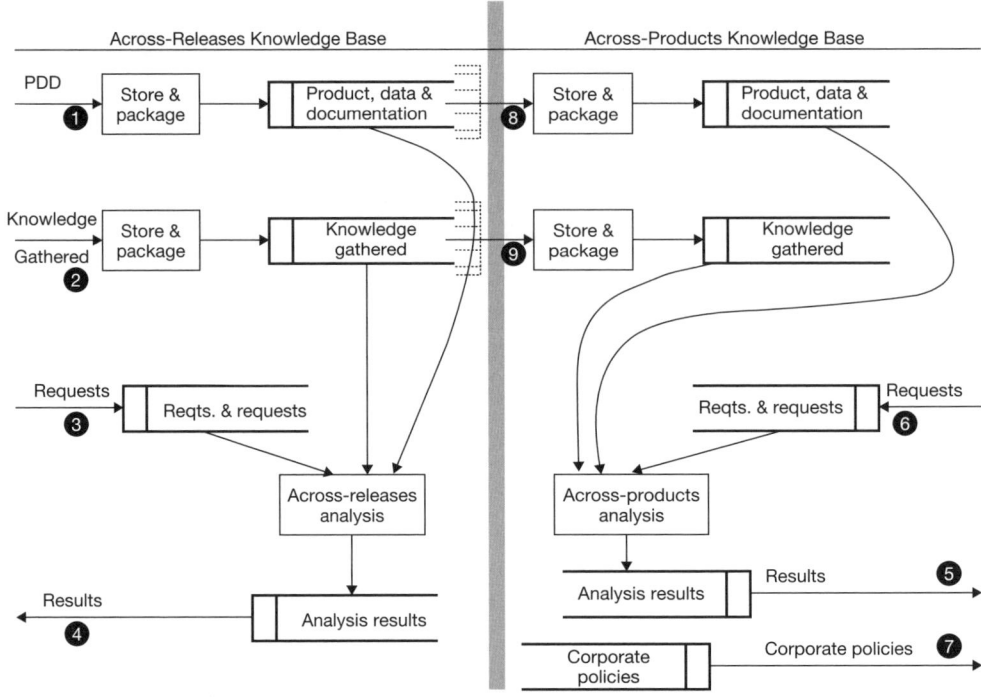

Figure 18.6 Knowledge bases: across releases and across products

time, defect quality over time and others) is either maintained under control or lost to system degradation. It is in this set of activities, at any given time, that *future* evolution of the system should be of primary concern and that the *professional* or *moral responsibility* of the new-release development team towards the future teams is most called upon.

18.3.2 Roles, Communication and Feedback

Apart from the technical matters described above, there are important *organisational* matters in the use of the framework. For example, we distinguish, at least logically, between the roles *release development* team and *evolution* team. Whereas the former role is expressly focused upon the *development* of the new release (as depicted in Figure 18.5), the latter role is expressly focused upon the *analysis* of how the system is evolving within the larger picture of (i) across releases and (ii) across products (as depicted in the partitioned Figure 18.6). For example, it is the development team's responsibility to ensure that system complexity is within the established limits. But it is the evolution team's responsibility to examine theories, data and other knowledge across releases and products, from which complexity policies may be designed or updated.

In making clear distinctions between the two role types, communication and feedback between them become crucial in their practical implementation. For example, some communication and feedback may be based on *explicit requests* made by the development team (e.g. outgoing links 3 and 6 in Figure 18.5 from the enacted process, *Develop & change process model*, or *Develop & change policies* to the respective destinations in

Figure 18.6). Yet another may be based on contractual *service-level agreements* between the two types of teams (e.g. periodic reports on complexity, defect-quality and size-growth trends and comparisons with previous releases and other products and processes). Both types of feedback, request-based and contractual, are returned to the developing team, from the evolution team, in the form of analysis results (e.g. input links 4 and 5 in Figure 18.5).

Finally, in keeping with the professional or moral responsibility of the current development team towards the future development teams, pertinent information and knowledge is gathered during current development for archival purposes (see the box *Gather knowledge* and link 2 in Figure 18.5). This information along with the product resulting from current development (link 1, Figure 18.5) form the primary inputs for processing *across-releases* evolutionary information in the left half of Figure 18.6 (box *Across-releases analysis*). Similarly, the right half of Figure 18.6 shows that information and knowledge from different products (each with all the releases) are packaged and stored (links 8 and 9) and subsequently used for *across-products* analyses. All analyses results are relayed to the development team (outgoing links 4 and 5 in Figure 18.6). In addition, there is a corporate policy base, created by corporate analysts, from which organisation-wide policies are relayed to the development projects (link 7 Figures 18.5 and 18.6).

We can clearly see the significance of (a) the complementary roles: *release-development* team and *evolution* team, and (b) the way they interact, in the evolution of a software system. The first role has the specialised knowledge and immediate concern for the development of the next release, guided by the policies that rest upon theories, findings from empirical analysis of previous releases, and upon prediction models resultant from the activities pertaining to the second role. They are essentially interlocked with each other to make evolution work.

18.3.3 The Framework Architecture

The numerous activities and interactions described above can be summarised in a framework architecture, as shown in Figure 18.7, in which there are three major components:

- *New-release development* (box 'A'), for the development of a new release;
- *Across-releases knowledge-base* (box 'B'), for storing and analysing past releases (if any) of the product being developed; and
- *Across-products knowledge-base* (box 'C'), for storing and analysing other products (with all their releases), if any.

This *separation of concern* among the three components is important because it permits specific focus on a given component with respect to its modularity, design, implementation, tools support, personnel training and selection and so on.

Behaviourally, there would be more frequent interactions between box 'A' and box 'B' than between box 'A' and box 'C' because, on a daily basis, a new-release development would generally benefit more from specific information pertaining to the past or predicted releases of the same product than from that pertaining to other products. Examples include size-growth trend, code complexity trend, testing effort to code change ratios and so on.

Whereas the impact of this information is *quite specific* on the release under development, that from box 'C' to box 'A' is likely to be *wide* because it would likely affect

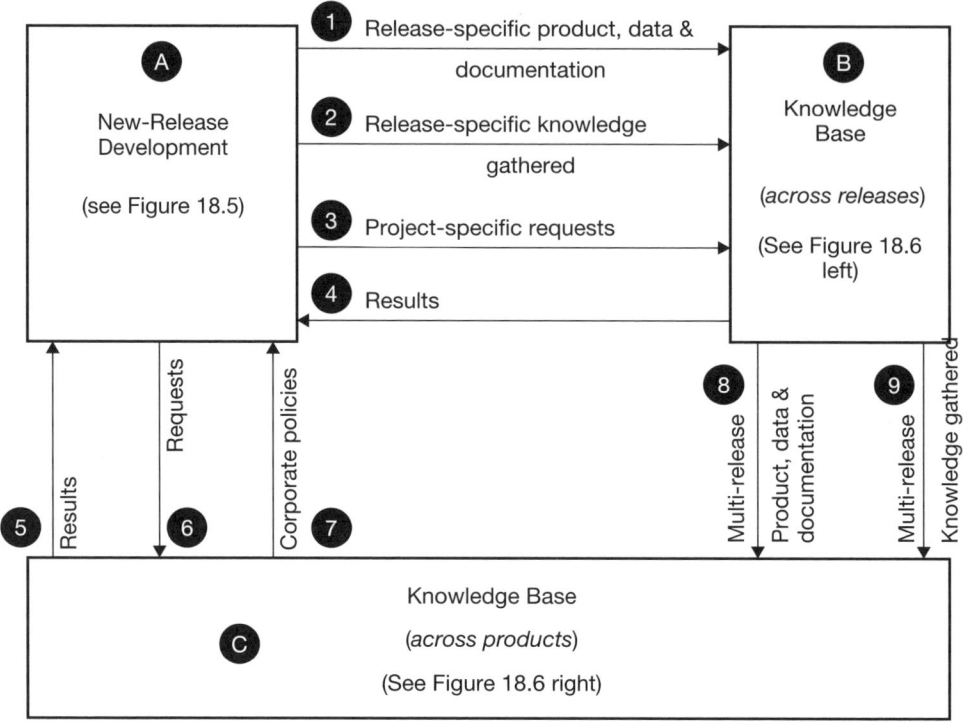

Figure 18.7 Framework-architecture: global components and interaction

such issues as product-wide quality control, work practices, tool usage, platform support, cycle-time, budget, resource constraints, standardisation and so on, which are potentially quite destabilising. Because of the high risk associated with these interactions, it clearly calls for extreme care as to when such perturbations are enacted from box 'C' to box 'A'. Past experience shows that lack of timely interactions of this nature can easily put the system out of use, not because functionally the system is defective (which too can occur) but because the system no longer satisfies key nonfunctional requirements [Nanda and Madhavji, 2002]. The information flow from box 'B' to box 'C' is broad range knowledge gathering from different products and projects so that information can be shared across projects (links 5 and 6) and corporate policies can be stipulated (link 7).

The benefits of modelling the described architecture are as follows:

- it acts as a *reference model* knowing well its lower-level details (as described in the subsections above), and
- it enables one to focus on the component interfaces, hiding the implementation details.

In turn, these have second-order benefits, such as portability of the framework, customisation, assessment, improvement, vision sharing and others.

Finally, note that Figure 18.7 depicts purely a *logical* view of the framework. That is, it could be tailored structurally and operationally to suit specific needs of an organisation.

For example, large organisations could adopt a *physical* separation between boxes 'A', 'B' and 'C' (as in Basili's experience factory concept [Basili *et al.*, 1992]) and have a more comprehensive evolution agenda; whereas, smaller operations, perhaps because of budget and resource constraints, may choose to adopt an *integrated* approach with time-shared role switching as well as selective agendas on policies and checking.

18.4 Technological Support

In this section, we describe the technological underpinnings of the two main issues presented thus far: one, the policy-checking mechanism (Section 18.2) and, two, the framework (Section 18.3).

18.4.1 Policy-Checking Mechanism

There are two tools of particular interest here:

- Policy-M for *specification* of a policy, and
- Policy-V for *verification* of a product model against the specified policy.

In Policy-M, a policy (e.g. see Policy 1 in Figure 18.2) can be specified either as a textual string, in a language based on first-order logic, or in a 'structured' manner using menu buttons for logical symbols, such as 'ThereIs', 'ForAll' and 'SetConstruct', which are then expanded to form the final policy string. The (partial) grammar for this language, in a BNF-like notation, is as shown in Figure 18.8.

In this language, entities of a product model or process model are elements of set 'E', and relationships are elements of set 'R'. These sets are used in specifying 'list expressions'. For a 'condition', the language contains all the arithmetic and logic operators, set

```
constraint     ::= ForAll  ( elementInSet , constraint )
               |  ThereIs ( elementInSet , constraint )
               |  condition
elementInSet   ::= ( elementVariable, listExpression )
elementVariable ::= entityVariable
               |  relationVariable
entityVariable ::= <name>
relationVariable ::= <name>( entityVariable,
                              entityVariable,stringVariable )
listExpression ::=
       Set(<name>)
    |  TypedEntSet(<set name>,<entity type>)
    |  TypedRelSet(<set name>,<entity type>,
                      <relation>,<entity type>)
    |  SetConstruct(elementInSet,condition )
    |  (listExpression listOperator listExpression)
listOperator   ::=  Union
               |    Intersection
```

Figure 18.8 Partial grammar for policy specification

functions, as well as *built-in* functions for such purposes as:

- accessing particular parts of a model (e.g. name or attributes of an entity);
- finding paths, even indirect ones, between given entities in a model;
- computing temporal values;
- comparing entities and
- computations on sets (e.g. cardinality, sum or average of the elements in the set).

The grammar consists of 31 production rules, and 66 built-in functions divided roughly equally between those for mathematical functions and those for operations on ERD models.

The Policy-V tool, on the other hand, accepts as input a policy string (specified using the Policy-M tool) and an ERD model, or part thereof, of a product or process[9]. The output is the verification result, as described in Section 18.2. Internally, a policy string is represented as an 'abstract syntax' tree; whereas, an ERD model is represented as a graph with type and attribute information. The model checking starts at the *root* node of the policy (the 'constraint' nonterminal symbol in Figure 18.8), with the call to an 'evaluate' function in this node. Basically, almost all nodes contain such a function (except list expressions, which are responsible for building, not evaluating, the list specified in the expression). These functions return a 'truth' value or other values (e.g. numbers, strings, char, etc.), and in the case of a nonterminal symbol, the result of evaluating the subtree nodes. Figure 18.9 shows an algorithm for the 'evaluate' function in a Constraint node. The algorithm's structure is based on the derivation chosen in the rule for 'constraint' (see Figure 18.8), making calls to the related objects down in the syntax tree. In the case of the `ForAll` clause, the algorithm goes through all elements in the set, retaining the values for which the rest of the constraint is not satisfied. In the `ThereIs` clause, a similar loop is used, but the evaluation stops as soon as the constraint is satisfied for one of the values. Finally, for a condition, the evaluation is just forwarded to the condition itself. The resultant list, containing all the values in the `ForAll` clause that do not satisfy the constraint, is displayed only after the entire verification is performed. That is, not incrementally in the 'evaluate' function because, say, in the case that the constraint contained two `ForAll` clauses in sequence then we would like to be able to show pairs of elements not satisfying the constraint.

18.4.2 Framework

Technological support for the verification of a new release rests on key functions (see Figure 18.5) such as Elicitation of product and process models, Measurement, Develop & change process models, Verify model against policies, Analyse verification results, Develop & change policies, and Gather knowledge. In support of these functions, already there are

- research prototypes for advanced elicitation (e.g. V-elicit) [Tassé and Madhavji, 2001] and simulation [Raffo *et al.*, 1999] of product or process models, and

---

[9] Both are provided as structured text files (format used in V-elicit [Tassé and Madhavji, 2001]), and it is assumed that the use of external tools (e.g. for process modelling) is possible through the implementation of a specific file/data translator.

```
constraint::evaluate
  if ''ForAll''
        result ← true
        call ElementInSet.buildSet()
        for each e ← call ElementInSet.getNext()
              eval ← call Constraint.evaluate(e)
              if eval = false
                    add e.name in result list
                    result ← false
        return result
  if ''ThereIs''
        call ElementInSet.buildSet()
        for each e ← call ElementInSet.getNext()
              eval ← call Constraint.evaluate(e)
              if eval = true
                    return true
        return false
  if ''condition''
        return result ← call Condition.evaluate()
```

Figure 18.9 Algorithm for the evaluation of a constraint node

- commercially available CASE tools (e.g. Rational Rose, Oracle Designer and Together ControlCenter for software; and Statemate, WebSphere Business Integration Modeler, ProVision and AI0 WIN for process modelling) based on ERD, UML, state transitions, petri-nets and other representations.

Likewise, for measurement there are tools such as Slim, Anova, SPC, TychoMetrics, Minitab, Metric ONE, McCabe and others. Verification tools such as Policy–V are currently experimental, as are tools for modelling policies such as Policy–M, both of which originally were integrated components of V-elicit [Tassé and Madhavji, 2001]. Similarly, with reference to Figure 18.6, metric tools, program analysis and understanding, and reverse engineering tools can support the function Across-releases analysis. For the function Across-products analysis, in addition to the mentioned tools, there are architectural description approaches and tools (e.g. patterns, UML and Searchable Bookshelf) and product-line approaches.

From all this[10], it is clear that there is no *technological* reason why the overall approach to software evolution as described in this chapter cannot be implemented in the software organisations. Indeed, much needed feedback would be gained to promulgate long-term thinking, while optimising short-term concerns, in software development and evolution.

18.5 Evaluation

There are several different types of evaluation of a concept, for example, *logical soundness*, as it might pertain to the components and their inter-relationships; *literature*

---

[10] A tabulated form of this description with commentary is accessible from: http://www.csd.uwo.ca/~nazim/Table.pdf (last access on 20/01/2006).

validation, based on published work; *technological* validation, that there is method and tool support; and *empirical* validation, based on case studies and industrial experience. Also, the concept, as a whole, may be composed of sub-components that have undergone different validation types.

In our case, the V-elicit tool [Tassé and Madhavji, 2001] (used for elicitation of product and process models – see 'Elicit & Measure' in Figure 18.5) has been validated through industrial-scale case studies [Turgeon and Madhavji, 2000a] involving actual models of the Preliminary Analysis (or Requirements Engineering) phase of software development and several laboratory-based case and control studies. The Policy-M and Policy-V tools (recently decoupled from V-elicit) have been used in specific case studies to verify models against 35 of Davis' 201 *principles* specified as policies [Davis, 1995]. From Lehman's *Laws* of Evolution [Lehman and Ramil, 2001], we have specified 42 policies, one of which, for example, is related to the law called *Self Regulation* (Policy no. 1, Section 18.2.1). We have also developed numerous policies from other third-party work, for example, [Mattsson and Bosch, 1999]: *'restructuring the change-prone modules could simplify the incorporation of future requirements'*; [Humphrey, 1996]: optimal value of *'Appraisal-to-failure ratio'*; and [Ramanujan *et al.*, 2000]: *'a standard for variable naming reduces maintenance effort in large projects'*. Such policies form a basis for model verification, as described in Section 18.2, and this demonstrates that evolutionary policies are possibly ubiquitous.

Zooming out to the level of the framework architecture (see Figure 18.7), the described support in Section 18.4.2 gives technological validity to the architecture. In addition, the *logical* separation of *development* activities (Figure 18.5) from *evolution* activities (Figure 18.6) is analogous to the *physical* separation of concern in Basili's experience factory concept [Basili *et al.*, 1992] between development and packaging, implemented at NASA.

While the degree of validation we have attained to date can be considered substantive, there are still many other challenges yet to overcome. For example, the fact that the tool can implement policies does not imply that the policies are guaranteed to have expected effect on the long-term evolution of the system. The on-going situation, such as the relevance and efficacy of the set of implemented policies, the effectiveness with which the feedback is analysed and the quality of the changes implemented are but three of many possible examples of factors that could influence the long-term health of a software system.

Another aspect is the acceptance of the technology by developers and managers. If the policies are authoritatively enforced, there is no doubt that the quality of the work environment would be adversely affected. For example, market pressures could easily dictate the need to release a system even though the system's indicators might suggest otherwise. This dilemma is similar to that faced in the automation of nonadministrative processes in an environment.

These considerations suggest that there are many aspects of the evaluation of the approach, which are difficult to tackle and progress is likely to come from empirically observing how the system delivers in different situations and from fine tuning the system parameters.

18.6 Related Work

The central issue in this research surrounds:

- whether the *development* in Figure 18.5 is in line with the *evolutionary* plans obtained from Figure 18.6 and
- taking corrective actions.

In this respect, we are not aware of any other alternative model to make direct comparisons against. However, the basic notion of process or product *deviations* from given specifications has been examined by other researchers.

In particular, Darwin [Minsky, 1991] had *rules* (in Prolog) about the exchange of messages, thus defining authorities and responsibilities of the different roles in a development process. Actions conducted by an agent that deviated from the applicable rules were thus flagged. In PROSYT [Cugola, 1998], deviations to the planned process are tolerated as long as the *invariants* on the states of the process and those on the artefacts are not violated. Also, Balzer [Balzer, 1991] has proposed the use of 'pollution markers' to isolate process components that have deviated from the policies until they are resolved. In [Cimpan and Oquendo, 2000], deviations are identified by measuring some process attributes and comparing them with expected values (representing expected behaviour). Alarms are sounded when specified threshold values are crossed.

Clearly, such systems can play an important role in software development, and it appears that their focus, explicitly or implicitly, is on the *detection* of violations. In contrast to this, while such detection is also possible in our approach (e.g. when checking a *descriptive* process model against a stated policy), it has also been designed to deal with *preventive* aspects of software *evolution*. For example, the projected 'size growth' of a planned new release (in Figure 18.2) can be checked against recommended growth limits (emanating from the analysis in Figure 18.6), and corrective actions taken to ensure, *prior* to its release, that the *evolution* goals are met. It is thus hoped that such a mechanism should increase user satisfaction with evolving systems and reduce evolution costs.

In [Emmerich *et al.*, 1999], the authors describe support for checking a document based on its structure against related standards (or policies). On the occurrence of specific events (e.g. opening or closing a file), the document is checked against the related standards (specified in first-order logic). The relevance of this work is significant in the area of quality control.

Also, in [Nuseibeh *et al.*, 2000], a conceptual framework is described for managing inconsistencies among software artifacts such as models, specifications, design and so on, which can be quite helpful for software development. Their framework overlaps with our verification loop where we check for policy violation and take corrective action. In their work, they provide guidance on the key steps (e.g. the inconsistencies identified may also be classified and their impact measured – although no technique is provided for performing such task). Our work covers additional aspects such as from where to obtain the information to be checked ('elicit and measure'), what should be stored for future analysis and the actual development of policies.

Finally, in contrast to the related work, our work has evolved, over a decade, from the notion of *process fitness* (based on discrete project variables and cause-effect relationships) in 1992, culminating in Perez's thesis in 1994 and a paper in 1996 [Perez *et al*., 1996]. We then used this idea in the verification of process models as early as 1994–1995, and initial ideas were published in [Turgeon and Madhavji, 1996], in Tassés thesis, and in [Tassé and Madhavji, 2001]. In 1999, we took this work a step further into the domain of *co-evolution* [Turgeon and Madhavji, 2000b], and more recently into the area of software evolution, as described in this chapter.

18.7 Conclusions

Software evolution is inevitable for the survivability of a software system and, in many cases, of the organisation owning the system. An 'ultimate challenge' is to be able to evolve a system such that:

- a succeeding release is always of a *superior* quality compared to the preceding ones, despite its aging, and
- the task actually gets *simpler* over time.

While we may someday aspire to rise to such a challenge, in this chapter we take a more humble, but novel, approach of architecting a model where evolutionary policies are used to keep the development of a new release under check as a way of *preventing* many avoidable problems with evolving software systems.

We are convinced that software does not evolve in a desired way simply by executing current release projects as best as possible, in much the same way that a wall does not evolve as desired simply by laying down individual bricks as best as possible. This condition is necessary but not sufficient. There is a need to focus explicitly on past and future releases of the software to *drive* the development of the new release, in much the same way as there is a need to 'stand back' from time to time and examine the evolving wall from a distance and project its evolution into the future according to some plans before laying down the next set of bricks. The described policy-checking mechanism and the framework architecture are precisely this type of mechanism. Further, the underlying technologies and our experimentation to date give validity to our approach. While this is an important step forward, future work will need to involve enhancing the multiple-policies features of Policy-V and Policy-M tools and their actual use in industrial software organisations.

References

Antoniol G., Casazza G., De Penta M. and Merlo E., "Modeling clones evolution through time series". *Proceedings of International Conference on Software Maintenance*, Florence, Italy, 2001, pp. 273–280.

Balzer R., "Tolerating inconsistency", *Proceedings of 13th International Conference on Software Engineering*, Austin, Texas, IEEE CS Press, May 1991, pp. 158–165.

Basili V., Caldiera G., McGerry F., Pojarski R., Page G. and Waligera S., "The software engineering laboratory – an operational software experience factory", *Proceedings of the 14th International Conference on Software Engineering*, Melbourne, ACM Press, June 1992, pp. 370–381.

Behm J.B. and Teorey T.J., "Relative constraints in ER data models", *Proceedings of 12th International Conference on the Entity Relationship Approach*, Arlington, Texas, Springer-Verlag, LNCS #823, 1993, pp. 46–59.

Cimpan S. and Oquendo F., "Dealing with software process deviations using fuzzy logic based monitoring", *ACM SIGAPP Appl. Comput. Rev. Arch.*, vol. 8, no. 2, Fall 2000, pp. 3–13.

Cugola G., "Tolerating deviations in process support systems via flexible enactment of process models", *IEEE Trans. Soft. Eng.*, vol. 24 no. 11, 1998, pp. 982–1001.

Davis A., *"201 Principles of Software Development"*, McGraw Hill, 1995.

Emmerich W., Finklestein A., Antonelli S., Armitage S. and Stevens R., "Managing standards compliance", *IEEE Trans. Soft. Eng.*, vol. 25 no. 6, 1999, pp. 836–850.

Humphrey W.S., "Using a defined and measured personal software process", *IEEE Softw.*, vol. 13 no. 3, 1996, pp. 77–88.

Lehman M.M. and Ramil J.F., "Rules and tools for software evolution planning and management", *Ann. Softw. Eng.*, vol. 11, 2001, pp. 15–44. Also in this volume.

Marshall A.D., "Supporting communications infrastructure evolution", *Proceedings of CAS conference (on CD-ROM)*, sponsored by IBM/NRC/NSERC/Industry Canada, Oct. 1994, paper available at www.cs.ubc.ca/local/reading/proceedings/cascon94/htm/english/abs/marshall.htm (last access on 20/01/2006).

Mattsson M. and Bosch J., "Observations on the evolution of an industrial OO framework", *Proceedings of the International Conference on Software Maintenance – 1999*, pp. 139–145, 1999.

Minsky N.H., "Law-governed systems", *Softw. Eng. J.*, vol. 6 no. 5, 1991, pp. 285–302.

Nanda V. and Madhavji N.H., "The impact of environmental evolution on requirements changes", *Proceedings of International Conference on Software Maintenance*, Montreal, October 2002, pp. 452–461. Also in this volume.

Nuseibeh B., Easterbrook S. and Russo A., "Leveraging inconsistency in software development", *IEEE Comp.*, vol. 33 no. 4, 2000, pp. 24–29.

Perez G., Emam K.E. and Madhavji N.H., "A system for evaluating the congruence of software process models", *Proceedings of the 4th International Conference on Software Process*, Brighton, UK, Dec. 1996, pp. 49–62.

Raffo D.M., Vandeville J.V. and Martin R., "Software process simulation to achieve higher CMM levels", *J. Syst. Softw.*, vol. 46, no. 2/3, 1999, pp. 163–172.

Ramanujan S., Scamell R.W. and Shah J.R., "An experimental investigation of the impact of individual, program, and organizational characteristics on software maintenance effort", *J. Syst. Softw.*, vol. 54 no. 2, 2000, pp. 137–157.

Tamai T. and Nakatani T., "An empirical study of object evolution processes", *Proceedings of International Workshop on Principles of Software Evolution*, Kyoto, Japan, April 1998, pp. 33–37.

Tassé J. and Madhavji N.H., "View-based process elicitation: a user's perspective", *Softw. Process Improv. Pract.*, vol. 6 no. 3, 2001, pp. 125–139.

Turgeon J. and Madhavji N.H., "A systematic, view-based approach to eliciting process models", *Proceedings of Fifth European Workshop on Software Process Technology*, Nancy, France, LNCS #1149, October 1996, pp. 276–282.

Turgeon J. and Madhavji N.H., "View-based vs Traditional modeling approaches: which is better?", *Proceedings of 7th European Workshop on Software Process Technology*, Kaprun, Austria, Springer-Verlag, LNCS #1780, February 2000a, 131–137.

Turgeon J. and Madhavji N.H., "A model for process congruence", *Proceedings of the International Workshop on Feedback and Evolution on Software and Business Processes*, Imperial College, London (UK), July 2000b. (http://www.doc.ic.ac.uk/~mml/f2000) (last access on 20/01/2006).

19

Feedback in Requirements Discovery and Specification: A Quality Gateway for Testing Requirements

Suzanne Robertson

19.1 Contents of the Requirements Specification

Effective feedback is received when somebody understands something well enough to be able to constructively react to it. The receiving stakeholder must be able to understand a requirement to be able to register agreement or disagreement and constructively point out flaws or misconceptions. If this is done successfully and continually, development time and cost and the probability of an unsatisfactory product is minimised. Given a well-specified understanding of the content of a requirements specification, then one can establish whether or not a given specification meets the standard for requirements specifications. In other words, one must be able to test a specification to establish whether or not it contains the expected requirements and whether those requirements are understandable from the point of view of all the relevant stakeholders.

To test successfully requires a set of criteria against which to test, and a choice of what is most appropriate to test. A good place to start is to consider what sort of information is needed in a requirements specification. This raises a problem because 'requirements specification' is one of the most elastic terms in current use. It is common experience that the individual specifications reviewed vary widely in the components that they contain and in the level of detail provided for each component. Some specifications contain purely functional requirements, others include nonfunctional or quality requirements, some contain all the project constraints, some specify the stakeholders, some include business goals, some

---

Software Evolution and Feedback: Theory and Practice   Nazim H. Madhavji, Juan C. Fernández-Ramil and Dewayne E. Perry
© 2006 John Wiley & Sons, Ltd

concentrate on the solution – and all these are expressed at differing levels of detail – the variations are endless. However, without some consistent agreement on what is intended in a particular specification it is impossible to test the quality of its contents.

Figure 19.1 is the table of contents of a requirements specification template [1] that has been built following the experience of working on many different projects. The template is intended as a guide for gathering and communicating the knowledge and understanding that is relevant to the project's requirements.

Requirements Specification Table of Contents

PROJECT DRIVERS
    1. The Purpose of the Product
    2. Client, Customer and other Stakeholders
    3. Users of the Product

PROJECT CONSTRAINTS
    4. Mandated Constraints
    5. Naming Conventions and Definitions
    6. Relevant Facts and Assumptions

FUNCTIONAL REQUIREMENTS
    7. The Scope of the Work
    8. The Scope of the Product
    9. Functional and Data Requirements

NONFUNCTIONAL REQUIREMENTS
    10. Look and Feel
    11. Usability
    12. Performance
    13. Operational
    14. Maintainability and Portability
    15. Security
    16. Cultural and Political
    17. Legal

PROJECT ISSUES
    18. Open Issues
    19. Off-the-Shelf Solutions
    20. New Problems
    21. Tasks
    22. Cutover
    23. Risks
    24. Costs
    25. User Documentation and Training
    26. Waiting Room
    27. Ideas for Solutions

Figure 19.1 The summary level table of contents for the Volere requirements template (downloadable from http://www.volere.co.uk) identifies the components of a requirements specification

One may consider the template as the basis for the requirements *content*, information that needs to be communicated for an effective specification that can lead to a satisfactory implementation. This is different from the *form* of the requirements, the medium chosen to communicate it. This latter is often a document or a series of documents, but it can also be discussions, demonstrations, simulations, emails, meetings, recordings or any mixture of these or other media that successfully communicate the relevant information to the relevant people. But though all these play a role, it is vital to avoid future conflict that an agreed record exists. In practice, therefore, however extracted, requirements information is recorded and communicated in the form of documents. But even then it is rare that all the information exists in one document or that the documents that exist are designated as requirements specifications. An organisation might, for example, publish a series of documents, a feasibility study, a business case, a functional specification, a project plan, a preliminary design specification, a detailed design specification and so on. Each of these documents will contain some mixture of requirements information and the latter will be at levels of detail depending on the way that projects in the organisation are conducted and the methodologies employed.

The template may be thought of as a gigantic filing cabinet containing 27 drawers. Each such drawer contains the necessary information relevant to a particular aspect of the system to be developed and the project that is to do this, along with suggestions for making that information accessible and understandable. The objective is, of course, to encourage early feedback from all stakeholders.

19.2 Project Drivers

Drawers number 1, 2 and 3 contain *Project Drivers*, information that is necessary in order to decide which requirements to gather and from where they should be gathered.

The contents of drawer number 1 explain the purpose of the product. A vital piece of requirements information is the reason for undertaking the project. This information must include measurable goals for building the product. Unless there is unambiguous understanding of the goals, subjective judgements will lead to an unsatisfactory, in many cases irrelevant, solution.

The *stakeholders* are also project drivers. They are, in fact, so important that two drawers of the cabinet have been allocated to them. Drawer 2 contains details about the client, the customer and the other stakeholders. The client is the person or the organisation who is paying for the development of the product, the person who is making the investment. The customer is the person or persons who can influence the purchase or adoption of the product. While the client and customer roles are different, in some cases they might be played by the same person or split between several people. Other stakeholders include all the people who have some kind of interest in the project. This might be because they have an active role in building or using it or it might be because their knowledge is necessary to make it fit into the world. The first step towards discovering all the requirements is to understand who all the stakeholders are, what roles they are expected to play, how much involvement they need to have and how committed they are to the project. Drawer 3 is devoted to potential direct users of the product. Here, one is talking about people who have hands on contact with the product. In short, one needs to understand the project's sociology.

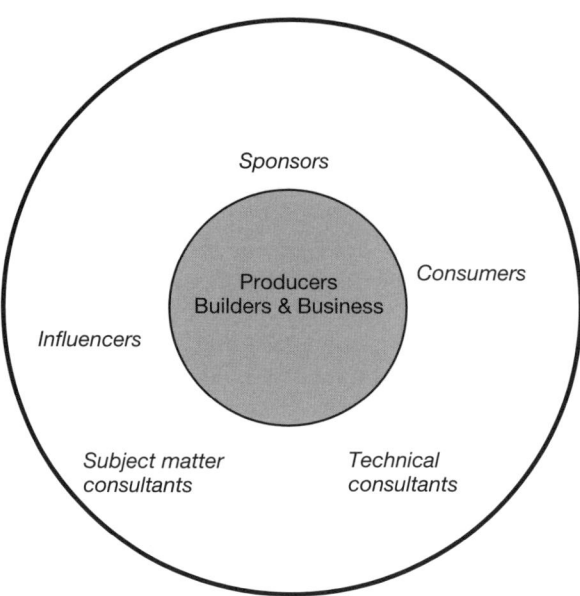

Figure 19.2 Different types of stakeholders make different contributions to the project

Participants in recent commercial workshops and projects have suggested that one needs a better way of classifying stakeholders than by referring to *users* and *developers*. Figure 19.2 develops this idea by identifying a number of different types of stakeholders whose participation is potentially necessary for a project's success. Each of these can provide feedback about his own particular knowledge and concerns. However, in order to stimulate that feedback the requirements engineer may have to provide a feedback mechanism that is appropriate for the particular stakeholder, possibly tuned to his needs.

19.2.1 Producers

Producers are the people who decide the precise details of what the product will be. They then work together to build it so that it satisfies the requirements within the stated constraints and that it is both technically and organisationally correct. In short, producers are actively involved in building a product that fits the real world. The producers are often referred to as the project team. Typically they include people like project managers, business analysts, key business people, marketing specialists, research and development specialists, designers, developers, programmers, testers and so on. Some of these will have business/subject matter/domain knowledge. Others will have technological knowledge. A producer who has participated in similar projects is likely to have a mixture of both. The nature of the product to be built will provide a guide as to who should be in the team of producers.

Any product is some combination of hardware and/or software components running on one or more devices, installed in one or more geographical locations, possibly needing to operate in a variety of environments, affecting a variety of people. Products now being built are growing more and more diverse. Software for a payroll system; a new web interface for a library; a vacuum cleaner containing mechanical, electrical and software components; a geographical positioning system for a car; a satellite guidance system; a portable personal organiser with an email interface; an automatic milking system for dairy farms; a new computer operating system; a building that controls its own temperature and lighting; the list is endless.

The common factor is that the products involve an evermore wider and deeper knowledge and understanding of increasingly different subject matters. And every different type of subject matter area brings with it a need for new, possibly specialist, stakeholder involvement. A frequently observed mistake is for producers to be limited to the people who play a technical role in product development. But, in order to build a product relevant, useful and satisfactory to its users, subject matter experts also need to join the producer team in one role or another. Without their participation the end product is likely to be a good technical solution that does not satisfy the needs of the real world. Each of the producers (both business and technical) should be committed to spending an agreed amount of effort on the project. Ideally, their involvement should be financed by the project budget in whole or in part. Producers should be people who form a gelled team [2] who are collaborating [3] to produce a shared product. They should be in close contact with each other, ideally located in the same workspace.

19.2.2 Consumers

Consumers are the people who make a decision to buy the product and/or use the product to do work. *Buyers* are an important consumer role that each project needs to identify and understand. People who play the role of *buyers* are those who decide whether or not to buy the product [4]. They might be individuals who decide to buy a new piece of software or a new hi-fi system. They might be people in an organisation who decide to commit part of their department's budget to buying a new piece of communications software or personal organisers for their staff. But the concept does not necessarily involve payment responsibility, money does not necessarily change hands. A buyer may simply be someone who influences the decision whether or not a product is to be used by some user or users. For example, suppose a product is being built to help children learn mathematics. The children's teachers will, generally, not be making the decision whether the product is or is not to be bought. The school boards will have decided that. Nevertheless, the teachers are buyers in the sense that they will decide whether the product will be used by their pupils. If teachers 'buy into' the product, it is far more likely to be successful in its market. So, part of understanding a project's sociology is to identify the people who can influence a purchase and the introduction of the product into its intended place in the world. The next step is to discover the factors that these buyers consider most important. In general, understanding of the buyers, their views and their feelings will help uncover relevant requirements. It will also help to prioritise the requirements when there is a need, for cost or time reasons for example, to prioritise implementation or delivery of requirements.

A further important *consumer* role is that of the people who will have direct contact with your product, the people who will actually use your product to achieve some specific task. These people are normally referred to as *users* of the product. Someone who uses a bank machine, air traffic controllers looking at radar screens, nurses monitoring heartbeats on a screen, the patient to whom the device is attached, bank clerks using on-line interfaces to make inter-bank transfers, householders entering a code into a home alarm system, software designers using a tool that records and evaluates a design are all *users*, each of specific products. Such users will rarely have a wide view of the product. They will have needs or express requirements related to the way that the product in use specifically affects them. Some users will tell you about specific requirements, others will have no ideas as to what their needs or requirements are. To be able to discover users' needs and transform them into well-defined and testable *requirements* requires understanding of the factors that give rise to their needs and influence their priority for implementation. The sorts of factors (the order of importance varies depending on each specific situation) that influence what people ask for:

- Understanding of the product to be built
- Awareness and appreciation of the project purpose and goals
- Subject matter experience
- Technological experience
- Skill in using similar products
- Intellectual abilities
- Attitudes to the producers of the product
- Attitude to job
- Attitude to technology
- Education
- Linguistic skills
- Age – older people have different life experiences to young people, and may not adapt as quickly to completely new concepts.
- Gender – men and women often have different viewpoints
- Disabilities/blind/deaf/Nonreaders
- Mood – the statement of need might be influenced by the mood of the user

Information about users of all types is recorded in drawer 3 of the template. For convenience, users have been separated from other stakeholders in this discussion because information about them will often be used by the producers to decide on very detailed aspects of the product. It is, for instance, impossible to discover appropriate usability requirements without consulting the direct users. Similarly, performance requirements require an understanding of why particular people require a particular response time. Knowledge of the users helps to build a product that fits into the users' world as it really is, not as the producers believe it to be.

19.2.3 Sponsors

The sponsors of a project are the people who have the organisational commitment to supporting the project. The role of the sponsor needs to be an official role and needs to be filled by a person who has enough influence to make the management decisions that affect the organisation and must be of a mind to help the project with problems or decisions outside the power of the project manager.

Suppose, for example, that a project is having trouble because the key stakeholders are unable to devote sufficient time and necessary involvement. It is up to the project manager to quantify the problem. When that has been done, the sponsor or his representative may be asked what can and should be done about it to 'preserve' the project, the project plan or the product quality, or its fitness for purpose for example. An example is provided by a project where producers were scattered around the organisation because of insufficient office space in, say, one location. The project manager went to the sponsor and explained the major impact of producers being unable to easily talk to one another and asked for some walls around the team. The sponsor understood the problem and agreed that it had a serious effect on the team's ability to meet the deadline. He, therefore, talked to other managers, located a Nissen hut in the organisation's grounds and fought the necessary battles to have it allocated to the producers. It was pretty basic accommodation but it did the trick. The team was together and they could talk to each other, they could get their work done, and the team was really gelled as a team. This would not have happened without the sponsor's political power.

The other side of the coin is that the sponsor's decisions are not always popular with other stakeholders, may be one person's view, biased by position, experience or personal factors. The sponsor needs to be a person who can take the view of the entire organisation while individual participants will tend to take a very local view in terms of their personal responsibilities and goals. The project team, on the other hand, is naturally looking at situations from the point of view of the project leader or, at best, from that of the project. It is the sponsor to be one who can take a detached view, based on an all-inclusive perspective of the application, its users, the project, its personnel and the organisations associated with the project. The sponsor needs to be a good analyst, a good decision-maker and a good leader – someone whom people have faith in. The ideal sponsor is someone who makes it possible for the project to flourish within the organisation and who makes sure that it remains relevant when there are changes within the organisation.

A common problem is, however, that the sponsor is too far removed from understanding of the project. Hence it is very difficult to have meaningful communication. A solution to this is to agree, at the start of the project, on some components of the project that the sponsor will be able to understand and review. Project goals are a good starting point. Suppose the sponsor can objectively verify that the project goals (in drawer 1) conform to the aims of the organisation. Then the producers can agree that they will use these goals to help them make choices and keep the project on track. In a situation where they cannot come up with a decision that conforms to the goals, then it is an indication that they need to ask the sponsor for some help.

19.2.4 Subject Matter Consultants

Subject matter consultants are people or organisations who are not producers but whose knowledge is necessary or beneficial in order to discover the requirements. A project for Polish railways, for example, used two consultants from British Rail and French SNCF respectively. Both these organisations had experience with similar projects and they agreed to contribute some of their subject matter knowledge to help the Polish project.

Very frequently, domain experts play the role of subject matter consultants. They might, as in the case of the railways, come from external organisations. Where an organisation has previously undertaken one or more projects concerned with the same subject matter they will often be able to locate *in-house* experts. If other in-house projects have built apparently relevant business data or business class models, it may be feasible and appropriate to use those as a source of subject matter knowledge.

19.2.5 Technical Consultants

Usually a project has need of technical knowledge additional to that available from the producers and members of the project team. The technical systems architect, the network specialist, an expert in the programming tools, a system software expert, a configuration management expert, a hardware supplier, a usability expert all exemplify technical specialists whose knowledge, understanding and skills are likely to be needed by the producers at some stage of a software or embedded system project. The greater the understanding of the requirements and constraints the more is it possible to identify the necessary technical consultants. Once a need for a particular sort of technical expertise has been identified, it is the responsibility of the project manager to investigate when need must be met, to identify a source of the necessary expertise and to determine how much will be needed or to delegate that responsibility to someone qualified to find the best answers.

19.2.6 Influencers

Are there others, apart from the consumers, who might influence the success or failure of the project? To help uncover all the requirements, this question must be addressed from the beginning of the project. Consider for example, whether there are others than those already identified with the project, individuals or organisations, that have or impose rules with which the system or the developing organisation is required to comply:

- Those within the project's domain, like client, customers and users, who have expectations from the proposed product
- Adjacent Systems – people or organisations adjacent to or affected by the project
- Auditors – does the process or its product have to pass any audit checks, including financial, technical or quality standards like ISO 2000?
- Operations/maintenance – people or organisations who expect our product to have particular operational characteristics
- Competition – products in competition with yours influence the success of your product Do competitive products have characteristics that buyers will expect from your product?
- Lawyers/police – what about the legal aspects?
- Professional Bodies – do professional bodies have any influence on whether the product will be accepted?
- Public Opinion/special interest groups – what special groups are there whose opinion will affect the acceptance of the product?
- Government – how might the government affect the product?
- Cultural Interests – are there any special cultural influences that might affect acceptance or use of the product?
- Is the product expected to meet specific security/safety/emergency services standards?
- Inspectors – who, if any, will have the right to approve/disapprove of the product?

The best approach to the discovery of influencers early on is to brainstorm to produce a list of the different people and organisations that might influence the project or the uptake and use of the product. The list is usually long because it opens a Pandora's box – it will appear that the whole world might have such influence. However, not all will require investigation. The list must be produced to facilitate identification of the most relevant, the ones that all or a majority – agree, should be considered influencers or even stakeholders, bearing in mind the goals of your project.

19.2.7 Project-Sociology Analysis

It has been found to be a good practice to undertake a project-sociology analysis at the beginning of a project. It begins with brainstorms above. This normally raises many questions about work context and product scope that would not otherwise occur to us until later in the project. To help discipline and direct this, a stakeholder analysis template has been developed. It may be downloaded from [http://www.volere.co.uk] and tailored to stakeholder roles as visualised or designed for any specific project.

Another reason for undertaking a project-sociology analysis is to prepare the ground for negotiation of relevant stakeholder involvement. If one can explain to stakeholders why the project needs their particular expertise in order to be successful, the chances that people will commit to being involved are greatly increased. This is further increased if one has the project understanding to be able to talk freely about the type of involvement visualised or desired, when it is needed and how much. People do not want to be tied up in meetings when partial involvement is sufficient to fulfil the purpose of their involvement, to provide the desired benefit. If the project can be so managed to focus on relevant involvement, then the chance of continuing the concerned stakeholder involvement is greatly increased. This is all part of sound management of stakeholder relationships and normally brings long term benefits.

Drawer 7 (The Scope of the Work) contains the information necessary to understand the details of the business problem and the scope of the study necessary to understand it. Drawer 8 (The Scope of the Product) contains all the details necessary to understand the scope of the product that we plan to build, and this scope will guide the gathering and specification of the requirements. The work and the product are separated because they are very different and, in order to make relevant choices, one needs to be able to understand them in parallel. The product identifies the users' needs and expectations from the product. The work has a wider scope – it deals with the part of the world needing to be investigated in order to identify the most advantageous product characteristics.

Drawers 9–17 contain detailed specifications of individual or atomic functional and nonfunctional requirements.

19.3 Contents of Individual Requirements

A requirement is a testable statement of some function or quality that the product must have. The issue is whether one can give each requirement a criterion such that it is possible to determine for alternate solutions whether or not they fit the requirement. The amount of work involved in writing the fit criteria varies tremendously depending on the understanding of the project and the sources of knowledge. A staged approach to identifying fit criteria by exploration of different aspects of the requirements helps in their determination. The requirements shell [5, 6] in Figure 19.3 illustrates the aspects that have been looked for.

The Requirement number is a unique identifier assigned to each requirement. The requirement type cross-references the requirement back to the list of types on the template. For example, if the requirement is type 12 then it is a performance requirement. The business event and product-use case numbers that are there to identify all the business events and use cases to which the requirement relates. This provides a traceable link between atomic requirements and object-oriented [7] development.

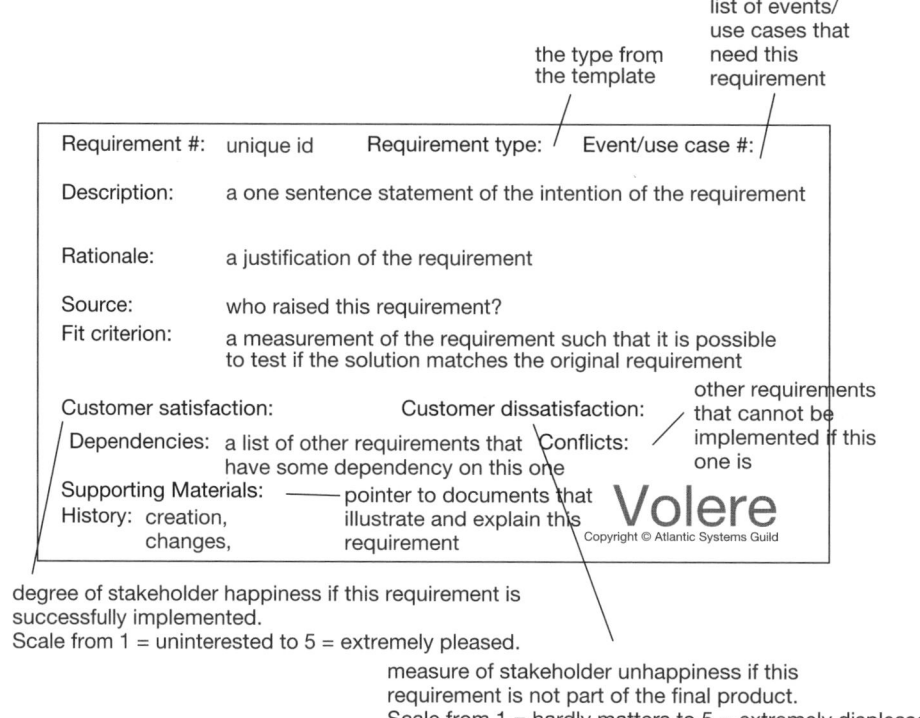

Figure 19.3 The requirement shell identifies the components of an individual requirement

The description might be very ambiguous, very vague or anything in between depending on who identified or isolated or developed it, or where it came from. The rationale is the first step to dealing with ambiguity because it indicates why this requirement is considered to be important. What does it contribute to the achievement of the goals of the product? Neither the description nor the rationale is testable, but they provide a basis for exploration of the requirement and for definition of the fit criterion. Once a requirement has a fit criterion then it can be tested to see whether either contain any ambiguity, whether all terminology is defined and whether it is possible to write a test that is capable of testing eventual solutions. Bear in mind that the intent is not to design the test. The requirement is being examined to determine whether it actually is well-defined, unambiguous and complete according to your project's completeness criteria. See [8] and [5] for further discussion on making requirements measurable and testable.

Another aspect of an individual requirement deals with customer value [4]. How satisfied will the customer be if the solution fits the fit criterion, how dissatisfied if it does not. An answer to this question represents the first attempt to understand the relative importance of the requirement. In addition, dependencies, conflicts, supporting material and History all serve to make the requirement coherent, make it possible to discuss the details of the requirement and to understand how it fits into the project as a whole.

Other sections of the template deal with individual functional and nonfunctional requirements and constraints and a variety of project issues. This chapter cannot discuss the complete contents of the template; however, a complete template can be found at http://www.volere.co.uk from where it may be downloaded.

The point of introducing the template is to illustrate that there are a number of components that one would expect to find in a requirements document. A requirements document might consist of a number of sections, chapters or parts, each of which addresses different components at different levels of detail. For instance many organisations produce an initial document that, effectively even if not in name, constitutes a feasibility study. One way of organising the initial document is to base it on the information included here in drawers 1-7 (drivers, constraints, work scope) and some of that in drawer 8 (product scope). The next version of the requirements document would then contain the detailed requirements taken from drawers 9 to 17 (individual requirements). Some organisations do not include the information from drawers 18-27 (project issues) in their requirements documentation because, strictly speaking, it is more related to project management. The selection of what to include really depends on how an organisation works and who needs to see what. The point is that project management decisions must be based on a common understanding of the requirements and their degree of completion. For this to happen, the parts of the specification need to have well-defined connections.

19.4 Keeping Track of Connections

The components listed in the requirements specification table of contents on Figure 19.1 indicate that there are many connections between the components. In order to build the product and, to subsequently deal with changes, one needs to be able to understand these connections. For example, which cases of product-use are addressed by each requirement and from which business events do the various product-use cases arise. To test the completeness and traceability of the requirements, it must be possible to identify these connections. Figure 19.4 is a requirements knowledge model that shows the connections between the components of a requirements specification.

Each class of knowledge, represented by a box, represents one or more of the components listed on the requirements specification table of contents. For example, the class called *Requirement* represents a collection of attributes about a class of business knowledge called a *Requirement*. The attributes that make up the requirement would be the same attributes that appear on the requirements shell in Figure 19.3. The attributes for each of the classes are defined [9] in a dictionary that supports the knowledge model. Incidentally, the triangle symbol that appears below the class called *Requirement* indicates a special relationship that identifies subclasses of knowledge. In other words, the classes; *Functional Requirement, NonFunctional Requirement* and *Mandated Constraint* are all subclasses of the class called requirement. This means that each of the subclasses inherits all attributes from its supertype (in this case the class Requirement) but each subclass also has some attributes that are unique to itself.

The numbers in the boxes correspond to the numbering scheme used in the requirements template's table of contents. The lines between the boxes indicate that there is a connection or relationship between them. For example, the line between Product-Use Case and Requirement is there because each product-use case can have a *Detailed Product Tracing* relationship with many requirements. Similarly, each requirement can have a *Detailed Product Tracing* relationship with many product-use cases. In other words, you can read the relationship between two classes in either direction. It does not matter how

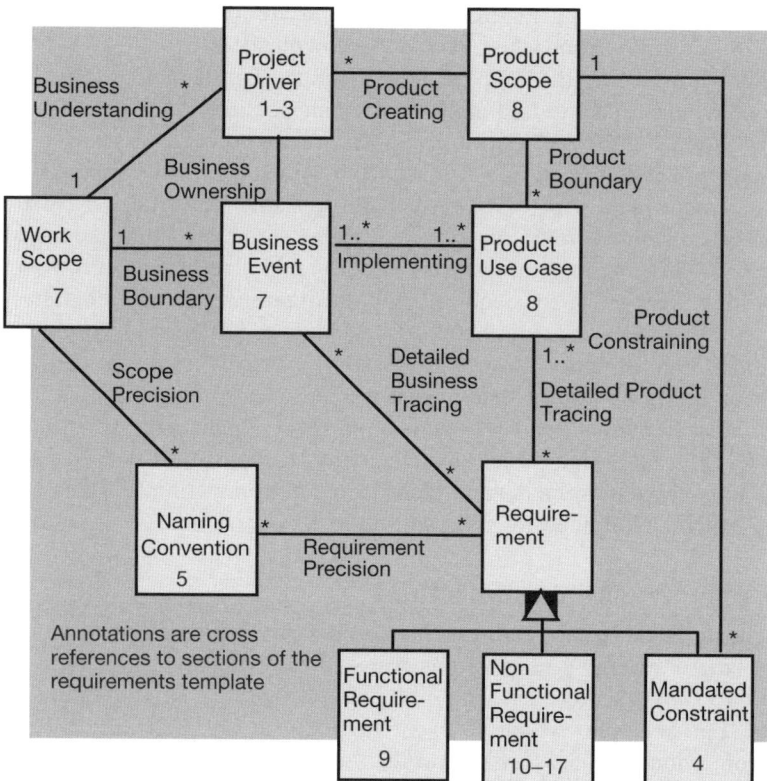

Figure 19.4 One test of a requirements specification is to verify that the connections between the components are traceable. This requirements knowledge model identifies the classes of knowledge that are related to requirements along with the relationships between them

these relationships are implemented within the requirements specification (many tools are available to help with this). What matters is that it is possible to keep track of the relationships between components and the quality of component content.

The requirements knowledge model exposes the often hidden expectations or assumptions of the stakeholders. Requirements knowledge that is gathered should conform to the content and relationships specified in the knowledge model. For example, the content of every requirement should be according to the definition of *Requirement* in the data dictionary. And every requirement should be traceable back to one or more product-use cases and one or more business events. Shared awareness of the knowledge model encourages feedback about all of the knowledge classes early in the project. In other words, requirements-related issues are forced to the surface early thereby saving time and cost.

19.5 The Quality Gateway

The purpose of the *quality gateway* is to provide a checkpoint where a series of tests can be applied to each requirement to determine whether it is ready to be accepted into the specification. The aim is to discover problems such as ambiguities, inconsistencies, missing requirements and so on, and to raise questions as soon as possible rather than later on in the development process when much more effort is required to deal with them. Provided the requirements have been defined in a consistent and testable way, all the stakeholders can be involved in applying the quality gateway tests. Here are examples of issues that can be addressed by the quality gateway:

- Does the specification contain all requirements components?
- Does the specification contain all relationships between components?
- Are all types of requirements defined?
- Is each requirement uniquely identifiable?
- Does each requirement contain all components on the shell?
- Is each goal measurable?
- Is the work context defined?
- Does the event list agree with the work context?
- Are all event inputs and outputs defined?
- Can one quantify why each constraint exists?
- Is each constraint measurable?
- Are stakeholders identified by name?
- Are users' characteristics defined?
- Are stakeholders' responsibilities defined?
- Can you trace product-use cases back to the business events?
- Are terms used in the fit criteria defined in the requirements specification?
- Are terms used consistently?
- Is it possible to write a cost-effective test to prove or disprove any solution to this requirement according to its fit criterion?
- Is each requirement really a requirement or is it a solution?
- Are conflicts between requirements identified?

If stakeholders are aware of these testpoints, then this awareness will help requirements engineers, systems analysts, designers, developers and business people to improve requirement quality. The quality gateway test is a point (or points) in the project where one can determine how well one is doing before a document is issued and errors pollute the product.

Like the knowledge model, the quality gateway drives out requirements-related negative feedback early in the development process. Thus, during design and implementation the team can focus on solving the problem rather than having to deal with expensive late feedback related to requirements.

19.6 Lessons Learnt

We have learnt a number of key lessons by applying these principles on a wide variety of projects.

- In order to encourage early feedback, one needs to make requirements into something visible and tangible rather than just a general idea. The key principle here is that a requirement is more than just a 'shall' statement, it has many attributes as illustrated on the requirements shell.

- The better defined the stakeholder roles and responsibilities, the more early requirements feedback will be generated. Time spent doing a project-sociology analysis leads to better understanding and contributes to generating earlier feedback.
- A requirements knowledge model [10] provides a connection point for diverse stakeholders. We have found it a good idea to start with the generic model and then tailor it so that the classes and relationships have names agreed by the project group. Thus, the model is owned by the project and people use it as a communication tool.
- The scope of an investigation for the discovery of requirements is wider than the scope of the product that is eventually built. Failure to realise this results in requirements that are not discovered until after implementation.

19.7 Conclusion

Consistent and *understandable* specification of requirements stimulates early feedback about errors, misunderstandings, misconceptions and, above all, assumptions and so reduces their occurrence and retention. This by itself is a worthwhile objective, with major long term pay-off and will, in general, fully justify the time and resources spent on their preparation and validation. This is all the more so if one is dealing with development and evolution of products with a life expectancy that may stretch over years or decades. It is almost essential for facilitating reliable and timely adaptation and evolution to ensure satisfactory operation in a forever changing world. If all stakeholders understand this fact of life and the requirements that define the product, and if they are not threatened by an incomprehensible document, then they are much more likely to be able to say what they really think and so help achieve this lifetime goal.

References

[1] Volere, *The Volere Requirements Template and other Requirements Resources* can be found at http://www.volere.co.uk [Accessed 2005].

[2] DeMarco, T. and Lister, T. *Peopleware: Productive Projects and Teams*, 2nd ed. Dorset House, New York, 2000.

[3] Highsmith, J. *Adaptive Software Development: A Collaborative Approach to Managing Complex Systems*. Dorset House, New York, 1999.

[4] Pardee, W. *To Satisfy & Delight Your Customer*. Dorset House, New York, 1996.

[5] Robertson, J. and Robertson, S. *Mastering the Requirements Process*. Addison-Wesley, London, 1999.

[6] Robertson, J. and Robertson, S. *Mastering the Requirements Process*, 2nd ed. Addison Wesley, Cambridge, MA, 2006.

[7] Leffingwell, D. and Widrig, D. *Managing Software Requirements - A Unified Approach*. Object Technology Series, Addison-Wesley, 2000.

[8] Gilb, T. and Finzi, S. *Principles of Software Engineering Management*. Addison-Wesley, Wokingham, England, 1988.

[9] Jackson, M. *Software Requirements & Specifications: A Lexicon of Practice, Principles and Prejudices*. Addison-Wesley Longman, Wokingham, England, 1996.

[10] Robertson, J. and Robertson, S. *Requirements-Led Project Management*. Addison-Wesley, Cambridge, MA, 2005.

20

Requirements Risk and Software Reliability

Norman F. Schneidewind

20.1 Introduction

While software design and code metrics have enjoyed some success as predictors of software quality attributes such as reliability [1–7], the measurement field is stuck at this level of achievement. If measurement has to advance to a higher level, attention must be shifted to the front end of the development process because it is during system conceptualization that errors in specifying requirements are introduced into the process and adversely affect the ability to develop the software. A requirements change may induce ambiguity and uncertainty in the development process that causes errors in implementing changes. Subsequently, these errors propagate through later phases of development and may result in significant risks associated with implementation of the requirements. For example, reliability risk, that is, the risk of faults and failures induced by changes in requirements, may arise from deficiencies in the process (e.g. lack of precision in requirements). Although requirements may appear to be correctly specified in terms of meeting user expectations, there could be significant risks associated with their implementation. For example, implementing user requirements correctly could lead to excessive system size and complexity, which, in turn, could have adverse effects on reliability. Equally, they might result in demand for project resources that exceeds the available funds, time and personnel skills. Interestingly, there has been considerable discussion of project risk (e.g. the consequences of cost overrun and schedule slippage) in the literature [8] but no corresponding attention to reliability risk.

Risk in the Webster's New Universal Unabridged Dictionary is defined as 'the chance of injury, damage or loss' [9]. Some authors have extended the dictionary definition as follows: 'Risk Exposure = Probability of an Unsatisfactory Outcome × Loss if the Outcome is Unsatisfactory' [8]. Such a definition is frequently applied to the risks in

---

Software Evolution and Feedback: Theory and Practice   Nazim H. Madhavji, Juan C. Fernández-Ramil and Dewayne E. Perry
© 2006 John Wiley & Sons, Ltd

managing software projects such as budget and schedule slippage. In contrast, *risk* as used here pertains to an alternative dictionary definition of *'the risk of executing the software of a system where there is the chance of injury (e.g. crew injury or fatality), damage (e.g. destruction of the vehicle) or loss (e.g. loss of the mission) if a serious software failure occurs during a mission'*. The term *risk factor* is used here to indicate the degree of risk associated with such an occurrence.

20.1.1 Requirements Changes and Software Evolution

The generation of requirements is not a one-time activity. It is, indeed, normal for changes to requirements to occur throughout the lifetime of a system that is being used. This is due, for example, to a need to constantly adapt the system to changes in the human activity it is being used to support and to changes in the real-world operational domain. The development of new software or change of existing software in response to new and changed requirements, respectively, carries with it potential reliability risks. Therefore, in assessing the possible effects of requirements on reliability, one must deal with changes in requirements throughout the evolution of the software. As Lehman points out, 'it is beneficial to determine the number of distinct additions and changes to requirements and assumptions over constituent parts of the system per release or over some fixed time period to assess domain and system volatility (i.e. *risk* (present author)). This can assist evolution release planning in a number of ways, for example, by pointing to system areas that are ripe for restructuring because of high defect rates or high volatility or where, to facilitate future change, extra care should be taken in change architecture and implementation.' [10]. Furthermore, as stated by Lehman, 'the growth in the difficulty of design, change and system validation, and hence in the effort and time required for system evolution, causes growth in costs and in the need for user support. Such increases will, in general, tend to be accompanied by a decline in product quality and in the rate of evolution, however defined and measured, unless additional compensatory work is undertaken.' [10].

In addition to the relationship between requirements and reliability, there are intermediate relationships between requirements and software metrics (e.g. size, complexity) and between metrics and reliability. These relationships may interact, putting the reliability of the software at risk because the requirements changes may result in size and complexity increases that may adversely affect the reliability of the software. Such interactions were studied for the space shuttle. For example, assume that the reliability of a requirements change is inversely related to the number of iterations, the 'mod level'; that is, a need for many revisions of a requirement before it is approved is indicative of a requirement that is hard to understand and implement safely, which, in turn, indicates the risk of direct adverse effects on reliability. At the same time, this complex requirement will also affect code size and complexity that will have further deleterious effects on reliability.

20.1.2 Objectives

The overall objective of this chapter is to identify attributes of software requirements that cause the resulting system to be unreliable. Furthermore, we seek to quantify relationships between requirements risk and reliability. If such attributes can be identified, then policies can be recommended to the software engineering community for recognizing these risks and avoiding or mitigating them during development. The objective of such policy changes is to prevent the propagation of high-risk requirements through the various phases of software development of the releases that contain them. In addition, it is important to provide feedback to the evolution planning and management process about the identification of high-risk requirements and fault-prone modules recognized in release i so as to mitigate these risks and fault proneness in release i + 1 [11].

Given the lack of emphasis in measurement research on the critical role of requirements, there is good reason to discuss the following issues:

- What is the relationship between requirements attributes on the one hand and reliability on the other? That is, are there any indicators that suggest a relationship between a requirement, the code that addresses it and the occurrence of defects and failures in the software?
- What is the relationship between requirements attributes and software attributes such as complexity and size? That is, are there requirements attributes that are strongly related to the complexity and size of the software?
- Is it feasible to use requirements attributes as predictors of reliability? That is, can static requirements change attributes such as the size of the change be used to predict reliability in the execution (e.g. failure occurrence) of the code?
- Are there requirements attributes that can discriminate between high and low reliability, thus qualifying them as predictors of reliability?
- Which requirements attributes pose the greatest risk to reliability?

An additional objective is to provide a framework that researchers and practitioners could use to

1. analyze the relationships among requirements changes, complexity, reliability and
2. assess and predict reliability risk as a function of requirements changes.

20.1.3 Methods

The approach described involves postulating several hypotheses about how requirements attributes affect reliability and then conducting experiments to accept or reject the hypotheses. Various statistical methods can be used to identify the major risk factor contributors to unreliable software. Selected methods are illustrated using requirements and reliability data from the NASA space shuttle.

Several projects have demonstrated the validity and applicability of applying metrics to identify fault-prone software at the code level [1–3, 12]. This approach is now applied at the requirements level to facilitate early detection of reliability problems. Once high-risk areas of the software have been identified, they would be subject to detailed tracking throughout the development process.

This discussion is presented under the following headings: background, selected measurement research projects, approach to analyzing requirements risk, risk factors, solutions to risk analysis example, future trends and conclusions.

20.2 Background

At present the field of software engineering lacks the capability to quantitatively assess and predict the effect of a requirements change on the reliability of the software as proposed in the previous section. A major focus of current activity in software metrics concentrates on the measurement of code characteristics [5, 13]. This is seen to be satisfactory for the evaluation of product quality and process effectiveness once the code is written. However, if organizations concentrate only on this class of measurements, they will miss out in a number of ways. It will, in particular, be incomplete excluding, for example, the coverage of requirements analysis and design. Basically it starts too late in the process. To be really effective, a measurement plan must start with requirements and continue beyond code generation to operation. After all, requirements characteristics directly affect code characteristics and, hence, reliability. It is, therefore, important to assess their impact on reliability when first specified and to demonstrate the feasibility of quantification of the risks to the reliability of requirements changes – whether new or changed.

Once requirements attributes that portend high risk for the operational reliability of the software are identified, it is possible to suggest changes in the development process of the organization. This is illustrated by a potential recommendation that all additions to, or changes of requirements for, mission critical software must be subjected to *quantitative* risk analysis. In addition to requiring such a risk analysis, the policy would have to specify the risk factors to be analyzed (for example, *mod level,* that is, number of modifications of a requirement). The validity and applicability of identifying critical values of metrics to identify fault-prone software at the code level [12] has been demonstrated. For example, on the space shuttle, rigorous inspections of requirements, design documentation and code have contributed more to achieving high reliability than any other process factor. Thus, it would be prudent to consider adapting this process technology to other NASA projects, Department of Defence (DoD) and other space and defense organizations because the potential payoff in increased reliability would be significant. The objective of these policy changes is to prevent the propagation of high-risk requirements through the various phases of software development. The payoff to these organizations would be to reduce the risk of mission critical software *not* meeting its reliability goals during operation. For example, if the risk analysis identifies requirements that appear risky, measurements could be made on a prototype of the design and code to verify whether this is indeed the case. If the risk is confirmed through rapid prototyping, countermeasures such as modularizing or simplifying the requirements can then be considered.

20.3 Selected Measurement Research Projects

A number of software reliability and maintenance measurement projects have been reported in the literature. For example, Briand *et al.* developed a process to characterize the latter [14]. They present a qualitative and inductive methodology for performing objective project characterizations that identify maintenance problems and needs. This methodology helps in determining causal links between maintenance problems and flaws in the maintenance organization and process. In summary, these authors have related ineffective maintenance practices to organizational and process problems.

Pearse and Oman applied a maintenance metrics index to measure the maintainability of C source code before and after maintenance activities [7]. This technique allowed the project engineers to track the 'health' of the code as it was being maintained and assess its maintainability.

Pigoski and Nelson collected and analyzed metrics on size, trouble reports, change proposals, staffing and trouble report and change proposal completion times [15]. A major contribution of this project was the use of trends to identify a relationship between the productivity of the maintenance organization and staffing levels.

Sneed reengineered a client maintenance process to conform to the ANSI/IEEE Standard 1219, a standard for software maintenance [16]. This project is a good example of how a standard can provide a basic framework for a process and can be tailored to the characteristics of the project environment and illustrates how the application of a standard is an appropriate element of a good process.

Stark collected and analyzed metrics in the categories of customer satisfaction, cost and schedule with the objective of focusing management's attention on improvement areas and tracking improvements over time [17]. This approach aided management in deciding whether to include changes in the current release, with possible schedule slippage, or in the next release.

None of the above work included any aspect of software risk assessment. A further indication of the back seat that software risk assessment takes compared to the role it plays in the hardware arena is provided by Fragola who reports on probabilistic risk management for the space shuttle. Interestingly, he says, 'The shuttle risk is embodied in the performance of its hardware, the careful preparation activities that its ground support staff take between flights to ensure this performance during a flight and the procedural and management constraints in place to control their activities.' [18]. There is not a word in this statement or in his article about software! Another hardware-only risk assessment is by Maggio, who says, 'The current effort is the first integrated quantitative assessment of the risk of the loss of the shuttle vehicle from 3 seconds prior to liftoff to wheel stop at mission end.' Again, there is not a word about software [19]. Pfleeger lays out a road map for assessing project risk that includes risk prioritization [20], a step addressed with some degree of confidence in the statistical analysis of risk (see Section 20.6).

20.4 Approach to Analyzing Requirements Risk

The approach to be described involves conducting experiments to see whether a mapping can be developed between changes in requirements and changes in software complexity and extended to changes in reliability. In other words, if R represents requirements, C represents complexity, F represents failure occurrence (i.e. reliability), it should be determined whether the implication $\Delta R \Rightarrow \Delta C \Rightarrow \Delta F$ is valid. Changes in size, documentation and complexity must also be considered. If such mappings can be achieved with the desired degree of statistical significance, the approach will be judged a success.

By retrospectively analyzing the relationship between requirements and reliability on the one hand and maintainability on the other, one is able to identify those risk factors that are associated with reliability and to prioritize them on the basis of the degree to which the relationship is statistically significant. In order to quantify the effect of a requirements change, various risk factors, defined as the attribute of a requirement change that can induce adverse effects on reliability (e.g. failure incidence), and project management (e.g. personnel resources) are used. This process is illustrated in Figure 20.1. Examples of space shuttle risk factors are shown in Section 20.5.

Table 20.1 shows the Change Request Hierarchyof the space shuttle. This involves change requests (CRs) (i.e. a request for a new requirement or modification of an existing requirement), discrepancy reports (DRs) (i.e. reports that document deviations between specified and observed software behavior) and failures. DRs can be written and failures

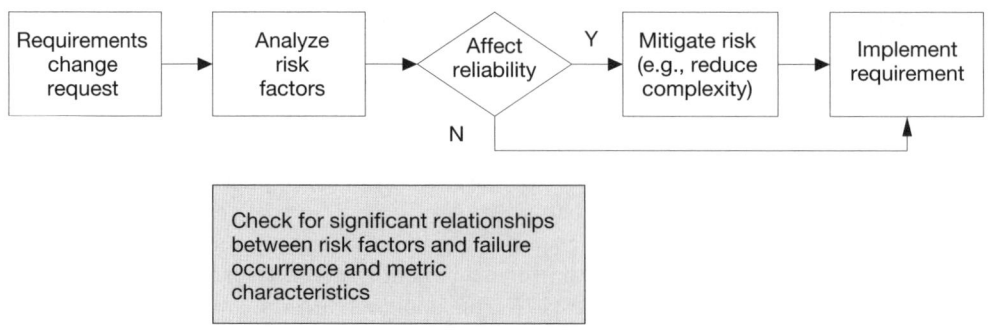

Figure 20.1 Risk analysis process

Table 20.1 Change request hierarchy

Change requests (CRs)
1. No discrepancy reports (i.e. CRs with no DRs)
2. Discrepancy reports or discrepancy reports and failures
2.1 No failures (i.e. CRs with DRs only)
2.2 Failures (i.e. CRs with DRs and failures)
2.2.1 Prerelease failures
2.2.2 Postrelease failures

can occur at any time during the life cycle. Categories 1 and 2 were analyzed with respect to risk factors to provide discriminants of the categories.

20.4.1 Categorical Data Analysis

Using the null hypothesis Ho: a risk factor is not a discriminator of reliability versus the alternate hypothesis H_1: a risk factor is a discriminator of reliability, categorical data analysis is used to test the hypothesis. A similar hypothesis was used to assess whether risk factors can serve as discriminators of metrics characteristics. The *requirements, requirements risk factors, reliability* and *metrics data* from the space shuttle *'Three Engine Out'* software (abort sequence invoked when three engines are lost) were used to test the hypotheses. Samples of these data are shown in the following text.

Prerelease and postrelease failure data from the space shuttle from 1983 to the present. An example of postrelease failure data is shown in Table 20.2, where an operational increment (OI) is a software system that is composed of modules and configured from a series of builds to meet the space shuttle mission functional requirements.

Risk factors for the space shuttle *Three Engine Out Auto Contingency* software. This software was released to NASA by the developer on 10/18/95. An example of a partial set of risk factor data is shown in Table 20.3.

Metrics data for 1400 space shuttle modules, each with 26 metrics. An example of a partial set of metric data is shown in Table 20.4.

Table 20.2 Post release of failure data

Failure found on operational increment	Days from release when failure occurred	Discrepancy report #	Severity	Failure date	Release date	Module in error
Q	75	1	2	05/19/97	03/05/97	10

Table 20.3 Risk factor data

Change request number	Source lines of code changed	Complexity rating of change	Criticality of change	Number of principal functions affected	Number of modifications of change request	Number of requirements issues	Number of inspections required	Manpower required to make change
A	1933	4	3	27	7	238	12	209.3 man weeks

Table 20.4 Partial set of metrics data

Module	Operator count	Operand count	Statement count	Path count	Cycle count	Discrepancy report count	Change request count
10	3,895	1,957	606	998	4	14	16

Table 20.5 Definition of samples

Sample	Size
Total CRs	24
CRs with no DRs	14
CRs with DRs only or DRs and failures	10
CRs with modules that caused failures	6
CRs can have multiple DRs, failures and modules that caused failures	
CR: change request	
DR: discrepancy report	

Table 20.5 shows the definition of the change request samples that were used in the analysis. Sample sizes are small owing to the high reliability of the space shuttle. However, sample size is one of the parameters accounted for in the statistical tests that produced statistically significant results in certain cases (see Section 20.6).

To minimize the effects of a large number of variables that interact in some cases, a statistical categorical data analysis was performed incrementally. Only one category of risk factor was used at any one time to observe the effect of adding an additional risk factor on the ability to correctly classify CRs that have *no DRs* versus CRs that have *DRs only* or *DRs and failures*. The Mann–Whitney test for difference in medians between categories was used because no assumption was required to be made about statistical distribution. In addition, some risk factors are ordinal scale quantities (e.g. modification level); thus, the median is an appropriate statistic to use. Furthermore, because some risk factors are ordinal scale quantities, rank correlation (i.e. correlation coefficients are computed on the basis of rank) was used to check for risk factor dependencies.

20.5 Risk Factors

One of the software process problems of the NASA Space Shuttle Flight Software organization is to evaluate the risk of implementing requirements changes and the degree to which they may affect the reliability of its software. To assess the risk of change, the software development contractor uses risk factors as described below. These were identified by agreement between NASA and the development contractor based on assumptions about the risk involved in making changes to the software. This formal process is called a *risk assessment*. No requirements change is approved by the change control board without an accompanying risk assessment. During risk assessment, the development contractor will attempt to answer such questions as, 'Is this change highly complex relative to other software changes that have been made on the space shuttle?' If this were the case, a high-risk value would be assigned for the complexity criterion. To date, this *qualitative* risk assessment has proven useful for identifying possible risky requirements changes or, conversely, for providing assurance that there are no unacceptable risks in making a change. However, there has been no quantitative evaluation to determine whether, for example, high-risk factor software was really less reliable than low-risk factor software. By doing a quantitative assessment, we were able to reduce the number of risk factors to four, which are statistically significant in their relationship with reliability. In addition, there is no model for predicting the reliability of the software, if the change is implemented. Both issues are addressed below.

We had considered using requirements attributes like completeness, consistency, correctness, and so on, as risk factors [21]. While these are useful generic concepts, they are difficult to quantify. Although some of the following risk factors also have qualitative values assigned, there are a number of quantitative risk factors and many of the risk factors deal with the execution behavior of the software (i.e. reliability), which is our primary interest.

20.5.1 Space Shuttle Flight Software Requirements Change Risk Factors

The following definitions of 19 risk factors categorize the risk factors and provide an interpretation of the question each is designed to answer. These factors are known during requirements analysis. If the answer to a yes/no question is 'yes', it implies that this is a high-risk change with respect to the given risk factor. The same holds true if the answer to a question that requires an estimate is an anomalous value.

Assessment of each risk factor provides an indication whether there is a statistically significant relationship between it and the reliability of the software version analyzed. An example of the details of the findings are shown in Section 20.6. In many instances, there was insufficient data to permit analysis (i.e. the data were missing or incomplete). These cases are indicated below. The names of the risk factors used in the analysis are given in quotation marks.

Complexity Factors

- *"complexity"*: Qualitative assessment of complexity of change (e.g. very complex).
  Not significant.
- *"mods"*: Number of modifications or iterations on the proposed change.
  Significant.

Size Factors

- *"sloc"*: Number of source lines of code affected by the change.
  Significant.
- *"mod chg"*: Number of modules changed. – Is the number of changes to modules excessive?
  Not significant.

Criticality of Change Factors

- *"crit func"*: Criticality of function added or changed by the change request.
  (Insufficient data)
- *"off nom path"*: Whether the software change is on a nominal or off-nominal program path (i.e. exception condition).
  (Insufficient data)

Locality of Change Factors

- *"critic area"*: The area of the program affected (i.e. critical area such as code for a mission abort sequence).
  (Insufficient data)
- *"recent chgs"*: Recent changes to the code in the area affected by the requirements change.
  (Insufficient data)
- *"new\ exist code"*: New or existing code that is affected.
  (Insufficient data)
- *"fails ex code"*: Number of system or hardware failures that would have to occur before the code that implements the requirement would be executed.
  (Insufficient data)

Requirements Issues and Functions Factors

- *"other chgs"*: Number and types of other requirements affected by the given requirement change (requirements issues).
  (Insufficient data)

- "*issues*": Number of possible conflicts among requirements (requirements issues).
  Significant.
- "*prin funcs*": Number of principal software functions affected by the change.
  Not significant.

Performance Factors

- "*space*": Amount of memory space required to implement the change.
  Significant.
- "*cpu*": Effect on CPU performance.
  (**Insufficient data**)

Personnel Resources Factors

- "*inspects*": Number of inspections required to approve the change.
  Not significant.
- "*manpower*" : Manpower required to implement the change.
  Not significant.
- "*cost*": Manpower required to verify and validate the correctness of the change.
  Not significant.
- "*tests*": Number of tests required to verify and validate the correctness of the change.
  Not significant.

20.6 Solutions to Risk Analysis Example

The solutions to the risk analysis example follow. They are based on the space shuttle data and the statistical analyses in a, b and c given below, as shown in Tables 20.6, 20.7 and 20.8 respectively. The process is illustrated in Figure 20.2. An important element of the figure is the feedback of the results of the risk and failure analysis to the software evolution process so that the development of *future* software can benefit from this knowledge. For example, the prioritized risk factors would be used to assess the risk of requirements changes on the next version of shuttle software. Furthermore, metric critical values would be used in the design process to avoid implementing modules with metric values that exceed the critical values.

Only those risk factors where there was sufficient data and the results were statistically significant are shown.

(a) Categorical data analysis on the relationship between CRs with no DRs versus DRs only or DRs and failures, using the Mann–Whitney test.
(b) Dependency check on risk factors, using rank correlation coefficients.
(c) Identification of modules that caused failures as a result of the CR, and their metric values.

20.6.1 Categorical Data Analysis

Of the original 19 risk factors, only 4 survived as being statistically significant (alpha $\leq$ 0.05); 7 were not significant and 8t had insufficient data to make the analysis. As

Requirements Risk and Software Reliability

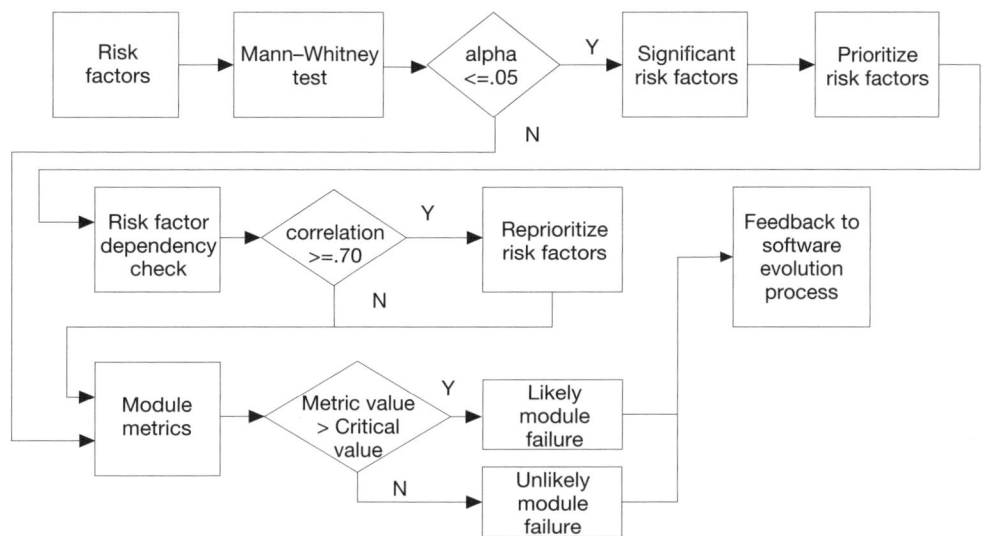

Figure 20.2 Statistically significant risk factors

Table 20.6 Statistically significant results (alpha ≤ 0.05). CRs with no DRs versus DRs only or DRs and failures. Mann–Whitney test

Risk factor	Alpha	Median value CRs with no DRs	Median value DRs only or DRs and failures
issues	0.0076	1	14
space	0.0186	6	123
mods	0.0401	0	4
sloc	0.0465	10	88.5

issues: Number of possible conflicts among requirements.
space: Amount of memory space required to implement the change.
mods: Number of modifications of the proposed change.
sloc: Number of source lines of code affected by the change.

Table 20.6 shows, there are statistically significant results for CRs with no DRs versus DRs only or DRs and failures for the risk factors 'mods', 'sloc', 'issues', and 'space'. The values of alpha in Table 20.6 are used as a means to prioritize the use of risk factors, with low values meaning high priority, the priority ordering being: 'issues', 'space', 'mods', 'sloc'.

The significant risk factors would be used to predict reliability problems for this set of data and this version of the software. Whether these results would hold for future versions of the software would have to be determined in validation tests on subsequent OIs.

The finding regarding 'mods' confirms the software developer's view that this is an important risk factor. This is the case because if there are many iterations of the change request, it implies that the change is complex and difficult to understand. Therefore, it is

Table 20.7 Rank correlation coefficients of risk factors

	CRs with no DRs			
	mods	sloc	issues	space
mods	–	0.370	**0.837**	0.219
sloc	0.370	–	**0.717**	0.210
issues	**0.837**	**0.717**	–	0.026
space	0.219	0.210	0.026	–

	DRs only or DRs and failures			
	Mods	sloc	issues	space
mods	–	0.446	0.363	**0.759**
•sloc	0.446	–	0.602	0.569
issues	0.363	0.602	–	**0.931**
space	**0.759**	0.569	**0.931**	–

likely to lead to reliability problems. It is not surprising that the size of the change 'sloc' is significant because previous studies of space shuttle metrics have shown it to be an important determinant of software quality [12]. Conflicting requirements 'issues' could result in reliability problems when the change is implemented. The on-board computer memory required to implement the change 'space' is critical to reliability because unlike commercial systems, the space shuttle does not have the luxury of large physical memory, virtual memory and disk memory to hold its programs and data. Any increased requirement on its small memory to implement a requirements change comes at the price of demands from competing functions.

In addition to identifying predictive risk factors, it would be desirable to plot failures against risk factors, as the CRs are implemented, to see whether failure occurrence (i.e. reliability risk) increases with increasing values of risk factors. If this were the case, it might be possible to develop predictive *functional* relationships between requirements change activity and reliability.

20.6.2 Dependency Check on Risk Factors

In order to check for possible dependencies among risk factors that could confound the results, rank correlation coefficients as in Table 20.7 must (or should?) be computed. Using an arbitrary value of 0.7, the results indicate a significant dependency among 'issues', 'mods' and 'sloc' for CRs with no DRs; that is, as the number of conflicting requirements increases, the number of modifications and the size of the change increase. In addition, there is a significant dependency among 'space', 'mods' and 'issues' for DRs only or DRs and failures; that is, as the number of conflicting requirements increases, the memory space and the number of modifications increase.

20.6.3 Identification of Modules that Caused Failures

In addition to CRs, code artifacts and their metric values can be used as important discriminants of quality. Table 20.8 shows modules in the present example that caused failures

Table 20.8 Selected risk factor module characteristics

Change request	Failed module	Metric	Metric critical value	Metric value
A	1	Change history line count in module listing	63	558
A	2	Noncommented sloc count	29	408
B	3	Executable statement count	27	419
C	4	Unique operand count	45	83
D	5	Unique operator count	9	33
E	6	Node count (in control graph)	17	66

All the above metrics exceeded the critical values for all the above change requests.

as the result of the CRs and those that had metric values that far exceed the critical values. The latter were computed in previous research [12]; the reader is referred to [12] for a more extensive coverage of this analysis. As already observed, a critical value is a discriminant that distinguishes high-quality software from low-quality software. A module with metric values exceeding the critical values is predicted as being most likely to cause failures. Although, because of the high reliability of the space shuttle, the sample sizes are small, the results consistently show that modules with excessive size and complexity lead to failures; the reliability is low. The application of this information is that there is a high degree of risk when changes are made to software that has the metric characteristics shown in the table. Thus, these characteristics should be considered when making the risk analysis.

20.7 Future Trends

Requirements risk analysis is another project in a series of software measurement projects that has included software reliability modeling and prediction and metrics analysis [22, 23]. The Naval Postgraduate School has been involved in the development and application of software reliability models for many years [24–26]. As is the case in general in software reliability, the models developed use failure data as the driver. This approach has the advantage of using a metric that represents the dynamic behavior of the software. This data is, however, not available until the test phase. Predictions at this phase are useful but it would be much more useful to predict at an earlier phase – preferably during requirements analysis – when the cost of error correction is significantly lower than at later stages of the process. Thus, there is great interest in the software reliability and metrics field in using predictive attributes of software in reliability modeling early on in a project or process. Moreover, such predictions would not only reduce the cost of error correction but also prevent poor-quality software from getting into the hands of the user. Thus, as future research should seek to identify and avoid, or at least minimize, software requirements attributes that cause the subsequent software to be unreliable.

On the basis of the premise that no one model suffices for all prediction applications, a future research goal is to develop an integrated suite of models for various applications. One type of model and its predictions have been described. Other potential members are quality metrics [11] and process stability models [27]. It is recommended that other researchers change their emphasis to the prediction of reliability at the earliest possible time in the development process – to the requirements analysis phase – that heretofore has been unattainable. In doing so, researchers would have the opportunity to determine whether there exists a 'standard' set of risk factors that could be applied in a variety of applications to reliability prediction.

20.8 Conclusions

The objective of the work described in this chapter has been to improve the safety of software, and particularly safety critical systems, by reducing its failures. By improving the reliability of the software which is directly related to safety, one contributes to improving system safety.

Risk factors that are statistically significant can be used to make decisions on the basis of a predictive assessment of the risk associated with making specific changes. These changes affect the reliability of the software. Risk factors that were not statistically significant had a valid and useful goal within the process. Moreover, risk factors that are statistical significant in one release may not be so in a future release. In one investigation, statistically significant results were found for CRs with no DRs versus DRs only or DRs and failures. The number of requirements issues ('issues'), the amount of memory space required to implement the change ('space'), the number of modifications ('mods') and the size of the change ('sloc') were found to be significant for the space shuttle, in that priority order. In view of the dependencies among these risk factors, 'issues' would be the choice if the organization using the software could only afford a single risk factor.

Metric characteristics of modules should be considered when making the risk analysis because metric values that exceed the critical values are likely to result in unreliable software.

The methodology described can be generalized to other risk assessment domains, but the specific risk factors, their numerical values and statistical results will not necessarily be the same. Future research opportunities involve, *inter alia*, application of the methodology described to the next version of the space shuttle software and identification of the statistically significant risk factors to see whether they match the ones identified in this chapter. In addition, researchers may apply our methodology to other domains to test its validity on other applications.

20.9 Acknowledgments

The authors acknowledge the technical support received from Julie Barnard, Boyce Reeves and Patti Thornton of United Space Alliance and the funding support received from Dr Allen Nikora of the Jet Propulsion Laboratory.

References

[1] T.M. Khoshgoftaar and E.B. Allen, "Predicting the order of fault-fault-prone modules in legacy software", *Proceedings of the Ninth International Symposium on Software Reliability Engineering*, November 4–7, 1998, Paderborn, Germany, pp. 344–353.

[2] T.M. Khoshgoftaar, E.B. Allen, R. Halstead and G.P. Trio, "Detection of fault-prone software modules during a spiral evolution of the software", *Proceedings of the International Conference on Software Maintenance*, November 4–8, 1996, Monterey, CA, pp. 69–76.

[3] T.M. Khoshgoftaar, E.B. Allen, K. Kalaichelvan and N. Goel, "Early quality prediction: a case study in telecommunications", *IEEE Software*, vol. 13, no. 1, 1996, pp. 65–71.

[4] D. Lanning and T. Khoshgoftaar, "The impact of software enhancement on software reliability", *IEEE Transactions on Reliability*, vol. 44, no. 4, 1995, pp. 677–682.

[5] J.C. Munson and D.S. Werries, "Measuring software evolution", *Proceedings of the Third International Software Metrics Symposium*, March 25–26, 1996, Berlin, Germany, pp. 41–51.

[6] M.C. Ohlsson and C. Wohlin, "Identification of green, yellow, and red legacy components", *Proceedings of the International Conference on Software Maintenance*, November 16–20, 1998, Bethesda, MD, pp. 6–15.

[7] N. Ohlsson and H. Alberg, "Predicting fault-prone software modules in telephone switches", *IEEE Transactions on Software Engineering*, vol. 22, no. 12, 1996, pp. 886–894.

[8] B.W. Boehm, "Software risk management: principles and practices", *IEEE Software*, vol. 8, no. 1, 1991, pp. 32–41.

[9] *Webster's New Universal Unabridged Dictionary*, 2nd Ed, Simon and Shuster, New York, 1979.

[10] M.M. Lehman, *"Rules and Tools for Software Evolution Planning and Management"*, International Workshop on Feedback and Evolution in Software and Business Processes, Sponsored by UK EPSRC, Imperial College, London, UK, July 10–12, 2000; Revised and extended version in *Annals of Software Engineering*, vol. 11, 2001, pp. 15–44.

[11] N.F. Schneidewind, "Software metrics model for integrating quality control and prediction, *Proceedings of the Eight International Symposium on Software Reliability Engineering*, November 4, 1997, Albuquerque, New Mexico, pp. 402–415.

[12] N.F. Schneidewind, "Software quality control and prediction model for maintenance", *Annals of Software Engineering*, Baltzer Science Publishers, Vol. 9, May 2000, pp. 79–101.

[13] A.P. Nikora, N.F. Schneidewind and J.C. Munson, *IV&V Issues in Achieving High Reliability and Safety in Critical Control Software, Final Report, Volume 1 – Measuring and Evaluating the Software Maintenance Process and Metrics-Based Software Quality Control, Volume 2 – Measuring Defect Insertion Rates and Risk of Exposure to Residual Defects in Evolving Software Systems, and Volume 3 – Appendices*, Jet Propulsion Laboratory, National Aeronautics and Space Administration, Pasadena, CA, January 19, 1998.

[14] L.C. Briand, V.R. Basili and Y.-M Kim, "Change analysis process to characterize software maintenance projects", *Proceedings of the International Conference on Software Maintenance*, Victoria, British Columbia, Canada, September 19–23, 1994, pp. 38–49.

[15] T.M. Pigoski and L.E. Nelson, "Software maintenance metrics: a case study", *Proceedings of the International Conference on Software Maintenance*, Victoria, British Columbia, Canada, September 19–23, 1994, pp. 392–401.

[16] H. Sneed, "Modelling the maintenance process at Zurich life insurance", *Proceedings of the International Conference on Software Maintenance*, Monterey, CA, November 4–8, 1996, pp. 217–226.

[17] G.E. Stark, "Measurements for managing software maintenance", *Proceedings of the International Conference on Software Maintenance*, Monterey, CA, November 4–8, 1996, pp. 152–161.

[18] J.R. Fragola, "Space shuttle program risk management", *Proceedings Annual Reliability and Maintainability Symposium*, 1996, pp. 133–142.

[19] G. Maggio, "Space shuttle probabilistic risk assessment methodology and application", *Proceedings Annual Reliability and Maintainability Symposium*, 1996, pp. 121–132.

[20] S.L. Pfleeger, "Assessing project risk", *Software Tech News, DoD Data Analysis Center for Software*, vol. 2, no. 2, pp. 5–8.

[21] A. Davis, *Software Requirements: Analysis and Specifications*, Prentice-Hall, Englewood Cliffs, NJ, 1990.

[22] N.F. Schneidewind, "How to evaluate legacy system maintenance", *IEEE Software*, vol. 15, no. 4, July/August 1998, pp. 34–42; Also translated into Japanese and reprinted in: *Nikkei Computer Books*, Nikkei Business Publications, Inc., 2-1-1 Hirakawacho, Chiyoda-Ku, Tokyo 102 Japan, 1998, pp. 232–240.

[23] N.F. Schneidewind, "Measuring and evaluating maintenance process using reliability, risk, and test metrics", *Proceedings of the International Conference on Software Maintenance*, October 2, 1997, Bari, Italy, pp. 232–239.

[24] N.F. Schneidewind, "Reliability modeling for safety critical software", *IEEE Transactions on Reliability*, vol. 46, no. 1, 1997, pp. 88–98.

[25] N.F. Schneidewind, "Software reliability model with optimal selection of failure data", *IEEE Transactions on Software Engineering*, vol. 19, no. 11, 1993, pp. 1095–1104.
[26] N.F. Schneidewind and T.W. Keller, "Application of reliability models to the space shuttle", *IEEE Software*, vol. 9, no. 4, 1992 pp. 28–33.
[27] N.F. Schneidewind, "An integrated process and product model", *Proceedings of the Fifth International Metrics Symposium*, November 20–21, 1998, Bethesda, MD, pp. 224–234.

21

Combining Process Feedback with Discrete Event Simulation Models to Support Software Project Management

David Raffo and Joseph Vandeville

21.1 Introduction

Effective project management is critical to the success of software development projects and involves, *inter alia*, two fundamental activities **Planning** and **Control**. The former looks ahead to determine what needs to be done, when it is to be done, how it is to be done and who is going to do it. Planning is usually undertaken prior to embarking upon a project or early in the project life cycle. **Control** is exercised to keep events on course by identifying and correcting deviations from the plan. This second activity has a narrow and immediate focus. It must alert managers to significant deviations from the plan while the project is in process. In combination, the two activities provide timely feedback to maintain the software development process on target.

In a domain where 'gut feel' and subjective estimates are common, software project managers have often looked for tools and an approach to provide quantitative data on current project status and quantitative estimates on potential project outcomes.

To provide an accurate picture of where a project currently is and to make predictions as to where the project is likely to go, the data from which the feedback information is derived must be timely and accurate. This can be facilitated by an ability to quantitatively monitor and assess software projects.

In a recent work, Raffo developed the Process Tradeoff Analysis (PTA) method. This method builds on previous work by Kellner *et al.* at the Software Engineering Institute (SEI) [1–3] by developing a quantitative approach to evaluating potential process changes

---

Software Evolution and Feedback: Theory and Practice   Nazim H. Madhavji, Juan C. Fernández-Ramil and Dewayne E. Perry
© 2006 John Wiley & Sons, Ltd

in terms of development cost, product quality and project schedule [4]. The core of the PTA method addresses the quantitative evaluation of process alternatives by developing stochastic simulation models of each. These models capture process-level details explicitly, including complex interdependencies as process components. The PTA method has been applied to real-world process change problems at leading software development companies [4–7]. This work has been primarily applied to the software project management *planning* function [4, 7].

The goal of on-going research is to develop a forward-looking approach that integrates metrics feedback with simulation models of the software development process in order to support software project management *control*. Such an approach provides predictions of project performance and the impact of various management decisions. By combining metric data with predictive models, a more comprehensive picture can be achieved than by using metrics alone. In addition, the predictive models can support managers as they attempt to re-plan and bring a project back on track.

It is often thought that the discrete event simulation paradigm does not facilitate the exploitation of feedback. This is due to the fact that parameters and calculations in the model do not change over time. In contrast, in continuous simulation models, many of the key parameter values of the model are functions of time. By linking the simulation model to a flexible metrics repository, and then updating model parameters, this potential limitation of DES is overcome in a very meaningful way. Timely process feedback is incorporated into the model in the form of updated model parameters that are based upon new data. These new data better reflect the current status of the project than the original estimates. This constant updating as new data items become available, provides an evolving and more accurate basis upon which to make predictions.

Section 21.2 of this chapter discusses the metrics repository and how it supports software project control by providing up-to-date information in a flexible manner. Section 21.3 provides an overview of a DES model. A distinction is made between the representation used by the DES model and other process modeling approaches that makes it highly compatible with the metrics repository. In section 21.4, software project control using OBCLs is discussed. This approach helps support the Quantitative Process Management and Software Quality Management Level 4 Key Process Areas (KPAs) of the Capability Maturity Model (CMM) [8]. This approach also supports the Organizational Process Performance and the Quantitative Project Management level 4 Process Areas (PAs) as well as Organizational Innovation and Deployment and Casual Analysis and Resolution level 5 PAs of the Capability Maturity Model Integration (CMMI) [9]. Finally, an illustrative example of a software process simulation model that has been applied at a leading software developer is presented.

21.2 Providing Up-to-Date Process Feedback

21.2.1 Feedback in Simulation Models

The concept of feedback in process simulation models to date has been limited to 'feedback loops' that are typically modeled in continuous simulation (a.k.a. system dynamics (SD)) models. In continuous simulation, model parameters are represented as functions that vary over time. These functions may also include terms that vary based upon the current value of a selected model parameter. For instance, let the *number of tasks completed* be a level of the continuous model and *productivity* be a time varying function that changes depending upon the *number of tasks completed* (as well as other parameters) as it is in [10]. Since *productivity* also affects the rate at which tasks are completed, we see that a feedback loop is created where both parameters affect the other.

The fundamental concepts being captured in this kind of feedback relationship are

1. the current state of the system is used to calculate the value of performance measures;
2. circular loops of causality can be represented; and
3. the value of functions change depending upon the current state of the system.

Using continuous models, the current state of the system is totally dependant upon the relationships determined *a priori* before the project executes. In short, the feedback is derived completely from the model. As a result, model predictions get less accurate as the project executes.

With the approach presented in this chapter, feedback is derived directly from updated parameters as the project progresses. These model parameters accurately reflect the current state of the system. As the project progresses, the time horizon of the model is reduced. This, coupled with the updated model parameters, provides increasing prediction accuracy.

21.2.2 Metrics Repository

An up-to-date source of project and process information is necessary to support project management and control decisions about a project. To collect, warehouse and report this information requires a flexible, extensible repository that can answer *ad hoc* queries. Such a repository also provides the critical link between raw project metrics and model parameters and must facilitate the collection of data on a 'real-time' basis.

The repository that was used in the application being presented in this chapter was developed by Harrison and is based on a *transformation view* of the software development process that permits flexibility in both information storage and in the types of queries it can accommodate [11]. The transformation model considers artifacts such as specifications, designs and code to be *transformed* by the application of a *transformation process* into a new artifact. For instance, a design artifact may be transformed into a code artifact by the application of a *programming transformation*.

Artifacts possess certain properties, such as *size*, *volatility*, *complexity*, and so on, and the transformation process properties such as *resources consumed*, *errors introduced* and so on. The transformation process as well as the artifacts themselves can be represented as in the simplified entity-relationship diagram of Figure 21.1.

That data model of the software development process denotes that an artifact is related to another one by some transformation *relationship*.

In order to provide a historical record of the state of the developing product as it progresses through the process, snapshots of project characteristics are recorded each time a *significant* transformation occurs.

A web-based prototype of the Metrics Repository is at: http://www.cs.pdx.edu/~reposit/. This site describes the schema and provides limited access to the prototype implementation.

The Prototype Repository contains the following tables or relations among others:

- Entities
    - *Artifact* (**id**, name)
    - *Event* (**id**, name)

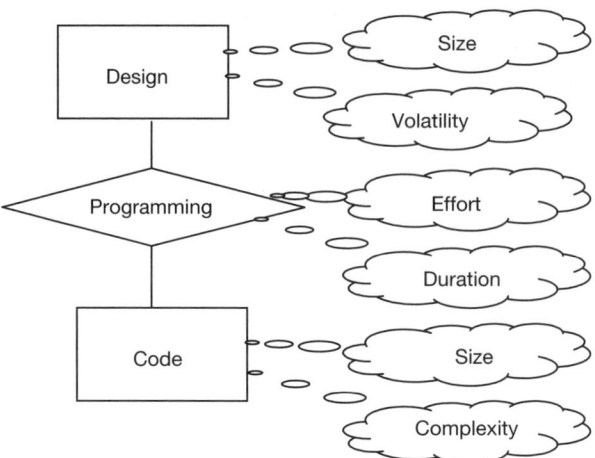

Figure 21.1 Entity-relationship diagram of a portion of the transformation process

- ○ *Resource* (**id**, name)
- ○ *Characteristic* (**id**, name, type, description)
- • Relationships (all are *n*-to-*n*, and the entire tuple comprises the key):
  - ○ *transforms* (Tid, Artifact.id, Artifact.id, Event.id, EndDate)
  - ○ *possesses* ({Artifact, Resource, Defect, Event}.id, Characteristic. id, qty)
  - ○ *consumes* (transforms.id, Resource. id, quantity)

All entity instances and transformation relationships are assigned a unique identifier (id). This facilitates the transformation of artifacts of the developing product and the retention of associated attributes. For instance, the transformation of a design specification, to another artifact such as a design structure or a section of code and the resources necessary to perform the transformation are captured.

Artifacts represent the *trackable* items under configuration control that make up a project such as code units, specification documents, design documents, test cases and so on. *Events* represent types of activities that occur, such as an inspection, a modification, an error correction, and so forth. *Resources* are consumables such as effort, calendar time, computer time that are of value to the project and that are used up by artifact creation. *Characteristics* represent types of information about the entities – size, complexity, number of defects, and so on, as appropriate and available.

Relationships connect entity instances to other entity instances. The most significant one is the *Transforms* relationship, which defines the transformation of one *artifact* into another as a result of an *Event*. One must also be interested in the *Resources* that are consumed by a particular transformation, so the *Consumes* relationship associates a particular transformation with a resource type or types as well as the amount consumed during the transformation. Every *artifact*, *event* and *resource possesses* a certain set of *characteristics*.

In the example discussed in this chapter, the repository represents things such as individual design documents and software code modules as artifact items. Events such as a code modification or corrections transform one artifact into another. For instance, a code module that is part of a larger CSCI[1] may be modified owing to an enhancement request. This enhancement is an event that triggers a transformation from the pre-change artifact into the post-change artifact.

Along with the record of each enhancement, the repository also maintains information on the resources expended in performing it (i.e. labor hours). If errors are detected, the repository links the particular version of the code module with the associated entries in the defect tracking system. Queries to the repository can aggregate information for the entire CSCI.

21.3 Discrete Event Simulation Models

Given the discussion above, it is clear that a detailed artifact-based process model of software development projects would fit very well with the metrics repository. This section briefly describes the on-going work with Northrop Grumman Corporation to develop such an artifact-based (entity-based) model with an interface to the metrics repository with parameterized links that are generated by a set of database queries. The parameters are updated, as appropriate, during significant project *transformations* to provide process feedback to the model to make improved predictions.

Northrop Grumman has been sponsoring research into the use of stochastic simulation models to support software process improvement and quantitative project management issues along the lines described above since 1996. They have recognized that such a quantitative, adaptive, simulation model can be used to simulate and predict the impact of proposed changes to the software development process prior to its deployment. In pursuit of this goal such a model has been developed. It reflects the artifacts and activities of one of Northrop Grumman's large-scale software development projects. The model uses cost, schedule and quality data collected from past projects. In order to maximize the benefit and long-term practical potential of this work, the investigation has been expanded to explore the integration of up-to-date metrics feedback extracted from a metrics repository with a discrete event simulation model of the software development process as proposed above.

The work has been based on the process being used to develop software for airborne radar surveillance and battle management systems (SBMS) at the Northrop Grumman's SBMS Melbourne site. The portion of the software development process modeled consists of 71 distinct development steps. The architecture of this model replicates that of the actual software development process. In both, some activities are executed sequentially, and others concurrently through the use of multiple entities.

The DES model can be viewed as a hierarchy of process steps with four distinct levels. The first three levels provide a detailed graphical representation of the process. At the top level, the model reflects the main life cycle phases of Preliminary Design, Detailed Design, Code and Unit Test and Computer Program Engineering Test (CPET) (– consists of internal integration and testing activities, which are not formally witnessed by the customer). In the second of the model levels, each of the life cycle phases is

---

[1] Computer Software Configuration Item (CSCIs) – see Air Force standard Department of Defense (DOD)-STD-2167A. A major software component of a system that is designated by the Buyer for configuration management to ensure the integrity of the delivered product.

decomposed into several main tasks. In the third level, the main tasks are, in turn, decomposed into sub-tasks. The fourth level implements the equations used to predict process performance in terms of quality, number of staff (equivalent manpower), person hours and schedule.

The overall duration of each simulation run is equal to the critical path schedule. Earned value is accrued by each activity as the project progresses. The amount of earned value assigned to each activity is based upon planned earned value allocations. A more detailed presentation of the actual simulation model or the data contained in the model is, however, not possible due to confidential disclosure limitations.

The equations used by the model were developed from detailed empirical analyses of past project data. Expert judgment was also used to estimate parameters for which sufficient data was not available. The model was then rigorously validated [12]. Taken together, the equations provide an integrated prediction of cost (development effort), quality (remaining defects), and schedule (project duration).

When the simulation model is run, parameters for each execution are drawn from populations of data that were collected in the repository from previous versions of this system. Thus, the distributions from which model parameters are drawn are derived empirically from previous projects. Using multiple runs, the model provides the mean and variance of performance results that may be experienced by different teams. Hence, the results of the simulation are stochastic, capturing the inherent uncertainty associated with real-world development. The process model was developed using Extend™ from Imagine That[2].

At SBMS Melbourne, the model has been used to analyze several process change problems and to evaluate alternative process configurations for a new project proposal. The analyses have also included flexible 'what if' assessments of several process change options.

One key distinction between the SD models as compared to a DES model is the handling of process artifacts. DES models permit the representation of individual artifacts with each able to retain distinct attributes. That is, rather than representing generic code or design artifacts, the discrete simulation model, represents a particular code module of some specific size, complexity, number of defects and so forth. This detail fits well with the structure and output of the metrics repository and accurately reflects what actually occurs on a project. By allowing for parameter variation, the added detail also expands substantially the scope for addressing interesting questions such as: How does the process react if only 20% of the modules contain 80% of the defects? How does the process react if some code modules are very large or highly complex rather than uniform throughout? What is the effect on the design of a high or low degree of fan-out of code modules? In short, this representation permits study of central and important issues related to project management.

Using active process feedback from the repository permits improved accuracy in the predictions, avoiding the need to base model predictions on estimates of key model parameters as stored in the repository some time earlier.

As will be discussed in the next section, this approach supports active planning and re-planning activities described earlier as part of the project management controlling activities.

---

[2] Extend is a registered trademark of Imagine That, Inc., San Francisco, California (http://www.imaginethatinc.com)

21.4 Combining Process Feedback with the Discrete Model

The feedback loops in a DES system are qualitatively different from those in an SD model. In an SD model, feedback loops are hypothesized and then represented explicitly in the model. In a DES system, feedback occurs as an extension of the project itself as shown in Figure 21.2 and is incorporated into the model by linking with the flexible metrics repository. The *values* of the *updated model parameters* incorporate the results of feedback as actually experienced, including, for example, reflections of schedule pressure, productivity changes resulting from a mix of experienced/junior programmers, and so on (i.e. factors explicitly represented in SD models [10, 13]). The feedback implied by the parameter updates is supplied continually from the repository and are then continually reflected in the project and the process performance. This provides a sounder basis and a reduced time horizon that improves prediction, precision and accuracy.

21.4.1 Comparing Statistical Process Control with Outcome Based Control Limits

The phrases *in control* and *out of control* are defined to mean that the project 'is' or 'is not' adhering to the plan within stated limits for performance measures under consideration.

Using statistical process control (SPC), control limits are derived statistically from previous measurements of the process [14]. The resultant limits are independent of the desired outcome. We define OBCLs, which are used as guides for assessing whether the project is 'in control' from a project management perspective. OBCLs can correspond to internal performance goals or can reflect contract performance requirements.

The decision as to whether a project is 'out of control' requires (a) constant monitoring of the current state of the project and (b) an objective, accurate and meaningful way to compare the current state to the planned state. Software process simulation models address this issue very well. In particular, they can identify changes that will have a significant impact on the project. Equally, they can distinguish deviations from the plan that will *not*

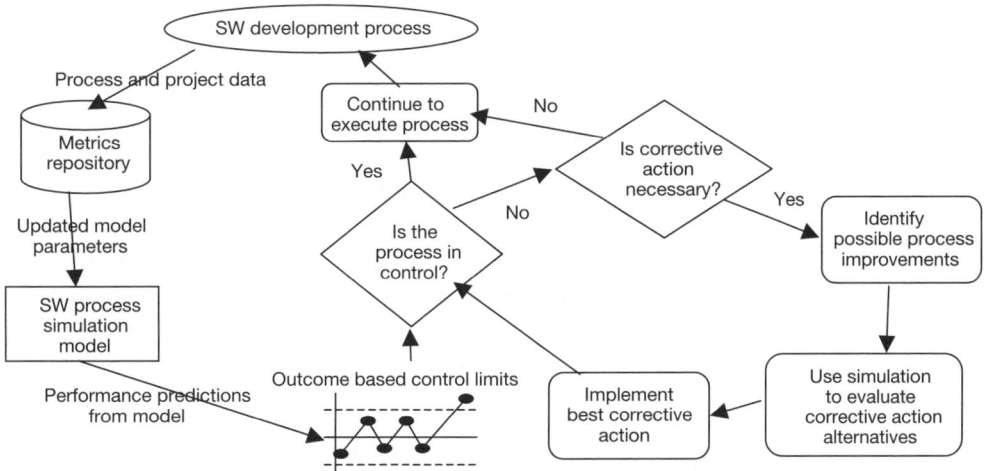

Figure 21.2 Integrating process feedback with simulation models

affect the project. For example, although coding on a particular enhancement may begin late, that may not have a noticeable impact on the project if it is not on the critical path.

By providing up-to-date metrics and other data to the simulation model on a continuing basis, the values of parameters can be maintained more accurately relative to a changing product and project domain. The time interval over which parameter estimates are sufficiently valid is extended and knowledge about the status of the project is more precise.

This performance would be compared with the OBCLs. If the project is within the OBCLs, confidence is increased that the current approach will achieve the desired performance targets. This is the primary feedback loop shown in Figure 21.2.

On the other hand, if performance is outside acceptable bounds, or any other significant deviation between planned and actual behavior is identified, management is alerted to the fact that action is required. Prior to taking action, it must be determined whether the deviation, is significant. Prediction of the final outcome of the project, given the apparent deviation can help determine whether the project is truly in trouble. Alternative actions to bring a project back into control and alternative remedial steps must then be identified.

If the apparent or suspected deviation is confirmed and indicates that the project may be in trouble, the project manager can change aspects of the model to reflect potential process step changes and explore their likely impact. Similarly, potential actions to bring the process back under control can be analyzed and compared for effectiveness, risk and cost. This use of the model is reflected in the secondary loop shown in Figure 21.2.

21.5 Illustrative Example

In this section, we present an illustrative example using the combined simulation model and metrics repository feedback framework. The model being used is based on one that has been applied by a leading software developer. The data has, however, been masked to maintain company confidentiality requirements. The purpose of this example is to show how updated information from the project (the process feedback) is gathered through the metrics repository and then used to support quantitative management of the software development process as discussed in this paper.

21.5.1 The Scenario Under Consideration

Consider a modified waterfall software development process that includes the life cycle phases: Requirements Analysis and Design, Preliminary Design, Detailed Design, Coding, Unit Test, CPET and System Test. The original development organization has been contracted to provide a 32 KLOC enhancement. It requires changes to six CSCIs with modifications to each ranging from 4 to 8 KLOC. A process model of the type discussed has been used to prepare the initial bid. Estimates for cost, quality and schedule performance for the proposed project were obtained from the model using, among others, measures of past project data augmented by updated estimates for productivity, efficiency and product size.

To illustrate how the model may be used to support project management, we now construct the following situation. The client organization has now accepted the bid. As a result, the bid estimates have now become the contracted project performance levels by which the project will be evaluated. The performance estimates developed by the

Table 21.1 Model estimates of project performance

	Mean	Std
Total effort (cost) in person months	418.5	5.54
Project duration (schedule) in months	26.2	2.03
Number of remaining defects (quality)	77.4	3.68

Table 21.2 Project performance targets and limits

	Target	Blue limits		Green limits		Yellow limits		Red limits	
		Upper	Lower	Upper	Lower	Upper	Lower	Upper	Lower
Total effort (cost) in person months	418.5	439.4	397.6	481.3	355.7	544.0	292.9	N/A	292.9
Project duration (schedule) in months	26.2	27.5	24.9	30.2	22.3	34.1	18.4	N/A	18.4
Number of remaining defects (quality)	77.4	81.2	73.5	89.0	65.8	100.6	54.2	N/A	54.2

simulation model are shown in Table 21.1 and the target performance levels for the proposed project in Table 21.2.

As can be seen, the *estimates* developed by the software process simulation model are expressed in the form of distributions with the expected values (means) and standard deviations shown. (Each of the performance measure outcome distributions from the simulation model were statistically tested and shown to be normally distributed.)

We define the *target values* for the project to be fixed levels that are set by management and may be contractually binding. In addition, as part of the *OBCLs* approach, management sets acceptable ranges or control limits for performance.

In some commercial or US DoD settings, the customer/client evaluates the software firm on a number of measures such as cost, schedule, quality, productivity and so forth using an appropriate system to indicate the degree to which the planned performance targets have been met. In this example, four colors are used to indicate the level achieved. Blue is the highest rating and is considered *excellent*. It indicates that the performance measure of interest is within 5% of the target value. Green is also considered to be good and indicates that the measure of interest is between 5% and 15% of the target value. Yellow is marginal performance and indicates that the measure of interest is between 15% and 30% of that value. Finally, Red indicates poor or unacceptable performance with a deviation of more than 30% from the target.

Different products addressing different markets will require different levels of performance to be successful. Using *OBCLs*, the target values and control limits are evaluated in relation to *outcomes* that *management has chosen* to aim for. Hence, OBCLs can be determined based upon the client's requirements, the client/supplier contract, contractor's strategic or financial objectives, and so on. The approach is very flexible and adaptable to the needs of an organization.

In DoD contracts, performance levels for cost, quality and schedule are contractually specified prior to beginning the project. In such situations, tight limits would be set for all of the performance measures based on standards and contractual obligations. Management would want a high level of certainty that these targets could and would be achieved. In commercial projects, schedule or time to market and product quality may be extremely important. Effort or cost may be less critical. In these situations very tight limits may be set around schedule performance, medium to tight limits would be set around quality and relatively looser limits might be set around effort or cost. The OBCL framework can easily accommodate these choices. In this example that follows, we can see that tight limits have been set around all three performance measures.

21.5.2 Determining the Performance of the Baseline Process

Continuing with the specific example: The next step is to evaluate the baseline performance of the project. To do this, the estimated project performance must be evaluated in terms of the OBCLs. As can be seen in Figure 21.3 and Table 21.3, predictions from the model indicate that the project has a 99.9% chance of achieving a blue rating for effort or cost performance; a 74% chance of achieving a blue rating for task duration or schedule performance; and a 70% chance of achieving a blue rating for target defect level or quality

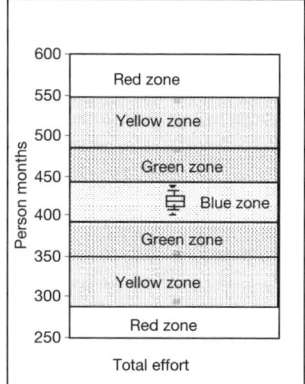 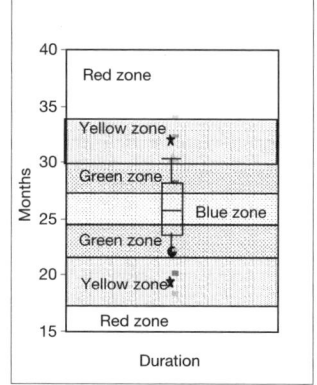 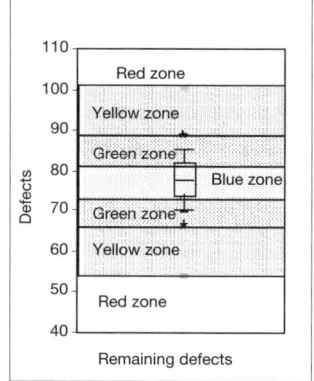

Figure 21.3 Bar and whisker charts of each performance measure with the appropriate OBCL.

Table 21.3 Probability of achieving blue/green performance for the baseline process

	Prob. of blue rating	Prob. of blue/green rating
Total effort (cost) in person months	99.9%	99.9%
Project duration (schedule) months*	74.1%	97.4%
Remaining defects (quality)	70.7%	99.8%

*Since there are multiple CSCIs being modified of various durations, the chance of the schedule reducing below the limits was assessed to be negligible

performance. Furthermore, the model predicts that there is a 99.9% chance of achieving a blue *or green* rating for effort or cost performance, a 97% chance of achieving a blue *or green* rating for task duration or schedule performance; and a chance of over 99% of achieving a blue *or green* rating for target defect level or quality performance. In this example, the management decided that it would be acceptable if all three performance measures had a 90% or better chance of being within 15% of the target, that is, achieving *a blue or green* level of performance.

If the baseline process does not yield satisfactory results (e.g. the level of certainty for achieving the desired outcomes is not sufficiently high), personnel, organizational or process changes may be required to ensure that the desired targets can (or will) be attained. That is, the OBCL approach can also be used for up-front planning.

21.5.3 Use of the Model and Metrics for Quantitative Process Feedback Management

As the project is initiated and work proceeds, the repository is automatically updated. For instance, modification of CSCI *a* to the enhancement request, is reflected in the repository by the adding of an entity occurrence for CSCI a' (the new version of CSCI *a*) and an enhancement transformation link that associates CSCI *a* with CSCI a' and the effort consumed in the process. At the completion of each major life cycle phase, or at other times (e.g. once a day) or when deemed timely, a current snapshot of the project is obtained from the metrics repository. This is done by aggregating all the data generated or changed since the last update and adding it to the repository. Thus, all events, transformations, artifacts, links, and so on, stored in the various project tracking systems since the last such snapshot are now represented in the information available to and accessible by the model. Updated model parameters are then generated using the new data. Among others, in the present example, these parameters include: detected defects, estimated size of the project, productivity, time and effort expended.

Incorporating the updated project information into the model is a two-step process. First, previously estimated model parameters and the new data from activities and phases of the project that have just been completed, are replaced. This improves the precision of the model and reduces variability of the estimated project outcomes. Second, the differences between actual observations and initial estimates may then be determined. The implications of the estimation errors may be assessed and project parameters that impact future phases may be modified accordingly.

Suppose, for example, that an increase in the number of detected defects primarily during the Preliminary Design life cycle phase, has been observed as shown in Table 21.4. It is possible that an increase in the observed number of defects for one or two phases

Table 21.4 Number of estimated and actual defects

Number of defects detected during	Initial estimates		Observed Values	Percentage Increase
	Mean	STD		
Requirements phase	112.9	3.77	113	0.1%
Preliminary design phase	67.5	2.06	78	15.5%

indicates a trend. If so, what will the impact be on overall project performance? Will it be possible to achieve the management's desired outcomes?

Depending on the extent of the differences between the initial project estimates and actual project data, management may *investigate* the causes of the differences. This investigation would include determination of possible reasons for the differences. If these suggest that such deviations will continue, model parameters dealing with future phases must be updated. The model is then run to provide a quantitative assessment of the implications of the updated parameter estimates. In the present example, it was observed that instead of an expectation of 67 defects detected during Preliminary Design, the actual number detected was 78 defects – a 15.5% increase. Upon further investigation, it was found that although the project was staffed by developers with more than five years experience with the firm, over half of them were new to the development of Internet applications. This suggests that higher than expected defect levels are likely to continue, at least for some time. It should be noted that other model parameters such as productivity, effort expended and so forth would be expected to change as well. This provides additional evidence for analysis of the cause or source of the problem. For the purposes of this example, however, the discussion is limited to the consideration of the observed differences in increased defects during Preliminary Design.

In this instance, after investigating the causes of the increased defects, management and the developers agreed that the number of defects would increase during the remainder of the project. As a result, the distribution of defects injected into the model was increased by 10%. The variability of the number of defects injected into the product was increased accordingly.

21.5.4 Assessing the Implications of Feedback and Developing an Action Plan (Is the Process in Control?)

The predicted outcomes for the parameter changes described in the previous paragraph are shown in Table 21.5. Depending upon how close predicted outcomes are to the target, the management will decide if *corrective action* needs to be taken in order to return the project back into the satisfactory performance range. Target values are shown in the first column of data. In columns two and three, the predicted outcomes (mean and standard deviation) for each of the three main project performance measures are shown. In column four, we show the probability that the project will achieve a blue performance rating.

Table 21.5 Project performance using observed defect levels for requirements and preliminary design

	Target values	Model predictions		Prob. of blue rating	Prob. of blue/green rating
		Mean	Std		
Total effort (cost) in person months	418.5	428.3	10.6	85.2%	99.9%
Project duration (schedule) in months*	26.2	28.1	3.9	43.8%	69.8%
Remaining defects (quality)	77.4	81.7	9.8	27.9%	71.7%

*Since there are multiple CSCIs being modified of various durations, the chance of the schedule reducing below the limits was assessed to be negligible

Finally, column 5 shows the probability that the project would achieve a green or blue rating. It will be observed that this rating for effort has a 99.9% chance of being achieved, but duration and delivered defects or quality have probabilities of about 70% and 72% respectively. The results, as shown in Table 21.5, were considered unacceptable by the management.

21.5.5 Taking Corrective Action and Assessing the Impact of the Changes

Once it is decided that action needs to be taken, a variety of potential process changes can be explored using the simulation model. If the simulation results indicate that with application of the corrective action, it is likely that the project will achieve the desired performance, action can be taken. The next major snapshot will then reflect the impact of the change.

Possible corrective actions in the present example could be the introduction of expert developers to help with development, the provision of additional testing, and so on. In general, a number of alternative of complementary corrective actions are possible. Using the simulation model, it is easy to assess the potential impact of each of these. Consider for example, the possibility of bringing expert developers to consult with the current developers and to inspect the larger, more complex CSCIs. The anticipated implications of this action are that the effectiveness of the detailed design and coding inspections would improve and the number of defects being injected would be reduced, by a certain estimated amount. The action would incur the additional costs and effort that would have to be expended by members of the original development team as well as experienced developers. The result of applying the corrective action is shown in Table 21.6. An additional 40 person months are included in the project costs for the additional effort for the corrective action. Whether these increases are acceptable in return for maintaining an acceptable performance level is a decision for management.

At this point, management selects and implements the corrective action alternative (best cost/performance balance) that appears optimal from the client's point of view and monitors the process to see that improvement is being achieved. The next project snapshot will be taken at the end of the Detailed Design Phase or other selected project event. Once again, model parameters will be updated with latest set of data and observations. The feedback cycle will then be repeated to determine whether the desired project behavior and performance is being achieved.

Table 21.6 Project performance using observed defect levels and incorporating the process change

	Target values	Model predictions		Prob. of blue rating	Prob. of blue/green rating
		Mean	Std		
Total effort (cost) in person months	418.5	457.2	7.7	1.1%	99.9%
Project duration (schedule) in months*	26.2	25.4	3.4	73.1%	91.7%
Remaining defects (quality)	77.4	74.8	5.8	45.4%	93.2%

*Since there are multiple CSCIs being modified of various durations, the chance of the schedule reducing below the limits was assessed to be negligible

21.6 Conclusions

Process feedback can make an important and valuable contribution to process change planning and software project management. This chapter has discussed on-going work with an industrial partner to integrate feedback from the software development process with a DES model to improve process performance predictions. The work follows earlier process modeling research that studied methods for predicting the impact of process changes in terms of cost, quality and schedule. A realistic example, derived from an actual project at a leading software development company has been described.

A flexible metrics repository provides feedback that is used to generate updated simulation model parameters at predefined project milestones. Model predictions using updated parameters and current project data are compared to Outcome Based Control Limits (OBCLs) defined for the project. If the expected performance is outside of the OBCLs, the management can be alerted to a potential problem and take corrective action. This is also the goal of methods based on SPC but it cannot be achieved using individual metrics alone. The predictive model is used to evaluate the outcomes of potential management decisions to bring the project back 'in control' and help the project meet its pre-determined goals.

This approach directly supports the ability to quantitatively monitor and assess software projects. As a result, this approach supports the KPAs and PAs of Levels 4 and 5 of the Capability Maturity Model (CMM) and Capability Maturity Model Integration (CMMI).

21.7 Acknowledgements

This work has benefited from discussion, comments and participation by Siri-on Setamanit and Rohit Rampal. Their contributions are gratefully acknowledged. In addition, the authors are grateful to the Software Engineering Research Center (SERC), a National Science Foundation Industry/University Collaborative Research Center for supporting this research effort.

References

[1] Kellner, M., *"Software Process Modeling: Value and Experience"*, Software Engineering Institute, Carnegie Mellon University, Pittsburgh, PA, SEI Technical Review 1989.
[2] Kellner, M., "Software Process Modeling Experience", presented at *The 11th International Conference on Software Engineering*, Pittsburgh, PA, 1989.
[3] Kellner, M.I., "Experience with Enactable Software Process Models", presented at *The Fifth International Conference on The Software Process*, Kennebunkport, ME, 1990.
[4] Raffo, D.M., *"Modeling Software Processes Quantitatively and Assessing the Impact of Potential Process Changes on Process Performance"*, Graduate School of Industrial Administration, Carnegie Mellon University, Pittsburgh, PA, UMI Dissertation Services #9622438, 1996.
[5] Raffo, D.M. and Kellner, M.I., "Using Quantitative Process Modeling to Forecast the Impact of Potential Software Process Improvements", *Proceedings of the 10th International Forum on COCOMO and Software Cost Modeling*, Held in Pittsburgh, PA, October, 1995.
[6] Raffo, D.M. and Kellner, M.I., "Field Study Results Using the Process Tradeoff Analysis Method", *Proceedings of the 1996 Software Engineering Process Group Conference*, Held in Atlantic City, NJ, May 20–23, 1996.
[7] Raffo, D.M., Vandeville, J.V. and Martin, R.H., "Software Process Simulation to Achieve Higher CMM Levels", *Journal of Systems and Software*, Vol. 46, No. 2/3, 15 April 1999.

[8] Paulk, M.C., Curtis, W., Chrissis, M.B. and Weber, C.V., "Capability Maturity Model for Software, Version 1.1", Technical Report SEI-93-TR-24, Software Engineering Institute, Carnegie Mellon University, Pittsburgh, PA, February, 1993.

[9] CMMI Product Team, *"Capability Maturity Model Integration: CMMI for Systems Engineering and Software Engineering (CMMI-SE/SW, V1. 1)"*, *CMU/SEI-2002-TR-002*, Software Engineering Institute, Carnegie Mellon University, Pittsburgh, PA, December, 2001.

[10] Abdel-Hamid, T. and Madnick, S., *"Software Project Dynamics"*, Prentice Hall, 1991.

[11] Harrison, W., "A Universal Metrics Repository", *Proceedings of the Pacific Northwest Software Quality Conference*, Portland, OR, October 18–19, 2000.

[12] Martin, R.H., "A Hybrid Model of the Software Development Process", Ph.D. Dissertation, Engineering Management Program, Portland State University, November, 2001.

[13] Martin, R.H. and Raffo, D.M., "A Model of the Software Development Process Using Both Continuous and Discrete Models", *International Journal of Software Process Improvement and Practice*, Vol. 5, No. 2/3, June/September, 2000, pp. 147–157.

[14] Summers, D., *"Quality"*, Prentice Hall, 1997.

22

A Feedforward Capability to Improve Software Reestimation

William W. Agresti

22.1 Introduction

This chapter is motivated by experiences of the author managing large software projects and advising the U.S. Government, especially the Department of Defense, on the progress/status/risks/health of many large software-intensive systems acquisitions. In every case, preproject estimates were generated for key measures, such as expected size, cost and schedule. In most cases, the estimates were based on the use of software cost estimation tools. Once a project began, a question of effective reestimation arose: How to incorporate, in a timely way, events, in-process measures, and qualitative information to improve the estimates.

This chapter examines the reestimation problem for the key software project characteristics of cost and schedule: specifically, the at-completion cost and the date when the software will be delivered. Other important aspects, such as delivered quality, could easily be addressed as well using the approach discussed here.

22.1.1 Reestimation: State of the Practice

It is widely acknowledged in the systems development community that the estimates produced at project initiation are often far off from their eventual, actual values. Boehm, *et al.* quote the Standish group study which found that 53% of software projects exceeded both their planned budget and schedule by 50% or more [1]. The reasons for this poor record are well known, if not easy to remedy, and include the following:

- Factors that are not under control of the project team turn out to have great effect
- Changes, often substantial, once the project is underway

Software Evolution and Feedback: Theory and Practice   Nazim H. Madhavji, Juan C. Fernández-Ramil and Dewayne E. Perry
© 2006 John Wiley & Sons, Ltd

- Lack of understanding at the start of a project as to what is really needed and practically attainable
- Increasing complexity of the task as more interrelationships emerge and must be considered

Acknowledging the difficulty of accurate estimation at the start of a project suggests that the estimates should improve as the project unfolds. Project management is then able to incorporate what it is learning into refinements of its original estimates. And, to varying degrees, the estimates do improve. Reestimation is currently handled in the following ways:

- *The modeling and estimating process recognizes learning explicitly*: For example, COCOMO II is a family of models, reflecting three stages of learning: the early prototyping state, early design stage, and postarchitecture stage. Each stage signals a milestone of learning, calling for a new round of estimates to accompany the increased knowledge [1]. The software engineering laboratory at NASA Goddard Space Flight Center uses a series of estimating relationships, based on what is known at the time of estimation [2]. Early in a project, cost estimation is based on the number of subsystems. Later on, estimation is based on the number of units or packages. In [3], Agresti, *et al.* show how size estimation is successively refined as the project team learns and incorporates more detailed information.
- *Providing for periodic reestimation as part of the project management process*: Project (or higher level) management may require reestimated cost, schedule and quality after a fixed time period (e.g. at monthly program reviews) or at project milestones (e.g. completion of systems requirements review).
- *The estimation model is recalibrated during the project*: The estimation model has a recalibration feature, a way for actual values and experiences to produce recalibrated model parameters, so the model in the future will generate estimates that are more reflective of the current project realities.
- *Reestimation is triggered by feedback from the ongoing project*: Feedback is obtained through regular metrics data collection, formal briefings, project reviews or informal reports from team members about the progress of their activities and the obstacles that remain. The comparison of actual data to plans and estimates can be quantified and formalized by reference to earned value or the proposed stakeholder value (see Chapter 24).

While these options for reestimation exist, cost and schedule keep exceeding even the reestimates. Forces that cause the deviation from the predicted behavior are still at play. Furthermore, the reality of systems development, especially early in a project, is that reestimation is not undertaken as frequently as it should be because managers must often attend to higher priority activities. Effective reestimation requires vigilance. In a typically high-pressure environment, managers must remain ever conscious of the assumptions that underlie the estimation models they use, so they are alert when their project experiences deviate from those assumptions. For example:

- As the users' needs become clearer, are the magnitude and complexity of requirements different from the size and difficulty of the job as assumed in the estimation model?

- The project was not able to use a programming support environment which it had planned to use: How does this new reality correspond to the parameter value used for the tool-support driver in the cost estimation model?

Because of the attention required to deal with reestimation, managers are inclined to perpetuate preproject estimates beyond their useful life. Revisiting the parameter values and assumptions to consider updating them takes management time that is typically in short supply during a project. In one particular project management review, the developers, after one year into a project, were still using the original preproject estimates. There are many reasons for this situation, including –

- *The original estimates appear more authoritative*: Software estimation tools frequently cover many of the key drivers of cost and schedule (and their interaction) in a systematic way, so they provide users with a sense of confidence and completeness in using them as the basis of estimation. Being computer based and often using well-known products (e.g. COCOMO [1], KnowledgePLAN [4], or SLIM [5]), the models produce output that has a ring of authority. By using these tools, the developer is sending a message that it is using due diligence and industry best practices.
- *There is no consensus industry best practice on how to update an estimate*: There are no prescribed ways to update the preproject estimate to include the variety and diversity of in-process data, measures and information. For some models and for some kinds of data, there may be guidance on updating the estimates. However, the updating task is not at all clear in many other cases, to incorporate, for example, the ongoing requirements elicitation, changes in the COTS marketplace, or the results of off-line technology and performance analyses.
- *Managers may be encouraged to copy previous estimates simply as a way to minimize the time spent updating estimates*: The development of the initial estimates takes effort to determine the proper setting of parameters. In a typical reestimation scenario, a manager will have the initial estimate, and be asked whether these are still the values that should be used for the next round of generating estimates. Granted, managers are understandably concerned when the accuracy of estimates reflects on their competence. However, with the press of other responsibilities and the need for 'context-switching' – that is, time needed for managers to get reacquainted with model parameters and their meanings – it is tempting for managers to simply reuse the existing values. In doing so, they perpetuate model parameters that may increasingly not be indicative of the current development project. An example in Section 22.3.2 illustrates the effect on multiple parameters when the composition of the team changes.

22.1.2 Objective

The purpose of this investigation is to explore the introduction of a feedforward capability into estimation models to improve the reestimation process. It is believed that reestimation can be improved by feedforward working as a complement to the feedback processes currently being used (e.g. to incorporate feedback on actual hours worked and units designed).

To clarify whether feedforward does indeed improve reestimation, consider a measure of effectiveness for the reestimation process to be the Estimating Quality Factor (EQF), introduced by DeMarco [6], which reflects the differences, at every point during the project, between current cost and schedule estimates and the at-completion values of these properties. In particular, EQF reflects the common-sense view that a project is adversely affected when inaccurate initial estimates continue to prevail after the project begins.

22.1.3 Related Research

This chapter fits the initiative on Feedback, Evolution and Software Technology (FEAST) [7] by addressing feedback in software processes, although the attention here is on an individual development process rather than a process that includes field use and changes to a product. However, the two processes are obviously related: the estimation and reestimation may be for the development of a given product release, while the collection of such releases characterizes the evolution of the product. The theme of this chapter is certainly consistent with the FEAST Hypothesis, that to achieve major process improvement of E-type processes, their global dynamics must be taken into account. The global dynamics are being taken into consideration in this chapter by analyzing the nature and content of early project experiences, such as requirements specification and high-level design activities in a development process. This investigation directly relates to the Eighth Law on feedback in E-type systems, and the 'need for continuing adaptation to exogenous changes.' [7]

This chapter is also consistent with the FEAST Uncertainty Principle. As discussed in [7], uncertainty is intrinsic to the development and evolution of E-type systems. The threat of error or failure due to uncertainty can be addressed by early detection of invalid assumptions through regular checking of the set of assumptions to detect ones that are invalid. Lehman cites the value of making assumptions more accessible and complete to facilitate their review [7]. This chapter discusses a technique for making assumptions more readily accessible, specifically by making it easier for project managers to recognize that early experiences are at odds with provisions of the estimation models.

Two papers from the FEAST 2000 Workshop discuss recalibration and feedback that have similarities with this chapter. Boehm presents a global organizational feedback cycle for coping with change during project execution, to support COCOMO II rescoping and recalibration. [8] Raffo and Harrison describe a forward-looking approach to use data from an ongoing project as input for simulation models that lead to adjustments in the model parameters for improved project control [9].

22.2 A Feedforward Capability

Given the state of reestimation, this chapter introduces the concept of a feedforward capability or model feature. This approach aims to improve the articulation between models and project experiences by proposing and specifying an enhancement to an estimation model so that it feeds its properties forward in time. For simplicity, an estimation model equipped with such a feedforward feature will be referred to as a feedforward *model*, even though it is more accurately a capability implemented as part of a more comprehensive estimation model and tool.

22.2.1 Feedforward Estimation in Other Domains

Estimation and prediction problems in engineering and other domains are often improved by the complementary use of both feedback and feedforward models, so it seems entirely natural that software resource estimation would benefit as well. As a simple example from a familiar domain, consider the problem of controlling the temperature in a building. It is well-known that the thermostat is a classic example of using feedback to control temperature. When the inside temperature deviates beyond a prescribed amount from a target level, a thermostat triggers a heating/cooling system to begin operating, thus bringing the temperature back within its target range. The addition of a feedforward model to complement the thermostat would measure the temperature *outside* the building. By obtaining this earlier indication of temperature change, the outside sensor can trigger the heating/cooling system before there is a deviation from the inside target level. The key recognition is that a change in the outside temperature is the primary cause of a temperature change inside the building.

Figure 22.1 illustrates the differences in the management control of a system when feedback is operating (a) alone and (b) in concert with a feedforward function. Feedforward takes advantage of the same sources of inputs as the system itself; that is, excitations

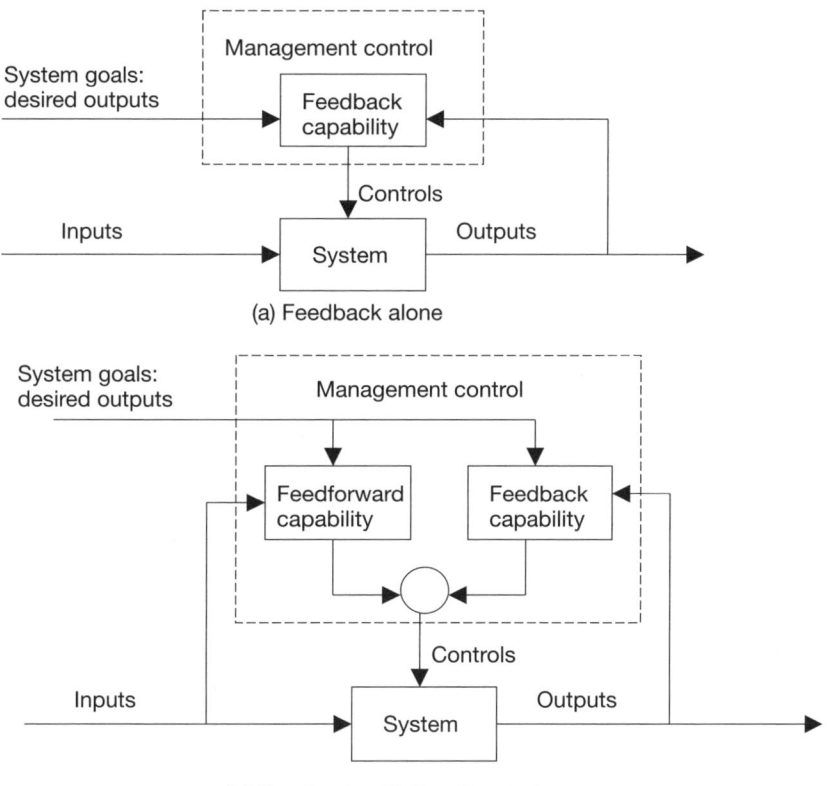

Figure 22.1 Management control of a system using (a) feedback alone and (b) feedback with feedforward

and stimulations from the organization and the surrounding environment. The management control element in the figure consists of two separate comparison activities when feedback and feedforward are used in a complementary fashion.

While the complementary use of feedback and feedforward models is in the best tradition of effective control engineering, it is also a desirable trait of an effective manager to anticipate deviations, not waiting until they have affected the system of interest and only then react. When a manager of a project team senses there is unhappiness in the ranks (a disturbance in the terminology used here), she is wise to talk to team members to determine the cause. Often the grumbling or dissatisfaction may be the result of a misunderstanding, or, in any case, may be entirely fixable by prompt action to uncover the reasons and deal with them. This early intervention stands in contrast to a management practice that waits for the unhappiness to manifest itself with poor performance or turnover that directly threatens project success. Management action at these later times must undo a lot to get the project back on track. The early detection of a disturbance, with quick and decisive attention to it, marks an effective manager.

The key distinction between feedback and feedforward processes – and the reason they are so effective in tandem – is summarized in [10] as:

- *Feedback*: 'Acts only when there are deviations'
- *Feedforward*: 'Acts before deviations show up'

22.2.2 Feedforward Estimation in Software Development

The engineering and management uses of feedforward principles illustrate several key features that can be mapped to a feedforward model for software resource estimation. First, the disturbance is measured at its source. In the building example, instead of waiting for the outside conditions to cause the inside temperature to vary beyond the desired level, the feedforward model provides an advance notice of the disturbance, so corrective action can be initiated earlier. Second, the feedforward model reduces the magnitude and duration of the deviation from the desired state. As a direct consequence of starting the corrective action upon early detection of the disturbance, the difference between the actual and desired inside temperatures can be reduced, and the duration of time that the actual inside temperature deviates (within some prescribed interval) from the ideal is likewise reduced.

As reflected in EQF, an indication of the effectiveness of the management control over a software project is how close the running estimates of cost and schedule – throughout the duration of the project – compare to their eventual values. By measuring disturbances at their sources, feedforward models can trigger updated estimates faster than if the project had waited until the disturbances caused deviations in outcomes that are being measured as part of the routine data collection process. More important, the early detection via feedforward models can cause an earlier start to risk reduction efforts. Boehm and Huang reinforce this theme that an organization benefits by transitioning from a process that instead of only reacting would proactively anticipate change (see Chapter 24).

For software projects, consider what happens when a key member of the development team leaves a project. This event affects both the software development process and the reestimation process. For software development, the event may easily have an immediate effect to reduce productivity and quality. However, without a feedforward model, there would typically be a delay before the disturbance manifests itself in the resource reestimation process. The data collection process would record the reduced staffing level, which would be translated into metrics for the next project management review. Meanwhile, the reduced productivity and quality would have caused unfavorable variances in the earned value accounting. For an explanation, the manager will cite the departure of the key person as a cause. Why wait that long? A feedforward model would signal that the current estimates were wrong as soon as the person walked out the door. This disturbance directly affected the resource model inputs and, therefore, its estimates. The departure affects previously computed values for input parameters such as those capturing the resource staffing level being applied, average overall experience of the team, its domain experience, its experience with the development environments, and its continuity. A feedforward model would have improved project reestimation and management by measuring this disturbance at its source. In this way, the effects on both the software development process and the reestimation process will be immediate.

It is only fair to note a few consequences of using a feedforward model as suggested here. First, turnover is a fact of life on projects, so it is important to understand what assumptions are already accounted for in the resource estimation models, and which events require special attention and reestimation. Second, the person departing may be replaced immediately by someone else. However, people are not interchangeable on projects. Although the new person may appear to be a reasonable match, there will be personal differences in strengths, weaknesses and overall effectiveness. More critical perhaps is the need to integrate with a working project team, including the ramp-up time required. Each of the factors will affect performance, compared to a project that has not experienced a key staff departure.

Another consequence of the operation of a feedforward model is the suggested volatility to every disturbance. If the feedforward apparatus is sensitive to every source of disturbance, then the estimates can be subject to continual fluctuations, as every event signals an updated estimate. When an outside software tool vendor goes bankrupt, it causes a revaluation of the parameter for 'stability of the development environment,' without waiting to see if there will be any effect at all on the project. The sensitivity of any feedforward model will need to be tuned to an appropriate level.

22.2.3 Operation of a Feedforward Model

The operational concept of a feedforward model draws on a distinction between M and P, where –

- M is the estimation model – specifically, the information intrinsic to its use, including the context, assumptions, parameters, estimating relationships, logical consequences and implications of estimation formulas, operating ranges in which the model is appropriate, and model outputs.
- P consists of the in-process experiences on the project – especially early experiences in the requirements, prototyping and design phases. The results of these early activities have an especially significant effect on project outcomes, and, therefore, offer a rich source of information to correct the original estimates in a timely manner and inject realism into the project management and oversight.

The defining characteristic of a working feedforward model is that it expresses the estimation model assumptions, parameters and consequences (the M information) in ways that more nearly match the form and nature of P, the information arising during the project. The intention is that reestimation will be more accurate and timely, thus scoring higher using EQF, because managers will find it easier to incorporate this vitally important information into revised estimates because they will more directly be able to match the information from M and P.

A feedforward model literally feeds forward in time the consequences of using the model, telling a project manager what events should be occurring and what the actual project metrics should look like. This projection forward in time may be based on the following information:

- *Parameters alone*: Are they the same values as they were when the current estimate was generated? A feedforward model may prompt the project manager, 'Is your team still averaging 7.2 experience years working in this domain?' In this way, the model is asking the manager to check if the parameters still hold. The current estimate was based on a parameter value of 7.2; if that value has changed significantly, the cost estimate will be affected. Ideally, the tool implementing the feedforward model would allow a manager to click on the phrase '7.2 experience years' to reveal how the number was calculated, that is, the individual team members with their years of experience. In this way, the manager could easily determine if the current composition of the team matches that used when the 7.2 figure was calculated. Again, this is not claiming anything new about the content of the model: Instead it is projecting the consequences and implications of the model in a form and interactive style that facilitate comparison to the actual data and experiences.
- *Model form alone*: Does the project look like it is adhering to the assumptions built into the cost estimation model? The mathematical form of the model carries with it a pattern for application of effort over time. For example, many cost estimation models (e.g. COCOMO [1] and SLIM [5]) can trace their origins to a Rayleigh distribution. As discussed in [6, p. 173–176], this curve was chosen because it matched empirical data on the rate of staff buildup and decline over time on engineering and development projects. A Rayleigh-based model with an added feedforward feature would be able to tell a manager, 'The effort level should have reached its peak last week, and you should notice a slight decrease beginning this week.'
- *Comparisons to actual data*: How does the actual project metric data compare to what is expected from the use of the cost estimation model? By comparing the actual data to values expected from the model, a feedforward model can indicate that the estimates must be updated: either by using a different model or using the same model with updated parameter values. A feedforward model could generate a message that 'Projecting the current actual effort values leads the model to estimate the total effort at-completion to be 755 Person-Months.'
- *Comparisons to actual experiences*: Are activities and events during the project reflective of the model being used for estimation? For example, after a Software Requirements Review (SRR), there may be a formal record of the action items generated. Each action item may be seen as a question about the requirements or a condition requiring off-line investigation, based on the presentation by the development team. This is a point in

time when the feedforward model can remind the manager what was assumed when the initial estimates were made. Do the action items and the overall experience of this SRR correspond to assumptions built into parameters that captured how precedented the project was envisioned to be (e.g. there was high uncertainty because this kind of system had not been built before) and the perceived degree of familiarity and experience of the team with this type of project? The model assumptions, as reflected in the parameters, may have been optimistic if there are a relatively high number of action items that show the current project is novel and the team is not experienced. An SRR may be the appropriate time for a feedforward model to check with the manager on the reality of these parameter values.

- *Alignment with project metrics data collection*: How will project information about assumptions be represented to the manager? A feedforward model will accept input on P, the specific form and content of qualitative and quantitative information that is likely to be available early in a project. This information will include the metrics data expected to be used in the project: data items, their definitions and reporting frequencies. A feedforward model will recast its M information in terms of P. As a simple example, suppose an estimation model has a driver for uncertainty due to requirements volatility, expressed in percentage terms. Each project has specific methods and practices to characterize properties of the requirements – Is it using function points? Is a tool being used to support requirements? What is the process for capturing requirements additions, changes and deletions? A feedforward model maps the volatility percentage to the P information and expresses future values of key properties of the requirements at specific milestones in the project using function points just as the project is doing. Through this reexpression, a feedforward model makes it possible for a manager to directly interpret incoming project data to determine if it is consistent with model assumptions.

Consider one of the experiences of the author in which advice from a feedforward model would have been helpful. It was on a project team that was following a waterfall-type development process. Management was using a cost estimation model and tool based on a Rayleigh distribution, which itself was a composite of individual Rayleigh distributions for separate activities of specification, design, code and test. The team was at the point of having passed a Critical Design Review (CDR), and was moving on to implementation. When the data was collected for team members' activities for the two-week period following the CDR, the manager discovered that almost all the effort had been spent on design, not coding. This was a serious blow to the project schedule. Upon investigation, the manager found that, although the CDR was passed, the team members had a lot of clean-up activities to put their detailed designs into proper 'code-to' format for implementation. The manager thought that two solid weeks of coding had been accomplished, when that was not the case at all. A feedforward model could make projections based on the point in time at which the design and code Rayleigh curves will first overlap. The model could issue a statement saying that this data collection period is the one for which the effort spent on coding should first exceed the effort spent on design – in this way, prompting the manager to be on guard for such an eventuality.

22.3 Example Uses of the Feedforward Concept

Several examples are intended to illustrate the use of the feedforward concept if it were integrated with a cost estimation tool and used as part of risk management.

22.3.1 Feedforward Capability Integrated with a Software Estimation Tool

To show how a feedforward capability may work with existing software estimation tools, COCOMO II is used for several reasons. It is very comprehensive and contemporary, really a family of models that are evolving in tune to the latest processes and technologies. The developers of COCOMO II have been very forthcoming to describe the background, rationale and operation of the models, especially through their book and accompanying CD [1]. COCOMO II also comes closest to providing feedforward estimation. It can generate milestone expectations: What the model expects actual values to be, at key milestones or anchor points.

The examples highlight the ways in which a feedforward capability may affect existing COCOMO II parameters, defined in [1]. The use of feedforward for reestimation may benefit project managers by detecting these specific disturbances in a software project:

- *Changes in the development platform*: The software infrastructure vendor shipped a new version of the operating system. Because it was advertised as providing compatibility with applications designed for the replaced earlier version, the support team did not believe it would cause any problems, so they installed it on the workstations of the developers. The project team began experiencing unexplained system crashes that were traced to the new operating system. When the resources were initially estimated, the manager characterized the platform parameter in the software estimation model as being very stable with low volatility. Estimates were generated with that parameter value in place. The reality is that the platform is changing and causing problems that are reducing productivity and quality. In COCOMO II, this change would affect the platform volatility parameter, PVOL and the derived early design cost driver for platform difficulty, PDIF.
- *Change to tool support*: A new tool becomes available and is adopted for use. As discussed in [1, p. 106] this event affects the parameter Use of Software Tools (TOOL), Language and Tool Experience (LTEX), and Process Maturity (PMAT).
- *Change to multisite development*: The management expected the development team to be entirely colocated. During the project, it was decided to split some development and testing to a different division in another part of the world. This decision affects SITE, which characterizes the physical location of the team members.
- *Change in product composition*: The project expected that the majority of the functionality of the delivered product would be provided from existing software components that could either be reused verbatim or adapted for reuse. Cost estimates were based on this assessment. As the project unfolded, the team evaluated the existing software in light of its requirements, and determined that its original estimate was optimistic. The existing software would not be a suitable source for as much functionality as the project initially believed. More functionality would need to be provided by custom development instead of COTS. If a feedforward model would quickly detect this change, it could have a significant effect. The origin of code (reused, reengineered, new) affects

the calculation for the equivalent lines of code, which is the influential size driver for cost estimation.

- *Change in team composition*: This event, in which a member of the development team leaves the project, has been discussed. With particular attention here to the effect on model parameters, this event is reconsidered to illustrate how singular events can affect more than one resource parameter. If a key project staff member leaves, it would affect multiple COCOMO II factors (some are composite parameters):
  o PCAP, Programmer Capability
  o ACAP, Application Capability
  o APEX, Application Experience
  o PLEX, Platform Experience
  o LTEX, Language and Tool Experience
  o UNFM, Programmer Unfamiliarity
  o TEAM, Team Cohesion
  o PERS, Personnel Capability
  o PCON, Personnel Continuity

These examples show the direct relationships between 'disturbances' (i.e. events and activities) in the project and parameters in the models.

22.3.2 The Role of a Feedforward Capability in Risk Management

One way to view this proposed introduction of a feedforward capability is to consider its relationship to project risk. COCOMO II has clear relationships between risks and model parameters. [1, p. 287] Essentially, a feedforward feature establishes another (lower) level of relationship, from occurrences of events during the project to model parameters. Just as COCOMO II discusses quantifying risk according to model parameter, this next layer would permit risk to be quantified by project events. The events affect parameters, which, in turn, affect risk. Working in this direction, it would be possible to develop a ranking of events by potential impact on risk. This ranking would play an important role in determining the priority of the need for early detection by a feedforward capability. This priority assignment to the feedforward-detection of various events would contribute to managing the costs of extra data collection and disturbance detection for the feedforward feature. For example, consider that the size and complexity of the emerging product, as reflected in the contents of various directories, are shown to be very influential factors. This determination may justify building a software agent to automatically measure the size and complexity and issue alerts as necessary. That is, the routine reporting of size and complexity may not be sufficiently timely.

To further relate the feedforward model to project risk, an appendix shows the most critical risks [11] and warning signals of problems [2] in software projects. Alongside each risk or problem is a description of the way that a feedforward model may contribute as part of an overall risk management approach. This attention to the truly critical risks and problems would also help focus the feedforward model on high priority targets.

The table shown in the appendix, which establishes relationships between project characteristics and the operation of an automated management aid (the feedforward model), is reminiscent of another effort. In [12], a much more comprehensive software tool was developed to help a project manager relate a process model to a project environment. A manager could create 'what-if' scenarios that would explore project risk areas and result in a set of process model attributes that would be most appropriate for a project.

Again, the examples are taken from COCOMO II because it is so comprehensive in its treatment of estimation, measurement and project risk. COCOMO II recognizes the need to respond to unanticipated changes and recommends a quantitative milestone plan or the use of an earned value or stakeholder value system. (see Chapter 24) What is discussed in this chapter may be seen as a more active capability to detect disturbances earlier in the process.

COCOMO II further recommends being aware of indications that the model needs to be recalibrated: 'The more management data you collect on actual project costs and schedules, the better you will be able to do this' [1, p. 297]. The extension to an active feedforward capability would extend this recommendation beyond actual costs and schedules to also collect data that directly informs the management about the model form, assumptions, parameters and drivers.

22.4 Conclusion

This proposal for a feedforward capability to work in concert with a feedback process is an aggressively proactive attention to risk: Detecting events and experiences so that threats to project success can be detected at their sources. With prompt and effective action to deal with the threats, the impact on the project can be minimized.

There is a technological analog for the feedforward model advocated here. Internet users are increasingly familiar with 'push' technology that will bring notices and alerts to their attention based on their described profiles and preferences. The cost estimation feedforward model will act in the same fashion. When informed about the project profile of planned milestones and metrics, the feedforward model can provide custom alerts and notifications to managers in terms that match the project. Certainly a significant implementation issue would be to ensure that the feedforward capability does not become a persistent, nagging and, therefore, an ignored feature for a manager.

There is one final lesson from the use of feedforward estimation in nonsoftware domains. It is vitally important to routinely remeasure the model inputs. The message for software cost estimation models is that it may not be sufficient to have managers periodically reenter model parameters. The parameters themselves must be actively measured as a routine part of the data collection process of the project. In this way, the parameter settings will receive appropriate attention for their impact on cost and schedule reestimation.

A topic for further research is to explore ways in which the feedforward capability would operate over an extended period of time in an organizational setting. Systems will be evolving over multiple releases in response to changing needs of the user community. A feedforward capability would focus appropriate attention on the evolution of the surrounding organization and environment by serving as an early warning process and providing advance notice of changes.

In summary, a feedforward capability is a novel strategy to address reconciling the estimation model with actual project experiences and data. This capability will help shift the burden of this reconciling task from the manager to the automation, namely, the software estimation modeling tool. A manager using a feedforward model will get information that will facilitate direct comparison with project experiences, leading to prompt, effective and realistic cost and schedule reestimation.

22.5 Acknowledgements

The constructive comments of reviewers are gratefully acknowledged.

Appendix

The role of a feedforward model to address project risks and problems

Topic area of risk	Project risk [11] or Warning Signal of Problem [2]	How a feedforward model would provide support to risk management
Requirements and specifications	Number of TBD (To Be Determined) requirements higher than norm or not declining [2]	Make projections from any parameters that relate to the extent to which users and customers know what they want; and make those projections in the same form as the data being used in the project, namely, tell the project manager the expected number of TBDs at various points in development. In this way, the manager could see how the actual TBDs compare to the projected number to know if the estimate is realistic or needs revision. This problem area from [2] is based on their practice of explicitly recording and tracking TBD requirements.
	High number of specification modifications received versus number completed [2]; continuing stream of requirement changes [11]	Make projections from the parameters it is using for requirements volatility, and make those projections in terms of the data being used in the project, namely, expected number of changes to requirements and specifications at various points in development. In this way, the manager could see how the actual changes compare to the projected number to know if the estimate is realistic or needs revision.

	Developing the wrong software functions and user interface [11]	Prompt the manager (e.g. on a biweekly frequency) with related questions, such as, 'When is the last time the current user interface and system functionality were checked with the customer?' 'Does the development process provide prototypes or other ways to gain early customer buy-in and agreement?' 'How do you know this is what your customer wants?'
	Gold plating [11]	Prompt the manager (triggered when requirements are added or functionality is reviewed) with key questions, 'What is the source of this feature or requirement – does the customer really want this?' 'Is this new requirement required by the contract?' 'Is the customer paying extra for this – for example, via a change order?'
System design and development	Number of completed units increases dramatically prior to the scheduled end of a build/release (the 'miracle finish') and/or effort drops dramatically just after a milestone is reached [2]	Issue alerts at each milestone for the manager to check if a miracle finish occurred or if effort dramatically drops off after the milestone, and, if so, to check the quality of the work completed during the miracle finish and the reason for the drop off.
Testing	Testing phase was significantly compressed [2]	Make projections on the needed length of the testing phase; alert the manager to the importance of not compressing the testing phase.
	The number of errors found during testing is below the norm [2]	Make projections from the model on the expected number of errors to be found; issue alerts to be on guard to check the actual error data, and, if lower than expected, to ensure that adequate resources and an effective process are being applied to testing.
Product assurance	More than one person controls the configuration [2]	Generate questions periodically for the manager to check on the number of people controlling the product configuration.

	Capabilities originally planned for one time period are moved to a later time period [2]	Make projections from the model on the estimated functionality (e.g. in function points or features) that is planned for each time period or product release; generate alerts for the manager to check actuals to ensure the plan is followed and to take action.
	Real-time performance shortfalls [11]	Make projections from the model if the system to be built is identified as one with real-time performance requirements, so the manager is alerted early in the project to conduct off-line studies (e.g. simulations and lab exercises) to ensure that real-time requirements will ultimately be met as the product takes form.
	'Corrected' errors reappear [2]	Issue an alert to check on the frequency of errors reappearing, from the error data being reported.
Project resources	Continual schedule slippage [2]	Make projections on expected numbers of components designed, coded, tested or integrated, and pose advisories to the manager to check against actual values.
	Personnel shortfalls [11] and turnover [2]	Monitor actively the size and composition of the team at all times; alert management when changes occur based on comparison to projected size and composition.
	Unrealistic schedules and budgets [11]	Prompt managers to check realism of parameter values; if the model parameters continue to be accurate, use the model to make schedule and budget projections; if actual resources are not sufficient based on projections, issue prompts to raise visibility of lack of realism

Development process	Straining computer-science capabilities [11]	Monitor action items from reviews for indications that there are science and technology shortfalls; prompt manager to consider review by external expert panel to get independent view of extent to which project is pushing state-of-the-art and relying on unproven technology.
	Change or decrease in planned use of methods or procedures occurs [2]	Make projections from model parameters on expected development platform, tools and maturity of development process; prompt manager to compare these projections to reality.
	Shortfalls in externally furnished components and tasks [11]	Monitor receipt and integration of externally furnished components; monitor completion of externally furnished tasks; compare to projected dates and issue alerts if differences exist.

References

[1] B.W. Boehm, C. Abts, A.W. Brown, C. Chulani, B.K. Clark, E. Horowitz, R. Madachy, D. Reifer and B. Steece, *Software Cost Estimation with COCOMO II*, Upper Saddle River, NJ: Prentice Hall PTR, 2000.
[2] Software Engineering Laboratory, *Manager's Handbook for Software Development*: NASA Goddard Space Flight Center, SEL-84-101, November 1990.
[3] W.W. Agresti, W.M. Evanco and W.M. Thomas, "Estimating Ada System Size During Development," Technical Report RL-TR-92-318, Rome Laboratory, Griffiss Air Force Base, New York, December 1992.
[4] KnowledgePLAN, "Software Productivity Research", Downloaded from www.spr.com, June 21, 2002.
[5] Software Lifecycle Management (SLIM), "Quantitative Software Management", Downloaded from www.qsm.com, June 21, 2002.
[6] T. DeMarco, *Controlling Software Projects*, New York: Yourdon Press, 1982.
[7] M.M. Lehman, "Rules and Tools for Software Evolution Planning and Management," *International Workshop on Feedback and Evolution in Software and Business Processes*, London, UK: Imperial College, July 10–12, 2000.
[8] B.W. Boehm, "Metrics-based Feedback Cycles for Software Life-Cycle Management and Process Improvement," *International Workshop on Feedback and Evolution in Software and Business Processes*, London, UK: Imperial College, July 10–12, 2000.
[9] D. Raffo and W. Harrison, "Combining Process Feedback with Discrete Event Simulation Models to Support Software Project Management," *International Workshop on Feedback and Evolution in Software and Business Processes*, London, UK: Imperial College, July 10–12, 2000.
[10] K.J. Astrom, *Introduction to Automatic Control*, Santa Barbara, CA: University of California, Downloaded on February 15, 2002. http://www.me.ucsb.edu/course_pages/course_pages_f01/me155a_f01/lecture1.pdf.
[11] B.W. Boehm, A Spiral Model of Software Development and Enhancement, *Computer*, Vol. 21, No. 5, May 1988, pp. 61–72.
[12] G. Perez, K. El Emam and N.H. Madhavji, "A System for Evaluating the Congruence of Software Process Models," *Proceedings of the Fourth International Conference on Software Process*, Brighton, UK, December 1996, pp. 49–62.

23

Modelling the Feedback Part of the Software Process in Software Resource Estimation

Juan C. Fernández-Ramil and Sarah Beecham

23.1 Introduction

It has been extensively argued in the literature that the processes of maintenance and evolution of software addressing real-world applications are feedback driven (see Chapters 1, 17 and 27 in this volume for further details). This view is supported by the interpretation of metric data collected over the years [bel72, leh85, leh94], and most recently during the FEAST (Feedback, Evolution And Software Technology) projects [www01]. To a certain extent, simulation process modelling [abd91, ma96, kel99, leh02] has permitted disciplined investigation of the software process. Such models do indeed reflect that feedback structure and have been applied to research into problems such as resource estimation [see, for example, ma96] and allocation of effort to different activities [leh02]. The approach has not difficulty burden associated with current process simulation modelling technologies that require a significant amount of effort before achieving useful results. The most popular cost estimation approaches are expert and algorithmic estimation [boe81]. However, none of these approaches take into account the feedback structure of the process. The influence of feedback in estimation modelling was recognised in a 1996 *in absentia* talk entitled 'Why COCOMO Works' [leh96a]. This chapter takes forward some of the ideas presented in that talk.

In this chapter, we concentrate on algorithmic models since these are objective and related to measurements taken from projects (empirical) or to theories about software process performance (theoretical). COCOMO [boe81, boe95, boe98, boe00] is one of these algorithmic models. There are others, such as Belady and Lehman's [bel72] estimation model; function points [abr02]; Sneed's work on Object Points and Life

Cycle cost management [sne95, sne04], Slim [put92] and our own work [ram00a, ram00b, ram03a, ram03b]. The latter focus on estimation for the evolution part of the life cycle. Though the specific measurements involved tend to vary from approach to approach, they do not explicitly account for the role and impact of feedback as a control mechanism.

The estimates may not consider feedback, but the actual estimates may become an information element as part of a feedback loop. For example, it is well known that estimates must be periodically revised to avoid unpleasant surprises [abd93] and feedback loops involving regular activities such as change analysis, re-estimation and re-planning are recommended (see Chapter 24 by Boehm and Huang in this volume). Other authors have argued that the success of the estimate can be rationalised, at least in part, by it becoming a *self-fulfilling prophecy*. In control system terms, this is equivalent to saying that the estimate becomes a *set point*, which guides the progress of a project. In general, the estimate and its sub-processes become a constituent part of the information feedback structure. Moreover, the estimation model is subject to evolution as the application, the software and the processes all evolve concurrently [leh06].

In [leh96b], the potential influence of feedback in the software process is discussed from a theoretical point of view. One of the characteristics of feedback systems is that small changes in the feedback loops can lead to large changes in the output. The considerations expressed in [leh96b] indicate that feedback has an impact on software process performance and hence in resource consumption that equates to cost. So feedback must be relevant in the context of cost estimation. The importance and relevance of feedback in cost estimation was addressed in a workshop paper [ram00a], a precursor of this chapter. The present contribution is a revised version of that paper.

23.2 The Evidence of Feedback

E-type software evolution [leh06] processes involve feedback mechanisms at many levels [leh94, leh85] with evidence emerging from several sources such as the following:

- The study of metric data as, for example, the observation of the presence of a self-stabilisation ripple in long-term growth trends of evolving software systems [bel72, leh85] and, in particular, in the interpretation of trends observed when one studies the growth and change of a software system over releases [leh85, leh94].
- Simulation modelling of software processes using *system dynamics* (SD) [for61], as in [leh02], and using other modelling techniques [kcl99].

Such evidence suggests that feedback is an important topic of study, though it involves some challenges [leh96b]. It follows that, in general, software evolution processes operate in a *closed loop*, as the operation under a feedback control is termed. Feedback mechanisms may also play an important role not only in long-term evolution [leh02] but also in shorter-lived software projects. Some system dynamics models have addressed cost estimation issues at the project level, for example, in [abd91, ma96]. However, such technology is not widely applied in industry. On the other hand, *algorithmic* approaches, which appear to be more popular, do not account, at least explicitly, for either the presence of feedback or the use of *closed-loop* data[1].

---

[1] Implications of the use of closed-loop data in statistical modelling are examined in [box78].

23.3 The Need for a Taxonomy

White-box modelling places the emphasis on the internal constituents of an entity of interest, as reflected, for example, by its internal mechanisms and their parameters. A *black-box model* reflects relationships and structure between externally observed attributes. A convenient way to study feedback influences is by performing white-box modelling of the entity of interest. Within a black-box view of an entity, the focus is on modelling the behaviour of the entity of interest as reflected by a set of externally observed attributes or measures. In black-box studies, the internal constituents of the entity being modelled are not of primary concern. However, algorithmic cost estimation models are essentially black box. How can one achieve an adequate reflection of feedback influences, maintaining the simplicity of a black-box view?

One can postulate that this achievement will be facilitated by codification of the feedback characteristics and their impact in a proper taxonomy, which is yet to be developed. In this regard, some concepts of a control theory offer an alternative to, hopefully, inspire empirical investigation which could trigger further advances in technology for software cost estimation.

23.4 Feedback as a Cost Factor

In modelling the behaviour of software processes, simulation process modelling exemplifies the white-box view [e.g. abd91, kel99, ma96, leh06]. On the other hand, the black-box perspective is exemplified by *algorithmic* cost estimation approaches [boe81] that involve models based on historical data reflecting software project cost performance and other attributes. The total cost and interval of the project, the size of the developed software and several *cost factors* or *drivers* are systematically recorded. Mathematical models are fitted to these historical data. In general, judged by the popularity and frequent reference of models such as COCOMO, these approaches are useful. There still is, however, a need for their improvement. This becomes apparent when one considers that the reported predictive accuracy of approaches such as COCOMO II is, for effort estimates, in the order of 30% of the actual values and 52% of the time [cla98].

Such improvement in accuracy may be pursued in several ways and, in particular, by investigating new attributes, new cost factors and assessing their contribution with regard to existing ones. Such factors may significantly influence software process performance and may not have been captured by current black-box approaches. The nature and other characteristics of the information feedback structure, also termed *feedback control*, an aspect that has been addressed in the context of white-box estimation [ma96, leh06] offers opportunities in this regard. To the knowledge of the present authors, it has not been *explicitly* addressed as part of an algorithmic cost estimation approach.

23.5 Cost Estimation as a 'System Identification' Problem

One way to achieve a cost estimation approach that explicitly considers the feedback control part of the process is to explore similarities between *algorithmic* software cost estimation and the *system identification* field [nor86]. The latter can be seen as a branch of applied mathematics, providing theory and procedures to achieve mathematical models of a system's input–output dynamic behaviour directly from input and output data. For example, suppose that as part of a control engineering application, one wishes to control the pressure and the temperature in a chemical reactor. The dynamic characteristic of the reactor may change as the product builds-up inside or as the amount of a catalyst varies. This can change the dynamics of the reactor. For control purposes, it may be important to model these changes, as they may impact on the optimal temperature or pressure that needs to be achieved to maximise production. Hence, it may be convenient to determine the mathematical characteristics of the model reactor on the basis of sensors which measure input and output variables such as flow of product in, flow of product out, pressure, temperature, and so on. Online system identification techniques are able to update the mathematical model of the reactor, used for control purposes, as the dynamics of the reactor change. This concept is very useful in many technological applications. Some of the ideas may be applicable to cost estimation and, in particular, if one sees the estimation model as a mathematical model which reflects process characteristics.

By referring to some system identification concepts, one may expect to identify some of the implications of the presence of feedback for *algorithmic* cost estimation.

Figure 23.1 depicts a system as generally seen in system identification. One seeks to express the output y (a scalar or a vector) as a function of the input u (a scalar or a vector) and of the system parameters, that is, vector Θ, expressed as

$$y = G(\Theta, u). \tag{23.1}$$

Θ may be determined as a function of y and u, that is, $\Theta = \phi(y, u)$ by some appropriate procedure. The discipline of system identification focuses on providing such procedures and in establishing their limits and the conditions for their application [gus98, nor86, wel91].

Now consider an *algorithmic* cost estimation model, for example, the widely mentioned Intermediate COCOMO 81[2] cost estimation model [boe81] in which the development effort is a function $f()$ given by

$$\text{Development effort} = f(\text{mode, 15 cost drivers, size})$$
$$= k_1 \times k_2 \times \ldots \times k_{15} \times A \times \text{size}^B \tag{23.2}$$

where the development effort is in person-months, the size of the software is expressed in thousands of delivered source instructions (KDSI) and the mode refers to one of the three development types (*organic, embedded, semidetached*) defined in the context of COCOMO. The multiplying factors $k_1, k_2, \ldots, k_{15}$ are a functions of the cost drivers. Constants A and B are functions of the development mode [boe81]. See [boe81] for

Figure 23.1 A typical control-theory representation of a general system with input u and output y

---

[2] COCOMO 81 has been superseded by COCOMO II [boe00]. This paper's discussion applies, in general, to all current algorithmic approaches.

details regarding COCOMO's drivers and modes. Equation 23.2 can be recast as follows, in the form of Equation 23.1, transforming the problem of estimation in a form that is similar to the one used in system identification:

$$y = \text{development effort}$$
$$u = \text{size}$$
$$\Theta = \{k_1, \ldots, k_{15}, A, B\}. \tag{23.3}$$

A similar transformation could be made with other estimation approaches. One could argue whether some cost drivers are project control variables and hence part of the input u or whether they must all be considered as process related and hence part of Θ. While this and other considerations may alter the final form of Equation 23.3, it will not alter the view that *algorithmic* cost estimation, as generally pursued, can be seen as an attempt to *identify* (in the system identification sense) an appropriate model for the system (the software process). As discussed in [leh94, leh96b] the software process operates under feedback control, with feedback not being properly accounted for in any of the existing methods of cost estimation.

Consider some of the consequences of feedback control seen from the point of view of *system identification*. Whether the system of interest (termed *plant*) operates under a feedback control law has been the focus of many studies since the 70s [gus98, sod75], if not before. It is well known, for example, that if feedback is not disconnected while system identification is performed, or accounted for in an appropriate way, one may face difficulties in obtaining a model that is an appropriate representation of the system studied. When feedback cannot be disconnected from the plant, such as in some unstable processes, or when feedback is somehow *embedded* in the plant being identified, one will obtain a model reflecting not only the plant but also the *aggregated* system formed by the plant and the feedback control; that is, the estimated model will reflect a *closed-loop* behaviour. The *closed-loop* system may behave very differently from the open-loop system. These observations become more evident when one considers Figures 23.2 and 23.3.

Figure 23.2 shows a system consisting of two components, the productive part, represented by G', and a feedback control H, representing, for example, management controls.

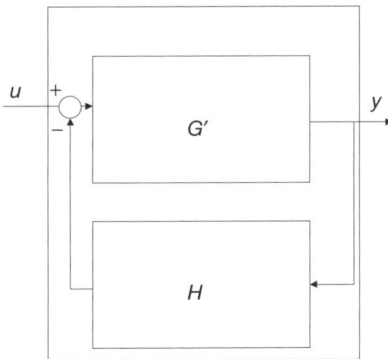

Figure 23.2 A closed-loop system in a black-box situation: only u and y are observable

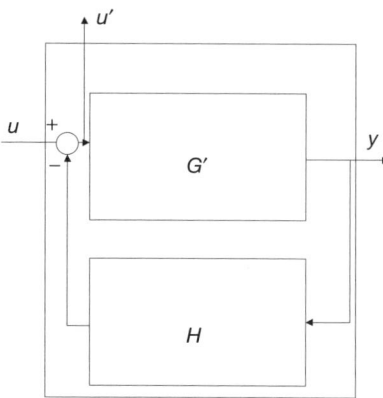

Figure 23.3 A closed-loop system in a white-box situation: variables internal to system such as u' are observable

As in the preceding text and owing to the presence of H, it may not be possible to obtain a dynamic model and the parameters of G' with knowledge of u and y only. (By the way, the choice of letters G and H to represent the 'plant' and the 'feedback control' is an established convention in control engineering which we follow here.)

Suppose now that the inside of the system is accessible to the investigator, so that, for example, she or he can measure u', the immediate input to G'. This situation is depicted in Figure 23.3. Still, in this case precautions may have to be taken if proper estimation of an appropriate dynamic model of G' has to be achieved [wel91].

Instead of considering such obstacles and whether they could be the basis of *new* cost estimation approaches, we draw some conclusions from the above observations in the context of *current algorithmic* software cost estimation. Consider the case of Figure 23.3 first in which one is able to distinguish between G' and H. This case implies that one is able to measure not only u, the input to the software process, but also u', the input to the forward paths of such a process. Current *algorithmic* models, however, only appear to be based on measures of the *aggregated* system, since no provision appears to be made for either H or u'. So, at least in principle, Figure 23.3 can be regarded as not being representative of current practice. On the other hand, Figure 23.2 appears to be a closer reflection of such practice. Given the limitations imposed by the presence of feedback to the situation in Figure 23.2, one may conclude that current estimation models are in this sense *biased*. They reflect the aggregated behaviour of G' and H. H is not reflected, at least explicitly, in the currently considered cost factors [boe81, boe00].

Before discussing how feedback could be taken into account, let us examine the rather surprising fact that existing algorithmic approaches work.

23.6 Why do Algorithmic Cost Estimation Approaches such as COCOMO 'Work'?

Having set up the scene and justified the importance of feedback in the software process, one may then ask, Why do existing approaches which do not consider effort estimation still work? In particular, why COCOMO [boe81, boe00] works? A number of answers, at present mere hypotheses, may be considered:

- *Feedback as a performance-equalising factor*: Feedback control may act as a regulating mechanism, forcing the performance (of otherwise different processes) to converge. The latter appears to have been initially suggested in [leh96a]. Moreover, as one of the anonymous referees has appropriately commented, COCOMO estimates may work, at least in part, owing to the fact that managers' actions are often based on a comparison of estimates with in-progress actual values. By doing so, as a project progresses, managers act as feedback controls that turn the estimates into self-fulfilling prophecies [boe81].
- *Feedback control influences can be factored out*: One may consider that the feedback control role is to a significant degree homogenous across projects and processes and hence can be safely factored out from the *algorithmic* cost estimation approaches.
- *Feedback control is yet to be accounted for*: This would imply that at least part of the still *unexplained* variance in the project cost data might be due to the absence of factors accounting for the role and impact of the feedback control.

The above list is not exhaustive and other reasons might be possible. The above reasons suggest that the topic deserves wider investigation. However, the fact that current approaches work should not stop us from trying to find ways of improving the software process, in particular, by explicitly taking feedback into account.

23.7 Approaches to Model 'Feedback' in Cost Estimation Models

This section considers the following ways in which feedback may be taken into account:

1. *Direct black-box modelling*: This would attempt to model G' and H from records of attributes of a process by, for example, system identification methods or adaptations of these. It is not evident how such methods may be applied to industrial software processes. For example, it is not clear how one could provide the experimental conditions, such as *persistent excitation* in the process inputs [wel91], to guarantee achievement of appropriate dynamic models. In order to fully explain and justify this, one needs mathematical arguments, which are beyond the scope of this paper.
2. *White-box modelling*: A second alternative would be, essentially, a white-box approach. It would try to model the dynamics of G' and H by the study of the process constituents and of the management control [eil79] over such process by using, for example, SD modelling and tools. As already mentioned, SD approaches have been applied to software cost estimation, as in [abd91, ma96]. However, SD modelling procedures do not force an immediate distinction between G' and H. The distinction between *process* feedback and feedback *control* must be imposed by the model builder, for example, by using multi-layers in the model. Such distinction may require the imposition of an extra discipline in the model-building process. Such discipline does not appear to be enforced by any of the existing SD modelling tools.
3. *Indirect black-box modelling (feedback control as a cost factor)*: A third possibility is to investigate by appropriate means, such as expert assessment of a process, where a given process and/or project stands in terms of feedback control. The result could be given

a set of appropriate levels or categories related to different project cost performances. These, in turn, may be considered as cost drivers.

Option 1 involves appropriate data and considerable modelling expertise, even if one uses sophisticated tools such as the MATLAB system identification toolbox [lju95]. It constitutes a line of further research, but its potential impact is difficult to predict. With regard to the second option, experience of one of the author as part of the FEAST projects [www01, leh02] indicates that white-box modelling is worth pursuing. It is possibly the best choice in terms of accuracy even though, as said, it is time and effort consuming. Ideally, for wider impact one would like to achieve generic SD models. Whether these are achievable is still a matter of investigation. Moreover in some processes, in particular in the less mature ones, feedback control may be undisciplined and/or undocumented; in short, it may be difficult to find, formalise and model [leh96b]. Here the intent is not to discuss the relationship(s) between feedback control and process maturity, which in itself could be an interesting topic of investigation. If successful, the second possibility would lead to a valid decomposition or separation between the process G' and its control H and of appropriate abstractions and representations of both. This in turn would lead, if and when achieved and applied, to a higher degree of software process mastery. This still seems far from being achieved though progress in this regard has been made in the FEAST projects [www01, leh02], for example. The third suggestion is briefly discussed in the next section.

23.8 Indirect Black-Box Modelling and Feedback-Related Cost Factors

In the context of *algorithmic* software cost estimation, one may wish to understand how software process performance, for example, may relate to the nature of H, the feedback control being applied to a given software process. For the sake of simplicity, one would like to do this without a detailed model of the dynamics of G' and H.

Under *appropriate* feedback control, the project is likely to keep on track even under significant external disturbances and changes. Under inadequate feedback, the project may run *out of target* more easily, even 'after the first bump in the road'. Can feedback control be considered as a cost factor and hence relate process or project performance to the type or degree of feedback control in operation in a given process? And if so, how can feedback control cost factors be measured/incorporated into the model?

No fundamental obstacles are foreseen, though the answer to the 'how' question is far from obvious. Both theoretical and empirical work might be required to understand the role of H in software processes and abstract its impact. In other words, map observed behaviour to a set of attributes that become feedback-related cost factors. The full achievement of this will require a considerable amount of empirical data (and might these attributes change from project to project, company to company?). One may, however, envisage an assessment procedure based on a procedure of systematic process observation and modelling that may lead to an overall assessment of the role of feedback control. This has already been achieved, for example, to assess the effect of process *maturity* [pau93] and later applied to investigate the relationship between maturity and software development effort [cla97].

An assessment procedure for feedback may have to involve assessment of attributes of the full or global software process[3] or organisation. This is due to the fact that software process is generally embedded in a larger organisation and interacts with other agents and processes from which dynamic influences stem and which sometimes are involved in across-organisational feedback control mechanisms.

Such assessment procedure may require the distinction between major types of feedback control emerging in industrial practice and their influences. One could use a classification of control systems in control engineering as a starting point [wel91]. Undoubtedly, any classification will require appropriate abstraction of the different types of feedback control in software and other industrial processes and their effects. Next, one would wish to distinguish between different feedback control adequacy levels such as *very low, low, medium, high, very high* or a similar set of values that will facilitate the assessment. All this will require a means for assessment. The assessment could be based on a systematic procedure that would take into account, for example (the listing order has no attached meaning):

- software project and organisation structure [eil79];
- number of hierarchy levels involved and, in general, the degree of management involvement [car95];
- size, structure, location and physical/cultural distance between the teams involved;
- control procedures, policies and other mechanisms;
- its degree of automation or computer support;
- alignment between the agents involved, for example, degree of *model clash* [box78];
- structure and other attributes of the global process and the information network involving developers, users, supporters, marketeers, their managers and others.[4]

The study of the role and impact of feedback control in domains different from software development and evolution (e.g. [lee00]), may provides clues for a better understanding of feedback control as cost factor in software processes. A study based on a survey in US software developing organisations suggests that involvement of upper management correlates with longer time to completion [car95]. This is consistent with Lehman's view that the outer organisational feedback loops have, in general, a constraining effect, where they become the dominant loops. If this is confirmed, one may have to focus the feedback control assessment on those loops, not so much in the detailed technical process.

Undoubtedly, the application of feedback control also involves a cost of its own. It consumes, for example, managerial resources. In an ideal world, one would like to not only quantify the total project or process cost but also distinguish between the cost of the feedback control H and the cost of running the productive process side G'. An organisation will want to improve its cost effectiveness by, for example, a decrease in managerial burden. In fact, this discussion does not intend to suggest *a priori* that increasing the number of feedback loops or mechanisms will lead to improved cost and schedule performance. For example, *lightweight* feedback may be more advantageous than other schemes that

---

[3] The full or global software process is seen as the process that encompasses the activity not only of developers and maintainers but also of others involved, such as support personnel, marketeers, users and their managers (For further details, see Chapter 27, Section 27.11).

[4] G. Kahen, Private communication.

rely on high degrees of prescription, communication and/or strong dependencies between the agents involved. This is what the above study [car95] appears to suggest. In this connection, the organisational structure seems to apply to *feedback control* in the software process. This is affirmed by Eilon who referred to organisational structures in general and wrote, '... It is not my intention to extol the virtues of one type of organisation as compared with another, but merely to underline the fact that structural choices may have far-reaching consequences for the enterprise [eil79]'. Senge, as well, is of the opinion that the role of structure and in particular, feedback loop structure, is crucial in the understanding of organisational performance [sen90]. Whether that structure can be characterised and reflected in a black-box model that is useful to a software organisation remains an open question that deserves further investigation.

The feedback structure may be particularly challenging to be subjected to scientific study and mathematical modelling in less *mature* [pau93] processes, in small size software development (however 'small' is defined) and/or where software development is a secondary or nonseriously pursued activity. This must be taken into account when selecting software organisations for study and when interpreting the results.

23.9 Final Remarks

This chapter has argued that feedback-related process characteristics appear to play an important role in determining process performance and may have to be explicitly considered in *algorithmic* cost estimation if the accuracy of the latter is to be improved. The arguments presented suggest that the feedback role must not be dismissed. Great progress has been made in the system dynamics modelling of software processes with application to cost estimation [abd91, ma96]. Although these models reflect feedback interactions it is uncertain how they can be applied to *algorithmic* estimation approaches to reflect feedback-related factors. Further work needs to be carried out in this area, with particular reference to seeking approaches to estimate the cost for software evolution processes [ram00b]. This chapter has given some suggestions for further study. It is hoped that if further pursued, it may lead to improved cost estimation approaches. To achieve this, however, one needs a taxonomy or, more broadly, an appropriate language or discourse to codify the feedback structure and its influences that allow for data gathering and subsequent model building and their utilisation. Last, but not least, to build on this topic one would need to address the role of individual humans, groups and teams, human agencies and organisations as feedback controls in software and wider business processes. This chapter tackles a very complex and difficult task of how to improve resource estimation in industrial software processes. Its approach to this problem is simplistic, where feedback control is mapped to behaviour in the software process. To gain a more in-depth understanding, this topic will necessarily require more than just mathematical models and modelling techniques. Further studies would therefore benefit from taking an interdisciplinary approach [leh94].

23.10 Acknowledgments

Grateful thanks are due to M Lehman, G. Kahen, L Barker and to anonymous referees for their comments. Financial support from the UK EPSRC, through the FEAST/2 project, grant no. GR/M44101. (1999–2001) and the CRESTES project, grant no. GR/S90782/1 (2004–2005) is gratefully acknowledged.

References

[abd91] Abdel-Hamid T and Madnick SE, *Software Project Dynamics – An Integrated Approach*, Prentice Hall, Englewood Cliffs, NJ, 1991, p. 263.

[abd93] Abdel-Hamid TK, Adapting, Correcting, and Perfecting Software Estimates: A Maintenance Metaphor, *IEEE Computer*, vol. 26, no. 3, March 1993, pp. 20–29.

[abr02] Abran A, Silva I and Primera, L, Field Studies Using Functional Size Measurement in Building Estimation Models for Software Maintenance, *Journal of Software Maintenance*, vol. 14, no. 1, January 2002, pp. 31–64.

[bel72] Belady LA and Lehman MM, An Introduction to Program Growth Dynamics, in *Statistical Computer Performance Evaluation*, W Freiburger (ed.), Academic Press, New York, 1972, pp. 503–511. Reprinted as chapter 6 in Lehman MM and Belady LA (eds.), *Software Evolution – Processes of Software Change*, Academic Press, London, England, 1985.

[boe81] Boehm B, *Software Engineering Economics*, Prentice Hall, Englewood Cliffs, NJ, 1981, p. 767.

[boe95] Boehm BW, Clark BK, Horowitz E, Westland C, Madachy R and Selby R, Cost Models for Future Software Life Cycle Processes: COCOMO 2.0, *Annals of Software Engineering*, vol. 1, 1995, pp. 57–94.

[boe98] Boehm B, Mini-Tutorial: Model-Integrated Software System Engineering (MISSE), *Proc. ICSE 98*, vol. 2, April 19–25, 1998, Kyoto, Japan, pp. 285–286.

[boe00] Boehm BW, Horowitz E, Madachy R, Reifer D, Clark BK, Steece B, Brown AW, Chulani S and Abts C, *Software Cost Estimation with COCOMO II*, Prentice Hall, 2000.

[box78] Box GEP, Hunter WG and Hunter JS, *Statistics for Experimenters – An Introduction to Design – Data Analysis and Model Building*, Wiley, New York, 1978.

[car95] Carmel E, Time-to-completion Factors in Packaged Software Development, *Information and Software Technology*, vol. 37, no. 9, 1995, pp. 515–520.

[cla97] Clark B, *The Effects of Software Process Maturity on Software Development Effort*, Unpublished PhD thesis, University Southern California, August 1997.

[cla98] Clark B, Devnani-Chulani S and Boehm B, Calibrating the COCOMO II Post-Architecture Model, *Proceedings of the ICSE 20*, April 19–25, Kyoto, Japan, 1998, pp. 477–480.

[eil79] Eilon S, *Management Control*, 2nd Ed., Pergamon Press, Oxford, England, 1979, p. 207.

[www01] FEAST Projects web site, Department of Computer, Imperial College, http://www.doc.ic.ac.uk/~mml/feast <as of Aug. 2005>.

[for61] Forrester JW, *Industrial Dynamics*, MIT Press, Cambridge, MA, 1961.

[gus98] Gustafsson F and Graebe SF, Closed-Loop Performance Monitoring in the Presence of System Changes and Disturbances, *Automatica*, vol. 24, no. 11, 1998, pp. 1311–1326.

[kel99] Kellner MI, Madachy RJ and Raffo DM, Software Process Simulation Modelling: Why? What? How?, *Journal of Systems and Software*, vol. 46, no. 2/3, April 1999, pp. 91–106.

[lee00] Lee S and Han I, Fuzzy Cognitive Map for the Design of EDI Controls, *Information & Management*, vol. 37, 2000, pp. 37–50.

[leh85] Lehman MM and Belady LA (eds.), *Software Evolution – Processes of Software Change*, Academic Press, London, England, 1985.

[leh94] Lehman MM, Feedback in the Software Evolution Process, Keynote Address, *CSR 11th Annual Workshop on Software Evolution: Models and Metrics*, September 7–9, Dublin, Ireland, 1994, also in Information and Software Technology, special issue on Software Maintenance, vol. 38, no. 11, pp. 681–686, 1996.

[leh96a] Lehman MM, Why COCOMO Works, Invited Talk (*in absentia*), *11th International Forum on COCOMO and Software Cost Modelling*, October 1996, USC, Los Angeles, CA.

[leh96b] Lehman MM, Perry DE and Turski WM, Why is it so Hard to Find Feedback Control in Software Processes? Invited Talk, *Proceedings of the 19th Australasian Computer Science Conference*, January 31–February 2 1996, Melbourne, Australia, pp. 107–115. A revised version in this volume.

[leh02] Lehman MM, Kahen G and Ramil JF, Behavioural Modelling of Long lived Evolution Processes-Some Issues and an Example, *J. of Software Maintenance and Evolution, spec. issue on Separation of Concerns*, vol. 14, 2002, pp. 335–351.

[leh06] Lehman MM and Fernández-Ramil J, *Software Evolution*, Chapter 1 in this volume.

[lju95] Ljung L, System Identification Toolbox – For Use with MATLAB, *User's Guide*, MathWorks Inc, Natick, MA, August 1995, http://www.mathworks.com/access/helpdesk/help/pdf_doc/ident/ident.pdf

[ma96] Madachy R, System Dynamics Modeling of an Inspection-based Process, *Proceedings of the 18th International Conference on Software Engineering*, March 25–29, 1996, Berlin, Germany, pp. 376–386.

[nor86] Norton JP, *An Introduction to Identification*, Academic Press, London, England, 1986.

[pau93] Paulk MC, Curtis B, Chrissis MB and Weber C, *Capability Maturity Model for Software, Version 1.1*, Softw. Eng. Inst. Rep., CMU/SEI-93-TR-24, 1993.

[put92] Putnam L and Myers W. *Measures for Excellence*, Prentice Hall, Englewood Cliffs, NJ, 1992, p. 28.

[ram00a] Ramil JF, Why COCOMO Works' Revisited or Feedback Control as a Cost Factor, *FEAST 2000 Workshop*, Imperial College, London, England, July 10–12, 2000, http://www.doc.ic.ac.uk/~mml/f2000 <<as of August 2005>>.

[ram00b] Ramil JF and Lehman MM, Metrics of Software Evolution as Effort Predictors – A Case Study, *Proceedings of the ICSM 2000*, October 11–14, 2000, San Jose, CA, pp. 163–172.

[ram03a] Ramil JF, *Continual Resource Estimation for Evolving Software*, PhD Dissertation, Department of Computing, Imperial College, London, January 2003.

[ram03b] Ramil JF, *Continual Resource ESTimation for Evolving Software (CRESTES)*, EPSRC proposal, Case for Support, Part 2, September 2003.

[sen90] Senge PM, *The Fifth Discipline-the Art & Practice of the Learning Organisation*, Currency/Doubleday Publishing, New York, 1990, p. 423.

[sne95] Sneed H, Estimating the Costs of Software Maintenance Tasks, *Proceedings of International Conference on Software Maintenance*, IEEE Computer Society Press, Opio, France, October 1995, p. 168.

[sne04] Sneed H, A Cost Model for Software Maintenance & Evolution, *20th IEEE International Conference on Software Maintenance (ICSM'04)*, Chicago, Ill, 2004.

[sod75] Soderstrom T, Gustavsson I and Ljung L, Identifiability Conditions for Linear Systems Operating in Closed Loop, *International Journal of Control*, vol. 21, no. 2, 1975, pp. 243–255.

[wel91] Wellstead PE and Zarrop MB, *Self-Tuning Systems – Control and Signal Processing*, Wiley, 1991, p. 579.

24

Value-Based Feedback in Software and Information Systems Development

Barry Boehm and LiGuo Huang

24.1 Introduction

The role of feedback control in software and information system development has traditionally focused on a milestone plan to deliver a prespecified set of capabilities within a negotiated budget and schedule.

Under the right conditions (capable people; realistic budgets and schedules), the traditional approach has been highly successful in project control. It has also created a legacy of project data that has been used to develop more accurate models for estimating future projects' budgets and schedules. These models have also been very helpful in supporting software capability/schedule/cost tradeoff analysis and in improving software development efficiency.

Section 24.2 of this chapter summarizes a set of four nested feedback and feedforward loops that have been successfully used to scope, estimate, control and improve the predictability and efficiency of software development and evolution. Section 24.3 summarizes one of the most powerful approaches available for controlling traditional software projects: the Earned Value (EV) system.

Three recent trends have, however, required information system development organizations to raise their sights above the level of managing and improving development efficiency using traditional capability/schedule/cost milestones. These trends are as follows:

1. The increasingly rapid pace of change in information system technology, market conditions and business value propositions, making prespecified plans and requirements ultimately unrealistic.

2. The increasing leverage that software project decisions have on an organization's competitiveness and profitability Boehm *et al.*, 1981. Most products and services are becoming increasingly software-intensive. Software project decisions are increasingly becoming of significant value, arising from their impact on the organization's bottom line.
3. The increasing need for organizations to rapidly adapt to changes in their marketplace, technology or structure. Where it exists, such adaptability becomes an increasingly valuable asset that enhances an organization's agility in the marketplace. But it also means that proposed adaptations and changes need to be evaluated in terms of their impact on both cost and value.

These trends make it increasingly important for organizations to evolve from purely project-efficiency-based decisions, plans and feedback control toward system value-based decisions, plans, and feedback control. Today's control systems that provide 'earned value' to project management can help to produce projects that are completely successful with respect to meeting cost and schedule targets. But they can still be completely unsuccessful in terms of the value they earn for their stakeholders.

Thus, today's 'EV' systems are misnamed. They have absolutely nothing to say about the stakeholder value of the system being developed. They serve a purpose, but need to be incorporated into feedback control systems that focus on the real stakeholder value being earned.

In Sections 24.4 and 24.5, an alternative approach for project feedback control is proposed. This focuses on the actual stakeholder value likely to be earned by completing the project. Section 24.4 provides a framework for monitoring and controlling value in terms of a Benefits Realization Approach Thorp and DMR's Center for Strategic Leadership, 1998 and business case analysis, using an order processing system as an example. Section 24.5 elaborates on the value-based feedback control mechanisms and illustrates them via an example. Section 24.6 presents the conclusions and directions for future research and development that appear promising.

24.2 Feedback Control of Software Development: Four Primary Feedback Cycles

This section presents four feedback cycles that have been successfully used to control software project scoping, project execution and continuous organizational improvement of project estimation accuracy and project execution efficiency. The specific techniques discussed here are based on the Constructive Cost Model (COCOMO) II Boehm *et al.*, 2000, but other software cost estimation models can be used as well.

24.2.1 Feedback Cycle 1: Project Scoping

Figure 24.1 shows how the COCOMO II model can be used to drive a feedback cycle that converges on a stakeholder-satisfactory definition of a project's scope in terms of its COCOMO II parameters. As shown by the arrows entering the COCOMO II box in Figure 24.1, these parameters address such system objectives as functionality (expressed as software size in COCOMO II), performance and reliability. Additional parameters cover project characteristics such as personnel and team capability and experience, multisite

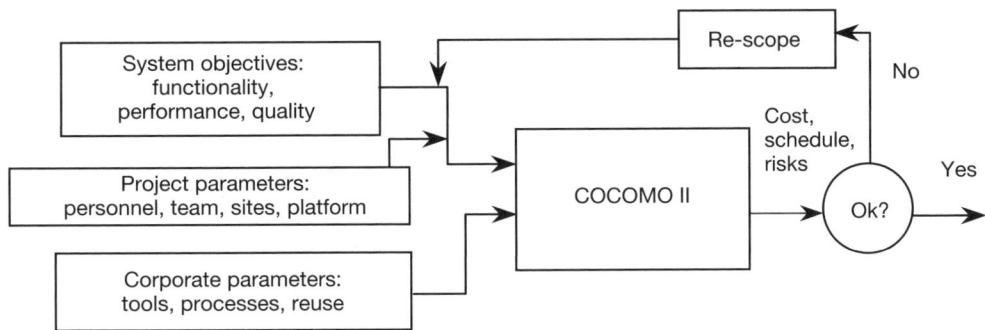

Figure 24.1 Feedback cycle 1: project scoping

development, and computing platform capability and volatility; and corporate parameters such as tool usage, process maturity and software reuse (expressed as a reduction in product size). COCOMO II will then estimate how these changes will affect the project's expected cost and schedule. It will provide developers and stakeholders with a framework for performing tradeoff analyses that involves the system, project and corporate parameters indicated in Figure 24.1, and a feedback cycle to re-scope the project until its estimated cost and schedule are satisfactory.

As COCOMO II includes a life cycle maintenance estimation model as well as a development estimation model, Feedback Cycle 1 as well as the subsequent three feedback cycles apply to software evolution projects as well as software development projects.

24.2.2 Feedback Cycle 2: Project Execution

Changes in project objectives, priorities, available componentry or personnel will occur frequently during project execution. If these are anticipated, COCOMO II can support a variant of the project definition process above to converge on a stakeholder-satisfactory re-scoping of the project.

A more serious case occurs when the changes are unanticipated and often unnoticed. This can frequently happen as a result of personnel changes; shortfalls in COTS products, reusable components or tools; requirements creep or platform discontinuities. In such cases, the COCOMO II phase and activity distributions can be used to develop a quantitative milestone plan or an earned value monitoring system for the project. Either will enable deviations from the plan to be detected, and appropriate corrective actions to be taken in a second feedback cycle (Figure 24.2). These again may involve the use of COCOMO II in project re-scoping.

At times, a need to make unanticipated project changes may be an indication that the COCOMO II model needs to be recalibrated or extended to better fit the changing conditions. For example, involving a new internal or external organization in a software project may result in different productivity rates than initially estimated. In such cases, one can recalibrate the COCOMO II model parameters and feed the resulting revised estimates forward into the project's milestone plans. This is essentially the technique discussed by Agresti in Chapter 22 "A Feedforward Capability to Improve Software Reestimation".

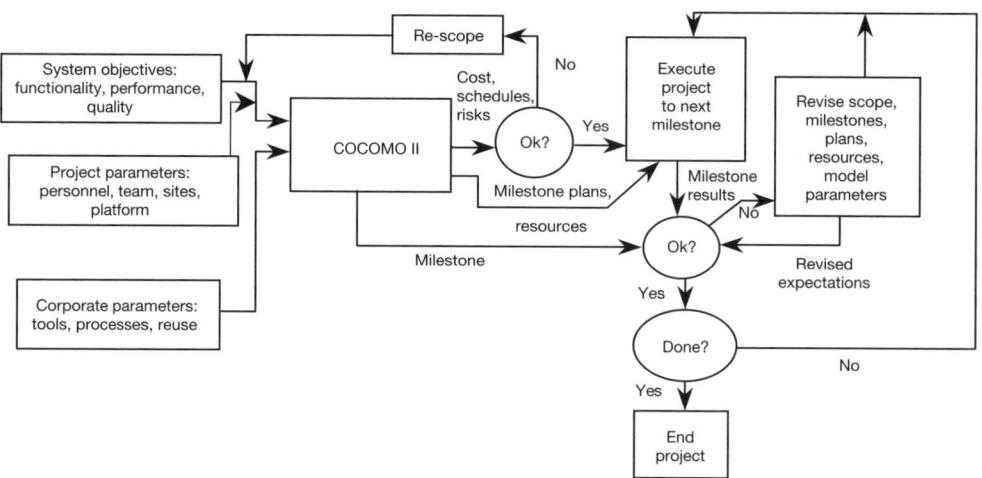

Figure 24.2 Feedback cycle 2: project execution

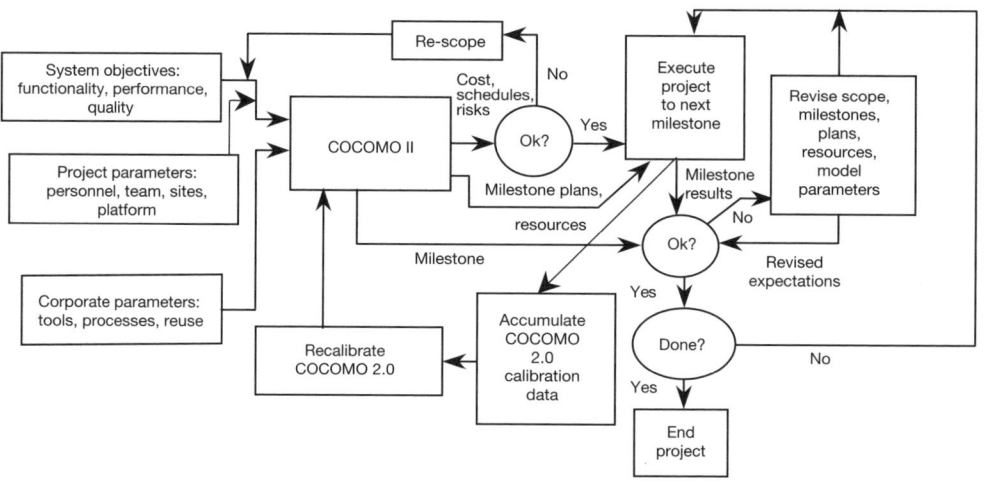

Figure 24.3 Feedback cycle 3: model update

24.2.3 Feedback Cycle 3: Model Update

The project-level feedforward approach becomes an organization-level feedback cycle as the organization recalibrates its COCOMO II parameters to reflect new organizational experience, as shown in Figure 24.3.

Recalibration might be appropriate, for example, if an organization is acquired by or merged into another with, for example, different definitions of project endpoints, or different definitions of which types of employees are directly charged to the project versus being charged to overhead. As described in Chapter 4 of Boehm *et al.*, 2000, techniques are available to recalibrate COCOMO II's base coefficients and exponents for cost and schedule estimation. Some COCOMO II tools such as USC COCOMO II and COSTAR provide such calibration features.

Extending the model will be appropriate if some factor assumed to be constant or insignificant turns out to be a significant cost driver. For example, additional cost drivers such as development for reuse, multisite development and process maturity were added to COCOMO 81 to produce COCOMO II, in response to user indications of need and our confirmation via behavioral analysis.

24.2.4 Feedback Cycle 4: Organizational Productivity Improvement

Any organization will be much better off once it evolves away from reacting to change, and toward proactive anticipation and management of change. This is what Level 5 of the SEI Capability Maturity Models are all about, particularly such key process areas as technical change management and process change management.

The COCOMO II model and parameters can assist the evaluation of candidate productivity improvements and change management strategies. For example, investing in sufficient software tool acquisition and training to bring a project's 'Use of Software Tools' rating from nominal to high will replace a 1.0 effort multiplier by a 0.90, for a 10% productivity gain. Similar investments in improving process maturity, architecture and risk resolution, team cohesion, multisite development, reuse or any of the personnel factors can also have significant benefits that can be investigated via COCOMO II (See Figure 24.4). A good example of the use of this approach is provided in Rational Software Corporation, 2001.

An integrated capability for using COCOMO II for evaluating the payoff of cost and schedule improvement strategies is provided by the COPROMO (Constructive Productivity Improvement Model) extension described in Boehm *et al.*, 2000. It enables one to start

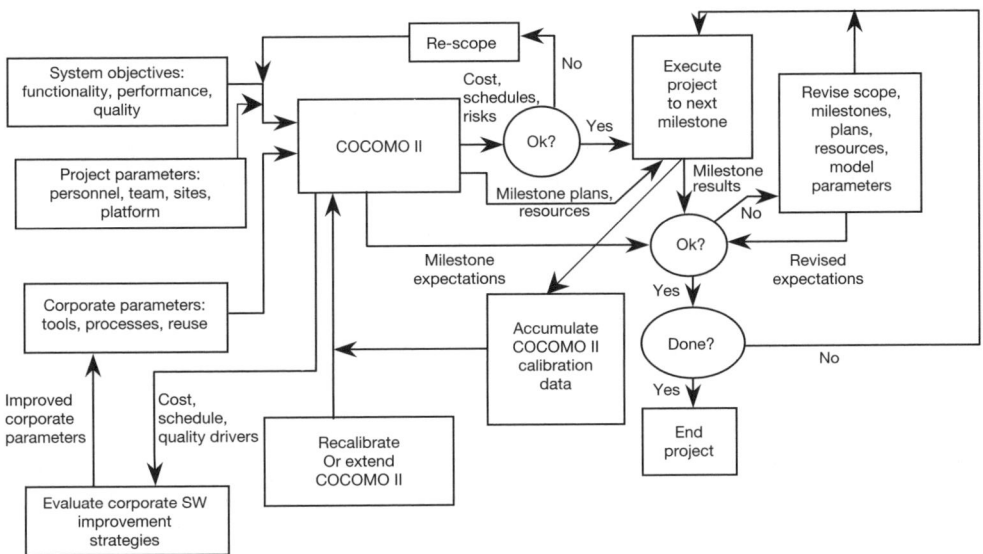

Figure 24.4 Feedback cycle 4: organizational productivity improvement

from a current baseline of cost and schedule drivers from either the organization's data or the COCOMO II database; and to express candidate cost and schedule improvement strategies in terms of achievable time-phased improvements in cost and schedule drivers. COPROMO will then generate the resulting estimates and provide time histories of cost and schedule improvements for each of the candidate strategies.

Together, the four COCOMO II feedback cycles in Figure 24.4 can enable an organization to determine and evolve project-level and organization-level sets of project analysis, management and improvement strategies based on their own quantitative metrics. These strategies will enable it to determine appropriate objectives and approaches for each project, and to manage projects to more successful completion. They are likely to improve its software development and evolution productivity, speed and quality by anticipating and capitalizing on change rather than by being a reactive victim of change.

24.3 Using 'EV' for Feedback Control of Software Development and Evolution

Performing feedback control of large software projects becomes very difficult, because there will be hundreds of tasks going on concurrently. Some tasks will be ahead on budget and schedule; others will be behind. Current 'EV' Forsberg *et al.*, 2000 systems do enable large-project managers to achieve better visibility and control of such complex situations.

Software cost and schedule estimation models such as COCOMO II include breakdowns of project budget and schedules by software component, life cycle phase, and task activity. This enables a project to set up an EV monitoring system in which the estimated cost for each task can be considered as the value earned for the project when the task is completed.

The EV monitoring system works as follows:

1. The project develops a set of tasks necessary for completion, and associated budgets and schedules for each.
2. Each task is assigned an EV for its completion, usually its task budget.
3. As a project proceeds, three primary quantities are reviewed at selected times T:
   (a) The Budgeted Cost of Work Scheduled (BCWS): The sum of the EV's of all tasks scheduled to be completed by time T.
   (b) The Budgeted Cost of Work Performed (BCWP), or project level EV: The sum of the EV's of all tasks actually completed by time T.
   (c) The actual cost of the project through time T.
4. If the BCWP (budgeted cost of work performed) is equal to or greater than the BCWS (budgeted cost of work scheduled), then the project is on or ahead of schedule.
5. If the BCWP is equal to or greater than the project cost, then the project is on or ahead of budget.
6. If the BCWP is significantly less than the BCWS and/or the project cost at the time T, then the project is significantly overrunning its schedule and/or its budget, and corrective action needs to be performed.

The six steps are summarized in the EV feedback process shown in Figure 24.5.

Value-Based Feedback in Software and Information Systems Development

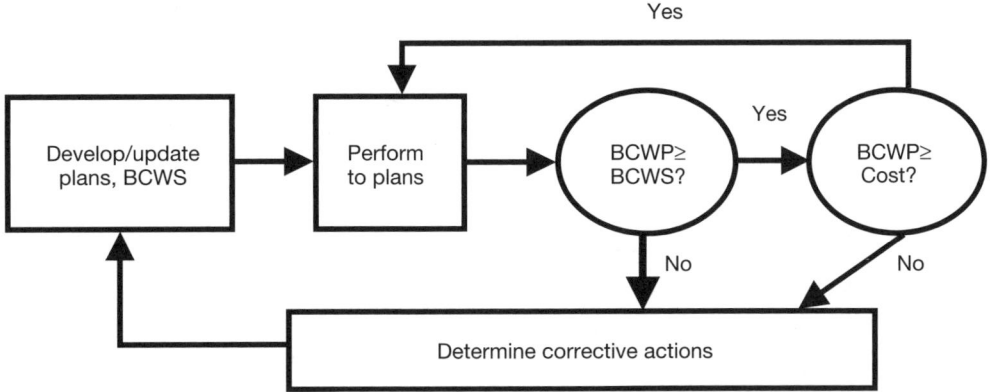

Figure 24.5 'Earned value feedback process'

24.3.1 An Earned Value System Example

Figure 24.6 provides an example to explain how the EV System can assist in assessing the project progress and likely cost to complete a software project. For simplicity, it is assumed that the project starts with four sequential tasks: prototypes, analyses, plans and specs.

The first step is to assign an EV to each task. Suppose it is estimated that the prototype completion will take two months and cost $15,000, the analyses one month and $10,000, the plans one month and another $10,000 and the specs one month and $15,000. Therefore, the cumulative EV obtained after successfully finishing the four tasks is $50,000.

Now let a snapshot be taken at the end of the fourth month to assess the status and actual cost of the project as shown in Table 24.1. At that time, the first three tasks, prototypes, analyses and plans, are scheduled to complete. The cumulative Budgeted Cost of Work Scheduled (BCWS) ($EV_{scheduled}$) is, therefore, $35,000. However, only the prototypes and analyses have been completed at that time yielding a Budgeted Cost of Work Performed (BCWP) ($EV_{performed}$) of only $25,000.

In this case, BCWP ($25,000) < BCWS ($35,000), and at the end of the fourth month, is therefore behind schedule. On the other hand, suppose that the actual cost to finish the prototypes was $14,000 and the actual cost to complete the analyses was $6000. Thus the cumulative actual cost of work performed at the end of the fourth month is $20,000, which indicates that the actual cost is below budget for the first two tasks.

Thus, in terms of the EV feedback process in Figure 24.5, BCWP > Cost ($25,000 > $20,000), so there is no need for corrective action on budget. On the other hand, BCWP < BCWS ($25,000 < $35,000), so the project is behind schedule and needs corrective action. This might involve slipping the schedule, or if that is infeasible, re-scoping the project to fit within the available schedule. Techniques such as the Schedule as Independent Variable (SAIV) process Boehm *et al.*, 2002b are available to accommodate such corrective action.

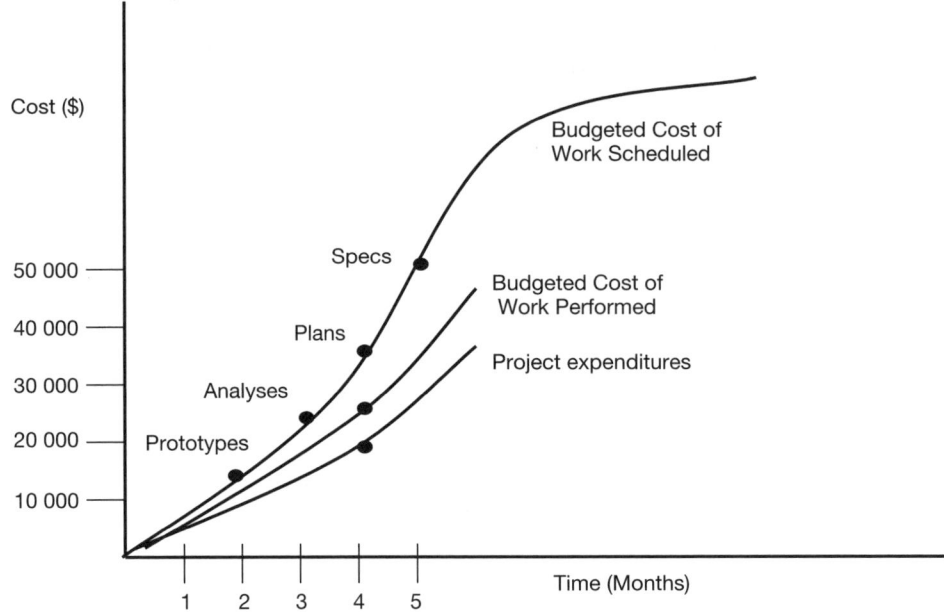

Figure 24.6 Earned value system example

Table 24.1 The snapshot of earned value and actual cost at the end of the fourth month

Project tasks	BCWS (EV$_{scheduled}$) ($)	BCWP (EV$_{performed}$) ($)	Actual cost ($)
Prototypes	15,000	15,000	14,000
Analyses	10,000	10,000	6,000
Plans	10,000	0	0
Specs	0	0	0
Total	35,000	25,000	20,000

24.4 Real Earned-Value Feedback Control

The EV management process is generally good for tracking whether a project is meeting its original plan. However, it becomes difficult to administer if the project plans change rapidly. More significantly, it has *absolutely nothing to say about the actual value being earned* for the organization by the results of the project. A project can be tremendously successful with respect to cost-oriented 'earned value', but an absolute disaster in terms of actual organizational value earned. This frequently happens when the resulting product has flaws with respect to user acceptability, operational cost-effectiveness or timely market entry. Thus, as already observed, it must be desirable to have techniques that support monitoring and control of the actual value to be earned by the results of the project, and the project's consequent return on investment:

$$ROI = (Benefits - Costs)/Costs, \text{ adjusted for inflation effects}$$

24.4.1 Business-Case and Benefits-Realized Monitoring and Control

A first step to achieve this is to use the business case as a means of monitoring the actual business value of the capabilities to be delivered by the project. This involves a continuing update of the business case to reflect changes in business model assumptions, market conditions, organizational priorities and progress with respect to enabling initiatives. Monitoring the delivered value of undelivered capabilities is difficult; therefore, this approach works best when the project is organized to produce relatively frequent increments of delivered capability. See Reifer, 2002 for further information and guidelines on software business case analysis.

In order to formulate the business case, it is necessary to determine and reconcile the value propositions of the project's success-critical stakeholders. This requires that one identify the success-critical stakeholders and their roles in realizing the project benefits.

An excellent technique for doing this is the Benefits Realization Approach Thorp and DMR's Center for Strategic Leadership, 1998. Its centerpiece is the Results Chain, as exemplified by Figure 24.7. The Results Chain establishes a framework linking Initiatives that consume resources (e.g. implement a new order entry system for sales) to Contributions (not delivered systems, but their effects on existing operations) and Outcomes, which may lead either to further contributions or to added value (e.g. increased sales).

A particularly important contribution of the Results Chain is the link to Assumptions, which condition the realization of Outcomes. Thus, in Figure 24.7, if order-to-delivery time turns out not to be an important buying criterion for the product being sold, (e.g. for stockable commodities such as soap and pencils), the reduced time to deliver the product will not result in increased sales.

The Results Chain is a valuable framework by which software project members can work with their clients to identify additional nonsoftware initiatives that may be needed to realize the potential benefits enabled by the software/IT system initiative. These may also identify some additional success-critical stakeholders who need to be represented and 'bought into' the shared vision.

For example, the initiative to implement a new order entry system may reduce the time required to process orders only if some additional initiatives or system features are pursued to convince the sales people that the new system will be good for their careers and to train them in using the system effectively. For example, if the order entry system

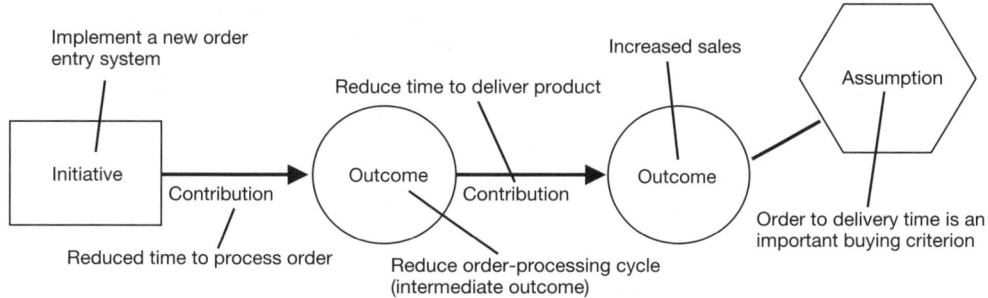

Figure 24.7 Benefits realization approach results chain

is so efficiency-optimized that it does not keep track of sales credits, the sales people will fight using it.

Further, the reduced order processing cycle will reduce the time to deliver products only if additional initiatives are pursued to coordinate the order entry system with the order fulfillment system. Classic cases where this did not happen include the late deliveries of Hershey's Halloween candy and Toys'R'Us' Christmas toys.

Such additional initiatives need to be added to the Results Chain. Besides increasing its realism, this also identifies additional success-critical stakeholders (sales people and order fulfillment people) who need to be involved in the system definition and development process. The expanded Results Chain involves these stakeholders not just in a stovepipe software project to satisfy some requirements, but in a *program* of related software and nonsoftware initiatives focused on value-producing end results.

Once the initiatives are agreed upon, they can be elaborated into project plans, requirements, architectures, budgets and schedules. The resulting budgets establish the cost inputs to the business case. The corresponding benefits for the business case are determined by a benefits analysis. The quantitative part of the benefits analysis will include the effects on the organization's profit-and-loss bottom line, either in terms of additional profit streams or cost savings.

The benefits analysis should also include qualitative analysis of such additional benefits as customer satisfaction, corporate reputation and supply chain controllability. For a public service organization, the benefits analysis needs to determine quantitative proxies for benefits wherever possible, such as improved health and safety records, reduced service delays and complaint rates or high-service–recipient satisfaction ratings. Such proxies are often worth tracking for commercial organizations, as they are frequently key competitive discriminators. A good example is the strategic profile approach presented in Kim and Mauborgne, 2002.

Figure 24.8 shows the resulting value realization feedback process. The Results Chain, business case and program plans set the baseline in terms of expected time-phased costs, benefit flows, returns on investment and underlying assumptions. If the projects and program perform to plans, but the actual or projected achievement of the cost and benefit

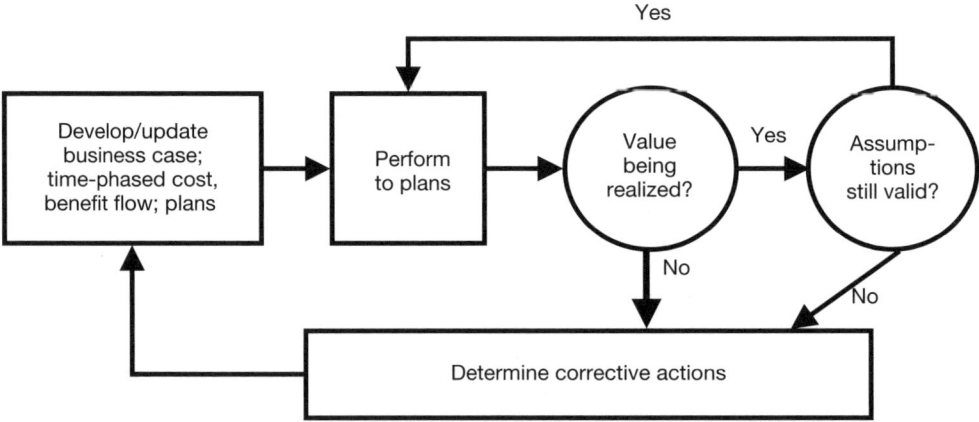

Figure 24.8 Value realization feedback process

flows and the realism of assumptions are becoming invalid, the project or program must determine and apply corrective actions in terms of changes in plans or initiatives, and associated changes in expected cost and benefit flows.

24.5 Value-Based Feedback Control: An Order Processing Example

Sierra Mountainbikes, Inc. has an outstanding reputation for high quality in their specialty area. However, an operations review confirmed that its retailers were highly dissatisfied with Sierra's order processing systems. They were encountering significant problems with delivery delays and mistakes; poor synchronization between order entry, order confirmation and order fulfillment; and disorganized responses to problem situations. The resulting crisis management mode of operation added to an already costly and inefficient order processing system. (This example is adapted from the experiences of a similar organization in a different specialty area.)

Sierra has entered into a strategic partnership with eServices, Inc., for joint development of a new order processing and fulfillment system. The partnership will continue to integrate the new system with an upgrade of Sierra's financial, production and human resource management informational systems. The incentive structure of strategic partnership is organized around the results chain and business case. Both parties will, therefore, share in the responsibilities and rewards of realizing the system's benefits and both are motivated to understand and accommodate each other's value propositions and win conditions. Each is thus motivated to use value-based feedback control to manage the program of initiatives involved in realizing the system's expected benefits.

Figure 24.9 shows the overall Results Chain for the program. Compared to Figure 24.7, it adds business process, outreach, training and order fulfillment initiative functions.

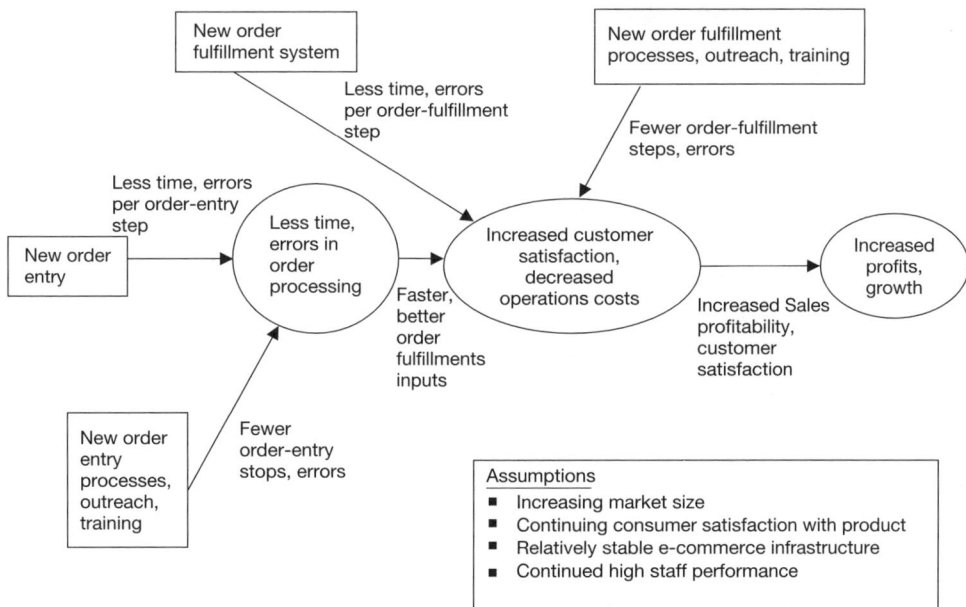

Figure 24.9 Expanded order processing system results chain

Besides involving its in-house stakeholders in these initiatives, Sierra has obtained commitments from its three leading distributors to participate in defining and beta testing the resulting new system, and in evaluating such expected outcomes as increased customer satisfaction and ease of use. It is worthy of note that it was the determination and planning how to monitor these aspects of benefits realized that led Sierra to recognize the distributors as additional success-critical stakeholders to be involved in the system's definition and development.

Figure 24.9 is about the right level of detail for a system of this complexity. It is sufficiently detailed to record the overall program vision and structure, and to identify the success-critical stakeholders. And it provides a sufficient framework for developing the new system's business case, and for feedback control that determines whether the initiatives are realizing the expected benefits. As most of its critical assumptions are program-wide, these are recorded in Figure 24.9 as a general list of assumptions to be monitored, rather than as additional hexagons.

24.5.1 Business Case Analysis: Costs, Benefits and Return on Investment

The overall development and evolution budgets and schedules for the order processing system are shown in Table 24.2. The project uses an evolutionary spiral approach Boehm and Hansen, 2001 involving overall strategic plans for an Initial Operational Capability (IOC). Subsequent extension to a Full Operational Capability (FOC) is initialized by prioritized sets of features, and by an architecture that supports growth to FOC and ease of dropping or adding features as their nature or priorities change.

Some additional key milestones are the Life Cycle Objectives (LCO) and Life Cycle Architecture (LCA) milestones used in the USC Model-based (System) Architecting and Software Engineering (MBASE) approach Boehm and Port, 2001 and the Rational Unified Process (RUP) Royce, 1998; Jacobson *et al.*, 1999; Kruchten, 2001, and the Core Capability Demonstration (CCD) milestone in the SAIV specialization of MBASE and RUP Boehm *et al.*, 2002b.

Table 24.2 Order processing system schedules and budgets

Milestone	Due date	Budget ($K)	Cumulative budget ($K)
Inception readiness	1/1/2004	0	0
Life cycle objectives	1/31/2004	120	120
Life cycle architecture	3/31/2004	280	400
Core capability demo	7/31/2004	650	1050
Initial oper. capability: SW	9/30/2004	350	1400
Initial oper. capability: HW	9/30/2004	2100	3500
Developed IOC	12/31/2004	500	4000
Responsive IOC	3/31/2005	500	4500
Full oper. cap'y CCD	7/31/2005	700	5200
FOC beta	9/30/2005	400	5600
FOC deployed	12/31/2005	400	6000
Annual oper. & maintenance		3800	
Annual O&M; old system		7600	

These milestones are also used in the COCOMO II cost estimation model to estimate the budget, effort, schedule and staffing level required to meet these milestones, as discussed in Section 24.2. Table 24.2 shows the resulting milestone due dates, budgets and cumulative development and evolution budget derived for the order fulfillment project from the COCOMO II estimates. They have been adjusted to cover the related business processes, outreach and training initiatives (covered under 'software') and to cover new purchased computer hardware and Commercial-Off-The-Shelf infrastructure software (covered under 'hardware' in the 9/30/2004 IOC milestone). These are used both for monitoring and controlling project progress using traditional EV techniques, and as the costs incurred in calculating the program's return on investment.

Overall, it will be seen that the IOC can start development on January 1, 2004. It will be installed for beta testing with the three key distributors on September 30, 2004, and cut over as a replacement for most of the old system on December 31, 2004, at a cumulative investment cost of $4 million. After an incremental release of the IOC responding to the most cost-effective initial IOC fixes and enhancements, the initial evolution to the FOC will also be beta-tested by the three key distributors, and then cut over as a full replacement for the old system on December 31, 2005, at a cumulative cost of $6 million. Thereafter, six-month increments and annual evolutionary releases will be installed at an annual investment level of $500 K.

Table 24.3 shows the corresponding expected benefits and return on investment, ROI = (Benefits − Costs)/Costs, annually for the years 2004 to 2008. For simplicity in this analysis, the costs and benefits are shown in dollars to avoid the complications of discounted cash flow calculations. Moreover, the 10% annual growth rate in estimated market size is not compounded, both for simplicity and conservatism.

As seen in Columns 2 to 5 of Table 24.3, if the new program is not executed, Sierra's current market share and profit margins are estimated to stay roughly constant over the 2004 to 2008 period, with annual profits growing from $7 M to $12 M. This is a conservative estimate, as problems with the current system are likely to increase with added sales volume, leading to decreased market share and profitability.

The next columns in Table 24.3 up through ROI show the expected improvements in market share and profit margins achievable with the new system due both to economies of scale and decreased operational costs, and the resulting ROI relative to continuing with the current system. They show that the expected increase in market share (from 20% to 30% by 2008) and profit margins have produced a 45% ROI by the end of the second year of new-system operation (2006):

$$\text{ROI} = \frac{\text{Benefits} - \text{Costs}}{\text{Costs}} = \frac{9.4 - 6.5}{6.5} = 0.45$$

The expected ROI by the end of 2008 is 297%.

The final four columns in Table 24.3 show expected 2004 to 2008 improvement in overall customer satisfaction and three of its critical components percentage of late deliveries, ease of use and in-transit visibility. The later capability was identified as both important to distributors (if they know what is happening with a delayed shipment, they can improvise workarounds), and one which some of Sierra's competitors were providing. Sierra's expected 2004 to 2008 improvements with the new system were to improve their

Table 24.3 Order processing system: Expected benefits and business case

Date	Market Size ($M)	Current system			New system			Cost savings	Change in profits	Cum. change in profits	Cum. cost	ROI	Late delivery (%)	Cust. statis. 0–5	In-tran. visib. 0–5	Ease of use 0–5
		Market share (%)	Sales	Profits	Market share (%)	Sales	Profits									
12/31/03	360	20	72	7	20	72	7	0	0	0	0	0	12.4	1.7	1.0	1.8
12/31/04	400	20	80	8	20	80	8	0	0	0	4	−1	11.4	3.0	2.5	3.0
12/31/05	440	20	88	9	22	97	10	2.2	3.2	3.2	6	−4.7	7.0	4.0	3.5	4.0
12/31/06	480	20	96	10	25	120	13	3.2	6.2	9.4	6.5	0.45	4.0	4.3	4.0	4.3
12/31/07	520	20	104	11	28	146	16	4.0	9.0	18.4	7	1.63	3.0	4.5	4.3	4.5
12/31/08	560	20	112	12	30	168	19	4.4	11.4	29.8	7.5	2.97	2.5	4.6	4.6	4.6

0 to 5 satisfaction rate on in-transit visibility from a low 1.0 to a high 4.6, and to increase their overall customer satisfaction rate for order processing from 1.7 to 4.6.

24.5.2 Value-Based Monitoring and Control

The expected benefits and business case in Table 24.3 are valuable not only as a means of justifying the program of initiatives. They are also valuable as a means of tracking actual progress in realizing the benefits and applying corrective action wherever the expected benefits are not being realized, wherever the assumptions in the results chain in Figure 24.9 are becoming invalid or wherever new opportunities may surface with a higher payoff than expected from the program (e.g. via acquisition of a competitor with an inferior product line but a superior existing order processing system).

Table 24.4 shows an example of the value-based monitoring capability for the order processing system. It is a simple, straightforward approach that can easily be implemented as a spreadsheet program. Some complications such as present-value discounting of future cash flows have not been included here, but can easily be added within a spreadsheet program. Most of the cells shown here compress two cells of information into a pair of numbers separated by a horizontal line. The number above is the expected value of the given elements at the given time, as expressed in the expected benefits and business case in Table 24.3. The number below is the actual cost or benefit actually realized at the given time in this hypothetical example. The following discussion is presented as if the project had been completed through the end of year 2005.

For example, consider the expected versus actual outcomes at the end of the program's first year. The Deployed IOC was expected to be completed by 12/31/04, but actually finished early on 12/20/04. Its cost was about 1% overrun ($4041 K actual versus $4000 K expected). A $200 K savings in hardware and COTS software acquisition kept the overrun from being serious. On the other hand, the knowledge and credibility of the order processing system enabled Sierra to land some new purchase contracts that actually raised their market share to 22% in the first year. This will enable Sierra to record a $600 K profit increase by the end of 2004 instead of the zero profit increase currently expected, and to repay $5.1 M of the $6 M investment by the end of 2005. The new system had decreased the late delivery rate to 10.8% versus the expected 11.4%, and had increased the systems ease-of-use rating to 3.2 versus the expected 3.0 by the end of 2004.

However, the new system's in-transit visibility rating had increased only to 1.6 versus the expected 2.5, pulling down the overall customer satisfaction rating to 2.8 versus the expected 3.0. The feedback control trail of this shortfall can be followed by looking at the Risks/Opportunities column. The LCA milestone requires all major risks to be either resolved or covered by a risk management plan. The project had identified a risk that Track Corp, the primary COTS-vendor offering an in-transit visibility package, would back off from its marketing promise to convert its ITV package to run on Sierra's selected UNIX platform in early 2004. The project's fallback plan was to develop an interim in-house ITV capability and search for alternative UNIX-based COTS ITV sources.

By the Core Capability Demo milestone on 7/20/04, the project had verified that TrackCorp would not deliver a UNIX ITV package in 2004 if at all. The project had therefore moved to its fallback strategy. The in-house ITV capability slowly increased the distributors' ITV rating. But it was only when the search for alternative UNIX COTS ITV packages turned up a viable new source at the end of 2004 that significant progress was

Table 24.4 Value-based expected/actual outcome tracking capability

Milestone	Schedule	Cost ($K)	O_T–Cost savings	Market share (%)	Annual sales ($M)	Annual profits ($M)	CumΔ profits	ROI	Late deliv (%)	Cust sat.	ITV	Ease of use	Risks/ opportunities
Life cycle Architecture	3/31/04 3/31/04	400 427		20 20	72 72	7.0 7.0			12.4 12.4	1.7 1.7	1.0 1.0	1.8 1.8	Increased COTS ITV Risk. Fallback identified.
Core Capability Demo (CCD)	7/31/04 7/20/04	1050 1096								2.4*	1.0*	2.7*	Using COTS ITV Fallback. New HW Competitor; renegotiating HW
Software Init. Op. Cap'y (IOC)	9/30/04 9/30/04	1400 1532								2.7*	1.4*	2.8*	
Hardware IOC	9/30/04 10/11/04	3500 3432											$200 K savings from renegotiated HW
Deployed IOC	12/31/04 12/20/04	4000 4041		20 22	80 88	8.0 8.6	0.0 0.6	−1.0 −0.85	11.4 10.8	3.0 2.8	2.5 1.6	3.0 3.2	New COTS ITV source identified, being protoyped
Responsive IOC	3/31/05 3/30/05	4500 4604	300 324						9.0 7.4	3.5 3.3	3.0 1.6	3.5 3.8	
Full Op. Cap'y CCD	7/31/05 7/28/05	5200 5328	1000 946							3.5*	2.5*	3.8*	New COTS ITV source initially integrated
Full op. Cap'y Beta	9/30/05 9/30/05	5600 5689	1700 1851							3.8*	3.1*	4.1*	
Full op. Cap'y deployed Release 2.1	12/31/05 12/20/05 6/30/06	6000 5977 6250	2200 2483	22 24	106 115	12.2 13.5	3.2 5.1	−0.47 −0.15	7.0 4.8	4.0 4.1	3.5 3.3	4.0 4.2	

ROI: Return on Investment; ITV: In-Transit Visibility; COTS: Commercial Off-The-Shelf Product; n*: Rating based on early trial use.

achieved on improving the distributors ITV rating. By the end of 2005, it had increased to 3.3 versus the expected 3.5, and overall customer satisfaction was at a 4.1 rating versus the expected 4.0. A good option when the project went to its fallback strategy would have been to use an Agresti-type feedforward approach to re-baseline the target ITV ratings, but this is not shown for simplicity.

The example illustrates how value-based monitoring and control capability provided by the MBASE/RUP life cycle milestones, the Benefits Realization Approach Thorp and DMR's Center for Strategic Leadership, 1998 and results chains, and the value-based outcome tracking capability shown in Table 24.4 can enable an organization like Sierra to proactively anticipate shortfalls in its benefits realization plans and initiate corrective action to recover from them. They could also enable organizations to proactively pursue opportunities to improve on a planned outcome, such as the emergence of a new hardware supplier becoming an opportunity to save on hardware costs and compensate from a software cost overrun. The above analysis indicates how the approach would have helped the company upon which the example is based. Full applications experience is needed from real projects to confirm the practicability of the approach.

24.6 Conclusions and Future Challenges

The increasing pace of change in the information technology field makes feedback control essential for organizations to sense, evaluate and adapt to changing value propositions in a competitive marketplace.

Traditional project feedback control mechanisms such as EV systems are effective for controlling the development and evolution efficiency of relatively stable projects in well-established value situations. But they have absolutely nothing to say about the actual value being earned by the project's results, and can lead to a highly efficient waste of an organization's scarce resources.

The value-based monitoring and control capability formulated and illustrated above can enable organizations to proactively monitor and control not only fast-breaking risks to project success in delivering expected value, but also fast-breaking opportunities to switch to even higher-value emerging capabilities.

Challenges for the future of value-based monitoring and control include the following:

- Integrating advanced financial instruments such as real options Amram and Kulatilaka, 1998 into the planning and control of software-intensive systems Sullivan *et al.*, 2001.
- Integrating the explicit information in plan-driven feedback control methods with the tacit information used in agile methods Highsmith, 2002 to support both agility and discipline in controlling software projects Boehm, 2002a; Boehm and Turner, 2004.
- Integrating project-level and organization-level feedback control of software-intensive projects, programs, portfolios and organizations, using such techniques as the Experience Factory Basili *et al.*, 1994, Balanced Scorecards Kaplan and Norton, 1996, the Benefits Realization Approach Thorp and DMR's Center for Strategic Leadership, 1998 and the CeBASE Method Boehm *et al.*, 2002a.
- Integrating value-based methods into the full range of disciplines involved in software engineering: requirements, design, development, test, COTS integration, planning and control Boehm and Sullivan 2000; Boehm, 2002b.

- Integrating the theoretical base of the approach into the proposed Theory of (Feedback Driven) Software Evolution as proposed by Lehman.

24.7 Acknowledgments

This paper is based on research supported by the National Science Foundation, the DoD Software-Intensive Systems Directorate, and the affiliates of the USC Center for Software Engineering.

References

Amram M. and Kulatilaka N., *Real Options*, Harvard Business School Press, 1998.
Basili V., Caldeira G. and Rombach H.D., "The experience factory", in Marciniak J. (ed.), *Encyclopedia of Software Engineering*, Wiley, 1994.
Boehm B., *Software Engineering Economics*, Prentice Hall, 1981.
Boehm B., "Get ready for Agile methods, with care", *Computer*, vol. 35, no. 1, pp. 64–69, January 2002.
Boehm B., *"The Future of Software Economics: Value-Based Software Engineering"*, USC-CSE Technical Report, March 2002b.
Boehm B. and Hansen W., "Understanding the spiral model as a tool for evolutionary acquisition", *Cross Talk*, vol. 14, no. 5, May 2001, pp. 4–11.
Boehm B. and Port D., "Balancing discipline and flexibility with the spiral model and MBASE", *Cross Talk*, December 2001. See also http://sunset.usc.edu/research/MBASE.
Boehm B. and Sullivan K., "Software economics: a roadmap", *The Future of Software Economics*, Finkelstein A. (ed.), ACM Press, 2000, pp. 319–343.
Boehm B. and Turner R., *Balancing Agility and Discipline: A Guide for the Perplexed*, Addison Wesley, 2004.
Boehm B., Port D., Jain A. and Basili V., "Achieving CMMI Level 5 improvements with MBASE and the CeBASE method", *Cross Talk*, vol. 15, no. 5, pp. 9–16, 2002a.
Boehm B., Port D., Huang L. and Brown A.W., "Using the spiral model and MBASE to generate new acquisition process models: SAIV, CAIV, and SCQAIV", *Cross Talk*, vol. 15, no. 1, January 2002, pp. 20–25.
Boehm B., Abts C., Brown A.W., Chalani S., Clark B., Horowitz E., Madachy R., Reifer D. and Steece B., *Software Cost Estimation with COCOMO II*, Prentice Hall, 2000.
Forsberg K., Mooz H. and Cotterman H., *Visualizing Project Management*, (2nd ed.), Wiley, 2000.
Highsmith J., *Agile Software Development Ecosystems*, Addison Wesley, 2002.
Jacobson I., Booch G. and Rumbaugh J., *The Unified Software Development Process*, Addison Wesley, 1999.
Kaplan R. and Norton D., *The Balanced Scorecard: Translating Strategy into Action*, Harvard Business School Press, 1996.
Kim W.C. and Mauborgne R., "Charting your company's future", *Harvard Business Review*, vol. 80, no. 6, June 2002, pp. 77–83.
Kruchten P., *The Rational Unified Process*, (2nd ed.), Addison Wesley, 2001.
Rational Software Corporation. *Driving Better Business with Better Software Economics*, Cupertino, CA, 2001.
Reifer D., *Making the Software Business Case*, Addison Wesley, 2002.
Royce W.E., *Software Project Management*, Addison-Wesley, 1998.
Sullivan K., Cai Y., Hallen B. and Griswold W., "The structure and value of modularity in software design", *Proceedings, ESEC/FSE*, 2001, ACM Press, pp. 99–108.
Thorp J. and DMR's Center for Strategic Leadership, *The Information Paradox*, McGraw Hill, 1998.

25

Expert Estimation of Software Development Cost: Learning through Feedback

Magne Jørgensen and Dag Sjøberg

Based on "Increasing Realism in Effort Estimation Uncertainty Assessments: It Matters How You Ask", by Magne Jørgensen which appeared in IEEE Transactions on Software Engineering, 30(4): 209–217, 2004. © 2004 IEEE.

25.1 Introduction

"How can experts know so much and predict so badly?" (Camerer and Johnson 1991)

Expert judgment (Boehm 1981) is one of the various techniques used to estimate the resource required in order to develop a software system. Several empirical studies report that expert estimation of software development and maintenance effort is the most popular estimation approach in industry (Heemstra and Kusters 1991; Hihn and Habib-Agahi 1991; Paynter 1996; Kitchenham et al. 2002). We were not able to find a single study that reported a dominance of non-expert-based (e.g. model-based) effort estimation. An important reason for this finding may be the flexibility of expert estimation. For example, while most formal estimation models require quantitative input on a pre-defined format, estimation experts are in general able to assimilate whatever information is available and produce, somehow, an effort estimate. Another reason for the dominance of expert estimation is the lack of substantial empirical evidence in favor of formal estimation models. We found fifteen studies comparing the estimation accuracy of expert estimates with that of model estimates for software development and maintenance work. Concerning the results of these studies, five found that expert estimation outperformed mode-based approaches (Kusters, Genuchten et al. 1990; Vicinanza, Mukhopadhyay et al. 1991; Mukhopadhyay,

Vicinanza *et al.* 1992; Pengelly 1995; Kitchenham, Pfleeger *et al.* 2002), five found no difference (Heemstra and Kusters 1991; Ohlsson, Wohlin *et al.* 1998; Walkerden and Jeffery 1999; Bowden, Hargreaves *et al.* 2000; Lederer and Prasad 2000), and five found that model-based approaches outperformed expert estimation (Atkinson and Shepperd 1994; Jørgensen 1997; Niessink and van Vliet 1997; Myrtveit and Stensrud 1999; Jørgensen and Sjøberg 2002). An analysis of the designs of these fifteen studies indicates that expert estimation leads to higher estimation accuracy when the experts possess important domain or project knowledge not included in the estimation models. A comprehensive review of expert estimation studies, including a description of situations when we can expect expert-based estimates to be more accurate than model-based estimates is provided in (Jørgensen 2004c).

The accuracy of formal estimation models can be improved through a proper assimilation of the feedback[1] from completed projects. For example, a regression-based effort estimation model tailored to enhancement tasks of a particular application and based on historical data should, in theory, improve its estimation accuracy as the amount of completed enhancement projects increases and as relations between the variables become clearer. In practice, however, there are many reasons for the improvement in estimation accuracy not to happen, for example, the productivity of different software developers and teams may vary much over time due, for example, to personnel turnaround, and, processes and tools may be changed, leading to changes in productivity and a decrease in the usefulness of historical data.

While this model-based estimation learning through feedback is explicit and the techniques to some extent well understood (see, for example, studies on calibration of estimation models (Cuelenaere *et al.* 1987; Ebrahimi 1999), the 'experts' estimation learning and processes are non-explicit and difficult to analyze. Consequently, there is a risk that the expert estimation feedback is not on a format, type and point-in-time that enables learning. The current state of learning estimation skills from on-the-job feedback and how to improve the learning are the topics of this paper. The remaining part is organized as follows:

- Section 25.2 examines how much software developers and maintainers improve the accuracy of their expert estimates from typical on-the-job estimation feedback and discusses the most important learning factors.
- Section 25.3 suggests and justifies four estimation learning guidelines. The guidelines are justified through the results from a survey of software effort estimation studies and compared with results from other domains.
- Section 25.4 illustrates through the results from an experiment on the use of the guidelines how they can lead to improved estimation learning.
- Section 25.5 presents a short summary of the message of this chapter.

25.2 Estimation Learning

Surprisingly, the experts' ability to learn from estimation experience seems to be disappointingly low for both maintenance and development of software applications. Jørgensen and Sjøberg (2002) report from a study of 54 software professionals' work on extending

---

[1] In the following, we interpret 'feedback' as all types of information about software development processes, products and those involved in the processes, enabling evaluation and understanding of reasons for estimation accuracy and also of reasons for the lack of that accuracy.

and maintaining large administrative applications. They found that the amount of application-specific experience did not lead to more accurate assessments of uncertainty of effort estimates, and that the lack of learning could not only be attributed to more complex tasks with increasing experience. This finding does, of course, not suggest that experience *never* improves the estimation or uncertainty assessment skills. Assume, for example, that two very similar maintenance tasks are conducted in sequence. Then, the feedback from the first task may be applied to increase the accuracy of the estimates and uncertainty assessments of the next task. The reported results indicate, however, that the amount of such estimation situations is low and even then the feedback from the first task is difficult to apply properly for estimation purposes. A similar lack of learning from estimation feedback seems to be present for project leaders developing new applications. A study of six software project leaders' estimates over a period of three years showed no significant improvement (Hill et al. 2000).

The observed lack of learning from on-the-job feedback is not unique to software effort estimation, but has been observed in many other domains. For example, studies on experts' clinical and financial predictions show no correlation between experience and estimation skills. For overviews, see (Garb 1989) and (Blocher et al. 1997). Hammond (1996, p. 278) concludes the issue of experts' learning from estimation experience based on a high number of empirical studies: *'Yet in nearly every study of experts carried out within the judgment and decision-making approach, experience has been shown to be unrelated to the empirical accuracy of expert judgments.'*

The two empirical studies (Hill et al. 2000; Jørgensen and Sjøberg 2002) reporting results on software development and maintenance estimation learning were not designed to investigate reasons for high/low learning from experience. This type of knowledge is, however, important to improve the learning. We should, therefore, try to identify and understand the factors that can positively impact the learning. The following list of such factors are based on our examination of project experience reports and interviews with software professionals in three organizations (Jørgensen 1995; Jørgensen and Sjøberg 2001; Jørgensen and Sjøberg 2002). Two of these companies are large software development organizations with mainly in-house development and the third company is a medium large web-development company developing software for clients:

- *Motivation*: There must be a motivation for collecting and learning from estimation feedback for it to happen. The software developers and maintainers we interviewed, however, did not feel that estimation was 'their main duty', although they all agreed that accurate estimates were important. Effort estimation was frequently perceived as an unpleasant task that they were told to conduct now and then. In addition, the software professionals were typically not rewarded for high estimation accuracy. On the contrary, they were rewarded for inaccurate effort estimates, since an over-optimistic estimate and an over-confident assessment of estimation uncertainty were believed to be interpreted, by the project leaders, as an indicator of high development skills. In an experiment (Jørgensen et al. 2004), we found that the project leaders actually evaluated software developers as more skilled when providing over-confident assessments of estimation uncertainty compared with more realistic assessments of estimation uncertainty, even after the actual effort was known, that is, even when they knew the level of over-confidence in the uncertainty assessments. Consequently, in order to provide the motivation for improved estimation, a change is needed in the standards by which

the software professionals are measured. There is also a need for increasing adherence to a 'code of practice' that encourages professionals to improve their skills.
- *Awareness of the impact from biases*: There are many human and situational biases that hinder learning from experience. Kahneman *et al.* (1982) provides an overview of several of them. A particularly interesting bias found in our examination of software project reports was related to how software professionals interpreted the reasons for high and low estimation accuracy (Jørgensen and Sjøberg 2001). It seems as if software professionals focused on *external* reasons, for example, problems with subcontractors, when explaining inaccurate estimates, but attributed accurate estimates to their own estimation and project management skills. This bias may easily lead developers to a too high confidence in their own estimation skills and to the perception that there is no strong need for improvement. Similar results are found in other domains. For example, Tan and Lipe (1997) found that: *'Those with positive outcomes (e.g. strong profits) are rewarded; justification or consideration of reasons as to why the evaluatee (sic) performed well are not necessary. In contrast, when outcomes are negative (e.g. losses suffered), justifications for the poor results are critical. . . . Evaluators consider controllability or other such factors more when outcomes are negative than when they are positive.'*
- *Easy evaluation and use of outcome feedback:* In (Jørgensen and Sjøberg 2001), we found a strong impact from the effort estimate on the development and maintenance work. One software maintainer stated, for example: *'If we find in the detailed requirement specification phase that the effort estimates have been too low, we simplify the software solution."* Similar impacts from the effort and time estimate on the software development work have been demonstrated in simulation experiments on system dynamics (Abdel-Hamid and Madnik 1983; Abdel-Hamid and Madnik 1986; Abdel-Hamid *et al.* 1999). This means that the estimation accuracy cannot always be evaluated as the deviation between estimated and actual effort, that is, that the outcome feedback (which frequently is the only explicit estimation feedback received) is not always reliable information. If we cannot easily and objectively assess the accuracy of an effort estimate, it certainly is more difficult to learn from the estimation experience than otherwise.
- *Training opportunities*: To learn from experience, there should be training opportunities and sufficient time should be allocated for learning (Ericsson and Lehmann 1996). However, the time a software professional spends on effort estimation seems to be low and fragmented. The time spent on writing experience reports, for example, understanding the deviation between estimated and actual effort, may be even lower.
- *Timely feedback*: When estimating software tasks, the feedback is frequently only possible several weeks (even months) after it was provided. Then, the estimation assumptions and important events are easily forgotten or are subject to 'hindsight biases' for example, the tendency to interpret consequences and events as more obvious after they happened than before (Fischhoff 1975; Stahlberg *et al.* 1995).
- *Availability of causal models*: Our interviews with software professionals have indicated that, in general, there was no explicit *causal* model to guide the estimation work. As reported in (Blocher *et al.* 1997), it is difficult to learn from experience without a causal model of the relation between important variables. Unfortunately, most current estimation models cannot be used as causal models, because they are based on correlations, not cause-effects, and do not include important task, application, developer and domain specific knowledge known by the software maintainers. For example, although there has

been much research on the shape of the software 'production function', that is, function-based relation between input and output parameters, for several years, no agreement on its shape has been reached. Dolado (2001), for example, investigated the relationship between software size and effort on 12 data sets using regression analysis and genetic programming. He reported that it was hard to conclude on a relationship between effort and size, and that we could only expect moderately good results of size-based estimation models. Currently, most software development effort estimation models are size-based. Frequently, one individual's or one project's on-the-job experience does not enable the building of causal models, either. For example, we interviewed a number of project leaders about the reasons for inaccurate effort estimates (Jørgensen *et al.* 2002). One important reason for cost overruns was, according to the project leaders, not sufficiently detailed requirement specifications. From the perspective of a project leader this opinion is easy to understand. A project may, for example, have had a lot of unexpected work on clarifying what the customer really wanted. However, when we compared the requirement specification information from the projects' experience reports with the cost estimation precision data in the experience database we found indications of the opposite, that is, high estimation accuracy was more frequently connected with the *lack* of highly detailed specifications. The experience report of the projects without detailed requirement specifications indicated that the amount of delivered functionality and the quality was lower than intended when the cost was estimated, but still within the (high-level) requirement specification. It appears that the less detailed, flexible requirement specification enabled the project implementers sufficient room for manoeuvre as to meet the estimate. The development of causal models relevant for estimation may therefore need analyses of a large set of projects, as well as deep analyses of single projects, that is, the development of causal models is a difficult task.

- *Standardization of the process*: Several well-known process improvement frameworks, for example, the Capability Maturity Model (Paulk *et al.* 1993), which promote standardization of the process are believed to lead to better predictability and less variation in use of effort. This belief is supported by opinions of project leaders we have interviewed (Jørgensen and Moløkken 2004), for example, that the lack of a standardized process makes learning from previous experience difficult.

Learning estimation skills from on-the-job experience is a hard task. The empirical studies and the learning hindrances discussed in this section suggest that in general we should not expect much estimation learning from typical on-the-job estimation feedback. Section 25.3 describes and validates several guidelines to improve this situation.

25.3 Estimation Feedback and Process Guidelines

This section discusses and evaluates the following four learning guidelines: (1) Increase the motivation for learning estimation skills, (2) Reduce the impact from estimation learning biases, (3) Ensure a fit between the estimation process and the type of feedback, and (4) Provide learning situations. The selection of the guidelines is based on the discussion of learning factors in Section 25.2. Our intention is not to provide a large number of guidelines, but only to discuss what we believe are the most important guidelines for improvement of the *feedback-oriented estimation learning process*. We do not, for example, address the role of estimation courses and self-instruction through textbooks.

25.3.1 Increase the Motivation for Learning Estimation Skills

Two important process actions to increase the motivation for learning estimation skills are the following:

- *Evaluate the estimation accuracy of the software professionals*: Lederer and Prasad (1998) report that the factor with the highest impact on the estimation accuracy was the use of the estimation accuracy in the evaluation of the performance of the software professionals. Similarly, the studies (Weinberg and Schulman 1974; Jørgensen and Sjøberg 2001) found that inducing estimation accuracy as an important performance measure improved the estimation accuracy compared with situations where the projects were evaluated according to other attributes such as schedule performance or quality. Higher motivation for learning from feedback may be only one out of many reasons for the measured improvement in estimation accuracy when evaluating the accuracy. Other reasons are, for example, more time spent on the estimation work and better project management to avoid effort-overrun. Nevertheless, the studies suggest that evaluation has an impact on the perceived importance of the estimation work. A perception of importance is, we believe, a precondition for learning estimation skills. It is important to be aware that evaluation may have negative consequences, as well. Several human judgment studies suggest that a high motivation for estimation accuracy, for example, when people feel personally responsible, perceive that the estimation task is very important or receive monetary rewards for accurate estimates, may *decrease* the estimation accuracy (Sieber 1974; Armstrong *et al.* 1975; Cosier and Rose 1977). A possible explanation for this phenomenon is that an increased awareness of being evaluated increases the level of so-called 'dominant responses' (instincts) on cost of more reflective responses (Zajonc 1965), that is, a strong perception of evaluation leads to more instinct and less reflection. It is, for this reason, important to ensure that evaluation of software estimation accuracy does not lead to a strong pressure in the estimation situation, but instead to more emphasis on analysis and proper use of previous project and estimation experience.
- *Avoid estimation rewards different from accuracy*: As discussed in Section 25.2, some of the software professionals felt that they were rewarded with positive evaluation feedback when providing optimistic and over-confident estimates. The 'estimation game' described in (Thomsett 1996) is a good example of this type of mixed rewards: *'Boss: Hi, Mary. How long do you think it will take to add some customer enquiry screens to the Aardvark System? Mary: Gee . . . I guess about six weeks or so. Boss: WHAAT?!!!! That long?!!! You're joking, right? Mary: Oh! Sorry. It could be done perhaps in four weeks . . .'*. This type of situation, obviously, does not stimulate learning. Another estimation accuracy evaluation practice that hinders the learning is the lack of proper distinction between 'estimated effort', 'planned effort' and 'bid', as reported in (Edwards and Moores 1994; Goodwin 1998; Jørgensen and Sjøberg 2001). The decisions on 'bid', 'planned effort' and 'most likely effort' have conflicting goals and should be rewarded differently. A bid should, optimally, be low enough to get the job and high enough to maximize profit, the planned effort should enable a successful project and motivate efficient work, and the estimate of the most likely effort should represent the most realistic use of effort. In order to stimulate estimation learning, we believe that the software developers' evaluation rewards should be on the estimated effort (not the planned effort

or the bid) and the managers should be trained to elicit estimates so that that hidden evaluation goals (e.g. to 'please the manager') are avoided.

25.3.2 Reduce the Impact from Estimation-Learning Biases

There are several learning biases that should be accounted for when supporting the learning process. Among the most relevant biases are the following:

- *The 'hindsight bias'*: Hindsight bias, that is, the tendency to interpret cause-effect relationships as more obvious after it happened than before (Fischhoff 1975; Stahlberg *et al.* 1995), is difficult to avoid. For example, it may not be sufficient to inform about it and instruct people to avoid it (Slovic and Fischhoff 1977).
- *The tendency to confirm rules and disregard conflicting evidence*: Empirical results suggests that learning processes easily lead to the mode of 'confirming theories on how to complete the project', rather than 'reject incorrect hypotheses and assumptions' (Brehmer 1980; Koehler 1991).
- *The over-confidence in own estimates*: A strong tendency to ignore previous feedback and persist in over-confidence in own estimates have been observed in software development and other domains (Koriat *et al.* 1980; Connolly and Dean 1997; Yaniv and Foster 1997; Jørgensen *et al.* 2004). We discuss reasons for this and how to overcome it when presenting the learning experiment in Section 25.4.

Probably, there is no easy method to avoid these learning biases. Although important, it is generally not sufficient to make software professionals aware of the learning biases. In addition to increased awareness, software professionals should be stimulated to document the estimation assumptions and criticize own causal models derived from experience (Silverman 1992; Brenner *et al.* 1996).

A change of the estimation process itself may also reduce an impact on the learning biases. For example, it seems as if estimation processes that use historical data more explicitly, for example, top–down, analogy-based estimation processes, are less biased than those relying on an 'inside-view' of the software to be developed, for example, bottom–up, work-breakdown structure-based estimation processes (Moløkken 2002). Similar results are reported in (Kahneman and Lovallo 1993).

25.3.3 Ensure a Fit Between the Estimation Process and Type of Feedback

Several human judgment studies show a disappointing lack of estimation improvement from outcome feedback, that is, feedback relating the actual outcome to the estimated outcome (Balzer *et al.* 1989; Benson 1992; Stone and Opel 2000). The single software effort estimation study on this topic that we were able to find (Ohlsson *et al.* 1998) shows the same result. That study reports no estimation improvement from outcome estimation feedback. In fact, the only situation where outcome feedback is reported to improve the estimation accuracy seems to be when the estimation tasks are 'dependent and related', for example, when the tasks are very similar, and the estimator initially was under-confident, for example, underestimated her/his own knowledge (Subbotin 1996).

The lack of improvement from outcome feedback should be no large surprise, since there is a lack of fit between the information needed when estimating and the type of feedback provided. For example, it is not easy to apply the feedback *'the effort estimate on your previous project was 30% too low'* when estimating a new project. Although not very useful for improvement of estimation accuracy, outcome feedback can be useful for the learning of estimation uncertainty assessments (Stone and Opel 2000). In the uncertainty assessment situation, there is a better fit between the estimation process and the type of feedback. For example, if all projects similar to that to be estimated were estimated within +/−50% of the actual effort, it is likely that the new project's estimate are likely to be within this uncertainty interval. Unfortunately, the typical estimation uncertainty process is not in general designed to make maximum benefit from the estimation outcome feedback. We discuss how to improve the fit between uncertainty estimation and feedback in Section 25.4.

To improve the estimation accuracy, several studies suggest that 'task relation oriented feedback', that is, feedback on how different events and variables were related to the actual use of effort, are required (Schmitt *et al.* 1976; Balzer *et al.* 1989; Benson 1992; Stone and Opel 2000). In other words, there seems to be a need for causal models, instead of shallow, correlation-based models to enable learning. Possible methods to move toward causal models are to use 'root cause analyses' or 'experience reports', for example, as part of an 'experience factory', or 'postmortem analyses' (Basili *et al.* 1994; Houdek *et al.* 1998; Jørgensen *et al.* 1998; Engelkamp *et al.* 2000; Birk *et al.* 2002).

25.3.4 Provide Learning Situations

As discussed in Section 25.2, it is not easy to learn from on-the-job estimation feedback alone. The time spent on estimation is low and fragmented, it is not easy to generalize cause-effects based on few projects, and the time from estimation to feedback is frequently long. We therefore recommend that software organizations, which can afford it introduce the 'cost engineer' role, that is, a position dedicated to analysis of all the estimation work, and 'deliberate learning', that is, artificial estimation situations designed for specific learning purposes to improve the individual and organizational learning. Our recommendations are based on the following justification:

- The importance of causal domain models for learning is emphasized in (Bolger and Wright 1994). See also discussion in Section 25.2. A person dedicated to analyzing and summarizing estimation relevant information, that is, the cost engineer is likely to do a better cause-effect estimating analysis than software professionals dedicating a low and fragmented part of their time to estimation. This argumentation is in line with the 'experience factory' organizational principles described in (Basili *et al.* 1994).
- It has been shown that immediate feedback is able to strongly improve the estimation accuracy (Bolger and Wright 1994; Shepperd *et al.* 1996). On-the-job estimation situations can seldom provide immediate feedback, and artificial learning situations may be necessary. We recommend that software organizations introduce the so-called 'deliberate training' as described by Ericsson and Lehmann (1996), for example, *'individualized training activities especially designed by a coach or teacher to improve specific aspects of an individual's performance through repetition and successive refinement'*. Ericsson and Lehmann (1996) found that it was not the amount of experience but the amount of 'deliberate training' that determined the level of expertise, for example, the estimation skills. The importance of designed training situations is also supported by the results

described in (Camerer and Johnson 1991), where it was found that while training had an effect on estimation accuracy, amount of experience had almost none. We suggest that software companies provide estimation training opportunities through creation and update of a database of completed projects. An estimation training session could, for example, include estimation of completed projects based on the information available at the point-of-estimation applying different estimation processes. This type of estimation training has several advantages in comparison with the traditional estimation training:
- Individualized feedback, the actual effort and the project's experience report, can be received immediately after completion of the estimates.
- The effect of not applying checklists and other estimation tools can be investigated on one's own estimation work. The estimator can, for example, use a checklist on the estimation of some projects and compare the estimation performance with situations without the use of checklists.
- The validity of the own estimation experience can be examined on different types of projects, for example, projects much larger than those estimated earlier.
- Reasons for forgotten activities or underestimated risks can be analyzed immediately, while the hindsight bias is weak.
- The tendency to be over-confident can be acknowledged and compensated for, given proper coaching and training projects.

As far as we know, there are no reported studies of organizations conducting estimation training in line following these or similar suggestions. However, the results from other studies, in particular, those summarized in (Ericsson and Lehmann 1996), strongly support that this type of training should complement the traditional estimation courses and learning-by-doing.

25.4 Experiment: Application of the Guidelines

The experiment[2] described in this section illustrates how the application of the Guidelines 2 (reduce the impact of estimation learning biases) and 3 (ensure a fit between the estimation process and the type of feedback) can lead to learning improvements. The idea of this experiment originates from studies on human judgment based uncertainty assessments in psychology, see for example, (Seaver *et al.* 1978; Yaniv and Foster 1997). The actual learning process evaluated in the experiment, however, is novel. The topic of the experiment is learning from feedback when assessing effort estimation uncertainty through effort prediction intervals. An effort prediction interval consists of a minimum and maximum value and the related confidence level (Moder *et al.* 1995). For example, a software maintainer may be 90% confident that the actual effort of a maintenance task will be between 20 and 40 work-hours. Then, the 90% effort prediction interval is [20, 40] work-hours.

---

[2] The experiment and results reported here are based on a subset of the data and analyses published in 'Increasing Realism in Effort Estimation Uncertainty Assessments: It Matters How You Ask', by Magne Jørgensen, which appeared in IEEE Transactions on Software Engineering, 30 (4): 209–217, 2004. © 2004 IEEE.

25.4.1 Background

There is strong empirical evidence that the prediction intervals, on average, are much too narrow to reflect the stated confidence level. For example, we observed the effort prediction intervals of a number of industrial software projects and found that the hit rate, that is, the proportion of tasks where the actual effort was inside the minimum–maximum values, was only about 30% (Jørgensen et al. 2004). Most of these projects did not state the confidence level, but, obviously, most meaningful interpretations of minimum–maximum values imply hit rates higher than 30%. Similarly, we found that the 90% prediction intervals of student projects had a hit rate of only 62%.[3] Similar prediction interval hit rates were found by Connolly and Dean (1997) on computer science students on programming tasks. The students and the software professionals had previous experience developing and estimating software tasks. Why were they not able to learn from this experience to achieve better, or at least make unbiased assessment of the uncertainty of their effort estimates?

By analyzing the learning process we found two main reasons for lack of learning: (1) The feedback they had received on previous tasks was difficult to apply in the next uncertainty assessment situation, that is, there was not a good fit between the estimation process and the type of feedback, (2) The situational and human biases stimulated the software professionals to remain over-confident, that is, not to learn from previous estimation outcome. The following example illustrates this. A software maintainer is asked to provide an effort estimate and a 90% confidence effort prediction interval for a new task. The maintainer estimates the most likely effort to be 20 work-hours based on experience with similar tasks, but is not sure how to decide on a 90% confidence effort prediction interval. On the basis of a search on previous estimation performance data on similar tasks, the software maintainer finds that the estimation accuracy varied from -10% to $+60\%$, that is, from 10% too high to 60% too low estimates. The median estimation deviation was a 30% too low estimate. Further, the maintainer knows that the previous 90% confidence prediction intervals included only 60% of the actual values, that is, the maintainer receives the feedback that he/she has previously been strongly over-confident. Even with all this estimation feedback, which is much more than typically received, the maintainer does not know how to determine the minimum and maximum value for a 90% confidence level. The maintainer knows that she/he, on average, should increase the width of the prediction interval, but does not know by how much. A formal calculation of the effort prediction interval is statistically complex[4] and a recent study suggests that statistically computed effort prediction intervals apply the uncertainty information inefficiently (Jørgensen 2004b), that is, formal uncertainty assessment models seem to provide meaninglessly wide minimum–maximum effort intervals. The lack of

---

[3] Just before the students estimated their projects they attended an estimation lecture emphasizing the typical too narrow minimum–maximum intervals. In spite of this lecture, the intervals were much too narrow as to reflect a 90% confidence level.

[4] The statistical definition of a prediction interval, assuming a single random sample of n independent observations from a normally distributed population, is Christensen, (1998). *Analysis of variance, design and regression. Applied statistical methods*, Chapman & Hall/Crc.: $\bar{y} \pm t(conf, df) \cdot s \cdot \sqrt{1 + \frac{1}{n}}$, where $\bar{y}$ is the sample mean, $t(conf, df)$ is the t-value for confidence level $conf$ and df degrees of freedom, and s is the standard deviation of the sample.

useful estimation feedback means that the maintainer has to base the uncertainty assessment on task knowledge, for example, through construction of scenarios leading to the different use of effort. Several studies on time-estimation, see (Buehler *et al.* 1997) for an overview, suggest that this strategy tends to lead to over-confidence and limited learning from experience.

In addition, there may be strong situational biases that lead to over-confidence, that is, to too narrow prediction intervals. For example, as described in Section 25.2, the maintainer knows that she/he will be perceived as more skilled when providing narrow prediction intervals. To be perceived as a skilled maintainer, may be perceived as much more important than a proper prediction interval. In particular, this is likely to happen if the maintainer expects that there will be no evaluation on the prediction interval.

In total, the feedback does not support the uncertainty assessment, that is, prediction interval, process and the situational biases provide stimulus to be over-confident.

The following experiment illustrates how a simple change in the uncertainty estimation process can lead to a large impact on the usefulness of the estimation outcome feedback and on the bias toward over-confidence.

25.4.2 Experiment Design

The *Traditional* prediction interval elicitation process, see for example, the PERT process described in (Moder *et al.* 1995) is the following:

1. Estimate the most likely effort.
2. Select a confidence level for the prediction interval to be estimated in Step 3. Typically, confidence levels reflecting a 90% confidence or more are selected, for example, the confidence level described as 'almost certain'.
3. Estimate the minimum and maximum effort so that the probability of including the actual effort is believed to equal the confidence level.

As discussed earlier this process does not enable an efficient use of estimation feedback and typically leads to over-confidence, that is, to too narrow effort prediction intervals. An *Alternative* uncertainty assessment process is the following:

1. Estimate the most likely effort.
2. Calculate the minimum and maximum effort as fixed proportions of the most likely effort, for example, apply the effort prediction interval guidelines from NASA (1990) where minimum effort = 50% and maximum effort = 200% of the most likely effort.
3. Estimate the confidence level, that is, the probability (likelihood) that the actual effort is between the minimum and maximum effort.

Formally, the difference between these two processes is not large. However, from an estimation learning perspective there are important differences. The described problems with the *Traditional* elicitation process may, to some extent, be removed by the *Alternative* process. Assume that a project leader is asked to provide the confidence level of a 50%–200% effort prediction interval of a software project and that there exists a number of similar, previously completed, projects that have been estimated applying this 50%–200% fixed-width effort prediction interval. A simple analysis of the previous prediction intervals gives, for example, that 70% of those intervals included the actual effort. Consequently, given that the history is relevant, the expected probability that the actual effort is included by the new 50% to 200% prediction interval is about 70%. As opposed to the *Traditional* process, no sophisticated statistical calculations are needed. Further, since the minimum and maximum effort values are calculated 'mechanically', it may also be easier to be realistic about the probability that the actual effort is inside the interval, that is, the over-confidence may be reduced. While minimum and maximum values provided by oneself, as in the *Traditional* process, may be used to signalize skill, those provided automatically may reduce the feeling of prediction interval ownership and consequently increase the focus on realism.

To test the effect of the *Alternative* uncertainty elicitation process we hired 29 software developers/project managers of a Norwegian, e-commerce software development organization to participate in an experiment. The participants were, randomly, divided into two groups: *Traditional* and *Alternative*. The participants of the *Traditional* group used the *Traditional* uncertainty elicitation process and those of the *Alternative* group used the *Alternative* uncertainty elicitation process. All participants should estimate the most likely effort and the uncertainty of the estimate of 30 software estimation tasks. The estimation work was completed in a Microsoft Excel spreadsheet. There was no interaction between the participants during the estimation work. The experiment was divided into two parts:

1. *Training*: Instructions and training in use of the estimation spreadsheet and how to provide effort prediction intervals. As training tasks, the effort and the effort prediction intervals of 10 real-world software development projects were estimated based on an 'experience database' of five similar projects. Feedback was given after each estimate. When the estimates were completed, the software developers were asked to analyze and reflect on their own performance, in particular, the correspondence between confidence level and hit rate.
2. *Estimation*: Estimation of 30 software enhancements tasks previously conducted in a large telecom company. Task 1 was estimated based on an 'experience database' including five previously completed tasks; Task 2 was estimated based on the five tasks and feedback, that is, the actual effort, on the Task 1 estimate; Task 3 was estimated based on the five tasks and the feedback on the Tasks 1 and 2 estimates, and so on.

The sequence of the 30 tasks was randomized for all the software developers, i.e., the software developers estimated the tasks in different sequences. The alternative, to let all the developers estimate the tasks in the same sequence, was avoided, because then the chosen sequence might have resulted in tasks with increasing or decreasing estimation complexity. Consequently, a measured improvement might have been caused by simpler tasks to be estimated, not necessarily a real learning from experience.

There are some factors that are different from a realistic estimation task. For example, in most realistic cases the estimators would have more relevant information about the application, for example, the complexity of the particular part to be changed, about the particular developer who carried out the task and about the necessary implementation, testing and integration activities. This means that we cannot expect very accurate predictions of the actual effort, that is, the effort prediction intervals probably get wider than those of real software task estimation situations. The learning opportunities, due to fast feedback, may be better compared with real life estimation tasks.

25.4.3 Results

Two of the participants who followed the *Traditional* prediction interval estimation process did not understand the task of estimating the prediction intervals properly and were removed from the data set, leaving 13 software professionals in the *Traditional* group and 14 in the *Alternative* group. To study the progress of the correspondence between hit rates and confidence, we divided the 30 tasks into three sets: Tasks 1–10, Tasks 11–20 and Tasks 21–30. There was no large difference in the accuracy of the estimate of the most likely effort, that is, there was no difference in estimation skills of the two groups. Both groups had a median deviation between the estimated and actual effort of about 50%.

Table 25.1 shows the differences in the correspondence between mean hit rates (Hit rate) and mean confidence levels (Conf.) for the two elicitation processes.

The participants who followed the *Traditional* process approached very slowly an acceptable correspondence between hit rate and confidence level. Even the data on Tasks 21–30 showed a tendency to over-confidence! The participants who followed the *Alternative* process, on the other hand, had a close to perfect correspondence between mean hit rate and confidence level on all groups of tasks.

In real software development organizations, there are rarely as much as 20–30 similar tasks that can be used as basis for new estimates. This means that the performance of the 10 first estimation tasks, based on a few earlier tasks, may be the most important criterion for comparing the two estimation process. The experiment indicates that the benefit of the *Alternative* elicitation process is at its largest on the first tasks. This strongly suggests that the effort prediction elicitation change from *Traditional* to *Alternative* based on the learning guidelines (2) and (3) was effective. The effect of the change is clearly visible also on an individual level, see Table 25.2. Pairs of hit rate and mean confidence level with deviation larger than or equal to 0.2 are printed in bold.

As expected, most of the hit rates of those who followed the *Traditional* process were too low to reflect a 90% confidence level, that is, the prediction intervals were strongly over-confident. The mean difference between the hit rate and the 90% confidence level was −0.2, that is, strongly biased. The participants who followed the *Alternative* process, however, had sometimes a too high and sometimes a too low confidence level. The mean difference between the hit rate and the confidence was −0.02, that is, there was no bias.

Table 25.1 Mean hit rate vs. mean confidence level

Group	Tasks 1–10		Tasks 11–20		Tasks 21–30	
	Hit rate	Conf.	Hit rate	Conf.	Hit rate	Conf.
Traditional	0.64	0.90	0.70	0.90	0.81	0.90
Alternative	0.67	0.73	0.69	0.71	0.73	0.71

Table 25.2 Hit rate vs. mean confidence level (individual data)

Person	Process	Training tasks		Task 1–10		Task 11–20		Task 21–30	
		Hit rate	Conf.	Hit rate	Conf.	Hit rate	Conf.	Hit rate	Conf.
T1	Traditional	**0,5**	**0,9**	**0,7**	**0,9**	0,8	0,9	1,0	0,9
T2	Traditional	0,9	0,9	0,9	0,9	0,9	0,9	**0,7**	**0,9**
T4	Traditional	**0,5**	**0,9**	**0,6**	**0,9**	**0,6**	**0,9**	0,9	0,9
T5	Traditional	**0,5**	**0,9**	**0,4**	**0,9**	0,7	0,9	**0,5**	**0,9**
T6	Traditional	0,8	0,9	**0,7**	**0,9**	**0,5**	**0,9**	1,0	0,9
T7	Traditional	**0,7**	**0,9**	**0,7**	**0,9**	**0,7**	**0,9**	0,8	0,9
T8	Traditional	**0,6**	**0,9**	**0,6**	**0,9**	**0,6**	**0,9**	0,8	0,9
T9	Traditional	0,8	0,9	0,8	0,9	0,8	0,9	1,0	0,9
T10	Traditional	**0,7**	**0,9**	**0,4**	**0,9**	0,9	0,9	**0,7**	**0,9**
T11	Traditional	**0,3**	**0,9**	**0,6**	**0,9**	0,9	0,9	0,8	0,9
T12	Traditional	**0,4**	**0,9**	**0,6**	**0,9**	**0,3**	**0,9**	0,8	0,9
T13	Traditional	**0,2**	**0,9**	**0,7**	**0,9**	**0,7**	**0,9**	**0,7**	**0,9**
A1	Alternative	0,9	0,9	**0,5**	**0,7**	**0,9**	**0,7**	0,7	0,7
A2	Alternative	**0,7**	**0,9**	**0,6**	**0,8**	0,8	0,7	0,9	0,9
A3	Alternative	0,7	0,8	0,6	0,6	0,6	0,5	**0,8**	**0,6**
A4	Alternative	n.a.	n.a	**0,5**	**0,9**	0,6	0,9	0,8	0,9
A5	Alternative	**0,8**	**1,0**	**0,6**	**0,9**	**0,5**	**1,0**	0,9	0,9
A6	Alternative	0,8	0,8	0,6	0,7	**0,5**	**0,7**	0,7	0,6
A7	Alternative	**0,6**	**0,9**	0,8	0,8	0,7	0,8	0,8	0,8
A8	Alternative	0,9	0,8	0,7	0,8	0,8	0,7	0,8	0,7
A9	Alternative	0,8	0,8	0,7	0,7	0,7	0,7	0,7	0,7
A10	Alternative	1,0	1,0	0,8	0,8	0,7	0,7	0,6	0,7
A11	Alternative	**1,0**	**0,8**	0,7	0,7	0,5	0,6	0,6	0,6
A12	Alternative	**0,9**	**0,7**	**0,9**	**0,6**	0,7	0,5	**0,8**	**0,5**
A13	Alternative	0,8	0,8	0,7	0,7	**0,9**	**0,7**	**0,4**	**0,7**
A14	Alternative	0,9	0,8	0,7	0,6	**0,8**	**0,6**	0,7	0,6

There are limitations regarding the generalizability of our results, for example:

- Only one level of confidence (*Traditional* process) and one interval width (*Alternative* process) were studied. These levels were chosen because they were typical (90% confidence) or recommended (50%–200% prediction intervals). It is, nevertheless, possible that other confidence levels and interval widths would lead to other results. For example, it is possible that the selection of a 70% confidence level would remove the bias toward over-confidence applying the *Traditional* process, and that an 80%–120% prediction interval would lead to over-confidence applying the *Alternative* process. Seaver et al. (1978) found no large difference between the two processes for the 'inter-quartile' interval, that is, the interval that should reflect a 50% confidence level. In other words, the improvements we found may depend on the chosen levels.
- The estimation process of the participants in the experiment was different from their normal process. Normally, they would know more about the task, the development environment, etc. than in the artificial experimental setup. There is, therefore, a need

for a replication of the study in more realistic estimation situations. We have recently finished a study comparing the *Traditional* and *Alternative* process in real industrial software development estimation processes. This study shows similar results as in the experiment (Jørgensen 2004a).

25.5 Summary

We conclude that on-the-job estimation learning opportunities is low and try to explain the reason for the observed lack of estimation learning. To improve the learning situation we propose the following four learning guidelines: (1) Increase the motivation for learning estimation skills, (2) Reduce the impact from estimation learning biases, (3) Ensure a fit between estimation process and type of feedback, and (4) Provide learning situations. On the basis of results from studies in software development and other domains we argue that the proposed learning guidelines are capable of improving the feedback-oriented estimation learning. To follow the guidelines means, for example, that software organizations should increase their awareness and understanding of how they motivate, evaluate and reward estimation, and what type of information the software professionals actually use when estimating effort and assessing uncertainty of effort estimates. While the majority of the learning enablers to be implemented may be simple, for example, to use estimation accuracy as an evaluation criterion, other changes may require more elucidation and research, for example, how to design 'deliberate estimation training' without incurring excessive costs. An experiment demonstrates the usefulness of the guidelines.

25.6 Acknowledgement

Thanks to Karl Halvor Teigen, Professor in Psychology at the University of Oslo, for his useful suggestions and interesting discussions.

References

Abdel-Hamid, T.K. and Madnik, S.E. (1983). "The dynamics of software project scheduling." *Communications of the ACM* **26**(5): 340–346.
Abdel-Hamid, T.K. and Madnik, S.E. (1986). "Impact of schedule estimation on software project behavior." *IEEE Software* **3**(4): 70–75.
Abdel-Hamid, T.K., Sengupta, K., et al. (1999). "The impact of goals on software project management: An experimental investigation." *MIS Quarterly* **23**(4): 531–555.
Armstrong, J.S., Denniston W.B. Jr., et al. (1975). "The use of the decomposition principle in making judgments." *Organizational-Behavior-and-Human-Decision-Processes* **14**(2): 257–263.
Atkinson, K. and Shepperd, M. (1994). Using function points to find cost analogies. *European Software Cost Modelling Meeting*, Ivrea, Italy.
Balzer, W.K., Doherty, M.E., et al. (1989). "Effects of cognitive feedback on performance." *Psychological Bulletin* **106**(3): 410–433.
Basili, V., Caldierea, H., et al. (1994). The Experience Factory. *Encyclopedia of Software Engineering*, J.J. Marciniak (ed), Wiley: 469–476.
Benson, P.G. (1992). "The effects of feedback and training on the performance of probability forecasters." *International Journal of Forecasting* **8**(4): 559–573.
Birk, A., Dingsøyr, T., et al. (2002). "Postmortem: Never leave a project without it." *IEEE Software* **19**(3): 43–45.
Blocher, E., Bouwman, M.J., et al. (1997). "Learning from experience in performing analytical procedures." *Training Research Journal* **3**: 59–79.

Boehm, B.W. (1981). *Software Engineering Economics*. Upper Saddle River, New Jersey, Prentice Hall.

Bolger, F. and Wright, G. (1994). "Assessing the quality of expert judgment: Issues and analysis." *Decision Support Systems* **11**(1): 1–24.

Bowden, P., Hargreaves, M., et al. (2000). "Estimation support by lexical analysis of requirements documents." *Journal of Systems and Software* **51**(2): 87–98.

Brehmer, B. (1980). "In one word: Not from experience." *Acta Psychologica* **45**: 223–241.

Brenner, L.A., Koehler, D.J., et al. (1996). "On the evaluation of one-sided evidence." *Journal of Behavioral Decision Making* **9**(1): 59–70.

Buehler, R., Griffin, D., et al. (1997). "The role of motivated reasoning in optimistic time predictions." *Personality and Social Psychology Bulletin* **23**(3): 238–247.

Camerer, C.F. and Johnson, E.J. (1991). The process-performance paradox in expert judgment: How can experts know so much and predict so badly?. *Towards a General Theory of Expertise*, K.A. Ericsson and J. Smith (eds), Cambridge University Press: 195–217.

Christensen, R. (1998). *Analysis of Variance, Design and Regression. Applied Statistical Methods*, Chapman & Hall/Crc.

Connolly, T. and Dean, D. (1997). "Decomposed versus holistic estimates of effort required for software writing tasks." *Management Science* **43**(7): 1029–1045.

Cosier, R.A. and Rose, G.L. (1977). "Cognitive conflict and goal conflict effects on task performance." *Organizational Behaviour and Human Performance* **19**(2): 378–391.

Cuelenaere, A.M.E., Genuchten, M.J.I.M., et al. (1987). "Calibrating a software cost estimation model: Why and how." *Information and Software Technology* **29**(10): 558–567.

Dolado, J.J. (2001). "On the problem of the software cost function." *Information and Software Technology* **43**(1): 61–72.

Ebrahimi, N.B. (1999). "How to improve the calibration of cost models." *IEEE Transactions on Software Engineering* **25**(1): 136–140.

Edwards, J.S. and Moores, T.T. (1994). "A conflict between the use of estimating and planning tools in the management of information systems." *European Journal of Information Systems* **3**(2): 139–147.

Engelkamp, S., Hartkopf, S., et al. (2000). *Project Experience Database: A Report Based on First Practical Experience*, PROFES. Oulu, Finland, Springer-Verlag: 204–215.

Ericsson, K.A. and Lehmann, A.C. (1996). "Expert and exceptional performance: Evidence of maximal adaptation to task constraints." *Annual Review of Psychology* **47**: 273–305.

Fischhoff, B. (1975). "Hindsight foresight: The effect of outcome knowledge on judgement under uncertainty." *Journal of Experimental Psychology: Human Perception and Performance* **1**: 288–299.

Garb, H.N. (1989). "Clinical judgment, clinical training, and professional experience." *Psychological Bulletin* **105**(3): 387–396.

Goodwin, P. (1998). Enhancing judgmental sales forecasting: The role of laboratory research. *Forecasting with Judgment*, G. Wright and P. Goodwin (eds). New York, John Wiley & Sons: 91–112.

Hammond, K.R. (1996). *Human Judgement and Social Policy*. New York, Oxford University Press.

Heemstra, F.J. and Kusters, R.J. (1991). "Function point analysis: Evaluation of a software cost estimation model." *European Journal of Information Systems* **1**(4): 223–237.

Hihn, J. and Habib-Agahi, H. (1991). Cost estimation of software intensive projects: A survey of current practices. *International Conference on Software Engineering*. Los Alamitos, CA, IEEE Computer Society Press: 276–287.

Hill, J., Thomas, L.C., et al. (2000). "Experts' estimates of task durations in software development projects." *International Journal of Project Management* **18**(1): 13–21.

Houdek, F., Schneider, K., et al. (1998). Establishing experience factories at Daimler-Benz an experience report. *International Conference on Software Engineering*, Kyoto, Japan: 443–447.

Jørgensen, M. (1995). "An empirical study of software maintenance tasks." *Journal of Software Maintenance* **7**: 27–48.

Jørgensen, M. (1997). An empirical evaluation of the MkII FPA estimation model. *Norwegian Informatics Conference*, Voss, Norway, Tapir, Oslo: 7–18.

Jørgensen, M. (2004a). "Increasing realism in effort estimation uncertainty assessments: It matters how you ask." *IEEE Transactions on Software Engineering* **30**(4): 209–217.

Jørgensen, M. (2004b). "Regression models of software development effort estimation accuracy and bias." *Empirical Software Engineering*, **9**(4): 297–314.

Jørgensen, M. (2004c). "A review of studies on expert estimation of software development effort." *Journal of Systems and Software* **70**(1–2): 37–60.

Jørgensen, M., Moen, L., *et al.* (2002). Combining quantitative software development cost estimation precision data with qualitative data from project experience reports at Ericsson design center in Norway. *Proceedings of the Conference on Empirical Assessment in Software Engineering.* Keele, England, Keele University.

Jørgensen, M. and Moløkken, K. (2004). "Reasons for software effort estimation error: impact of respondents role, information collection approach, and data analysis method." *IEEE Transactions of Software Engineering* **30**(12): 993–1007.

Jørgensen, M. and Sjøberg, D.I.K. (2001). "Impact of effort estimates on software project work." *Information and Software Technology* **43**(15): 939–948.

Jørgensen, M. and Sjøberg, D.I.K. (2002). "Impact of experience on maintenance skills." *Journal of Software Maintenance and Evolution: Research and Practice* **14**(2): 123–146.

Jørgensen, M., Sjøberg, D.I.K., *et al.* (1998). Reuse of software development experience at Telenor Telecom Software. *European Software Process Improvement Conference (EuroSPI'98)*, Gothenburg, Sweden: 10.19–10.31.

Jørgensen, M., Teigen, K.H., *et al.* (2004). "Better sure than safe? Overconfidence in judgment based software development effort prediction intervals." *Journal of System and Software* **70**(1–2): 79–93.

Kahneman, D. and Lovallo, D. (1993). "Timid choices and bold forecasts: A cognitive perspective on risk taking." *Management Science* **39**(1): 17–31.

Kahneman, D., Slovic, P., *et al.* (1982). *Judgment Under Uncertainty: Heuristics and Biases.* Cambridge, United Kingdom, Cambridge University Press.

Kitchenham, B., Pfleeger, S.L., *et al.* (2002). "A case study of maintenance estimation accuracy." *Journal of Systems and Software*, **64**(1): 57–77.

Koehler, D.J. (1991). "Explanation, imagination, and confidence in judgment." *Psychological Bulletin* **110**(3): 499–519.

Koriat, A., Lichtenstein, S., *et al.* (1980). "Reasons for confidence." *Journal of Experimental Psychology: Human Learning and Memory* **6**(2): 107–118.

Kusters, R.J., Genuchten, M.J.I.M., *et al.* (1990). "Are software cost-estimation models accurate?" *Information and Software Technology* **32**(3): 187–190.

Lederer, A.L. and Prasad, J. (1998). "A causal model for software cost estimating error." *IEEE Transactions on Software Engineering* **24**(2): 137–148.

Lederer, A.L. and Prasad, J. (2000). "Software management and cost estimating error." *Journal of Systems and Software* **50**(1): 33–42.

Moder, J.J., Phillips, C.R., *et al.* (1995). *Project Management with CPM, PERT and Precedence Diagramming.* Wisconsin, WI, Blitz Publishing Company.

Moløkken, K. (2002). *Expert Estimation of Web-Development Effort: Individual Biases and Group Processes*, Master Thesis. Department of Informatics, University of Oslo.

Mukhopadhyay, T., Vicinanza, S.S., *et al.* (1992). "Examining the feasibility of a case-based reasoning model for software effort estimation." *MIS Quarterly* **16**(2): 155–171.

Myrtveit, I. and Stensrud, E. (1999). "A controlled experiment to assess the benefits of estimating with analogy and regression models." *IEEE Transactions on Software Engineering* **25**: 510–525.

Niessink, F. and van Vliet, H. (1997). Predicting maintenance effort with function points. *International Conference on Software Maintenance*, Bari, Italy, Los Alamitos, CA, IEEE Computer Society: 32–39.

Ohlsson, N., Wohlin, C., *et al.* (1998). "A project effort estimation study." *Information and Software Technology* **40**(14): 831–839.

Paulk, M.C., Weber, C.V., *et al.* (1993). *The Capability Maturity Model for Software: Guidelines for Improving the Software Process (SEI)*, Addison-Wesley.

Paynter, J. (1996). Project estimation using screenflow engineering. *International Conference on Software Engineering: Education and Practice, Dunedin, New Zealand.* Los Alamitos, CA, IEEE Computer Society Press: 150–159.

Pengelly, A. (1995). "Performance of effort estimating techniques in current development environments." *Software Engineering Journal* **10**(5): 162–170.

Schmitt, N., Coyle, B.W., *et al.* (1976). "Feedback and task predictability as determinants of performance in multiple cue probability learning tasks." *Organizational Behaviour and Human Decision Processes* **16**(2): 388–402.

Seaver, D.A., Winterfeldt von, D., *et al.* (1978). "Eliciting subjective probability distributions on continuous variables." *Organizational Behaviour and Human Decision Processes* **21**(3): 379–391.

Shepperd, J.A., Fernandez, J.K., *et al.* (1996). "Abandoning unrealistic optimism: Performance estimates and the temporal proximity of self-relevant feedback." *Journal of Personality and Social Psychology* **70**(4): 844–855.

Sieber, J.E. (1974). "Effects of decision importance on ability to generate warranted subjective uncertainty." *Journal of Personality and Social Psychology* **30**(5): 688–694.

Silverman, B.G. (1992). "Judgment error and expert critics in forecasting tasks." *Decision Sciences* **23**(5): 1199–1219.

Slovic, P. and Fischhoff, B. (1977). "On the psychology of experimental surprises." *Journal of Experimental Psychology: Human Perception and Performance* **3**(4): 544–551.

Stahlberg, D., Eller, F., *et al.* (1995). "We knew it all along: Hindsight bias in groups." *Organizational Behaviour and Human Decision Processes* **63**(1): 46–58.

Stone, E.R. and Opel, R.B. (2000). "Training to improve calibration and discrimination: The effects of performance and environmental feedback." *Organizational Behaviour and Human Decision Processes* **83**(2): 282–309.

Subbotin, V. (1996). "Outcome feedback effects on under- and overconfident judgments (general knowledge tasks)." *Organizational Behaviour and Human Decision Processes* **66**(3): 268–276.

Tan, H.-T. and Lipe, M.G. (1997). "Outcome effects: the impact of decision process and outcome controllability." *Journal of Behavioral Decision Making* **10**(4): 315–325.

Thomsett, R. (1996). "Double dummy spit and other estimating games." *American Programmer* **9**(6): 16–22.

Vicinanza, S.S., Mukhopadhyay, T., *et al.* (1991). "Software effort estimation: An exploratory study of expert performance." *Information Systems Research* **2**(4): 243–262.

Walkerden, F. and Jeffery, R. (1999). "An empirical study of analogy-based software effort estimation." *Journal of Empirical Software Engineering* **4**(2): 135–158.

Weinberg, G.M. and Schulman, E.L. (1974). "Goals and performance in computer programming." *Human Factors* **16**(1): 70–77.

Yaniv, I. and Foster, D.P. (1997). "Precision and accuracy of judgmental estimation." *Journal of Behavioral Decision Making* **10**(1): 21–32.

Zajonc, R.B. (1965). "Social facilitation." *Science* **149**(July): 269–274.

26

Self-Adaptive Software: Internalized Feedback

Robert Laddaga, Paul Robertson and Howard Shrobe

26.1 Introduction

This chapter presents self-adaptive software as software that internalizes some of the feedback processes of software development and maintenance. In the normal development process, programs are produced, which run open-loop[1] in an environment that can either closely or poorly resemble the environment that the program's designers expected. Various forms of response to program behavior (i.e. bug-reports, feature requests) are then treated as modifications of the original requirements, specifications or program design, and are implemented and deployed.

The development and postdevelopment processes have an industrial 'feel'. The processes are similar to the processes used to develop and maintain automobiles. Excluding mechanical wear (the most significant aspect of automotive maintenance and irrelevant to software) if a car is performing poorly at high altitudes or in very dusty conditions, we can retrofit the car with modules designed to improve performance in those environments.

An alternative class of models for development and maintenance are biologically inspired models. In a biological organism, for example, the maintenance processes are driven by the same design plans, and use many of the same processes as that of the development process. There are of course other interesting biological models including symbiosis, ecological models and immune response. We are motivated by a loose biological analogy of the self-maintenance of organisms. We call this self-maintenance notion self-adaptive software.

---

[1] By 'open-loop' the authors mean that bug-reports, anomalous behavior and requested features are all feedback that cannot be accommodated within running applications. Instead, the feedback is processed inside a more comprehensive loop including the software development and maintenance process.

Software Evolution and Feedback: Theory and Practice   Nazim H. Madhavji, Juan C. Fernández-Ramil and Dewayne E. Perry
© 2006 John Wiley & Sons, Ltd

Self-adaptive software is software that incorporates monitoring and evaluation functions, and can rapidly (at runtime) respond to some sorts of need for change. Thus, in many cases it can run a closed-loop feedback process, where traditional software only closes the loop 'back in the shop'.

The rest of this chapter covers the following topics, in order to give the reader an understanding of the context and substance of self-adaptive software.

- We first discuss the historical and conceptual roots of self-adaptive software. Those roots are deeply related to the evolution in programming language and compiler design of the process of binding function call to function value. The relationship between self-adaptive software and dynamic languages is a strong one, and there is a sense in which self-adaptive software is a kind of late binding.
- We next present a description of the technological underpinnings of self-adaptive software, and the research directions that seem promising today. A broad selection of technologies can be brought to bear to make ever more capable versions of self-adaptive software. We discuss component technologies and their relationship to self-adaptive software and each other as well as discussing some collections of such components as examples.
- Finally, we discuss the sort of applications to which it has been applied, especially including our own work on vision systems, and on a perceptually enabled environment.

26.1.1 Some Software Life Cycle Concepts

Several biologically motivated analogies have been applied to software with a significant degree of acceptance by the software development and engineering communities. The authors believe that many of these analogies are somewhat forced, but that they can serve a useful communicative purpose, even as rather loose and suggestive analogies.

One such loosely analogous concept is that of a 'life cycle' for a software artifact [IEEE, 1995]. Another is the very high profile concept of software evolution. Both of these concepts are motivated largely by the significant complexity of software systems, including the inherently complex relationship between local and global properties of software components.

The software life cycle concept is intended to help organize the structural and dynamic properties of the different modes (or phases) of software effort. These modes include (nonexclusively) conception, requirements definition, specification, design, development, coding, testing, component integration, deployment, maintenance, revision and versioning.

The main concern addressed by early software life cycle concepts was that of sequencing modes of software effort [Royce, 1970]. The simple waterfall models [Boehm, 1981; Boehm, 1978] supposed that software effort moved purely sequentially through stages, such as the following:

Requirements definition, specification, system design, module design, detail design, coding, module testing, integration, system testing, documentation, deployment and maintenance.

This simple sequencing model did not allow for a robust concept of software evolution, and alternatives to the waterfall model have largely addressed adding evolutionary properties to the life cycle concept. An early modification of the waterfall approach was the cyclic approach [Boehm, 1985; Boehm, 1997]. In its simplest form, the cyclic approach simply says that the maintenance phase is followed by a new waterfall beginning with requirements revision.

An alternative notion of how to break software development down into simpler steps is the concept of top–down structured programming [Wirth, 1971]. The main concept here is that programming proceeds from the overall requirements down to the actual code by stepwise refinement.

A different alternative to the waterfall approach is that of fast, full function prototyping [Yeh, 1994]. This life cycle is characterized by roughly parallel effort in all of the traditional modes of effort, with a gradual increase in functional coverage and functional refinement. This concept suggests that software is not built like a car, but grows like an organism, except that the growth is directed by an outside agent: the software development team.

26.1.2 Brief Introduction to Self-Adaptive Software

Self-adaptive software begins (as with many revolutionary computer science concepts today) with the realization that computer systems processing and memory capacity are characterized currently by plenty, rather than the poverty of resources with which we used to struggle. In this climate of resource excess, we can ask questions like the following:

1. What if we have extra cycles to do more redundant checking of function, performance, progress, reliability and stability?
2. What if we have enough disk and memory to store many variations of algorithms, modules, functions, data tables and historic traces of program execution?
3. What if we have both the memory capacity to include in the running program all the design and descriptive documents used in the software development process, and the processing capacity to use that data in our redundant checking processes?

Self-adaptive software is an attempt to answer those provocative questions, and one more over-arching meta design question is the following:

4. What does it take to run software change processes closed-loop rather than open-loop?

Briefly, self-adaptive software envisions including many variants of the code that would normally go into a running program. The purpose of the variants is to allow the program designer to move the time of making engineering trade-offs from program design time, when we can at best guess the program's environment and inputs, to runtime, when the environment is manifest and the inputs are known. Significant evaluation functionality is required in addition to the normal functional code, in order to control the process of revision and selection of code. The evaluation functions and code variants then can be fashioned into a form of feedback control process.

Although we have entered an era of plenty with respect to computing resources, the same cannot be said about knowledgeable human resources. The lack of resources in the human area makes all the more attractive an approach, like self-adaptive software, that reduces the requirements for direct maintenance by human programmers.

A good introduction to self-adaptive software is [Robertson *et al.*, 2000]. The significant technological requirements to support this approach and the opportunities for improvement of software development and maintenance processes opened by this approach, are discussed in Section 26.3.

26.1.3 Introduction of Binding of Function Call to Function Value

One of the powerful abstraction methods that we use in many different ways and places in computer science is the function call. It is a powerful concept that can provide many useful and diverse advantages. Historically, it was first valued for the ability to save memory by not having to duplicate redundant code blocks. Shortly thereafter, computer pioneers realized the advantages this concept provides during program modification. Adding parameters increased the utility and applicability of the concept.

The general concept is that we have linguistic and execution entities that are program calls, and these program calls must be bound (paired) with the value of the call, namely, the source and binary code that implement the desired function. This concept has several properties that provide implementation design choices, chief among them the algorithm for doing the binding, and the time that the binding happens.

As we will see in the next chapter, this concept is central to the development of self-adaptive software.

26.2 Historical Perspective

26.2.1 Dynamic Versus Static Binding

In the earliest days of computer programming machine, instructions were written down in numeric form and trivially written to a binary file that could be loaded into the computer's memory for execution. Unfortunately, making even small changes to a program written in this way was excruciatingly difficult because adding or removing anything addressed would require changes to all subsequent location references to places in program code and to variable locations.

Assembly languages were soon developed that permitted the numeric codes of the old machine code to be replaced by symbolic names for both variable locations and machine instruction locations such as subroutines entry points and branch targets. This permitted the layout of memory to be changed easily in the assembly language program both for variables and for subroutines and labels. These were the earliest forms of variable and function binding and it was clear from the outset that delaying the time at which a programmer's concept of a place is bound to a machine location was beneficial to both readability and the process of software evolution. Whereas the machine code programmer had to do his own binding of conceptual places to machine locations in his head, the binding was now delayed until the time when the assembler was run. This delay in binding, while producing exactly the same machine codes, provided enormous facility for software development and evolution.

As programs grew in size, so did the problems of managing the code base that was being developed. It became useful to add another delay. For a variety of reasons programs would not always load into the same location in memory. There were two principle reasons for this. One reason was that the operating systems began to manage program memory and so the place where the program would be loaded would vary from run to run. In most cases, this was solved by having the hardware implement mechanisms for binding memory locations specified in the program to locations provided by the operating system. This had the great benefit of allowing the program to be moved in memory without having to change any of the instructions. This execution time binding of program location to machine address was part of the notion of an operating system providing a virtual machine. The programmer was given the illusion that his program would execute at fixed locations in memory, but the operating system would put it wherever it wanted and let hardware address mapping take care of binding the program addresses to physical memory locations. The result of this delay in binding was to significantly improve performance of programs and simplify the operating system. The reason for the performance improvement was that by allowing programs to be run at any location in physical memory allowed the swapping of programs in and out of memory to be much more efficient in its use of the available memory.

Even with this hardware mapping of program location to machine location programs would not always execute from the same location. The notion of subroutine had given rise to the idea of code reusability. By putting a collection of subroutines into a separate file and by making subroutines of general usefulness by appropriate use of parameters the same collection of subroutines could be used in many different programs. Of course, the locations of these subroutines would not be the same in each program because each program would contain different components and be of different sizes. This problem was solved by the introduction of another program: the linker. The linker would relocate the locations assigned by the assembler, assemble a collection of separately assembled program parts and link references of names in one program part to the definition of those names in other program parts. This led the way to program libraries and program reuse. By separating generally useful subroutines from the program that used them, it allowed greater modularity that in turn supported easier software evolution.

Let us summarize the binding mechanisms in place at this point in the story. The programmer writes an identifier in the program representing the name of a storage location (variable) or a program location (subroutine start or label). The assembler binds these names to relocatable addresses. The linker binds the relocatable addresses to virtual addresses. Finally, the machine hardware in conjunction with the operating system maps the virtual addresses onto physical machine addresses. Delaying the binding of a conceptual place to a physical machine location has resulted in performance improvements (owing to more efficient use of the memory resources by the operating system) and improved software development and evolution.

The mechanisms for binding discussed so far are all static. They do not change while the program is running[2]. The conceptual idea of why we would like to delay binding is that binding involves making a decision. We can make a better decision by waiting until we have more information on which to base the decision. Perhaps the most important piece of information that we do not have early on is the knowledge of the future life in

---

[2] Actually, of course, a page swapping operating system will swap programs out of one location, and into another location when they are swapped back in to memory.

the evolution of the program. Binding too early adds rigidity to software that impedes its future evolution.

Not surprisingly, more benefit can be derived by delaying binding even further. When binding occurs during the execution of the program, it is called dynamic binding. Taking binding into the runtime of the program involves making the jump to high-level languages, which we discuss next.

26.2.2 Language and Compiler Development

Variable locations in a program fall into two categories: those that are determined statically as discussed above and those that are determined dynamically. A procedure will often allocate its local variables dynamically because it makes the procedure (or function or subroutine) reentrant and permits more general use of the procedure (such as recursion). The binding mechanism in such cases is a combination of memory allocation and indexed addressing. In the early days of high-level languages, Fortran [ANSI, 1966] allocated all variable locations statically but as a result did not support recursion. With the introduction of Algol-60, [Naur, 1963] procedures and functions dynamically bound their local variables permitting more general use including recursion. Instead of deciding before the program is executed how the locations are to be assigned, they are assigned (bound) at runtime at the point when the procedure is called. Most modern languages now support dynamically bound variable locations and most processors include instructions designed to minimize the runtime cost of delaying binding until runtime. The support in question includes index registers so that variables can be referenced relative to the start of a piece of dynamically allocated memory in the same number of machine cycles (or close to) that the statically bound reference would require, support for fast runtime allocation of local memory, such as instructions for manipulating stacks and detecting when they overflow using hardware interrupts.

The more complex and interesting parts of programs are the instructions, rather than the variables, and consequently there is much more scope for late binding of procedures than for variables. The general idea with procedure binding is that instead of hardwiring the function address into the references to the function, a runtime mechanism is provided that decides what function address to transfer control to at the time the call is performed. One of the first languages to use dynamic binding of functions was Lisp. Lisp provided dynamic binding of functions by introducing a level of indirection to the function call. The name of the function would be represented at runtime as a symbol and the symbol has local storage that contains the address of the function definition. When a function is called, the address of the called function is computed dynamically by looking up the address of the function in the symbol.

Dynamically binding function names in this way allows the function definition to be easily changed at runtime. This is particularly useful for incremental development of the code and allows, among other things, the changing of a function (for example, to fix a bug) within a running program. Other uses include installing break points and instrumenting functions to support performance monitoring. Perhaps the most interesting idea is to use it to support pushing back the binding even further. If the function definition contains a function that computes what function to call and then calls it, then we would have pushed the decision of what function to call all the way back to the point of the call itself.

In 1967 Simula-67 [Dahl et al., 1970] introduced this very idea. The choice of function would be made by putting the function in a data structure that was selectable based on the type of an argument. A few years later that idea was the fundamental basis for a new language called *Smalltalk* [Goldberg, 1989] soon to be followed by C++ and later Java. These languages support what is known as the *message-passing paradigm*. Since a special argument is responsible for selecting the function to run, it is convenient to think that these languages send the function name and arguments to that special argument as if it was a message and that argument then selects the function to run. The idea is that the special argument is an object and that object 'knows' what function is appropriate to implement the named function.

In parallel with the development of these languages, Lisp introduced two different notions that extend these ideas. The first was the idea that the chosen function should be chosen on the basis of all of the arguments to the function rather than just one 'special' argument and the second was the idea of 'mixins' and method combination [Cannon, 1982]. Both of these ideas involved generalizing the ideas developed in Simula-67 in fairly natural ways. In the case of selecting the method to be run based on all of the arguments rather than just one (called 'multiple-argument dispatch'), the generalization is in the arguments used to make the dispatch. In the case of mixins, the generalization involves moving from a class hierarchy (tree structured) to a class structure that is a directed acyclic graph (DAG). With each generalization comes trade-offs, which we will discuss below. First, however, we will look at another innovation that relates to the late binding discussion: method combination.

One aspect of late binding of a function leads directly to one of the most powerful ideas of object-oriented programming : specialization. Consider a class called *Employee* that implements a method that calculates an employee's total compensation based upon salary. At some point in the evolution of the system, a special class of employees called *key employees* is introduced. These key employees are given, in addition to their salary, a bonus and incentive stock options. The evolution of the software can be accomplished without disrupting the existing implementation of Employee. A new class called *KeyEmployee* is defined that is a subclass of Employee, and a new implementation of the total compensation method is implemented that does the following:

1. Call the existing total compensation to get the base amount
2. Calculate the additional compensation that key employees get
3. Combine the two results by adding them.

When you have a straightforward hierarchy of classes, it is fairly easy to write the above logic into the specialized methods. When the class structure is a DAG, it becomes much more complicated and some form of automation is required if the software is to remain readable and maintainable. The flavors system developed at MIT for its Lisp in the late 70s introduced the notion of method combination that allows inherited methods to be combined in the way outlined above automatically by specifying the manner in which the method return values are to be combined (addition in the case given above). Other languages (such as C++) incorporate a limited kind of method combination that works only for constructors. Lisp, the language most associated with rapid prototyping and perhaps best described as an evolution oriented programming language, remains the only language in widespread use that supports general method combination.

The trend toward late binding is clear. We have come from the point where a function or subroutine was referenced by planting its address directly into the call, to the point where the function refers to a piece of code that implements an algorithm that constructs a solution from a collection of available parts (methods) by considering not only what methods are available but by considering what is appropriate for the collection of arguments provided by the caller. The benefits to software have been enormous. The power of specialization described above has been the driving force of the object-oriented programming revolution. It allows new incremental functionality to be added by specializing an existing capability with a minimal requirement for understanding how the existing capability works.

26.2.3 Performance Trade-Offs

When we discussed delaying binding in the context of static binding, it was always the case that the benefits came without runtime cost. Whether by hardware support or by the final stages of preparing the binary program for execution, the benefits of late binding came either for free or resulted in a performance improvement. When we began discussing dynamic binding, we carried some of the binding cost into runtime. If good use is made of the late dynamic binding, performance can be improved because when more is known about the data (at runtime), choosing the appropriate algorithm dynamically can result in a more efficient implementation. Sometimes, however, the overhead imposed by the late dynamic binding carries a fixed burden to the cost of a call. Some languages attempt to allow the user to decide how to make this trade-off by providing different binding time choices. For example both Lisp and C++ support simple functions that are statically bound and therefore have no runtime overhead for binding and dynamically bound functions that support varying degrees of support for the facilities described above.

With computational power getting cheaper and with software evolution issues becoming more expensive, it is reasonable to expect that except for the most performance sensitive of applications the trend toward late dynamic binding of functions will continue.

Much of the computer science community still has a mind set inherited from the earlier days of static binding. In this mind set, the most important thing is correctness, the second most important thing is performance, and flexibility comes up a poor third in priority. For most real-world and embedded applications, correctness and performance are not absolutes. Instead, we must make trade-offs among precision, performance and flexibility. Late dynamic binding provides a capability to apply more useful information to the task of making that trade-off than can be made at program design time.

26.2.4 The Concept of Software Application Evolution

The history of software evolution has shown that almost all programs evolve throughout their lifetime. They begin to evolve during their design and implementation and continue to evolve throughout the use of the program. The programs that do not have to evolve are so few that they can be ignored. The cost of software evolution is also well understood to be very high and in most cases so high as to dwarf the original development cost of the program. Nevertheless the early focus on the cost of the computer hardware has remained with us stubbornly. Even today when the cost of software development is skyrocketing and the cost of computation is so cheap that it might as well be free, there still remains a stubborn focus on efficiency over evolvability. The trends in costs for computer equipment versus programmers will at some point force issues of evolvability and maintenance to take on a more important role than that of absolute performance.

Most of our discussion about software evolution has centered around the idea that human programmers are the ones doing the software evolution but toward the end of our discussion of late dynamic binding of functions we were talking about functions that were to some extent synthesized automatically at runtime and functions that were to some extent chosen as a function of the data they received in their arguments. This discussion has primarily been historical but it is important to recognize that when software is generated automatically at runtime in response to the data, we open the door to considering automatic software evolution of a program in response to the data that it is being applied to.

As we mentioned under performance above, doing binding at runtime involves computational cost. If the binding involves synthesizing and compiling new code at runtime, the cost can be substantial. However, if dynamic synthesis results in more efficient algorithms being applied, it can result in a program that operates robustly where a static program would fail. It may actually result in an application so closely tuned to the needs of the data that it is actually faster overall than its static counterpart. This runtime automatic evolution is the focus of self-adaptive software – the focus of this chapter – and is the natural extrapolation of the trend toward later binding in the function space with greater computation involved in the binding process.

Runtime evolution brings into runtime a lot of what has historically lived in the compile time world including the evaluation of the performance of the existing software, determination of how it needs to evolve, the development of evolved software, the testing of the evolved software and the smooth transition to the new version with backward compatibility performed without stopping the running program. The cycle of evolution described above is strikingly similar to that of a conventional control system and many of the issues of building control systems carry over to self-adaptive software even though, unfortunately, the methods in designing control systems do not appear to be directly useful to self-adaptive software.

26.2.5 A Note about Software Ecology

Lehman provides a comprehensive theory of software evolution. The theory includes a natural division between analytic (S-type) and embedded (E-type) software, and covers much of our knowledge about the evolution of E-type applications. Lehman has proposed eight laws of software evolution, plus the Feedback, Evolution and Software Technology (FEAST) hypothesis and the uncertainty principle.

In a discussion of these laws, and particularly of law VIII, one recognizes that evolution does not occur in a vacuum, but instead occurs in the context of a global feedback system.

Law VIII, the feedback System, says that: 'E-type evolution processes are multilevel, multiloop, multiagent feedback systems' [Lehman, 2000]. As soon as one recognizes that software evolution is occurring in a complex global feedback system, one should immediately think of the concept of ecology. This is because, broadly speaking, ecology deals with complex relationships among individuals that are each structurally and behaviorally complex. Software and its users in the real world clearly fall into the same category.

At least one definition of Ecology is the following [Academic, 1992]:

> 'the branch of the biological sciences that deals with the relationship between organisms and their environment, including their relationship with other organisms'.

The following extended quote from [Lehman *et al.*, 1998], provides a clearer picture of the reason for thinking of the multilevel, multiloop system as an ecology:

> In referring to the software process, numerous publications reporting the work of the FEAST/1 project ... apply the adjective global. The term is used to include in that process more than just the people, technical analysis, decision taking and implementation activity required to develop a system *ab initio* or to make a change to an already existing system. It also involves those who influence the process, in one way or another, by their decisions and actions at many levels of management, marketing and application. They fuel the process, determine, set and adjust objectives, define new needs, change goals, fit the development into other organizational activities, control progress in the context of changing organizational circumstances and evolving application domains, explore and serve the marketplace and so on. Formal and informal communication and control paths between these numerous groups and individuals, with their technical, managerial, marketing or user orientation, provide information flow and control paths. The flow may be in forward activity paths, transmitting, for example, specifications to designers, designs to implementers, implementations to testers, validated elements to integrators, shippable subsystems or systems to user organizations. Equally, information may flow from corporate management defining changing targets or budgets to line managers for allocation to individual activities. Marketeers may communicate details about future products or changes in policy to users. As the project progresses, information and control from many sources will be fed back to management who, in turn, pass directives or other information to technical management for implementation, thus influencing process activities.

What this means for our concept of software evolution is that we must take account of the fact that all the organisms and processes connected with software are evolving, and simultaneously seeking new states of dynamic stability. Not only do our changing needs result in changes to software, but new software capabilities can change our views and requirements.

We have called this subsection a note, because we cannot now present a theory of software ecology. We can however, present one more piece of evidence that there is relevance between ecology and software evolution. One of the concepts studied in ecology is that of biodiversity. The amount of diversity, both phenotypic and genotypic, has an enormous bearing on the survivability and adaptability of an ecosystem and its species. In a similar vein, computer scientists have speculated about the need for diversity of software (operating systems and applications) as part of a process of protecting users from attacks by viruses and worms. There are many questions about how much diversity, and at what level of abstraction, is needed for appropriate adaptability, without overly complicating the processes maintaining software and of learning to use it.

We suspect that someone with more expertise in Biological Ecology may be able to suggest some useful principles and concepts to transfer from Biological Ecology to Software Ecology.

26.3 Self-Adaptive Software

26.3.1 Concepts

Software design consists in large part in analyzing the cases that the software will be presented with and ensuring that requirements are met for those cases. It is always difficult to get good coverage of cases, and it is impossible to assure that coverage is complete. If program behaviors are determined in advance, the exact runtime inputs and conditions are not used in deciding what the software will do. The state-of-the-art in software development is to adapt to new conditions via off-line maintenance. The required human intervention delays change. The premise of self-adaptive software is that the need for change should be detected, and the required change effected, *while the program is running* (at runtime).

The goal of self-adaptive software is the creation of technology to enable programs to understand, monitor and modify themselves. Self-adaptive software understands the following: *what it does; how it does it; how to evaluate its own performance; and thus how to respond to changing conditions*. We believe that self-adaptive software will identify, promote and evaluate new models of code design and runtime support. These new models will allow software to modify its own behavior in order to adapt at runtime, when exact conditions and inputs are known, to discovered changes in requirements, inputs and internal and external conditions.

A definition of self-adaptive software was provided in a DARPA Broad Agency Announcement on self-adaptive software (BAA-98-12) in December of 1997 (see www.darpa.mil/ito/Solicitations/PIP_9812.html) [Laddaga, 1997]:

> Self-adaptive software evaluates its own behavior and changes behavior when the evaluation indicates that it is not accomplishing what the software is intended to do, or when better functionality or performance is possible.

> ... This implies that the software has multiple ways of accomplishing its purpose, and has enough knowledge of its construction to make effective changes at runtime. Such software should include functionality for evaluating its behavior and performance, as well as the ability to replan and reconfigure its operations in order to improve its operation. Self-adaptive software should also include a set of components for each major function, along with descriptions of the components, so that components of systems can be selected and scheduled at runtime, in response to the evaluators. It also requires the ability to impedance match input/output of sequenced components, and the ability to generate some of this code from specifications. In addition, DARPA seeks this new basis of adaptation to be applied at runtime, as opposed to development/design time, or as a maintenance activity.

Self-adaptive software constantly evaluates its own performance, and when that performance is below criteria, changes its behavior. To accomplish this, the runtime code includes the following things not currently included in shipped software:

1. descriptions of software intentions (i.e. goals and designs) and of program structure;
2. a collection of alternative implementations and algorithms (sometimes called a *reuse asset base*).

Three metaphors have been useful to early researchers on self-adaptive software: coding an application as a dynamic planning system, or coding an application as a control system, or coding a self aware system [Laddaga, 2000]. The first two are operational metaphors, and the third deals with the information content and operational data of the program.

In programming as planning, the application doesn't simply execute specific algorithms, but instead plans its actions. That plan is available for inspection, evaluation and modification. Replanning occurs at runtime in response to a negative evaluation of the effectiveness of the plan, or its execution. The plan treats computational resources such as hardware, communication capacity and code objects (components) as resources that the plan can schedule and configure.

In program as control system, the runtime software behaves like a factory, with inputs and outputs, and a monitoring and control unit that manages the factory. Evaluation, measurement and control systems are layered on top of the application, and manage reconfiguration of the system. Explicit models of the operation, purpose and structure of the application regulate the system's behavior. This approach is more complex than most control systems, because the effects of small changes are highly variable, and because complex filtering and diagnosis of results is required, before they can serve as feedback or feed-forward mechanisms. Despite the difficulties of applying control theory to such highly nonlinear systems, there are valuable insights to be drawn from control theory, and also hybrid control theory [Branicky *et al.*, 1996], including, for example, the concept of stability [Passino and Burgess, 1998]. Adaptive Control [Åström, 1989] and Reconfigurable Control [Shamma, 1996] approach some of the concepts of self-adaptive software from within the control theory community.

The key factor in a self-awareness program is to have a self-modeling approach. Evaluation, revision and reconfiguration are driven by models of the operation of the software that are themselves contained in the running software. Essentially, the applications are built to contain knowledge of their operation, and they use that knowledge to evaluate performance, to reconfigure and to adapt to changing circumstances. The representation and meta-operation issues make this approach to software engineering also intriguing as an approach to creation of artificial intelligence.

26.3.2 Technology Requirements and Opportunities

We view self-adaptation as a complex feature, and have attempted to identify its component features [Laddaga *et al.*, 2000]. In Figure 26.1, the central core components of self-adaptive software are shown as a library of alternative functions (or procedures or methods, a method of dynamic dispatch, and a method for choosing between alternatives. The simplest sort of self-adaptivity requires only a library of alternative functions, and

Self-Adaptive Software: Internalized Feedback 519

some simple form of explicit choice at runtime among alternatives. One form of elaboration is using dynamic signature driven dispatch, where some kind of matching is done on context or call parameters, in order to determine the appropriate method or rule to be invoked on any given occasion [Laddaga, 1997]. This type of system is common today, in the form of Dynamic Object Languages (e.g. Common Lisp), and in rule-based systems.

In general, in Figure 26.1, as you move further from the center, the technologies become more difficult to implement, and their contribution to self-adaptive software is therefore more speculative. All of these components can be extended in interesting ways to provide greater self-adaptation.

For example, one can elaborate the library of alternatives, by improving the description of alternatives. In the lower part of the diagram, we see semantic and syntactic self-description. These involve the incorporation in running code of what was once design time information about our programs and systems. Semantic self-description includes goals,

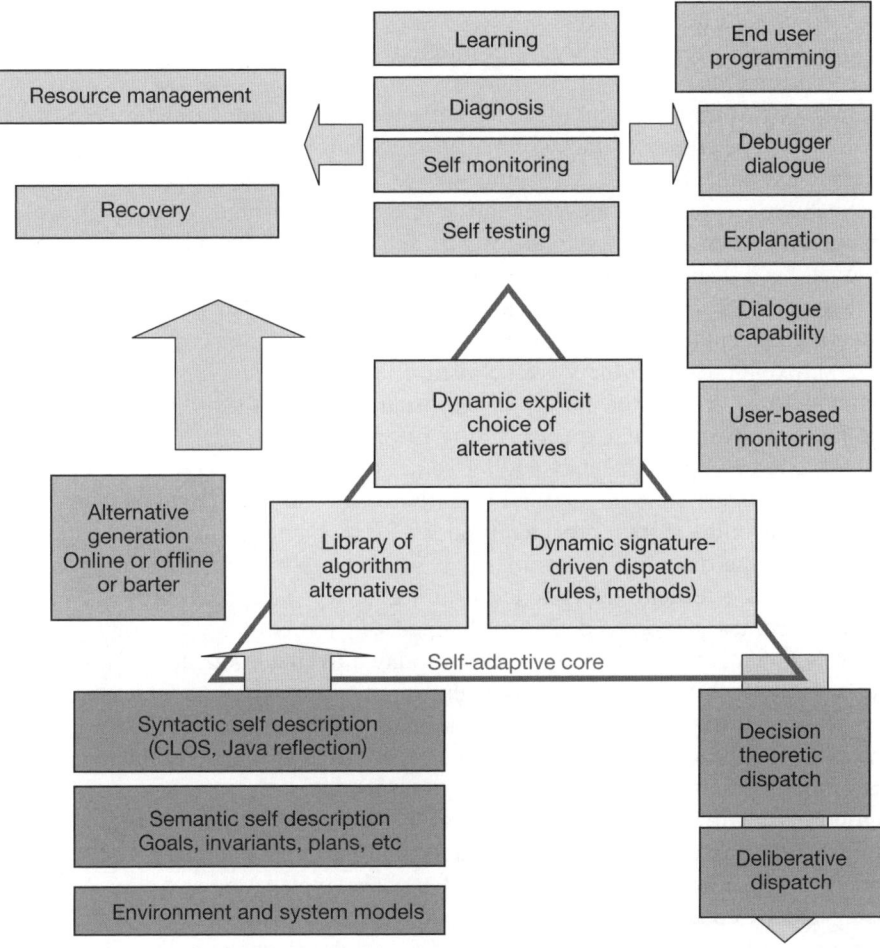

Figure 26.1 Self-adaptivity components

plans, designs and semantic dependencies of both the overall system and the function, method or module of each. Syntactic self-description includes necessary dispatch, calling and storage requirements.

In addition to significant elements of semantic and syntactic self-description, we also need the appropriate reflective programming technology so we can use the descriptions to revise structural and behavioral features of our programs or systems. With these three capabilities in place, all the features indicated in blocks above this base, including the base functionality middle blocks, can be implemented with enhanced functionality. The more semantic and syntactic description we provide, the greater the possible self-adaptivity.

The block labeled 'environmental model' covers application or domain-specific models of the program's or system's environment. These would include physical models for embedded systems, statistical models of behavior, and models of relations among external states, program inputs and program outputs. Where the rest of the self-adaptive framework provides the description of the structure and functionality of the program or system itself, the environmental models provide description of structure and behavior of the world with which the program deals [Shrobe, 2003].

Another modification to the library of alternatives is the generation or discovery (analogous to resource discovery) of alternatives.

Another axis of improvement, dispatch improvement, is represented by the two blocks in the lower right corner of the figure. By deliberation, we mean the ability to reason from evidence and values to a specific course of action. Deliberation can take many forms, including voting schemes, deductive inference, reasoning by analogy, case-based reasoning, and others. One particular form of deliberative choice has been singled out for a box of its own, because of its generality and popularity, both in practice and research. That method is decision theory, in which probabilities are used to weigh evidence via a common metric, and utilities are used to weigh preferences by a common metric [Laddaga et al., 2003]. With decision theory, all evidence is commensurable, as are all preferences. A common form of decision theory is Bayesian Decision theory, in which actions are undertaken to maximize the expected utility of results.

A third axis of improvement is adding some kind of self monitoring, to determine if there is a need to switch to an alternative method. Self monitoring can be elaborated with self testing, where the system proactively looks for problems at runtime. Diagnosis allows us to single out the functions or modules that are at the root of misbehavior. A level above that is diagnosis of crucial dependencies during correct and incorrect behavior, and the ability to in some cases extend that to diagnosis in terms of a causal analysis [Shrobe, 2003]. It is a relatively trivial matter, given today's available memory, to make libraries of alternatives accessible at runtime. We also already know how to evaluate some of our system functionality. The laborious part is in hand coding transducers to fix input–output mismatches, in calling chains of alternative algorithms, and hand coding the evaluation of performance of alternative algorithms at runtime.

A fourth axis of improvement is 'recovery'. Recovery largely consists of noting a functional or performance discrepancy, diagnosing the problem, and replacing the failing components with correct components. Our diagnosis, explanation and dynamic alternative choosing blocks cover this behavior reasonably well. However, recovery also involves determining and repairing or remediating side effect damage, rolling back operations as needed and finding a clean place to restart operation. This sort of behavior is well understood in database operation, where the practice is common, but not well understood or practiced in general software.

One significant problem that self-adaptive systems will need to deal with is management of their own computational and communicational resources. So, for example, they will need to trade-off time to compute and configure a better solution against the time needed to compute solutions with old or new configurations. Of course, resource management is, in general, a portion of the solution to many real-world problems, and as such, contributes to the environmental models component of self-adaptive systems.

The final access of improvement covers user interface issues, and is represented by the five upper blocks along the right edge of the figure. For example, another form of monitoring is accepting advice from the user, when the user determines that things are not going well. Such advice could be as simple as 'try something else', or could be a fairly complex dialogue. Most of the remaining UI boxes are based on some form of dialogue capability (natural language, speech, etc.).

By explanation, we mean the ability to usefully characterize the behavior of the program, both when it is working well, and when the program is misbehaving. This involves the coordination of self monitoring behavior with the high-level functional and goal descriptions of the program, and related library alternatives. If we combine the explanation capability with some sort of natural dialogue management (audio, text or graphic based), we can provide behavioral and alternative behavioral explanations to human users or designers.

One of the most important tools for the software developer is an interactive debugging tool. Current debugger technology provides a text and graphical-based presentation of evidence concerning program behavior. The evidence presented is based purely on general behavioral properties of programs in a specific language, and some structural properties of the programming language implementation. Given an ability to diagnose and explain behavior, as well as modify it in experimental ways, one could imagine building a debugger dialogue tool, capable of communicating with a programmer in terms of high-level expressions about the goals and methodology of a program or system. The tool could further engage in dialogue about probable causes, diagnostic hypotheses, experiments designed to narrow in on a conclusive diagnosis, and having diagnosed a problem, suggest alternatives.

Learning and end user programming denote very advanced capabilities, well beyond what is possible today. By learning, we mean that programs and systems will record failures and attempted fixes, and learn better approaches. This would also include generalizing principles from specific experience. Human-assisted learning would also be a possibility, given the dialogue capabilities we have posited before. Those same dialogue capabilities make end user programming possible. Self-adaptive software knows a great deal about itself, its organization and structure, and its alternative capabilities. We imagine a partnership in which users indicate how they would like programs to work better, and programs indicating what changes they could make, and the resulting dialogues producing better outcomes for the user.

26.4 Applications of Self-Adaptive Software

In this section, we briefly describe several self-adaptive software applications. We then describe three separate applications of self-adaptive software that were developed by the authors and their students and colleagues. Two of these are vision applications, and one is an application to perceptually enabled environments. Problems of coordinating perception and interpretation from low-level control to high-level interpretation, in noisy real-world situations, provide an ideal context for demonstrating the effectiveness of self-adaptive software.

26.4.1 Recent Application Work

The Second International Workshop on Self-adaptive software (Balatonfured, Hungary, May 2001) had papers on self-adaptive software applications in areas such as information survivability, communication protocols, perceptual applications and control systems [Laddaga et al., 2003].

Two applications use self-adaptive software to create systems that survive malicious attacks by responding autonomously. One uses model-based diagnosis and recovery [Shrobe, 2003], the other describes using explicit trust management to make survivable systems [Doyle and McGeachie, 2003].

A collection of papers describes application of self-adaptive software to communication protocol definition and testing [Tarnay, 2003, Harangozo and Tarnay, 2003] and [Adamis and Tarnay, 2003].

One paper presents the use of self-adaptive software in a hard real-time controller [Goldman et al., 2003], while another presents a soft real-time controller [Bakay, 2003].

26.4.2 Vision Systems

Image understanding programs have tended to be very brittle and perform poorly in situations where the environment cannot be carefully constrained. Natural vision systems in humans and other animals are remarkably robust. The applications for robust vision are myriad. Robust vision is essential for many applications such as mobile robots, where the environment changes continually as the robot moves, and robustness is essential for safe and reliable operation of the robot.

Currently, there are many vision systems that work spectacularly well in constrained situations; but in natural environments, where lighting and other environmental and subject variables can vary widely, they perform poorly.

In this section we give an overview of a robust and self-adaptive vision system architecture [Grounded reflective adaptive vision architecture (GRAVA)][3], and its application to two different recognition problems: satellite image interpretation and face recognition.

GRAVA was first successfully applied to satellite image interpretation [Robertson and Brady, 1998, Robertson, 2001] and is now also being used to identify faces in video images with unconstrained pose and lighting [Robertson and Laddaga, 2002].

We first present the GRAVA architecture as used in the context of satellite image interpretation, and then present the face recognition application.

26.4.2.1 Grounded Reflective Adaptive Vision Architecture

Logical Components of the System

We present a self-adaptive system called *GRAVA* that segments and labels aerial images in a way that attempts to mimic the competence of a human expert. Figure 26.2 shows

---

[3] GRAVA is the work of one of the authors, Paul Robertson.

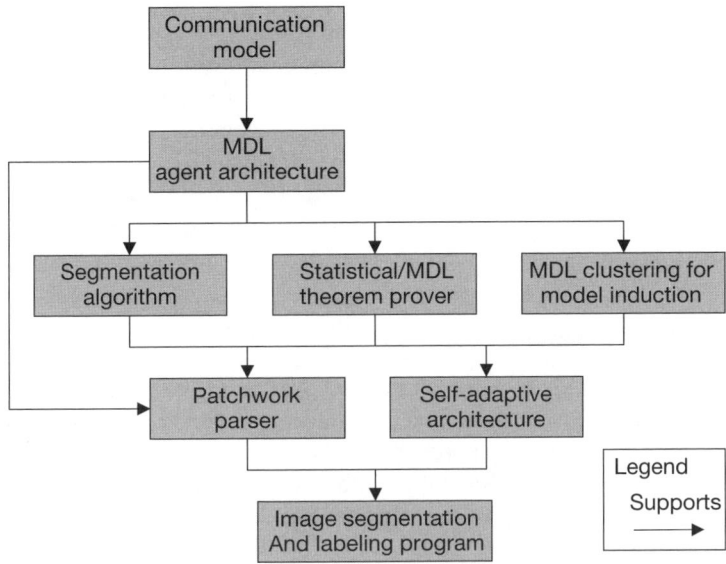

Figure 26.2 Logical components

the logical components of the system along with the supporting relationships between the parts. We now sketch the roles of these components.

26.4.2.2 Image Segmentation and Labeling Program

To produce an image interpretation, a variety of tools need to be brought into play. First, the image is processed by various tools in order to extract texture or feature information. The selection of the right tools determines ultimately how good the resulting interpretation will be. Next, a segmentation algorithm is employed in order to produce regions with outlines whose contents are homogeneous with respect to content as determined by the chosen texture and feature tools. The segmentation algorithm also depends upon tools that select seed points that initialize the segmentation. The choice of tools to initiate the segmentation determines what kind of segmentation will be produced.

Labeling the regions depends upon two processes. The first tries to determine possible designations for the regions by analyzing the pixels within the regions. The second is a statistical parser that attempts to parse the image using a 2D grammar. Our application currently does not make use of the parse; but it could be used as the basis for further image interpretation. An important side effect for our application is that contextual information, mobilized by the parse process, enables good labels to be chosen for regions when there may be several ambiguous possibilities if one only looks at the pixels within the region.

At any point, a bad choice of tool – for initial feature extraction, seed point identification, region identification or for contextual constraints – can lead to a poor image interpretation. The earlier the error occurs, the worse the resulting interpretation is likely to be.

26.4.2.3 Minimum Description Length Agent Architecture

The problem of interpreting the real world is inherently ambiguous. A speech or vision program must select the most likely interpretation from the ambiguous candidates. Selecting the most likely interpretation is equivalent to selecting the interpretation with the minimum description length (MDL). We developed, apparently for the first time, an agent architecture based on the MDL principle, and supporting a conjecture of Leclerc [Leclerc, 1989] that MDL can apply to higher-level semantics. In the GRAVA system, as a result of the MDL architecture, cooperation between agents is an emergent property.

26.4.2.4 Semantic Segmentation

The region competition algorithm of Zhu and Yuille [1996] is probably the leading approach currently to segmentation, and it produces reasonably good segmentations on the basis of a purely low-level approach; but since there is no provision for combining evidence from higher-level semantics, the approach performs poorly when there is poor low-level discrimination between regions. By developing an MDL algorithm similar to the region competition algorithm, using the MDL agent architecture, interaction between agents at differing semantic levels allows evidence from higher-level semantics to influence the segmentation.

The use of MDL in a segmentation algorithm is not unique [Zhu and Yuille 1996, Leclerc 1989]; but the use of MDL as a coordination device for bringing high-level semantics to bear on the segmentation *is* new.

The algorithm produces good results. Figure 26.3 shows an image that has been segmented without any high-level semantics. Seed points were selected and the base segmenter was allowed to proceed without any image semantics. The results are as good as those achievable using the Zhu and Yuille [1996] segmenter.

When semantics are introduced, difficult segmentations in which the boundaries are not evident at all such as the Marr example of overlapping leaves shown in Figure 26.4 are possible. Although the leaves can easily be segmented by human sight, analysis of the pixels along the overlapped leaf region shows that there are no intensity changes from

Figure 26.3 Segmented image

Figure 26.4 Marr's overlapping leaves example

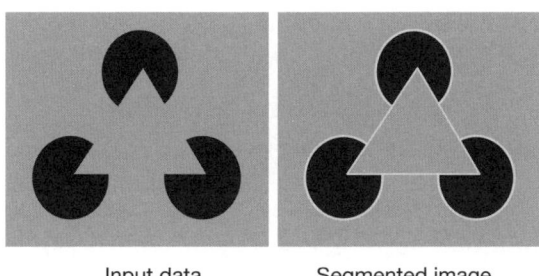

Input data   Segmented image

Figure 26.5 Segmenting Kanizza's triangle

which the edge could be found using low-level techniques. The edge that we perceive is a kind of subjective contour. We can illustrate this point by demonstrating a traditional subjective contour example.

Figure 26.5 shows Kanizza's triangle as a traditional subjective contour. The description length is shorter with the triangle than without it, and so the segmentation produces the occluding triangle. It may be that human perception of subjective contours is produced by an entirely different mechanism but the fact that our segmenter can produce segmentations of this kind is very encouraging.

26.4.2.5 Patchwork Parser

In our test case, what we have been calling semantics in the foregoing is a meaningful *parse* of the image. The patchwork parser is a statistical 2D parser. The parser takes as input a segmented image with content descriptors assigned to the segments. The parser builds a structural description of the image. Difficulties in producing a good parse can cause self-adaptation that results in the segmentation program producing different segmentations that may parse better.

Two corpora were developed using aerial images imaged from a satellite, and from a plane. Annotations were made to the images of the corpora by an expert, and the image grammar is induced from the corpus. The image parser attempts to make structural sense out of the segmentation produced by the semantic segmentation algorithm. This results in the propagation of contextual information, assignment of labels to the segments indicating region contents, and interaction with the semantic segmentation algorithm to refine the segmentation on the basis of evidence from the parse.

The parser is a structure-generating application that interprets the image contents. Both the parse structure and the synthesized program structure for the application are generated by a common structure-generating theorem prover.

26.4.2.6 Statistical/Minimum Description Length Theorem Prover

If image understanding is defined in part as the problem of building a description of the scene depicted in the image, there is a need for some apparatus that can assemble such descriptions. While the components of the description are generated by special purpose agents, the task of building a structurally complex description out of these components is a problem that belongs to no one component. Similarly, the problem of synthesizing the program within the self-adaptive framework described above requires some mechanism capable of assembling the individual agents into a form of a program.

We have developed a common structure-building component in the form of a theorem prover, and incorporated it into the architecture to address structure-building needs. The proof that has the shortest description length is judged to be the best proof. In this kind of proof, the theorem is a valid solution. In the case of a parse, it is a syntactically correct structure for the set of lexical items (a lexical item in the case of a patchwork parse is a region). In the case of a program, it is a legal program that addresses the details of the program's design; in the case of a plan, the theorem would be a legal plan that addresses the details of the goal structure for which the plan seeks to find a solution. While the parse, program or plan may be legal, none is guaranteed to be correct. The execution of the program may fail at some point. A plan may not succeed. Checkpoints are added to the generated structure whenever a component has a probability of success less than one. These checkpoints provide a mechanism whereby self-adaptation can be initiated.

26.4.2.7 Minimum Description Length Clustering for Model Induction

GRAVA is grounded because it applies models that are *grounded* in experience with the real world. We developed a corpus of images annotated by a human photo interpreter as the basis for grounding the models used by the system. We developed an MDL-based clustering algorithm that supports the automatic induction of statistical models from the corpus. We call this algorithm principal component decomposition (PCD). It works by searching in decreasing order of eigenvalue for ways of dividing the input space along principal components in order to decompose a complex set of data points that constitute positive examples of a phenomenon for which we wish to induce models. The resulting clusters can be modeled using principal component analysis (PCA) so that the resulting set of models can be described with a MDL. As such, the resulting model is the most probable interpretation of the data points.

26.4.2.8 Self-Adaptive Architecture

The goal of the architecture is to support self-adaptation. When the self-assessment determines that the program is doing poorly, the program should seek some way of adjusting its structure so as to do better. The self-adaptive architecture is a collection of supporting capabilities that permits this simple approach to self-adaptation to work. The supporting components are as follows:

1. *Self-assessment* – the ability of a computational agent to evaluate how well it is doing its current task. The GRAVA architecture provides a protocol for supplying self-assessment functions.
2. *Structure building* – the mechanism that constructs a program from a collection of computational agents. This structure-building apparatus is invoked whenever self-assessment indicates poor performance; the system tries to improve by resynthesizing its program code, using the statistical theorem prover.
3. *Reflection* – the support for self-understanding within the system. By inspecting the state of the embedded semantic account, the system can reason about what the system is doing in terms of a goal that its actions are intended to achieve.

26.4.2.9 Reflection

The role of reflection in the GRAVA architecture is to allow the system to modify itself. The way that this goal is achieved in GRAVA is by having the meta-level goal of the program be described in a specification. GRAVA Agents interpret that specification to produce a design for a program that would satisfy the specification. Agents then interpret the design in the form of a program. The number of levels of *meta* that lay between the meta-goal of the system at the top and the program code at the bottom is arbitrary. When the ultimate program code is run it interprets the image in order to produce its description. This arrangement generates a tower of interpreters. At each point in the decomposition, from meta-goals to image interpretation, the components at one level are linked to those components at a higher level that played a role in defining the semantics of the low-level component.

26.4.2.10 Results

GRAVA was based on the idea that if vision programs knew what they were doing, and knew when they were doing poorly, then they could adjust their assumptions and thereby do a better job. It seemed that the idea of reflection, developed in AI, offered a way to do this. That approach leads us to utilize reflection in a novel way – to support self-adaptation.

We were able to get positive results from all phases of the research on GRAVA, including the final step of making the program self-adapt in order to produce an acceptable interpretation of images. The problem domain involved segmenting, labeling and parsing aerial images. We had no consumer for the image parse and so it is difficult to access the success or usefulness of the parse for any particular use. The parses that were generated seemed plausible when inspected by hand. The parse process was certainly useful as a mechanism for propagating nonlocal context in arriving at plausible region labeling. We did not collect enough data to quantify the benefit to labeling that the parser provided, but anecdotally there are many cases where otherwise ambiguous regions were correctly labeled.

The size of the corpus, though large by the standards of much vision research, was really too small (the color corpus consisted of 105 images). The color corpus included a number of different imaging modalities and some variation in geographical location and image content. There were too few examples of some of the contexts to make separate parse rule contexts and inadequate sequences of images to support the initial goal of handling sequences of consecutive images. Nevertheless, the data that we were able to develop was sufficient to test all phases of the architecture and the special purpose agents that we developed along the way.

We are encouraged by the success of the architecture within the limitations discussed above. We have succeeded in building a segmentation algorithm that is capable of using higher-level semantics in order to produce appropriate segmentations [Robertson, 1999]. We have produced an image parser that produces structural descriptions of the image in terms of labeled regions, and we have shown how models can be induced from an annotated corpus and used as the basis for the segmentation, labeling and parsing of an aerial image.

26.4.3 Face Recognition

Most of the face identification and recognition systems work by measuring a small number of facial features that are given a canonical pose and matching them against a database of known faces. Frequently, however, in practical applications few frames show a full frontal face. Furthermore, lighting may vary significantly. These factors frustrate attempts to identify a face. Many applications have much more relaxed recognition goals. If the task is to track people as they move throughout a monitored space, the task may be to identify the individual from a relatively small set of people. For face profiles, different models involving ear, eye and nose may prove successful. By building a face recognizer that can seamlessly switch between different contexts such as pose and lighting we can construct a recognizer that is robust to normal changes in the natural environment. This permits a much wider application of face recognition technology.

Our application[4] involves recognizing people as they move about an intelligent space [Brooks, 1997] in an unconstrained way. To better understand contexts consider the face 'pose' contexts:

Figure 26.6 Four pose contexts

---

[4] The face recognition application was developed by Paul Robertson and Robert Laddaga, based on Robertson's earlier work on GRAVA.

Figure 26.6 shows four pose contexts: 'profile', 'oblique', 'off-center', and 'frontal'. The profile view is supported by agents that measure points along the profile of the face, the corner of the eye, and the lips. The oblique view with ear supports measurements of the ear and measurements of the position of the ear, eye and nose. The triangle formed by the eye, ear and nose help determine the angle of the face to the camera that allows measurements to be normalized before recognition. The off-center view permits measurements of points on the eyes, nose and mouth. The shape of the nose can be measured but the width of the base of the nose cannot be measured because of self-occlusion. The frontal view allows nose width to be measured, but the nose shape cannot be measured. There are other contexts that include/exclude ears. The different contexts control, among other things, what models can be used for matching, what features can be detected and what transformations must be made to normalize the measurements prior to matching. This example shows contexts for pose, but there are also contexts for lighting, race, gender and age.

The recognizer supports a collection of face candidate finders, face models, feature finders and normalization algorithms implemented as agents. The face recognition process is shown schematically in Figure 26.7. Face candidate finder agents look for face-like shapes in the image and generate evidence that supports the selection of a set of contexts based on the shape and shading of the face candidate. Agents appropriate to the context are selected to make a special purpose face recognizer. If the recognizer does not succeed in finding appropriate features where they are expected to be then the system self-adapts by using available evidence to select a more appropriate context, constructing a new recognizer, and trying again. The system iterates in this manner until appropriate lighting, race, age, gender and pose contexts have been chosen and the best match has been achieved. Convergence on the right set of contexts is rapid, because evidence in support of a context is collected each time an agent runs.

What is unique about the recognizer outlined above is that it has multiple ways of recognizing faces, it divides up a complex space of lighting, age, race, sex and pose into contexts that can be composed in a huge number of ways and self-adapts the recognizer at runtime. In the following section we describe the self-adaptive architecture that supports this capability.

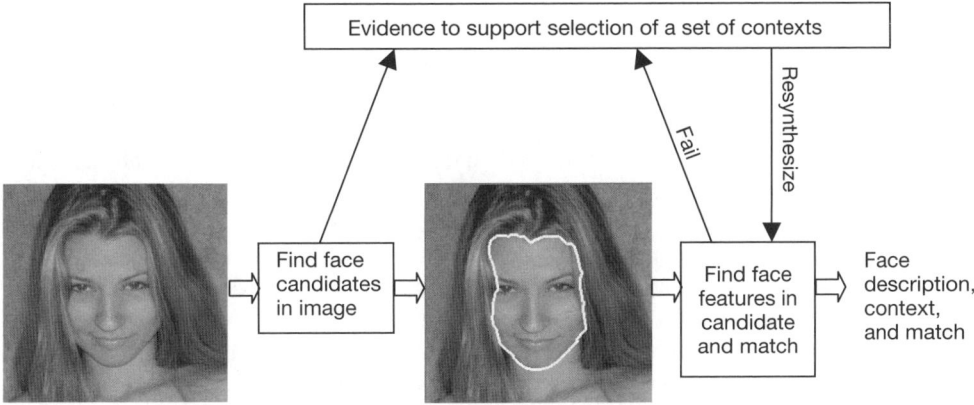

Figure 26.7 Recognizer schematic

26.4.3.1 Results

Most papers on face recognition describe a single way of modeling a face and an algorithm that fits the model to images of faces in a canonical pose and compares those models to known faces in a database. In our system, there are many models for faces and many agents for locating each of the features that may be used by each model. Our models are similar to those that are in widespread use involving measurements of key points on the face and using principle component analysis to produce a face model from a corpus of training faces. Rather than trying to use one model to cover all cases, however, we first divide the complex space up into multiple contexts and then provide multiple methods for modeling and matching faces. The self-adaptive architecture described in this paper is the key to the robustness of the system.

Although there are many more feature recognizers than on most face identification programs, only a small subset are configured into the interpretation program at any point in time; so, the system performance is not degraded by the multiplicity of approaches.

26.4.4 Pervasive Computing

Our vision of ubiquitous computing is that our environment will be heavily populated by devices under computer control, and that these devices will be interconnected and interfaced with each other and with us. Many of the devices under computer control will be sensors that provide a window from the world of interconnected computation into the physical world around us. Today, cars are run by microcontrollers that can sense acceleration, engine performance, breaking action and so on. Tomorrow's cars will have even more processors, connected with each other, sensing ambient temperature, weather conditions, other cars, roadside facilities and communicating with other cars, traffic controllers, roadside facilities and with us.

The major importance of ubiquitous, pervasive, connected computing will be the ability for computationally empowered devices to sense the world around us, and to respond by changing that world. There will be a tremendous need for these devices to take direction, explain their behavior, and modify their behavior in accord with our directions. They would not need to communicate with us all the time, but they will always need to be able to communicate in those instances when they are unsure or we wish to override. Needless to say, it would not work (for a variety of reasons) to communicate with these devices via a keyboard on our person, or dangling from the device. Our machines will need to use vision and auditory capability to see and hear what is going on in the background in order to establish context, and they will need to understand and generate speech to engage in dialogue with humans.

Our view of ubiquitous computing makes it clear that moving ahead in the sensor, affector arena is not sufficient, we also need our computers to be able to dialogue, and understand both command and context. We understand our world, and communicate with each other via seeing, hearing, speaking and gesturing. If we are not to become enslaved by our ubiquitous computing environments, they will need to communicate with us in the same manner, and understand the context in which such dialogues occur. We focus on what is required of software development tools and methods for building the comprehensive vision systems of the embedded computing future.

26.4.4.1 The Intelligent Room

For several years, our research group in the MIT AI Lab has been developing an 'Intelligent Room' [Coen, 1997, Coen, 1998, Brooks, 1997], a space that interacts with its users through sensory technologies such as machine vision, speech recognition and natural language understanding. Our room also is equipped with a rich array of multimedia technologies. These technologies are intended to provide a natural, human-centered interface to its users[5].

The Intelligent Room is designed to be a utility that must always be available and it must provide reasonable services to its users even though their needs are not easily predicted. It must continue to provide these services even if there are equipment failures or if there is contention for the use of resources among the users or applications. It is also desirable that it be able to provide improved and additional services if higher quality equipment is added.

Finally, and most crucially, to be truly human-centered it must be able to do all these things seamlessly while running, without intervention by programmers and systems wizards. In other words, the Intelligent Room must be a self-adaptive system in the spirit of [Laddaga *et al.*, 2000, Laddaga, 2000]. It must monitor the environment as well as its own state, have a variety of techniques for accomplishing its goals, and make intelligent choices about which technique to use in the current context. In addition to this moment to moment adaptation to environmental conditions, an intelligent environment should be able to evolve over longer time periods as new equipment and computational capabilities become available. Our experience is that the same architectural features that allow for rapid adaptation to small variations in the environment also allow for longer term evolutionary accommodations to larger changes in the resource base.

This section describes our experience with building such a system. The key insights are:

1. People should interact with the Intelligent Room not in terms of resources, but rather in terms of *abstract services* (e.g. 'show me this information' rather than 'print this on that printer').
2. The Intelligent Room should be capable of mapping a service request to a variety of different solutions ('project the information', 'display it on a PDA', 'print it on a printer')
3. The Intelligent Room should choose a solution dependent both on how well the solution meets the users' needs and how well it minimizes the use of costly or rare resources and
4. The Intelligent Room should make this decision at runtime so that it can respond to a changing set of requests and a changing environment.

This leads us to provide a rich set of representations describing the abstract services, the methods for achieving them and the resources required to support those methods. These descriptions are consulted dynamically as service requests arrive; the binding between service request, method and resources is made as late as possible. It is this late binding of these decisions that facilitates both adaptation to changing conditions and evolution as the resource base changes.

---

[5] The perceptual environment research group, led by one of the authors (Howard E. Shrobe), is now called *Agent-based Intelligent Reactive Environments* (*AIRE*). See http://www.ai.mit.edu/projects/aire/.

26.4.4.2 What Is a Resource Manager For a Smart Space

What we mean by a resource manager is a system capable of performing three fundamental tasks: *service mapping, resource matching*, and *arbitration*.

Service mapping is the process of deciding which of several alternative methods for realizing a service are relevant to the current request. Resource matching (also called match-making) is the process of finding out what actual resources can be taken into consideration given a specific service request and a method for realizing the service.

Arbitration is the process of selecting which method should be used to meet a service request and which resources should be allocated to that method. The choice of method and of resources to support the method determines the quality of service that is rendered to the user; the goal is to make an optimal (or nearly optimal) choice balancing off the cost (or scarcity) of the specific resources against the service quality provided to the user.

Our concern is with the management of higher-level resources. While OS level management (memory, CPU time, etc.) is of course important, and load-balancing of computationally intensive agents over multiple machines is also important, we limit our focus to higher-level resources such as physical devices and large software components (see [Yamane, 2000] and [Roman and Campbell, 2000] for an example of a system that deals with resources in smart spaces at the OS level). Our concerns lie with, for example, projectors, multiplexors, wires, displays, modems, user-attention, software programs, screen real estate, sound input and output devices, CD players, drapes and lamps.

26.4.4.3 Some Definitions

For clarity, we define here some potentially ambiguous or unfamiliar terms.

- *Metaglue* [Coen *et al.*, 1999] is the multiagent system forming the software base for all work at the Intelligent Room Project. Metaglue manages agent-to-agent communication via Java's RMI system. Agents are also aggregated into societies so that multiple users and spaces can have distinct name-spaces. Metaglue makes it easy to coordinate the startup and running of agents on any number of machines with differing operating systems.
- *Agents* are distinct object instances capable of providing services and making requests of the resource manager. This means agents themselves are considered to be a type of resource (refer to the following text) because they provide services.
- A physical or logical *device* is something akin to a projector, screen or user-attention; devices are often, but not necessarily, represented by agents. Devices provide services and so are resources.
- *Services* are provided by agents and devices; a single agent or device can provide more than one service and any kind of service can be provided by a number of agents or devices.
- A *resource* is a provider of a service. Both agents and physical devices are resources. For example, a physical LED sign is a resource (providing the LED sign hardware service) obtained and used by the LEDSignText Agent, which is in turn a resource (providing TextOuput service and LEDSign service) that can be obtained and used by any other agent needing such a service.

26.4.4.4 Resource Management

Rascal [Gajos, 2001] is our current resource manager; it provides the three basic services of Arbitration, Resource Matching and Service Mapping. Currently, Rascal does not deal with issues of privacy and access control although we believe that these issues can be dealt with within the framework.

Rascal maintains a knowledge representation, describing the types of service, methods, resources and agents that are available. This knowledge base is dynamic and may be updated while the system runs. The addition of a new description allows an evolutionary expansion of the capabilities of the system. These descriptions include a list of startup needs, for each agent, a list of provided services (each with a list of its own needs) and descriptions of all possible requests for resources that the agent may make during its life cycle.

These representations allow Rascal to ensure that before it assigns a particular agent to provide a service in response to a request, all of the needs of that new agent (and its underlings) can be satisfied. For example, if some agent requests a TextOutput device and the possible candidates are SpeechTextOutput and GuiTextOutput, Rascal will ensure that either speech generation is available for SpeechTextOutput or a computer screen is available for GuiTextOutput, before assigning either candidate to the requester. Additionally, knowing agent's startup needs also allow us to dynamically choose what particular machine an agent should be started on.

Rascal can autonomously instantiate an agent on-demand and consequently it must be able to reason about agents that do not currently exist but could be brought to life if needed. The approach of providing a rich set of representations in a knowledge base facilitates this reasoning process. For example, it allows us to make multiple instances of an agent class when we want to perform several versions of the same task. Furthermore, it allows us to have very complex interrelationships between agents and to support very large collections of agents. Without on-demand startup, one needs to craft elaborate startup scripts or hand-start all the agents in the system; both of these are infeasible when talking about collections of forty agents or more, especially when considering that the particular agents change depending on who is starting the system, the various tasks the system is to accomplish, and the room the system is being started in. Starting a single high-level agent is sufficient to obtain a service provided by that agent. This agent will then request and, cause to be started, all other agents it needs in order to do its job well. This modularization facilitates evolution; new capabilities can be added in modular, incremental chunks that can interact in novel ways.

The following examples illustrate these points:

Let us assume that there is an abstract service called the *remote dialog service* and that one method for providing this service is the 'phone method', which uses a voice modem to initiate an outgoing voice call. This method needs a computer with a voice modem hooked up to a phone line in order to provide its services. Imagine a system consisting of several machines with voice modems hooked up to a single phone line (e.g. in a shared graduate student office).

Within our framework, Rascal would decide that the phone method is one way to provide the service; furthermore, it would reason that the method can use any of the pairs of connected computers and modems. However, it would also realize that regardless of which computer-modem pair it selects it still needs the single phone line. If the phone line is available, it might select this method and pick a computer-modem pair that is currently not being used. It would then instantiate agents of the appropriate types to manage the computer, modem and phone line. If, however, there was already a call using the phone line, then Rascal would realize that it cannot find a resource set for the phone method and would instead try some other method of realizing the remote communication service. If this were happening several years ago, then it might decide that it has no other method available and would give up. However, as new capabilities arise (e.g. e-mail, instant messaging or a chat room), they can be added to the system's knowledge base and described as providing remote dialog service. Once this happens, the next request for this service may be realized using one of these alternative techniques. Similarly, if additional phone lines are made available, then Rascal is free to realize the request using the phone method but with one of the new phone line resources. In each case, Rascal would have to evaluate whether the quality of service provided by the particular method and supporting resources are worth the expense of using that set of resources.

In the absence of this architecture, we would have to do one of the following:

- Start the phone agent on a prespecified machine, running a risk that if that machine goes down the service is no longer available.
- Start an instance of the phone agent on every machine with a voice modem and a connection – a rather misleading solution because each of the agents would be advertising phone service but only one of them would be able to provide it at a time because all of the machines share a single phone line.
- Miss the interchangeability with other methods of meeting the user's needs such as E-mail or chat rooms.

Finally, we note that this approach provides far greater robustness in the face of failure. If a modem breaks or a computer crashes, the system can recover by initiating the same service with a different set of resources. If all the resources capable of supporting the phone method crash, then the system can recover by attempting to use a different method altogether. Thus both adaptation to short-term changes and failures and evolution as new capabilities arise is provided for.

26.4.4.5 Implementation

Rascal uses explicit utilities and costs, for both users and the system, in order to calculate resource allocations. In the formula below, the utility of a request r, satisfied by a resource s, is a monotonically increasing function (fu) of the degree of need attached to the request, and the extent to which the request and resource match.

$$utility(r; s) = fu(need(r); match(r; s))$$

Rascal's arbiter needs to make sure that the cost of reassigning resources never exceeds the utility of the new assignment. If the resource is simply taken away from a current user, that cost is the utility of the resource to the current user, plus some change penalty, to account for the system overhead in implementing the change. If the resource taken away from the current request is replaced by a different resource, then the cost will be the change penalty, plus the difference in utility of the request satisfied by the old resource, and the request satisfied by the new resource.

A constraint satisfaction engine is used to make optimal or nearly optimal allocations relative to the utility assignments.

26.4.4.6 Results

So far our software has been installed in six spaces of four different kinds: three small offices, one small living room, one large office (also used for small meetings), and a twelve-seat conference room. The instrumentation of these spaces varies widely; we have a single dilapidated projector and a couple of lights in one of the small offices on one hand, and six projectors and a large number of A/V devices in the conference room on the other. Our living room has two projectors, a TV, several cameras and A/V equipment.

26.5 Conclusion

We have discussed the history of binding in software engineering, and explained the relationship between binding and software evolution. We predict that delayed binding will become increasingly popular as human costs continue to dramatically exceed computational costs of software. We further predict that useful measurement of software evolutionary properties will give rise to a multidisciplinary study of Software Ecology encompassing Software Engineering, Business Management and Economics, Sociology and Psychology.

We also described self-adaptive software, the next major step in the direction of delayed binding. We presented motivation and research objectives for this new field of study. Finally, we presented some example applications of self-adaptive software.

The authors have to date developed several vision systems using a self-adaptive vision architecture, and also have applied self-adaptive software to resource management, and information intrusion diagnosis and response. We have developed support for probabilistic dispatch, as a first step toward decision theoretic method dispatch.

It is quite clear that the applications of self-adaptive software are far reaching and significant. We expect such application work to continue, particularly with respect to embedded software applications. However, there is also a great deal of work remaining to be done in several foundational areas:

1. Programming language, developmental environment and automatic programming technology in support of automating or semiautomating the production of evaluation code.
2. Technology for representing and manipulating software specifications, designs and structural descriptions.
3. Technology for capturing, representing and manipulating goals, requirements and decision justifications.
4. Theory and technology on providing behavioral guarantees for self-adaptive software (i.e. stability, convergence properties, etc.).

References

Academic Press Dictionary of Science and Technology, Academic Press, 1992.
Adamis, G and Tarnay, K. "Frame-based Self-adaptive Test Case Selection", in *Self-Adaptive Software: Applications*, eds. Laddaga, R., Robertson, P and Shrobe, H. *Volume 2614 Lecture Notes in Computer Science*, Springer-Verlag, 2003.
ANSI, *American National Standard Fortran*, ANSI, New York, 1966.
Åström, K.J. *Adaptive Control*, Addison-Wesley, Reading, MA, 1989.
Bakay, A. "Model Based Adaptivity in Real-Time Scheduling", in *Self-Adaptive Software: Applications*, eds. Laddaga, R., Robertson, P and Shrobe, H. *Volume 2614 Lecture Notes in Computer Science*, Springer-Verlag, 2003.
Boehm, B. *Software Engineering Economics*, Prentice Hall, 1981.
Boehm, B. "A Spiral Model Of Software Development and Enhancement", *ISPW2*, Trabuco Canyon, 1985.
Boehm, B., Brown, J.R., Kaspar, H., Lipow, M., McLeod, G. and Merritt, M. *Characteristics of Software Quality*, North Holland, 1978.
Boehm, B., Egyed, A., Kwan, J. and Madachy, R. "Developing Multimedia Applications with the WinWin Spiral Model", *Proceedings, ESEC/FSE 97 and ACM Software Engineering Notes*, Zurich, Switzerland, November 1997.
Branicky, M.S., Borker, B.S. and Mitter, S. *"A Unified Framework for Hybrid Control: Model and Optimal Control Theory"*, 1996.
Brooks, R.A. "The Intelligent Room Project", *Proceedings of the Second International Cognitive Technology Conference (CT'97)*, Aizu, Japan, 1997.
Cannon, H. *"Flavors: A Non-Hierarchical Approach to Object-Oriented Programming"*, 1982.
Coen, M. "Building Brains for Rooms: Designing Distributed Software Agents", *Ninth Conference on Innovative Applications of Artificial Intelligence (IAAA97)*, Providence, RI, 1997.
Coen, M. "Design Principles for Intelligent Environments". *Fifteenth National Conference on Artificial Intelligence (AAAI98)*, Madison, WI, 1998.
Coen, M., Phillips, B., Warshawsky, N., Weisman, L., Peters, S. and Finin, P.. "Meeting the Computational Needs of Intelligent Environments: The Metaglue System", *Proceedings of MANSE'99*, Dublin, Ireland, 1999.
Dahl, O., Myrhaug, B. and Nygaard, K. *Simula 67 Common Base Language*, Publication No. S-22, Norwegian Computing Center, Oslo, Norway, October 1970.
Doyle, J and McGeachie, M. "Exercising Qualitative Control in Autonomous Survivable Adaptable Systems", in *Self-Adaptive Software: Applications*, eds. Laddaga, R., Robertson, P and Shrobe, H. *Volume 2614 Lecture Notes in Computer Science*, Springer-Verlag, 2003.
IEEE 1074-1995, *IEEE Standard for Developing Software Lifecycle Processes*.
Gajos, K. "Rascal – A Resource Manager for Multi Agent Systems in Smart Spaces", *Proceedings of CEEMAS 2001*, Cracow, Poland, 2001.
Goldberg, A. *Smalltalk-80: The Language*, Addison-Wesley, Reading, MA, 1989.
Goldman, R.P., Musliner, D. and Krebsbach, K.D. "Managing Online Self-Adaptation in Real-Time Environments", in *Self-Adaptive Software: Applications*, eds. Laddaga, R., Robertson, P and Shrobe, H. *Volume 2614 Lecture Notes in Computer Science*, Springer-Verlag, 2003.
Harangozo, S. and Tarnay, K. "FTDs in Self-Adaptive Protocol Specification", in *Self-Adaptive Software: Applications*, eds. Laddaga, R., Robertson, P and Shrobe, H. *Volume 2614 Lecture Notes in Computer Science*, Springer-Verlag, 2003.
Laddaga, R. *Self-Adaptive Software DARPA BAA 98-12*, December, 1997.
Laddaga, R. "Active Software", in *Self-Adaptive Software*, eds. Robertson, P., Laddaga, R. and Shrobe, H. *Volume 1936 Lecture Notes in Computer Science*, Springer-Verlag, 2000.
Laddaga, R., Robertson, P and Shrobe, H. "Results of the First International Workshop on Self Adaptive Software". in *Self-Adaptive Software*, eds. Robertson, P., Laddaga, R. and Shrobe, H. *Volume 1936 Lecture Notes in Computer Science*, Springer-Verlag, 2000.
Laddaga, R. Robertson, P. and Shrobe, H. (eds.) *Self-Adaptive Software: Applications*, Volume 2614 Lecture Notes in Computer Science, Springer-Verlag, 2003.
Leclerc, Y.G. Constructing simple stable descriptions for image partitioning. *International Journal of Computer Vision*, Vol. 3, 1989, pp. 73–102.

Lehman, M. Rules and Tools for Software Evolution Planning and Management, Position Paper, *FEAST 2000 Workshop*, Imperial College, 10–12 July, 2000.

Lehman, M., Ramil, J.F. and Wernick, P.D. *The Influence of Global Factors On Software System Evolution*, Research Report 98/11, Department of Computer, Imperial College, London, England, October 1998.

Naur, P. "Revised Report on the Algorithmic Language ALGOL 60". *Communications of the ACM*, Vol. 6, No. 1, January 1963, pp. 1–17.

Passino, K.M. and Burgess, K.L. *Stability Analysis of Discrete Event Systems*, John Wiley, 1998.

Robertson, P. "A Corpus Based Approach to the Interpretation of Aerial Images", *Proceedings IEE IPA99*, IEE, Manchester, NH, 1999.

Robertson, P. A Self-Adaptive Architecture for Image Understanding. PhD thesis, University of Oxford, 2001.

Robertson, P. and Brady, J.M. Adaptive image analysis for aerial surveillance. *IEEE Intelligent Systems*, Vol. 4, No. 3, May/June 1998, pp. 30–36.

Robertson, P. and Laddaga, R. "A self-Adaptive Architecture and its Application to Robust Face Identification", *Pacific Rim Conference on Artificial Intelligence 2002*, Springer-Verlag, 2002.

Robertson, P., Laddaga, R. and Shrobe, H. *Self-Adaptive Software*, *Volume 1936 Lecture Notes in Computer Science*, Springer-Verlag, 2000.

Roman, M. and Campbell, R. "Gaia: Enabling Active Spaces", *Proceedings of 9th ACM SIGOPS European Workshop*, Kolding, Denmark, September 2000.

Royce, W.W. "Managing the Development of Large Software Systems: Concepts and Techniques", *Proceedings of WESCON*, IEEE Computer Society Press, Los Alamitos, CA, 1970.

Shamma, J.S. "Linearization and Gain-Scheduling", *The Control Handbook*, CRC Press, Boca Raton, FL, 1996.

Shrobe, H. "Model-Based Diagnosis for Information Survivability", in *Self-Adaptive Software: Applications*, eds. Laddaga, R., Robertson, P. and Shrobe, H. *Volume 2614 Lecture Notes in Computer Science*, Springer-Verlag, 2003.

Tarnay, K. "Self -Adaptive Protocols", in *Self-Adaptive Software: Applications*, eds. Laddaga, R., Robertson, P. and Shrobe, H. *Volume 2614 Lecture Notes in Computer Science*, Springer-Verlag, 2003.

Wirth, N. Program development by step-wise refinement. *Communications of the ACM*, Vol. 14, No. 4, April 1971, pp. 221–227.

Yamane, T. The Design and Implementation of the 2k Resource Management System. Master's thesis, University of Illinois, Urbana, Ill, 2000.

Yeh, R.T. "Rapid Prototyping", in *Encyclopedia of Software Engineering*, ed. Marciniak J. Wiley, 1994.

Zhu, S. and Yuille, A. Region competition: unifying snakes, region growing, and bayes/mdl for multiband image segmentation. *IEEE Transactions on Pattern Analysis and Machine Intelligence*, Vol. 18, No. (9), 1996, pp. 884–900.

27

Rules and Tools for Software Evolution Planning and Management

Meir M. Lehman and Juan C. Fernández-Ramil

This chapter is a revised version of the paper by Lehman MM and Ramil JF, Rules and Tools for Software Evolution Planning and Management, Annals of Software Engineering, vol. 11, special issue on Software Management, 2001, pp. 15–44, with kind permission of Springer Science and Business Media.

27.1 Introduction

The software *evolution phenomenon* manifests itself in the common need, since the beginnings of electronic computing, for continuing maintenance and periodic upgrades of software used in real world applications[1]. Though studied for over thirty years [Lehman 1969; Belady and Lehman 1972] (both papers included in [Lehman and Belady 1985], the phenomenon and its economic and social importance have only recently been *widely* recognised and accepted as worthy of serious study [e.g. PSE 1998–2001; Pfleeger 1998b].

One may consider and study software evolution from different points of view. The principal issue of concern may be with the *what* and the *why* of evolution. One focuses on the properties of the phenomenon, its causes and identification of the drivers underlying development and maintenance activity. This is the view adopted by several groups (including the present authors) [e.g. Cook *et al.* 2000; FEAST 2001; Godfrey and Tu 2000; Hsi and Potts 2000; Kemerer and Slaughter 1999; Shepperd 2000]. A complementary view is primarily concerned with the *how* of evolution, that is, with the methods, tools and technology to facilitate disciplined and efficient software change [e.g. PSE 1998–2001; FFSE 2001]. Clearly the two views supplement each other, though the latter is, by far,

---

[1] By application we understand the actual problem being solved (e.g. word processing, web browsing) for a group or community of users.

the more common. But to master the technology and to justify the deployment of good practice in industrial processes, understanding the *what* and *why* are essential [Lehman 1980b; Lehman and Ramil 2000]. Such insight and understanding [Lehman 1980a] provide an opening for developing means for achieving the goals of effective evolution in a given development, application domain or specific technology, the *how* of evolution.

This chapter, a substantially revised version of an earlier contribution [Lehman 2000a], summarises practical implications of the results of the FEAST (Feedback, Evolution And Software Technology) and earlier studies, their observations, models derived from them and their interpretation, as determined in extensive discussions amongst themselves and with collaborator personnel. It presents some fifty or so recommendations, by no means exhaustive, of software evolution *planning* and *management* and identifies some of their implications. Recommendations are only good to the extent that they can be reliably and cost-effectively implemented. Proposals for project planning and management tools are therefore also included though much development is required in that area.

Overall, the recommendations must, clearly, be applied intelligently. This requires insight into the relevant general observations, the data, the models and the interpretations on which the conclusions are based. This chapter cannot provide such detail and is restricted to a general review of the relevant phenomenology. Where appropriate, references to additional sources of information, for example, possible modelling approaches and structures, are provided.

Observations and rules relevant to software system evolution planning and management were first identified during studies of the evolution of OS/360–70 and other systems between 1968 [Lehman 1969] and 1985 [Lehman and Belady 1985]. They were first summarised in a 1978 paper [Lehman 1978]. More recently the FEAST/1 project (1996–1998) [Lehman and Stenning 1996], with the collaboration of ICL, Logica, MoD-DERA and Matra-BAe Dynamics, has been able to confirm, refine and extend the earlier results. This was made possible by analysis of data on the evolution of their respective systems, VME Kernel, the FW Banking Transaction system and a Matra-BAe defence system. Data on a large real time system also became available for analysis during this time. FEAST/2 (1999–2001) [Lehman 1998b], which includes BT Labs as a collaborator, advanced the conclusions and understanding of the evolution phenomenon reached in FEAST/1 and in earlier work. Broadly speaking, the long-term evolutionary behaviour of the *release-based*[2] systems studied was qualitatively equivalent, though varying in detail. This, despite the very different application and implementation domains in which the systems were developed, evolved, operated and used, and to which the respective data sets related. Moreover, the results were broadly compatible with and supportive of those obtained in the earlier studies [Lehman and Belady 1985].

The systems studied so far have been evolved applying paradigms as used for the past thirty or so years. Extending the results obtained to the products of newer paradigms such as OO design and component-based systems and open source software requires further investigation. Thus, for example, the more significant role of *integration* may change evolutionary characteristics significantly. Hypotheses concerning the evolution phenomenology of component and COTS-intensive processes [Lehman and Ramil 1998]

---

[2] The term *release-based* refers here to systems evolved over a sequence of releases to end-users, termed *level II evolution* in a paper [Lehman and Ramil 2001]. A revised version of this paper is available in this volume as a separate chapter.

have been proposed but await empirical investigation. The results of a study of the evolution of Linux, a popular open source operating system [Godfrey and Tu 2000], reveals commonalities with earlier evolution studies but also differences. This result provides an opportunity for the development of deeper insight by seeking understanding for the source of both commonalities and differences. That said, the many similarities observed in the long-term evolutionary behaviour of the systems studied over a period of rapidly evolving technology suggests that the observed behaviour and the rules derived there from are not primarily dependent on specific technologies, application areas or environments employed. It seems likely that they have more fundamental explanations shared by all of the systems. This suggests that it may be possible to extend the conclusions presented here to yield results of wide validity in the field of software, and ultimately more general, evolution.

In presenting the practical implications of the FEAST work, the chapter follows the order in which the *laws of software evolution* [Lehman 1974, 1978, 1997; Lehman and Belady 1985; Lehman et al. 1998; Lehman and Ramil 2001] and other concepts and principles [Lehman and Belady 1985; Lehman 1989, 1990] were formulated. This ordering has, however, only historical significance. It is now recognised that the laws are not independent of one another. The dependencies and relationships between them are currently being investigated and formalised. An introductory description of that investigation is now available [Lehman and Ramil 2000]. The relationship is, unavoidably, reflected in this chapter by a degree of overlap and repetitiveness between sections. In any event, its use in structuring this chapter is a matter of convenience and has no other implications.

27.2 Laws of Software Evolution

The laws of software evolution are listed in a companion Chapter 1 [Lehman and Ramil 2001]. They first emerged from a follow-up of the 1969 study of the evolution of IBM OS/360 [Lehman 1969] and were strengthened by the results of other evolution studies in the seventies. Additional support came from an ICL study in the eighties [Kitchenham 1982]. The present wording incorporates minor modifications that reflect new insights gained over the years [Lehman and Belady 1985; Lehman 1994, 1997; Lehman et al. 1998; FEAST 2001].

Over the years, the laws have gradually become recognised as providing useful inputs to understanding of the software process [e.g. Pfleeger 1998a, b] and have found their place in a number of software engineering curricula. Analysis of the release-based data obtained from FEAST collaborators has indicated that six (I, II, III, V, VI and VIII) of the eight laws are, in general, consistent with the processes reflected by the data [Lehman et al. 1998; Lehman et al. 2000; FEAST 2001]. Law IV has been refined to reflect the presence of segment or stages in evolution, a phenomenon described in [Rajlich and Bennett 2000]. With regards to the remaining law (law VII), it was neither supported nor negated by the FEAST data[3].

The laws have been subject to verbal criticism from the moment of first formulation of laws I–III [Lehman 1974]. Expressed concern included the absence of precise definitions or statement of assumptions, their being based on a single and atypical data

---

[3] Note of the editors: A chapter included in this volume, by Nanda and Madhavji, provides independent support for law VII.

source (OS/360), an allegation that OS/360 represented unique (IBM) development and marketing domains and, more recently, that it reflected outmoded technology. Further criticism was based on an alleged lack of significant support when applying statistical tests [Lawrence 1982]. However, proper 'testing' of the laws will need to address issues related to the identification of qualitative patterns in quantitative data sets having the characteristics of the data being analysed [Ramil 2002]. Such research will also need to address how statistical tests could be applied or interpreted when applied to very small data. Finally, critics expressed concern about use of the term *laws* in relation to observations about phenomena directed and managed by humans and reflecting human activity. This was countered by one of the present authors (Lehman) who noted that it was precisely such human involvement that justified use of the term. The term was selected just because each law encapsulates organisational and other factors that lie outside the realm of software engineering and the scope of software developers. From the perspective of the latter they must be accepted as laws. This reasoning is supported by the analogous application of the term law to, for example, the forces of supply and demand in economic systems.

27.3 S- and E-Type Program Classification

27.3.1 Basic Properties

The laws *apply*, in the first instance, to E-type programs and the associated *global* processes. The latter includes all activities involved in system evolution including, but not limited to, those undertaken by technical, management, marketing, user support personnel, users, and so on [Lehman 1994]. As indicated earlier, type E refers to programs actively (and regularly) used to solve a problem or address an application in a real world domain. A key characteristic of such systems is that their *acceptability* depends on the results delivered to users and other stakeholders. E-type properties include expectations that, at least for the moment, stakeholders are *satisfied* with the system as is. Over and above *functionality*, factors such as *quality* (however defined), *behaviour* in execution, *performance*, ease of use, *changeability*, and so on, will also be of concern.

Evolution is intrinsic to E-type systems. They must be continually enhanced, adapted and fixed if they are to remain effective in a changing world and an evolving application environment. The study of E-type systems is important because the majority of systems upon which businesses and organisations rely for their operation are of this type.

The following section assumes that the reader is also familiar with the definitions of S- and P-type programs and other relevant characteristics. See Section 3 in the companion chapter in this volume [Lehman and Ramil 2001].

27.3.2 Implications of the SPE Program Classification Scheme

Guidelines that follow from the *SPE* classification scheme are listed in this section, with others under the headings that follow. Note that this list (and all others that follow) is to be considered as randomly ordered. No implications, for example, in terms of relative importance, are to be drawn from the position of any item.

(a) All properties and attributes required to be possessed by software products created or modified by individual developers should be explicitly identified in a specification that then serves as the task definition.

(b) Assumptions must be captured and recorded when incorporated into a program specification, a program or into their documentation. This is so even if, at the time they are adopted and embedded in them, they are compatible with the application domain.
(c) The (long-term) goal should be to express specifications formally.
(d) It must be a goal of every process to capture and retain assumptions underlying the specification, both those that form part of its inputs and those arising during the subsequent development process.
(e) When *validating* any specification or program, a conscious effort must be made to identify, document and validate all assumptions implied by an individual statement or combinations of statements, ensuring also their continued validity in the circumstances of the moment, that is, the state of the application domain, the execution domain and the software system itself.
(f) It must be recognised and agreed by the assignor that whatever is not so included is left to the assignee, who must ensure that the decision is not inconsistent with the specification and is either
   1. documented in an *exclusion* document or
   2. formally approved and added to the specification and to all supporting and appropriate user documentation.
(g) Tools to assist in the implementation of these recommendations and to support their systematic application should be developed and introduced into practice.

Practical implications of the laws and the tools suggested by them are dealt with in the following text. Many of the items will appear self-evident. What is new is the unifying conceptual framework on which they are based.

27.4 First Law: Continuing Change

An E-type system must be continually adapted or else it becomes progressively less satisfactory in use.

The need for change reflects a need to *adapt* the system as the outside world, the domain being covered and the application and/or activity being supported or pursued changes. Such exogenous changes are likely to invalidate assumptions made during system definition, development, validation, installation and application or render them unsatisfactory. The software reflecting such assumptions must then be adapted to restore their validity.

Every *E*-type system is a *model-like* reflection of the application in its operational domain [Lehman and Ramil 2001]. Both the real world and every application have an unbounded number of attributes or properties, however defined. Being part of the real world, the operational domain in which the system operates is initially undefined and is, therefore, also intrinsically unbounded. Software systems, on the other hand, are essentially finite in the number of properties. Therefore, the process of abstraction and transformation defining and developing the application concept and its software involves *assumptions* about, for example, what capabilities are to be included in the final program and what properties the latter should display in execution. This process of abstraction, in fact, maybe called *finitisation*, excludes all elements/attributes of the operational domain and the application not specifically included. As a model of the real world, the system is incomplete [Lehman 1976, 1989, 1990; Lehman and Belady 1985]. As briefly discussed earlier, some of the assumptions will be explicit while others will be implicit and some will be by inclusion and others by exclusion. They will be reflected in the system, by the choice of theories and algorithms, codes, lists, parameters, call sequencing, documentation, and so on. Exclusions may be explicit or by omission, and omissions are as real in impacting system operation as are inclusions. Thus, every E-type system has embedded in it an infinite assumption set whose composition will determine the domain of valid application in terms of execution environments, time, function, geography, the detail of many levels of the implementation, and so on.

It may be that the initial set of assumptions was *valid* in the sense that it defined a system that had all the required and desired properties. Any limitations it imposed and the system behaviour it assumed did not render the system unacceptable in operation at the time of its introduction. However, with the passage of time, user experience increases, user needs and expectation change, new opportunities arise, applications expand in terms of numbers of users, details of usage, and so on, new needs and constraints arise in the operational domain, and so on. Thus, a growing number of assumptions may become invalid. This is likely to lead to less than acceptably satisfactory performance in some sense and hence to requests for change. There will also be changes in the real world that impact the operational domain, thus requiring changes to the system to restore it as an acceptable model of the operational domain. Taken together, these facts lead to the unending maintenance that has been the universal experience of all regular computer users since the start of serious computer applications by all regular computer users.

An upper limit for the number of changes implemented per release is likely to exist, above which quality attributes such as safety, for example, and potential for success will be at serious risk. As the number, magnitude and orthogonality to system architecture of changes implemented in a release increases, complexity, assumption and defect injection rates grow, probably more than linearly, with respect to that number.

A partial listing of practical consequences of this unending need for change to every E-type system in continuing use to adapt it to changing stakeholder views and changing operational domains is provided:

(a) Change validation should address the change itself, the actual and potential interaction with the remainder of the system and impact analysis [Bohner and Arnold 1996] on the remainder of the system.
(b) Comprehensive documentation should be created and maintained up to date as changes accumulate.
(c) As the design and implementation of changes proceed, all aspects including, for example, the issue being addressed, the reasons why a particular implementation design/algorithm is being used, details of explicit assumptions adopted, and so on, should be recorded in a way that will facilitate subsequent review.
(d) The assumption set should be reviewed as an integral part of release planning and periodically thereafter to detect any inconsistencies, domain and other changes that conflict with the existing set or that violate constraints.
(e) Releases concentrating primarily on defect removal, performance enhancement and structural cleanup will be required from time to time to maintain system viability. Strategies that have been applied in industry include daily stabilisation with internal release (the *synch-and-stabilise* process [Cusumano and Selby 1995]) and alternating change/growth and stabilisation releases [e.g. Woodside 1980].

(f) Models should be developed to determine the effect of system age and change rate on release stability and to provide an indication of limits to *safe* change rates. Such models may, for example, be based on numbers of changes per release over a sequence of releases or in real time. Another useful metric is the fraction of elements changed or *handled* per release or over a given time period. Metrics and models that maybe used in this context are discussed elsewhere [Ramil *et al.* 2000].

(g) It is beneficial to determine the number of distinct additions and changes to requirements and assumptions over constituent parts of the system per release or over some fixed time period to assess domain and system volatility. This can assist evolution release planning in a number of ways, for example, by pointing to system areas that are ripe for restructuring because of high defect rates or high volatility or where, to facilitate future change, extra care should be taken in change design and implementation.

27.5 Second Law: Increasing Complexity

As an E-type system is changed its complexity increases and becomes more difficult to evolve unless work is done to maintain or reduce the complexity.

Complexity increases because of the injection and the super-positioning of changes to achieve, for example, growth in functionality or satisfaction of the needs of changing operational domains. This leads to increasing internal inter-connectivity and, hence, to deteriorating system structure, thus increasing disorder. Similarly, it results in increasing complexity of internal and external interfaces at all levels. These effects are amplified because, as the system ages, changes are more likely to be orthogonal to existing system structures. However, effective interaction with the system, whether as a developer or a user, requires one to *understand* it in its entirety, so as *to be comfortable* with it. As the system ages and as changes and additions to the system become even more remote from the original concepts and structures, increasing effort and time will be required to understand and implement the changes, to validate and use the system and to ensure that the untouched portion of the system continues to operate as required. The original system architects or experts with in-depth knowledge of the software and of the application may have already left the organisation [Rajlich and Bennett 2000]. Changes and additions take longer to design and to implement, errors and the need for subsequent repair become more likely, and comprehensive validation is more complex.

It follows that, for example, the number of *potential* connections and interactions between elements (objects, modules, subsystems, etc.) is proportional to the *square* of the number n of elements. Thus, as a system evolves, and with it the number of elements, the work required to ensure a correct and adequate interface between the new and the old, the potential for error and omission, the likelihood of incompatibility between assumptions, all tend to increase as n^2. The increasing remoteness of changes from the existing design will also contribute to increased inter-connectivity. All these factors contribute to an increase in system complexity.

The growth in the difficulty of design, change and system validation, and hence in the effort and time required for system evolution, causes increase in costs and in the need for user support. This will, in general, tend to be accompanied by a decline in product quality (see Section 27.10) and in the rate of evolution (see Section 27.8), however defined and measured, unless additional compensatory work is undertaken. FEAST observations indicate directly that, in the long term, the average software growth rate measured in elements such as modules or their equivalent tends to decline as a function of the release sequence number as the system ages. With the partial exception of OS/360, the long-term growth trends of the release-based systems studied in FEAST tend to follow declining growth rate trajectories (inverse square, see [Turski 1996]) with one or two recovery points.

Complexity control effort is largely *anti-regressive* [Lehman 1974], and has no immediate value but constrains or reduces future increases in costs due to future increases in effort required or quality deterioration. The activity includes elimination of so-called *dead* or *repetitive* code, re-structuring, documentation updating, and so on. In general, these activities have minor or no impact in functionality, performance or other properties of the software in execution. In any event, *immediate* benefits are generally relatively small. Long-term impact is, however, likely to be significant and may, at some stage, make the difference between system survival and its demise or replacement. Anti-regressive work is exemplified by code *re-factoring* activities [Fowler 1999].

Determining the level of effort for *anti-regressive* activity, such as complexity control in a release or sequence of releases, presents a major paradox. If the level is reduced or even abandoned to free resources for *progressive* [Baumol 1967] activity such as system enhancement and extension, system complexity is likely to increase, and *productivity* and evolution rates likely to decline. This is likely to lead to stakeholder dissatisfaction, increases in future effort and cost and decline in system quality (see law VII). If, on the other hand, additional resources are provided for complexity control, resources for system enhancement and growth are likely to be reduced. Again the system growth rate is likely to decline. In the absence of process improvement that is based on the principles examined in this chapter, decline in evolution rate appears inevitable.

On the basis of the second law, which reflects these observations, and the measurement, modelling, analysis and other supporting evidence obtained over the years, the following observations and guidelines may be identified:

(a) The many aspects of system complexity must be considered in process design, improvement and planning and, when possible, actively managed and controlled. They include, but are not limited to, the following:
   1. application and functional complexity – including that of the operational domain;
   2. specification and requirements complexity;
   3. architectural complexity;
   4. design and implementation complexity;
   5. structural complexity at many levels (subsystems, modules, objects, calling sequences, object usage, code, documentation, etc.).
(b) There must be a conscious effort to control and reduce complexity and its growth, wherever possible, as modifications are made locally and in interfaces with the remainder of the system.
(c) Complexity control is an integral part of the development and maintenance responsibility. Activity to address it must be considered whenever changes to a system or new releases are being planned.
(d) In planning release content for one or a series of releases, the timing, degree and distribution of complexity control activity must be carefully considered. One must

evaluate alternative complexity control strategies [e.g. Hops and Sherif 1995] and approaches [e.g. Fowler 1999] and select the one that is most likely to help achieve corporate business goals or whatever else requires to be optimised.

(e) In general, it appears to be a sound strategy to alternate releases between those focusing primarily on complexity reduction and restructuring and those implementing major enhancement and adding new function or significant functional extension [e.g. Woodside 1980].

27.6 Third Law: Self Regulation
Global E-type system evolution is feedback regulated.

Patterns of incremental growth observed in FEAST and before can be explained in terms of the presence of self-regulatory feedback mechanisms (see Section 27.11) [e.g. Lehman *et al.* 1998; FEAST 2001]. It is unlikely that these patterns are exclusively a reflection of conscious management control or the management's desire for *stability*[4]. These mechanisms should be identified to permit improvement in control. As a first step to their identification, one may search for properties common to several projects or groups or for correlations between project or group characteristics such as size, age, application area, team size, organisational experience or behavioural patterns. One then may seek behavioural invariants associated with each characteristic. To identify the feedback mechanisms and controls that play a role in performance self-stabilisation and to exploit them in future planning, management and process improvement, the following steps will be helpful:

(a) Employing measurement and modelling techniques as used, for example, in FEAST [Lehman *et al.* 2000; Ramil *et al.* 2000], determine typical patterns, trends, rates of growth and rates of change implementation of a number of projects within the organisation. To obtain meaningful results, data reflecting at least 6 to 10 past releases in the systems studied are required.

(b) Establish *baselines*, that is, typical values for process rates such as growth, defects, changes over the entire system, units changed, units added, units removed, and so on. These may be counted per release or per unit time. Our experience has been that the former yields results that are more regular and interpretable because of the fact that some of the feedback mechanisms operate over releases. Initially, however, and occasionally thereafter, results over release sequence numbers and over real time must be compared and appropriate conclusions drawn. Incremental values, that is the difference between values for successive releases or standard time intervals should also be determined, as should numbers of people working with the system in various capacities, person days, for example, in categories such as specification, design, implementation, testing, integration, customer support, and so on. A third group of measures relates to quality factors. These can be expressed, for example, in pre-release and user reported defects, user take-up rates, installation time and effort, support effort, and so on.

---
[4] Stability, as sought by management, means *planned* and *controlled* change, not constancy. Managers, including software managers, in general, abhor surprises or unexpected changes. They all desire, for example, constant workloads and increases in productivity; software managers desire a steady decline in defects; senior management desire a decline in costs and growth in profit and, for example, market share and sales.

(c) New data that becomes available as time passes and as more releases are added should be used to re-calibrate and improve the models or to re-validate them and test their predictive power.

(d) An analysis of FEAST/1 data, models and data patterns suggests that, in planning a new release or the content of a sequence of releases, the first step must be to determine which of three possible scenarios exists. Let m be the running average of the incremental growth of the system in going from release to release over a series of perhaps five or so releases and s the standard deviation of the incremental growth over the same interval. The scenarios may, for example, be differentiated by an indicator $m + 2s$ that identifies a release plan as *safe, risky* or *very risky* according to the conditions listed in the following text. Note that the rules are expressed for release-based measures. For observations based on incremental growth per standard real-time unit, analogous safe limits are likely to exist but will be a function of the interval between observations in a manner that remains to be determined.

1. The FEAST studies suggest a *safe* level for the planned release content m (where m may decline as the system ages, see Section 27.8). If the desired release content is less than or equal to m, growth at that rate may proceed with good potential for success. Growth at that rate over a sequence of releases is likely to be achievable.

2. The desired release content is greater than m but less than $m + 2s$. The release is *risky*. It could succeed in terms of achieved functional content but serious *delivery delays* (or a perceived need to significantly increase the planned interval between releases) may result. Quality or other problems could arise. If pursued, it would be advisable to plan for a follow-on clean-up release. Even if not planned, such a small growth release is likely to be required. Note that $m + 2s$ has long been identified as a threshold value, for example, in statistical process control and monitoring [Box and Luceño 1997].

3. The desired release content is close to or greater than $m + 2s$. A release with incremental growth of this magnitude is *very risky*. It is likely to cause major problems and evolution instability over one or more subsequent releases. At best, it is likely to require that it be followed by a major clean-up, that is, a *recovery release* in which the main emphasis is on defect fixing and *anti-regressive* work (see Section 27.5).

(e) An appropriate *evolutionary development* strategy [Gilb 1981] should be considered whenever the number of items on the *to be done* list for a release being planned would lead, if implemented in one release, to incremental growth in excess of the levels indicated earlier. It should prove appropriate whenever the size and/or complexity of the required addition is large. In this event, strategies to be considered include spreading the work over two or more releases, *delivering* the new functionality over two or more releases with mechanisms in place to return to older version if necessary, reinforcing the support group, preparing for the release by means of one or more clean-up releases or, if the latter is not possible, preparing for a fast follow-on release to rectify problems that are likely to appear. In either of the last two instances, provision must be made for additional user support.

(f) It would seem that this law implies that the characteristics of the process are influenced by its system dynamics [Forrester 1961] as demonstrated by the self-stabilisation postulated in this law. That being so, the construction of system dynamic models could make an important contribution to better planning and management of the release process.

27.7 Fourth Law: Conservation of Organisational Stability

The work rate of an organisation evolving an E-type software system tends to be constant over the operational lifetime of that system or phases of that lifetime.

The observations on which this law is based date back to the late seventies. Further data gathered in FEAST suggests that the activity rate (e.g. elements *changed, handled* or *handlings* per release or unit of time [Lehman and Belady 1985; Ramil *et al.* 2000]) tends to remain constant over periods or phases of system lifetime. Behaviour may, in the long term, be seen to display an abrupt change from time to time, breaking the overall, otherwise smooth (e.g., constant average and variance), trajectory into two or more segments. This is reflected in the most recent formulation of the fourth law as stated earlier.

This 'piecewise' behaviour of long-term evolutionary attributes is consistent with Boehm's statement that '... *Once an organization has determined its desired level of maintenance for a software product ... the organization's social, economic, and political inertias will generally make it difficult to make significant changes in the level of effort or mode of operation. In some situations, major increases in demand from the investment segment (such as conversion) or significant increases or redirections in demand ... may cause instabilities or reorientations. But in most cases, the maintenance activity will settle into a fairly predictable equilibrium*' [Boehm 1981, p. 546]. For example, Boehm recently referred to the activity triggered by the Y2K issue in many organisations as an anomaly to the original statement of the fourth law that did not account for segments in previous formulations. Other possible triggers of anomalies mentioned by Boehm are mergers, acquisitions, downsizing and a move into e-commerce [Boehm 2000]. This view is consistent with that of Rajlich and Bennett [2000], who have discussed the presence of stages in software maintenance and evolution. In the present context, the fourth law leads, among others, to the following recommendations:

(a) Process plans should allow for work rates that do not exceed the activity rate of the immediate past, unless appropriate adjustments to the process, policies and resource allocation, to support the new desired activity rate are considered and appear to be attainable and maintainable.
(b) Use activity rate metrics, such as elements *handled* per release [Lehman and Belady 1985; Ramil *et al.* 2000], to characterise process performance in association with appropriate *change impact analysis* tools [Bohner and Arnold 1996] and to provide a basis for work planning models [Ramil *et al.* 2000].
(c) As discussed earlier, activity rate can, under some circumstances, be forced to change. Each segment of equilibrium may benefit from its individual, though in all likelihood not dissimilar, model for release planning and effort estimation [e.g. Ramil and Lehman 2000], for example. This requires ongoing monitoring for structural changes in the trends reflecting attributes of the product, process or related domains. Model

re-calibration or adjustment during or after any such change will be required to ensure that they remain a valid tool. Tools for metric tracking and analysis that enable both monitoring of changes in evolutionary trends and detection of segments of equilibrium would be a desirable management aid.

(d) Rajlich and Bennett [2000] suggest that individual stages in product evolution will require application of *stage-specific* methods and tools to adequately perform software maintenance and evolution. This view has also managerial implications that cannot be discussed here. The interested reader is referred to the source [Rajlich and Bennett 2000].

27.8 Fifth Law: Conservation of Familiarity

In general, the incremental growth (growth rate trend) of E-type systems is constrained by the need to maintain familiarity.

With the partial exception of OS/360, and of intermediate periods or segments where the net growth rate appears to be increasing, a long-term decline in incremental growth and growth rate appears to dominate the growth of all release-based systems studied. It might be thought that this could be due to a reduction in the demand for correction and change as the system ages but anecdotal evidence from the marketplace and from developers, for example, indicates otherwise. In general, there is always more work in the *waiting attention* queue than in progress or active planning. Other potential sources of declining growth rate include increasing mismatch of system structure and interfaces with the operational domain and the application addressed (see Section 27.10), decreasing interest in the system, its move into a servicing stage in which only essential fixes are done or progressive system phase-out [Rajlich and Bennett 2000].

It is not appropriate here to speculate further on the source of the behaviour described by the fifth law. We restrict our comment to what emerged from the FEAST studies. This analysis has suggested that the most likely source of the declining incremental growth rates observed is, primarily, the increasing complexity as the system ages (Section 27.5).

Given the growing complexity of the system, its workings and its functionality, achieving renewed familiarity after numerous changes, additions and removals and restoration of pre-change familiarity after change becomes increasingly difficult. This reasoning suggests that the rate of change and growth of the system be slowed down as it ages. This trend has been observed in nearly all the data studied in FEAST but there is no available evidence at that time that the slowdown is the result of such reasoning on the part of those involved. It was, instead, interpreted as a reflection of the feedback-driven software process dynamics.

Further analysis, in phenomenological terms, of distributed mechanisms that control evolution rate together with models of related data, suggest the following guidelines for determining release content:

(a) Collect, plot and model system growth and change data as a function of real time or release sequence numbers (*rsn*) to determine system evolution trends. Elements that may be counted include objects, lines of code (*locs*), modules, inputs and outputs, interconnections, subsystems, features, requirements, and so on. As a start, it is desirable to record several or even all of these measures so as to detect similarities and differences between the results obtained from the various measures and to identify

Rules and Tools for Software Evolution Planning and Management 551

those from which the clearest indications of evolutionary trends can be obtained. Once set up, further collection of such data is trivial. Procedures for their capture may already be a part of configuration management or other procedures. Once data is available, models that reflect historical growth trends may be derived and indicators derived.

(b) On the basis of the observations reported in Section 27.6, in planning further releases the following guidelines should be followed:
1. Seek to maintain incremental growth per release (or the growth rate in real time) at or about a level m (Section 27.6). Such a running average will follow the long-term system growth trend, that is, m will tend to decrease. Alternatively, m could be derived from the trend model(s) obtained following the recommendation (a) and periodically adjusted.
2. When the growth per release needs to be significantly greater than the level m indicated, seek to reduce it by, for example, spreading over two or more releases.
3. If limiting the growth to the recommended level is difficult or not possible, plan and implement a *preparation release* that pre-cleans the system.
4. Alternatively, allow for a longer release period. This will help to prepare for handling problems at integration, higher than normal defect injection rates – hopefully, also higher detection rates – and some user discontent.
5. If the required release increment is near or above some upper limit of safe growth (see Section 27.6), the steps in 2–4 must be even more rigorously applied. Prepare to cope with and control a period of system instability, provide for a possible need for an increase in customer support and accept that a major *recovery release* may be required.
6. Plan to periodically clean-up, re-structure or re-engineer the software and/or adopt other measures to avoid the, otherwise likely, decline in system growth rate.

(c) Develop automatic tools to help in collecting, modelling and interpreting data as it builds up over a period of time to derive, for example, the dynamic trend patterns. A scripting language such as *Perl* [Wall *et al.* 1996] can be used to extract data from sources such as change-logs to estimate, among others, element growth and change rate. Adoption of a fixed standard format for change-log data will facilitate data extraction.

27.9 Sixth Law: Continuing Growth

The functional capability of E-type systems must be continually enhanced to maintain user satisfaction over system lifetime.

This law must be distinguished from the first law, which asserts 'continuing change'. It reflects the fact that all software, being finite, limit the functionality and other characteristics of the system (in extent and in detail) to a finite selection from an infinite set. The domain of operation has also infinite attributes, but the system can only be designed and validated, explicitly or implicitly, for satisfactory operation in some finite part of it. Sooner or later, excluded features, facilities and domain areas become bottlenecks or irritants in use. They need to be included in some manner to fill the gap. The system needs to be evolved to satisfactorily support new situations and circumstances.

Though they have different causes and represent, in many ways, different circumstances, the steps to be taken so as to take cognisance of the sixth law do not, in principle, differ radically from those listed for the first law (Section 27.4). There are, however, some differences owing to the fact that the former is, primarily, concerned with functional and behavioural change, whereas the latter leads, in general, directly to additions to the existing system and therefore to its growth. In practice, it may be difficult or inappropriate to associate a given activity[5] with either law. Nevertheless, since the two laws are due to different phenomena, they also are likely to lead to different, though overlapping, recommendations. These are therefore listed together in Section 27.4.

In general, the cleaner the architecture and structure of the system to be evolved, the more likely it is that additions may be cleanly added with firewalls that permit only the exchange of appropriate information between the old and the new parts of the system. There must, however, be some penetration from the additions to the existing system. This will, in particular, be so when one considers the continued evolution of systems that were not, in the first instance, designed or structured for dynamic growth by the addition of new *components*. Sadly, the same remarks, limitations and consequent precautions are likely to apply when one is dealing with systems that are component based or that made widespread use of COTS [Hybertson *et al.* 1997; Lehman and Ramil 1998] from the start. Future growth is inevitable and a sound architectural and structural base will reduce the effort that will inevitably be required when extending or re-engineering the system. Careful attention must be paid at all times to the points made in Section 27.4.

(a) It appears, in general, to be a sound strategy to alternate releases between those concentrating primarily on defect removal, complexity reduction and minor enhancements and those that implement performance improvement, provide functional extension or add new functions [e.g. Woodside 1980]. Incremental growth and other models provide indicators to help determine if and when this is appropriate.

27.10 Seventh Law: Declining Quality

Unless rigorously adapted and evolved to take into account changes in the operational environment, the quality of an E-type system will appear to be declining.

This law follows directly from the first and sixth laws. As discussed in previous sections, an *E*-type system must undergo changes and additions to adapt and extend it if it is to remain satisfactory in use in a changing operational domain. Functionality must be changed and extended. To achieve this, new blocks of code, modules, components and subsystems are attached and new interactions and interfaces are created, sometimes one on top of the other. If such changes are not made, embedded assumptions become falsified, and mismatch with the operational domains increases. As already observed, the complexity of the system in terms of the interactions between its parts, and the potential for such interaction, all increase. Performance is likely to decline and the potential for defects will increase as earlier embedded assumptions are inadvertently violated and the potential for undesired interactions created. Without compensatory action, adaptation and growth effort tend to increase, whether the direction of evolution emphasises functionality or

---

[5] For a recent discussion on the topic of classification of activity into types, see [Chapin *et al.* 2001].

emphasises performance. Growing complexity and mismatch with operational domains, declining performance, increasing numbers of defects, increasing difficulty of adaptation and growth will all cause stakeholder satisfaction to decline unless the work to maintain quality in every respect is undertaken.

There are many approaches to defining software quality [e.g. Boehm *et al.* 1978; Sommerville 2001]. The causes of decline in terms of some of the more obvious sources and causes were listed, though there are many others. It is not proposed to discuss the possible viewpoints, the impact of circumstances or the more formal definitions. The bottom line is that quality is a function of many factors whose relative significance will vary with circumstances. Users in the field will think of it in terms such as performance, reliability, functionality and adaptability. A CEO, at the other extreme, will be concerned with the contribution the system is making to corporate profitability, its market share, the corporate image, resources required to support it, the support provided to the organisation in pursuing its business, and so on.

In summary, we observe that the underlying cause of the seventh law, the decline in software quality with age, appears to relate to a growth in complexity that must be associated with ageing. It follows that in addition to undertaking activity from time to time to reduce complexity, practices in architecture, design and implementation that reduce complexity or limit its growth should be pursued:

(a) Identify aspects of quality that are of concern in relation to the business or task being addressed.
(b) Quantify the aspects identified in (a) so that they become adequately controllable. Subject to being observed and measured in a consistent way, the associated measures of quality can be defined for a system, project or organisation. Their value, preferably normalised, may then be tracked over releases or units of time and analysed to determine whether levels and trends are as required or desired. One may, for example, monitor the number of user generated defect reports per release. A fitted trend line (or other model) can then indicate whether the rate is increasing, declining or remaining steady. One may also observe oscillatory behaviour and test this to determine whether sequences are regular, randomly distributed or correlated to internal or external events. Time series modelling may be applicable to extract and encapsulate serial correlation [e.g. Humphrey and Singpurwalla 1991]. One may also seek relationships with other process and product measures such as the size of or the number of fixes in previous releases, subsystem or module size, testing effort, and so on. When abundant metric data is available, and the process is sufficiently mature, models such as Bayesian nets may be useful to predict defect rates [Fenton and Neil 1999]. The above examples all relate to defect-related aspects of quality. Other measures may be defined, collected and analysed in an analogous manner.
(c) Design changes and additions to the system in accordance with established principles such as information hiding, structured programming, elimination of pointers and GOTOs, and so on, to limit unwanted interactions between code sections and control those that are essential.
(d) Devote some portion of the evolution resources to complexity reduction of all types, restructuring and the removal of *dead* system elements, unnecessary replications, and so on. Though primarily *anti-regressive* [Lehman 1974], without immediate revenue

benefit, such activities help ensure future changeability and have the potential for providing reliable and cost-effective evolution in the future. Hence, in the long run, they contribute to profitability.
(e) Train personnel to capture and record assumptions, whether explicit or implicit, at all stages of the process in a standard form and in a structure that will facilitate their review.
(f) Review relevant portions of the assumption set at all stages of the evolution process to avoid design or implementation action that could invalidate even one of them. Methods and tools to capture, store, retrieve and review them and their realisation, a nontrivial action, must be developed.
(g) Monitor the appropriate attributes to identify or predict a need for clean-up, restructuring or replacement of parts [e.g. Hops and Sherif 1995] or the whole software.

As indicated earlier, the definition, measurement, modelling and monitoring of software quality–related characteristics are very dependent on application, organisation, product and process characteristics and goals. Interested readers who seek details of the various aspects of quality monitoring, modelling and control beyond those discussed in the present chapter are referred to the literature in this field [e.g. Boehm *et al.* 1978; Sommerville 2001].

27.11 Eighth Law: Feedback System

E-type evolution processes are multi-level, multi-loop, multi-agent feedback systems.

The behaviour of complex feedback systems is not and cannot, in general, be described *directly* in terms of the local behaviour of its forward path activities and mechanisms. Feedback will constrain the ways in which the process constituents interact with one another and will modify their individual, local and collective, global, behaviour. According to the eighth law, the software process is such a system. This observation must, therefore, be expected to apply. Thus, the contribution of any activity to the global process may be quite different from that suggested by its open loop characteristics. If the feedback nature of the software process is not taken into account when predicting its behaviour, unexpected, even counter-intuitive, results must be expected both locally and globally.

Consider, for example, the growth and stabilisation processes described by the first and third laws (Sections 27.4 and 27.6). Positive feedback conveys the desire for functional extension, leading to pressure for *growth* and a need for continuing *adaptation* to exogenous changes. If the resultant pressure is excessive, it may lead to instability. Management, exercising its responsibility to manage change and the rate of change will, in response to information received about progress, system quality, and so on, induce *negative* feedback, in the form of directives and controls to limit change, contain its side effects and drive it in the desired direction. Stabilisation may result. The FEAST and earlier studies have provided behavioural evidence to support this analysis and the eighth law.

Figure 27.1 illustrates the global process. The indicated activities are simply illustrative since the operational program could be achieved following a different set of steps, even with parallel activities. What the figure seeks to convey are the learning, communication and iteration that are integral parts of each step and between steps. It portrays a snapshot of the global software process as the complex multi-agent, multi-loop, multi-level feedback system previously mentioned. The cloud surrounding the graphic, symbolising the bound

Rules and Tools for Software Evolution Planning and Management

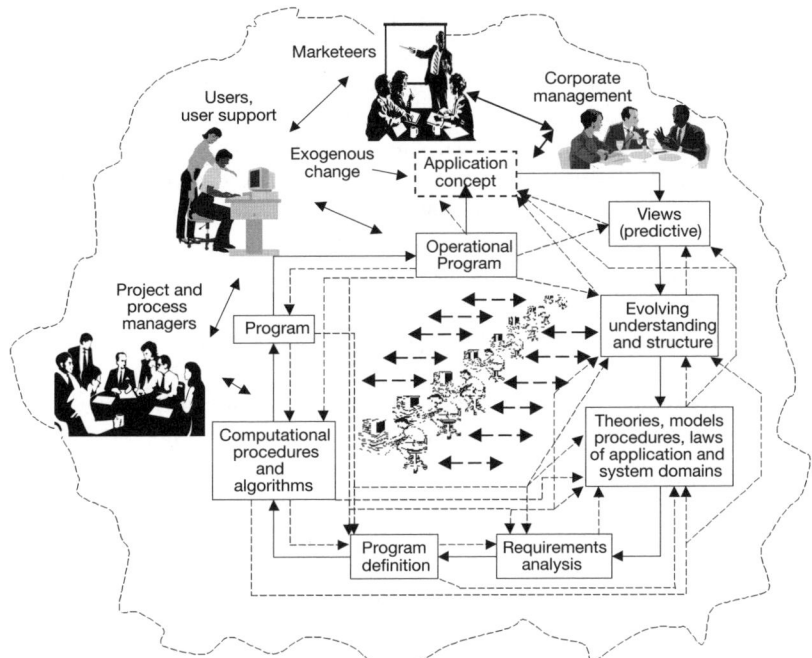

Figure 27.1 Feedback in the global software process

of the operational domain at some moment, now encompasses the entire process that, through its execution of the different aspects of the evolution process, becomes part of the operational domain. As indicated above, and as implied by the first (continuing change) and sixth (continuing growth) laws of software evolution, a fundamental property of E-type applications is that the bounds change as the system is adapted to support a changing environment and is expanded to remove functional and performance limitations. The figure, however, does not reflect the unceasing evolution that could, for example, be portrayed by a sequence of such pictures, one behind the other, enveloped in clouds of ever-increasing size.

The positive and negative feedback loops and control mechanisms of the global E-type process involve activities in the many domains, organisational, marketing, business, usage, and so on, within which the process is embedded and evolution is pursued. The process develops a dynamics that drives and constrains it. Many of the characteristics of this dynamics are rooted in and will be inherited from its history and the wider, global domains. As a result, there are significant limitations to the control that management can achieve in the process. The basic message of the eighth law is, therefore, that in the long term managers are not free to adopt any action considered appropriate from some specific business or other local point of view. Reasonable decision can, generally, be locally implemented. The long-term, global consequences that follow may not be what was intended or anticipated.

It follows that fully effective planning and management require that one takes into account the dynamic characteristics of the process and the limitations and constraints they impose, as outlined above and elsewhere [FEAST 2001]. To achieve this, models that reflect the dynamic forces and behaviour are required. FEAST and other sources [e.g. JSS 1999; ProSim 2000] have made progress in such modelling but more work is required, much of it interdisciplinary, to achieve a systematic, controlled and usable discipline for the design and management of global software processes. From the FEAST work it appears that feedback loops involving personnel outside the direct technical process may have a major impact on the process dynamics and, therefore, on the behaviour of the software evolution process. The interactions of, for example, maintenance, planning, user support, marketing and corporate personnel need at least as much thought and planning as do technical software engineering and other low level issues and activities.

These observations lead to the following recommendations:

(a) Determine the organisational structures and domains within which the technical software development process operates, including information flow, work flow and management control, both forward and feedback, and monitor changes.
(b) In particular, seek to identify the many informal communication links that are not a part of the formal management structure but play a continuing role in driving and directing the system evolution trajectory, and seek to establish their impact.
(c) Model the global structure using, for example, system dynamics approaches [Forrester 1961], calibrate and apply sensitivity analysis to determine the influence and relative importance of the paths and controls.
(d) In planning and managing further work, use the models as simulators to help determine the implications of the influences that are implied by the analysis [e.g. Woodside 1980; Wernick and Lehman 1999; Chatters *et al.* 1999; Kahen *et al.* 2000].
(e) In assessing process effectiveness, use the models as outlined in (c) above as a guide to identify interactions, improve planning and control strategies, evaluate alternatives and focus process changes on those activities likely to prove the most beneficial in terms of the organisational goals.

27.12 The FEAST Hypothesis[6]

To achieve major process improvements of E-type processes other than the most primitive, their global dynamics must be taken into account.

The FEAST hypothesis extends the eighth law by drawing explicit attention to the fact that one must take the feedback system properties of the complex global software process into account when seeking effective *process improvement*. The adjective *complex* used to qualify the process is an understatement. It is a multi-level, multi-loop, multi-agent system. The loops may even be dynamically changing and need not be hierarchically structured. The implied level of complexity is compounded by the fact that the feedback mechanisms involve humans, whose actions cannot be predicted with certainty [Lehman 1976]. Thus, analysis of the global process, prediction of its behaviour and determination of the impact of feedback are clearly not straightforward. One approach to such investigation uses simulation models [Forrester 1961; Vensim 1995]. FEAST/1 has made

---

[6] One of a number of alternative statements given since its first formulation

Rules and Tools for Software Evolution Planning and Management   557

some progress in this regard and FEAST/2 continued this line of work [FEAST 2001]. A number of system dynamics models [Forrester 1961] using the Vensim tool [Vensim 1995] were calibrated and investigated [e.g. Kahen *et al.* 2000]. Many of their variables reflect organisational characteristics and it may be possible to derive generic versions. Modelling and analysis *methods* are already emerging [Ramil *et al.* 2000; Lehman *et al.* 2001]. Available evidence [Lehman 1994; Lehman *et al.* 1998; FEAST 2001] supports the validity of the hypothesis. Much effort must, however, still be applied if full understanding of the role of feedback in software development and maintenance is to be achieved and fully exploited. In any event, the recommendations made in the previous section may be extended as follows:

(a) When seeking disciplined process improvement, use models as outlined in Section 27.11 to guide the analysis of the global process, investigation of potential changes and evaluation of alternatives, focusing implementation on those changes likely to prove the most beneficial in terms of the organisational goals.

27.13 The Principle of Software Uncertainty

The real world outcome of any E-type software execution is inherently uncertain with the precise area of uncertainty also not knowable.

This principle was first formulated in the late 1980s [Lehman 1989, 1990]. It asserts that the outcome of the execution of an E-type program is not absolutely predictable. The likelihood that execution will not satisfy the stakeholders may be small but a *guarantee* of *satisfactory* results (from the point of view of the stakeholders, and of the operational domain) can never be given no matter how impeccable the previous operation has been or whether the program *satisfies* a formal specification. This statement may sound alarmist or trivial (after all there can always be unpredictable hardware failure) but that is not the issue. By accepting the statement and taking appropriate steps, even a small likelihood of unsatisfactory results may be further reduced.

There are several sources of software uncertainty [Lehman 1989, 1990]. The most immediate and the one that can be at least partially addressed in process design and management relates to the assumptions reflected in every E-type program. Some will have been taken consciously and deliberately, for example, to limit the geographical range of the operational domain to a specific region or to limit the scope of an air traffic control system. Some may be unconscious, for example, ignoring the gravitational pull of the moon in setting up control software for a particle accelerator [CERN 1998]. Others may follow from implementation decisions taken without sufficient foresight such as adopting a two-digit representation for years in dates. These examples illustrate circumstances where errors can eventually arise when changes in the user or machine world, or in associated systems, invalidates assumptions and their reflection in code or documentation.

As indicated in Section 27.4, a real world domain has an uncountable number of properties. Once any part of that real world is excluded from the system specification or its implementation, the number of assumptions also becomes infinite. Any one of this infinite set can become invalid, for example, by extension of the operational domain, by changes to the problem being solved or to the activity that the system implements or supports or by changes in the system domain under and with which the program operates. Uncertainty is therefore intrinsic since an invalid assumption can lead to behavioural changes in the program. Awareness of that uncertainty can, however, reduce the threat of error or failure if it leads to systematic search for and early detection of invalidity through regular checking of the assumption set. The better the records of assumptions, the simpler they are to review, and the greater the frequency with which they are reviewed, the smaller the threat. Hence, it was recommended in earlier sections to incorporate conscious capture, recording and review of assumptions of all types into the software and documentation processes.

The discussion on software uncertainty has focused on *assumptions*. There are also other sources of uncertainty in system behaviour on execution but the likelihood of their contributing to system failure is small in relation to that stemming from invalid assumptions embedded in the code or documentation. They are, therefore, not further considered here.

As implied earlier in this chapter, it follows that the list of recommendations [Lehman 1998a] below needs to be considered, and if possible, adopted:

(a) When developing a computer application and associated systems, estimate and document the likelihood of change in the various areas of the application domains and their spread through the system, to simplify subsequent detection of assumptions that may have become invalid as a result of changes.
(b) Seek to capture by all means, assumptions made in the course of program development or change.
(c) Store the appropriate information in a structured form, related possibly to the likelihood of change as in (a), to facilitate detection of any that have become invalid in periodic reviews.
(d) Assess the likelihood or expectation of change in the various categories of catalogued assumptions, and as reflected in the database structure, to facilitate such reviews.
(e) Review the assumptions database by categories as identified in (c), and as reflected in the database structure, at intervals guided by the expectation or likelihood of change or as triggered by events.
(f) Develop and provide methods and tools to facilitate all of the above.
(g) When possible, separate validation and implementation teams to improve questioning and control of assumptions.
(h) Provide for ready access by the evolution teams to all appropriate domain specialists with in-depth knowledge and understanding of the application domain.

Finally, and as already noted, the uncertainty principle is a consequence of the unboundedness of the operational and application domains of E-type systems and the fact that the totality of *known* assumptions embedded in it must be finite. However much understanding is achieved and however faithfully and completely the recommendations listed in the previous sections are followed, the results of execution of an E-type system will always be *uncertain*. There is no escape. Adherence to the recommendations will, however, ensure that unexpected behaviour and surprise failures can be reduced, if not completely avoided. In view of the increasing penetration of computers into all facets of human activity, organisational and individual, often in life, societal or economically critical applications, any reduction in the likelihood of failure is important.

27.14 Conclusions

It is appreciated that some of the above recommendations may be difficult and/or costly to implement but the potential long-term benefit of their implementation in terms of productivity and predictability, process effectiveness and system maintainability, for whatever reason and by whatever means, makes their pursuit worthwhile. The selection and application of individual recommendations and their combination becomes a matter of management judgement in terms of their relative efficacy, cost-benefit evaluation and business objectives.

Determination of a product evolution strategy is a management responsibility that must take into account many technical and business-related factors. Circumstances may, for example, arise where business or technical considerations suggest a release policy in the interests of the business as a whole that may have undesirable consequences for the system whose evolution is being planned. Global and local, *black-box* and *white-box* process models [FEAST 2001; Ramil *et al.* 2000] reflect, among others, the role and mutual impact on one another of the evolving system, the organisation, the system evolution and usage domains and the actors and activities in all these domains. Their systematic use, together with full understanding of the technical alternatives and their likely consequence in the short, medium and long term, will facilitate a well founded decision that optimises the overall organisational benefit, reducing risk and increasing the long-term aggregate benefit.

Lengthy though it is, this chapter gives at best an overview of the topic. The reader is advised not to apply the recommendations blindly. To appreciate, and apply them fully, requires understanding of the human and technical backgrounds, usage and organisational, that underlie the observations from which the conclusions were derived. For real progress, some understanding of the phenomenology is necessary. References have been provided and the reader is encouraged to explore these and to seek to understand the models and the reasoning that underlies them. Above all, note that this chapter is based primarily on an ongoing investigation by a single group. For further advances, many more people must become involved in the search for even more effective approaches to software process management and, more generally, to the development and evolution of computerised systems and the software that is crucial to their satisfactory and safe performance. Moreover, since many of the conclusions relate directly to the behaviour of people (implementers, managers and all stakeholders), and organisations, such studies demand inter-disciplinary collaboration.

To which degree an evolution process planned and managed with full awareness of the laws will or will not ultimately conform to the behaviours implied by them is an open question. The present authors have reason to believe that such awareness has not been part of the processes studied by the present group or those studied in earlier works. Whether the full or partial application of the recommendations in this chapter will significantly affect the evolutionary behaviour will also need to be addressed.

Finally, it must be stressed that the evolution studies, source of the recommendations in this chapter, have been based on the well-tested scientific method. The real world has been observed, patterns of behaviour identified, measured and quantified, observations modelled, hypotheses formulated, support sought and theories developed or planned. This process must, of course, be pursued iteratively. This would apply to any further study of the topic. The addition of a theoretical framework is now being planned [Lehman and

Ramil 2000; Lehman 2000b]. Eventually such a theory might be broadened to comprise a theory of the software process or generalised to address a wider group of business processes. It is hoped that this effort will provide significant benefit to a world and a society relying evermore on computers and, therefore, on the software that provides their functionality.

27.15 Acknowledgements

Sincere thanks are due to our colleagues Dr Goel Kahen and Ms Siew Lim for their support. Equally to Professors Perry and Turski, to our collaborators at BT Labs, DERA-MoD, ICL, Logica and Matra-BAe and to their respective staffs who provided data, process insight and constructive criticism. Thanks are also due to the anonymous referees for their comments. Finally to the UK EPSRC and its reviewers for funding provided under grant numbers GR/K86008 (FEAST/1), GR/M44101 (FEAST/2), GR/L07437, GR/L96561 and GR/N02412 (SVFs).

References[7]

Baumol W.J. (1967), "Macro-Economics of Unbalanced Growth – The Anatomy of Urban Cities," *American Economics Review*, LVII(3), June, pp. 415–426.

*Belady L.A. and Lehman M.M. (1972), "An Introduction to Program Growth Dynamics," In *Statistical Computer Performance Evaluation*, Freiburger W. (ed.), Academic Press, New York, pp. 503–511.

Boehm B. (1981), *Software Engineering Economics*, Prentice Hall, Englewood Cliffs, NJ.

Boehm B. (2000), "Value-Based Feedback in Software/IT Systems," Joint Invited Keynote Presentation, *ProSim 2000 and FEAST 2000 Workshops*, Imperial College, London, UK, 12 July, available from http://www.doc.ic. ac.uk/~mml/f2000/program#presentations.

Boehm B., Brown J.R., Kaspar J.R., Lipow M., MacCleod C.J. and Merritt M.J. (1978), *Characteristics of Software Quality*, North Holland.

S.A. Bohner and R.S. Arnold (eds.) (1996), *Software Change Impact Analysis*, IEEE Computer Society Press, Los Alamitos, CA, p. 376.

Box G. and Luceño A. (1997), *Statistical Control by Monitoring and Feedback Adjustment*, Wiley, p. 327.

CERN (1998), "The Earth breathes on LEP and LHC", CERN Bulletin 09/98, 23 February 1998, http://bulletin. cern.ch/9809/art1/Text_E.html.

Chapin N., Hale J.E., Khan K.M., Ramil J.F. and Tan W.G. (2001), "Types of Software Evolution and Software Maintenance," *Journal of Software Maintenance and Evolution: Research and Practice*, 13(1), January-February, pp. 1–30.

Chatters B.W., Lehman M.M., Ramil J.F. and Wernick P., (1999), "Modelling a Software Evolution Process," In *Proceedings of ProSim'99, Software Process Modelling and Simulation Workshop*, 28–30 June, Silver Falls, OR; A revised version as "Modelling a Long Term Software Evolution Process," *Journal of Software Process – Improvement and Practice*, 5(2/3), July 2000, pp. 95–102.

Cook S., H. Ji and R. Harrison (2000), *Software Evolution and Software Evolvability* working paper, University of Reading, August.

Cusumano M.A. and Selby R.W. (1995), *Microsoft Secrets*, The Free Press, New York, p. 512.

FEAST (2001), *Feedback, Evolution And Software Technology*, Projects Web Site, Department of Computing, Imperial College, London, UK, http://www.doc.ic.ac.uk/~mml/feast/ <<as of August 2005>>.

Fenton N.E. and Neil M. (1999), "A Critique of Software Defect Prediction Models", *IEEE Transaction on Software Engineering*, 25(5) September/October, pp. 675–689.

FFSE (2001), *International Session on Formal Foundations of Software Evolution, FFSE 2000*, Lisbon, Portugal, 13 March, http://prog.vub.ac.be/poolresearch/FFSE/.

Forrester J.W. (1961), *Industrial Dynamics*, MIT Press, Cambridge, MA.

---

[7] Papers identified with a '*' have been reprinted in [Lehman and Belady 1985].

Fowler M. (1999), *Refactoring: Improving the Design of Code*, Addison-Wesley, New York.

Gilb T. (1981), "Evolutionary Development," *ACM Software Engineering Notes*, 6(2), April, p. 17.

Godfrey M.W. and Tu Q. (2000), "Evolution in Open Source Software: A Case Study," In *Proceedings of the International Conference on Software Maintenance, ICSM 2000*, 11–14 October, San Jose, CA, pp. 131–142.

Hops J.M. and Sherif J.S. (1995), "Development and Application of Composite Complexity Models and a Relative Complexity Metric in a Software Maintenance Environment," *Journal of Systems and Software*, 31(2), November, pp. 157–169.

Hsi I. and Potts C. (2000), "Studying the Evolution and Enhancement of Software Features," In *Proceedings of the International Conference on Software Maintenance, ICSM 2000*, 11–14 October, San Jose, CA, pp. 143–151.

Humphrey W.S. and Singpurwalla N.D. (1991), "Predicting (Individual) Software Productivity," *IEEE Transactions on Software Engineering*, 17(2), February, pp. 196–207.

Hybertson D.W., Anh D.T. and Thomas W.M. (1997), "Maintenance of COTS-intensive Software Systems," *Journal of Software Maintenance: Research and Practice*, 9, pp. 203–216.

JSS (1999), *The Journal of Systems and Software*, Special Issue on Software Process Simulation Modelling, 46(2/3), 15 April, pp. 89–216.

Kahen G., Lehman M.M., Ramil J.F. and Wernick P.D. (2000), "Dynamic Modelling in the Investigation of Policies for E-type Software Evolution," *ProSim 2000*, Imperial College, London, UK, 12–14 July; a revised version to appear in *Journal of Systems and Software*, 2001.

Kemerer C.F. and Slaughter S. (1999), "An Empirical Approach to Studying Software Evolution," *IEEE Transaction on Software Engineering*, 25(4), July/August, pp. 493–509.

Kitchenham B. (1982), "System Evolution Dynamics of VME/B," *ICL Technical Journal*, May, pp. 42–57.

Lawrence M.J. (1982), "An Examination of Evolution Dynamics," *Proceedings of the 6th International Conference on Software Engineering*, IEEE Computer Society, Tokyo, Japan, 13–16 September, pp. 188–196.

*Lehman M.M. (1969), "The Programming Process," IBM Research Report RC 2722, IBM Research Centre, Yorktown Heights, NY, September.

*Lehman M.M. (1974), *Programs, Cities, Students, Limits to Growth?*, Inaugural Lecture, *Science and Technology Inaugural Lecture Series, vol. 9*, Imperial College, 1970, 1974, pp. 211–229; Also in D. Gries (ed.) (1978), *Programming Methodology*, Springer-Verlag, pp. 42–62.

Lehman M.M. (1976), "Human Thought and Action as an Ingredient of System Behaviour," CCD Research Report 76/12, Imperial College of Science Technology, July 1976; Also in R. Duncan and M. Weston-Smith (eds.) (1977) *Encyclopaedia of Ignorance*, Pergamon Press, Oxford, England, pp. 354–397.

*Lehman M.M. (1978), "Laws of Program Evolution – Rules and Tools for Programming Management," In *Proceedings Infotech State of the Art Conference, Why Software Projects Fail?*, London, England, April, pp. 11/1–11/25.

Lehman M.M. (1979), "The Environment of Design Methodology," Keynote Address, In *Proceedings Symposium on Formal Design Methodology*, T.A. Cox (ed.), Cambridge, UK, 9–12 April 1979, pp. 17–38; STL Ltd, Harlow, Essex, UK, 1980.

*Lehman M.M. (1980a), "On Understanding Laws, Evolution, and Conservation in the Large Program Life Cycle," *Journal of Systems and Software*, 1(3), pp. 213–221.

*Lehman M.M. (1980b), "Programs, Life Cycles and Laws of Software Evolution," In *Proceedings of IEEE, Special Issue on Software Engineering*, September, pp. 1060–1076; With more detail as "Programs, Programming and the Software Life-Cycle," *System Design, Infotech State of the Art*, Rep, Se 6, No 9, Pergamon Infotech Ltd, Maidenhead, England, 1981, pp. 263–291.

Lehman M.M. (1989), "Uncertainty in Computer Application and its Control through the Engineering of Software," *Journal of Software Maintenance: Research and Practice*, 1(1), September, pp. 3–27.

Lehman M.M. (1990), "Uncertainty in Computer Application," Technical Letter, *Communications of the ACM*, 33(5), p. 584.

Lehman M.M. (1994), "Feedback in the Software Evolution Process," Keynote Address, In *CSR Eleventh Annual Workshop on Software Evolution: Models and Metrics*, 7–9 September, Dublin, Ireland; and In *Information and Software Technology*, special issue on Software Maintenance, 38(11), 1996, Elsevier, pp. 681–686.

Lehman M.M. (1997), "Laws of Software Evolution Revisited," *Proceedings of EWSPT'96*, LNCS 1149, Springer-Verlag, Nancy, France, pp. 108–124.

Lehman M.M. (1998a), "The Future of Software – Managing Evolution," Invited Contribution, *IEEE Software*, 15(1), January-February, pp. 40–44.

Lehman M.M. (1998b), *FEAST/2: Case for Support*, Department of Computing, Imperial College, London, UK, July. Available from links at the FEAST project web site http://www.doc.ic.ac.uk/~mml/feast.

Lehman M.M. (2000a), "Rules and Tools for Software Evolution Planning and Management," position paper, *FEAST 2000 Workshop*, Imperial College, London, UK, 10–12 July. Available from links at http://wwwdoc.ic.ac.uk/~mml/f2000.

Lehman M.M. (2000b), *These – An Approach to a Theory of Software Evolution*, Project Proposal, Department of Computing, Imperial College, London, UK, December.

Lehman M.M. and L.A. Belady (eds.) (1985), *Program Evolution – Processes of Software Change*, Academic Press, London, UK.

Lehman M.M., D.E. Perry and J.F. Ramil (1998), "On Evidence Supporting the FEAST Hypothesis and the Laws of Software Evolution," In *Proceedings of the Fifth International Metrics Symposium, Metrics '98*, 20–21 November, Bethesda, MD.

Lehman M.M. and J.F. Ramil (1998), "Implications of Laws of Software Evolution on Continuing Successful Use of COTS Software," Technical Report 98/8, Department of Computing, Imperial College, London, UK, incl. panel pos. statement, ICSM '98, Washington DC, 16–18 November; A revised version as "Software Evolution in the Age of Component Based Software Engineering," *IEE Proceedings – Software*, Special Issue on Component Based Software Engineering, 147(6), December 2000, pp. 249–255.

Lehman M.M. and J.F. Ramil (2000), "Towards a Theory of Software Evolution – and its Practical Impact," Invited Lecture, Pre-prints of the *International Symposium on Principles of Software Evolution, ISPSE 2000*, 1–2 November, Kanazawa, Japan, pp. 1–9. Also as a revised version, in this volume.

Lehman, M.M. and J.F. Ramil (2001), "Software Evolution", Invited Keynote Lecture, Pre-prints *IWPSE 2001*, September 10–11, Vienna, Austria; a revised and extended version of an article in J. Marciniak (ed.), (2002), *Encyclopedia of Software Engineering*, 2nd Ed., Wiley.; Further revised versions were published as "Software Evolution and Software Evolution Processes", *Annals of Software Engineering*, special issue on Software Process-based Software Engineering, 14, 2002, pp. 275–309, and in this volume.

Lehman M.M. and V. Stenning (1996), *FEAST/1: Case for Support*, Project Proposal, Department of Computing, Imperial College, London, UK, March. Available from links at the FEAST web site http://www.doc.ic.ac.uk/~mml/feast.

Lehman M.M., J.F. Ramil and G. Kahen (2001), "Experiences with Behavioural Process Modelling in FEAST, and Some of its Practical Implications", *Proceedings of the 8th European Workshop on Software Process Technology, EWSPT-8*, 19–21 June, Haus Bommerholz, Witten, Dortmund, Germany, LNCS 2077, Springer-Verlag, Berlin, Germany, pp. 47–62.

Lehman M.M., J.F. Ramil and P.D. Wernick (2000), "Metrics-Based Process Modelling with Illustrations from the FEAST/1 Project," In *Systems Modelling for Business Process Improvement*, D. Bustard, P. Kawalek and M. Norris (eds.), Artech House, April, Chapter 10.

Pfleeger S.L. (1998a), *Software Engineering – Theory and Practice*, Prentice Hall.

Pfleeger S.L. (1998b), "The Nature of System Change," *IEEE Software*, 15(3), pp. 87–90.

ProSim (2000), *Workshop on Software Process Simulation and Modelling*, Imperial College, London, UK, 12–14 July 2000, http://www.prosim.org.

PSE (1998–2005) *Series of International Workshops on Principles of Software Evolution (IWPSE) and 2000 International Symposium on Principles of Software Evolution*, ISPSE. Most recent Proceedings: M. Saeki, G. Canfora, and S. Yamamoto (eds.), (2005) *Proceedings of IWPSE 2005*, Sept. 5–6, IEEE Computer Society Press, Lisbon, Portugal.

Rajlich V.T. and K.H. Bennett (2000), "A Staged Model for the Software Life Cycle," *Computer*, 33(7), July, pp. 66–71.

Ramil J.F (2002), "Laws of Software Evolution and their Empirical Support", Invited Panel Statement, In *Proceedings of ICSM 2002*, 3–6 October, Montreal, Canada, p. 71.

Ramil J.F. and M.M. Lehman (2000), "Metrics of Software Evolution as Effort Predictors – A Case Study," In *Proceedings of ICSM*, 11–14 October, San Jose, CA, pp. 163–172.

Ramil J.F., M.M. Lehman and G. Kahen (2000), "The FEAST Approach to Quantitative Process Modelling of Software Evolution Processes," *Proceedings PROFES'2000*, LNCS 1840, 20–22 June, Springer, Oulu, Finland, pp. 311–325.

Shepperd M. (2000), "Dynamic Models of Maintenance Behaviour," In *Workshop on Empirical Studies of Software Maintenance, WESS 2000*, 14 October, San Jose CA, http://members.aol.com/_ht_a/geshome/wess2000/metricsandmodels.htm.

Sommerville I. (2001), *Software Engineering*, 6th Ed., Addison-Wesley & Pearson Education Limited, Harlow, UK, Chapter 24.

Turski W.M. (1996), "Reference Model for Smooth Growth of Software Systems," *IEEE Transactions on Software Engineering*, 22(8), August, pp. 599–600.

Vensim (1995), *Vensim Reference Manual, Version 1.62*, Ventana Systems Inc., Belmont, MA.

Wall L., Christiansen T. and Schwartz R.L. (1996), *Programming Perl*, O'Reilly & Associates, Sebastopol, CA, p. 645.

Wernick P. and Lehman M.M. (1999), "Software Process Dynamic Modelling for FEAST/1," *Journal of Systems and Software*, 46, 193–201.

*Woodside C.M. (1980), "A Mathematical Model for the Evolution of Software," *Journal of Systems and Software*, 1(4), October, pp. 337–345.

Index

Abstraction 19, 20, 320, 510, 543
Action plan, development of
  corrective action 438
Adaptation 58
Adaptive maintenance 224
Agents 532
Agile methods 124
Algorithmic cost estimation 464–465
Algorithms 44
Alternate releases strategy 552
AMEISE 86–88, 91
Analytical model 277–278
Anomalous behaviour, causes of 131
Anti-regressive activity 224
Anti-regressive work 546
Application
  evolution of 27–28
Architectural impact 288
Architecture 77, 79–80, 88, 104–105, 269–280
  and risk resolution 475
  deterioration 227
Architecture, system 105–106
Artefact, technical 72
As needed strategy 238
Assembler 511
Assignment 255
Assumption 103, 105, 112, 113, 347–349
  embedded in software artefacts 558
Assumption reviews 554
Average effort per release 133

Balanced scorecards 487
Baseline process 436
Baselines 547
Bayesian decision theory 520
Behavioural stability 283
Benchmarking 283, 306
Benefits realization approach 472, 479
Benefits-realized monitoring and control 479–481
Bernoulli trial 149, 153
BGW framework 285
Binding 510
  dynamic 512
  dynamic vs static 510
  static 510
Biological evolution 194–197
Black box modelling 465–466
  control theory 461
Black-box framework 285, 300
Black-box models 559
Blackmore 144
Bounding 20–21
Bricolage 191, 193
Budgeted cost of work performed (BCWP) 477
Budgeted cost of work scheduled (BCWS) 477
Business case analysis 482–485
Business event 405
Business processes 54, 56, 60

C++ 236, 514
Calibration 277

Software Evolution and Feedback: Theory and Practice Nazim H. Madhavji, Juan C. Fernández-Ramil and Dewayne E. Perry
© 2006 John Wiley & Sons, Ltd

Call depths 236
Calling structure 230
Capability Maturity Model (CMM) 343, 428
Capability Maturity Model Integration (CMMi) 343
Capability/schedule/cost tradeoff analysis 471
Cash receipts transaction management system 145, 148, 149
Categorical data analysis 416–418, 420
Causal models 493
CeBASE 487
CES. *See* Congruence Evaluation System
Change 249–251, 254, 260, 265
 gradual 75, 85
 radical 78, 79, 85, 91
Change drivers 75, 85
Change impact analysis 283, 306
Change logs 228
Change rate 287, 288
Change request 415, 417
Change request forms 228
Change request hierarchy 415
Change ripple effects 238
Change-prone modules 282, 305, 308
 re-engineering of 381
Chidamber & Kemerer 145
Class of knowledge 407
Class tree 149, 151–153
Clean-up releases 548
Closed source software 181
Closed source systems 194, 200
Closed-loop system 463
Co-evolution 54, 56–58, 60, 199, 270
COCOMO 464–465
Code characteristics 414
Code decay 226
Code structure 212
 code components 212
 evolution of 213–218
 folders and levels 212
Commercial Off The Shelf (COTS) 12, 344, 346
Communication gap 61

Compiler 512–514
 development, choice of function 513
Complexity 53–68, 98, 99, 107, 109, 210, 219, 249, 261–263, 265, 545–547
 measurement of 254, 257, 263
Compliance 270–271
Components 78, 79, 89
Composition 318, 322–324, 334
Computational models 199, 201
Concept of large in software 8–10
Confidence level 501
Configuration 273–277
 trade-offs in 275
Conflicting evidence 495
Conflicting requirements 'issues' 422
Congruence 164
Congruence Evaluation System (CES) 162–176
 capabilities, analysis of 165
Connectedness 57, 58, 67
Connectors 84
Conservation of familiarity 226, 263–264
Conservation of organisational stability 263
Constant effort law 80
Constraint 400
 mandated 407
Constructive Cost Model II (COCOMO II) 444, 472
Consumers 401–402
Continuing change 261–262
Continuing growth 264
Control theory 461
Control-flow 251, 260
COPROMO 475
Core Capability Demonstration (CCD) 482
Corrective action 438
Corrective maintenance 223
Correctness 11, 13, 17–19, 29
Cost 482–485
Cost effective process 225
Cost estimation 444, 493

Cost factors 461
  feedback-related 466–468
COTS. *See* Commercial Off The Shelf
Coupling 83–85, 90
Cultural context 50

Darwinian evolution 143, 144
Data complexity 238, 244
Data level 228, 236–240
Data refinement 316
Data-flow 251
De-localisation 238, 240
Declining quality 264
Deliberate training 496
Dependency check 422
Derivation 319
  feasibility 320
Design 106, 121, 123
  vs production 372
Design history 314
Design patterns 124
Design processes 372
Design recovery 219
Design unit 78–79, 84, 88–90
Detailed product tracing relationship 407
Developers 400
Development effort
  distribution of 300
Development process 411
Developmental biology 194
Diagnosis 520
Dimensions of evolution 41–49
Discrepancy reports (DRs) 415
Discrete event simulation 431–432
Discriminants 422
Distribution model 153–159
Document 399
Documentation 227, 236
Domains
  nonparadigmatic 112
  paradigmatic 113–114
  pre-paradigmatic 113–116
  real-world 105, 113
Dominant design 195

E-type applications and software 12
E-type software 339, 344, 349, 350, 549
  E-type specification 350
E-type systems 75, 115–123, 161, 164, 171, 176, 278, 279, 446, 460
  uncertainty 117–118
Earned Value (EV) 471, 476–477
Earned Value feedback process 476, 477
Earned Value system 477
Ecologies
  informational 196
  organizational 195, 199
Ecosystem 57
Effort estimation 497
Elements 'handled' or 'touched' 213, 549
Emergence 65, 66, 68
Emergent properties 65, 67
Empirical studies 30, 182–184, 207, 208, 210, 220
  of software change processes 246
  of software evolution 225
Enabling environment 54, 64–68
Engineering experiments 46
Environment 161, 163
Environmental changes 163, 168, 170, 171
Environmental characteristics 170, 171
Environmental evolution
  impact of 167
  requirements changes 171
Ephemeral process 31
Epistatic interaction 57, 67
Error correction
  cost of 423
Estimation 459–468
Estimation experience 490
Estimation feedback 491, 493–497
Estimation game 494
Estimation learning 490–493
  effort estimation 491
  evaluation of outcome feedback 492
  guidelines 493–497
  motivation for 491

Estimation learning (*continued*)
   timely feedback   492
   training opportunities   492
Estimation models   444
Estimation skills   494–495
Evaluation   494
   of performance   494
Evolution   270–271
   aspects of   71–91
   colloquial   75
   definition of   75
   generic theories of   96, 125
   in vitro   83
   in vivo   83
   inevitability of   13
   laws of   76, 82
Evolution control   90
Evolution drivers   76
Evolution dynamics   9, 210
Evolution identification method   287, 305–307, 310
Evolution management. *See* Evolution control
Evolution model   194–197
Evolution pattern   146–153
Evolution planning   413
Evolution studies
   open source   186–194
Evolution theories   194–197
Evolutionary biology   194
Evolutionary burst   79, 84
Evolutionary development   269, 271, 273, 278, 548
Evolutionary pattern   184–194
Evolutionary processes   17
Evolutionary spikes   80
Evolutionary trends   215, 217
Evolutionistic models   194
Experience   500
Experience factory   487
Experience, forms of   44–47
   experimentation   46
   feedback   45
   understanding   46
Expert estimation   489–503
Expert judgment   491

Exploration of the space of possibilities   66, 68, 69
Exponential   187

F/OSS   181, 185–186
Face recognition   528
Failure occurrence   422
Far-from-equilibrium   66–68
Fault-prone modules   413
FEAST   23, 367, 446
FEAST hypothesis   556–557
Feature interaction   329, 332
Feature interaction, telephony   330
Feature level   80
Feature-oriented systems   329
Feedback   45–46, 54, 56, 68, 107, 118, 210, 219, 269, 275, 278, 279, 397, 460–468, 507–535
   nonlinear   54, 56
   positive   103
   in simulation models   428
   sociology of   366
Feedback characteristics
   taxonomy of   461
Feedback control   277, 365–366, 373, 472–476
   adequacy, assessment of   467
   mechanisms of   371
Feedback control system   197–198
Feedback cycle   472–476
Feedback effects
   in software evolution   140
Feedback loop   269, 277, 279
Feedback overload   371
Feedback properties   76
Feedback system   264
Feedforward capability   446
   role in risk management   453
Feedforward model
   operational concept of   449
Feedforward systems   447
Fitness   161, 162
   external factors   161
   internal factors   161
   threats to   161
Flexible architecture   269

Folder structure evolution   207, 213–218
Formal estimation models   490
Formal methods   354
Formal specification   11, 557
Framework   85
Framework assessment   283, 309
Framework deployment   282, 306
Framework development effort   301, 304
Framework evolution   282, 284, 287, 291
Framework instantiation   282, 285, 300, 304, 307
Framework instantiation effort   304
Framework stability indicator   284, 298, 306, 307, 309
Free software   194
Function   512
Function call   510
Function level   228, 233–236
Functional requirements   407
Full Operational Capability (FOC)   482

Gene   144
Global software process   106–108, 118–119
GNOME   186–188
GNU software   229
GNU/Linux   181, 186
Godfrey   186–188, 190
Goodness of fit   269
Granularity   228, 233, 236
GRAVA   522
    role of reflection in   527
Growing complexity   262–263
Growth rate   287, 288
Guarded commands   315

Heat exchange simulation system   145, 148, 151, 152, 155
Hermeneutics   108–113
    methodological   109
    phenomenological   109, 114, 116
High-risk requirements   413, 414
Hindsight bias   495

Impact analysis   250–251
Incremental effort   132
Influence
    vs control   370
Influencers   404
Information   74–75
Information content   74, 77, 83
Information technology   53–68
Infrastructure   195
Initial Operational Capability (IOC)   482, 483, 485
Instantiation effort   304, 307
Instantiation process   301
Intellectual reach   77
Intellectual span   77, 78, 81, 83
Intelligent room   531
Inter-release intervals   136
Interactions   272, 275, 277
Intermodule change propagation   256, 257
Interpretation   108–110
Interpretative processes   108, 109
Intramodule change propagation   255, 257
Invariant   325
Inverse square law   133, 136
IT legacy systems   53
    complexity of   53–68

Judgmental bias   497
Jun   157

Knowledge model   408
KnowledgePLAN   445

Labeling program   523
Large software systems   8
Laws of software evolution.   *See* Evolution, laws of
Laws of system evolution   132
Layered architecture   272
Learning biases   495
    over-confidence in own estimates   495
    reducing the impact
        conflicting evidence   495
Learning from experience   491

Learning situations 496–497
Legacy properties 225, 232, 242–244
Legacy systems 53–68
Legacy tendencies 225
Lehman's Laws 100–101, 116
  of software evolution 346
Libre 201
Life Cycle Architecture (LCA) 482
Life cycle objectives (LCO) 482
Lines of code (LOC) 149, 211, 550
  total number of 132
Linker 511
Linux Kernel 186, 188
Lisp 512
Load bearing walls 77, 79, 80
Localised redevelopment 236
LST paradigm 17–18

Madey 190, 192
Magic 319
Maintenance 252–254
Maintenance costs 53, 55
Management planning and controlling 427, 432
Management process 413
Mature requirement 166, 177
McCabe's cyclomatic complexity 257
Measurement 249, 261, 263
  of ripple effect 250, 261, 262, 266
Mechanisms 270–272, 279
Mega-system 81, 85
Memes 144, 194, 199
Metaglue 532
Methodological hermeneutics 110
Metrics 146, 233, 242, 243, 250, 252, 253, 263
Metrics data 416
Metrics repository 429–431
  transformation model 429
Metrics-based assessment 283
Minimum description length 524
Model parameters
  evolution of 155
Model validation 131
Model-Based (System) Architecting and Software Engineering (MBASE) 482

Models 194–197
Modification 322–324
Module-clustering principles 138
Modules 77
  changes in 83
  easy to modify 137, 138
  evolution of 90
  hard to modify 137, 138
  relative frequencies of 137
  total number of 132
Monitoring 271, 274, 279
Most likely effort 501
Motivation 491, 494–495
  for learning estimation skills 494–495
  most likely effort 494
Mozilla 181, 186, 191, 202

Natural selection 144
Negative binomial distribution 149, 153–155
Networking 64, 65
Nondeterminism 314
Nonfunctional requirements 407
Normal science 110–113
Normalized-extent-of-change-metric 295, 297, 299

Object-orientation 83, 90
Object-oriented framework 281–309
Observational level theory 344
On-the-job feedback 491
Ontology 197–200
Open source software 181–200, 207, 540
Open source systems 190, 196
Open-loop 507
Operation refinement 316
Operational increments 416
Order processing system 481–487
Organisational context 50
Organisational performance 468
Organisational restructuring 59, 63
Organisational structure 468
OSS. *See* Open source software
Outcome based control limits 433–434
Over-confidence 499

Index

P-type situations and software 13
P-type systems 120
Paradigm 108, 110–115
   characteristics of 111
   formation processes 111
Paradigmatic domain 113–114
Parameterisation 85
Parameters 263, 274–276
Patchwork parser 525
Pattern 75, 77, 80, 85
Pearson's test 149
Perfective maintenance 223
Performance targets 435
Persistence 272, 276
Pervasive computing 530–535
   intelligent room 531
Policies 270, 271, 273, 276, 279
Policy-checking mechanism 379–384, 389
Postcondition 315
Precondition 315
Prediction interval 497
Predictive power 134
Predictive risk factors 422
Preparation release 551
Preventative maintenance 224
Process evolution 28–32
Process feedback 363–374, 428–431
Process improvement 28–29, 342–343, 371, 556
Process maturity 466, 475
Process model evolution 32
Process modelling techniques 459–468
Process models 32, 272, 431
Process regulation 366
Process stability 424
Process systems 367
Process Tradeoff Analysis Method 427
ProcessWeb 272–273, 277–278
Producers 400–401
Product lines 84, 195, 196
Product-use case 405
Productive unit 195
Program classification 10
Program conjunction 322
Program disjunction 324

Program modification 322–324
Program refinement 314–320
Program size distribution 153
Program slicing 259
Program volume 77
Programming language 513
Programming methodology 29
Project drivers 399–405
   influencers 404
Project management 138, 140, 444
Project planning 427
Project sociology 405
Proneness-to-change 283, 287
Propagation 254–256
Properties
   structural. *See* Structural properties
Prototyping 509
Pseudo-time 136

Quality gateway 408–409
   testpoints 409
Quality metrics 424
Quantitative project management 431

Rational Unified Process (RUP) 482
Rationale 79
Re-factoring 546
Real earned-Value feedback control 478–481
Real world 42–43
Real-world program relationship 346–347
Recovery 520
Reengineering 229
Reestimation 443–455
Refactoring 150, 159, 191, 210, 224
Refinement 17, 314–320, 325, 327
   modification of 320
   requirements 328
   weakest preconditions 319
   wide-spectrum language 314
Reflections 71, 74, 76
Regression coefficient 152, 153
Relationship 407, 410
Relative-extent-of-change-metric 293, 296, 297, 299

Release   15, 16, 22
Release planning   545
Release Sequence Numbers (RSN)   132
Reliability risk   411
Replication   144
Replicator   97–99, 116–117, 121, 123
Representation   73, 326
Requirements   103, 107, 109, 110, 113, 114, 116, 123, 397–410
   environment-specific   166, 167
   system-specific   166, 167
   volatility of   82
Requirements analysis   113–115
Requirements attributes   414
Requirements changes   161–177, 412
Requirements component   407
Requirements discovery
   feedbacks in   397–410
Requirements document   407
Requirements evolution   162
Requirements management   283, 307
Requirements risk   415
Requirements shell   409
Requirements specification   397–399
   feedbacks in   397–410
   project constraints   397
   testing requirements   397
Requirements template   407
Resource manager   315
REST.   *See* Ripple Effect and Stability Tool (REST)
Restructuring   208, 210, 216, 217
Results chain   479
Retrenchment   324–335
   within   331
Returns on investment (ROI)   480
Reusable asset   281, 309
Reverse engineering   229
Revolutionary modification   79
Rigorous inspections   414
Ripple   460
Ripple effect   249–265
   computation of   255
Ripple Effect and Stability Tool (REST)   258

Ripple effect measurement   250, 261, 262, 265, 266
Ripple pattern   134, 136
Risk analysis   420–423
Risk factors   418–419
   dependency check on   422
Risk management   453–454
Robustness   228
Roles   272–273
   scheduled   276
   timed out   274, 276
RUP.   *See* Rational Unified Process

S-curve   200
S-type applications and software   10
S-type systems   122
Schedule As Independent Variable (SAIV)   477
Scheduling   270–274
   focus of   275
Science
   philosophy of   96, 108
Scientific experiments   46
Scientific knowledge   110, 121
Scope of product   405
Scope of work   405
Securities management system   146
Segmentation   523
SEI Capability Maturity Models   475
Self regulation   263, 547–549
   establishing baselines   547
Self-adaptive architecture   527
Self-adaptive software   509, 517–521
   agents   532
   applications of   521–535
   binding of function call to function value   510
   internalized feedback   507–535
   internalizing monitoring and evaluation functions   508
   technology requirements
      diagnosis   520
Self-organisation   64, 65, 67, 68
Semantic focus   72
SESAM   86, 87, 91
Seventh law, Lehman   171, 177

Sierra mountainbikes   481
Sierra's order processing systems   481
Simula-67   513
Simulated evolution   136
Simulation   326
Simulation modelling   460
Simulation models   209, 431–432
SLIM   445
Smalltalk   147, 157, 513
Social ecosystem   54, 57–58, 60
   adaptation   58
Software
   categorisation of   77–82
   definition of   72–75
   as information   74–75
   nature of   73, 74
   open source   124
Software adaptation   554
Software aging   75
Software application   543
Software architecture   269, 270
Software complexity   415
Software component   99
Software defects   552
Software development
   expert estimation of cost   489–503
   feedback control of   472–476
      process maturity   475
Software development technologies   48
Software development tools   48
Software documentation   558
Software ecology   515–517
Software engineering   100, 116
   methods   47–48
   processes   47–49
   techniques   48
Software evolution   7–37, 96–104, 162, 171, 177, 208–210, 313–336, 368, 420, 460
   dimensions of   41–49
      domains   42–44
      experience   44–47
      process   47–49
   empirical studies   30, 182–184
   evidence of feedback
      self-stabilization ripple   460

formal methods   313–336
global views of
   process improvement   342–343
how of   341
laws of   100–101, 182–183, 260–265, 541–542
   complexity of   545–547
   self regulation   547–549
Lehman's laws of   30–31
management   539–560
monitoring of
   policy-checking mechanism 379–384
retrenchment for   332
risk factors   226
stages in   16–17, 550
strata of   77
theories of   18–19, 99–101, 211, 339–355
   good practice   345
   scientific method   340
   theory formation   345–346
what, why and how of   8, 539
why of   344
world view of
   assumptions   347–349
Software life cycle   245, 508
Software maintenance   252–254
Software maintenance models   252–254
Software metrics   412, 549
Software process   28, 35, 36, 373, 459–468
   difficulties with feedback control 363–374
      step functions vs regulation 371–372
   feedback in   13–14, 23, 25, 33, 34
   nature of   32
   need for theory
      formal methods   354
   theory of   560
Software process models   33
Software quality   355, 553
Software reestimation   443–455
Software requirements analysis   418
Software reuse   121–122, 124, 285

Software size 412
Software system 95–126
　architecture of 104–105
　assumptions about 113
　environmental changes, impact of 162
　evolution 270
　and interpretation problem 108
　interpretative processes 108
　P and S categories 120
　real world 42
Software system evolution 22–27
　causal theory of 131
　dynamic model of 131
Software system growth 131–141
Software systematics 198
Software uncertainty
　principle of 22, 346, 557–558
Software, self-adaptive 507–535
Software-related evolution
　levels of 14–16
Software-size 77
Source code 249, 251
Source code size 211
Space shuttle flight software 418
　complexity factors 419
　criticality of change factors 419
　locality of change factors 419
　metric critical values 420
　performance factors 420
　personnel resources factors 420
　requirements issues and functions
　　factors 419
　size factors 419
SPE 95, 101–104
SPE program classification 542–543
　validation of 543
SPE software classification 10
SPE+ 96, 115–124
　validation of 123
Specification 101–104, 122–123, 350
Specification statement 315
Spherical model 138
Splitting 233, 235, 236
Sponsors 402–403
Stability 254, 255, 265, 266

Stability assessment 283, 284, 293–300, 306, 307
Stability indicator 298
Stakeholders 104–108, 399
　policies of 123
　satisfaction of 102, 117, 119, 120, 122
Stakeholders' concerns 104, 119
Standardisation 85
Static binding 510–512
Statistical clustering 526
Statistical experiments 46
Statistical modelling 143–149
Statistical process control (SPC) 433
Statistical significance 415
Statistically invariant effort 133
Step functions 371–372
Stratification 72, 91
Structural patterns 208, 213
Structural properties 79
Structural stability 283, 288
Subject matter consultants 403
Subroutine 511
Subsystems 138, 140
Success-critical stakeholders 479, 480
Successive versions 228, 229
Superlinear 186, 187, 193
System 80
　S-type 101, 102–103, 122–123
　E-type 101, 103–104, 115–120
　P-type 101, 103, 120–122
System architecture 105–106, 270, 271, 277
　compliance of 270
　ProcessWeb 272
System complexity
　growth of 133
System dynamics 460, 548
System function 270, 271
System heterogeneity 138
System identification 461–464
System level 228, 230–233
System size 132, 136, 139
System volatility 412
System-level evolution 84
System-of-systems 80–81

Index 575

Systemic viewpoint 269, 270
Systems-of-systems
    evolution of 85

Technical consultants 404
Technical system 195
Technological change 62
Technological infrastructure 60–62
Technology
    vs sociology 366
Teleological perspective 73
Terminology
    in software evolution 71
    object-oriented 90
Test 397
Testable requirements 402, 405
Testing 406
Testpoints 409
Theorem proving 526
Theory evolution 43–44
Theory formation 345–346
Time of a release 132
Timely feedback 492
Total-extent-of-change 296
Trade-offs 275–277
Training opportunities 492
Transformation 429

Ubiquitous computing 530
Uncertainty elicitation process 500
Uncertainty, in E-type systems
    117–118

Undecidability 20
Users 400, 401

Validation 11, 545
Validity
    threats to 176
Value 472, 476, 479
Value-based feedback control 481–487
    business case analysis
        cost 482–485
Value-based monitoring and control
    485–487
Variable definitions 254, 256–258
Variable occurrence 256
Verification 18–19
Version 146, 150, 157
Viewpoints, architectural 104, 106
Virtual machine 272, 273, 275
Vision system 522–528
    image segmentation 523
Visual builder 285
Volatility management 84

Waterfall model 508
White-box framework 285
White-box models 559
Wicked system 75

χ^2 test 149

Z schema calculus 314